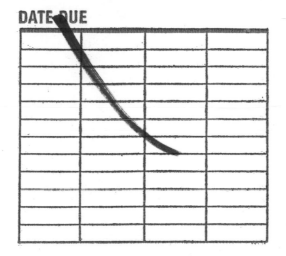

Early Quaker Writings, 1650-1700

Early Quaker Writings 1650-1700

edited
by

HUGH BARBOUR

and

ARTHUR O. ROBERTS

WILLIAM B. EERDMANS PUBLISHING COMPANY
Grand Rapids, Michigan

TO OUR STUDENTS AND COLLEAGUES
AT EARLHAM COLLEGE AND GEORGE FOX COLLEGE

We owe thanks to other Quaker scholars who have advised us in the selecting of the works included in this volume: Edwin Bronner, Henry Cadbury, Maurice Creasey, Michael Graves, T. Canby Jones, and Frederick Tolles.
We owe yet more to those who have faithfully transcribed the original editions and manuscripts or intermediate copies: Jeff Allen, Robert Atwood, Clarissa Barker, David Brassfield, Lois Burleigh, Susan Burnam, Jill Crollick, Sally Dimschultz, Penny Marsh Eastman, Pamela Gibson, Jane Herrold, Michael Jackson, Barbara Miller, Mary Myton, Lettie Pack, Martha Pennington, Martha Schulwolf, and Jerilyn Thomas.

Foreword

While it is never possible to discover precisely how things were in the past, we generally assume that the more we know about the events, the thoughts, the beliefs, and the feelings of a period, especially as expressed through the written and printed word, the more likely we are not to be misled in our understanding. Thus we welcome most enthusiastically the publication of this volume of relevant, though relatively unknown writings of seventeenth-century Quakers, which are presently available in only a few select libraries.

Friends published 3,750 titles by 1700. In his earlier book, *The Quakers in Puritan England,* Hugh Barbour estimated 2,000 manuscript letters and documents preserved from the same period. After omitting those in print, the best-known works, such as Fox's *Journal,* Barclay's *Apology,* and Penn's *No Cross, No Crown,* Barbour and his collaborator, Arthur O. Roberts, have painstakingly gone over this vast collection and selected a few dozen items that serve to illustrate and illuminate five aspects of early Quakerism for today's reader. Anyone familiar with this literature might make other selections, but one should willingly admit that the editors have made a conscientious effort to present representative examples of seventeenth-century Quaker writing and thought.

It would be an interesting exercise to compare the quantity of published material produced by members of the Society of Friends today, with the number of words published by seventeenth-century Quakers. Those of us who are responsible for collecting and preserving contemporary Quaker writing in special libraries are overwhelmed by the amount of paper now generated by Friends. But if one were to take into account the difference in numbers, and the difference in average educational level, between the first generation of Quakers and the Society three centuries later, the results might be surprising.

When one attempts to compare the quality of writing then and now, one cannot avoid the conclusion that the first Quaker authors displayed a passion, a sense of commitment, and an obedience to the "Christ Within" not often revealed today. Some contemporary writers may display more erudition than many of their forebears, but a handful of the seventeenth-century authors measure up on that count as well, when one looks for logic, for clear thinking, quality of prose, and reliance upon classical learning.

It would appear that this book represents only one facet of a multi-sided effort to republish early Quaker writings. Dean Freiday's *Barclay's Apology in Modern English* (1967) was the first volume, and it differed from the others in that the editor attempted to present this Quaker classic in contemporary language. Phillips Moulton's *The Journal and Major Essays of John Woolman* (1971), a definitive edition of the New Jersey Quaker's writings, followed conventional lines of scholarly re-editing, as he reproduced Woolman's precise words, fully annotated. Henry J. Cadbury is presently making another major contribution to Quaker scholarship with his volume of *The Narrative Papers of George Fox,* largely unpublished before, and the balance available only in rare seventeenth-century tracts. The William Penn Papers project, headed by Professor Caroline Robbins, falls into a slightly different category, but is not unrelated to these other efforts.* One is reminded of the great outburst of new editions of Quaker writings which followed the so-called Hicksite Separation of 1827, when the fourteen-volume *Friends Library* was assembled, and all of George Fox's major writings were reprinted. Penn's writings had just been reissued, and a few years later came the multi-volume *Friends' Miscellany.*

This collection of documents has been enhanced by extensive introductory essays to the entire volume and to each of the five sections. In addition, it is fully annotated, with an extensive "biographical index" giving pertinent details about the persons mentioned in the book. The Introductions will be most helpful to

---

*In deference to it, Penn's writings are less fully represented than one could wish in this present volume.

the average reader as well as to scholars, and the notes will be invaluable to students. The editors are steeped in the religious history of the seventeenth century, have spent many years in preparing this collection of Quaker sources, and have been encouraged by their publisher to share the results of their research with the readers.

The first section of the book, in which "Truth is Proclaimed," contains selections from James Nayler, Edward Burrough, William Dewsbury, a manuscript message written by Fox, and the appealing essay by Marmaduke Stephenson, written as he faced hanging on the Boston Common. A view of early Quakers through the unfriendly eyes of Puritan Francis Higginson is also included. The self-confident tone, the vibrant, triumphant message, the complete dedication to a God revealed by the "Christ Within," give immediacy to the words.

The second part contains materials written by various Quakers to describe their experiences as they lived the Truth that had been revealed to them. Some of the selections are what the editors call "forerunners of the journal," and the balance are from full-fledged journals. The writings of a farmer, John Banks, are quoted along with those of Cambridge man Isaac Penington. The graceful prose of Thomas Ellwood enhances this section. In the third part, "Truth Defended," Quaker efforts to explain and defend their theology are printed along with the slashing attacks of Richard Baxter. Writers whose works were quoted in the first section are joined here by Samuel Fisher and Barclay, whose "Catechism and Confession of Faith" is reproduced.

As the social implications of the Truth are discussed in the fourth part it is clear that some Quakers developed strong social concerns even while they were primarily involved with changing people's lives. The first step in this direction was the defense of individual conscience and a person's understanding of divine will, against the power of the state. The second step was the struggle for toleration. In 1659 Edward Billing (Byllynge) advanced a number of proposals for social justice, which found direct application in the "Concessions" for West New Jersey. John Bellers, acclaimed as an early socialist, is also quoted. One of Penn's political tracts is included, and a gay Ellwood poem on women's dress is used.

The organization of the Society to preserve Truth is discussed in the final portion. The tempo, the words used, seem quiet and measured when contrasted with the vitality of the first section.

Nevertheless, this is an interesting study of the way in which a spontaneous movement begins to take shape and become institutionalized. Margaret Fell is quoted more than once here, the only woman whose writings have been used, aside from Elizabeth Hooton. Fox plays a key role in this area too, along with Barclay and a new voice, that of George Whitehead.

Clearly there is great variety in the material selected for this volume, just as there was a wide variation in the manners, styles, and beliefs of early Friends. The vision of Humphrey Smith, prophesying the great London Fire, will intrigue some, while the descriptions of the sufferings of early Friends by Joseph Besse and George Bishop will touch the hearts of others. The mysticism of Penington contrasts with the evangelical zeal of Nayler's description of the "Lamb's War." The logical expositions of Barclay seem far removed from the argumentative tone of Fox's *The Great Mistery of the Great Whore Unfolded.* . . . Few readers will enjoy equally everything in this volume, but anyone interested in the beginnings of Quakerism, whether as a scholar or an amateur, will find the book informative, challenging, sometimes exciting, and always enlightening.

Haverford College   Edwin B. Bronner

Contents

General Introduction

The Quaker movement has always been more powerful than its books. Four of its works remain in print as classics: the *Journals* of George Fox and John Woolman, the *Apology* of Robert Barclay, and various groupings of William Penn's ethical aphorisms and pleas for toleration.[1] Yet these books are all loved more for

[1] Of many recent editions of Fox's *Journal*, the most complete and scholarly is that edited by John L. Nickalls (Cambridge: Cambridge Univ. Press, 1952). Most paperback and older hardback editions are abridged reprints of the first printed edition (1694) as edited after Fox's death by Thomas Ellwood. Most university libraries include Norman Penney's definitively annotated editions of the original manuscripts of the *Journal*, as dictated by Fox in 1673-74 (Cambridge: Cambridge Univ. Press, 1911; hereafter given as Fox, *CJ*), and of the *Short Journal and Itinerary Journals* (Cambridge: Cambridge Univ. Press, 1925).

The much later (1775) *Journal* of John Woolman, often reprinted in the "Whittier edition" text (sometimes with other Woolman tracts), has recently been re-edited from the manuscripts by Phillips Moulton (Oxford: Oxford Univ. Press, 1971).

Robert Barclay's *Apology*, the most often reprinted of all these among Friends (at least thirty-one English, three Latin, and eleven other editions up to 1909), is less read among non-Quakers. Though widely available, it is currently in print only in the modern-English private edition of Dean Freiday and in a Pendle Hill pamphlet selection.

The newest scholarly edition to print more than fragments of William Penn's works is *The Witness of William Penn* by Frederick B. Tolles and E. Gordon Alderfer (New York: Macmillan, 1957), though AMS Press recently photo-reproduced the first (1726) edition of Penn's complete *Works*. Penn's *Fruits of Solitude* and *No Cross, No Crown* each saw at least thirty editions apiece, though only one of each in the twentieth century.

By contrast with these four classics, most works included in the present

their writers' character than for their style or logic. None of these books, moreover, belongs to the first explosive decade of Quakerism, though all of these authors but Woolman had shared in those years, when the Friends were the most vital and fastest-growing religious community in the Puritan commonwealths of England and America. This volume is intended as a shelfmate for those four familiar classics—to round out their witness, to present more fully the earliest periods of Quaker writing, and to show the emergence of the special genres that came to be typical of Friends: the journal, the epistle, and the prophetic tract.

Quaker experience spoke through many voices. In their first fifty years (1650-1700), which are covered here, close to 650 Friends (at least 82 being women) wrote "as each felt led," and 3100 new writings were published, besides 650 reprints and memorials.[2] Friends rarely quoted or consciously echoed the writings of Fox, even though they shared many outlooks rooted in their common encounter with the Spirit. Each man wrote out of his own experience. There was no Quaker canon of definitive books. Hence, though some tracts of Fox and Barclay are included here, more place is given to James Nayler, Edward Burrough, and Isaac Penington, who were almost equally important in their own day and have become so again in ours.

All early Quaker writings reflected personal involvement in a cosmic struggle. Friends saw their movement as "Primitive Christianity Revived"[3] by the same Spirit that began to work before

volume have not been reprinted since the seventeenth century, though most were widely influential then. Obvious exceptions are the parts given here from the often-reprinted journals of Crisp and Ellwood, and certain epistles of Fox, of the Yearly Meeting and of Isaac Penington (printed in the nineteenth century only). More notably, Barclay's *Anarchy of the Ranters* saw six English and American editions and his *Catechism* thirty-three (the latest being 1878), besides those in Latin, French, and Dutch. The complete works of Fox, Barclay, Nayler, Penn, and Penington were also reprinted about 1830.

[2] The standard Quaker bibliography is Joseph Smith's *Descriptive Catalogue of Friends' Books* (London, 1867), useful in conjunction with Donald Wing's *Short-Title Catalogue . . . 1641-1700* (New York: Index Society, 1945-51). John Whiting's *Catalogue of Friends' Books* (1708) was for its day remarkable. Luella Wright, in *The Literary Life of Early Friends* (New York: Columbia Univ. Press, 1932), p. 8, assesses from Whiting's and Nathan Kite's researches that by 1725 440 Quaker authors had produced 2678 titles. But see the Appendix, p. 575.

[3] The title of William Penn's tract of 1696.

14

the fifteen hundred years of apostasy; hence they cared less about restoring New Testament church patterns than about responding to the Spirit's present power to transform the world and bring Christ's kingdom. Like Martin Luther and Jonathan Edwards in the early-blossoming days of their movements (and like some outward revolutionaries, too), early Friends expected the fulfillment of the Christian hope within their lifetime. Even Quaker apologias defended the power of the Spirit working through Friends, not doctrine as such.

Inner experience and world transformation were thus fused in early Quaker life. Within themselves, Friends knew the work and victory of the Spirit through the laborious conflict with inner evil, and only later through peace and joy. Yet each man's inner change was shared with a local "Meeting" and with the world community of "Children of Light," who gave his struggle its place within a cosmic victory. Thus Friends' distinctive experience has always been simultaneously of radically inward worship and ethics and of apocalyptic social change.

This blend of history and inwardness sets Friends apart from most pietist and mystical groups (including many nineteenth-century Quakers) and from most religious revolutionaries (even among twentieth-century Friends). Early Quakers' stories are vivid and their lives speak: they have more often been well portrayed than clearly understood. Mystics, secular radicals, and modern-day "Anabaptist" ethical reformers have each seen early Friends in their own image. All these groups do indeed share a central concern for intense and joyful directness of experience and for ethical commitment and creativity. Yet the forms of inner experience and outward radicalism vary widely among these present-day groups, and each tends to describe that fraction of original Quakerism which corresponds to its members' own experiences, using its own terms for it, and claiming for its view the dynamism of early Friends.

Meanwhile, for four decades English-speaking scholars have been reexamining the Puritan world out of which Quakerism came and reassessing the early Quakers in its light.[4] Their results must

---

[4] The tradition of great British liberal historians such as Trevelyan produced within Quakerism the "Rowntree Series" of William Braithwaite and Rufus Jones, still the most accurate and thorough histories on Quaker events. Their view was compatible with the liberals' view of Quakerism as mysticism plus social reform. Though the questions these books asked now seem limited, their answers were reliable. To the precision and intended objectivity

be summarized here and applied for the first time to early Quaker writing. If some of the conclusions surprise the reader, he is urged to test them out against the material itself, comparing the selections given here with the whole body of Quaker writing rather than with favorite fragments, and to help also in further reinterpretation of them.

The Setting and Experience of Early Quakerism

When Quakerism began as a mass awakening sweeping from the North of England southwards and overseas in 1651-56, the Puritans saw current events, the victories of Cromwell and Parliament, as sacred history. Biblical hopes and a hundred years of dreaming and working within England were finally being fulfilled. For the century after Elizabeth became queen, all Englishmen concerned for vital faith, total dedication in worship, and Christian remaking

of these works belongs the tradition still kept alive by Henry Cadbury and Geoffrey Nuttall, and until his death by Elbert Russell.

Basically similar approaches, with more cordiality toward theology and churchmanship, underlay the first generation of great twentieth-century students of Puritanism: William Haller, Marshall Knappen, Perry Miller, and others. When such men turned their attention to Quakerism they saw its dominant Puritan, rather than its mystical, aspects and saw Friends in their environment of daily history in the Puritan Revolution. They saw Puritanism itself in personal and cultural terms more even than as theology and, despite some critics like George Marsden, have been widely influential.

Meanwhile the German scholarly tradition was blending two quite different strains. The Marxists such as Bernstein and Kautsky taught us to see Quakers and Baptists as the proletarian wing of a revolutionary alliance with the bourgeois Presbyterians, from whom they split at the crisis of the Puritan commonwealth, just as did the Jacobins from the Girondists in the French Revolution or the Anabaptists and peasants from the Lutherans and Calvinists in Germany. Such scholars taught us to call Anabaptists "the radical reformation" and to see English Separatists and Quakers as "left-wing Puritans." Secondly, the great German church historians Harnack and Ernst Troeltsch taught us to see ethical world-outlooks underlying even theology. Through Richard Niebuhr an American generation of historians has begun from this viewpoint.

Renewed efforts first to see early Quakerism in terms of personal and Christian experience and hence to tie it up on the one hand with traditional biblical doctrines, and on the other with insights from psychology and the descriptive sciences, have especially concerned Maurice Creasey in England and, in this country, T. Canby Jones and the editors of the present volume, who nevertheless are indebted to all these viewpoints.

16

of the social order and the church had been drawn into the Puritan fellowship. The exceptions were only a handful of earnest Catholics and a slowly growing minority of Anglicans, most of them highly educated sacramentarians like John Donne, Lancelot Andrewes, and Archbishop Laud. The Puritans had seen a new godly order of church and state in Calvin's Geneva and the English-language Bible. For three generations after the death of "Bloody Mary," the Tudor Catholic, all human hopes for carrying out this divine commission to re-order England had been repeatedly thwarted as the Puritans were excluded from power by Elizabeth and her Scottish successor, James I, Protestants though these monarchs claimed to be. Some impatient Puritan congregations opted individually for "Reformation without Tarying for Anie":[5] they were the first groups deliberately to leave the national Church of England and the unintended forerunners of modern denominations such as the Congregationalists and Baptists.

To most Puritans, as well as to Anglicans better satisfied with the middle-of-the-road position of the Church of England, such "Separatism" amounted to an antisocial rejection of the ancient dream of a Christian nation sharing Christian laws under Christian rulers, a dream that all Europe had shared in varying forms since the rising Middle Ages. Ruler and nation combined to harry the "Brownists" out of the land and eventually to Holland and Plymouth Rock. Some of them picked up from Dutch sects the practice of baptizing by immersion only fully committed adult Christians, which identified the English "Baptists" with the once revolutionary Anabaptists of Europe.

The majority of Puritans throughout the period clung to the parish churches of the Church of England, which until this time had included all Englishmen, even while they argued and were burnt to death over whether the theology and worship of that church should be Catholic, Calvinist, or an "Anglican" compromise. The Puritans wanted thorough purification of the national Church from all "Papist" ceremonies and superstitions. They maintained a network of pastorships and congregations, sparked by key colleges and professorships at Cambridge. Until 1640 they accepted endless unhappy compromises with the royal bishops over liturgy and priestly robes. They developed Bible study, prayer meetings, and sermon reading in homes and neighborhood circles.

5 The title of Robert Browne's tract of 1582, from which the "Brownists" or English Separatists were nicknamed.

They wrote diaries and books on ethics so that the standards of a godly life and the evidences of God's converting power, which were expected ultimately to transform England, could meanwhile shape the lives of individuals. They never lost hope of reforming the nation, nor did even the English Separatists, as became clear when both types of Puritan happened to meet in Massachusetts and by God's providence and clever charter-juggling were free to set up a New England within the legal bounds but not the practical control of the English nation and government.

Toward 1640 Charles I's arbitrary rule and taxation united the English merchants, Parliament, and the Scots and Irish against him. Apart from Ireland, most of these would also be called Puritans, though not all favored the tightly knit church pattern of Scottish Presbyterianism. After 1640 there was increasing freedom for all sorts of sects and free congregations within England itself. Yet even the loose links between local congregations did not follow lines distinguishing "Baptists" from "Independents," "Separatists," or "Congregationalists." Other issues such as predestination proved much more divisive. Still less should we regard as a distinct fellowship or denomination the scattered "seeker" groups that had rejected all sacraments and clergy as without spiritual power and met to wait in silent worship. Reluctantly, the more strictly Calvinist and presbyterian Puritans accepted all the Separatists as allies except for "Ranters" and "Familists" who put inner freedom above good and evil.

As political deadlock gave way to the Civil War in England, regional and even local loyalties formed a checkerboard. The strongly Puritan areas were around London, up the eastern lowlands as far as York, and across through the hill mill-towns of Halifax and Manchester to Liverpool. Most of these areas were easily held by militia armies loyal to the Parliament. Elsewhere the king held the loyalty of whatever men were religiously indifferent and of the feudal nobility and country gentry and their tenants (see map, p. 34). Two years of military standoff were broken only when Oliver Cromwell raised "New Model" regiments of "Ironside" volunteers among the east-coast Puritans. His officers were mainly gentry like himself, but the rank and file believed increasingly in the autonomy of local congregations even in a land ruled by "the saints," and in their freedom to accept untrained "mechanick preachers" from their own working-class ranks. These men won the war and refused to go home until their demands for reforms and for overdue pay were met.

By the end of the war in 1646, bishops, the House of Lords, and the king's right to tax and arrest by fiat had been easily swept away; but no one yet saw how to build a constitutional monarchy around a king who refused to concede any power even when a captive. Conservative Puritans and the Scots would have accepted the changes in taxes and the Church that the king would grant. He rallied them to his side for a second Civil War, which revealed and opened the breaches between conservative "Presbyterians" and radical "Independents" in church policy, and between advocates of a Parliament limited by wealth and birth and those "Commonwealthsmen" or "Levellers" who wanted either universal suffrage or a "rule of the saints." Cromwell triumphed again. He identified himself with the Independents, and agreed with the political radicals except on their two key issues: suffrage for all freeholders and the abolition of the old parish system with its sense of community responsibility. Cromwell appointed outstanding Puritan pastors as committees of "tryers and ejectors" to screen and supply parish pulpits. One great minister out of this tradition, Richard Baxter, was indifferent all his life regarding congregational, presbyterian, or even episcopal Church linkages; but he was Calvinist in theology and always pastor to all of Kidderminster. He appears later in this volume through his conflict with the Quakers (see p. 262). Cromwell was willing and even eager to tolerate independent separatist and baptist congregations alongside the parish churches. Both in the church and in electoral policy he tried throughout his career to reconcile the many minorities, none of which could rule England alone—separatist, Independent, presbyterian, and even anglican; radical and old-style Parliamentarians; and even Royalists. The inability of these groups to trust each other, however, and the logic of Cromwell's victories drove his officers in 1647 to purge Parliament of its conservative faction, and in 1649, with the remaining "Rump," to try to execute the beaten but still uncompromising king.

For the radical Puritans it was the high-water mark of their hopes and of their assurance that God himself through these simple men had overthrown the proud and mighty. After yet another round of battles against Scottish and Irish Royalists, in which Cromwell's victories at Dunbar and Drogheda seemed more than ever beyond human power, he dissolved the remainder of the Puritan "Long Parliament" and allowed the Puritan congregations themselves to select a "Nominated Parliament" of "Saints" in 1653. Cromwell shared their dreams of forming a simpler and

19

more just code of English law, promoting local self-government and building a new Jerusalem in England's green and pleasant land; but he refused to let them abolish the parish churches. When the "Parliament of Saints" disbanded itself in frustration, he announced a Commonwealth under a Council of State and ruled through old-style Parliaments and the support of his army, taking for himself the title of Protector from England's first fully Protestant rulers, the regents for young Edward VI a century before.

The radical Puritans felt the betrayal of their hopes so bitterly that they prepared an abortive revolt in 1654 and others later; they formed a "Fifth Monarchist" faction who hoped that one more revolution would complete the timetable of five cosmic monarchies in Daniel 7. Other men who left or were mustered out of Cromwell's regiments, however, had come to feel already in the peak period of Puritan hopes that civil wars and parliaments had failed to transform England and that the conquest of evil and shaping of Christ's kingdom must come by some more deeply inward power. Alienation from the political hopes and distance from national events only strengthened their inner hunger.

Emphasis upon inner transformation was part of the Reformation from the beginning. Its protest against the outwardness of Catholicism was rooted in the attack of Luther and Calvin on the do-good self-righteousness they found in Catholic "works of merit" even at their best. Instead they preached total self-surrender to the love and power of God, and this implied a deeper faith than orthodoxy, a change of heart. Man's relation to God was an issue that went beyond any dualism of inward intent and outward action: men could not even attain or claim credit for trust within themselves. Faith itself was a gift of God. Yet only from it could come outward actions of true love or obedience. Thus the Puritans' campaigns for the simplification of worship and their earnestness about social and political conduct for the glory of God did not cut them off from the inner root. Indeed the Puritans stressed *consciousness* of conversion more than did Lutherans or other Calvinists and in New England even made it a prerequisite for church membership.[6] It was balanced by the Puritans' concern to see God's power also in the outward remaking of the whole society and nation. Even the individualistic and plebeian Baptists and Separatists, who measured the genuineness of a conversion

6 Cf. Norman Pettit, *The Heart Prepared; Grace and Conversion in Puritan Life* (New Haven: Yale Univ. Press, 1966).

20

especially by its emotional intensity, expected God would rule through his saints. It is not easy to separate such emotionalism from concern about moral earnestness nor from the deeper mysticism in a group of "spiritual Puritan" writers and ministers: John Everard, William Dell, John Saltmarsh, Walter Cradock, and to lesser degrees Hugh Peters and Peter Sterry. Yet all these men served fervently in Cromwell's cause, many as his chaplains. All looked to outward as well as inward events for immediate guidance from God, as did Cromwell himself. One of these "spiritual Puritans," Sir Harry Vane, who was briefly governor of Massachusetts, was to head the English government in 1659.

Sermons by "spiritual Puritan" parish pastors were widely read in Cromwell's England. It is hard to know, therefore, how consciously mystical ideas were distinct, within the rich thought-world in which Friends grew up, beside the radical Puritan emphasis on the inner experience of conversion, which made them reject the professional clergy as lacking in moral and emotional power. In exactly the same way, Anabaptist doctrines of ethical perfectionism mingled in the mainstream of radical Puritanism with a very unseparatist enthusiasm toward war and political power. Direct links through sects, books, or teachers between Friends and European Anabaptists were far fewer before 1654 than Mennonite historians may wish. The links Rufus Jones sought to show between Quakers and continental mystics like Boehme—mainly by way of the Ranters, who deified themselves above morality in free-love communes—were also few.

Thus it was in a pervasive climate of radical Puritanism, where Calvinist outlooks overshadowed those from mysticism and perfectionism, that most early Quaker leaders arose. They tended geographically as well as in doctrine to be on the fringes of parish Puritanism. George Fox,* Nayler, Dewsbury, Howgill, Burrough, and many others had wandered from vicar to preacher and on through informal prayer groups before they learned to rely on the inward voice of God rather than the ministers'. Most had been leaders of local separatist circles, and some brought their whole group into the Quaker movement.

The breakthrough for Quakerism did not come from the newness of Fox's doctrines. It came when Fox turned north, out of the Midland region where his separatist friends had long met, into the largely untouched hill country of Yorkshire, Westmorland, and

*For the lives of Friends, see the Biographical Index, pp. 580ff.

Cumberland, including Wordsworth's "Lake District," and there proclaimed Christ present within men as teacher, priest, and Lord. Of all England the northwestern region had been least reached by good schools, adequate pastors, and even by Puritan and Anglican thought. As often happens in new movements, there too the leaders were those who had already tasted some new experiences and, in this case, Puritan zeal for righteousness. The whole region also had a tradition of yeomen's independence and of ethical protest going back to the Viking settlers. Here hunger for religious vitality moved not just individuals but crowds. The early witnesses saw these mass awakenings into "experimental knowledge," like those in Acts, as clearly the work of God.

From Fox's encounters with the small separatist groups in the far Northwest developed a regional movement that emptied the few churches and drew thousands to outdoor meetings. The region's isolation allowed a sense of newness of experience. The new emphasis in Fox's message reinforced the personal crisis each man went through. The power of the mass meetings and the spirit of "the camp of the Lord" called to recapture England helped the Quaker fellowship grow to a "critical mass" whose chain reaction was self-sustaining. The momentum they gathered freed them from being merely one more Puritan sect among others and drove them out across England and the New World as an independent, world-changing movement. The open-air gatherings and the intensive after-sessions of the "convinced" in small, quiet "Meetings" presaged John Wesley's early days in Cornwall, or the "Great Awakening" under Whitefield and Edwards on the American frontier, both of which (contrary to their founders' intentions) were such dynamic and locally concentrated movements that like Friends they broke loose from the established churches, finally to form new denominations. Friends combined the spontaneity and lay leadership of the urban revivals of mid-nineteenth-century America and Scandinavia with the sermonic authority of Wesley or Billy Graham. Lacking the support of established clergy, they gathered in the alienated like the Jesus movements of the 1970's.

The rank-and-file Quaker often first heard the message of the power of God's Spirit in such mass meetings. The Light, a metaphor which suggests a searchlight into a well or a candle in a dark closet and not man's own mental power, is not to be distinguished in early Quaker experience from Christ or the Spirit within men. The Light searched out sin and brought into sight all of a man's inward motives and outward acts, showing a man who he was, as

22

through long evenings alone or at Quaker gatherings the hearer opened himself to Christ's Spirit for redemption. In the silence, *every* act and motive was branded as the fruit of self-will. This brought men close to despair, since (as Crisp describes on p. 203) even a man's efforts to understand or move out of this situation by repentance or self-commitment are acts of self-will too. An impasse followed, which led often to physical quaking, when "the tall cedars were shaken" and pride's "mountains were broken down." In the little groups or Meetings those who had gone through the experience could help those still wrestling with deeper discoveries of self-deception. They could warn against conventional but inadequate ways of reassuring oneself, such as by reliance on doctrines.

In the journals we find Friends describing how the same Light that revealed all self-willed acts and motives as evil, began after a period of waiting and openness to prompt positive acts just as specifically. The basis of new life is often pictured as total openness to wait for and obey such "leadings." Yet Friends also speak of "the Seed," sometimes as something planted within each man able to respond positively to the Light when the hard soil of the heart is broken, and at other times expressly as a Seed of God, not of human nature, and as Christ (the "Seed of the woman" of Gen. 3:15 and Rev. 12:1-5). This Seed is the "new man" to replace the crucified "old Adam" within.

No theology and no psychological theory can easily do justice to the new life that a man enters after such an experience. Friends rarely used Calvin's or Augustine's approach of seeing conversion as recommitment, redirection of the will, or empowering of the will through grace. Perhaps this was because Friends knew the uselessness of self-made commitment and had discovered how self-will continued to rebel against "leadings" of the Spirit even when new life had begun. In the light of William James's conception that a period of inner conflict leads to conversion by reintegration around new values,[7] it is clear that Friends did achieve a new synthesis of impulse, emotion, values, and conscience. Yet James's account does not interpret the intensity of power to act in new ways that Friends showed as well as felt. Clearly there were some impulses and emotional strengths from within, which Friends were now free to accept and act on—for instance, anger against

[7] William James, *The Varieties of Religious Experience* (1901-2), chs. VIII-X.

23

injustice. In this respect early Quaker experience has some parallels with psychotherapy or "sensitivity training." The central role of conscience and of openness to its positive leadings is the distinctive feature of Quaker "convincement." Early Friends were clearly describing "experimentally" (we would say, existentially) what the later, more rationalistic Methodists would systematize in their doctrine of sanctification. Quakers did not imagine that they had been given instant sanctification at any time. But they had seen perfect obedience to the Light as ever a possibility, and they could announce this possibility as a doctrinal truth. This firm conviction, and the growing habit of openness and obedience despite renewed conflicts between self-will and "leadings" to new decisions, missions, or messages to be given, represent what we may see as a new character or personality pattern in the "established" Friend. Quakers themselves rarely dared try to delineate this "new man," since its center and power was always outside the self in the Spirit of Christ. Part of the vitality and creativity of Quakerism may lie in the way its "new life" was an ever-open pilgrimage, not mere conformity even to human images of Christ. Yet at each stage self-will and evil were overpowered.

At each stage Friends claimed also to have been led by the Spirit into new "Truth," and their claim is supported by their new responsiveness and perceptiveness about previously overlooked evils such as slavery, war, and cruelty to the insane. Outward as well as inward realities were integrated by the Spirit shaping the "new life," and Friends were brought by it into unity with each other in seeing truth, as well as in emotions.

The joy and love that "broke through" in early Quakers' experience, whereby the whole earth had a new smell and Adam's purity was within man's experience, is clearly close also to that in the Methodists' sanctification. The emotional barometer of an early Friend fluctuated at first as wildly as did John Bunyan's.[8] The Quaker preacher aimed to break men open, driving them to despair about the bright, tight image of themselves by which they had tried to live. In the same way, Jonathan Edwards tried to preach men into despair, and the psychotherapist finds his role as

---

[8] Cf. John Bunyan, *Grace Abounding* (1666). The intensity of early Friends' struggle and the power of their life as "established" Friends are underestimated in sociological studies; cf. Richard Vann, *The Social Development of English Quakerism, 1655-1755* (Cambridge, Mass.: Harvard Univ. Press, 1969), ch. I.

a "head shrinker." All these guides stirred up such intense emotions that they knew that they risked driving the neurotic into insanity; and the same overwhelming emotional release, joy, and spontaneity followed their various processes for reuniting the self one ought to be and the self one knows one is. However much richer and more powerful a synthesis was the Quakers' "new life" than a Freudian's acceptance of life-drives or even a Calvinist's acceptance of grace, we cannot separate such inner resources of released love from the love given by Christ's Spirit in Friends' experience. Yet Friends' immediate letters reflect even more intensely than their later journals their sense of victory over sin through Christ, their freedom to face whatever outward suffering lay before them, and their embarrassingly outspoken love for each other.

Rufus Jones and many others after him have asserted that Quakerism is a form of mysticism. Friends' depth of silent worship, their vital openness to what is within, and their delight at what may spring up there are clearly experiences common to Quakers and mystics. So is the negative attitude toward outward worship and outward sources of truth, unless given inward meaning. Certain by-products of ecstasy, such as an intuitive sense of understanding all things and of love to all creatures, are also shared. As we press deeper, we may ask whether the differences lie in experience or in terminology that lead one man to describe his encounter with God as an "I-Thou relationship" in which the "otherness" of God and the self is enhanced, while another man describes total losing of the self in the abyss of the divine Spirit in an experience of ineffable "Union." Rufus Jones clearly included all of these experiences in what he meant by mysticism. But it is clear that early Friends did not typically experience "mystical union." An important exception is Isaac Penington, who in the early 1650's, before encountering Friends, wrote a series of pamphlets such as his *Light or Darkness* (1650) (cf. p. 226) in which he does describe encountering, just as Eckhart did, a "godhead" deeper than the personal God and surrendering the self into a reality beyond good and evil. Yet it also may be significant that when Penington joined the Friends, he turned back precisely at this point and came to believe that the deepest levels of the true experience of the Spirit did involve the judging and overcoming of evil and being led out into action. Fox himself was held back from an earlier acceptance of the Light within by knowing Ranters like Salmon and Bauthumley of Leicester, who believed pantheistically that god was equally in all things, was the only reality, and was beyond good and evil.[9]

This should probably be the criterion by which most Quakers would be better classified with the prophetic tradition than with the mystical: for Friends the conquest of evil is not a mere means for achieving spiritual realization. Quaker mystics today recognize early Quakerism as "ethical mysticism." God himself is not beyond good and evil and conquers evil in and through men. There is a paradox here, of course; for evil and good cannot be defined by the dogma of a code of law: they are to be measured by openness to the Spirit's leading and freedom from self-will, if not from human limits. Nevertheless, in the prophetic experience, unlike that of most mystics, the Spirit leads men in concrete human life and within history. The truth it leads to is always in terms of human relationships and action; the whole of which each man is a part is no formless, timeless absolute but rather the forward-moving people of God.

Little has been said so far about the role of Christ in early Quaker experience. For some, particularly Fox himself, it was more natural to speak of "Christ within" than of the Spirit; yet we do not know that he ever prayed to Christ as distinct from the Father. All early Friends believed in atonement for past sins through the death of Jesus. Yet some Friends stressed the relative unimportance of Jesus' physical body, and many asserted the inadequacy of belief about a past external act of ransom without the inner spiritual experience of transformation. Early Friends' inner experience, as we have seen, had less to do with forgiveness and reconciliation than with surrender to the Light and truth, crucifixion of self-will, and responsiveness to leadings. The Quakers' willingness to trust all these, their identification of the inner cross with love, their confidence that from inner conflict in seeming weakness a cosmic victory was coming—these traits showed more plainly than their doctrine that early Friends indeed knew the spirit of Jesus. They expected that the experience each had passed through could be shared and trusted by everyone. In some areas where mass meetings swept whole villages of the Northwest, this seemed nearly to have happened. It would happen throughout the world, they expected. Christ had come, they said, to teach his people himself and at last to bring in his kingdom by the inner

[9] Y. T. S. Elkins, "The Ranters Ranting," *Church History*, XL (March, 1971), 91ff.

26

Armageddon, "the Lamb's War," through which they had themselves just come.

Types of Early Quaker Writing

The use of biblical perspectives and biblical patterns for the writing of appeals, epistles, and narratives was inherent in early Quakerism. Quotation of specific biblical texts was not. There was also less mimicry of biblical phrases and titles than in most Christian movements with prophetic claims, such as the Mormons. The basic Quaker assumption went deeper: the same Holy Spirit who moved the early Christians was still guiding God's people, and inspired Quaker pronouncements as it had the Bible writers. The Spirit, they thought, was likely to be more clearly recognized when the grammar and messages were akin to those which had been inspired long before. Hence a biblical style often seemed natural to Friends. Yet except in debate their biblical quotations were as often unconscious as deliberate, for since childhood they had steeped themselves in the Bible.

Early Quaker writings can seldom be neatly classified within the traditional genres of religious literature—the sermon, the poem, the catechism, the theological treatise—until Barclay set himself to match such models.[10] Most Quaker tracts can be pinned down to a precise date and audience, and indeed must be to be fully understood; month-by-month Puritan history is often an essential clue. In writing or speaking, Quakers rarely stressed their divine authority to proclaim timeless doctrines or eternal ethical commands. To such the Spirit would eventually lead the hearers directly if each responded individually to the Quaker summons to the Light. Without such a turning to the Light, men would hold even true doctrines only as ideas or "notions," mental possessions but not testimonies of experience.

Hence the earliest and most central and authoritative form of Quaker writing was the *tract of proclamation*, usually a message of warning or appeal to a particular group and situation. An analysis

10 Luella Wright faithfully hunted out poems, essays, maxims, and other Quaker writings of conventional genres (chs. 9-12), and some are worth noting (see also p. 437 of this volume); yet most such styles (e.g., aphorisms) emerge late and atypically in early Quaker life. Often such works (e.g., biographies) are best understood not in conventional terms but in their roles in Quaker communities.

of all early Quaker writings, as listed in the Appendix: Types of Quaker Writings,[11] shows that up to 1660 about 341 out of 1094 took the form of prophetic proclamations. Some were to individuals, some to a town or community, some to soldiers or merchants or other vocational groups, some to the government in all its echelons, some to all England. They grew over the years from a few lines to a hundred or more pages. The longer and more reflective works were mostly written in prison or enforced retirement, and they, too, had specific targets. Often a proclamation tract was only written at all because a verbal message had been rejected or had been impossible to deliver.[12]

As an agent of truth, not simply of power, the Spirit was expected to be consistent as it showed specific desires and habits as good or evil within and guided men to concrete outward acts and words. Yet early Quaker preachers insisted on the infallibility of the Spirit within them, not to defend doctrines but to warn their hearers lest they doubt the Quakers' judgment proclaimed against them personally. Even the Day of the Lord, which Friends proclaimed from the top of Pendle Hill or Cader Idris and in many a marketplace, was not a future date prophetically forecast. It was the individual hearer's "Day of Visitation," which in each case meant today. Friends applied Judgment Day imagery to the heart. There would indeed be a physical Day of Fire for those whose hardened heart or "seared conscience" made inner purging impossible; yet Friends never assumed that any hearer was already hopelessly reprobate. Friends shared the Christian hope for cosmic restoration as a future event but had no clear picture of how the Quakers' own state might then change, except that the saints would then rule the earth. For the Quaker who had been through the inner fires, the Day of Judgment was already past. To new hearers it was often announced that by sending the Quaker preacher the Spirit had thereby made this their Day of Visitation. Such seeming arrogance may explain why Friends were angrily accused of blasphemy in claiming to be indwelt by Christ's Spirit. Yet this intense, immediate "nowness" of each moment of decision has

---

11 Smith, *Descriptive Catalogue* (Smith also edited the *Bibliotheca Anti-Quakeriana* [London, 1873]); Whiting, *Catalogue of Friends' Books;* and Donald Wing, *Short-Title Catalogue.*

12 Cf. Samuel Fisher, *To the Parliament* (1659), afterward printed in his *Works* (*The Testimony of Truth Exalted*, 1679), pp. 25ff.

been taken by Rudolf Bultmann and Douglas Steere as the essence of Jesus' ethic.[13]

Friends kept their awareness that the future fulfillment of the kingdom was genuinely future by seeing the seeming weakness of the Spirit in the present. Quakers had known inner suffering in their submission to the Light, and they expected physical suffering from those against whom they witnessed. They said more about bearing the Cross than about standing in its debt: it is the "old Adam" as well as the new who must be crucified in the present age. At times Friends seemed to glory in suffering as a sign that the conflict of good against evil was taking place. (Fortunately their joy in the physical world as "the Creation" kept them from dualism.) But for this reason it is not easy to separate the *tract of testimony to suffering* from other kinds of proclamation by word or tract. Clearly these, too, were meant to reach the hearts of the hearers in a way that would challenge pride. Like Quaker speech and dress, they were part of the total assault by which the Spirit, through the Friends, would bring the world to submission.

Other narratives were often part of a proclamation tract: a summary of the Quaker writer's previous effort to warn the addressee, the events of his call to do so. The framework could include all of world—or at least Commonwealth—history. The story of the Massachusetts martyrs, for instance, shows that proclamation and history cannot be separated in the earliest Quaker writing. The Quaker proclamation tracts, though often short and rarely republished, represent the heart of the movement. They were among the most compact and incisive statements of the Quaker world-view and shaped the other Quaker genres of writing.

The Quaker journal evolved out of the autobiographical elements in these proclamation tracts. Such accounts served to authenticate the preacher; they also showed his readers what they might expect and to what they might attain. Quakerism demanded a protracted struggle, and the individual in the midst of it might find comfort even in the long narratives of soul-searching. Unlike most Puritan conversion narratives full of gratitude for free grace, Friends told matter-of-factly what happened in a process that was still continuing. The journal developed into devotional or travelogue literature only later, when Quaker journals came to be

---

[13] Rudolf Bultmann, *Jesus and the Word* (New York: Scribner's, 1958); Douglas Steere, *On Being Present Where You Are* (Wallingford, Pa.: Pendle Hill Pamphlet No. 151).

written mainly for Quaker readers and "convincement" into Quakerism required fewer struggles of will. Even then, as was true of biblical histories and the Acts of the Apostles, the telling of the past acts of God was relevant because of the assurance that he was still acting. Fox's own role here as recorder and as letter-gatherer was crucial. Apart from the influence of his own journals, we will see his initiative in collecting accounts of "miracles" and "judgments" on persecutors, and in prompting local Meetings to send in reports on their beginnings and on sufferings.[14]

Friends were neither surprised nor deflected by hostility, persecution, or outright violence. Since their inner experience had focused on struggle, they expected the pride and self-will of other men, too, to resist the Light fiercely when it confronted them through a Quaker preacher. We noted the tone of onslaught in proclaiming "Visitation." Fox would tell a hearer, "To the Light in thy conscience I appeal . . . thou child of the devil . . . which will witness me eternaly and thee condemne."[15] Hence the Quaker *theological tracts* were often polemic in mood. They were often defenses, too. Friends had attacked the parish pastors for their compromises with evil and externalism, and they in return had to parry the Puritans' doctrinal charges. Friends felt that for the honor of Truth every attack must be answered. Many a verbal argument developed into a *debate in print*, continuing through two or three rounds on each side (see p. 262). The historian of theology feels frustrated that creative expositions of Quaker thought appear so late in the first generation's writing and, except for Robert Barclay's and Penn's books, were so little read. Yet the characteristic Quaker doctrinal tract throughout the first fifty years was a debate or refutation, often phrase by phrase, of a Puritan's attack. Except for an occasional overall apologia to demonstrate Quakers' Christian orthodoxy, the key issues were the doctrines on which Puritans called Friends unsound, not necessarily the heart of Quakerism. As a basis of doctrinal authority Friends borrowed the Puritans' reliance on biblical texts and even on classical authors. Even so the debate often touched fundamentals, as when Quakers appealed to the Puritans' own witness to the inner and ethical work of Christ and the Spirit. This kind of debate appeared from the very start of Quakerism (cf. pp. 251 and 575) and reappeared in every interval between periods of

14 See p. 57 on *First Publishers of Truth.*
15 Fox, *CJ*, I, 90, 99.

intense persecution until it died away about 1720. Some were long tracts: Fox's *Great Mistery* (1659) and Samuel Fisher's *Rusticus and Academicos* (1660) were over 750 folio pages each, and such writings form the largest volume in the collected works of Penn, Penington, and Nayler. Yet they rarely varied from the pattern of sentence-by-sentence reply.

To group the Quaker *tracts on ethical "testimonies"* topically thus cuts across other groupings, the genres or forms of writing. Some tracts of prophetic warning or proclamation focused on specific ethical issues involved in their addressee's lifework. Some Quaker epistles within the fellowship also centered on such issues. Yet in the early years each ethical issue must be seen as part of Friends' total assault on evil in men's hearts, whether expressed through attack on a specific evil or through commending the Quaker way. Quaker dress and language, for instance, were more concerned with challenging men's pride than with achieving social equality for its own sake. Luxury in dress or furniture showed pride of status first of all, only secondly the economic exploitation of the poor. Quakers seldom cared whether other men adopted their ethical customs unless they sprang from total inner submission to the Light. Just for this reason, few early Quaker ethical tracts stuck to a single issue. It is fairly common for early prophetic messages to spend a paragraph apiece on each of the main social evils as they reflected the individual heart's evil.

The issue of *toleration*, however, and to some extent the linked issues of nonviolence and rejection of parish churches, parsons, and forced tithes, drove Friends to a more systematic type of thought and writing. They had to frame arguments that would appeal not only to their persecutors' consciences for eventual conversion, but to specific common beliefs and assumptions that even a cavalier judge might meanwhile share with Friends. This was somewhat a new experience for Friends, and early statements were often naive, groping, or narrow, and later ones dangerously broad, in defining the bases of the claim for toleration. Yet just because Quakers had not begun from dogmatism, rationalism, or naturalism, their answers to the problems of violence and freedom were more creative than those of other besieged nonconformists or strife-weary scholars. The combination of inner experience and universal expectation was still the source of Quaker vitality in approaching each new area or issue.

Quakers wrote letters before they wrote *epistles*. We will show how notes between traveling Quaker preachers were built up into

31

ENGLAND IN 1660
WITH PARTS OF SCOTLAND
AND IRELAND

Centers of Puritan
Strength – 1600-60
in CAPITALS

Centers of Quaker
Strength – 1650-60
underlined

Aberdeen

Dundee

Perth

Dunbar

Edinburgh

Glasgow

Berwick

LONDONDERRY

Newcastle

BELFAST

Carlisle

Durham

Lurgan

Pardshaw

Isle of
Man

Kendal

Richmond

Cavan

Ulverston
(Swarthmoor
Hall)

Sedbergh

Malton

Settle

YORK

Drogheda

Skipton

Preston

Wakefield

HULL

DUBLIN

BOLTON

MANCHESTER

Doncaster
(Balby)

LIVERPOOL

WARRINGTON

SHEFFIELD

Lincoln

Chester

Mansfield

WREXHAM

Derby

BOSTON

Swannington

Nottingham

LYNN

Shrewsbury

Litchfield

Waterford

Wexford

Leicester

NORWICH

(Birmingham)

PETERBOROUGH

HUNTINGDON

ELY

KIDDERMINSTER

CAMBRIDGE

Worcester

NORTHAMPTON

BEDFORD

IPSWICH

Ross

Evesham

COLCHESTER

GLOUCESTER

HERTFORD

Pembroke

Nailsworth

Oxford

ST. ALBANS

CHELMSFORD

Cardiff

LONDON

BRISTOL

READING

KINGSTON

ROCHESTER

CHATHAM

Canterbury

Winchester

DOVER

Bridport

Poole

EXETER

Launceston

St. Austell

Plymouth

Land's End

0   50   100 MILES

followed, and continued through the summer of 1653. This was the year of Cromwell's "Parliament of Saints," the peak period of radical Puritan hopes, despite angry mobs and vindictive Royalist Justices of the Peace. Friends then were safe from the national government. In an environment polarized but often cordial, Quakerism flourished throughout the Northwest.

In the summer of 1654, probably responding to letters from individual Friends who had been to London, sixty-odd newly established Quaker men and women went out in apostolic pairs to carry the movement to the rest of Britain (see p. 84). Fox and Nayler stayed for a time in the North, and the younger preachers found a curiously uneven but usually hostile reception in the old Puritan parishes of southeast England and in Presbyterian Scotland. Among former Baptists and Separatists, especially in London and Bristol, and in the western counties that had been little touched by previous religious fervor, mass meetings again developed, and strong little groups were "convinced" to become permanent Meetings and to press together toward transformation by the Light. Late in the year, a meeting of the wandering "ministers" that Fox had called together seems to have agreed to report regularly by letters to Swarthmoor Hall, whence a fund collected at Kendal (cf. p. 474) could be sent out for their special needs. Friends still submitted each new campaign and each step individually to the Spirit's leading; how well coordination and spontaneity interacted was shown in the Massachusetts campaigns and in the Irish trip of Burrough and Howgill in 1655 (see p. 476).

Most of the early Quaker leaders had been yeomen or craftsmen, as had Fox and Nayler and the Yorkshiremen. In the Northwest, Camm and Audland, Burrough, Howgill, and Hubberthorne were at most prosperous local farmers, and half a dozen of the sixty itinerants of 1654 were household servants. The northwestern Quakers of social prominence, Gervase Benson and Margaret Fell of Swarthmoor, stayed at home for the time being. In the South, however, along with weavers and tradesmen, the Quakers opened contact with men much closer to public life: George Bishop and John Crook in Puritan politics, the families of the printers Calvert and Simmons, and the country gentlemen Penington, Ellwood, and later Penn.[18] Thus while some of the north-

18 The only really thorough study of Friends' economic and social backgrounds is the analysis of Buckinghamshire, Norfolk, and Norwich in southeast England by Richard Vann: *The Social Development of English Quakerism*, ch. II.

country Quakers began idealistic but often fruitless expeditions across Europe, certain of these better-educated southern Friends, notably Stubbs and Ames, began quiet but effective work in Holland.

In 1656, Nayler and Fox, who had come south to reinforce the steadily growing work in London and Bristol, felt drawn into the west country, and in Devon and Cornwall they ran into a storm of opposition. Long and exhausting imprisonments there left Fox, Nayler, and other Quakers bitter and divided just at the moment when some of Nayler's wilder women followers persuaded him to reenact at Bristol, in honor of the inner Christ, the Palm Sunday ride into Jerusalem. Nayler's resulting trial for blasphemy was carried all the way to Parliament. National opinion was turning conservative, and Cromwell himself had to bow to it in part. Despite Nayler's courage under unearned and savage mutilation and imprisonment, he had brought national disgrace upon the Quaker movement. For the next four years, English Friends turned increasingly to the srengthening of their local Meetings, and carried out their preaching missions mainly overseas. In the pastorless backwoods of Virginia and the Carolinas and the Chesapeake inlets of Maryland, little Quaker groups formed which often dominated the neighborhood.[19] Rhode Island, and Long Island beyond the Dutch claims around Nieuw Amsterdam, were also outside the effective control of New England and became Quaker refuges. Puritan Massachusetts and Connecticut, however, had been set up at great cost to all their committed settlers as biblical commonwealths. Individualists were consigned to Providence and the Narragansett Indians, and all Quakers and Anabaptists were given "free liberty to stay away." The barriers aroused the consciences of some dozens of Friends in England and the colonies, whose coordinated efforts to break them down finally succeeded at the cost of four lives (cf. p. 136). The Quaker onslaught and the simultaneous collapse of the English Puritan Commonwealth in 1660 broke the Boston Puritans' spirit.

In 1658 Cromwell had died, leaving power in the hands of the officers in his Council of State and of his well-meaning son Richard. Oliver's patient policy, balancing and protecting the various Puritan and other factions against each other, was more than these men could achieve or in many cases wished to achieve.

[19] Kenneth Carroll, *Quakerism on the Eastern Shore* (Maryland Historical Society, 1970).

The Council, led by its more radical officers such as Lambert, overcame the conservative Puritan Parliament and forced Richard Cromwell's resignation. It recalled the "Rump" of the "Long Parliament" of the 1640's, led now by Sir Harry Vane, and finally clashed with them, too. So long as the government moved in the direction of radicalism and thereby toward greater toleration, Friends thought they saw "the hand of God in all these overturnings" (cf. p. 395), but other Englishmen saw simply military coups and chaos. Conservative Puritans began secret negotiations with the son of Charles I, already in Holland claiming his title as Charles II, by which he would be restored to the throne, and a national church broad enough to include Presbyterians as well as bishops would be established, with some toleration outside it. When General Monk, commanding the Cromwellian garrison in Scotland, marched south in support of the scheme, the opposing radicals evaporated. 1659 had been a dramatic year.

Charles II probably meant to keep the agreement he had announced at the Declaration of Breda, but the Presbyterians awoke with horror to find two successive Parliaments ("Restoration" and "Cavalier") packed with the previously silenced and dispossessed Royalist country squires, thirsty for Puritan blood. Of toleration there was now no hope, and within the restored Church of England the Act of Uniformity would allow only ministers pledged to use the full episcopalian liturgy. By 1662 some two thousand Puritan pastors had left or been ejected from their parish pulpits, taking many followers. With brutal shrewdness the Parliament aimed at them the whole "Clarendon Code": a Conventicle Act that forbade even prayer meetings outside the established Church (an aristocratic student, William Penn, was expelled from Oxford for this); Corporation and Test Acts that closed to the Puritans all posts in city or national government, the army, and the universities; and even a Five Mile Act to exile the Puritan pastors from their former flocks.

Meanwhile a wild plot by a fanatical circle of Puritan radicals, the "Fifth Monarchists," had drawn the government's vengeance not only upon them and upon the survivors of the "Rump" that had killed Charles I, but also upon the Quakers. Friends' refusal on biblical grounds to swear, even for the Oath of Allegiance, made outlaws out of every Quaker, from Margaret Fell to the poorest shepherd anxious to validate his marriage and his son's inheritance rights. Even before the Clarendon Code a special "Quaker Act" ensured that for the next twenty-five years all the Quaker leaders would be in prison more than they were free. By 1670 Nayler and Hubberthorne, Howgill and Burrough, Camm and Audland, Will Ames and Will Caton had died in prison or from its effects. Before the storm was over, about 450 Friends died among the eleven to fifteen thousand jailed.[20] Newly won Friends such as William Penn and Thomas Ellwood were swept into Bridewell or Newgate prisons along with whole Quaker congregations. Crammed by dozens or hundreds into small rooms, they had only what food and bedding the fee-hungry jailors would let relatives bring in.

Friends had always expected opposition and anger against the onslaught of the Spirit against pride. Violence they had understood as the devil's diversion, by which evil men were distracted from conquering the true evil within themselves. Friends seldom were either surprised by physical violence or tempted to it. In the last days of the Commonwealth the radical Puritan government had appealed to Friends to serve as Commissioners of the Militia to forestall Royalist plots. Though so much of English hopes and history hung in the balance, Friends had refused (with a few doubtful exceptions). Already in 1660, Fox and Margaret Fell had each gathered groups of leading Friends to reassure the new Restoration government that the Spirit within them in its self-consistency could be relied on never to lead Friends to outward violence or rebellion (cf. p. 405). Since Friends had not given up nonviolent resistance to the church laws nor their confidence that through their movement the Spirit would yet conquer the world, the Anglicans at first gave no truce. Parliament made Charles II rescind his two efforts to allow limited toleration by his Declaration of Indulgence of 1672 and an earlier more informal pause between the First and Second Conventicle Acts, 1667-70.

The English people at large, however, had learned the deeper lesson. When the persecutions were renewed, the Quakers—like the Jehovah's Witnesses in our day—felt a growing popular sympathy. Under persecution the Puritans had lain low and met secretly, producing only a few visible prison martyrs like Baxter and Alleine,[21] but the Friends had continued to hold their public Meetings for Worship as a witness to the world. In Reading their

[20] Cf. John Whiting, *Persecution Exposed*, p. 33; William C. Braithwaite, *The Second Period of Quakerism* (Cambridge: Cambridge Univ. Press, 1919 and 1961), p. 115.

[21] Cf. Gerald R. Cragg, *Puritanism in the Period of the Great Persecution* (Cambridge: Cambridge Univ. Press, 1957); and Harry Grant Plum, *Restoration Puritanism* (Chapel Hill: Univ. of North Carolina Press, 1943).

children (exempt under the Conventicle Act) continued the Meeting during their imprisonment. The Second Conventicle Act's harsher penalties often could not be enforced; neither could old-style riot acts, as the jury's response showed in the Penn-Meade trial. Hence the government switched to ruinous fines and deportation, reinforced by paid informers. In the end the fines drove many Friends from their farms to cities or the colonies, and a few to bankruptcy. Informers and deportation to America, on the other hand, were so unpopular with the public that these tactics largely failed.

After 1675 there arose against the Royalists a "Whig" political party that depended on Puritan votes and the toleration issue, though it was led by Church of England members. Penn worked for them, risking his own and the Quakers' reputation. The Whigs, though they dominated one brief Parliament and worked toward power in others, refused to make common cause on toleration with the king and the Catholics, whom they suspected of intending to use toleration as a stepping-stone to power and persecution: French Protestants were just then losing all the rights granted them in the previous century by the hard-won Edict of Nantes, and Charles II of England was half French and a secret Catholic. The king was driven back into the arms of the French king and the Anglican "Tories" in Parliament, and the Whigs suffered. Both parties became involved in plots and blunders, and the last years of Charles II's reign saw as many Quakers as ever in prison. Political persecution could be as deadly as religious persecution, but it did not divide Friends from their neighbors.

Charles II died in 1685, and his brother and successor, the Duke of York now become James II, announced himself for toleration. William Penn, who had worked with him through the previous decade for the charters of New Jersey and Pennsylvania, was one of the few Englishmen who believed he meant it permanently: James II was an open Catholic. In 1688 James achieved a blunder that his brother had never made: he sired a legitimate son, who would inevitably have become a Catholic king, too, some day. Whigs and Tories united in instant and bloodless revolution and replaced James with his Protestant daughter Mary and her husband and cousin, William of Orange, leader of Holland's struggle against Catholic France. Within a year Parliament passed a Toleration Act that allowed full freedom of worship. The established parish church system remained, of course, with bishops and liturgy unchanged, and kept its monopoly of the right to enter government, the army, and the universities. The Quakers remained free "on their good behavior," for the Toleration Act had to be renewed annually. Friends' right to use affirmations instead of oaths was not legally validated until 1722.

During the decades of conflict, Friends had gradually shifted their goals from the call to share in Christ's kingdom to a call to maintain the standards and freedom of God's little flock, and from the conquest of all human evil and the transforming of England to achieving toleration and purity of life. Once they had achieved these goals, they aimed at respectability and a low profile (silhouettes of the era show an increasingly rounded one). Friends passed on to the Whigs much of their tradition of wholehearted but nonviolent political struggle, and on this attitude of "loyal opposition" the workability of a two-party political system rests. In the reign of Queen Anne, Mary's sister and successor from 1702 to 1714, the ability of Whigs and Tories to relinquish power to each other without executions or revolutions was bitterly strained. Yet the loyalty of both groups to the new king, George I, in face of the attempt of James's son, "the Old Pretender," to regain the throne in 1715, showed that the new spirit had taken root.

Except in the colonies, Friends had meanwhile largely withdrawn from political life. The Quaker community became an end in itself. Quaker dress and speech had originally been part of Friends' total assault on all status as a bulwark of human pride, part of the campaign to bring all men to submit to the Light. But each "testimony" was also seen as Truth and as a leading of the Spirit, often undergirded with scripture. For instance, refusal to say "your humble servant" to strangers, and to say "you" instead of "thee" and "thou" to individuals of social standing, were both correct grammar and true to human equality, quite apart from their shock value to the propriety of the proud. Under persecution, Friends maintained such "testimonies" doggedly, in loyalty to the Spirit and also to the Spirit-led fellowship. Friends encouraged uniformity in refusing tithes and oaths by getting all members in an area to sign joint statements.

When the persecution ended, this group loyalty continued. Styles and customs of dress and speech had meanwhile changed. "Thee" and "thou" were decreasingly used toward anyone but children. Quaker dress had simply been "working-class Puritan," but there were no more Puritans. Quaker ways that had once been marks of honesty and simplicity had now become merely the badges of a "peculiar people," a special sect.

40

Those who admired Quaker ways and worship and wished to join the "Society of Friends" were accepted, as were the children of Friends, but missionary journeys became rarer, and some who undertook them, like George Keith, ended up outside Quakerism. The inner struggle to submit to the Light still took place, but more quietly, and not always on first entering the Quaker community. Worship after 1700 reflected "quietism," a drastic setting aside of any word or thought that could be linked to self-will or reason, and Friends remained partly isolated from the rationalism that dominated eighteenth-century religion. But their Meetings were often in total silence for months on end. Whatever messages were given there were chanted—and thus sharply distinct from ordinary speech.

A few Friends, like John Woolman in the New Jersey taverns, still reached out to non-Quakers. On ethical issues that were new "testimonies" and had played less crucial roles in the Quakers' struggle for identity, appeals to the public at large were as keen as those on toleration had been, and the same kind of limited argument was used. Slavery, war, and mistreatment of the insane seemed contrary to the conscience of all humanity, not simply to the Quaker Light. Friends had established their role as "reformists," as lobbyists for ethical issues; yet in the process a split had opened between what could be argued for universally and the supposedly absolute, Spirit-led Quaker "Truth." Even among Friends, the work for the wider social causes was at times taken up as a "testimony" bound upon the conscience of all Friends, as when in 1757 John Woolman persuaded the Philadelphia Yearly Meeting that the whole Quaker community must clear its stand regarding slavery. Yet often it was individual Friends who were left to carry such concerns to the outside world.

After thirty years of struggle, Quakers in 1688 were weary. The survivors among the original leaders—Fox, Crisp, Dewsbury, and Burnyeat, and also Richard Richardson—were all to die within four years. Except for Penn and Barclay (both busy with estates and colonies), the new leaders were much quieter men: George Whitehead, Thomas Ellwood, Ellis Hookes, and Thomas Lower all made their marks mainly as "clerks," organizing and overseeing business affairs for the Quaker community as a whole and crystallizing and recording the groups' decisions.

Quaker organization, as will be shown in the last section of this volume, owed more than any other aspect of the movement to George Fox. He had attempted to coordinate, without overruling,

41

the various leadings Friends had felt about mission trips in the earliest days and the spontaneous forming of Meetings. In the process of arranging for the printing of the tracts Quakers felt led to write, he arranged that the London Friends who saw the manuscripts through the printers' hands would screen the tracts, edit them, and distribute them to Friends throughout England. As persecution intensified, individuals whose ideas or actions seemed to discredit Quakerism were formally "disowned" before society, though the men misled were not "handed over to Satan" spiritually. The repentant, after a statement for the public's benefit, were restored.

The authority such "disowning" implied on the part of Quaker leaders and groups was not unchallenged. Fox's own effort to devolve such responsibilities on local Meetings collectively, and in particular his efforts to separate Men's and Women's Meetings for business, were targets for the more individualistic Friends, notably John Perrot, John Wilkinson, and John Story. The protesters in the 1660's and 1670's, however, were visibly less responsible than Fox's faction, both for meeting the needs of Friends in trouble and for sharing their stand under persecution. In order to regulate Friends' marriages and burials and inheritance rights and to establish which attenders in Meeting held valid claims for aid in prison or poverty or for educating their children, Friends moved toward formal recognition of local Quaker *groups*, since many leaders were dead or in prison. Apart from consultations of leaders and mass rallies, the earliest Quaker organization on regional and national levels grew out of the physical needs of imprisoned Friends. The projects of Kendal, Swarthmoor, and London Friends were concentrated and regularized in the "Meeting for Sufferings" and the Monday or "Second Day Morning Meetings." These eventually took on a representative character. The formal gathering of the London Yearly Meeting and of "Quarterly Meetings" on roughly a country-wide basis had been preceded by less business-centered gatherings of all Friends within a region—in New England, Carolina, Maryland, and Virginia and, as their settlements developed after 1680, in Philadelphia and adjacent New Jersey. In gathering all these groups Fox took a hand, at least by letters of advice, but there was never a formal charter of organization. Friends have always insisted on the key role for Christian life of the fellowship of "Children of Light," but have never seen the church in terms of organization; and "gospel order" existed only as a channel for the Spirit. Friends have always been free to make and to "lay down" organizations, service committees, and even forms of worship, as they found they were led. Once again, however, the need for unity and uniformity under persecution created a loyalty to established patterns that after 1689 froze the names and patterns of Quaker organizations. As with worship and the "testimonies," Quaker business meetings kept their basic dependence on the leading of the Spirit, now expressed in the group collectively, now in the summing up of "the sense of the Meetings" from the interweaving and coordinating of the fragmentary leadings of all its members. But the price, once again, was often relative inactivity by Friends as a whole where a common sense of the Spirit's leading was not felt.

In the same way, Quaker documents arose from the keeping of informal records of experiences inward and outward, especially of how the Spirit reached out to new groups, and of Friends' suffering under persecution. Fox again played a key role in collecting these. Such collective or collected works are the Quaker documents that come closest to being official: books of Yearly Meetings' advices, queries, and epistles and resulting "Books of Discipline" to guide local Meetings, Besse's *Collection of the Sufferings*, and the officially authorized editions of the collected works of each major Quaker. In such projects, the leading Friends such as Ellwood and Whitehead appear as the editors. But there has never been a canon of authoritative Quaker writings.

The first fifteen years after the Toleration Act of 1689 saw a renewed burst of theological debate by pamphlet. Even in the intervals of the persecution years this had continued, and Friends such as Penn and Penington had replied to barrages from all sides, from Anglicans to Baptists, including final salvos from Baxter and the orthodox Puritans. Some of these anti-Quaker writers, such as Anglican Charles Leslie, continued after 1689 their attacks on the Quaker "snake in the grass," and were answered with equal venom. A new group of debaters were ex-Quakers Charles Pennyman, Francis Bugg, William Rogers, and later George Keith himself, who spent much of their time thereafter writing thundering tracts against Friends. Much of this tract literature, and the Quaker replies to it, despite vivid titles, is repetitive and nowadays uninteresting, though some specific criticisms, for instance of early Quaker Christology, deserve to be taken seriously. Fox and Penn felt increasingly obliged to stress the orthodoxy of Friends regard-

43

ing the Christian credal doctrines: Fox's letter to the Governor of Barbados has been used as a key document among Evangelical Friends since the 1880's.

Most of this controversy died away in the early decades of the eighteenth century, as we pass beyond the period of this volume. Friends' respectability was established, and their lives were relatively quiet. English Friends, who had evidently declined in both wealth and social status during the persecution decades, began to recover prosperity and at the same time to cluster more closely together, moving to towns or overseas colonies with viable Quaker communities.[22] Intermarriage among Quakers had already been long expected for the sake of the children's practice of the Quaker testimonies. The resulting concentration of social and business interactions within Quaker circles became for a while almost inescapable, until increasing Quaker respectability made outsiders more regularly seek them out. Quaker schools, except for Waltham Abbey School and day-schools in local Meetinghouses, also belong to the latter half of the eighteenth century, when Quaker communities were larger and richer and apprenticeship was no longer enough education. (Early Meetinghouses themselves had suffered so much pillage in persecutions that they had legally been listed as the property of individuals; the oldest Meetinghouses now found belong to the 1680's.) These, too, fostered the tendency of Friends to cluster and become ingrown.

American Friends felt two pulls more strongly than English Quakerism. On the one hand, the backwoods frontier homestead was so isolated that each Quaker family had to be more self-sufficient and any neighbor, Quaker or not, was welcome. In the end, as settlements grew, thorough mixing of the Quaker and non-Quaker communities often resulted. Worldliness and wealth were not synonymous, nor did poor rural Quakers give up their Meetings; but many drifted out of Quakerism, and others unconsciously picked up the dress, modes of worship, and theological expressions of their neighbors. On the other hand, Friends settled in Pennsylvania, West Jersey, and parts of New York State by communities. Though Swedes and Dutch were already there, and German Mennonites and Brethren settled alongside them,[23]

---

[22] Cf. Vann, *Social Development*; and Frederick B. Tolles, *Meeting-House and Counting House* (Chapel Hill: Univ. of North Carolina Press, 1948).

[23] Cf. Donald F. Durnbaugh, "Relationships of the Brethren with the Mennonites and Quakers, 1708-1865," *Church History*, XXXV (March,

Friends were the dominant social and political group, as nowhere else except for a brief period in Rhode Island and Carolina. Even political conflicts in Pennsylvania tended to be between Quaker groups, notably between the poorer farmsteaders under David Lloyd and the wealthy families of Penn's coterie, "The Free Society of Traders" and the Logans. By the 1750's, however, when English and Irish Friends were more secure in their own identity through their schools and business enterprises, and were reentering the non-Quaker world vigorously, Pennsylvania Quakers found the outside world thrust upon them as their power waned. No longer a majority in their own colonies, Quakers found that their friendly and fair policies with the Indians and French still kept them in mediating roles. After somewhat humiliating efforts to compromise—since every colonial government was answerable to the London ministries—Friends largely withdrew from politics, though perhaps not as suddenly and totally as was once thought.[24]

So it was mainly in the second half of the eighteenth century that east-coast American Friends made the turn toward quietism and mysticism that had occurred in England some decades earlier as a defense of the authority of the Spirit against rationalism and worldly power. Except where frontier life kept them in the mainstream, American Friends were equally slow to emerge from isolated Quaker-community perspectives. The American Revolution overclouded the social status of Quakers, who refused to fight on either side, but after 1800 the Friends of Philadelphia, Boston, New York, and Baltimore were increasingly pulled into the marketplace and the literary society, and into the evangelical and social concerns of their business associates. They found the eastern rural Meetings much less ready to follow their new, wider interests than were English Friends in a similar position. Harsh use of leaders' authority helped bring on the "Hicksite" and later "Wilburite" splits of 1827 and 1845. The rural followers of Elias Hicks kept much of both the isolationism and the social radicalism of early Friends, along with the mysticism, quietism, and unacknowledged rationalism that had grown on them in their seventy-five years of

1966), 35-59; and Gary B. Nash, *Quakers and Politics: Pennsylvania, 1681-1726* (Princeton: Princeton Univ. Press, 1968).

24 Cf. Isaac Sharpless, *A Quaker Experiment in Government* (Philadelphia, 1902); and in reply Richard Bauman, *For the Reputation of Truth: Politics, Religion and Conflict among the Pennsylvania Quakers, 1750-1800* (Baltimore: Johns Hopkins, 1971).

45

self-sufficient Quaker life. The "orthodox," though they may have picked up their Bible-centered theology and their dress-styles from their non-Quaker neighbors, found unexpected allies in the Quakers of the small-town Midwest: both "orthodox" groups had maintained the early Quaker concern with world and national history and the call to live with and serve all men. Both also emphasized the common Christian doctrines that Fox and early Friends had kept since boyhood but had not stressed. The split has continued until today: the "orthodox" in the Friends United Meeting and the Evangelical Friends Alliance have intensified their evangelicalism and have moved still more fully into the mainstream of Protestantism in accepting pastors, programed worship services, and revival meetings. The "Hicksites" of the Friends General Conference have become a haven for theological liberals in university communities who are drawn by Quaker openness to ethical issues and inner experience.

Thus the problems of combining inner experience with a dynamic understanding of world history and God's work in it have remained near the heart of Quakerism from the earliest writings represented here until our day. Some radical ethical challenges, such as the needs of runaway slaves and American Indians, of refugees after two world wars, and of Friends' own peace testimony during them, have reunited the branches of Quakerism and reminded all the branches of their common roots. Theological confrontation has begun to lead to a larger unity.

PART A:

Tracts to Proclaim
the Day of Visitation

Introduction

Quaker writing began with short, urgent prophetic messages. The oldest surviving Quaker documents seem to be a group of hand-written notes sent from Derby jail in 1650-51. One is a letter from Fox's fellow-prisoner and fellow-member of the Mansfield separatist group, Elizabeth Hooton, to the magistrate, Noah Bullock, who had imprisoned them (cf. p. 381). Another seems to be Fox's own "fair copy" of that letter, a rare case when Fox's spelling and writing are better than another Quaker's (cf. Illustration facing p. 383). Two notes in his own handwriting Fox later identified only as "to professors" (cf. p. 55). All of these are messages of personal warning and calls for repentance to resisters of Fox's mission.[1] The oldest Quaker printed tracts seem to be those from Thomas Aldam and his fellow-prisoners in York Castle, 1652-53 (cf. p. 358); they are similar in aim and tone. We may assume that they also closely parallel the spoken Quaker messages in the same period. Fox's notes in his *Journal* and other summaries of sermons (cf. p. 80) from the early mass meetings carry similar tones of urgency and warning.

Friends' spoken messages, being prompted by the inner voice of Christ or the Spirit, were seldom written down beforehand, unless the Quaker could not leave prison to deliver it. Occasionally, part of the "leading" itself was to print and "give out" a broadsheet, for instance at the door of Parliament.[2] Nevertheless a "procla-

---

[1] Source for these facts and for Quaker research generally is the *Annual Catalogue of George Fox's Papers Compiled in 1694-97,* as edited, identified, and supplemented by Henry J. Cadbury (lithoprinted at Ann Arbor, Mich., by Edwards Bros.), 1939.

[2] Cf. Samuel Fisher, *To the Parliament* (1659), afterward reprinted in his *Works, The Testimony of Truth Exalted* (1679), pp. 25ff.

Fox preaching against the "bloody city of Lichfield" (*from lithograph by Robert Spence; used by permission*)

mation tract" addressed as "A Warning from the Lord to the Inhabitants of Underbarrow" (1654) or as "The Visitation of the Rebellious Nation of Ireland, And a Warning from the Lord proclaimed to all the Inhabitants thereof" (1656) may represent an actual sermon as later expanded; supporting evidence is that their author, Edward Burrough, had in each case just left the distant area named when the tract was published in London.

Except where God is clearly the speaker in a Quaker tract, we can rarely tell how much the writer felt his words came verbatim from the Spirit. The message clearly did, as the Quakers experienced it. That early Friends did not themselves clearly understand such prophetic experiences is shown by Fox's puzzlement, even afterward, at having been commanded to "cry woe to the bloody city of Lichfield"[3] just after his release from Derby jail, and also by the journals of Crisp and Banks presented in this volume. That

3 Fox, *CJ*, I, 15.

Lichfield cathedral today (*from photograph by Hugh Barbour*)

a modern post-Freudian might ascribe some impulses out of sub-conscious depths to human rather than divine sources is also evident. To one brought up in Puritan England, the very thought of "going naked for a sign" to warn a wicked city against its "spiritual nakedness" would horrify his self-esteem and would have clear biblical models (cf. Isa. 20:2-3); hence a Friend like Robert Barclay would find his own resistance to the impulse the clearest proof that he must go.[4] Yet it was also the frequent discovery of Fox and other Friends that in a message they had felt impelled to give they had unknowingly "spoken to the condition" of a hearer almost miraculously. Though these prophetic leadings may seem closer to psychotic "compulsions" than to mystical meditations, their substance was often a message of truth. Perhaps we must simply accept the early Friends' certainty that the inner voice was divine as one of the facts in these cases, and respond personally however we are able. These Quakers and all experiential Christians accept risks of self-deception in opting for the obedience of faith.

The typical Quaker message was one of judgment, and this earned Friends a reputation for being "sour," especially during the backlash from Puritan earnestness of the Restoration years. A "tract of proclamation" would begin with general wrath but would then list the special points at which the hearer's faults grieved God, and might include a summary of the Quaker's efforts to warn the addressee personally. We have seen that the Quaker message was an attack on pride and self-will more total than any Puritan's. The essence of idolatry, as Luther, too, had said, was that a man should choose how he would conceive of God and how he would worship him. Men naturally like to believe that God has reason to love them. Hence Friends had almost nothing to say about love in their message to the world, for fear of any word that would cater to men's self-esteem. True love, they said, consists of honestly showing men as precisely as possible where they truly stand in God's eyes. Friends assumed that love between the brethren, and grateful awareness of God's love given in Jesus, would be discovered by their hearers for themselves once they had wholly submitted to the judgment.

Hence, as we saw, the target of a Quaker mission was usually the hearer's conscience. Though early Friends never considered

[4]Cf. Robert Barclay, *A Seasonable Warning to the Inhabitants of Aberdeen* (1672).

any man's conscience divine and recognized the social and personal forces that darkened and limited it, they did assume that it could become the Light's instrument. The ultimate disappointment for itinerant Friends, for instance on meeting Oliver Cromwell, came when they "could not fasten anything upon his conscience," since he seemed to "stumble at the Cross."[5]

Despite early Friends' greater perceptiveness and detail in spotlighting evils, their stirring up of their hearer's guilt may seem to twentieth-century folk to make their tracts too similar to terror-based forms of revivalism; the difference lay in the sense of hope and power. Within individuals, Christ would guide and move as well as judge and atone; throughout the world he would spread the Light and the kingdom. The hearer was called not so much to repentance as to self-surrender, not to obedience without first openness and waiting for Light. He was not called to turn inward to watch his own spiritual growth except as a preparation for his place in the ranks of a task force with a world mission. The intersection of inner experience and world-sweeping kingdom is the "Day of Visitation" that these tracts proclaim as judgment, call, and promise.

It is not easy to describe a single line of development in the style or form of Quaker prophetic tracts. Though most describe the whole compass of a pride-based life and call for surrender along the whole front, some of the earliest tracts (cf. p. 358) and many later ones (cf. p. 363) are so focused on single issues that they are best listed among ethical tracts; always the specific life-problems of the particular addressees are central. Among "proclamation tracts" we may notice two subgroups, each with its own line of growth.

The tracts of prophetic judgment became rarer and more strident after 1660. Some included visions or dreams of the future (cf. p. 141), but others were mainly thunder and woe with few targeted lightning bolts except upon persecutors. After 1672, as some recent studies have shown,[6] the "Morning Meeting" in

[5] Cf. Swarthmore Manuscripts (hereafter SMS) 3:34, Anthony Pearson to Margaret Fell, July, 1654. Catalogued as No. 70 in *Early Quaker Letters* (hereafter *EQL*, ed. Geoffrey F. Nuttall); also the A. R. Barclay Manuscript (hereafter ARBMS) No. 20, March, 1654, from Camm and Howgill (see p. 384).

[6] Arnold Lloyd, *Quaker Social History, 1669-1783* (London: Longmans, Green, 1950), ch. 11; Wright, *Literary Life*, chs. VI and VIII; Vann, *Social Development*, pp. 214-15.

London screened out the most lurid prophecies of doom before they saw print; some of these were nevertheless given orally.[7]

Secondly, the persuasive appeal, the tract that called men to decision by reminding them of their spiritual needs more than by judgment, became increasingly common. It became typical of Nayler's later writings, such as *The Lamb's War* (cf. p. 104), and many works of Penn and Penington. Howgill early and Barclay later combined this mood with theological argumentation from the context of debates to produce the best of Friends' few systematic doctrinal treatises. Fox's own first published tract, *To All That Would Know the Way to the Kingdom* (1653 or 1654), is this kind of appeal to seekers, yet begins and end with warning and call.

In the General Introduction, it was shown that two other genres of Quaker tract may conveniently be grouped with "proclamation tracts," with which they often overlapped in style and function—though these also overlap with journals and autobiography.

The *record of sufferings* had in each case a specific and limited aim, as well as to convince the hostile and witness to God's power in his faithful saints. Records of sufferings were closely related to formal group petitions and individual appeals to rulers (cf. p. 385), and to general tracts concerning toleration. Some of these records of persecution, with the letters and messages included in them, played crucial historical roles in breaking down persecution in Boston, and later in England itself, by popular demand or outside pressures on the governments. Other lists were used by already sympathetic governments, notably Cromwell's and Vane's, to ensure the release of individual Quakers imprisoned by local magistrates. After 1680, the detailed collecting of cases of sufferings, originally compiled for political reasons, was continued for the sake of encouraging new and wavering Friends and became a kind of devotional literature, just as happened also to autobiography.

The *general historical narrative*, by which Fox (and occasionally Penn and other Friends) characteristically summed up the Acts of the Spirit through the Quaker apostles, also has its roots in the prophetic proclamation, which often describes in single paragraphs (cf. p. 93) the call and mission of "the Camp of the Lord in England." Some of these survey-narratives, like Penn's "Rise and Progress," were written to preface journals; some as separate

---

[7] Cf. Russell Mortimer, "A Guide to the Administrative Records of the Society of Friends in Bristol, 1669-1869" (Thesis, University of London, 1937).

histories of Friends (e.g., Croese's and Sewel's). Some collections of specialized narratives (e.g., collections of "miracles," "examples," and "passages" or voyages"), which were never printed, have recently been studied by Henry J. Cadbury.[8]

Thus we find again that the printed tracts and broadsides of prophetic proclamation can never be separated from spoken preaching, and have included in this section three accounts, one by a non-Friend, of Quaker preachers in action.

1. Fox's Message to a Professing Puritan (SMS 7:173), probably written in 1650 and among the oldest surviving Quaker documents. A good sample of Quaker prophetic messages—short, intense, personal:

O friend, Thou that preachest Christ and the scriptures in words: when any cometh to follow that which thou hath spoken, and to live the life of the scriptures, and doth not live their lives according, doth persecute them that doth mind the prophets and apostles and Jesus Christ and all the holy men of God. What they spake was from the life, and they that had it not, but words, persecuted and prisoned and bondaged them that lived the life they backslid from. [endorsed on verso] G. ff. to priests and professors, an old epistle.

2. Local Memories of Quaker Beginnings in Northwestern England (1652-54)

Quakerism emerged as a distinct and powerful movement when George Fox turned northward from Mansfield, Notts, in the summer of 1651 and drew around him from the separatist groups in Yorkshire the most effective of his fellow-preachers, James Nayler and William Dewsbury, along with Farnworth, Aldam, and others. As the group preached through Yorkshire that summer and the next, and especially when they reached the dales of Westmorland, Cumberland, and Furness in 1652, mass meetings became common. Separatist congregations still formed the nucleus, notably on Firbank Fell, but large groups of previously untouched yeomen

[8] Henry J. Cadbury, *Narrative Papers of George Fox* (Richmond, Ind.: Friends United Press, 1972).

and shepherds first found active religious life through the movement.

Except for the events described, Quaker historiography does not really belong so early in our story. After the full-grown Quaker movement had begun to fulfill its early sense of a unique role in history, but also had lost a majority of its early leaders, who died in prison in the early 1660's, Fox's feeling that a new "Acts of the Apostles" would be needed led him to ask for local reports:

Friends,

All my dear friends everywhere who have been moved of the Lord God to speak in steeplehouses, to priests or markets or fairs, or courts or assizes or towns, for all to be drawn up together in a book in every county & sent up to London & put together in one book standing to generations with all the words that you spoke in the power of God. So this would be a book that would fasten over all & stand as before to generations that they might see their testimony, and what strength God did ordain out of the mouths of babes and sucklings, & what Friends have been moved to go to sectary meetings, & so that they may not be lost, those pure motions, & with all the examples that have fallen upon the persecutors, & so to every Quarterly Meeting you may bring them.

Such Friends that be deceased, such some may remember, that so the testimony of the Lord may not be lost, that he raised up in his people by which they were carried on through great tribulations & sufferings: many laid down their lives & their goods spoiled & they persecuted to death, to keep up their testimony what the Lord moved them to speak forth by the power may not be lost. And they that cannot write ye may help them to write so that the power & spirit may be exalted; so the account may be taken of that which hath been spoken & done by the Spirit of God from the first, as above mentioned, & so if you be but diligent & those that can write help them, this may easily be done.

The 1st, 11th month, 1669.   G.ff.

Clear evidence of direct response to Fox's plea is lacking,[9] but similar pleas were made at the Yearly Meetings of 1676 and 1680

---

[9] Instead, the impending passage of the Second Conventicle Act seems to have led Friends to assemble lists of sufferings and imprisonments, as had been done in 1660, for Parliament; this time they reported that eight thousand Quakers had been imprisoned under the Restoration government, of whom 173 had died and 138 been banished (C. E. Whiting, *Studies in English Puritanism*, 1931, p. 136).

and by the Meeting for Sufferings in 1682. As the few survivors of the first Quaker generation also began to disappear in 1720, Benjamin Bealing, the first clerk of the Yearly Meeting, again asked each county and, where possible, each local Meeting to record its beginnings in Quakerism, and coordinated the resulting manuscripts. Under his title of *The First Publishers of Truth*, these manuscripts finally saw print in 1907, as edited by Norman Penney of London, the most important single scholar in the assembling of Quaker source materials. From these materials is reproduced here the story of the crucial outburst of Quakerism in 1652 in Yorkshire, Westmorland, and Furness, to set alongside the record in Fox's *Journal* and the anti-Quaker record that follows.

[The report from the oldest Yorkshire Meetings]

It appears by the accounts within our Monthly Meeting belonging Brighouse, as followeth:

That about the year 1651, George Fox came to a place called Wood Kirk, near Leeds (accompanied with Willm. Dewsbury), and preached truth in the steeple house (whereat the priest raged, and threatened putting them in the stocks). The same day, Richard Farnworth preached Truth amongst some high professors at Tong. Several were convinced by the above said friends. William also preached Truth at Leeds, and meetings were settled thereabouts; William also preached Truth at Halifax and a meeting was settled there. Also that Wm. Dewsbury and Thomas Taylor severally, about the years 1652 or 1653, came to Christopher Taylor, a priest of a chapel, called Chapel in the Briars, betwixt Brighouse and Halifax, who was convinced of the Truth, and bore testimony to it, and was instrumental in settling a meeting at Bradford; also one was settled at Brighouse. And that Thomas Goodaire and Thomas Taylor preached Truth about Mankinholes, where a meeting was settled. In the year 1657, we find that Dan'l Thackra, of Holdback, was by John Dawson and Martin Iles, of Leeds, Aldermen, sent to the House of Correction in Wakefield for witnessing the kingdom of heaven is within, and was at Leeds Session fined ten shillings, and afterwards sent by Wm. Fenton, and John Payton, John Davison, and said Martin Iles, to York jail.

In Luke the 17th and 21st may be seen the blindness of those Leeds magistrates.

The 9th of the 11th month, 1704.

[From Kelk Monthly Meeting in the moorland of northeastern Yorkshire]

In the year 1651, George Fox was ordered first into these parts, and came to Cranswick, where Richard Pursglove received him. There he abode some time, and preached the Gospel unto the people. Afterwards, in the first month, called March, 1651/2, he came to Ulrome, and was received by George Hartas, and tarried about six days, preaching the Truth and publishing the Gospel of glad tidings to many that came to see and hear him; and many were convinced of the Truth while he was there, and were made to bless the Lord who sent his servant and faithful labourer to turn the minds of people from darkness to light and from the power of Satan to the true and living God. From thence he passed towards the east parts of Holderness.

Now though many were convinced and did believe the Truth, and divers did no longer join with the priests of the world in their public worship, yet we had no settled or appointed meetings, but on the first days of the week it was the manner of some of us to go to some town where were friendly people, and there sit together, and sometimes confer one with another of the dealings of the Lord with us.

In the latter end of the eighth month of the same year, William Dewsbury was moved to come into these parts, and travelled much from town to town, sounding the trumpet of the Lord. His testimony was piercing and very powerful, so as the Earth shook before him, the mountain did melt at the power of the Lord, which exceedingly, in a wonderful manner, broke forth in these days in our holy assemblies, to the renting of many hearts, and bringing divers to witness the same state, measurably, as the prophet or servant of the Lord did in ancient times, whose lips quivered and belly shook, that he might rest in the day of trouble. Oh! It was a glorious day, in which the Lord wonderfully appeared for the bringing down the lofty and high-minded, and exalting that of low degree. Many faces did gather paleness, and the stout hearted were made to bow, and strong oaks to bend before the Lord.

[From Selby Meeting, Yorkshire]

Dear Friends, unto whom these few lines may come, it is in my heart to give this small testimony concerning the breaking forth of this blessed Light and Truth in this our town of Selby.

Dear John Leake, and Ann, his wife, and Richard Tomlinson, and Elizabeth, his wife, (with whom I was then apprenticed), were the first convinced, and the first families which received the Lord's blessed messengers in the town at that day. And William Dewsbury was one of the first that came with a public testimony into the said town, who lodged at our house. And then the said Elizabeth Tomlinson was made to go out into the streets in the mighty power of the Lord, which carried her almost off her feet, and her testimony was, "Repent! Repent! for the day of the Lord is at hand. Woe to the crown of pride. Woe to the covetous professors. Woe to the drunkards of Ephraim," and struck a great astonishment in the people. And William Dewsbury was then a blessed instrument in the Lord's hand, of my convincement, who was wild and wanton at that day, though not outwardly profane, but without God in the world, as too many are at this day; and the power of God was mightily upon William, and fixing his eyes upon me, declared what the Lord put into his mouth to me in particular, and I did truly witness the word of the Lord to be quick and powerful, which cut me to the heart, that I fell down in the house floor as dead to all appearance as any clog or stone. When I came to sense again, he had got me up in his arms (it was about the year 1652); so that I can truly say I was smitten down to the ground by the living power of the Lord, as surely as ever Saul was, in his way to Damascus, and my beastial will at that time got a deadly wound that through the loving kindness of the Lord was never healed to this day. Although I had a time of halting betwixt God and the world, yet a cry was raised (almost continually) in my heart, "Oh! that men would praise the Lord for his goodness, and magnify him for his wonders amongst the sons of men; what is man that thou art so mindful of him, or the sons of men that thou visitest them," and I can truly say that the Lord's time was a time of love, for his love was so shed abroad in the hearts of his gathered, that overcame all the love of this world, and made a clear separation (as people of another nation), not only from the friendships, fashions, and customs, and worships of the world, but in a large measure from the spirit of it. And although at that day we were scoffed and scorned, and not only so, but beaten, and stoned, and hailed to prisons, the Lord did administer a suitable support, which carried over all with cheerfulness in what exercise soever. And I can further testify that the Holy Ghost was showered down upon the meetings of the Lord's people at that day, as sure as ever it was at Jerusalem when the cloven tongues did appear, and many were made to utter things in a wonderful manner that they were altogether strangers to, and some there were that did things by imitation, which I have seen to fall away as untimely fruit.

And now having a living sense of those things upon my heart, and being both in eye and ear witness of them, I was desirous to commit them to writing, although with a shaking hand, and leave the perusal and disposal of them as in the wisdom of God you may see meet. And it is the desire of my heart that the Lord may have the glory of his own works, who alone is worthy forever, and remain

your loving friend in a measure of Truth,

George Canby
Selby, the 8th day of the 7th month, 1704.

[From Sedbergh Monthly Meeting: Concerning Fox's arrival in the Northwest]

In the beginning of the year 1652, he came into the northwest part of Yorkshire, into the dales and hilly country there, and particularly to the house of Richard Robinson, at Brigflats, near the town of Sedbergh in Yorkshire, near the borders of Westmorland, upon the seventh day of the week, in the latter end of the third month, or beginning of the fourth, being the day called Whitsuneve. And the said Richard Robinson received him and his testimony in great love, with whom G. F. lodged that night. And the morrow, being the first day of the week, he and the said R. R. went to a meeting of religious people separated from the common national worship, at the house of Gervase Benson, at Borrat, near Sedbergh aforesaid, who some time before had been commissary in the archdeaconry of Richmond in the diocese of Chester, but those courts being laid aside in the late domestic wars, in which he became a soldier, and was advanced to the place of a colonel, so then bore the name of Colonel Benson, and was also then justice of peace in the county of Westmorland, and some time before had been mayor of the town of Kendal. At whose house there was a great meeting from several adjacent places, both of Yorkshire and Westmorland, in which meeting G. F. did powerfully preach the Gospel of the kingdom, which had an entrance into, and reception by many hearts there. And the said Gervase Benson and his wife were convinced, and gladly received him into their house, and the said Richard Robinson, and Major Bousfield, Thomas Blaykling and wife, their son, John Blaykling, and wife, all of Draw-well, near Sedbergh, Joseph Bains, of Strangerthwait in Westmorland, and many others, who several of them afterwards received him joyfully into their houses, and believed in the Truth by him preached, and became obedient to the same, and lived and died faithful witnesses and faithful testimony bearers thereto, who are all now dead, except Joseph Bains.

Upon the 4th day of the same week, being a fair at the town of Sedbergh, commonly called Whitsun Wednesday, where the said G. F. powerfully declared Truth in the steeple house yard, and although some opposed him, yet many received his testimony, and were convinced and turned to the way of Truth. After which, G. F. went to the house of Thomas Blaykling and John Blaykling, his son at Draw-well aforesaid, who gladly and in great love received him. And upon the first day following, G. F., being accompanied with the said John Blaykling, went to Firbank Chapel, where F. Howgill and John Audland preached in the forenoon to a seeking and religious people there separated from the common way of national worship. The said G. F. bore till they had done, and when the meeting broke up, gave notice of a meeting afternoon the same day intended, hard by the said chapel; whither many did resort, and then and there the said G. F. was opened in a living testimony by the word of life to the reaching God's witness in many hearts, and the said J. A. was then fully convinced of the Truth, with many more.

And the said J. A. invited G. F. to his house, at Crosslands in Westmorland, whither he came the second or third day of the same week, and J. A., and his wife, Ann, joyfully received him into their house. And on the fourth day morning, came with G. F. to the house of John Camm, at Camsgill in Preston Patrick, who with his wife and family gladly received G. F.

[From *Lancaster Quarterly Meeting Minutebook*, ed. Henry J. Cadbury: on Swarthmoor Meeting]

G. F. was the first that brought the message of glad tidings unto us and first preached the everlasting Gospel at Swarthmoor again being Judge Fell's house, and upon the fifth day of the week in the fifth month 1652, he went to Ulverston steeplehouse, it being their Easter day, and there he preached the Gospel in the mighty power of God saying that he was not a Jew that was one outwards; nor that was not circumcision which was outwards in the flesh; but he is a Jew that is one inwards and it is the true circumcision which is in the heart by the Spirit; that he continued preaching the Gospel for some time, till he was haled out of the steeplehouse. And on the first day of the week following he went to Dalton steeplehouse and he preached the Gospel. And on the second day of the week following he went to Dendron Chapel and there preached the Gospel and at Auldenham steeplehouse and Rampside Chapel and at Walney Island, and at several other places of worship he went upon the first days and Easter days to preach the Gospel as aforesaid.

Margaret Fell then the wife of Judge Fell was the first in Lancaster named aforesaid that received George Fox and the rest, and the joyful message and the Gospel of peace and of reconciliation again unto God; by Christ Jesus the light of the world who hath enlightened every man that cometh into the world. Unto which light of Christ they were turned and in which they believed and M. F. aforesaid and her seven daughters and most of their servants, and Thomas Salthouse, Will Caton, Leonard Fell, Mary Askew, Anne Clayton, and others received the Gospel and most of them became able ministers thereof unto others soon after. Also James Lancaster of the Island of Walney, and Thos. Hutton of Rampside and Richard Myers and Thomas Goade of Beakliffe all of low Furness aforesaid, received G. F. and the Gospel preached again by him. And Thomas Lawson priest of Rampside Chapel hearing that G. F. had been at Auldenham steeplehouse, the first day aforesaid in the morning said to his congregation when their forenoon sermon was ended that he was credibly informed that G. F. purposed to be at their Chapel the afternoon unto whom he purposed to resign his place; the said Thomas Lawson went a mile to meet the said G. F. and conducted him to his chapel at Rampside aforesaid and offered him his pulpit to preach in, which the said G. F. refused, but stood up on a form, and livingly declared and held forth the way of salvation to the people for about three hours' space; and when he came forth into the yard, some of the people would have laid violent hands on him, but the said Thos. Lawson forbade them, saying he was greatly satisfied with G. F.'s preaching; and said if our worship and doctrine cannot be maintained without fear and violence, 'tis time to leave it. So the people were quieted and an old woman aged 80 years said she never heard such good doctrine out of the mouth of any black coat all the days of her life. And the said Thos. Lawson soon after laid down his public ministry, being satisfied that the call of man made not a minister of Christ.

G. F. after he had preached the Gospel at Ulverston steeplehouse as aforesaid at which time he was only haled out the second time when he came upon a lecture day, one John Sawrey, then called a justice of peace, called to the officers and rude multitude to have him out, and after they had pulled him out into the yard the said Jo. Sawrey cried "away with him," whereupon the rude multitude fell upon him, and beat him with forks and staffs and threw stones at him, thrusting, pulling and pushing him till they had haled him to the common or moss side and then they knocked him down with clubs and staffs. But the said G. F. soon got up again and held forth his hands to the people exhorting them to more sobriety and one of the rude multitude struck him over the back of the hand with a long cut staff and wounded and bruised him so sorely that his fingers felt as if they were broken, and his arms and other parts of his body remained black with the blows, knocks and bruises for many days after. And several other Friends that were with G. F. and accompanied him were beaten also. And Thos. Salthouse had his head broken and one William Pool's head was broken; and James Lancaster's cloak was pulled off his back and torn in pieces; and several other Friends were beaten and bruised at the same time. And in their fury and madness they threw Judge Fell's only son George Fell into the water, who only stood by the Friends that were so abused. And when some Friends would have had G. F. to have gone away to Swarthmoor on the back side of the town aforesaid, the said G. F. refused to do (it), but came back again through the town and market then held. And when the rude multitude saw him, they cried "A Fox, a Fox", and began to be rude again; but there was a soldier, one Leonard Pearson, who having seen or heard these former barbarous usages of him, drew his sword and said "let me see whether any dog in the market dare catch this Fox," whereupon G. F. passed quietly through the market, none daring then to lay violent hands on him, and so he went up to Swarthmoor. And sometime after, G. F., with James Nayler, went to the Island of Walney to preach the Gospel. And then James Lancaster fetched them out in a boat, and they had no sooner landed upon the island but the inhabitants came with clubs and staffs of purpose to have destroyed G. F., and fell upon him and knocked him down. And the said James Lancaster, seeing their cruelty and wicked intentions, lay along upon G. F. to save him from their blows, crying out bitterly, "What, will you kill this good man that came in love to your souls?" And they pushed at him with pitchforks and poles and the women threw stones at him when they could find or spy a place bare to hit him and miss the aforesaid Ja. Lancaster that lay upon him to defend him from their blows and stones. And at last they pulled James Lancaster by the leg to get him off him, and so sprained one of his thighs in pulling of him, as he felt the strain and hurts thereof a long time after. And then the said James Lancaster desired to let them go with their lives, and they should take all he had amongst them. And then G. F. got up, and they thrust him towards the sea with intent to have drowned him. And the boat which brought them over, being near, James Lancaster put G. F. into it and then threw it off into the water and they took up a fishing pole of the said James Lancaster about 6 or 7 yards long, and struck again at G. F. but missed him. And when they were got out of the reach of the pole, they again threw stones at them; and the said James Lancaster stood up betwixt G. F. and them to defend him from the stones, and some of the stones lit on James Lancaster's cheek and made it bleed; and then they rowed off by the seaside to seek for James Nayler, who had walked off into the island whilst they were beating G. F. as aforesaid, being unknown to them. But they after perceiving he was a Quaker also, they hunted him out, and fell upon him, and with clubs and staffs beat him sorely also. . . .

3. Early Friends in Puritan Eyes: Francis Higginson's *The Irreligion of the Northern Quakers* (1653)

The handful of dedicated Puritans in the wide parishes of northwestern England were inevitably more hardworking, anxious, and lonely than those elsewhere. They sought each others' support and that of the Puritan pastors and justices clustered around Newcastle and Manchester. Some had welcomed Quaker preachers into their back-country areas, only to find them tearing down, not supporting, their work. Being thoroughly exposed to the Quaker movement, these pastors could give a picture of its ways and beliefs more vivid and accurate than any of the later descriptions.

Francis Higginson returned to Europe for schooling after sailing as a boy of ten to Massachusetts Bay with his father, who had been called as a pastor with the first Puritan shiploads of 1629.

worship of God, to embrace their doctrines of devils, and follow their pernicious ways.

This sort of people are vulgarly, and not unaptly, distinguished from others by the name of Quakers, the reason of which appellation I shall show you hereafter.

Now to the end it may be as apparent as the day, that the guides of this sect, notwithstanding their fair pretensions of an immediate, and extraordinary mission, and the great opinion their deluded [2] followers have conceived of them, are not the servants of the Lord Jesus, but in very deed the emissaries and ministers of Satan, and that their way is not the good old way, the way of God, but as contrary to it as the darkness to the light, I shall take some pains to acquaint my reader,

1. With the cursed blasphemies which George Fox, Grand Master of the faction, and some others, have uttered.

2. With some of those doctrines of devils, damnable heresies, and dangerous errors, which their speakers have disseminated, and wherewith they have infected their unhappy disciples.

3. With the bitter and rotten fruits of their doctrine; such of their strange, impious, seditious, suspicious, insolent, and barbarous practices as have come to my knowledge; some of which do in the judgment of the most sober and intelligent Christians, strongly savor of sorcery, and the immediate cooperation of the devil.[16]

Of the horrid blasphemies of the Quakers against God and his Christ

George Fox, the father of the Quakers of these parts, hath avowed himself over and over to be equal with God; being asked by Doctor Marshall, in the presence of Master Sawro, Colonel Tell, and Colonel West, Justices of the Peace in the county of Lancashire, at a private session in the town of Lancaster,[17] whether or no he was equal with God, as he had before that time been heard to affirm; his answer was this, "I am equal with God."

This blasphemy hath been attested upon oath by the foresaid Doctor Marshall, and Master Altam,[18] schoolmaster of Lancaster, before the justices

16 On the linking of Quakerism and witchcraft see p. 269.

17 Thomas Fell, husband of Margaret Fell (later Fox) of Swarthmoor Hall, and John Sawrey were Puritan Justices of the Assize or circuit court for Lancashire and Cheshire, and took opposite stands in regard to Fox. Both had been members of the "Parliament of Saints," as had Colonel William West, Clerk of the Assize, who with Fell took Fox's side and refused to draw up a warrant of blasphemy (cf. Fox, *CJ,* pp. 408, 412; BBQ, p. 108).

18 On William Marshall, pastor at Lancaster, see Fox, *CJ,* I, 62-68, 412; on Michael Altham, see *ibid.,* I, 65.

at the last sessions, held at Appleby, January 8, 1652/ [53], and before Judge Puleston at the last assizes held at Lancaster, March 18, 1652/ [53].

This Fox, in a book entitled *Saul's Errand to Damascus*, endeavours to purge himself of this and other such cursed speeches laid to his charge, but he doth it so woodenly and ambiguously, that if there wanted sufficient witnesses, his own bungling answers would to a rational man declare him guilty.

[Two paragraphs omitted]

[3] At the last assizes above mentioned at Lancaster, Mr. Sawro, a Justice of the Peace in that county, and an honest gentleman, told Judge Puleston in the open court that he could produce many who would witness that Fox had affirmed himself to be the Christ. The same also he had said in the hearing of an honest minister in Westmorland, who will be ready to attest to it when called to it.

This Fox hath also professed himself to be the judge of the world. George Bickett, Adam Sands, Nathaniel Atkinson witness.[19] Yea, the eternal judge of the world: George Bickett witnesses.

[Four paragraphs of similar charges against Nayler and James Milner are omitted.]

[4] *Of the erroneous opinions of the Quakers.*

Hitherto of their blasphemies. Now for the doctrine which the leaders of this sect have avouched and taught, and the principles they have instilled into their credulous adherents. . . .

1. They hold that the holy scripture, the writings of the prophets, evangelists, and apostles, are not the word of God, and that there is no written word of God; but they say, using a foolish distinction of their own coining, that they are a declaration of the word only in those that have the faith.

2. They hold their own speakings are a declaration of the word (Christ) in them, thereby making them, though they be for the most part full of impiety and nonsense, to be of equal authority with the holy scriptures.

3. They hold that no exposition ought to be given of the holy scripture, and that all expounding of scripture is an adding to it, and that God will add to such a one all the plagues written in that book. Opening, and applying the scripture, is one thing they mainly declaim against, wherever they come.

4. They teach poor people that whosoever takes a text of scripture and makes a sermon of or from it is a conjurer, and that his preaching is conjuration.

[5] Fox, in his printed answer to this (*Saul's Errand*), page 7, says thus:

---

19 Adam Sandys was chief constable of Ulverston, a Puritan, and a gentleman; cf. *ibid.,* I, 406. About George Bickett and Nathaniel Atkinson no information is available.

All that study to raise a living thing out of a dead, to raise the spirit out of the letter, are conjurers, and draw points and reasons, and so speak a divination of their own brain. They are conjurers and diviners, and their teaching is from conjuration, which is not spoken from the mouth of the Lord, and the Lord is against all such, and who are of God are against all such. For their doctrine doth not profit the people at all, for it stands not in the counsel of God, but it is a doctrine of the devil, and draws people from God.

5. They affirm that the letter of the scripture is carnal.

6. That he that puts the letter for light is blind.

[The following twenty-two propositions attacked as Quaker doctrine mostly concern atonement and the afterlife.]

[7] 29. They hold that Fox and all the rest of their speakers are immediately called. *Saul's Errand*, p. 4, Fox says they were moved to come into these parts by the Lord, and the Lord let them see he had a people here before they came. Nayler also at the last sessions at Appleby, January 1652, affirmed in the face of the court, that when he was at plow in barley seed time, meditating on the things of God, he suddenly heard a voice commanding him to go out from his country, and from his father's house, and had a promise given with it. And being demanded whether he heard the voice, he said he heard it himself, but those who were with him heard it not. Being asked again whether it was an audible voice, he answered, "No, friend, it was not a carnal voice, audible to the outward ear." A little after, going on in his relation, he said that, going agateward, (they are his own words) with a friend from his own house, the voice came to him again, commanding him to go into the west, not telling him where he should go, or what he was to do there, but when he had been there a little while, it was given him what he was to declare.

If my reader please to be detained with another short story to this purpose, he shall have it.

Fox, with one or two other men, his companions, as I heard it, came to an honourable gentleman's house in Cumberland. One of the house came to them to the door to know their business. They asked if the gentleman of the house was within, calling him by his name, for they gave no title of respect to any man whatsoever; they were answered affirmatively. Being called in, the gentleman took them aside, to know what they would with him. They told him they were sent to him from God. He inquired of them how they certainly knew it. They answered that a voice came to them, commanding them to come to him. He asked them again where this voice came to them. They replied, T.F.'s [Thomas Fell's] garden in Lancashire. He demanded again what that voice commanded them to say to him. They answered it was not yet given in to them. [8] The gentleman then told them if they knew not what they had to say to him, he knew not what he had further to say to them. That night, being towards evening, they were entertained in that gentleman's house, and being desired by the servants to supper, they refused to eat, but called for a little water only. The next morning also they refused to eat anything, but offered to one of the servants money for their lodging. He told them they did not well to come thither to abuse his master, he kept no inn. In the return towards their old rendezvous a few miles from this gentleman's house, they called at a little alehouse that stands alone, where desiring the hostess to provide for their breakfast, they ate and drank heartily. The poor old woman told one of the aforesaid gentleman's servants that had occasion that way that two or three notable trenchermen had been at her house, who, inquiring what manner of men they were, knew them to be the same men that had been at his master's.

30. They deny all ordinances, and their practice is suitable to this their wicked tenet. An honest minister in Westmorland, discoursing with Fox, asked him whether he did believe prayer, preaching, the sacraments, meditation, holy conference to be ordinances of God. No, says he, away with them, I deny them all.

31. They call the worship of God used in our public assemblies a beastly worm-eaten form, a heathenish way; and worship fleshly, carnal, etc.

32. They hold that the sprinkling of infants is Antichristian, and their baptism the mark of the beast, spoken of in the Revelation, which those that worship the beast receive in their foreheads.

33. They affirm that there is not one word in scripture that speaks of a sacrament, and that they are unlawful; that a little bread and a little wine in a sacrament is the world's communion, and that in the true church of God there is no talk of such carnal things.

[The six propositions omitted here criticize the Quakers' rejection of singing Psalms, church-houses, and magistrates' authority.]

[10] 40. They are of the opinion that it is unlawful to call any man Master, or Sir.

41. They hold it unwarrantable to salute any man by the way.

42. They account it unlawful to use the civility of our language in speaking to a single person in the plural number. . . .

Of the wicked practices of the Quakers
and first of their meetings and speakings.

Hitherto of their errors that are come to our knowledge; I shall now go on to present my reader with a brief view of their black wicked practices, the natural fruits of such corrupt principles as are above mentioned. In doing of which I shall principally take notice of their meetings, speakings, quakings, fastings, revellings, censoriousness, lyings, inconstancy in their own opinions, enmity to learning, idleness, incivilities, bloody, barbarous, and turbulent practices, for their ways have not been altogether in the clouds, nor their deeds of darkness always done in corners.

[11] For the truth of this relation—let me say this much beforehand for the previous satisfaction of my reader—the particulars of it are most of them so notoriously known to the whole country where these degenerated people live, that no sober man can deny them. Many of them are, and will be owned by themselves, for they make some of these horrid practices hereafter mentioned a part of their religion, and glory in them. And there is, I think, few particulars contained in it which we shall want witnesses to attest, if need be, upon oath.

And first for their meetings, and the manner of them. They come together on the Lord's Days, or on other days of the week indifferently, at such times and places as their speakers or some other of them think fit. Their number is sometimes thirty, sometimes forty, or sixty, sometimes a hundred or two hundred in a swarm. The places of their meetings are, for the most part, such private houses as are most solitary and remote from neighbors, situated in dales and by-places. Sometimes the open fields, sometimes the top of a hill, or rocky hollow places, on the sides of mountains are the places of their rendezvous. In these their assemblies, for the most part they use no prayer, not in one meeting of ten. When they do, their praying devotion is so quickly cooled that when they have begun, a man can scarce tell to twenty before they have done. They have no singing of psalms, hymns, or spiritual songs— that is an abomination. No reading or exposition of holy scripture, this is also an abhorrency. No teaching or preaching—that is in their opinion the only thing that is needless. No administration of sacraments—with them there is no talk, they say, of such carnal things; not so much as any conference by way of question is allowed of: that which asks, they say, doth not know, and they call propounding of any question to them a tempting of others. They have only their own mode of speaking (that is all the worship I can hear of) which they do not call, but deny to be, preaching, nor indeed doth it deserve that more honourable name. If any of their chief speakers be among them, the rest give place to them; if absent, any of them speak that will pretend a revelation. Sometimes girls are vocal in their convent, while leading men are silent. Sometimes after they are congregated, there is (altum silentium) not a whisper among them for an hour or two or three together. This time they are waiting which of them [12] the Spirit shall come down upon in inspirations and give utterance to. Sometimes they only read the epistles of Fox and Nayler, which according to their principles are to them of as great authority as the epistles of Peter and Paul.

They exceedingly affect night meetings, which are usually of both sexes very lately, and not infrequently continued all night long. Their holies, they think, are best dispersed while others are asleep. These unseasonable dark assemblies of theirs, much like the night meetings of the Anabaptists in Münster,[20] which afterward proved fatal to that city, in a time of peace and liberty, considering the constitutions of the spirits of this people, have been in some places a just cause of affrightment to the neighboring inhabitants that are not of their way, who have professed they could scarcely sleep in their beds without fear.

These night meetings were therefore forbidden by the justices at the sessions at Appleby, January last, where one of them pleaded stiffly for this liberty of the subjects, as he called it.

For the manner of their speakings, their speaker for the most part uses the posture of standing, or sitting with his hat on, his countenance severe, his face downward, his eyes fixed mostly towards the earth, his hands and fingers expanded, continually striking gently on his breast. His beginning is without a text, abrupt and sudden to his hearers, his voice for the most part low, his sentences incoherent, hanging together like ropes of sand, very frequently full of impiety and horrid errors, and sometimes full of sudden pauses, his whole speech a mixed bundle of words and heap of nonsense. His continuance in speaking is sometimes short, sometimes very tedious, according to the paucity or plenty of his revelations. His admiring auditors who are of his way stand the while like men astonished, listening to every word, as though every word was oraculous, and so they believe them to be the very words and dictates of Christ speaking in him.

Sometimes some of them, men or women, will more like frantic people than modest teachers of the gospel, or like the prophets of Münster or John of Leyden's apostles, run through or stand in the streets or market place, or get upon a stone and cry "Repent, repent, woe, woe, the judge of the world has come, Christ is in you all, believe not your priests of Baal, they are liars, they delude you." Kendal, and many other towns in these northern [13] parts, are witnesses of these mad speakings and practices.

The matter of the most serious and ablest of their speakers is *quicquid in Buccam venerit,*[21] and for the most part of this nature. They exhort people to mind the light within, to hearken to the voice and follow the guide within

---

[20] At Münster in 1535 a community of hard-pressed German Anabaptists took over the city as a "new Jerusalem," under the rule of John of Leyden and other Dutch visionaries. During the bitter siege by the armies of the nobles and the Bishop of Münster they proclaimed community of property and even polygamy. Though bloodily crushed, they gave Anabaptism a "bolshevik" image that was used later to discredit all Separatists and radical Protestants.

[21] "Whatever comes into their mouth."

them, to dwell within, and not look forth, for that which looks forth tends to darkness. They tell them that the Lord is now coming to teach his people himself alone, that they have an unction and need not that any man should teach them; that all their teachers without, the priests of the world, do deceive them, away with them; that they speak the divination of their own brain, and everyone seeks for gain from his quarter; that they take tithes which are odious in the sight of the Lord; that they teach for lucre and the fleece, and live in pride, covetousness, envy, and in great houses; that they sit in the seat of the scribes and Pharisees, go in long robes, are called of men masters; that they scatter people, and delude them with notions of fleshly wisdom, and ways of worship according to their own wills, and not according to the mind of the Lord. They [i.e. Quakers] call them out of all false ways and worships and forms, and false ordinances—so they call all the ordinances of God used in our public assemblies. Such stuff as this all their speakings are, for the most part, stuffed with. Something also they speak of repentance, of living under the cross, against pride in apparel, and covetousness. But the main subject and design of their speakings is to inveigh against ministers and ordinances, to bring ignorant country people to hate or forsake them, to mind only their light within for teaching, which they tell them is sufficient to salvation.

[Paragraph omitted]

[14] If the devil himself (whose Mercuries these speakers of whom I am now speaking, are) could with his seductions prevail upon unstable souls but thus far, what would he desire more?

I have related in part what is, and will now tell you according to the best intelligence I could gain, what is not the subject of their speakings. I once heard Nayler speak awhile myself, I have inquired of divers who have been the auditors of others of them, I have read very many of their epistles and papers that are common in the country, which I think I can produce. I could never see, or hear, or learn, that they speak almost anything of the miserable estate of all men by nature, of Jesus Christ our redeemer, of his two natures, of the reality of his deity and humanity, of his office of mediatorship, especially of his sacerdotal office, of his meritorious death and resurrection, of the satisfaction he hath given to God for us, of his intercession for us, of remission of sins, and justification to life to be obtained through faith in his blood. . . .

[Paragraph omitted]

And for propagation of such their erroneous opinions as are heretofore recited, their speakers and others of their way, that have nothing else to do but follow them, wander from one parish and part of the country to another, sometimes ten or twenty, sometimes a whole troop of them together; and by their agents and letters which they send beforehand to those who are friends to their sect, or that they hear are opinionative, and addicted to novelties in religion, gather people together. And sometimes they are invited by such as hanker after their way. Where their places of meeting are, many resort, some out of curiosity to see their persons that are so famous, or infamous rather, in these parts for their [15] seductions, some itching to hear how and in what manner of doctrine they speak. In these conventions, they tell people they are sent from God to declare what he hath revealed in them, and begin such preachments as are above deciphered. Where this swarm hives, they are generally more chargeable in two or three nights than the payment of their tithes, which they so eagerly declaim against, would be in two or three years.

Of their quaking fits, and the manner of them.

Now for their quakings, one of the most immediate notable fruits and accidents of their speakings. Though their speakings be a very chaos of words and errors, yet very often while they are speaking, so strange is the effect of them in their unblest followers, that many of them, sometimes men, but more frequently women and children, fall into quaking fits. The manner of which is this: those in their assemblies who are taken with these fits fall suddenly down, as it were in a swoon, as though they were surprised with an epilepsy or apoplexy, and lie groveling on the earth, and struggling as it were for life, and sometimes more quietly as though they were departing. While the agony of the fit is upon them their lips quiver, their flesh and joints tremble, their bellies swell as though blown up with wind, they foam at the mouth, and sometimes purge as if they had taken physic. In this fit they continue sometimes an hour or two, sometimes longer, before they come to themselves again, and when it leaves them they roar out horribly with a voice greater than the voice of a man—the noise, those say that have heard it, is a very horrid fearful noise, and greater sometimes than any bull can make.

The speaker, when any of them falls in this fit, will say to the rest (that are sometimes astonished at this sight, especially if they are incipients), "Let them alone, trouble them not, the Spirit is now struggling with flesh, if the Spirit overcomes they will quickly come out of it again, though it is sorrow now, it will be joy in the morning," etc. And when they have said a few words to this effect, they go on with their speaking.

Sometimes they carry those wretched patients to beds, when [16] they are near them, and let them lie on them till their fit is over. These quakings they maintain (*Saul's Errand*, page 5) and in their books and papers call them the marvelous works of the Lord. . . .

[Paragraph omitted]

Some are of opinion that these quaking fits are mere feignings, but others look upon them as real passions. I hope my reader will not be displeased if I freely deliver my own opinion. In plain English, I do heartily believe these quakings to be diabolical raptures immediately proceeding from the power of

Satan, if not from his corporal possession, or obsession, of the parties so passive.

[Then follow three pages of argument distinguishing "divine and satanical trances."]

[18] George Fox, the ringleader of this sect, hath been and is vehemently suspected to be a sorcerer.

The presumptions of his wickedness in this kind are not weak. Some persons of good quality that came out of Nottinghamshire to Kendal told them of note in that town what pranks this Fox had [19] played and what disturbance he had caused in that county before he came into these more northern parts. With all he credibly reported to them a very strange story of the devil's discovering this Fox to be one of his vassals and agents, while he was there in a certain house together with many of his disciples, speaking to them. This accident he said caused many of his followers to desert both him and his wicked way, and principally procured this Fox's apprehension and imprisonment in Nottingham castle, till he ran away, and his keeper with him.[22]

It has been his custom in these parts to fix his eyes earnestly on such strangers as came into his company a good while together, as though he would look them through. If anyone please to look on him steadfastly again, it is his manner impudently to outstare them. His followers say he can outlook any man, and that he does it to know what is in them, but if there is such a thing as fascination by an evil eye, I should rather suspect him guilty of that than of any ability to discern the complexions of men's souls in their faces.

When such as have conceived of any liking of their way come to their meetings, or any young men or women or others are by their proselyted friends who desire to make them as bad as themselves, brought to hear him speak or discourse with him, it is another of his customs to talk and hold them awhile by the hand, and it is confidently reported that many he has thus handled, though some of them before their coming to him did exceedingly disaffect both him and his impieties even to hatred, and though they stayed but a while with him and heard nothing from him that might either morally persuade or rationally convince them of the evil of their former way, or of any greater excellency in his new way, yet so strangely have they been wrought upon and altered that they have been all on the sudden earnest, fierce, impetuous, in both for it and him, and do now much more violently affect his wicked religion than ever before they did distaste it. Such heady, fiery diverters of many men and women to their way makes sober Christians

---

[22] For Fox's own account of this episode, which involved an insane woman whom Fox later healed, see his *Journal* (Nickalls), pp. 42-43.

think that though there be nothing that is divine, either in it or the propagators of it, yet there is much diabolical attraction and art in both.

Many have professed that, having left their society after dislike of their ways, they have been for a while so distempered both in mind and body that their bodies have been all wet with sweat in [20] their beds, and they could not get a wink of sleep.

[Paragraph omitted]

Of their fastings

They use also fastings, which are sometimes prescribed by their speakers to their novices, and continued by those that observe them for many days together. But their fasts are, as the apostle calls, the humility of will-worshippers, a voluntary humility, not savouring of religion, not joined with prayer, but undertaken as a foolish imitation of the miraculous forty days' fasts of Moses, Elias, Christ, and the long three weeks' abstinence of Daniel, and three days' fast of the apostle Paul, and as is conceived for the procuring of revelations and inspirations, as they think, of the Spirit. [One tale of fasting omitted] But where are such ungodly murderous fasts as these prescribed in the Word? David George of Delft,[23] a blasphemous imposter, whom George Fox resembles as much as one egg another, had frequently his three days' fasts. The heathen priests in China use abstinence sometimes for thirty days together, to procure ability to prophesy. The savage Indians in New England who are trained up for powwows (so they call their wizards) use to fast many days before the devil appears to them, and they make their compact [21] with him. And some maids there are who know what St. Agnes' fast means; and Papists, we know, have their fasts as well as Quakers. All fasts are not holy fasts, some are superstitious, and some are diabolical. No more of them.

Of their railings.

They are also as horrible railers as ever any age brought forth, a generation whose mouths are full of bitterness, whose throats are open sepulchers, etc. The Billingsgate oyster-women are not comparable to them. It is ordinary with them in the letters they write to other men to call them fools, sots, hypocrites, vain men, beasts, blasphemers, murderers of the just. It is a customary thing with this gang of people in their discourse with others, to tell them they are dogs, heathen, etc. One of Kendal, going to the burial of a minister of his acquaintance, met a woman of the sect by the way, and asked her if she had seen the corpse go by. "I saw," says she, "a company of

23 David George or Joris was a "spiritual" Anabaptist who made apocalyptic prophecies. Cf. R. H. Bainton, *David Joris* (1937).

heathen go to bury a dead dog." Such language is common in the mouths of their principal speakers, and none more notorious this way than Fox, their prime oracle.

If any man in their meetings speaks anything in opposition to what they deliver, or asks questions wherein he desires to be satisfied, not agreeable to their humours, or manifests the least disrelish of what they say, it is enough to provoke such terms. To give one example, Nayler at a private meeting in Sedbergh asked an honest Christian, Samuel Handley, whether he was without sin or no? Handley replied he was a sinner. Hereupon Nayler called him a thief, a murderer, a Cain, and justified himself to be without sin.

[Paragraph omitted]

[22] They affirm that all the ministers in England who preach in steeple-houses are liars of Jesus Christ; they uphold the kingdom of Antichrist, that they do all for filthy lucre. . . .

They accuse them of being brought up at Oxford and Cambridge; they say, they know nothing but natural books and natural things, the scripture letter, Hebrew and Greek, which is all natural; that the ungodly, unholy, proud priests and professors must be scorned who know not the power of the word. Reader, I coin or add no expression of mine own, I repeat only their words, which such books and papers of theirs as I can produce are full of.

They apply all that is spoken to idolatrous, ignorant, profane persecuting priests, and false prophets, either in the Old or New Testament, to the ministers of England. . . . They exhort people not to hear them, to cease from them, and not to hold them up, and tell them they will never be profitted by them. . . .

[23] They say the Lord is coming to beat up their quarters, the son of thunder is coming abroad to sound trumpets, to call to battle against the great day of the Lord, and their kingdom must be taken from them, and that their downfall is near at hand. Some of them have said they hope within a year's time to see never a minister left in England.

[Paragraph omitted]

Reader, I do verily believe that if these wicked men had power in their hands, there would be no toleration of any true minister of Jesus Christ in England, and one of the first things they would endeavour would be, if not to raise a tempest of persecution by raining blood, yet at least to raise and extirpate the sacred callings, I say sacred calling of the ministry, being the institution of Jesus Christ in the church.

. . . They presume to take this liberty to themselves, because they are apt to conceive that ministers are now almost friendless, that [Cromwell's] authority will not appear for them [the pastors], and that they are the object of the wrath of divers soldiers in the army, whom they foolishly suppose to incline to their, as to them, unknown sect. But I hope, yea, I am confident, that . . . [24] those worthies that by divine Providence do or will sit at the stern to guide the ship of the Commonwealth, and the godly officers of the army, will not only disown and detest, but also manifest themselves to be enemies to all their impieties, and enormous practices, of this turbulent faction.

[Paragraph omitted]

[There follows here a section titled "Of their censoriousness, instability in their own errors, and enmity to learning."]

Of their idleness, savage incivilities, and their irreligious, bloody, barbarous, and turbulent practices.

To what has been hitherto related of their impieties and disorderly walkings, it may be added that they are many of them notorious for idleness in their callings, working not at all sometimes for whole weeks and months together.

Some of them leave their wives, children, families, vocations, and turn all journeyman speakers. Others, regardless of all at home, wander after them, compassing the country from place to place, and live upon those of their fraternity where they light, to their excessive charge.

[Paragraph omitted]

A son, if turned a Quaker, will not use the usual civility of the world that is Christian in putting off his hat to his father or mother, will give them no civil salutations.[24] To bid him goodmorrow that begat him, or farewell, that brought him forth, is with them accounted a wickedness.

None of the Quakers will give the common respects to magistrates, or to any friends or old acquaintances. If they meet them by the way, or any stranger, they will go or ride by them as if they were dumb, or as though they were beasts rather than men, not affording a salutation, or resaluting though themselves be saluted.[25]

They do not give any title or colour of respect to those who are their superiors in office, honour, estate—such as Master or Sir, etc., but call them by their naked name—Thomas, or William, or Gervase, or Dorothy, and ignorantly mistake it to be disagreeable to the word of truth.

They go to their meals for the most part like heathen, without any prayer or thanksgiving.

[29] When meat or drink is set on the table, the master of the house, if he is anything skillful in their way, invites none of his guests to it, but they fall to one after another, as their appetite serves them. When they go to bed,

24 See Thomas Ellwood's *History of the Life of T.E.* (1714), p. 76.

25 See William Penn, *Rise and Progress of . . . Quakers* (1694), also printed as preface to Fox's *Journal* (1694), ch. II, point § 8.

when they rise in the morning, when they depart from a house, they use no civil salutes, so that their departure and going aside to ease themselves are almost undistinguishable. It is the opinion of many honest men who have observed the ways of this society, that there are none professing Christianity more irreligious than they are, Ranters excepted.

[Paragraph omitted]

James Nayler . . . used only in his prayer three or four sentences, whereof this was one: "Oh, Lord," says he, "raise up thy Son from under corruption in us."

[Paragraph omitted]

It was a strange bold piece of impiety in George Fox in commanding a cripple in a place near Kendal to throw away his crutches, as though he had been invested with a power to work miracles, but the cripple remained a cripple still, and George Fox impudently discovered his own folly.

Many of them who had good clothes, as soon as they joined themselves to this sect, burned their bravery, and some of them, as one says, as a part of their first zeal, burned their Bibles.

[Four paragraphs on Quakers "going naked for a sign" omitted]

[30] One of their gang in Westmorland, on Friday the eighth of April last, ran like a mad man naked, all but his shirt, through Kendal, crying "Repent, repent, woe, woe, come out of Sodom, remember Lot's wife," with other such stuff. His principal auditors were a company of boys who followed him through the town. . . .

[Eleven paragraphs on pp. 30-31 omitted; most deal with a supposed attack of Quakers on Justice Burton, which actually sounds more like the work of highwaymen. "A Copy of a Scurrilous Paper affixed to the Church Door at Lancaster" concludes Higginson's text.]

4. Charles Marshall on the Bristol Mass Meetings of 1654-55, from his "Testimony Concerning John Camm and John Audland"; written as a preface for their collected works published as *The Memory of the Righteous Revived* (1689)

Despite the arrest and imprisonment of Nayler and Howgill, and the following summer of Fox at Carlisle, the Quaker movement continued almost unchecked through 1652 and 1653 in the English Northwest. The great sweep southward in 1654 began in London (see p. 84), but soon afterward and more decisively took hold in Bristol, then the second city of England, where within a few weeks thousands were meeting to hear Camm and Audland. Among those convinced were George Bishop (cf. p. 481), Barbara Blaugdone (cf. p. 479), Walter Clement, Josiah Coale, and Thomas Curtis of Reading as well as Charles Marshall himself. Howgill and Burrough took over from Camm and Audland in October, but the latter after a trip home to Westmorland returned in November and continued until after their strength gave out, Camm's in April and Audland's late in 1655. At the height of their meetings in September their letters to Burrough and Howgill, then still in London, reflect the same mood as Marshall's description:

E.B., F.H.   Bristol, this 13 day of 7 month . . .

We were yesterday 3 miles out of the town where we had a gallant meeting, above 500 people as they were numbered, and truly they were very pretty people as ever I saw since I came out of the north. The witness of God was raised in many of them, and much love did breathe out from them to usward. . . .

John Camm

Dear and precious brethren, our love & life is to you and with you. . . . Never such service were we in. Night & day we even labor & travail continually. We came into this city the 7 day of this month. We have every day a meeting. . . . We had a great meeting upon the 1st day in the morning. The house & all was filled, & the street. So the voice went forth for a field, . . . and we went to it like an army. My dear brother J.C. spoke. Then before he had done the Word of the Lord came to me, & when he had done I stood up, & all my bones smote together & I was like a drunken man because of the Lord. . . . Such a dreadful voice ran through me as I never felt before, and the terror of the Lord took hold upon many hearts, & the trumpet sounded throughout the city. The afternoon we met at the fort, where soldiers are, the greatest meeting that ever I saw. It far exceeded the greatest when I was with you. . . .

John Audland[26]

Charles Marshall's Testimony Concerning John Camm and John Audland

John Audland, with dear honourable John Camm, was instrumental in the hand of the Almighty God of our gatherings; and the spending of their lives and strength was most in their labours and travels among us, in the city, and

26 ARBMS § 157; cf. *JFHS*, L, 177-80. Cf. also BBQ, pp. 165-69.

adjacent parts, of which I was an eye and ear witness, being with them frequently. These two faithful ministers of Christ Jesus came to the city of Bristol, in the 5th Month 1654, and first they came among a seeking people,[27] who kept one day in the week in fasting prayer, waiting for, and breathing in spirit after the morning and visitation of God, and day of redemption. Among us they spoke the powerful Word of Life, in the dread of his Name that lives forever; and we were seized on, and smitten even to the heart; and that Day, and the visitation of it overtook us, which we had longed and waited for, and from darkness to the marvelous light of the Lord we were turned. Some meetings we had before the more general gathering in and about that city, which began on this wise: On a first day in the morning I went with these two servants of God, about a mile and a half from the city, to a little spring of water, where I often had spent many solitary hours in my tender years, seeking the Lord: where we sat some time, and drank of the spring. After some hours of the morning were spent, I saw in them a great travail in spirit. Trembling, J.A. said, "Let us be going into the city;" so we came to the street called Broadmead, to a house where were several people met together, inquiring after these two men of God. John Audland was under a great exercise of spirit and said, "Is anyone here who has an interest in any field?" An ancient man said, "I have, in a field pretty near." Notice being given to the people in the house, they came forth; and as we went along, people in the streets went also to the field called Earlsmead,[28] so that we came to a pretty number, where some seats or stools were brought. Dear John Camm began to speak tenderly, and in great zeal, directing to the heavenly grace of God, and testifying against sin and iniquity fervently; to which some were attentive in this season. I perceived a great exercise of spirit on my dear friend and father in Jesus Christ, John Audland, who very much trembled. After dear John Camm stood down, he stood up, full of dread and shining brightness on his countenance, lifted up his voice as a trumpet, and said, "I proclaim spiritual war with the inhabitants of the earth, who are in the fall and separation from God, and prophesy to the four winds of heaven." And these words dropped among the seed, and so went on in the mighty power of God Almighty, opening the way of life. But, ah! the seizings of souls and prickings at heart which attended that season; some fell on the ground, others crying out under the sense of opening their states, which indeed gave experimental knowledge of what is recorded, Acts 2:37. Indeed it was a notable day, worthy to be left on record, that our children may read, and tell

[27] Most of these separatist or seeker congregations broke up as their members became Friends, of course, or broke up at the Restoration, leaving no records. The records of the Broadmead Baptist Congregation have survived, however, from about 1655 onward.

[28] This may refer to joint ownership in a medieval-style "open field."

to their children, and theirs to another generation, that the worthy noble acts of the arm of God's salvation may be remembered, which have been the way of the Lord, leading his servants through generations, etc.

At this meeting many were effectually convinced, and from darkness to light turned, after which our meetings grew larger and larger. They visited the meetings of them called Independents, and Baptists, testifying among them in great power the things given them of God, directing the poor and needy in spirit, who saw their want of the Lord Jesus Christ, no longer to seek the living among the dead, but look from the mountains and hills dead ways and worships, unto Christ Jesus the foundation of life and salvation. And there was added unto the gathering daily, and great dread was round about, and in our meetings, under the seasonings of the Holy Ghost.

Oh, the tears, sighs, and groans, tremblings and mournings, in the sight of the middle wall of partition, that we saw then in our awakened states, that stood between us and the Lord, and in the sight and sense of our spiritual wants and necessities. Oh, the hungerings and thirstings of soul that attended daily, and great travails of spirit, to obtain through the working of the mighty power of God's dominion, and spiritual victory over the enemy of our souls, who has led us in the paths of death and darkness. Indeed, as the visits of God's holy and ever blessed day was signal and unexpressible, as aforesaid, so I testify in the fear and dread and awe of God Almighty, we received the gospel with a ready mind, and with broken hearts, and affected spirits; and gave up to follow the Lord fully, casting off the weights and burdens, and the sin that easily besets, and from the evil ways and vanities of this world departed. Oh, the strippings of all needless apparel, and the forsaking of superfluities in meats, drinks, and in the plain self denying path we walked, having the fear and dread of God on our souls, that we were afraid of offending in word or deed. Our words were few and savory, our apparel and houses plain, being stripped of superfluities; our countenances grave, and deportments weighty among those we had to do with. Indeed we were a plain, broken-hearted, contrite spirited, self-denying people; our souls being in an unexpressible travail to do all things well pleasing in the sight of God; for our great concern night and day was to obtain through Jesus Christ the great work of salvation, and thereby an assurance of the everlasting rest and Sabbath of our God. In those days, oh, the unexpressible labour, travels, and spending of the strength of all these servants of the most high God, in great assemblies in that city, and countries round about. Our meetings were so large that we were forced to meet without doors, and that in frost and snow; in which meetings, oh, the extending of voices of these servants of God, to reach over these great multitudes, when several thousands have been assembled together, and as the work of the Lord increased, so the enemy was at work in priests, and people, in those days, who stirred up the youth of the city into a

81

tumulting, like the men of Ephesus. Once we had a very great tumult that the streets were crowded, and these two servants of the Lord were seized upon by the multitude, and were in great hazard.

[One paragraph omitted]

And now, dear friends everywhere, but more particularly in and about the city of Bristol, who have seen the morning of the day of God break forth in our age, as aforesaid, and by the divine light thereof, have seen the darkness that has covered the people expelled, in which darkness people have been ignorant of the true and living God, and his precious work of salvation, in which ignorance they have performed their worship, even in the same nature that they are sinning and rebelling, and grieving the good spirit of God, which all ought to be subject to; now it pleasing the divine being, in his infinite love and tender pity and compassion to look down upon us, whilst in the land of Egypt, and house of bondage spiritually, and to send forth his light and truth, to give us a sense inwardly of the deplorable states of our souls in the separation from, and depravation of the enjoyments of the Lord, which sense and sight begat in us living breathings, and a holy cry after the knowledge of him we saw ourselves ignorant of; and he in the fullness of the dispensation of time visited us, as afore mentioned, of which, dear friends, we were right glad, although when the Lord discovered our states, he laid judgment to the line, and righteousness to the plummet, and gave to us the cup of trembling, in which was the wine of astonishment.

5. The Rise of London Quakerism: William Crouch's *Posthuma Christiana* (London, 1712)

Though appearing in print only after Crouch's death fifty-odd years later, his account is our only first-hand story (apart from letters to Swarthmoor and a report in *FPT*) of the first London Quakers. It may have been inevitable that London should become the eventual center of Friends, being already five times the size of Bristol and Norwich, the next biggest English cities, and a center of radical Puritanism and working-class preachers from Queen Elizabeth's day. Where so much happened daily in Parliament and the churches to catch the public eye, Friends did not arouse the immediate mass response that had turned out in Bristol and the Northwest. Yet within twenty years London had five Monthly Meetings (one per county was usual) and over a dozen Meetings for Worship each Sunday.

The need for a major preaching mission in London, such as Howgill and Burrough began, had presumably been seen by Howgill and Camm on their visit to Cromwell four months earlier (cf. p. 384). Yet for a year previously, Amor Stoddart, Isabel Buttery, and the Dring brothers had been shepherding Quaker tracts through their printing. Isabel Buttery and Captain Stoddart had encountered Friends near Nayler's South Yorkshire home (but perhaps only partly convinced; cf. p. 473). Crouch omits from his account the preaching of James Nayler in London in 1655 while Howgill and Burrough were in Ireland (cf. p. 476)—the high-water mark of Quaker impact in London, but the opening for results so tragic (cf. p. 480) that Crouch may mean to disown Nayler even sixty years later.

After 1660 London also became the focal point for the persecution of Friends (cf. p. 213) and the scene of mass arrests and of the trial of Penn and Meade that unexpectedly vindicated the rights of juries. After 1670 London replaced Swarthmoor as the center for Quaker organization and for aid to Friends in prison or in need.

William Crouch

POSTHUMA CHRISTIANA

LONDON, 1712

[Section I is a rambling autobiography.]

SECT. II

[12] As it pleased the Great Disposer of all things, according to his own goodwill and pleasure, to order his servants and handmaidens into divers and sundry parts of this nation, so according to his own secret will and counsel, he moved in the hearts of many of his servants to visit foreign nations, as Holland and Germany, and other of those eastern countries, and also the English colonies and plantations abroad. For particular accounts of all which, and of the services, labours, and travels they had, and underwent, and what progress truth made by the ministration of the spirit in and through them, and how they were received and treated, as also of the great sufferings and harships they endured; more especially in New England, I refer the reader to a book entitled, *New England Judged*, etc.[29] as also of the sufferings and

[29] Cf. pp. 123-124.

travels of two of the Lord's handmaidens, to wit, Kath. Evans and Sarah Chivars,[30] in the Isle of Malta.

About the beginning of the year 1654, some workings of the power of truth came to be felt amongst some tender people in and about the city of London, and some few were convinced, and turned unto the Lord.[31] About this time, two women coming out of the north to the city, viz. Isabel Buttery and her companion, who (by what providence I cannot tell) became acquainted with Amor Stoddart, sometime a captain in the parliament army, who when convinced of truth had left his command, and Simon Dring of Moor-Fields. These [13] women having an epistle or testimony given forth by George Fox ... To All That Would Know the Way to the Kingdom,[32] to direct people to turn their minds within, where the voice of God is to be heard. Which epistle or testimony being printed, they delivered, or dispersed abroad to such as would receive it. This Isabel Buttery, and the other women, being in company with Amor Stoddart and Simon Dring, walking in the fields towards Stepney, were overtaken by Ruth Brown, then about sixteen years of age, who afterwards became my wife. Isabel Buttery steadfastly looked on her, gave her one of the said printed epistles, in the reading whereof she was convinced of the truth, and added to the small number who then did believe. After this these women had private meetings at Robert Dring's house in Watling Street, and at Simon Dring's in Moor-Fields, where they did now and then speak a few words. To which places my wife went with great expectation, and there met with Anne Downer, afterwards Anne Whitehead, a worthy young woman, who became an eminent instrument of the Lord's hand in her day. . . .

Moreover in the fifth month of this year, 1654, it pleased God to send two of his faithful messengers and able ministers to the city of London, viz. Francis Howgill and Edw. Burrough, who were the first that declared truth

---

[30] Katharine Evans of Englishbatch near Bath, and Sarah Cheevers from Wiltshire, both housewives, traveled together to Scotland in 1662 and later to Ireland, but are best known for their voyage toward Jerusalem, permanently interrupted at Malta, where their efforts to preach landed them in the prisons of the Inquisition. After three and a half years and a fruitless but risky visit of Daniel Baker to try for their release, they were finally sent home by the intercession of the English queen's Lord Almoner (cf. BBQ, pp. 428-32).

[31] Little is known of this London separatist group, whose members may have included the names later mentioned. Some may have been the "tender people" Fox met on his boyhood visit to London (*Journal* [Nickalls], p. 4).

[32] Though placed first in the collected edition of Fox's tracts (Doctrinals) this "proclamation of 1653" tract may not have been Fox's first published writing, if Smith is right that "A Paper sent forth into the World" had an edition before 1654 (no copy of which survives), or if *Saul's Errand* (cf. p. 251), the same spring, came out first.

publicly there, whom he made instruments in his hand for the gathering many. . . .

Now as the Lord was pleased to visit a tender seed in and about the city of London, by these his chosen instruments, and as he opened the hearts of a remnant to receive the word of life, and believe in it, such opened their doors for meetings in their houses; and for some time it so continued, that they met from house to house.

And now they having sounded an alarm, and proclaimed the great and notable day of the Lord, in the city and parts adjacent, the Lord moved them to visit the nation of Ireland, and the time being come for their departure, and leaving the city, a meeting was appointed at Robert Dring's in Watling Street, there to take their leave of their friends and brethren. At which time there was great brokenness of heart, and the melting power of God was amongst them, which caused great sorrow, and abundance of tears to flow from the eyes of many tender plants. . . .

In the time of their absence and stay in Ireland, the Lord was pleased to send others of his messengers and servants to the city of London, viz. Thomas Aldam, Christopher Atkinson, Richard Hubberthorne, George Fox, Alexander Parker, John Stubbs, Thomas Salthouse, and some others, who published and declared the word of the Lord freely. . . .

The Lord having increased the number of his people, about this time, in the year 1655, some part of an ancient great house, or building within Aldersgate, was taken for a meeting place, the other part of it, with a yard, etc., being before made a public inn for carriers and travellers. Which having for a sign the Bull and Mouth, occasioned the meeting held there, to be known and distinguished by the name of Bull and Mouth, or Bull-Meeting, which was the first public meeting place taken and set apart for that service; where meetings were held on every first day of the week, in the forepart of the day, and on the fourth day of the week, in the forepart of the day, and so continued until the dreadful burning of the city, when the same was laid in ashes.

And being now come to time in some degree within my own knowledge and remembrance, to wit, the year 1656, when I find the two aforementioned friends, to wit, Francis Howgill and Edward Burrough returned from Ireland, and frequenting the meetings in and about the city of London, where their service was very great, and I may say in the words of Paul, (Rom. 11:13), They were the apostles of this city in their day, by whom many were gathered, both sons and daughters, and were settled through the grace of God in the faith of the Gospel, by the effectual working of the word of life throughout their ministry, and of others, the servants of the Lord, as aforesaid. And the Lord opened the mouths of some of the inhabitants of this city, to bear witness to the truth now made known. The first of which that had a public testimony to bear, was Ann Downer aforesaid, who was followed by Richard Greenway, John Giles, Sarah Blackberry, Ann Gold, Rebecca Travers, Richard Davis, William Bayly, Mary Booth, and some others.[33]

Now those meetings which I found and frequented at my first convincement, were at the Bull and Mouth, at Sarah Yates' in Aldersgate Street, at Humphry Back's [Bache's] a goldsmith in Tower Street, held on the first, and on the sixth days of the week, both in the afternoon. And at the house of Gerard Roberts in a street called Thomas Apostles, where sometimes resorted travelling friends, who came out of the country upon the service of truth, and there was also a meeting on the first day of the week. . . . [Note: He then describes nine other sites of weekly meetings in and around London in 1658, mostly in private homes, and the permanent meeting houses later built at four of these.]

In the year, 1656, or near that time, a meeting was set up in John's Street, called the Peel Meeting, which still continues there, and the meeting in Westbury Street, bearing the name of Wheelers Street meeting, which first began in the house of John Oakly, in an upper room. And being increased in number, another room was added, but the meeting still increased, and both rooms being too strait, the meeting was sometimes without doors, and after a tent covered with canvas, or sailcloth, was set up in the garden, where the meeting was kept for some time, till a meeting house was there erected, which has been since enlarged for the convenience of the meeting.

About this time also, meetings were set up at Hammersmith, Hendon, Kingston, Wandsworth, Barking, Ham, since at Plaistow, and at Waltham Abbey.[34]

During which time and season, the Lord in a plentiful manner did shower down his blessings and favors upon his heritage, in and about the city of London, and places adjacent, by sending many of his messengers and servants to visit them, to water and refresh his plantation, that they may grow and flourish, and bring forth fruit to his praise, viz. George Whitehead, William Dewsbury, Stephen Crisp, John Crook, Josiah Coale, Samuel Fisher, John Whitehead, Richard Farnworth, George Fox the younger, and many others, whom he fitted and prepared for his work and service in their day. These

[33] In addition to Nayler, the names of his coterie are omitted here, notably of Martha Simmonds, Calvert's sister and wife of another printer of Quaker tracts; nor is anything said about Nayler's influence on members of Cromwell's court such as Lady Darcy and the Earl and Countess of Pembroke.

[34] Waltham Abbey school, the only important Quaker boarding school in the seventeenth century. (Though Arnold Lloyd, *Quaker Social History,* p. 168, speaks of fifteen others by 1671, some were day-schools or short-lived.) It was the scene of a religious revival in 1679.

published deliverance by and through repentance to poor captive souls enslaved in sin, through the lusts of the flesh reigning in their mortal bodies, through the temptations of Satan.

Now many of these meetings which were set up and added in these years, and about this time, are sufficient testimonies to the progress of truth at that time made, by the messengers and servants of the Most High, and how it pleased the Great God to prosper his own work, through such, whom he had chosen, and made faithful laborers and ministers, in the word and doctrine of the Gospel, whereby many more were brought to believe in, and return to the great bishop and shepherd of their souls, Christ Jesus the True Light. And although with great love and goodwill to their countrymen and neighbors, they did thus labor and travel in divers parts of this nation, as well as the city of London, and parts adjacent, and were gladly received by many well disposed people; but were often evil entreated by the wicked, and as primitive Christians were of old, sometimes beaten, stoned and imprisoned, and everywhere evilly spoken of, and the people often in uproars and tumults, when the servants or messengers of God were sent amongst them. Even like the Jews of Thessalonica, who when Paul preached to them, and reasoned with them out of the Holy Scriptures, of the sufferings and resurrection of Jesus, and that he was the Christ. And as it was then, even so now, those that "believed not," (Act. 17:5), "lewd fellows of the baser sort," did gather together, and assault houses, and bring friends there met before the rulers, crying, "These that have turned the world upside down, are come hither also." Ver. 6. Whom many of the priests and hireling teachers did often incense, for fear their craft, by which they get their wealth, should be set at nought.

From the year; 1654, (in the time of Oliver Cromwell, who died, Anno 1658), and from thence to 1660, the sufferings and exercises of many of the people of God called Quakers, were great and manifold, although no law was enacted against us in that time. Yet besides the sufferings inflicted by the rude people, we were made great sufferers by the magistrates and rulers, and that only for the sake of a good conscience towards God. For some were imprisoned for refusing to swear; some for using the plain and proper language of "thee" and "thou" to a single Person; and others for wearing their hats, and not putting them off when brought before magistrates, or in courts of judicature, have been both fined and imprisoned. Some for not paying tithes to the hireling priests, have been imprisoned and made great sufferers; and for testifying against them, and their formal worship; and others for publishing and declaring the day of the Lord in steeplehouses, markets, etc.

And although the enemy of our peace and prosperity did prevail over some particular persons, who made some show for a time amongst us; yet the Lord was pleased to preserve a remnant steadfastly in the truth, and who turned not either to the right hand, or the left, but their minds and hearts were kept upright to the Lord, over all the devices of Satan within, and the malice of enemies without.

SECT. III

Shows what care and good order the believers in the truth were led and directed into, both men and women, and how they answered their particular care and service in the church, in those early days. . . .[35]

After the taking of the house, called Bull and Mouth for a meeting place, as aforesaid, the ancient men-friends about the city did sometimes meet together, to the number of eight or ten, sometimes a few more were added, in an upper room belonging to the place, there to consult about and consider the affairs of truth, and to communicate to each other what the Lord opened in them, for the promotion thereof. And also to make such provision to supply all necessary occasions which the service of the church might require.

And now also some ancient women-friends did meet together, to consider of what appertained to them, as their most immediate care and concern, to inspect the circumstances and conditions of such who were imprisoned upon truth's account, and to provide things needful to supply their wants. And what did or might more immediately concern men-friends, the women would acquaint them therewith. And all was done in great love and unity, no jar or discord amongst them, no repining or murmuring; but a sweet harmony and agreement was preserved in all things. These women did also inquire into, and inspect the wants and necessities of the poor, who were convinced of the truth. And they sat not still until the cry of the poor came to their houses. But where they did suppose or discover a want of help, their charity led them to inquire into their conditions, and to minister to their necessities.

And thus things were carried on with cheerfulness and brotherly kindness, in the infancy of the church. All whisperings and backbitings were shut out, and love and goodwill to all were promoted and cherished.

And afterwards as truth grew and prospered, and many came to be added to the faith, the meetings came, through the providence of God, to be settled in that order and method as at this day.

SECT. IV

Of the coming in of King Charles the Second, and what ensued thereupon. Of the act for banishment, and great imprisonments, with something concerning Edward Burrough.

In the year, 1660, in the third month, King Charles the Second returned to

---

[35] On Fox's account of the Women's "Box" and "Morning Meetings," cf. p. 147.

England, at which time the water swelled mightily, and overflowed the banks; the winds blew and the sea raged. For the people were in uproars and disorders, and had great expectations, that now they should have opportunity to destroy and lay waste the whole heritage of God. The roaring, swearing, drinking, revelling, debauchery, extravagancy of that time I cannot forget, with the menacings and threats of the rabble against all sobriety, and against religious people and their meetings, which they expected now should be totally suppressed and brought to nothing. Soon after the King's return, he was visited by sundry epistles, written in great love and goodwill unto Him, and his council, from several servants of the Lord (of the people called Quakers) who were moved thereto through the spirit of His Son, to admonish and counsel him in the fear of the Lord, to avoid those judgments which had fallen upon those princes, who, following the advice of evil counsellors, had persecuted the people of God. Which wholesome counsel had little or no place in his heart. Although upon Richard Hubberthorne's delivering the epistle written by George Fox the younger unto him, called, *A Noble Salutation, and a Faithful Greeting, Unto Thee Charles Stuart, now Proclaimed King, etc.,*[36] he did promise that none should be molested, or called in question for their opinions in religion, who did not disturb the peace of the kingdom.[37] Yet he had little or no regard to his promise; for although not one of the people called Quakers, was at any time found in any plot, or contrivance against the King and government, nor could in any wise be suspected in the least of any confederacy, or combination of evil against him or the government, yet in a little time a law was made to banish us out of our native country, for the exercise of a good conscience towards God, and meeting together to worship Him, according to our persuasion.

And so very severe and cruel was the prosecution of this law, that many were taken up at our peaceable religious meetings in and about the city of London, and elsewhere, and actually banished, and sent out of their native country. Husbands from their wives, fathers from their children, and housekeepers from their habitations and families, for no other cause than as aforesaid. And thus the King did violate his promise.

During this persecution, great were the sufferings of the Lord's people in this city, and elsewhere in the nation. In many places the jails were filled with the innocent; but the Lord was always near to preserve them, and to keep up

36 See below, p. 389.

37 Hubberthorne's own account, *Something that Lately Passed in Discourse Between the King and R.H.* (1660), was intended to publicize Charles II's statement, following a long discussion of Quaker claims to be guided by the Spirit: "Well, of this you may be assured, that you shall none of you suffer for your opinions of religion so long as you live peaceably; and you have the word of a King for it. And I have also given forth a declaration to the same purpose," i.e., the Declaration of Breda.

their heads, so that the water-floods did not cover nor overwhelm them. He supported them with strength; He opened the springs of life; He made them to drink of the brook by the way, and refreshed their weary souls, so that they fainted not, nor were dismayed. Everlasting honor and praise be given to his excellent name forever.

Amongst the many others, who were at this time shut up in nasty holes and prisons, in this city, was that eminent and worthy servant of the Lord, Edward Burrough; of whom I think myself obliged to say something in particular, with respect to that spiritual relation in which I stood to him, even as a child to a father. Upon which account he was very dear to me, I loved and honored him in the Lord, and for the truth's sake. I had many times an opportunity of conversing with him, and wrote several things from him, as he dictated them, which were since printed in the collection of his works. He was a man (though but young) of undaunted courage; the Lord set him above the fear of his enemies, and I have beheld him filled with power by the spirit of the Lord. For instance, at the Bull and Mouth, when the room, which was very large, had been filled with people, many of whom have been in uproars, contending one with another. Some exclaimed against the Quakers, accusing and charging them with heresy, blasphemy, sedition, and what not; that they were deceivers and deluded the people; that they denied the Holy Scriptures, and the resurrection. Others, endeavoring to vindicate them, and speaking of them more favorably. In the midst of all which noise and contention, this servant of the Lord has stood on a bench, with his Bible in his hand, for he generally carried one about him, speaking to the people with great authority from the words of John, 7:12. "And there was much murmuring among the people concerning him, (to wit, Jesus), for some said He is a good man; others said, nay, but he deceives the people." And so suitable to the present debate amongst them, that the whole multitude were overcome thereby, and became exceedingly calm and attentive, and departed peaceably, and with seeming satisfaction.

As his service was great in this city, so he had a share in suffering also. In the year, 1662, he was taken from a meeting at the Bull and Mouth aforesaid, and committed to Newgate, where after some time he fell sick, and in a few months finished his course, being gathered to his fathers. . . .

6. Edward Burrough: *The Visitation of the Rebellious Nation of Ireland* (London: Giles Calvert, 1656)

Crouch's narrative introduced us to Edward Burrough's power as a preacher, and to his mission to Ireland with Francis Howgill in

1655, for which each (to their mutual delight) felt led independently (cf. SMS 6:6, 15). Ireland under Cromwell's garrisons was the unhappiest part of Britain, and its native population, Catholic and still largely illiterate, had been driven not only "beyond the pale" around Dublin, but from all valuable lands and castles. (In the long run, only the older Protestant settlement planted in Ulster by Queen Elizabeth endured, but the Penns were among many English who received Irish estates.) The Quaker mission therefore found a hearing mainly within the garrisons and English settlements. Here Burrough and Howgill were sufficiently successful (cf. p. 476) to lead to their expulsion by the governor, Cromwell's son Henry. Irish Quakerism has endured to the present day, mainly among the radical Puritan English families of the Southeast rather than the Ulster Scots-Irish.

Burrough's tract, like his *Trumpet of the Lord* written about the same time against England, was evidently written in Ireland but printed only after his return to London in 1656. Both include long warnings addressed successively to various ranks and groups leading the church, the government, and the army. Each is called on to repent in the Lord's name and told what he expects of them in remaking England or Ireland, from Oliver Cromwell or his son, down to Baptists and Catholics. The sections of these tracts, like many Quaker writings, are noted as having been received as separate "motions of the Lord" at differing times and places. We include here only the last section of *The Visitation of . . . Ireland*, as presenting unusually clearly the Quaker use of Judgment Day language for their own "Visitation" of their hearers with the call to repent, their attitudes toward war and guard duty in these early years, and early Quaker language about the "inward Light" and its work in men's consciences.

An Invitation To All The Poor Desolate Soldiers To Repent,
And Make Their Peace With The Lord, And Their Duty
Showed Them What The Lord Requires Of Them.

To all you poor desolate soldiers of the lowest rank, who are scattered up and down in this desolate land of Ireland and live a careless and a desolate life without the fear of the Lord, in lying, in swearing, in drunkenness, in whoredom, in oppression, and in the wickedness of the world, and are past feeling, and senseless of the operation and power of God, careless of your eternal happiness. The dreadful day of the Lord God is coming. In power the Lord is risen, and the wrath of the Lord is gone forth. With the strength of indignation and fury you will be besieged, and fearfulness will surprise you. Repent of your transgressions, and fear and tremble before the presence of the Living God, who is commander in chief over heaven and earth. Prize your souls; this is the day of your visitation, and make your peace with the Lord. The righteous judge, the Lord, sees you in your darkness, and searches you in your desolate obscurity, and his soul is pressed under your iniquities, and he has not disrespected any of your persons or desolate places.

God is light, and has lightened every one of you with the true light of life eternal, if you love it and be guided by it; or of death everlasting, if you hate it, and disobey it, and walk contrary to it. That is the light which convinces you of sin, of lying, of swearing, and cursed-speakings, and drunkenness, which are the fruits of the cursed tree, which burdens the ground of the Lord, which the ax is now laid to the root of, to cut it down and cast it into everlasting burning. While you act against this light in your consciences, you crucify the life of Christ Jesus, and are enemies to him, and servants of the devil, and love your evil deeds, and upholders of the devil's conquests, which is the dominion of sin. The light reproves you in secret of violence, and false accusing, and all unjust words and actions which are contrary to God. So, turn your minds to the light, which will lead you to repentance from dead works, out of the broad way of destruction, which many are in (as Christ Jesus' faith) and it will teach you in your place to serve the Living God, and to do violence to no man, but to be terrors, and reprovers, and correctors of all violence, and of such who live in it. And it will teach you not to strengthen the hands of evil-doers, but to lay your swords in justice upon everyone that does evil. And it will teach you not to make war, but to preserve peace in the earth. This is your place and duty required of you from the Lord God, commander in chief, to whom you must all give an account, and receive a just reward according to your deeds. Everlasting punishment to him that does evil; but if you stand in the fear of the Lord, your sword will be a terror and dread to them that do not fear him. But live contrary to the light in their own consciences, which light if you love, it is your command to march by, and your rule to judge by, and weapon to fight with, and your chief commission for duty.

And now take heed to yourselves, do not go in your course of evil, nor take your pleasure in unrighteousness, but to the light in your conscience take heed, it is your teacher to God if you love it, or your condemnation from God if you hate it. And this is your terms with the Lord, prize the acceptance of his love to your souls, and the day of your visitation, for fear that you will perish in your rebellion eternally.

7. William Dewsbury's *True Prophecy of the Mighty Day of the Lord* (1655)

Virtually a Quaker before he met George Fox in 1651, Dewsbury had already passed through the Parliamentary army into disillusionment with violence and the beginning of his career as a forceful preacher. Though his letters show him as a wise and gentle counselor, his tracts are mainly fiery and prophetic, as his sermons before huge crowds must also have been. His *True Prophecy* may thus fairly provide a sample both of his writing and of Quaker thought about the Day of Visitation as they announced it in each new town. It catches the fervor of "the Camp of the Lord," the Quaker preachers who set out to sweep England and Europe in 1654-55. Yet it was probably written in Northampton jail, where he spent all of 1655 and also wrote many of his other works, including *To All You that Rule England* and *The Mighty Day* which preceded and followed our tract, which has the distinction of having been seized (along with Lilburne's *Resurrection*) in the Massachusetts home of William Marsden in 1658; the word had spread even from prison.

A TRUE PROPHECY OF THE MIGHTY DAY OF THE LORD

Which is coming, and is appeared in the North of England, and is arising toward the South; and shall overspread this nation, and all nations of the world.

WHEREIN

The Lord is redeeming Sion forth of her long enthralled captivity in Babylon's kingdom, where she hath been fettered in the cloudy and dark day, into forms and observations, and there kept by the priests, and teachers of the world, who ran when God never sent them.

Now is the Lord appearing in this day of his mighty power, to gather His elect together, out of all forms and observations, kindreds, tongues and nations; and is making up his jewels, his mighty host, and exalting Jesus Christ to be King of Kings, to lead his Army he hath raised up in the North of England;[38] and is marched towards the South, in the mighty power of the

---

[38] The pride of the "valiant sixty," the Quaker preachers of 1654, in the North of England included even south Yorkshiremen like Dewsbury, and is found in many of Burrough's tracts.

living Word of God, which is sharp as a two edged sword, to cut down the high and low, rich and poor, priests and people: and all the powers of the land, and all the world over, that are fruitless trees that cumbers the ground, defiles the flesh, and walks in disobedience to the righteous law of God, the pure light in the conscience; For who falls on this stone shall be broken, but on whom it falls shall be ground to powder: So shall this Nation, and all the nations of the world be conquered; and the victory witnessed, neither by sword nor spear, but by the Spirit of the Lord.

A Word from the Lord to all the inhabitants of England, rulers, priests and people, to haste to meet the Lord with speedy repentance, and returning within, to hearken diligently to his counsel, the pure light of Christ in your conscience, to be guided by his power, else you shall perish in your gain-sayings; For if his anger be kindled a little, blessed are all they that trust in him.

From the Spirit of the Lord, written by one whose name in the flesh is William Dewsbury, called Quaker with the people of the World, who live in the perishing nature. London, printed by Giles Calvert at the Blackspread Eagle at the west end of Paul's, 1655.[39]

A true prophecy of the mighty day of the Lord, &c.

Hos. *14*:1[40] O England, who lies in the fallen and lost estate, separated from the true and living God, by thine iniquities, notwithstanding all thy profession in his Name, in outward forms and observations: Repent, repent, and turn unto the Lord God Almighty, who waits on thee, to be gracious unto thee, and to

Isa. *30*:18 make thee the glory of all the nations of the world, if thou wilt diligently hearken unto his counsel, the light that is in the conscience of everyone, to

John *1*:9 wait in it upon the Lord God, that he may guide thee by his power.

And this I have to declare unto thee from the Lord, which he hath made known unto me, concerning thee O England: certain years ago, when the

Isai. *55*:3, everlasting covenant of life was confirmed unto my soul in the Lord Jesus

35:10 Christ, that I should go with the ransomed of the Lord unto Sion, I enquired

[39] The present St. Paul's Cathedral was built by Christopher Wren on the site where the medieval Cathedral, along with most of the central city, had been destroyed in the great fire of September 2-5, 1666 (cf. p. 141). Calvert's press was therefore near the present beginning of Fleet Street. Notice that his Puritan avoidance of the term "Saint," in connection with churches or places, is common for publishers (cf. pp. 65, 264).

[40] The biblical references are from the original edition, and though copious are by no means complete; like Fox and most other early Friends, Dewsbury seems to have received his messages in the form of a patchwork of Bible phrases and current equivalents.

of my God, to manifest unto me where Sion was, that I might return thither
to worship him in spirit and in truth, there being so many confused cries in   John *4*:24
thee O England, who professes to worship the only true God, some saying, Lo
here is Christ in the Presbyterian practice so called: and the Independent so
called cries, "Lo he is here;" and the Anabaptists so called saying, "Lo he is
here;" and others in outward form saying, "He is here;" according as Christ
foretold, that the time would come when they shall say, Lo here is Christ and
lo there, as it is fulfilled in thee. But Christ saith, Believe them not, look not
forth, for the Kingdom of Heaven is within. And as the lightning that shineth   Luk. *24*:23,
out of the one part under Heaven, and shineth unto the other part under the   27
Heaven, even so shall the Son of man be in his day. And this I witness. And
while I was waiting on my God, to make known unto me where Sion was, the
Word of the Lord came unto me with witness to my spirit, that Christ was   I Cor. *1*:3
not divided, and that there was no rent in his garment, for the Lord is one   Zech. *14*:9
and his people one; and that all thy outward forms of worship, O England,
where thou art waiting for Christ in observations, is contrary to his Will; (for
Christ saith, The Kingdom of God is not in observations; neither shall they   Luke *1*7:20,
say lo here, or lo there, for behold the Kingdom of God is within you); and   21
that all thy strict observing of thy outward forms, is but imitating the Saints'
practices, in thy Babylonish and heathenish wisdom, so there is nothing but
confusion in thee. . . .

[2] And this glory of the Lord was by the Lord made known unto me,
which [3] shall be made manifest to the inhabiters of England, if you will
harken diligently to the counsel of the Lord, which is the light in your
consciences, and in it wait on the Lord to be guided by his power. I waited in
the counsel of my God, in the calling where I was placed, until the year 1652
and in the eighth month of the year, as it is accounted of men the Word of
the Lord came unto me, saying: "The leaders of my people causes them to   Isa. *9*:16
err, in drawing them from the light in their consciences, which leads to the
anointing within, which the Father hath sent to be their teacher, which would   I John 2:27
lead them into all truth, to seek the Kingdom of God in observations, where   Luke *1*7:20
it is not to be found. So my people perish for want of bread. Freely thou hast
received, freely give, and minister; and what I have made known unto thee in
secret, declare openly." Which Word constrained me by the power of it to
leave my wife and children, and to run to and fro to declare to souls where   Hos. *4*:6
their teacher is, the light in their consciences, which the Lord hath given unto   Dan. *10*:4
everyone a measure to profit withal, for the exercise of the conscience
towards God and men, and waiting in the light for the power of Christ. He   Rev. 7:17
would lead them up to the living fountains of water, where their souls would
find refreshment in the presence of the Lord, and their bread should be sure,
and their water never fail, (as the Lord hath made manifest to my soul), and
to worship him in truth at New Jerusalem, to sing Hallelujahs and praises   Isa. *35*:10

Rev. *5*:13 among the redeemed sons and daughters of God, in the beauty of holiness, unto the Lord God that sits upon the throne, and to the Lamb for evermore.

To you rulers of England, whose names will be honorable: if you will honor the Lord in obeying his counsel, which is the light in your consciences, that he may guide you in all your ways, to you I am moved to write: Thus Eze. *21*:27 saith the Lord God Almighty, I will overturn, overturn, overturn until I have given it unto him whose right it is, and he will give it me. As you have seen the power of the Lord manifest on many that are in the place where you are, a cloud of witnesses: the bishops and the king, the lords and the late Parliament,[41] who all professed the name of Christ, but they would not obey Jer. *9*:13, 14 his counsel, the light in their consciences, but walked after the counsel of their own hearts, and improved their power for their own ends, and would Dan. *12*:2 have dissembled with God and the country. But our righteous God hath overturned them, to their everlasting shame and contempt.

Now if you will not obey the light in your consciences to rule in the power Isa. *58*:6 of the Spirit, to break every yoke of unrighteousness, and put every filthy and abominable thing out of the sight of the Lord, that the oppressed may be Rev. *13*:16 set free; but you will cause both small and great to worship the image of the beast, in forcing them to obey the heathenish and unrighteous laws made by Nebuchadnezzar's natureproud flesh who set up himself a king, to oppress all under his power, and set up whom he would to rule and reign with him over others in tyranny, cruelty and oppression in all unrighteousness. . . .[42]

[4] O be valiant for the truth upon earth, ye rulers of England, and give Mica. *3*:10, 11 over building up Sion with blood, and Jerusalem with iniquity, as it hath been in this nation, by all that upheld this image, which the Lord hath overturned, Mic. *3*:11 cast out before you, and is still held up by you: The heads thereof judge for rewards, and the priests teach for hire, and the prophets thereof divine for money: yet will they lean upon the Lord, and say, "Is not the Lord among us? no evil can come upon us." O prize your time, and stand stedfast in the counsel of the [5] Lord. The Light in your consciences, hearken unto it: let it alone guide you in all your counsel, that Christ may be head in you all. Then will the glory of God be the end of all your undertakings, and you will remove this filthy and abominable thing out of the sight of the Lord, the judges that judge for rewards, and the lawyers that plead for money, and the Exod. *18*:25 priests that teach for hire; and set over the people, to judge their causes, men Isa. *55*:1 fearing God, and hating covetousness, to judge their causes without rewards,

41 The "late Parliament" is presumably the "Long Parliament" of 1641-53, whose "Rump" Cromwell had recently dissolved (cf. p. 19).

42 This sentence (grammatically incomplete) refers, as does the following paragraph, to Cromwell's failure to abolish the tax- or "tithe"-supported parish church system in 1654.

and that the people may be taught freely, without money or price, by the free Spirit of Christ in the hearts of his saints, who cannot but declare freely, as we have freely received. Then will the mighty power of God go along with you in all your ways, if you will stand in his counsel, and walk in his fear, to depart from all evil, which is the beginning of wisdom. And your names will become a sweet savour through the power of the Lord among his saints, as all the names of the righteous are; and you shall partake of the glory of the Lord, which he is manifesting to his chosen people in this nation, which he hath chosen to make known his power, in exalting the Kingdom of Jesus Christ, and will make it the glory of all the nations in the world, and the mighty God of power will be unto us Salvation for walls and bulwarks, and we shall sit under our vines and figtrees, and none shall make us afraid. And this shall be the portion of your cup, if you will deny yourselves, and diligently hearken to the counsel of the Lord, the Light in your consciences, to which I speak, which shall eternally witness me the truth declared unto you. For the mouth of the Lord of Hosts hath spoken it, who hath raised up his own seed in his people in this nation, which cannot cleave to this great Image, which was set up by those that were in the place where you are, which the Lord hath overturned, and cast out in his indignation; and is not yet taken away by you; and while you uphold it the anger of the Lord is kindled against you. There is no peace to the wicked, saith my God.

Mat. 10:8

Pro. 8:13

Isa. 26:1
Mic. 4:4

Dan. 2:43

This is the day that the God of Heaven will set up his own Kingdom, which shall never be destroyed; and the Kingdom shall not be left unto other people, but it shall break into pieces and consume all these kingdoms, and it shall stand for ever and ever.[43] Here I have cleared my conscience, in declaring unto you what my God hath made known unto me concerning you and the nation, which shall shortly come to pass: He that hath an eye to see, let him see; and he that hath an ear to hear, let him hear.

Dan. 2:44

To all you unrighteous judges, that judge for rewards, and lawyers that plead for money, who devour the Creation, and set people at variance, destroy many families, and delight in unrighteousness; and to all oppressors, high and low, who grind the faces of the poor, and cause them to groan under your cruelty and oppression, hear the word of the Lord:

Mic. 3:10, 11
Pro. 6:19
II Thes. 2:12

Thus saith the Lord God, "Howl and weep for the misery which is coming upon you, for the cry of the oppressed hath entered into the ears of the Lord, and he is coming to render vengeance upon you, and set the oppressed free: For the trust of your money and gold shall eat your flesh, as it were fire, for you have heaped [6] up treasures for the last day; and ye shall be cut down, ye

Jam. 5:1, 2

Isa. 5:8, 6

---

43 This is the language of Daniel 7, etc., much beloved of the "Fifth Monarchist" radicals whom Cromwell had just put down in their effort at a theocratic putsch.

Jam. *5*:3 fruitless trees, that cumber the ground, and cast into the lake, for it is the place prepared for you, and for all fearful and unbelieving; and the abomi-
Luk. *13*:7 nable, and murderers, and whoremongers, and sorcerers, idolaters, and all liars
Rev. *21*:8 shall have their part in the lake which burns with fire and brimstone, which is the second death."[44] Repent, repent, now while you have time, put away the
Isa. *55*:3 evil of your doings, turn to the Lord, and hearken diligently unto his counsel, the light in your consciences, which lets you see the evil of your doings.
John *3*:19 Loving the light and giving yourselves up to be guided by it, it will lead you to life: hating it, and disobeying it, it is your condemnation. This is the Day of your Visitation; prize it, lest you perish in the mighty day of the Lord's
Joel *2*:1 anger, which will speedily come upon the children of disobedience. To the pure Light in your consciences I speak, which witnesses against the evil of your doings, and will witness me eternally, when the Book of Conscience is opened. . . .[45]

[Two paragraphs that follow pronounce destruction on "the fruitless trees which cumber the ground."]

[7] To all you who have professed yourselves to be ministers of Christ, and
Mat. *23*: walk contrary to the Doctrine of Christ, in having the chiefest places in the
5, 6, 7 assemblies, standing praying in the synagogues and having uppermost rooms
Isa. *56*:10, at feasts, greetings in the markets, and of men called masters, as the scribes
11 and Pharisees did, which Christ cried Woe against; and every one of you seeking your gain from your quarters, as the false prophets did, when the Lord sent Isaiah the true prophet to cry against them.

And you hold up the horrible filthy thing committed in the land, in bearing rule by your means, as the false prophets did, when the Lord sent Jeremiah the true prophet to cry against them.

Jer. *3*:30, And you seek for the fleece, and clothe yourself with the wool, and feed
31 with the fat, and make a prey of the people, as the false prophets did, which
Ezek. *34*:2, the Lord sent Ezekiel the true prophet to cry against, Thus saith the Lord, "I
3 will require my flock at their hands" . . . when the Lord sent Micah the true prophet to cry out against them. And you cry peace, as they did, and he that puts not into your mouths, you even prepare war against him. And this is fulfilled by your going to law with poor people for your wages; and others, in
Jer. *23*:30 raising persecution against everyone that will not obey you in your vain traditions; wherein you steal, every one, the Word of the Lord from his

44 Quaker doctrines of the afterlife (cf. also p. 310) usually included a well-stoked hell-fire, but this was usually subordinated to the present experience of the inner judgment-fire in those who were willing to submit to it.

45 This characteristic sequence of phrases may have been begun by Fox, and is found in the writings of many Friends. Notice the implicit divine authority claimed in assuming that "the Light in thy conscience will witness *me.*"

neighbor, in taking a part of the Scripture, and adding unto it your wisdom, and so speak of the saints' conditions, which you cannot witness fulfilled in yourselves; a false vision, a divination and deceit of your own heart, and so cause the people to err by your lies, and by your lightness, as the false prophets did, when the Lord sent Jeremiah the true prophet, who knew the word of the Lord to be as a fire and a hammer, to cry against them:[46] and all the saints that know the word of the Lord, knows it to be a fire and a hammer in them, in transforming them by its power from under the powers of darkness, into the glorious light and liberty of the sons of God. See you, how you daub up the people with untempered mortar, seeming vanities, divining lies unto them, saying, "Thus saith the Lord, as you may find it written in such a place of Scripture," which was spoken by the Lord in them which gave it forth. And thus you steal the saints' words to speak of, when as the Lord never spoke by you. . . . *Jer. 1:14   Jer. 23:29   Ezek. 13: 10, 11*

[9] There is no Scripture for your call into the Ministry of the Gospel of Christ, by humane wisdom; nor for your making bargains with the people for so much a year.   *I Cor. 1:26, 27   Acts 20:33   Mat. 10:3*

There is no Scripture for your sprinkling water on the face of a child calling it Baptism.

There is no Scripture for your stealing the Saints' words in taking a part of Scripture, and adding to it your wisdom, tearing it in sunder, in doctrines, reasons, uses, helps, motives, according unto the fancies of your brains.

There is no Scripture for your particular houses that you have, to creep into, where none must come but yourselves, and whom you please to declare your sermon as you call it; which is a divination of your own hearts, one day after another, one year after another.

There is no Scripture for your putting David's words into the mouths of poor ignorant people,[47] to sing praises unto the Lord (as, "O Lord, I am not puffed in mind;" "I have no scornful eye;" "I water my couch with my tears, all the night make I my bed to swim; all my bones do tremble") when they cannot witness these conditions; and so you cause them to blaspheme the Name of God. And when the Light in their consciences cries against them, for lying in the presence of God, and blaspheming his great and glorious Name, you tell them it is the light of a natural conscience, and so murder their souls in shutting them out of the Kingdom of God as the scribes and Pharisees, and   *Psa. 131:1   Psa. 6:6   Psa. 119:120   Mat. 23:13*

---

46 The explicit quotation of Jeremiah 23:28 shows that Friends understood the basic experience of Old Testament prophecy as "existentially" applying to the prophet himself as well as to his audience.

47 Quakers, like other radical Puritans, rejected singing during worship, even of the Psalms most Puritans were willing to allow, since all worship must be led by the Spirit and express the worshippers' actual situation.

John *1*:9 all the false prophets did, that denied Christ to be the light, who enlightens everyone that comes into the world:

Here I have cleared my conscience, dealing plainly with you, declaring [10] unto you where you are, as the Lord hath made known unto me, that you may be without excuse in the mighty day of the Lord, which will speedily come upon you, wherein you shall give account for the blood of souls that have been shut out of the Kingdom, and destroyed by you: To the Light in every one of your consciences I speak, which shall eternally witness me, when the Book of Conscience is opened.

Repent, repent, and give over deceiving the people, and destroying their
Psa. *2*:12 souls, and haste, haste to meet the Lord, in returning within, to be guided by his counsel, the light in your consciences, which you have rejected, lest ye perish in your gainsayings: Kiss the Son, in obeying his counsel, the Light in your conscience, that lets you see the evil of your doings, lest you perish in the way; for if his anger be kindled a little, blessed are all they that trust in him. . . .

[Three paragraphs follow, condemning the luxury of priests' lives.]

Rev. *18*:4 [11] To every particular inhabiter of England I write: Come out of Babylon, all forms, and observations, and traditions, which are set up by the will of man: Return within everyone in particular; examine your hearts, and mind the Light in your conscience, and it will always let you see where your hearts are, and what they delight in, for it is the heart the Lord requires; He will no
John *4*:14 longer be worshipped in words, forms, and observations, but in spirit and in truth, and in sincerity in the inward parts: therefore everyone be faithful in taking heed to the light in your consciences, which the Lord hath given to
Mat. *25*:15 everyone a measure to profit withall, for the exercise of the conscience towards God and men; in minding your watch to wait in the light in measure, it will bring to judgment all the powers of darkness in you; and the righteous law of God will cry through your earthly and carnal hearts, till judgment be
Isa. *42*:2 brought forth into victory, and your wills will be brought in subjection into
Luk. *1*:53 the Will of God, to wait on him for refreshment from his presence, who satisfieth the hungry with good [12] things, and take heed of consulting with flesh and blood, for that leads into pride and disobedience, there is your teacher within you, the light in your consciences; loving it and obeying it, is your life; hating it and disobeying it, is your condemnation:[48] To that pure light in your consciences I speak which will eternally witness me, when the Book of Conscience is opened in you: Now you have time, prize it, in waiting on the Lord in the light, to make your calling and selection sure, in putting off the old man and his deeds, and putting on the Lord Jesus Christ in

---

[48] Another series of characteristic Quaker phrases from Zechariah and Malachi shows Quaker theocratic ideas of government (see also p. 391).

righteousness and holiness without which no man shall see the Lord; in so | II Pet. *1*:10
doing you shall escape the wrath of God, which is coming upon the children | Isa. *51*:3
of disobedience in this nation and elsewhere; for the Lord will make the
Earth as the Garden of Eden, and hath begun His great and strange works in | Joel 2:3
this nation, which shall make the ears of them that hear to tingle, wherein He | I Sam. *3*:11
is exalting the Kingdom of the Lord Jesus, which Kingdom shall break down
all the kingdoms of the world and shall fill the whole Earth; for the mighty | Dan. 2:35
day of the Lord is coming that shall burn as an oven, and all you that are
proud, and all you that do wickedly shall be stubble, and the day that cometh | Mal. *4*:3
shall burn you up, saith the Lord of Hosts, and it shall leave of you neither
root nor branch. But unto you that fear the Name of the Lord shall the Sun
of righteousness arise with healing in his wings, and ye shall go forth and grow
as calves of the stall, and ye shall tread down the wicked, and they shall be as
ashes under the soles of your feet, in this day that I do this, saith the Lord:
wherein he is now gathering his Elect together, His scattered sheep, that have | Mat. *24*:31
been scattered in the cloudy and dark day, and will bring them from the | Eze. *34*:12
people, and gather them from the countries, and will bring them to their own
land. And I will feed them upon a good pasture and upon the high mountains
of Israel shall their fold be, and there shall they lie in a good fold, and in a fat
pasture shall they feed upon the mountains of Israel; and none shall make
them afraid: Thus shall you know that I the Lord your God am with you, and
that the house of Israel is my people, saith the Lord God.

England, here I have cleared my conscience, in declaring to thee what the | Isa. *33*:2
Lord hath made known to me of his love and mercy he will manifest to thee,
if thou wilt hearken diligently to his counsel, the Light which is in the
conscience of everyone, and wait upon him to be guided by his power: and all
you that disobey the righteous law [13] of God, the Light in your con- | John 3:20
science, you shall be swept away with the beesom of his wrath, and your
place shall be no more, for the mouth of the Lord of Hosts hath spoken it.
And whether you hear or forbear, I am clear of the blood of all men, in | Acts 27:26
making known to you what the Lord hath revealed to me; he that can receive
it, let him.

W. D.

A WORD FROM THE LORD.

To all saints and children of the most high God, whom he hath called and
chosen out of the world, and all their customs, fashions, worships, forms,
observations and traditions, which are set up by the will of man, to wait upon | I Pet. 2:9
him in the light, the counsel of Jesus Christ, the Captain of our salvation;
every one in your measure stand valiant soldiers, and be not discouraged, | Isa. *55*:2

101

neither at the enemy within nor without, lift up your heads, and behold your King Jesus Christ, who is present with you, to dash in pieces and destroy all your enemies for you. Stand faithful in his counsel, and walk in his power, everyone in your measure; and be bold in the Lord, for you are the Army of the Lord God Almighty, his mighty Host, whom he hath chosen out of the world to make known his eternal power in, to sound out his eternal and powerful Word, which shall make the ears of all the inhabitants of the Earth that hear, to tingle. And at the sound and hearing thereof shall their hearts fail, and paleness shall gather into all faces in the mighty day of the Lord's power, which is begun in this nation, wherein he is exalting the Kingdom of Jesus Christ our King, who is riding in his majesty and mighty power, conquering all the powers of the Earth in the hearts of his saints, and will overturn and dash in pieces all the powers in this nation, and all the world over, that will not submit to his scepter, to be guided [14] by his counsel, the pure Law of God, which is the light in the conscience. Now is He coming with ten thousands of his saints to judge the world, and to give to everyone according to their deeds: and the kingdoms and dominions, and the greatness of the kingdoms under the whole heavens, shall be given to the saints of the most high God, and all nations shall serve and obey him. Rejoice, rejoice, ye saints and children of the most high God, stand fast in the counsel of Jesus Christ, the light in you, and walk in his power, and you shall walk as kings upon the Earth, and shall sing the new song that none can sing, but the hundred forty four thousand, whose minds are redeemed from the Earth, who stand before the Throne of God day and night singing Hallelujahs and praises to the Lord God omnipotent, who is taking to him great power to sit upon his throne, and to the Lamb for evermore.

Marginal references: Isa. *13*:9 · Joel 2:2, 3 · I Sam. *3*:11 · Joel 2:4, 6, 7, 8, 10, 12 · Rev. *1 7*:14 · Jud. *14*:15 · Dan. 7:27 · Rev. 5:9 · *14*:13 · *19*:6 · *5*:13

William Dewsbury

FINIS

8. James Nayler: *The Lamb's War* (1658)

Nayler is perennially the most fascinating of Friends. His intense sensitivity, leading to unbalance, evokes in our time, as in his own, passionate and partisan writing for and against.[49] He

49 Emilia Fogelklou (Norlind), *James Nayler, the Rebel Saint, 1618-1660* (1931) and *The Atonement of George Fox* (Pendle Hill, 1969); M. Brailsford, *A Quaker from Cromwell's Army* (1927); and Geoffrey Nuttall, *James Nayler, A Fresh Approach* (FHS, 1954), in our own time, and in his own, *True Narrative* (1654), etc., have spoken for Nayler. George Bishop (cf. p.

had already been the best-known Quaker preacher and considered the Friends' "chief leader" before his Bristol adventure (cf. p. 36) made him a national target in Parliament's effort to refute Cromwell's toleration policy.[50] He was the most prolific early writer (even by 1700 surpassed only by Fox, Burrough, Penn, and Keith). He was also probably the most alert Quaker theologian before Barclay, thanks to his intensive Puritan preparation among the Woodkirk Separatists whom Anthony Nutter had nurtured within his Yorkshire parish,[51] and to his years as preacher as well as quartermaster in Lambert's Cromwellian regiment. Yet Nayler's new call to go west as a Quaker preacher came with dramatic suddenness some months after meeting Fox (cf. p. 68), and his sense of Christ within him was much stronger than any other Friend's except Fox's. The paradoxes of his spirit converge on his messianic sense, for which he was pilloried in ballad and cartoon.[52] This sense also runs through his famous "dying words," taken as the key-lines for Kenneth Boulding's *Nayler Sonnets*.[53]

481) and other Friends privately, and a host of Puritan and Anglican anti-enthusiasts, plus French and German heretic-haters in the seventeenth century, and (with balance and restraint) Elisabeth Brockbank (*JFHS*, XXVI [1929], 11ff.) in our own, have written against him. Nayler is also a subject of current fiction and drama (cf. Jan de Hartog, *The Peaceable Kingdom* (1971); and Judson Jerome, "Candle in the Straw," in *Religious Theatre*, No. 1 [1964]).

50 Cf. W. K. Jordan, *Development of Religious Toleration in England* (1932-40)

51 Cf. Ronald A. Marchant, *The Puritans and the Church Courts in the Diocese of York, 1560-1642* (London: Longmans, 1960), pp. 42, 108, etc. Nutter was chaplain to Sir John Savile, Baron of Pontefract.

52 See the undated contemporary tract reproduced facing p. 482 by kind permission from the copy in the Quaker Collection, Haverford College Library.

53 Cf. James Nayler, *A Collection of Sundry Books* (1716), p. 696:

His Last Testimony, said to be delivered
by him about two Hours before his
Departure out of this Life; several
Friends being present.

There is a spirit which I feel, that delights to do no evil, nor to revenge any wrong, but delights to endure all things, in hope to enjoy its own in the end: its hope is to outlive all wrath and contention, and to weary out all exaltation and cruelty, or whatever is of a nature contrary to itself. It sees to the end of all temptations: as it bears no evil in itself, so it conceives none in thoughts to any other: if it be betrayed it bears it; for its ground and spring is the mercies and forgiveness of God. Its crown is meekness, its life is everlasting love unfeigned, and takes its kingdom with intreaty, and not with contention, and keeps it by lowliness of mind. In God alone it can rejoice, though none else

The same spirit speaks through *The Lamb's War*, whose title (thanks to *The Quakers in Puritan England*, and T. Canby Jones) has become the watchword of the nonviolent activists among young Quakers and Mennonites across America. This tract was published anonymously in 1658 by the husband of the Martha Simmonds who played the central role in the Bristol "entry"; a shorter version was printed in 1657, and the original must have been written in the earliest months of Nayler's long imprisonment, following his brutal flogging, branding, and humiliation by Parliament. He had suffered for the Lamb, and his "fall" itself may partly be credited to his unwillingness to quench the "smoking flax" of the confused light in his followers.

This tract is a compact summary of Friends' understanding of the basic conflict of good and evil. It is thus full of apocalyptic symbols from Daniel and Revelation, which had been used much more violently in the Puritans' warfare against Popery and Anglicanism. The Beast, the Enemy, and the "god of this world" are all Antichrist or Satan, easily identified with Babylon, "the scarlet woman" or "whore" who was Rome. Nayler, however, finds the power of darkness within each heart. He retains a Puritan sense that "fleshly pleasures" lead to being "at peace in the flesh"; that true love in a deadly conflict of good and evil consists in denouncing and overcoming evil; and that at the same time suffering is the Spirit's weapon. Just as Satan attempts to make men destroy "the creation" rather than the true evil within, so the Spirit bears this suffering using "spiritual weapons." This is the root of Quaker doctrines on persecution and war (cf. pp. 374, 406, etc.). The creation itself is God's work and therefore good, yet also rightly the servant of the Spirit, never loved for itself. The bitterness of suffering is also a sign of the bitterness of Satan's plight, and thus of the nearness of "the End."

THE LAMB'S WAR AGAINST THE MAN OF SIN

The end of it, the manner of it, and what he wars against.
His weapons, his colors, his kingdom.

regard it, or can own its life. It's conceived in sorrow, and brought forth without any to pity it; nor doth it murmur at grief and oppression. It never rejoiceth, but through sufferings; for with the world's Joy it is murthered. I found it alone, being forsaken: I have fellowship therein, with them who lived in dens, and desolate places in the earth, who through death obtained this resurrection and eternal holy life.

J.N.

And how all may know whether they be in it, or no: and whether the
  same Christ be in them, that is, was, and is to come, and their
  faithfulness or unfaithfulness to him.
London, printed for Thomas Simmons, at the Bull and Mouth near
  Aldersgate, 1658.

The Lord God Almighty, to whom belongs all the kingdoms in heaven and earth, does nothing therein but by his Son, the Lamb. By him he creates and governs, by him he saves and condemns, judges and justifies; makes peace, and makes war: and whatsoever he does he is at his right hand in all places, who in him has long suffered the burden of iniquity, and oppression of wickedness that has abounded for many generations, till it be come to the full measure, as in the days of old.

And now his appearance in the Lamb (as ever it was when iniquity was full) is to make war with the god of this world, and to plead with his subjects concerning their revolt from him their creator, who ordered their beginning, and gave them a being; and their breaking the order that was in the beginning, and giving up their obedience to the worldly spirit, and the inventions thereof, till they become so far one with it, as that it had . . . defiled their souls and bodies, blinded their eyes, stopped their ears, and so made the creature utterly unprofitable to God. . . . They are also become open enemies to every check and reproof of that Spirit which should lead them to God, and does testify against their evil deeds, and are not afraid to speak against it as a thing not worth minding, nor able to lead them in the way of truth. Thus has God lost the creature out of his call and service, and he is become one with the god of this world, to serve and obey him in ways that defy the Spirit of grace; and now use the creation against the creator. Now against this evil seed, and its whole work brought forth in that nature, does the Lamb make war to take vengeance of his enemies.

The End Of His War Is: to judge this deceiver openly before all the creation showing that his ways, fashions, and customs are not what God ordered for man to live in, in the beginning; to bind him, and to redeem . . . out of his captivity all who will but believe in the Lamb and are weary of this service and bondage to his enemy, and who will but come forth and give their names and hearts to join with him and bear his image and testimony openly before all men; . . . and all that follow him to redeem them to God; and the rest who will not believe and follow him and bear his image, them to condemn with the destroyer into everlasting destruction; and to restore all things, and make all things news as they were in the beginning, that God alone may rule in his own work.

The Manner of His War Is: first, that he may be just who is to judge all men and spirits, he gives his light unto their hearts even of man and woman, whereby he lets all see (who will mind it) what he is displeased with, what is with him and what is against him, what he owns and what he disowns, that so all may know what is for destruction, to come out of it, lest they be destroyed with it; that so he may save and receive all that are not wilfully disobedient and hardened in the pleasures of this world against him, all who are deceived who are willing to be undeceived, all who are captivated who are willing to be set free, all that are in darkness and are willing to come to light. In a word all that love righteousness more than the pleasures of sin, that he may not destroy them (nor fight against him and know it not) but that he may receive them to be one with him against that which has misled and deceived them. And as many as turn at his reproof he does receive and give them power in spirit and life to be as he is in their measure, (but all in watching), and wars against that which has had them and now has the rest of the creation in bondage, that he may restore all things to their former liberty.

What They Are To War Against: and that is, whatever is not of God, whatever the eye (which loves the world) lusts after, whatever the flesh takes delight in, and whatever stands in respect of persons (as says the scripture) the lust of the eye, the lust of the flesh and the pride of life, these are not of God; and whatever the god of the world has begotten in men's hearts to practise or to plead for, which God did not place there. All this the Lamb and his followers war against, which is at enmity with it both in themselves and wherever they see it. For in the work of God alone is his kingdom and all other works will he destroy. So their wars are not against creatures, they wrestle not with flesh and blood which God has made, but with spiritual wickedness exalted in the hearts of men and women, where God alone should be, . . . by which they become enemies to God and their souls are destroyed. Indeed their war is against the whole work and device of the god of this world, his laws, his customs, his fashions, his inventions, and all which are to add to or take from the work of God which was in the beginning. (This is all enmity against the Lamb and his followers, who are entered into the covenant which was in the beginning). And therefore no wonder why they are hated by the god of this world, and his subjects, who come to spoil him of all at once and to destroy the whole body of sin, the foundation and strength of his kingdom, and to take the government to himself that God may wholly rule in the heart of man, and man wholly live in the work of God.

What Their Weapons Are: as they war not against men's persons, so their weapons are not carnal nor hurtful to any of the creation; for the Lamb comes not to destroy men's lives nor the work of God, and therefore at his appearance in his subjects he puts spiritual weapons into their hearts and hands; their armor is the light, their sword the Spirit of the Father and the

Son, their shield is faith and patience, their paths are prepared with the gospel of peace and good-will towards all the creation of God; their breastplate is righteousness and holiness to God, their minds are girded with godliness, and they are covered with salvation, and they are taught with truth. And thus the Lamb in them, and they in him, go out in judgment and righteousness to make war with his enemies, conquering and to conquer. Not as the prince of this world in his subjects, with whips and prisons, tortures and torments on the bodies of creatures, to kill and destroy men's lives, who are deceived, and so become his enemies; but he goes forth in the power of the Spirit with the Word of Truth to pass judgment upon the head of the Serpent which does deceive and bewitch the world (and covers his own with his love, while he kindles coals of fire on the head of his enemies). For with the spirit of judgment and with the spirit of burning will he plead with his enemies. And having kindled the fire and awakened the creature, and broken their peace and rest in sin, he waits in patience to prevail to recover the creature and stay the enmity by suffering all the rage, and envy, and evil entreatings that the evil spirit that rules in the creature can cast upon him, and he receives it with meekness and pity to the creature, returning love for hatred, wrestling with God against the enmity with prayers and tears night and day, with fasting, mourning and lamentation, in patience, in faithfulness, in truth, in love unfeigned, in long suffering, and in all the fruits of the spirit, that if by any means he may overcome evil with good, and by this his light in the sight of the creature that the eye may come to be opened, which the god of this world has blinded, that so the creature might see what it is he hates and what fruits he himself brings forth, that the creature may be convinced he is no deceiver but has with him the life and power of innocency and holiness, in whom he rules. And this preaching has a power in it to open the eye of all that are not wilfully blind, because they love the deeds of darkness, and such are left without excuse forever. And thus he in his members many times wrestles and preaches to the spirits in prison, with much long suffering towards the world, a nation, or a particular person before he gives them up and numbers them for destruction; yea, sometimes till their rage against him and cruelty exercised upon his members be so great that there be no remedy, as in the days of old, (II Chron. *36:*15, 16).

And These Fruits Are His Colors He Holds Forth To All The World, In Such As He Reigns In: as they come to obey him, he covers them with love, gentleness, faith, patience and purity, grace and virtue, temperance and self-denial, meekness and innocency all in white, that follow him, in whom he is, who walk themselves as he walked in all things conforming to God, with boldness and zeal owning the Lamb to be their leader, with him testifying against the world that the deeds thereof are evil; themselves the mean-while covered with his righteousness, against all the storms and tempests that they must be sure to meet with all; who bear that testimony which the Lamb has ever borne, in whom he appeared to the convincing of the world: that he is the same that ever he was from the beginning; that all that will believe and love holiness may see where it is to be found and come forth to him, and be saved; that the whole world become not as Sodom in the day of wrath, which ever comes upon a people or a nation after Christ has appeared and been rejected thereof.

What His Kingdom Is: The power, the glory and compass of it is not comprehended with mortal understanding, which was before all beginnings and endures forever, who orders and limits all spirits in heaven and earth, who rules in the rulers of the earth and in all heavenly places, though many spirits know him not till they have felt his reproof for their rebellion against him. His sufferings are free for love's sake, which is naturally in him to the creation, being his offspring. For which cause he becomes meek and lowly, that he may bear the infirmities of the creation, which does in no way take from his power, who is equal with the father, but does manifest his power to be unlimited, in that he bears all things.

His dominion he has amongst the heathen, and his hands are in the counsels of the kings of the earth, and there is no place where he is not, who descends below all depths and ascends far above all heavens that he may fill all things. But his kingdom in this world, in which he chiefly delights to walk and make himself known, is in the hearts of such as have believed in him, and owned his call out of the world, whose hearts he has purified, and whose bodies he has washed in obedience and made them fit for the Father to be worshipped in. And in such he rejoices and takes delight; and his kingdom in such is righteousness and peace, in love, in power and purity. He leads them by the gentle movings of his Spirit out of all their own ways and wills in which they would defile themselves, and guides them into the will of the father by which they become more clean and holy. Deeply he lets them know his covenant,[54] and how far they may go and be false, he gives them his laws and his statutes, contrary in all things to the god of this world, that they may be known to be his before all his enemies. If they keep his counsel they are safe, but if they refuse he lets them know the correction of the Father, his

---

[54] This, though loosely phrased, is one of the best Quaker statements regarding "the eternal covenant," about which they often preached. The conception goes back to William Ames's Puritan "covenant theology" whereby God covenants to guide the righteous, whom he has predestined, elected, and called by pure grace, in order that they shall also do righteous works.

presence is great joy to them of a willing mind, but with the froward he appears in frowardness; the kisses of his lips are life eternal, but who may abide his wrath? The secrets of the Father are with him, and he makes all his subjects wise. He makes them all of one heart, and with himself of the same mind. His government is wholly pure and no unclean thing can abide his judgments. As any come into his kingdom they are known, and their change is to be seen of all men. He keeps them low in mind, and a meek spirit does he generate in them; and with his power he leads them forth against all the enmity of the evil one, and makes all conditions comfortable to them who abide in his kingdom.

Now these are the last times, and many false Christs there must appear and be made manifest by the true Christ, with their false prophets, false ways and false worships, and false worshippers, which though they be at wars one with another, yet not the Lamb's War. Now seeing he has appeared who is from everlasting and changes not, here is an everlasting trial for you all, all sorts of professors, whether you profess him from the letter or the light; come try [test] whether Christ is in you. Measure your life and weigh your profession with that which cannot deceive you, which has stood and will stand forever, for he is sealed of the father.

Now, in truth to God and your own souls, prove your work in time lest you and it perish together. First, see if your Christ be the same that was from everlasting to everlasting, or is he changed according to the times: in life, in death, in peace and wars, in reigning, in suffering, in casting out and receiving in. And if you find the true Christ then prove your faithfulness to him in all things. Does he whom you obey as your leader lead you out to war against this world and all the pride and glory, fashions and customs, love and pleasures, and whatever else is not of God therein; and to give up your lives unto death rather than knowingly to yield your obedience thereto? Does he justify any life now but what he justified in the prophets and apostles and saints of old? Does he give his subjects liberty now to bow to the god of this world and his ways, in things that he has denied in the saints of old, and for denying whereof many, both then and now, have suffered? Is he at peace in you while you are in the fleshly pleasures, or while you have fellowship with the unclean spirits that are in the world? Does he not lead out of the world, and to strive against it in watchings, fastings, prayers, and strong cries to the Father that you may be kept and others delivered from the bondage and pollutions of it? Is his kingdom the same in you? And does he give out the same spiritual laws against all the laws and customs of the man of sin in you, as he has done in his subjects in all ages? Does he beget in your hearts a new nature contrary to the world's nature in all things, motions and delights like himself, whereby he works out the old nature that inclines to the world and can be at peace therein?

And now your peace is wholly in him, and that which crucifies the world to you, and you to it, is your joy and delight. Has he called you out of this world to bear his name before the powers thereof, and put his testimony into your hearts, and the same weapons into your hands as were used by the saints of old against the powers of darkness, whereby you have power given to overcome evil with good? And many other fruits you may find which he ever brought forth in his chosen, whereby they were known to be in him and he in them, for which the world hates them. By all which you may clearly know, if he be the same in you today as he was yesterday in his people, and forever. For he changes not, nor conforms to the world, nor the will of any creature, but changes all his followers till they become in all things like himself; for they must bear his name and image before all men and spirits.

Now if you profess the same as was, and is, and is to come, the same for evermore, the same Christ, the same calling in you that was in all the people of God, then prove your faithfulness in answering and obeying. Who is it that sees not what wars are begun? And to whom has not the sound gone forth? The children of light have published the gospel of light throughout the world, and the Prince of Darkness has shown his enmity against it. The Lamb has appeared with his weapons as before mentioned, in much long suffering. The god of this world has appeared to withstand him with his weapons, and has prevailed unto blood with much eagerness, and the Lamb has prevailed unto suffering with much meekness and patience, each of them in their subjects, in whom these contrary spirits act one against another; and now see what part you take, who has hired you, and whose work you are in. Or are you idle, looking on? Or are you gone out with the beast of the field and regard nothing but your bellies and pleasures? Does it not greatly concern you to try your spiritual states, seeing all must come speedily to an account for their lives and service? Are you such as spend your time and strength in watching and praying to the Father of Spirits, for yourselves and the people of God, that they may be kept in the time of temptation and assaults of the Evil One, who seeks his advantage on the weak brethren; and for your enemies, that they may be delivered from under his power, who are captivated by him at his will to fulfill his lusts and envy and satisfy his wrath upon the innocent?

And do you deny yourselves of your pleasures, profits, ease and liberty, that you may hold forth a chaste conversation and conduct in the power and life of gentleness, meekness, faithfulness and truth, exercising a conscience void of offence towards God, and all men, that thereby you may shine forth in righteousness, so as to convince your enemies whom you pray for; thus following him who laid down his life for his enemies? Is this your war and these your weapons? Is this your calling and are you faithful to him that has called you hereto, so as you can by no means bow to the God of this world, nor his ways, though it were to save your lives or credit in the world, or

110

estates, and yet can serve the meanest creature in God's way, though to the loss of all? I beseech you be faithful to your own souls herein. Do you find nothing in you that calls or moves this way or reproves the contrary? If there be, are you not such as quench the spirit, and put out your own eye, and deny the Lamb's call against your own lives? And if there be not, then are you not dead members cut off from Christ and all your profession is but a lie, and without Christ you are in the world? O that you would prove your own selves, for there be many deceitful workers at this day of his appearance who do the work of the Lord negligently and deceitfully. Many do their own work instead of his, and many are called and for a while abide, but in the time of hardship prove deceitful, and return to serve in the world again and take pleasure therein. Others are called and convinced, but come half out of the world, even as far as they can do it without loss or shame, but keep their covenant therewith still, in what makes most for their gain, or earthly advantage or credit. Others have answered their call and been faithful in the covenant of the Lamb against the Prince of this world, so far as they have seen; but not minding the watch against the enemy, and not keeping low in the fear, and zealous in the light, have suffered the simplicity to be deceived, and are led back to the old beggarly rudiments of the world again, and take that for their perfection and growth which once they had vomited up. These expect great things in their work, but they are blinder than the rest and more to be pitied because of the simplicity that is deceived.

Many other grounds there be that bring not fruit to perfection, who are not faithful to him that has called them therein; so that now the truth is, that many are called but few chosen faithful. Many are ashamed at the Lamb's appearance, it is so low, and weak, and poor, and contemptible, and many are afraid seeing so great a power against him. Many be at work in their imaginations, to compass a kingdom, to get power over sin, and peace of conscience, but few will deny all, to be led by the Lamb in a way they know not, to bear his testimony and mark against the world, and suffer for it with him. Now deceit has taught you to say, and maybe you think it also, God forbid but you should suffer with Christ till death; but come to the trial in deed and truth. Does not he suffer under all the pride and pleasures of the flesh, by all manner of excess, by all manner of customs and fashions, not of God but of the world? Is not all against him that is not of him and the father? Is not the lust of the eye, and of the flesh, and pride of life, his oppressors? And do you that live in these things, and fashions, and plead for them, suffer with him by them, or war with him against them? Then would you be weary of them, and not practice nor plead for them against him: this you will find true in the end, you cannot suffer with him, and serve his enemies.

Can you live at ease, and in your pleasures and profits, and cover yourselves with worldly glory, while Christ Jesus is glorified in his temples with mock-

111

ings, stockings, stonings, whipping, and all manner of evil intreatings; cast into holes, pits and dungeons, having none on earth to take his part, nor plead his righteous cause, nor once to take notice of his innocent sufferings? But who as will, may tread down his precious life in the open streets, without resisting; and this for no other thing, but for testifying against the deeds of the world, that they are evil. The pride and oppression, false ways and false worships, never set up by him but in the will of man, and so maintained against him, which he must judge with a contrary appearance, ere he come to his kingdom. Do you suffer with him herein, who have a heart consenting to these things, if not a hand deeply in them; secret or open, either in this cruelty acting or contriving, or in cursed and scornful speeches condemning them that bear witness, as a foolish ignorant people, and that they bring their sufferings upon themselves, by their own wills. So shoot your poisoned arrows one way or other against that Spirit which leads, and has ever led such as do not resist and disobey him, into the same testimony, and so in secret you become worse than open persecutors. Or it may be some few become as far as Pilate, who washed his own hands, while others shed the innocent blood; and these are few indeed, who thus far will openly confess the just and innocent Lord before his accusers, in what soever vessel he is thus honored.

But will the best of these stand in judgment as sufferers with him? Or will he know you at his appearance, by this mark? Are these his steps you follow? Or is this his image, or power, war or weapons? Will this suffering bring you to reign with him, or he in you to your peace? Or will this cross crucify you to the world, and the world to you? Do you walk as he walked, or has he left you such example to follow? Search the Scriptures, and read the life of them, and your own lives, with the light of Christ Jesus. Cease to blaspheme any longer in saying you are Christians, while in Christ you are not, but in a contrary spirit, and contrary life, and your fellowship is not with him in suffering, but with them by whom he suffers.

Were ever Christians at their ease and worldly delights while Christ has not where to rest his head; thrust out of your meeting places, towns, and markets, and every assembly, if he does but testify against the evil thereof? Are you asleep in the world, and does it not awaken you to see or hear how sudden a return that bloody spirit has made, lately in part cast out? And with what power he is now entering, like to exceed seven-fold what he has this many generations, making daily havoc of the lambs? Is it a time for you to riot in, to satisfy your lusts, to eat and drink, and rise up to play, and spend your time and strength (many of you) so as modest heathens would blush at, and then say you are Christians and suffer with Christ. Surely were you members of that body, or sensible of his sufferings herein, you would not add thereto a greater weight, nor join to his adversary the Devil whose works these are. . . . [sentence omitted]

112

How long shall it be ere the life of what you profess be seen in the face of your conversation, teachers and people? When will you teachers approve yourselves as the ministers of God and sufferers with Christ, (as says the Scripture which you profess). . . .

[Here Nayler quotes most of II Corinthians 6:4-10, I Corinthians 9:18, and Jude 11.]

Surely he that has a living conscience may much admire how you get over these Scriptures in your teaching of others, and not to wound yourselves, or pierce your hearts with fear, and your faces with blushing, who are found so absolute in contradiction thereto, in conversation, and unlike in your lives, in the sight of every open eye. Or how can you muzzle your consciences while you pass your prayers, that your own mouth does not condemn you? It's no wonder why you are such enemies to the Light within; everyone that does evil hates the light.

And you hearers of all sorts, how long will it be before you hearken to what the Lord says to your soul, who is no respecter of persons; but everyone that bears not the image of his son in well-doing he hates, though with Cain you sacrifice, or with Esau you pray with tears; that with the Light of Christ in your own hearts you may see how the world's lusts have spoiled your souls of that heavenly image, and has captivated your minds into itself and likeness, and how you lie dead in sin covered with earth and daubed over with the words of men. Oh! that you would awake before wrath awaken you, and put on the armor of God, not relying any longer on men that beat the air, to fight your battles against him who is got into your hearts;[55] but that yourselves as soldiers of Christ may all come to use the spiritual weapons against the spiritual wickedness exalted in the temple of God, so that you can neither see nor serve God therein, being filled with wicked and worldly cumbrances.

That's the spiritual weapon which captivates every thought to the obedience of Christ, and this is the true warfare, and is mighty through God, to cast down the strong holds of the man of sin in you; and having a readiness to revenge all disobedience; knowing that he that will not be led by the spirit of God is for condemnation. And only these weapons are effectual to cleanse the heart of all that exalts itself against the life and knowledge of God, and to make way for his appearance; which no man's words who is in the same evils has power to do; for this power is only in Christ his Light and life. And only blessed are they who feel and find this treasure working in the earthen vessel; such shall approve their own work to God and have praise, not of man. So should you come to see what others have said in scripture, concerning the Lamb of God, who takes away the sins of the world, and savingly feel the

---

[55] This summarizes the usual form of the Quaker peace testimony until it was specifically focused upon bearing arms in 1659.

power of his cross, of his death and resurrection, and the everlasting purity of his life, and that eternal love the father bears thereto, an everlasting inheritance to all who learn him, and attain his appearance, whose beauty is blessed forever.

Called, chosen and faithful are the servants and subjects of Christ's kingdom, in whom this day, he maintains war against the Prince of this World, the Beast and his seat, with the false prophet, and all that serve under his dominion and obey his laws which he has set up.

Now you that cry, "the kingdoms of this world are become the kingdoms of the Lord and of his Christ;" see that it be truth in you, and that you lie not within yourselves. *The Lamb's War you must know* before you can witness his kingdom, and how you have been called into his war, and whether you have been faithful and chosen there or no. He that preaches the kingdom of Christ in words, without victory, is the thief that goes before Christ. So take heed that your own words do not condemn you, but mind your calling and how you have answered, and whether you have been faithful to that which you have been called, the *war*. Christ has a war with his enemies, to which he calls his subjects to serve him against all the powers of darkness of this world, and all things of this old world, the ways and fashions of it will he overturn, and all things will he make new, which the god of this world has polluted, and where his children have corrupted themselves, and do service to the lust, and devourer. This the Lamb wars against, in whomsoever he appears, and calls them to join with him herein in heart and mind, and with all their whole might. And for that end he lights his candle in their hearts, that they may find out every secret evil that the man of sin has treasured, even to every thought and intent of the heart, to cast out the enemy with all his stuff, and to subject the creature wholly to himself that he may form a new man, a new heart, new thoughts, and a new obedience, in a new way, in all things to reign, and *there is his kingdom*.

Now many are called to this war, but few are chosen and faithful. They that are faithful in their calling he chooses, and in them he reigns, and with them he makes war against his enemies on every side under what color soever they appear. If they are not subjects to him, all in whom he reigns are at war with them in Christ. The sword of his Spirit he has put into their hands, his word into their mouths, where they are at wars with all the world and the world with them, and he that's faithful will make no peace or agreement, neither will he bow nor yield agreement till there be a subjection to Christ. These are faithful to him that has called them.

So you that are much in words, prove your own selves; if you be in his kingdom, or of his subjects, then are you at work with him in this his day, where he is coming in thousands of his saints to take vengeance into his hands and inflict it upon his enemies.

114

Now you who are asleep and at ease in the flesh are not of his kingdom; for by suffering in the flesh does he make war and slays the man of sin. You that are at peace in the world's ways and fashions, invented and maintained by the Man of Sin, you are not in his kingdom. He has given an alarm against all those things which has caused the Dragon to whet his teeth, and all the devouring spirits are stirred up, their Lord's kingdom to defend, every one with such weapons as they have, against the Lamb in his kingdom, in what vessel soever he reigns; and he is but one in all his, against all these.

Now you that are making peace where these things are upholden, you are false-hearted and betray the Lamb, as that of God in you will witness; you are at peace-making with his enemies.

But you say, God is love and we are commanded to love all and seek peace with all.

I say, is God's love in you otherwise than it has ever been in Christ and all his saints, whom the world ever hated, whom God loved, and in whom he testified against the world unto death, and unto bonds, and persecution? Were they not in God's love? Did they not keep his commandments? Will you take their words in your mouths, and condemn their lives by your practices?

The Lamb's War is not against the creation, for then should his weapons be carnal, as the weapons of the worldly spirits are, for we war not with flesh and blood, nor against the creation of God, that we love, but we fight against the spiritual powers of wickedness, which wars against God in the creation and captivates the creation into the lust which wars against the soul, and that tho creaturo may bo dclivcred into its liberty, prepared for the sons of God. And this is not against love, nor everlasting peace, but that without which there can be no true love nor lasting peace.

Love in God and man constrains us to be faithful in this war. Nor is God's love to that seed of bondage, nor did he ever command you to seek the peace of it. For the love of the world is enmity with God, as says the Scripture.

And were you not fallen into self-love which is utterly blind (as to the love of God) you would see a great difference between the creature, and that which keeps the creature in bondage and out of the love of God. Can you love that and not hate the creature, and God also? This all who fight in the Lamb's battles know, who are in the true love. Does not the spirit of pride, gluttony, drunkenness, pleasures, envy and strife, keep that in bondage which you should love by the command of God? Does not the creature groan to be delivered from the vanity, customs and fashions of this generation? Is not the whole time of man taken up in service of the lusts and inventions which the Man of Sin has found out: inventions in meats and drinks, inventions in apparel, inventions in worships, in sports and pleasures, etc.? Is not the whole creation captivated under the spirit of whoredom, and so man's whole life spent in vain, so that men and women come into the world, and depart out of

115

it again as though they were made for no other end but vanity and selfishness? Hardly one of ten thousand knows any call from God to any service for him, or has an ear to hear his voice; but if any do hear, and obey, they all conclude him deceived and are ready to devour him, because he testifies against the evils which destroy men's souls and make void man's service to his creator, and devours the creation.

And can you love this spirit, bow and conform to it, or suffer it to reign in yourselves or your brethren, and you be silent under a pretence of seeking love and peace, and obeying God's command; and boast in high words about Christ's kingdom, counting it a low and foolish thing in such as faithfully and zealously bear testimony for God, and against these evils? And will not God find you out, and your deceit and unfaithfulness in your generation; will not God break your peace and disannul your covenant, which you are making with the world to settle yourselves in ease and pleasure, and bring you out with true judgment, where it shall be seen what nature your love is of, whose kingdom you are in, and whom you love and serve.

The day is dawned, and the sun is risen to many that will not set, nor will he cease his course until he has rightly divided between the precious Seed, and the children of whoredoms and deceit. And now the holy Seed is called forth to appear in its colors against the Man of Sin; and with the sword of his mouth does he make war, and with the spirit of judgment and the spirit of burning does he consume the filthy and unclean spirits. And all that are faithful have their armor on, ready day and night to follow the Lamb as he moves, counting nothing hard to undergo, so that they may have hopes of reconciliation between God and the creature that is fallen to the Prince of the world and led captive at his will. And this is love indeed, to lay down all for such as are yet enemies.

Go on and prosper in the name of the Lord, and in righteousness make war; and all that are zealous for truth and purity shall say amen. But the slothful, the lukewarm, and all unclean persons, shut themselves out as not for this work, nor worthy to be counted faithful nor chosen.

9. Quaker Martyrology: The Visitation of Massachusetts (1656-61)

The literature of sufferings has long been recognized as a special form of Quaker writing.[56] Joseph Smith's *Catalogue of Friends'*

[56] Cf. BSP, pp. 281-85, as used here; Lloyd, *Quaker Social History,* ch. XI; and Henry Cadbury, *Narrative Papers of George Fox* (1972), ch. VII.

Books (1867) groups 224 titles before 1689 under the heading *Sufferings* (and others for later years); most of these are also listed by author or title. The biggest groups came from the Commonwealth (66) and Restoration (89) decades. (Our list includes 90 in the 1650's and 118 in the 1660's when 42 were also appeals for toleration.) Smith's earliest is *Saul's Errand* (cf. pp. 64, 259), but there continued to be reports on fines and imprisonment for tithe-refusers well into the eighteenth century.

Smith's list includes many types of document, from petitions to tract debates, but is important for showing a gradual shift in the types and moods predominating from one decade to another. In the Commonwealth years the sufferings tracts were clearly a form of the literature of proclamation: they are theocratic, even apocalyptic, with strong appeals for the reader's repentance. The linking of the first English Protestants with Mary Tudor's Smithfield fires and the Massacre of St. Bartholomew's Day in France had made martyrdom and victory against anti-Christian rulers the heritage of all Huguenots and Puritans; these were bound to be embarrassed when Friends turned this tradition against them. Typical Quaker titles are *The Saints Testimony Finishing through Sufferings* (1655), describing the Banbury trial of Anne Audland and her fellow-preachers, and *The West Answering the North, in the fierce and cruel persecution of the Manifestation of the Son of God . . . in George Fox, Edward Pyot and William Salt at Lanceston* (1657), each also preserving the records of a key collision in which Friends converged to challenge the hostility of local powers. The most famous such writings are the ten of 1659-61 presenting the Massachusetts martyrology, two of which follow here. [57]

[57] Priority is usually given to Humphrey Norton's *New England's Ensign* (1659), though Robert Fowler's account of the voyage of his little ship *Woodhouse* to carry English Friends to New England came out the same year, as did *New England, the Degenerate Plant,* by the newly won (and banished) Massachusetts Friends Samuel Shattuck, Nicholas Phelps, and Josiah Southwick, with John Rous and John Copeland. In 1660, the *Call from Death to Life* provided the main letters and documents of Robinson and Stephenson, reworked in the more influential *Declaration of the Sad and Great Persecution* of Edward Burrough, while Penington's *Examination of the Grounds* and Humphrey Smith's *To New England's Pretended Christians* refuted the Bostonians' self-justifications. Finally, in 1661, George Bishop in the first two parts of *New England Judged* assembled all these materials into the fullest and best known of all these New England martyr-tracts. Later retellings of the story have leaned mainly on these sources, notably Besse's *Sufferings* (Vol. II, 1753); James Bowden, *History of the Society of Friends in America* (Vol. I,

Toward the end of the Commonwealth, Quaker proclamations began to blend with pragmatic data-gathering aimed to influence the government to end Friends' sufferings at specific issues and localities. *The Record of the Suffering for Tythes in England: the Sufferers are the Seed of God* (1658) is one such title; another is *A Declaration of the Present Sufferings of Above 140 Persons of the People of God (who are now in Prison) called Quakers, with a brief Accompt of above 1900 more . . . delivered to Thomas Bampfield, then Speaker of Parliament; . . . Also a Cry of Judgement at Hand upon the Oppressors of the Lord's Heritage* (6/2/1659).

Such rosters of sufferings continued to be common throughout the Restoration years, particularly at times when toleration or indulgence seemed in sight, such as 1669, 1672, and 1676. The Meeting for Sufferings, which crystallized as a monthly national clearing-house for Quaker prisoners' needs, also worked to collect such records. The forty-four folio volumes of manuscript evidence, which the Yearly Meeting wanted to digest for printing as early as 1676, were finally only published by Besse eighty years later. [58] Meanwhile the lists of imprisoned Friends were used for appeals and pardons, so that the Friends' Meeting clerks in each county were urged to send them accurately and fully to Ellis Hookes in London.

In the 1660's, therefore, Quaker tracts on sufferings were mostly appeals to the general public. They were still often personal cases, for these were the years when those who worshipped in Conventicles were sentenced on the third offense to be transported and banished, and when the plague and overcrowding killed five hundred Friends in prison. So titles like *A Hue and Cry against Bloodshed* (1662) predominate. But Friends no longer expected to convince their readers wholly for Quakerism; titles like *The Cry of the Innocent and Oppressed for Justice* (five supplements, 1664-76) became ever commoner, especially after the Penn-Mead trial of 1670 showed that, even if justice could not always be won in the courts, injustice would be fought by non-Quaker citizens. While there was a *Cry of the Oppressed* (by Thomas Rudd) as late as 1700, the 1680's and '90's turned Quaker sufferings literature away from public pleading and toward the

1850); Rufus M. Jones, *Quakers in the American Colonies* (1911); and Mary Hoxie Jones, *The Standard of the Lord Lifted Up* (New England Yearly Meeting, 1961).

[58] Cf. BSP, p. 282; *JFHS,* I, 15; XXIII, 1-11.

pattern of mutual encouragement among Friends that had begun with James Parnell. The records of imprisonment became memorials to deceased Friends and examples for their easier-going descendants. Joseph Besse, who otherwise wrote mainly theological refutations, produced the all-inclusive and definitive *Collection of the Sufferings* (1753), twenty years after his first summary *Abstract of the Sufferings* and forty after John Whiting's *Persecution Exposed.* These were written for Quaker readers. The Massachusetts martyrology, by contrast, was not only written for non-Friends, but still keeps its setting as part of the Day of Visitation.

The confrontation in Massachusetts has the dimensions of a classic tragedy. The Boston Puritans had given up homes, careers, and homeland to build a new Commonwealth on a Calvinist (they would have said biblical) model. Their hopes that it would be a "pilot model" for England itself had been frustrated just in the moment of Puritan victory over the king, when Cromwell's regiments, and the Separatists and Independents generally, had overridden their attempt at Westminster to set up a single uniform English church. Now the worst of the same radical sects had appeared in New England with the explicit intention of overthrowing their constitution there, the Cambridge Platform of 1647. They were desperate, too, because individualism and moral radicalism were always ready to burst out in their own population, as they had already found with Roger Williams and Ann Hutchinson. Their life-work was at stake; hence the death penalty. Yet this penalty confirmed in the minds of Friends and the internal rebels the conviction that the Massachusetts Commonwealth was founded upon Antichrist and justified the giving of their lives to break it. The Quakers from within and without succeeded, and from 1660 onward the Massachusetts government was of necessity ever more secular; the only attempt to turn back to religious ideals led to the worse disaster of the Salem witch trials. By the end of the century a royal governor ruled the biblical Commonwealth.

—DOCUMENTS ON QUAKERS AND THE GOVERNMENT OF MASSACHUSETTS—

A COLLECTION OF THE SUFFERINGS
Of the PEOPLE called QUAKERS.
FOR THE TESTIMONY OF A GOOD CONSCIENCE. FROM
The TIME of their being first distinguished by that NAME in the Year 1650,
to the TIME of the Act, commonly called the Act of Toleration, granted to

119

Protestant Dissenters in the first Year of the Reign of King WILLIAM the Third and Queen MARY, in the Year 1689.

Taken from ORIGINAL RECORDS and other AUTHENTIC ACCOUNTS, by JOSEPH BESSE.

VOLUME II
London:
Printed and sold by Luke Hinde at the Bible in George-Yard, Lombard-Street, 1753.

[p. 177] CHAP. V

NEW ENGLAND[59]

In that province they had, long before any of the Quakers came thither, *viz.* in the year 1646, made a law or order for Uniformity in Religion by imposing a penalty of five shillings per week on such as came not to hear the established ministers. Thus they early began to entrench themselves against any farther discoveries of truth and religion by a penal law. And as to the Quakers, they had received an unreasonable prejudice against them, as appears by their rigid treatment of the first of them who came into that country.

ANNO 1656. When in the fifth month, called July, two women of that persuasion arrived in a vessel from Barbados in the road [-stead] before Boston: intelligence of their arrival being given to Richard Bellingham, the Deputy-Governor (the Governor himself being out of town), he immediately ordered them to be detained on board, and sent officers, who searched their trunks and chests and took away about a hundred books, which they carried on shore. The danger which was apprehended from the arrival of these women and the spreading of their books, produced the following order, *viz.*

"At a Council held at Boston, the 11th of July, 1656.

"Whereas there are several laws long since made and published in this jurisdiction, bearing testimony against heretics and erroneous persons, yet notwithstanding Simon Kempthorn, of Charles-Town, Master of the Ship Swallow, of Boston, hath brought into this jurisdiction, from the Island of Barbados, two women, who name themselves Anne, the wife of one Austin, and Mary Fisher, being of that sort of people commonly known by the name of Quakers, who upon examination are found not only [p. 178] to be

---

[59] Most of this material had also been printed in Humphrey Norton, *New England's Ensign* (1659).

transgressors of the former laws, but do hold very dangerous, heretical and blasphemous opinions; and they do also acknowledge that they came here purposely to propagate their said errors and heresies, bringing with them and spreading here sundry books, wherein are contained most corrupt, heretical, and blasphemous doctrines, contrary to the truth of the Gospel here professed among us.

"The Council therefore, tendering the preservation of the peace and truth enjoyed and professed among the Churches of Christ in this country, do hereby order,

"First, that all such corrupt books as shall be found upon search, to be brought in and spread by the aforesaid persons, be forthwith burned and destroyed by the common executioner.

"Secondly, that the said Anne and Mary be kept in close prison and none admitted communication with them without leave from the Governor, Deputy-Governor, or two Magistrates, to prevent the spreading of their corrupt opinions, until such time as they be delivered aboard of some vessel to be transported out of the country.

"Thirdly, the said Simon Kempthorn is hereby enjoined speedily and directly to transport, or cause to be transported, the said persons from hence to Barbados, from whence they came, he defraying all the charges of their imprisonment; and for the effectual performance hereof, he is to give security in a bond of one hundred pounds sterling; and on his refusal to give such security, he is to be committed to prison till he do it."

In consequence of this order, their books were burnt by the hangman in the market-place, and they, being brought on shore, . . . in prison they were kept close, and an order given that none should speak with them, no not through the window. . . .

A few days after sending away these women, *viz.* on the 7th of the month called August, eight others of the same persuasion, namely Christopher Holder, Thomas Thurston, William Brend, John Copeland, Mary Prince, Sarah Gibbons, Mary Wetherhead, and Dorothy Waugh, arrived at Boston from London in a ship whereof Robert Lock was master. He would not let them go on shore till he had given a list of their names to the Governor, who sent officers on board to search their boxes, chests, and trunks for books, and to bring those eight, together with Richard Smith, an inhabitant of Long Island, before the Court, then sitting at Boston. After some examination they were sentenced to banishment and to be kept in prison till they might be sent back whence they came by the same ship: the master of which was required to give security to carry them back at his own charge, which he refusing, was sent to prison; but after some days confinement, fearing the loss of his voyage, he complied. They were kept in prison about eleven weeks.

121

[p. 179] While they were yet in prison, a law was made to punish them, being the first general law made expressly against Quakers; for the two women had been sent away by particular orders respecting them only. This law was as follows:

"At a General Court held at Boston, the 14th of October, 1656. . . . What-[ever] master or commander of any ship, bark, pink, or catch shall henceforth bring into any harbor, creek or cove within this Jurisdiction any Quaker or Quakers or other blasphemous heretics, shall pay or cause to be paid the fine of one hundred pounds.

[p. 180] If any person within this Colony shall take upon them to defend the heretical opinions of the Quakers or any of their books or papers as aforesaid, if legally proved, shall be fined for the first time forty shillings; if they shall persist in the same and shall again defend it the second time, four pounds. . . .

"This is a true copy of the Court's Order, as attests
Edward Rawson, Secr."

[Besse then describes the arrivals and punishments of Anne Burden, Mary Dyer, and Mary Clark in 1657, and of the *Woodhouse* shipload via Nieuw Amsterdam—ten Quakers including Christopher Holder, Mary Wetherhead, Dorothy Waugh, Humphrey Norton, and William Robinson, under Captain Robert Fowler. Citizens of Massachusetts sympathetic with Friends were also punished or banished (see p. 138). Many Friends came to Boston and Salem via Rhode Island, like William Leddra from Barbados; so did Rhode Islanders like Mary Dyer who had been convinced by English Quakers in transit. In Boston, William Brand was brutally flogged, and Holder, Copeland, and John Rous had their right ears cut off. William Marsden of Salem was fined £10 for possessing two Quaker tracts, John Lilburne's *Resurrection* and Dewsbury's *Mighty Day.*]

[p. 190] John Norton and the other priests petitioned the magistrates to cause the Court to make some law to banish the Quakers upon pain of death. The magistrates, thus excited by the priests, made the less scruple in this bloody business. However, it was carried with no little opposition; for the Court, where this law was made, consisted of twenty-five persons, and when it was put to the vote, twelve were against it, so that it was carried only by one vote. This so troubled one Wozel, a deacon of their church, when he heard it, having through sickness been absent, that he got to the Court, and weeping for grief that his absence should occasion such a law to pass, said, if he had been able to go, he would have crept thither upon his knees rather than such a law should have passed. Thus the persecuting party carried their point; yet there was great difference in the Court, and the twelve, who had voted in the negative, resolved to enter their dissents to that law.

Thus their sanguinary law for banishment on pain of death, was passed on

122

the 20th of October, 1658, being as follows. . . . Notwithstanding all former laws made upon the experience of their arrogant and bold obtrusions, to disseminate their principles amongst us, prohibiting their coming into this Jurisdiction, they have not been deterred from their impetuous attempts to undermine our peace, and hazard our ruin.

"For prevention thereof, this Court doth order and enact that every person or persons of the cursed sect of the Quakers who is not an inhabitant of but is found within this Jurisdiction, shall be apprehended without warrant, where no magistrate is at hand, by any constable, commissioner, or select man, and conveyed from constable to constable, to the next magistrate, who shall commit the said person to close prison, there to remain (without bail) unto the next Court of Assistants, where they shall have a legal trial; and being convicted to be of the sect of the Quakers, shall be sentenced to be banished upon pain of death. . . .

−From: George Bishop, *New England Judged.* (1661)−
Marmaduke Stevenson's paper of his call to the work and service of the Lord. Given forth by him a little before he was put to death, and after he had received his sentence.[60]

In the beginning of the year 1655, I was at the plough in the east parts of York-shire in Old England, near the place where my outward being was, and as I walked after the plough, I was filled with the love and the presence of the Living God, which did ravish my heart when I felt it; for it did increase and abound in me like a living stream, so did the love and life of God run through me like precious ointment, giving a pleasant smell; which made me to stand still; and as I stood a little still with my heart and mind stayed on the Lord, the Word of the Lord came to me in a still small voice, which I did hear perfectly, saying to me in the secret of my heart and conscience, "I have ordained thee a prophet unto the nations." And at the hearing of the Word of the Lord, I was put to a stand, being that I was but a child for such a weighty matter. So at the time appointed, Barbados was set before me, unto which I

60 George Bishop of Bristol was evidently a local Puritan politician as well as an ex-captain of Cromwell's army and in 1651 in Cromwell's secret service as secretary of a "Committee of Examination." His sympathies were with the Levellers and radicals, both in 1654 when they lost influence, and again in 1659 when they briefly regained it. Since Bristol was the port through which Fox and most Friends sailed for America, Bishop was a natural person to collect and edit their reports and to add the weight of his name to their publication. The report of Stevenson (more usually Stephenson) is also in Besse, II, 201-2. Henry Fell in Barbados played a key role in transmitting news.

was required of the Lord to go, and leave my dear and loving wife and tender children. For the Lord said unto me immediately by his Spirit that he would be as a husband to my wife and as a father to my children, and they should not want in my absence, for he would provide for them when I was gone. And I believed that the Lord would perform what he had spoken, because I was made willing to give up myself to his work and service, to leave all and follow him, whose presence and life is with me, where I rest in peace and quietness of spirit (with my dear brother) under the shadow of his wings, who hath made us willing to lay down our lives for his own name sake, if unmerciful men be [p. 108] suffered to take them from us; and if they do, we know we shall have peace and rest with the Lord forever in his Holy Habitation, when they shall have torment night and day. So in obedience to the Living God, I made preparation to pass to Barbados in the fourth month, 1658. So after some time I had been on the said island in the service of God, I heard that New England had made a law to put the servants of the Living God to death if they returned after they were sentenced away, which did come near me at that time. And as I considered the thing and pondered it in my heart, immediately came the Word of the Lord unto me, saying, "Thou knowest not but that thou mayest go thither." But I kept this word in my heart and did not declare it to any until the time appointed. So after that a vessel was made ready for Rhode Island, which I passed in. So after a little time that I had been there, visiting the seed which the Lord hath blessed, the Word of the Lord came unto me, saying, "Go to Boston with thy brother William Robinson." And at his command I was obedient and gave up myself to do his will, that so his work and service may be accomplished; for he had said unto me that he had a great work for me to do, which is now come to pass. And for yielding obedience to and obeying the voice and command of the Everliving God, which created heaven and earth, and the fountains of waters, do I with my dear brother suffer outward bonds near unto death. And this is given forth to be upon record, that all people may know who hear it, that we came not in our own wills but in the will of God. Given forth by me, who am known to men by the name of

Marmaduke Stevenson.

Written in the Boston prison in the 8th month, 1659	But have a new name given me, which the world knows not of, written in the Book of Life.

A CALL FROM DEATH TO LIFE, AND

Out of the dark ways and worships of the world where the Seed is held in bondage under the merchants of Babylon, written by Marmaduke Stephen-

son:[61] *Who (together with another dear Servant of the Lord, called William Robinson) hath (since the writing hereof) suffered death for bearing witness to the same truth, amongst the professors of Boston's jurisdiction in New England. With a true copy of two letters, which they writ to the Lord's People a little before their death. And also . . . a brief relation of the manner of their martyrdom, with some of the words which they expressed at the time of their suffering.*

John 16:2, 3 [quoted]

London: Printed for Thomas Simmons, at the Sign of the Bull and Mouth near Aldersgate. 1660.

(p. 2) To the READER.

But especially to you that are professors (one in doctrine and discipline with the professors in New England) do we write these things, that the witness of God may arise in you to judge between the Lord's people called Quakers and your Brethren the professors in New England, whether they have not forgotten God and his goodness towards them, and lost their first love which was stirring in them when they were little amongst the families of the earth. . . . [They have become children of Antichrist.] Oh! how are they fallen that once seemed so tender in conscience, as that they would rather leave their native country than practice things contrary to their conscience. . . . For they have taken two of God's dear servants and hanged them on a tree for no matter of fact committed by them against any law which is just, but because they were found by their words and actions to be Quakers, and did (contrary to the sentence of banishment, which upon pain of death, the Court passed upon them) return into their Jurisdiction as they were required of God to bear witness unto the truth . . . and that they [A-2] might be clear from the blood of all men, in giving them warning to repent and walk in the Light of the Lord, their lives were not dear to them. . . . [But those born after the flesh persecute the Spirit.]

And here we do appeal to the witness of God in you all, professors and people, whether the professors in New England have not acted quite contrary to God in imprisoning, scourging, banishing and killing those that tremble at his Word. . . . And again we say, let the witness of God in you judge, whether they have not acted directly contrary to Christ in destroying men's lives, seeing he comes not to destroy men's lives but to save men's lives. . . .

[61] This tract is listed by Wing under Peter Pearson's name, but the collecting of these letters was evidently the work of John Whitehead and other Yorkshire Friends.

[p. 4] That it may appear that these two (which the professors of New England have taken and by wicked hands put to death) were the servants of Christ Jesus and of the Household of God, we do here present to thy view these things following, which were writ by their own hands, and sent unto us not long before their death; together with a letter which was writ from Plymouth in New England by Peter Pearson, relating the manner of their death, with some of their words which they did express a little before their martyrdom; all which we desire may be seriously weighed and laid to heart, that the witness of God may rise in judgement against the spirit of persecution in whomsoever it appears. . . .

Written in York-shire,
the 23rd. day of
the 3rd month.
1660.

John Whitehead.
Marmaduke Storr.
William Padley.
Gregory Milner.
Thomas Leemin.

[p. 5] *A Call from Death to Life, and out of the dark ways and worships of the world, where the seed is held in bondage under the merchants of Babylon.*

M.S.

Oh you, my dear neighbors and people in the town of Shipton and Wighton and elsewhere where this may come, who have been spending long your money for that which is not bread, and your labor for that which doth not satisfy, as I have done; oh come buy wine and milk without money and without price, while it is held forth to you, lest the day come that you be deprived of it; for long hath the Spirit of the Lord been striving with you (as it did with me), but you have resisted it time after time, because it testified against you when you went on in sin, and reproved in secret for the evil of your doings; therefore you do not regard it, but flies[62] from it. So in bowels of tender love to you all do I speak, and in love and pity to your souls, prize the love of God and his tender mercy and forbearance to you, that he did not cut you off in the height of your iniquity but hath spared you until this day, though you have long taken pleasure in sin, not regarding God that made you;

---

[62] Such use of "singular" verb-ending with a plural subject is a north-of-England dialect form, and part of the process by which medieval forms like "he goeth" changed to modern speech. It seems to underlie both modern colloquialisms like "says you" and "I says" and the American Quaker traditions such as "Thee says" (for "thou sayest"). We have kept these forms throughout our text where differences of speech, rather than spelling, seem to be involved.

126

yet hath his Spirit been striving with you many days and years (as it did with me) and hath reproved you time after time, for the evil of your doings, but you regarded it not, though it often called upon you in love and meekness to depart from your iniquity and that which you have been addicted to. It hath reproved and called you that have been addicted to drunkenness, lying and swearing to depart from these things, for they are evil; and it hath called upon you that are proud and covetous to depart from them; and hath reproved you that have been wild and wanton and given to sports and pleasures, to depart from them and run on no longer in vanity; but you did not regard it, but took pleasure in sin. Oh consider dear neighbors and people, what you have been doing ever since you came to years of maturity, and let the witness of God which is faithful and true in you all arise and answer, to which I speak, and it will let you see that you have provoked the Lord.

[This epistle, which was his last word to his home and friends, continues entirely as earnest exhortation, with no personal comments about his own situation. It concludes:]

[p. 18] Yet truth is truth and will stand forever over the heads of all its enemies, and here comes the Scriptures to be fulfilled, for many are called but few are chosen. And this hath appeared in our generation, that many have had a true taste of the love of God and of the Powers of the World to come, but they are gone from it again and are turned aside into the crooked path, like the dog to his vomit and like the sow that was washed into the mire again, where they are defiled with the flesh-pots of Egypt, which they lusted after. Oh! is not the unclean spirit entered into them again and become worse than he was before; so none rejoice at the hearing of those that turns from the truth, which they were once in, for verily it will not ease you of your misery and torment which will come upon you if you go on in sin and despise the day of your visitation. So to you all I have cleared my conscience in the sight of God.

Written in the Common Jail	From a friend of truth, and a
of Boston in New England,	sufferer for the seed's sake
in America, in the beginning	which is kept in bondage under
of the seventh month, 1659.	Pharaoh and his Taskmasters,
	my name in the flesh is[63]
	Marmaduke Stephenson.

63 This is a phrase much used in early Quaker writings; while it clearly refers to the "new name" written in the Lamb's "Book of Life" in Revelation (2:17; 3:5), it may reflect some actual use of secret names among early Friends (who wrote about each other usually only with initials: J.N., E.B., ff.G [for Fox, etc.]).

These are copies of letters sent from William Robinson and Marmaduke Stephenson (after they were banished) unto Christopher Holder, a prisoner in Boston Common Prison.

Christopher Holder,

O my dearly beloved of my father, my soul and life salutes thee, for thou art dear to me in the love which changeth not, but doth endure forever; am I one with thee in the life and power of truth, where we are joined together as members of his Body who is our Head, and our preserver night and day, where we are kept safe under the shadow of his wings, where we feed together in the green pastures [p. 19] by the pleasant springs, where thou may feel me, my beloved one, at the living fountain which doth refresh the whole city of our God, where we are daily refreshed together in the banqueting house, where we do receive strength and nourishment from him who is our life and fills us with his living virtue day by day, which is as precious ointment poured forth giving a pleasant smell, and is pleasant to behold. For it hath ravished our hearts whereby we are constrained to leave all to follow it, who gathers our hearts in one, where I am joined and sealed with thee in the covenant of life, where we shall forever remain the bosom of the father, after our testimonies are finished. Then shall we lay down our heads, in peace with all the faithful. Even so the Lord keep us all as witnesses of his truth, so that we may be armed with his power and strength in the hour of temptation, and in the day of trial to support us and bear us up in his arms, that so he may be honored by us who alone is worthy of all glory and honor, to whom it doth belong now and forever, Amen. So with my love to thee I rest, who am thy dear brother in the truth.

Marmaduke Stephenson.

C. Holder,

Dearly beloved brother, whom my soul dearly loves, and my spirit and life doth dearly embrace in God's love and life, power and truth, thou may feel me with thee in the arms of the Lord where we are kept, who is our strength and the portion of our cup forever. God knows how my life doth flow forth unto thee, from the river of our God which daily runs through us, wherewith we are daily refreshed, and whereby our strength is daily renewed; for surely the Lord is with us, and who shall be able to stand against us. Dear heart, in the sweet and pleasant habitation of our God, in the mansion house of my father and thy father, feel me with thee, for surely we have all one God to our Lord, who is our king and our law-giver; for truly out of one womb

128

have we all come, and at one fountain do we all drink and are daily nourished, dear heart; where thou may feel me with thee in the life, where we are sealed together for evermore. Oh! my dear beloved, my soul doth greatly love thee. Oh! I cannot express it, but thou may feel it in the covenant of everlasting love, where we are united by the spirit of truth and holiness in the power and heavenly peace of God; feel me with thee where neither [p. 20] length of time nor distance of place can separate us, nay all the powers nor strength of darkness it cannot break it. In the same life and love and authority of God, the Lord forever keep us and grant that it may be with us for evermore, Amen. Which I know the Lord God will perform: even so be it, saith my soul. Dear heart, the remembrance of thee doth ravish my soul, and by it is my heart filled with pure love and joy. Oh! the Lord God knows how greatly I long to see thy face, but dear heart, I have not the freedom in the Lord to accomplish it, for I see some service I have to fulfill before I come to Boston, if the enemy hinder not, for truly hitherto I have seen the hand of the Lord greatly with us.

William Robinson.

[Three more letters follow, in similar spirit and language.]

[p. 21] This was written by William Robinson to the Court of Boston.

On the 8th day of the 4th month, 1659, in the after part of the day, in traveling betwixt Newport (on Rhode Island) and Daniel Gould's house with my dear brother Christopher Holder, the Word of the Lord came expressly to me, which did fill me immediately with life and power and heavenly love, by which he constrained me and commanded me [p. 22] to pass to the town of Boston, my life to lay down in his will, for the accomplishing of his service that he had there to perform at the day appointed; to which heavenly voice I presently yielded obedience, not questioning the Lord how he would bring the thing to pass, being I was a child and obedience was demanded of me by the Lord, who filled me with living strength and power from his heavenly presence, which at that time did mightily overshadow me. And my life did say Amen to what the Lord required of me and had commanded me to do, and willingly was I given up from that time to this day, the will of the Lord to do, and perform, whatever becomes of my body: for the Lord hath said unto me, [that] my soul shall rest in Eternal peace, and my life shall enter into rest, for being obedient to the God of my life. I being a child, and durst not question the Lord in the least, but rather willing to lay down my life than to bring dishonor to the Lord; and as the Lord made me willing, dealing gently and kindly with me, as a tender father towards a faithful child whom he

129

dearly loves, so the Lord did deal with me in ministering of his life unto me, which gave and gives me strength to perform what the Lord hath required of me. And still as I did and do stand in need, he ministered and ministreth more strength and virtue and heavenly power and wisdom, whereby I was and am made strong in God, not fearing what man shall be suffered to do unto me, being filled with heavenly courage, which is meekness and innocence; for the cause is the Lord's that we go in, and the battle is the Lord's; . . . Friends, the God of my life and the God of the whole earth did lay this thing upon me, for which I now suffer bonds near to death. He by his almighty power and everlasting love constrained me and laid this thing upon me, and truly I could not deny the Lord, much less resist the Holy One of Israel. Therefore all who are ignorant of the motion of the Lord in the inward parts, be not hasty in judging in this matter before you hear the truth of the matter, lest you speak evil of the things you know not; for of a truth the Lord God of heaven and earth commanded me by his Spirit, and spoke unto [p. 23] me by his Son, whom he hath made Heir of all things. And in his life I live, and in it I shall depart this earthly tabernacle, if unmerciful men be suffered to take it from me. And herein I rejoice that the Lord is with me, the ancient of days, the life of the suffering Seed, for which I am freely given up, and singly do stand in the will of God. . . . I can say in truth and from an upright heart, "Blessed be the Lord the God of my life, who hath counted me worthy, and called me hereunto, to bear my testimony against ungodly and unrighteous men, who seek to take away the life of the righteous without a cause," as the rulers of the Massachusetts Bay doth intend, if the Lord stop them not from their intent. Oh! hear ye rulers, and give ear and listen all ye that have any hand herein to put the innocent to death: for in the name and fear and dread of the Lord God, I here declare the cause of my staying here amongst you, and continuing in your jurisdiction, after there was a sentence of banishment upon death (as you said) pronounced against me . . . with my companion, unto whom the word of the Lord God came unto him saying, "Go to Boston with thy brother William Robinson"; unto which command he was obedient . . . it is in obedience to the Lord the God of the whole earth that we continued amongst you, and that we came to the town of Boston again in obedience to the Lord the creator of heaven and earth, in whose hand your breath is. . . . If you do this act and put us to death, know this, and be it known unto you all ye rulers and people of this jurisdiction, that whosoever hath a hand herein will be guilty of innocent blood, and not only upon yourselves will ye bring innocent blood but upon this town and the inhabitants thereof, and [p. 24] everywhere within your jurisdiction that had the least hand therein; therefore be instructed ye rulers of this land, and take warning betimes, and learn wisdom before it be hid from your eyes.

Written in the common
jail, the 19th of the
8th month, 1659, in
Boston.

Written by one who feareth the Lord,
who is by ignorant people called a
Quaker, and unto such am only known
by the name *William Robinson*; yet a
new name I have received, which such
knows not.[64]

A relation from the two innocent servants of the Lord concerning the (bloody) sentence of death passed on them by John Endicott in the Court of Boston.

On the 20th day of the 8th month, 1659, I with my beloved companion, Marmaduke Stevenson, and Mary Dyer of Rhode Island, was had into the Court, where John Endicott with others of his Council were assembled; and soon after we were come to the Bar before them, John Endicott called to the keeper of the prison to pull off our hats, which was done accordingly. Then did John Endicott begin to speak unto us as a man out of the dust, whose life is departing from him, so faintly did he utter his words unto us, to this effect: that they had made several laws, and tried and endeavoured by several ways to keep us from among them, and neither whipping, nor imprisoning, nor cutting off ears, nor banishing upon pain of death would not keep us from amongst them. And he said also, he or they desired not the death of any of us; yet notwithstanding, his following words were, "Give ear and hearken now to your sentence of death," said John Endicott their Governor. So after these words were spoken by him he stopped, the words being uttered very faintly out of his mouth. Then I did make way to speak to John Endicott and the rest of the Court, which was, as I remember, to this effect: I desired I might read a paper to them and the people there present (which was many), which was a declaration of my call, wherein was declared the reasons and causes of my staying in their jurisdiction with my companion after banishment upon death which had been pronounced against us and two more friends [p. 25] (the one of which is a sufferer now with us) on the 8th day of the 7th month last; at which words speaking, John Endicott their Governor in a furious manner (for rage and madness like Nebuchadnezzar was got up in him) said, I should not read it, neither would they hear it read: which thing only at that time I desired before the sentence of death was pronounced against us; yet he would not grant it. So I seeing, and being sensible of their

64 Robinson's letter is also in Bishop (pp. 103-6) and in Besse (II, 199-201).

131

hardness of heart that they are given up to work wickedness and commit murder in laboring to take the lives of the innocent from the earth, I said unto them, seeing that I could not be suffered to have it read unto the people that then was present. I said I should leave the paper with them, which I did soon cast upon the table amongst them; and the secretary or some other handed it to the Governor, who read it himself, but would not let it be read in the hearing of the people. And when he had looked a certain time on it, he called me by my name and said I needed not have made such ado or desired to have it read; for he said I had spoke more than that unto them the day before concerning it; which I had not, for there is many words in the paper which I did not then utter unto them, so that I desired the thing again, that all that was there present might hear it, but he would not suffer it; but soon after in envy called me by my name and said unto me, "Hearken unto your sentence of death," which he uttered forth to this effect (in which time I was silent), he said, "William Robinson, this is your sentence: you shall be had back from the place from whence you came, and from thence to the place of execution, to be hanged on the gallows till you are dead." This was the sentence of death John Endicott their Governor pronounced against me, and soon after called to the jailor to have me away, which he did accordingly.

William Robinson.

Soon after my dear brother W.R. was taken away out of the Court, the Governor being partial, spoke unto me, saying, "If you have anything to say, you may speak;" but I was silent and gave him no answer then, so that when he saw that I would not speak, when he required of me, then he pronounced the sentence of death against me, as he had upon my brother before: "You shall be had to the place from whence you came, and from thence to the gallows, and there to be hanged until you be dead." Then did these words following run through me: "Give ear ye magistrates, and all who are guilty, for this the Lord hath said concerning you, who will perform his promise upon you, that the same day that you put his servants to death shall the day of your visitation pass over your heads, and [p. 26] you shall be cursed for evermore; the mouth of the Lord of Hosts hath spoken it. Therefore in love to you all take warning before it be too late, that so the curse might be removed, for assuredly if you put us to death, you will bring innocent blood upon your own heads, and swift destruction will come upon you." So after these words were spoken unto them, I was had to prison again, where my brother was.

Marmaduke Stephenson.

The like sentence did John Endicott their Governor pronounce against Mary Dyer, after M.S. was had away: "Mary Dyer, you shall go to the place from whence you came, namely the prison, and from thence to the place of execution, and be hanged there till you are dead." I said, "The will of the Lord be done." "Take her away, marshal." I said "yea, and joyfully I go:" and in the way to the prison often used such speeches with praises to the Lord for the same. I said to the marshal, "Let me alone," for I should go to prison without him. "I believe you, Mrs. Dyer," said he, "but I must do what I am commanded."

Mary Dyer.

[Omitting a letter from Stephenson]
[p. 28] This is a copy of W.R., his letter to the Lord's people.

The streams of my father's love runs daily through me from the holy fountain of life to the seed throughout the whole creation. I am [p. 29] overcome with love, for it is my life and length of my days, it's my glory and my daily strength. I am swallowed up with love, in love I live, and with it I am overcome, and in it I dwell with the Holy Seed, to which the blessing of love is given from God who is love, who hath shed it abroad in my heart which daily fills me with living joy from the life from whence it comes. You children of the living God, feel me when you are waiting in it, when your hearts and minds are gathered into it, when in the strength of it you are traveling feel me, when it runs from the fountain into your vessel, when it issues gently like new wine into your bosoms, when the strength and power of it you feel, when you are overcome with the strength of love (which is God), then feel me present in the fountain of love, wherein are many mansions. You children of the Lord feel me wrapped up with you in the pure love which destroys the love which is in enmity with God, which warreth against the Seed which proceedeth from the father of love, the God of truth. Let nothing separate you from this love which is my life, neither words nor thoughts nor nothing else enter betwixt which is contrary to it, for that will stain the place of its abode. . . . With the life of it I am filled, and with it I shall depart with everlasting joy in my heart and praises in my mouth, singing Hallelujah unto the Lord, who hath redeemed me by his living power from amongst kindreds, tongues and nations. And now the day of my departure draweth near, I have fought a good fight, I have kept the holy faith, I have near finished my course, my traveling is near at an end, my testimony is near to be finished, and an eternal crown is laid up for me, and all whose feet are shod with righteousness and the preparation of peace, even such whose names are written in the Book of Life, wherein I live and rejoice with all the faithful Seed for evermore.

The 23rd day of the 8th month was this given forth, and he	Written by a servant of Jesus Christ,

suffered the 27th day of the   William Robinson.
same month at Boston in New
England, 1659.

This is a copy of Peter Pearson's letter, wherein is a relation of M.S. and W.R.'s suffering.[65]

Dear brethren unto whom my life is united in the invisible unlimited power of the Lord God Almighty: I give you a relation of diverse [p. 30] passages, wherein is tidings of heaviness and joy. Our dear brethren, the two servants of the Lord, William Robinson and Marmaduke Stephenson, have finished their course in the pure dominion and eternal majesty of the almighty God, and are laid down in Abraham's bosom in the heavenly kingdom of endless felicity, where the life of all the upright is united with their life to all perpetuity; so that their memorial shall never rot, for their name, their life, is left upon heavenly record and shall never be blotted out from the life of the Tribe of the Faithful. Upon the 9th day of the 4th month, 1659, the 4th day of the week, had all us English Friends that were abroad in this country a meeting upon Rhode Island, the 6th day following of the same week at a ferry side upon Rhode Island, did one friend whose name is William Leddra and I part with Christopher Holder, Marmaduke Stephenson, and William Robinson, we being about to pass over the ferry, to travel into this part of the country called Plymouth Colony. At the end of two days' journey we came to a town therein called Sandwich, and the day following had a pretty peaceable meeting, and it was with us, if we did escape apprehending in this colony, to have traveled into Boston's jurisdiction; but the second and last meeting that we had determined to have at Sandwich, in which we were apprehended and had before the Governor and magistrates, and by them committed to this prison, where we have remained five months and upward. And being we deny to defray the charges that they have brought themselves into by meddling with us (namely their wicked officers' fees) and also refusing to make an engagement to come into the government no more, we are by their law to remain close prisoners during the Court's pleasure. But well content we are, rejoicing that we are worthy to suffer as witnesses for the Lord against them, and their law, and the thick power of darkness by which they did establish it; this knowing that for our testimony's sake bonds must abide us during the Lord's pleasure. The day after we were taken prisoners was William Robinson and Marmaduke Stephenson imprisoned at Boston, where they remained until the 7th month; in the forepart of the 7th month they were had before their Court of Assistance, and after diverse passages in their examination, the jury (whom they witnessed against as unfit men to try their cause, being out of

---

[65] This is the earliest printed account of the two men's death, though later used by Burrough, Bishop, etc. The letters are given in full nowhere else.

the doctrine of Christ) when they gave in their verdict, said they had found them to be Quakers. So when they were found and judged by their ungodly law to be guilty of the sentence of banishment upon pain of death, they were returned to prison again, and after a little time were had again before their judgment seat, and the sentence of banishment upon pain of death passed upon them, against which their life did arise in power and dominion, being the Lord had commanded them to stay; and William Robinson declared unto them how it stood between them and God. . . . And although they had passed the sentence of banishment upon them, yet this overplus to vent their furious minds in torturing the outward man whilst they had it, they made a decree to have William whipped, and commanded the constable to get a man that was able to do it. So a man being prepared and had before their Court, and judged a man fit for their purpose, they had William Robinson into the open street, and there stripped him and put his hands through the holes of the carriage of a great gun, where the jailor (a member of their Church) held them till the whipper gave him twenty stripes with a threefold cord whip with knots at the ends, which stripes he laid upon his body without mercy or pity. . . . Then they returned him with Marmaduke Stephenson again to prison, and wrote an order to the jailor to discharge the prison of them forthwith. The jailor, when he had taken W.R.'s great coat from him, turned them out of the prison, and after some stay in the town according to their freedom, passed abroad into the country within their jurisdiction, entering into great service and sounding through a dark cloudy country which had not been broken through before, wherein was found honest desires, and divers were convinced the power of the Lord accompanied them, and with astonishment confounded their enemies before them. Great was their service abroad in that jurisdiction for four weeks and upwards, and having acquitted themselves like men, upon the 13th day of the 8th month, they returned again to Boston with six friends that did accompany them, and one friend that went out of this government and met them near Boston, where they were all apprehended and had before the Governor and some of the Counsel. The seven friends were all committed to prison, and M.S. and W.R. were delivered to the custody of the jailor to be kept in chains in a room by themselves, the which was done, they were shut up in a room by themselves, and chains laid upon their right legs. The next week their general Court began, before which they were had and sentenced to die, and so returned to prison again. Upon the 27th day of the same month was the day appointed that they were to be executed; the night before they had notice given of it; then the latter part of the 27th day, being the 5th day of the week after their lecture so called,[66]

---

[66] Puritan churches had two services on Sunday and the second might be called a Lecture, as was the talk or sermon on Thursdays. Most Puritan parishes had a second minister or Teacher for these presentations.

W.R. and M.S. were had forth of the prison into the open street, where was one James Oliver, who was made captain over a band of armed men, by information two hundred, which were prepared to guard them to and at the place of execution, with drums and colors and halberds, guns, swords, picks and half-picks, besides many others on horseback, to keep off the multitude of people. So they set the [p. 32] two dear lambs near the hinder part, and the chief marshal and the drummer next before them, then command being given to march to the place of execution, W.R. spake these words, saying, "This is your hour and the power of darkness." Then the drummer beat up his drum, and after a little space ceased again. Then M. Stephenson spake, saying, "This is the day of your visitation, wherein the Lord hath visited you." Other words passed which were not clearly heard, by reason of the sound of drums. So they walked along in pure retired cheerfulness to the place of execution, triumphing in the strength of the Lamb over all the wrath of man and fury of the beast, in the pure retired heavenly dominion of the invisible God. And when they were come to the ladder's foot, they took their leave each of other, and W.R. stepped up the ladder and spake to the people, saying, "This is the day of your visitation wherein the Lord hath visited you, this is the day the Lord is arisen in his mighty power to be avenged on all his adversaries": and the rope being about his neck, as he spake the executioner bound his legs and hands; and his neck cloth being tied about his face, he said, "Now ye are made manifest." So the executioner being about to turn him off the ladder, he uttered this expression, saying, "I suffer for Christ in whom I live, and for whom I die." So he being turned off, M.S. went up and spake to the people, saying, "Be it known unto all this day that we suffer not as evil-doers but for conscience sake." Then he being bound according to the former manner, as the executioner was about to turn him off the ladder, he uttered these words, saying, "This day shall we be at rest with the Lord." Thus the faithful witnesses sealed their testimony for the Lord against the Dragon's power, and blessedly departed with praises in their mouths, entering joyfully with their beloved into Everlasting Rest.

Written in Plymouth Prison in New England,   Peter Pearson.
the 6th day of the 10th month, 1659.

Mary Dyer, an inhabitant in some part of that country, was likewise sentenced to die when these two friends were, only for coming a second time to Boston, to visit her imprisoned brethren there, and was carried with them to the place of execution; and after they two was executed, she stepped up the ladder and had her coats tied about her feet, and the rope put about her neck, with her face covered; and as the hangman was ready to turn her off, they cried out stop, for she was reprieved; and loosing her feet and bid her come down. But she was not forward to come down, but stood still, saying she was there willing to suffer as her brethren did. Unless they would null their wicked law, she had no freedom to accept their reprieve; but they pulled her down, and a day or two after carried her out of town by force. And yet the rulers of Boston had the impudence to affirm (in their Apology published to vindicate their barbarous proceedings against the innocent) that this Mary Dyer accepted her life, promising or consenting that she would depart their jurisdiction in few days and return no more; thus do they make lies their refuge, and add iniquity to sin.

THE END

The Death of Mary Dyer [from Edward Burrough, 15/1/1660/61] :[67]

A DECLARATION OF THE SAD AND GREAT PERSECUTION AND MARTYRDOM
Of the People of God, called Quakers, in New-England, for the Worshipping Of God, Whereof

22 have been Banished upon pain of Death.

03 have been *Martyred*

03 have had their Right Ears cut

01 hath been burned in the Hand with the letter H.

31 Persons have received 650 stripes

01 was beat while his Body was like a jelly.

Several were beat with Pitched Ropes

Five Appeals made to England were denied by the Rulers of Boston

One thousand forty four pounds worth of goods hath been taken from them (being poor men) for meeting together in the fear of the Lord, and for keeping the Commands of Christ.

One now lyeth in Iron-fetters, condemned to dye.

ALSO

Some Considerations presented to the King, which is in Answer to a Petition and Address which was presented unto Him by the General Court at Boston: Subscribed by J. Endicott, the Chief Persecutor there; thinking thereby to cover themselves from the Blood of the Innocents.

Gal. 4.29

London, Printed for Robert Wilson, in Martins Le Grand.

[67] Burrough's tract is the earliest to describe Mary Dyer's death; it was soon overshadowed by Bishop's, but Burrough himself, by taking Samuel Shattuck to see Charles II, procured "the King's Missive" (see Whittier's poem) that saved Wenlock Christison and later Quaker prisoners from death in Boston.

137

[The first section answers the claims of the Boston General Court's Petition, justifying their persecution of the troublers of their peace; it is fourteen pages. The second section, signed by John Rous and John Copeland (who had lost their ears), Samuel Shattuck, Josiah Southwick, Nicholas Phelps, Joseph Nicholson, and Jane Nicholson—these latter all Boston residents, banished from their homes and families—expands the summary of sufferings on the title page. The third section—on the sentencing of Robinson, Stephenson, and Mary Dyer, and execution of the first two—is taken almost verbatim from *A Call from Death to Life*. The final section, written by Burrough, seems to be taken from the account of the Nicholsons, and is the first printed report on Mary Dyer's death.]

[27] Mary Dyer, being freed as aforesaid, returned to Rhode Island, and afterwards to Long Island, and there was [28] most part of the winter, over the Island, where she had good service for the Lord; and then came to Shelter Island, whence she thought she might pass to Rhode Island. And being there, sometime she had movings from the Lord to go to Boston, and there she came the 21st of the 3rd Month, 1660. And the 30th day was their Governor chosen, and the 31st of the 3rd Month, in the former part of the day, she was sent for to the General Court.

The Governor said, "Are ye the same Mary Dyer that was here before?" . . .

Mary Dyer: "I am the same Mary Dyer that was here the last General Court."

The Governor said, "You will own yourself a Quaker, will you not."

M.D.: "I own my self to be so reproachfully called." The bloody minded Jailer, having now opportunity to have his bloodthirsty will fulfilled, said "she is a vagabond."

The Governor said, "The sentence was passed upon her the Last General Court, and now likewise: 'you must return to the prison from whence you came, and there remain until tomorrow at nine of the clock, then from thence you must go to the gallows, and there be hanged till you are dead.' "

Mary Dyer said, "this is no more than that thou saidst before."

"Aye, aye," the Governor said, "and now it is to be executed. Therefore prepare yourself tomorrow at nine of the clock," (being the first day of the 4th Month, 1660).

Mary Dyer answered and said, "I came in obedience to the will of God, the last General Court, desiring you to repeal your unrighteous laws of banishment upon pain of death; and that same is my work now, and earnest request, because ye refused before to grant my request, although I told you that if ye refused to repeal them the Lord will send others of his servants to witness against them."

John Endicott asked her whether she was a prophet.

She said she spake the words that the Lord spake in her; "and now the thing is come to pass." She beginning to speak of her Call, J. Endicott said, "away with her, away with her."

So she was brought to the prison-house, where she was before, close shut up until the next day. About the time prefixed, the marshal Michaelson came and called hastily for her. When he [29] came into the room, she desired him to stay a little, and speaking mildly to him she said she should be ready presently, even like a sheep prepared for the slaughter. But he in the wolvish nature said he could not wait upon her, but she should now wait upon him. Margaret Smith, her companion, hearing him speak these words with others from the Cain-like spirit, was moved to testify against their unjust laws and proceedings, being grieved to see both him and many others in such gross darkness and hardheartedness. Then he said, "you shall have your share of the same," with other violent words.

Then they brought her forth, and drums were beat before and behind her, with a band of soldiers, through the town, and so to the place of execution, which is about a mile, the drums being that none might hear her speak all the way.

Some said unto her, that if she would return she might come down and save her life (Bonner- and Gardner-like).[68] She answered and said, "Nay, I cannot. For in obedience to the will of the Lord God I came, and in his will I abide faithful to the death."

Their Captain, John Webb said, She had been here before, and had the sentence of banishment upon pain of death; and had broken this law in coming again now, as well as formerly; and therefore she was guilty of her own blood. To which M. Dyer said, "Nay, I came to keep blood-guiltiness from you, desiring you to repeal the unrighteous and unjust law of banishment upon pain of death, made against the innocent servants of the Lord. Therefore my blood will be required at your hands, who wilfully do it; but for those that do it in the simplicity of their hearts, I do desire the Lord to forgive them. I came to do the will of my Father, and in obedience to his will I stand even to the death."

John Wilson, their priest of Boston, said, "M. Dyer, O repent; O repent, and be not so deluded and carried away by the deceit of the Devil." M. Dyer answered and said, "Nay, man, I am not now to repent."

[30] Some asked her whether she would have the Elders to pray for her. She said, "I know never an Elder here." They asked whether she would have any of the people to pray for her. She said she desired the prayers of all the People of God. Some scoffingly said, "It may be she thinks there is none

68 Stephen Gardner and Edmund Bonner were bishops through whom Mary Tudor tried to bring back the Church of England to Catholicism by burning the Protestant leaders.

here; this is a mock." M. Dyer looked about and said, "I know but few here."

Then they spake to her again, that one of the Elders might pray for her. She replied and said, "Nay, first a child, then a young man, then a strong man, before an Elder of Christ Jesus." Some charged her with something that was not understood what it was. But her answer was, "It's false; it's false; I never spoke the words."

Then one said she should say she had been in Paradise. And she answered, "Yea, I have been in Paradise several days." And more she spake of her eternal happiness, that's out of mind. And so sweetly and cheerfully in the Lord she finished her testimony and died a faithful martyr of Jesus Christ.

And still they are going on in acting their cruel laws: for the same day, in the former part of it, they sent for Joseph Nicholson and his wife Jane Nicholson, and banished them on pain of death. Then sent for three more, and whilst they were examining them, there came one to the Court spake to this purpose, and one scoffingly said "she did hang as a flag for them to take example by." (But precious in the sight of the Lord is the death of his saints) .... These are the people that say their churches are the purest churches in the world, and that their magistrates are godly magistrates, and godly ministers. A fair show to the world! Even "another Beast coming up out of the earth; and he had two horns, like a lamb, and he spake as a dragon; and he exerciseth the power of the first Beast before him." [Rev. 13:11-12]

And their General Court being ended, they left nine of us still remaining in prison, it seems looking for encouragement from England that more may follow their Ensign. And we have a further account also, that one of our Friends, named William Leddra, being banished upon pain of death, he not departing the colony but being moved to return again to Boston, was apprehended and cast into prison, and there lieth chained to a log with a horse-lock, condemned to die.

[Burrough's appeal to the king, presented by this tract and in a personal interview, was not in time to save the life of Leddra, but induced the king to order the transfer of all accusations against Quakers in Massachusetts to courts in England. Thereby the lives of Wenlock Christison and others were saved; but the struggle continued nevertheless for five years more.]

10. *The Vision of Humphrey Smith Concerning London* (1660)

Most early Friends could claim to be prophets: they felt directly led by God to deliver specific messages to specific hearers. But predictive prophecy among Friends was rare; Quaker preachers were more concerned with the present-tense Day of Visitation than with foretelling the act of the Spirit. Exceptions such as

Fox's sense of Cromwell's impending death in 1658 often do not prove much; neither do general forewarnings of judgment, though sometimes dramatically fulfilled by disasters to persecutors.[69]

Humphrey Smith, however, published a vision of London afire before his death in 1663 which seemed to Friends dramatically fulfilled in the great fire that destroyed all central London in September, 1666, at the height of the Conventicle Act persecutions. Smith is also one of the relatively few Friends who seems to be describing a daylight trance vision. Fox had several famous ones, "the oceans of darkness and light" and the "great people to be gathered" being the most famous.[70]

Banks had both a dream and a sort of vision (cf. pp. 194, 186). Yet the common Quaker experience was hearing, not seeing: "It was said to me," "it was given me to say . . . ," "it was opened to me that. . . ." Humphrey Smith's vision stands out in its visual intensity and detail.

Humphrey Smith himself, apparently well educated and a separatist free preacher before becoming a Friend, was after his convincement in 1654 a prolific writer. If his spoken messages centered on judgment thunder as fiercely as did his tracts, his frequent imprisonments and death in prison (1663) are understandable. Our text is from Smith's works, *A Collection of the Several Writings,* printed only in 1683.

THE

VISION

OF

HUMPHREY SMITH

Which he saw concerning

LONDON

In the 5th Month, in the Year 1660,

being not long after the King came in.

The prophet speaking of the "pouring forth of the Spirit in the latter days," saith, "That then the young men shall see visions," Joel 2.28. And the wise

[69] Cf. Henry J. Cadbury, ed., *George Fox's Book of Miracles* (Cambridge: Cambridge Univ. Press, 1948).

[70] Cf. Fox, *CJ,* I, 346 for Fox's own vision about London in ruins; II, 175 about liberating men by digging in the earth. Fox seems to have had recurrent visions about "mastiffe doggs" (I, 37, 291; II, 22); it approached hysteria about the "ugly slubering hound." Some of these, and many others (cf. *CJ,* I, 291; II, 275), may have been dreams, or even delirium (II, 169).

King said, "Where there is no vision the people perish," Prov. 29.18. And the true minister of Christ said, "I will come to visions and revelations of the Lord," 2 Cor. 12.1.

Concerning the Great City of LONDON

I beheld all her waters, which belonged to her, frozen up, and that exceeding hard, and the vessels which went upon them, so that I had others passed over her waters without the least danger and over the greatest vessels which had carried her merchandise; for all was frozen with a mighty freezing, whereby all her goodly merchandise were stopt, and her mighty swift [194] waters were turned into a mighty thick frozen ice, which stood still, so that her pleasant streams ran not.

And as for the city herself and her suburbs and all that belonged to her, a fire was kindled therein, but she knew not how, even in her goodly places; and the kindling of it was in the foundations of her buildings, and there was none could quench it, neither was there any able, and the burning thereof was exceeding great, and it burned inward in a hidden manner, which cannot be expressed. And the fire consumed foundations which the city stood upon, and the tall buildings fell, and it consumed all the lofty things therein, and the fire searched out all the hidden places, and burned most in secret places: but the consumation was exceeding great, wherewith it consumed.

And as I passed through her streets, I beheld her state to be very miserable, and very few were those that were left in her, who were but here and there one, and they feared not the fire, neither did the burnings hurt them, but they were (and walked) as mournful, dejected people, and the fire burned everywhere, so that there was no escaping of it. And thus she became a desolation and as an astonishment; for the burning was suffered of God for her chastisement and could never be quenched nor overcome; and in the midst of her waters was the vessel of her merchandise frozen up, that none could move it, and there were none that could stop the burning; and the fire consumed all things, both stone and timber, and it burned under all things and under all foundations, and that which was lifted above it fell down, and the fire consumed it, and the burning continued; for though the foundation was burned up, and all the lofty part brought down (by the fire) yet there was much old stuff and part broken, desolate walls and buildings in the midst, which the fire continued burning against; and that which was taken as to make use of, which yet escaped the fire, became useless in man's hand, as a thing of nought. And the vision hereof remained in me as a thing that was secretly showed me of the Lord.

And now let her wise men find out the matter, and her prudent men read, and her divines (so called) interpret the vision (and let her know, that her day is at hand) and let every one of them look to their own ways.

142

And as for thee, O city of London, thy sin hath been exceeding [195] grievous, and thy iniquities beyond measure. Who can number thy daily transgressions or set before thee the multitude of thy abominations? Oh! thy ways have grieved the Lord, and thy works have oppressed the just, and the Lord will surely plead with thee, whom thou hast long rebelled against and walked in thy pride and nourished thyself in voluptuousness, as a beast for the slaughter, and in arrogancy hath thy steps been found. Oh! thy heart hath been defiled, and thy ways are ways of grievousness, and thy paths are polluted before the Lord, and thou hast not done the thing that is just in his sight, but hast chosen thy own ways and trusted in thy own wisdom.

Take heed now therefore, O city of London, for God will be too strong for thee, and thy strength shall fall before him, and thou must come to an account for thy deeds; and then where will be thy refuge, or what shall be thy shelter? Will thy multitude of men deliver thee from God, or the greatness of thy strength prevail against the Almighty? If so, then mayest thou stand in thy ways, O city of London:[71] But if not, thy misery will be great; and who shall bemoan thee in that day or pity thee in the time of thy distress? Forasmuch as thou hast refused the counsel of the Lord and rejected the voice of his servants in the midst of thee and hearkened not to his word in thy own bowels, but also slighted the many warnings of the Lord by his servants, who were sent of him in love to thee, that thou mightest come to serve him, and not thy own pleasure, proceeding on from year to year like a monstrous woman, who regardeth not the voice nor person of husband nor friend: Oh! what shall be said unto thee? And must thou needs be left for desolation? And must thou be left as a woman forsaken? Will thy lovers help thee in the day of trouble? or thy delightsome pleasures preserve thy heart from judgment, or thy glorious riches hide thee from the burning torments? If thou lovest thy wages of vanity more than God and thy heart's lust more than thy Maker and wilt not turn speedily from it to seek the Lord in thy heart, then mayst thou post on (as thou art going) hastily to the Pit and with much eagerness to the Gulf of Misery, where none can help thee. And then will thy feasting be turned into famine, thy beauty into dust, thy glory into shame, and thy honour [196] into contempt, as thou hast seen it come to pass upon others, whose glory and strength was as great as thine, by whom thou hast not taken warning by a thorough and speedy returning unto the Lord with all thy heart.

Therefore will God search thee and judge thee according to what is found in the midst of thee, and thou shalt be awakened in the day of God's anger and be sensible of the torment when it cometh. For though God hath also

[71] Certain phrases suggest acquaintance with Bishop Hugh Latimer's "Sermon the Plough" against London, 18th Jan., 1548 ("the Fourth Sermon" in 27 *Sermons* [1562], fol. 15).

tried thee with giving thee thy heart's desire, yet hast thou not been thereby humbled. And though the Lord hath visited thee in loving kindness, yet hast thou walked loftily; nay, moreover thou hast taken occasion thereby to be the more exalted and art going in the steps of them that the Lord so lately (for such things) overturned before thee, that it cannot yet be forgotten. And dost thou or the rule[r]s in thee think to establish yourselves by acting such things, for which God overturned many mightier than you? Therefore, O city, think not to establish thyself by blood, nor to be settled by way of revenge; for though some men may have done some things unjust against some of you, (and others) so that God may justly by you scourge them forth for it; yet wherein you do it in the way of revenge or to avenge your own cause or to set up yourselves in self-ends, like them before you, therein God will also find a scourge for you. And this I have seen, that the great men of the earth stand in slippery places, and their great strength before the Lord is as smoke before the wind.

My counsel is, therefore, that thou fear the Lord and turn from the way thou art in; and let thy judges know that the Lord will judge them; and let thy rulers understand that the Lord will rule over their strength and wisdom; and let thy teachers perceive that God is come to teach his own children. And let the King's heart be upright before the Lord in this the day of his Trial and time of visitation from God, (the shortness or length thereof being hid from him, over whom God ruleth as it pleaseth him) who is cutting his work short in righteousness. Therefore, let all thy inhabitants, O thou great city, from the highest to the lowest, take good heed unto their ways and intents which are in them, for the Lord seeth the secrets of all your hearts.[72]

H.S.

11. The Beginnings of Quaker Historiography: Fox's Fragments

Quaker narratives were written at first as an additional weapon in the Lamb's War; they also became important as witnesses, showing those who had accepted the inner Light of Christ the power with which it had worked. This became especially important in the persecution years after 1660. Fox began then to sort and supplement the papers and letters that had originally been sent in for the sake of contact and coordination by the Quakers on mission. At least three times he dictated narratives of the rise of Quakerism: one form, the *short journal*, was dictated in Lancaster

[72] Smith's tract continues with the description of an earlier vision, where the great trees on a hill were broken to let in light, but the land was covered

prison in 1664 but printed only in 1925; the "Great Journal" manuscript referred to in other papers of Fox seems to be lost; the Spence Manuscript of 1673-76 (which in its present form begins only with 1650) formed the basis of Ellwood's and all standard editions of Fox's *Journal*. But other fragments also survive.[73] One of these, bound up with the journal manuscript and printed with it in the *Cambridge Journal* edition of 1911, includes several very early fragments: Ellwood included much of it in his edition of Fox's *Epistles* (1698), pp. 2ff. We include the opening, which makes an interesting parallel to the now-lost source from which Ellwood took the *Journal* narrative of Fox's boyhood and Fox's description of the setting up of Women's Meetings.

Beyond personal narratives like Fox's, Friends did not at first go. But opponents were fond of cartoon-sketches of the rise of Quakerism; and one of these non-Quaker histories, by Gerard Croese in Holland (1696), was full and objective enough to draw on Quaker as well as anti-Quaker documents. Its English translation (1698), by the printer's consent, was rounded out by comments both from George Keith, once a leading Quaker and then returning to Anglicanism, and from his still-Quaker opponents in Pennsylvania. The logical end-product was the Dutch Quaker Willem Sewel's *History of the People Called Quakers*, in two folio volumes, which falls outside our period (1722) but from which Whitehead's "Christian Doctrine" is taken (cf. p. 558). This carries us far from Fox's first fragments.

Concerning the First Spreading of the Truth, and How that Many Were Imprisoned, & c.

And the truth sprang up first in Leicestershire in 1644, and in Warwickshire in 1645, and in Nottinghamshire in 1646, and in Darbyshire in 1647, and in the adjacent countries [=counties] in 1648, 1649 and 1650,[74] and in

---

with briars, which he sees as those "who covered the earth with . . . raging, swearing, roaring and drinking the health of their king at his coming."

73 Cf. Cadbury, *Narrative Papers*, Ch. I, and *Annual Catalogue*.

74 How to understand what Fox meant by "the Truth sprang up" in the years before 1650 is still argued. The dates and places named here are close to those of Fox's own wanderings. Yet he himself spoke of "divers meetings of Friends . . . gathered to God's teachings" (*Journal* [ed. Nickalls], p. 27), and Ellwood too (*Epistles*, p. 2) assumes that "the People of God" are meant here, not just Fox. Later Fox journeyed repeatedly to visit what were evidently well-established groups in Leicestershire, Staffordshire, Derbyshire, and Nottinghamshire. Besse reports numerous Friends who suffered in

Yorkshire in 1651, and in Lancashire and Westmorland in 1652, and in Cumberland, and Bishopric, and Northumberland in 1653, and in London, and most parts of the nation of England, and Scotland and Ireland in 1654 &c.

And in 1655, many went beyond seas, where truth also sprang up.

And in 1656, truth broke forth in America, and many other places.

And the truth stood all the cruelties and sufferings, that were inflicted upon Friends by the Long-Parliament . . . and then by O. Protector, and all the acts that O. Protector made and his Parliaments, and his son Richard after him; and the Committee of Safety. And after, it withstood and lasted out all the acts and proclamations since 1660, that the King came in. And still the Lord's truth is over all, and his seed reigns, and his truth exceedingly spreads unto this year, 1676.

And Friends never feared their acts, nor prisons, nor gaols, nor houses of correction, nor banishments, nor spoilings of goods; nay, nor life itself. And there was never any persecution, that came, but we saw, it was for good; and we looked upon it to be good, as from God: And there were never any prisons, or sufferings, that I was in, but still it was for the bringing multitudes more out of prison: For they that imprisoned the truth, and quenched the spirit in themselves, would prison it, and quench it without them. So that there was a time, when there were so many in prison, that it became as a byword, truth was scarcely anywhere to be found, but in jails. . . . [Para-

these counties, but beginning only from 1653 except for Fox's own imprisonments. The local records of Quaker origins collected in *FPT* do not include these counties (Benjamin Bealing, who first assembled them, notes them as unreported as of 1682; *JFHS*, XXXI [1934], 1ff.). No major "publishers of Truth" came from there, though in the eighteenth century the ironworks and potteries had turned these counties into centers of Quaker industry. What is needed is a careful study to find how many of the later Quaker Meetings in the region had roots before 1650, which if any Fox himself founded or gathered, and which predated him or treated him as an added member. This was an active region for Separatists. A comparison of the twenty-three Nottinghamshire parishes where Puritan pastors refused to conform in 1662 with the twenty-six where Nonconformists congregations asked for licenses during the interim of 1672 shows only eight overlaps, suggesting that half of the latter had been nonparish groups from the start (*Vict. County Hist.*, pp. 72-75). But Marchant (*Puritans and the Church Courts in the Diocese of York, 1560-1642* [London: Longmans, 1960] has found 245 Yorkshire parishes with 398 Puritan pastorates (often the same man in several) before the Civil War, and in much smaller Nottinghamshire 75 with 127 pastorates. Many pastors are familiar names as later Independents and Separatists, like Nutter of Woodkirk and Brerely of Grindleton; yet few are firmly linked to Quakerism as were similar men in the Northwest. Clearly only detailed work will interpret Quaker origins.

146

graphs omitted cover sufferings for refusing to drink to the king's health, for tithes, and for oaths.]

And many have suffered to death for their testimony, both in England and beyond the seas, both before and since the King came in; which ye may see, as followeth:

This was given to the king and both houses of parliament, being a brief, and plain, and true relation of some of the late and sad sufferings of the people of God in scorn called Quakers, for worshipping God and exercising a good conscience towards God and man by reason whereof 89 have suffered till death, 32 of which died before the king came into England, and 57 since, of which, 57 by hard imprisonment and cruel usage, 43 have died in this city of London and Southwark since the act were made against meetings. They have thus suffered as you may see it at large in the paper that was given with their names that did suffer to the king and Parliament 1661. . . .[75]

And the governor of Dover Castle, when the King asked him, if he had dispersed all the sectaries' meetings? he said, That he had; but the Quakers, the Devil himself could not: For if that he did imprison them, and break them up, they would meet again; and if he should beat them, and knock them down, or kill some of them, all was one; they would meet, and not resist again. —And thus the Lord's power did support them, and keep them over their persecutors; and made them to justify our patience and lamb-like nature. This was about 1671. . . . [The preceding and following paragraphs are on unjust sufferings.]

And when the glorious Gospel and truth was spread over the nation, and they had received the word of life, then first the quarterly, and some monthly Meetings, were settled throughout the nation; and then after, as truth more and more spread, the monthly Men's Meetings, in 1667 and 1668.

And then also some Women-Meetings were set up; and after, the Women's-Meetings throughout the nation, and other nations were exhorted unto, and set up and established throughout the nations. For I was sent for to many sick people: And at one time I was sent for to White Chapel, about the third hour in the morning, to a woman, that was dying, and her child; and the people were weeping about her. And after a while I was moved (in the name and power of Jesus Christ) to speak to the woman; and she and her child were raised up; and she got up, to the astonishment of the people, when they came in, in the morning; and her child also was healed. And when I came to Ger. Roberts' house, about eight in the morning, there came in Sarah Blackbury to

---

[75] The preceding paragraph survives in Fox's own handwriting on a fragment in the Haverford collection, and is dated by Henry Cadbury to 1664 (*Bulletin of Friends Historical Ass'n* [hereafter *BFHA*], XL [1951], 98; XLI [1952], 133).

complain to me of the poor, and how many poor Friends were in want; and the Lord had showed me, what I should do, in his eternal power and wisdom. So I spoke to her to bid about sixty women to meet me about the first hour in the afternoon, at the Sign of the Helmet, at a Friend's house: And they did do accordingly, such as were sensible women of the Lord's truth, and fearing God. And what the Lord had opened unto me I declared unto them, concerning their having a Meeting once a week, every second day, that they might see and inquire into the necessity of all Friends who was sick and weak, and who was in wants, or widows and fatherless in the city and suburbs. . . .

And afterwards the same Women's-Meetings were settled up and down the nation, and beyond the seas in the power of the Lord.

Upon the fourth day of first month, the power of the Lord in me spread over all the world in praise.[76]

Praise, honour and glory be to the Lord of Heaven and Earth, Lord of life, Lord of peace, Lord of joy! Thy countenance maketh my heart glad, Lord of glory, Lord of mercy, Lord of strength, Lord of life and power over death, and Lord of lords, and King of kings! In the world there are lords many, but to us there is but one God the Father, of whom are all things; and one Lord Jesus Christ, by whom are all things: To whom be all glory, who is worthy: . . . For everyone (in that state) doth strive to be above another; few will strive to be the lowest. O that everyone would strive to put down (in themselves) mastery and honour, that the Lord of Heaven and Earth might be exalted!

G.F.

[76] This sentence is in Fox's handwriting and is set apart at the foot of a fragment that contains his letter of 1650 "to a professor" (probably Justice Barton; SMS 7:93). It is found in *Ellwood's Epistles* but not in the Spence MS (=*CJ*); in Ellwood it is followed by the prayer, part of which is given here, whose source is not known.

PART B:

Journals of Lives
Led by the Light

Introduction

Both in form and in detail, the journal has been more carefully studied than any other form of Quaker literature. Several scholars have undertaken to read and analyze all the sixty-five-odd surviving autobiographies from the first generation of Friends, and their pre-Quaker parallels.[1]

The spiritual autobiography, which dates from Augustine and Jeremiah, became the special forte of the Puritans, who stressed conversion experience as the clearest of many events in which they had seen God's grace work in their lives. The classic fruits of this tradition, John Bunyan's *Grace Abounding* and *Pilgrim's Progress* (1666 and 1678), the *Life and Diary of David Brainerd* by Jonathan Edwards (1758), and John Wesley's *Journal* (d. 1791) were well into the future when Friends wrote. But the Puritan age was thoroughly familiar with a basic understanding of Christian life centering on a change of heart and will based on man's relationship to God. The Puritan had heard frequent sermons on "How to Live and That Well" and read many books on "The Plaine Man's Pathway to Heaven," and the pilgrim metaphor was as crucial to his vision of life as was "spiritual warfare" against inner evil.[2] The anxiety over salvation kept Puritans writing diaries for their own reassurance. The need to reassure others, which led to publishing

[1] Cf. Wright, *Literary Life,* chs. XVIII-XX; Vann, *Social Development,* ch. I; Howard H. Brinton, ed., *Children of Light* (New York, 1938), pp. 383-406, and especially Owen Watkins' unpublished thesis for the University of London, "Spiritual Autobiography from 1649 to 1660" (1952) and resulting book.

[2] Cf. William Haller, *Rise of Puritanism* (New York: Columbia Univ. Press, 1938), ch. III; Marshall Knappen, *Tudor Puritanism* (Chicago: Univ. of Chicago Press, 1939), ch. XXII.

diary narratives in the writers' own lifetimes, rarely moved orthodox Puritans, and first became a custom through the Quakers
themselves and the Ranters before them, who needed to authenticate their claims of authority for their messages through telling
their spiritual experiences.[3] Nevertheless, enough individual and
collective spiritual biographies by the children and disciples of
Puritans and enough posthumous diaries had been published by
1650 to afford ample models for Friends.

Four specific types of Puritan writing became ingredients of the
Quaker journal, and were not even fused among Friends until the
1680's. First, pastoral counseling of individuals formed a daily
part of Puritan parish ministry and led to books on "cases of
conscience" answering common problems. Some of these, such as
the best-known and much later *Christian Directory* (1673) of
Richard Baxter, provided detailed ethical answers to economic and
political dilemmas. But such books usually began with the inward
and basic agonies: "the maine Question teaching assurance of
salvation: How a man may be in conscience assured of his owne
salvation."[4] Such guidebooks and kindred sermons clearly belong
in the same thought-world as spiritual autobiography, and this was
equally true among Quakers. We can only partly reconstruct what
early Quaker preachers told their mass audiences about the spiritual pilgrimage to which they called them, or how in the small
gatherings of the "convinced" they "spoke to the conditions" of
those struggling (cf. p. 183). We do have, however, many letters of
counsel from William Dewsbury, Isaac Penington, Margaret Fell,
and others, and include some here (cf. p. 234). Fox's letter to
Lady Claypoole[5] may be the most famous.

The memorial or spiritual obituary was a second custom Friends
adopted from the Puritans. It had often taken the form of a funeral
sermon or the preface to a posthumous volume of sermons, and from
1650 onward there were frequent collections of such holy lives into
devotional books or martyrologies (the model here had been John
Foxe's *Book of Martyrs,* climaxed by the Protestants burned under
Mary Tudor). In such books fragments of autobiography out of
letters or sermons were readily included, as well as unpublished

[3] Cf. Owen Watkins, *Puritan Experience: Studies in Spiritual Experience*
(1972), and Haller, *Rise,* p. 103 on William Cowper.

[4] William Perkins, *Works,* Vol. II: *The Cases of Conscience* (Cambridge,
1609), p. 21.

[5] Cf. *Journal* (Nickalls), pp. 346-48.

spiritual diaries. We have seen early Friends producing three such books from the letters and papers of the Massachusetts martyrs (p. 117), and have included here the earliest careful Quaker memorial, that for James Parnell.[6]

Thirdly, as was noted, Friends had used the concise accounts of their own convincement within "proclamation tracts"[7] to authenticate the prophetic message and prove how unnecessary were ministerial ordination and university education for true ministry. Such a personal narrative might include the first experience when the writer received a leading to carry a message, or might go on to the specific call that had brought the Quaker to his audience of the moment.

In any case, the Quaker was no more satisfied than the Puritan to limit his record of the Spirit's work to inner transformations. Among the types of historical records that Fox collected were apparently transcriptions of which only the indexes survive, the "Book of Miracles," which included healings, outward deliverances from danger, and disasters to persecutors, and a book or collection of "passages" or "gospel journeys."[8] On Fox's American journey of 1672 and the Irish trip of 1669, he dictated almost daily notes, printed in recent though not early editions of his *Journal.*[9]

Fox's *Journal*, in telling the full story of his outward life, sufferings, and travels,[10] as well as inner experiences, set a pattern for other Friends. Later journals used letters to make up the bulk of the story where narratives were lacking, for instance for the travels of John Banks; much briefer summaries had been used in the combined memorials and writings, for instance of Parnell (1662), Hubberthorne (1663), Burrough (1672), Howgill (1676), Fisher (1679), and Penington (1681). The new style of full-length journals is already found with Stephen Crisp (1694) and Burnyeat

6 The earliest in print, that prefacing the works of George Fox "the Younger" in 1661, is more formal, but opened the way for printing Parnell's death-story with his own writings the next year.

7 Luella Wright (*Literary Life*, pp. 203-4) counts nineteen such narratives by 1660, and a dozen more before the first full-length journals around 1690. Her list does not exactly match our Appendix, which assigns some of these to sufferings or proclamation tracts.

8 Cf. Wright, *Literary Life*, p. 156, and Henry Cadbury's book on Fox's *Narrative Writings*.

9 For discussion of these see preface to *Journal* (Nickalls) and the introductions by T. Edmund Harvey and the editor to Penney's *Short Journal.*

10 Early Friends spelled the words "travail" and "travel" interchangeably.

(1691), and an intermediate form with Will Caton (1689), Miles Halhead (1690), and Joan Vokins (1691), who must all have written before Fox's *Journal* was in print but may have known of Fox's manuscripts during his lifetime (except for Caton). Finally we find William Edmondson and Thomas Ellwood, when they got around to writing their own life-stories early in the next century, producing for Friends a far more literary narrative in that era of increasing peace. It was designed for enjoyment and remembrance and was full of adventure for its own sake, but basically it was for the kindling of Friends not outsiders. So were the increasingly devotional books of memorials and of dying words that embalm and bury the active lives of the next Quaker century.

The influence of a common pattern on Quaker journal writers will naturally make us ask how far individual Friends shaped and screened their memories to fit the stages of an expected pilgrimage.[11] Fortunately, we have a good test case, since we have Richard Hubberthorne's letters to Fox from the midst of his spiritual struggle in 1652 to lay beside his published autobiographical account in a pamphlet three years later. Despite its greater emotional pain, the letter is more stereotyped in phrases and outlooks than the later tract. This still does not rule out the probability that the crisis experience, even while it was happening, was partly understood in borrowed terms. This is a commonplace of conversion experiences where strong expectations have been built up; none of us escape our culture nor do we come to religious rapture without experience. Most Friends who wrote journals were leaders who had already gone on long pilgrimages through branches and sects of Puritanism. On the whole it is surprising how few of the variety of images and phrases handy they actually used. Moreover, there is no escaping the element of surprise with which some of these spiritual veterans such as Howgill, Crisp, and Penington (none of them strongly dependent on Fox as teacher) experienced unforeseen depths and later heights of experience in Quakerism.

To erect a standard chart for the Quaker pilgrimage is therefore, even in sensitive hands like Howard Brinton's,[12] easier in the

---

[11] The same question arises about Puritan conversion accounts, Satori experiences in Zen, experiences of mystical union, etc. Strong group expectation is sometimes ascribed a major role among Friends, e.g. by Vann, Melvin Endy's work on Penn, etc.

[12] *Children of Light*, pp. 388-406.

eighteenth than in the seventeenth century. Many Friends were evidently trying to tell, in the best tradition of Quaker diaries, of a childhood owing much to the unappreciated grace of God and strict parents, followed by intervals of wild oats (the Quaker variety being no more puffed up than the Puritans') and other periods of legalistic righteousness. Most of these men also went through a full conversion experience of the Calvinist type, in which they learned to trust fully in the vicarious atonement of Christ for salvation. This they never later denied, and their reasons for later finding it inadequate or slipping back from it vary. The hypocrisy of so-called Christians is often mentioned, as is the emptiness of mere doctrines even about Christ, but more deeply they were usually touched by their own hypocrisy in accepting forgiveness while still sinning.

Clearly their Quaker "convincement," when it came, was neither a conversion to new doctrines (which the journals indeed rarely spell out, as if already self-evident) nor complete inward change. It was convincement or conviction of sin, an often rebellious commitment to accept what the Light showed. It was the beginning, not the end, of struggle. For every Friend who seems, like Will Caton, to have entered the Quaker stream without thrashing, or one like Edmondson or Fox himself, whose accounts pass over the inward pain, we find several other narratives flooded with imagery from Job. Banks had to quit his job and Ellwood his home, like many young folk in turmoil today, being in no condition to face them. If we take this early Quaker experience seriously, it illuminates for us Quaker teachings about pride and judgment and the cross, and also the sense of newness and wonder with which each Quaker proclaimed his inner freedom from all teachers and traditions.

1. The Convincement and Establishment of Richard Hubberthorne, from Swarthmore Manuscripts 4:4 and 3:1, and his *True Testimony of Obedience to the Heavenly Call* (1654), in *A Collection of the . . . Writings of . . . Richard Hubberthorne* (1663)

By having three first-hand reports on the convincement experience of this early Friend, we can test how far later outlooks might have shaped early memories in full-length Quaker journals—

apparently not much. Richard Hubberthorne is also typical among early Quaker leaders: a yeoman of the Northwest and a former Cromwellian soldier, one of the separatist group who together first encountered Quakerism when Fox spoke on Firbank Fell. He was short, weak, and soft-spoken but a mediator and leader among Friends. He was less unrestrained in emotion than many Quakers, and was called by a Puritan opponent in debate "the most rational calm-spirited man of his judgment that I was ever publicly engaged against" (cited in *EQL,* p. 64). His first letter (SMS 4:4=*EQL* No. 1) may be only two or three weeks after meeting Fox, and his second later in July, 1652; both are addressed to Fox:

Dear Brother:

The eye being opened, which was blind, now comes to witness thee, and reads thee within me. "I was in prison and thou hast visited me." The conscience opened, thy words found there are my life, and I live in thee in measure. Now "the earth with its bars compasseth me about" and "weeds and pollutions are often wrapped about my head" [Jonah 2:6, 5], even these things that thou said: lust and thoughts; fleshly lusts wars against the soul; strong enemies, wily and cunning foxes which have holes and dens in the earth comes forth to devour that young vine and tender plant which is planted by the Lord. Now, dear brother, pray for me, that the spoiler may be taken, and be spoiled, and the pure which hath been led captive and kept in prison by the bands of wickedness may be delivered, and the Lamb overcome. All the inhabitants of the earth within me do now give their glory and their power unto the Beast; and the more this grows which is pure, the more cunning formings and transformings doth Antichrist present within. And as this riseth to be a prophet within me, to prophesy death from the mouth of the Lord, so the deceit and false prophet presumes to prophesy in the same name. Pray for me, that the pure which witnesseth thee may grow to overcome all his enemies; for he is a servant made under the Law in me, often clouded over and a veil drawn; and then thou art hid, yet within me pressed down, and I am led into the wilderness to be tempted, and strong temptations compass me about. But thou art above them all, and not ignorant of his wiles, but art in the liberty of the Son; and that which the son desires of the father is according to his will and in his name, and is granted. Pray that the tender plant may grow up to be the Son, to have power and strength over all his enemies, that that which hath hated him may both within and without come bending unto him, and that I may come out of all, to live in him who is invisible, pure and spiritual, which I have had a taste and sight of, through the visible and carnal which is yet uncrucified, causing plagues, woes and miseries.

And the Son yet as a servant learning obedience, under sufferings; and he is calling me to forsake all, to take up the daily cross to all that which is carnal and natural, and to be not of this world, nor know no man after the flesh, own no relations but those who are called by the same power into the same path which man treads not in. And pray for me that that which is pure may draw me out of all [?] ; which is the true Son of the eternal God; but there is the bondwoman, and her son, and he pleads for freedom because he is of Abraham; but that he may be cast out, and the true seed, the pure birth, may grow. Pray that I may be kept not to boast above my measure, but may stand in the easy and gentle leadings of the Lamb, and may drink of those rivers in which thou swims.

And to you all the dear family of love my love is run into you all. You are my relation, father, mother, sisters and brothers, which I must now own and dwell with in amity and love eternally. Farewell in the same love.

Yours in the eternal love,
Richard Hubberthorne.

Hubberthorne's second letter (these two being the earliest surviving letters between Friends) does not make clear whether he had in the interim seen or heard from Fox, ten miles away across the Morecombe Bay quicksands. Both letters are typical of those written to Fox in these ecstatic months—in their personal adulation of the Spirit within him, in their intensity of emotion, and in their incessant use of biblical phrases and stories as allegories of inner experience. This last was a strong Puritan tradition, but specific symbols may have been learned from Fox's preaching. This letter, too (SMS 3:1=*EQL* No. 2), has apparently not before been transcribed or printed.

Dear heart:

My dear and tender love, wherewith I am beloved of the Lord, I remember unto thee and to all the rest of the precious hearts which hath tasted of the powerful love of the Lord, which cometh to redeem their souls from death, which the world knoweth nothing of. Therefore keep your souls in that same power, separate from the world, and touch no unclean thing, that ye may be received of the Lord and dwell in his everlasting power.

Dear heart, since I saw thee, the hand of the Lord hath been mightily exercised upon me, and his terrors hath been sharp within me. The consumption determined upon the whole earth hath and is passing through me; which hath been terrible unto the brutish nature, which could not endure the devouring fire, it being so hot and unquenchable that I saw nothing that could live or pass through it, but that all as stubble must be destroyed. Then that which was to be burned struggled to keep itself alive, and resisted the power of the Lord, which was mighty and did whatever it pleased, and was stronger than all. And that same power continued tormenting, and giving no rest day nor night; he spared not, neither had he pity of his enemy; which made the carnal impatient nature cry out because its torment was upon it. "When evening came I waited long for the morning, and when morning came the night was as much desired" [Job 7:4], for blackness and darkness covered me: the day was very black, and no light in it, full of woe and misery, insomuch that I sought death, but it fled from me; for I desired death rather than my life. And this same power caused a flame to enter to within me, to destroy the lust which had fed upon stolen waters and bread gotten by deceit; for I have fed upon vanity and lies, and made refuges of such things as could not secure in the day of trial. But all that which was my life, and that which had fed and nourished it, must now all perish together. I see the death of all determined, though the death of all be not fulfilled, for his angels minister, the deliverance shall be brought forth, and judgment shall come forth to victory; though the day of redemption be not come, but is yet to be waited for; for the end is not yet. In the midst of his terrible judgments there was a mercy hid which I saw not, which was the cause why I was not consumed; and his compassions failed not, though at that time I could see neither mercy nor compassion, for it is hid from the eyes of all living; and the fowls of the air must not meddle with it. All things which is pure and holy is hid from man, for he is separate from God and knoweth not any of his ways; but when the Lord revealeth any of his ways within man, man must die and know his own ways no more, but must "be led in a way which he knoweth not," contrary to his will, contrary to his wisdom, contrary to his reason, and to his carnal mind. For none of these must enter, but must be cast out into the lake which burneth. Precious and pure is that love of the Lord which reveals these things in man, things which are eternal and everlasting. All the ways of God is eternal and "whatsoever he doth is forever" [Eccles. 3:14]; dwell in his power, in measure manifested. For the least measure of his power is eternal, and leads to eternity. Now the love and power of the Lord keep thee to himself, and all my brethren and sisters dwelling in the truth in thy family, and about thee. Remember my dear love to Richard Myers. I desire greatly to see thee, but I must wait upon the Lord, which bringeth things to pass according to his will. For he is worthy to rule and to be praised by all those who have tasted of his power.

Thy brother in the Lord,
Richard Hubberthorne.

158

Most of the same outward metaphors of inward struggle and of the pain and death of the "old carnal nature" within, which we will also find in many later Quaker descriptions of convincement, were used again by Hubberthorne himself when he published his story as an appeal and warning to his persecutors:

A True Testimony of Obedience to the Heavenly Call, for which I suffer the loss of all things, that I may be found in obedience to him who hath called me.

A servant of the Lord, and a prisoner for the testimony of Jesus, whom he hath called by his grace to deny the world, . . . who hath called me out of my own country, and from my father's house, and to go in obedience to his command whithersoever he shall call me. While I was young, I girded myself, and went whither I would, and then I yielded obedience to my own will and to the will of man, and was a manpleaser, but the Will of God I knew not; . . . but when the Lord was pleased to reveal his Son in me, and make known his will unto me, . . . when his Power was made manifest and his Word spoke within me, which Word was in my heart, and was as a fire or a hammer; and this Word being made manifest within me, and my Conscience being awakened by the Light of God, which did convince me of sin, and did testify against all my words and actions, and that just judgments of God were revealed from heaven against that nature I lived in, and the trumpet of the Lord was sounded within [2] me, and the earth did tremble, and the vials of the wrath of the Almighty were poured down upon me, . . . the foundation of wisdom and earthly knowledge was shaken. And the judgments of God were upon the outward man, and my flesh wasted off my bones, and the bones smote one against another, and I knew the Lord to be terrible, and this Word powerful in burning up and hammering down the lustful nature I lived in, in pleasure and wantonness, in pride and fulness. . . . Which made my flesh and bones to tremble exceedingly, and did cause pain in all my loins, and paleness of face. . . . And I was brought to the bed of sorrows, where I cried out in the bitterness of my spirit, and I had no ease nor rest day nor night. . . . In my trouble, I cried in the evening "would God it were morning," and in the morning, "would God it were evening." And, the terrors of the Almighty being upon me, my acquaintance and familiars stood afar off me, for they knew not the power of the Lord, nor the judgments of my God. . . . And by this Word was I called to go and declare it, as I had received it from the Lord, to those who lived in the same heathenish nature, without the knowledge of God, and to declare the judgments of God against sin and ungodliness, as they were made manifest in me.

And by this Word was I called to forsake Father and Mother, lands and living, to go in obedience to the Lord, who commanded me not to take thought what I should eat, or what I should drink, or wherewith I should be clothed, but cast my care upon him. And this I witness the Lord's care; and those whom the Lord calls into his work . . . need not complain to the world for want. And for yielding obedience to the Lord and his commands, and not giving obedience to the corrupt will of man, who commands [3] me contrary to what the Lord hath commanded, do I suffer under the persecution of those who are set in the place of rulers and magistrates, professing themselves to be ministers of the Law of England to act justice according to that Law.

Those who are rulers of the city, . . . say this is their Law, that if I will home into my own country, and to my father's house, and stay there, and depart this city, I may be free upon this account; else I shall remain in prison. . . . [4] And you who say I have no lawful calling,[13] I do witness the same Word of God the true prophets of the Lord were commanded by, to declare against all sin and ungodliness. . . . Elisha was a ploughman, and when the Word of the Lord came to him, he left the plough, and obeyed the Word of the Lord. And his call was lawful. Amos was a herdsman. . . . And I do witness the same call, who was a husbandman.

[5] O wicked and adulterous generation, thy woe and misery is coming upon thee, for the Lord is appearing, who is come and coming to cleanse the land of evil-doers.

This I was moved to declare from the Spirit of my Father dwelling in me . . . who is a prisoner for the Truth's sake, whose earthly name is

Chester, the 12. day of the   Richard Hubberthorne
12th Month, called February,
1653[/54].

I came to Chester about the 29th of the 9th Month.

2. Letters Reporting Ministry as Material for Later Journals: James Parnell, Letter to Burrough and Howgill (1655)

(A. R. Barclay MS No. 29, to Francis Howgill and Edward Burrough, May 18, 1655). Few if any Friends kept daily diaries, but many reported regularly by letter to each other or Margaret

---

13 Clearly Hubberthorne had been sentenced under the "Poor Law" against vagabonds, which provided that men without work should be sent from town to town (whipped en route, if need be) to their home parishes, which were responsible for giving them work and shelter.

Fell at Swarthmoor Hall (see p. 469). Journals and the collected works of Friends that were published after Fox's in 1691 regularly included such letters; earlier ones did not. James Parnell, a fiery little teen-ager brought into Quaker circles, perhaps by the Aldam clan in 1653, was a year later preaching the new message in Cambridge, and had been through three months in jail and six of ministry in that region when he wrote this letter.

Dear

Friends and brethren: In the eternal unchangeable love and life and the new covenant am I with you, and there do salute you, where we are one in our measures though ten thousand, all children of one father, brethren and sisters of one family, and heirs of the promise every one, in the measure of the gift of grace given unto us, for to be good stewards therein. And herein doth our joy abound, and is made full in one another. In the light of the new covenant you read me, where I am present with you, and do embrace and salute you, though absent in body; for we, being all begotten by one immortal word and bornage, and we come to bear the one image of our Father; so that hereby we know one another to be the children of our Father, and do see and read and enjoy one another in this same unchangeable covenant of love and light. And here is the blessed union and communion and fellowship, and the glorious liberty of the children of the new covenant, who are sealed down in this everlasting covenant of life. And this is the great riches of the love of God bestowed upon us, that we should be found worthy of this high calling.

Dear Brethren: the letter which you sent from Cambridge I received with the same that sent it, and did own it as your care and wisdom; and I shortly went into the Isle of Ely, and I had meetings at Ely town, and was moved to go to the steeple[-house]; but the rude people would not suffer me to speak. But mightily by the power of God I was preserved, and I had a great meeting in the town that day; and in much power was I carried forth to the binding and chaining of the heathen and the reaching of the witness; so that many was convinced. But the town is much hardened against the Truth; but yet I see a further work to be done in it. There is a pretty people a coming on at Littleport in the Isle. I remained there a certain space among them, and there is about 60 that are brought to meet together alone in that town. There was one of them was [?] moved to go naked, and to go so to a captain's house, an Independent professor; and the town was much enraged and set him in the stocks all night.[14] And on the first day following I had a meeting at a place

14 This is one of the earliest cases of a Friend who was "moved to go naked for a Sign," as did later both William Simpson and Robert Barclay.

called Soam, within 3 miles of Col. Russell's, and there was J. Loud,[15] a priest, gotten up into the seat of the Pharisee; and he was a right Pharisee, for he was much painted [?]; and I was suffered to stay until he had done, and then I was carried out in a mighty power to speak to him and to the people, and which bound them all under; and they was a very great people, and rude; but the power of God was wonderfully seen in delivering me, so that I know not that they gave me a stroke. And the throng was great, so I pressed forth into the yard, and there they made way for me; and I was moved to speak in much power; and they stood even like lambs about me. And at last there came one Robert Hammond, called a Justice, who had been at the steeple-house, and he said that there was a proclamation that all who disturbed the minister in the time of his Public Exercise should be apprehended as disturbers of the peace;[16] so if I would not pass away, he said, I should be apprehended; so I was free to pass from that place. But I told him and the people that I should declare the truth in the town that day. And so upon these conditions I was set free, and I had a great meeting in the town that day; and there was several of the people that belonged to those people at Chippenham;[17] but I heard of none that came out of the town. But those that was there received the truth willingly; and there was many people convinced that day. . . . And there was a man that was moved to come from Littleport, and stand naked among the people in the meeting, as there was of all sorts. But I knew nothing of it until it was done; and many of the world stumbled, and the Enemy got some advantage there; but the people was much silent and quiet, though there was some startling among them of the world. But I was made to clear it much to the people, so that many was satisfied, who had a capacity to receive. But this went to Hammond's ear, and stirred up his spirit against the truth. So the priests and he consulted together against me; and the next morning he sent a warrant for me and committed me to Cambridge jail, for speaking to the priest, whereas he had set me free from that among a hundred people. So this was on the last Second Day, that I was come to Cambridge, and there I was put into the low jail, among the thieves. . . . And on the next day, Justice J. Blackley[18] sent out his warrant and set me

This particular man may be Samuel Cater, who also may be the "Friend from Ely" who later figured in Nayler's "Fall" (cf. p. 484). On Friends at Littleport cf. *CJ*, I, 9; Besse, I, 93. The "Steeple of Ely" is presumably the glorious stone "lantern" topping the cathedral tower.

15 No data at hand on Col. Russell or J. Loud.

16 This refers to an edict of Cromwell's Council of State in 1654.

17 Perhaps from the household of Justice Edward Stokes; cf. *CJ*, I, 444; SMS 181=*EQL* No. 321.

18 On Alderman James Blackley of Cambridge, cf. *FPT*, pp. 13-14; *JFHS*, XXXI (1934), 56.

free from the tyrants' bonds; but I was made very willing to remain, if it had been the Lord's will; but in his large wisdom he ordered it according to his good will and pleasure. For I did not motion it unto Blackley, but he did it of his own accord. And the next day, I went to a meeting six miles from Cambridge, where I met with my dear sisters Anne Blaykling and Dorothy Waugh. They do remain in those parts awhile, but my sudden releasement and going into the country proved very serviceable; for the heathen was much exalted and rejoiced at my imprisonment. It is like, if the Lord will, I shall pass shortly back into those parts where I was taken, for there is a people there to be brought forth (I heard Russell was then at London). But the heathen, I perceive, is plotting together to get me into prison again. For the jailer hath been with Blackley about it, and is troubled in mind, because he let me go without bail. And there went to get another warrant for me; but according to the good will of God be it as it stands, to his glory. I am content whether in bonds or out of bonds. But I have thoughts to be hereabouts until the next return,[19] if you have movings unto anything. Jollie the scholar[20] is come to the town, but he is in little service. He is come to see about some means that is due to him in the College, for they have not yet put him out, and he hath gotten some means of them.

Salute me dearly to my dear brother G.F., and all the rest of my dear brethren and sisters and fellow laborers in the vineyard of the Lord. Salute me dearly to all my dear and tender hearts whom the Lord hath chosen out of that great city Sodom, for to bear his image, and to glorify his name, and to be as signs and wonders in that old adulterous generation. The Lord God prosper and increase the power to beat down their enemies before them.

This from C.B.	I shall be glad to hear from	
18th day of 3 month	George or any of you.	James Parnell

3. Posthumous Testimony: *Stephen Crisp's Testimony Concerning James Parnell* (1662)

Tracts describing the death of the Massachusetts martyrs have been presented among the proclamation writings of early Friends.

[19] I.e., the next return mail-coach; if Burrough or Howgill wrote in reply, the letter is lost.

[20] James Jollie of Trinity College, Cambridge, protested against the need for formal ministerial training, and praised the Quaker ministry, "cut his name from the butteries" of the College fellows, but after a day offered to sign on again to teach "any other Art or Science professed there which is not curious but necessary" (Aldam MSS, quoted in *JFHS*, XXV [1928], 54).

Even the death of Parnell himself became the subject of a small tract debate (cf. BBQ, p. 192).

But the printing of the collected writings of Friends who had recently died opened the way for another type of biographical writing, the testimony, usually written by a colleague in ministry or a member of the family. Typically five to ten such testimonies preceded a collection of works in later years, but the earliest, John Pennyman's "Epistle to all Friendly Readers" of the works of George Fox "the Younger" (1662), and that for Richard Hubberthorne (1663), were single, short, and austere. Since, however, both these Friends died in prison, as did Edward Burrough (whose works appeared in 1672) and Francis Howgill (1676), there was room for eulogy. As a model for later writers and the best source for his life stands Stephen Crisp's memorial to Parnell, who had first won him for Quakerism (cf. p. 203).

STEPHEN CRISP
HIS
TESTIMONY
CONCERNING
JAMES PARNEL

It was the care of the holy men of old, to keep in remembrance the words and works which sprang from the blessed power of God, and therefore did record the words of many prophecies, and the histories of many battles and wars, in which the Arm of God was manifest; and whenever God crown'd any with worthiness and honour, as his witnesses of his word and power, this was commonly added unto the renown of their noble acts and faithful testimonies, that their name and manner of life was committed unto the generations that followed after; insomuch as one said, "The righteous should be had in everlasting remembrance"; and another said, "the name of the righteous was precious"; and many other such like sayings are there in the Holy Scripture: Christ said to her that anointed him with the box of oyntment, wherever the Gospel should be preached, this charity and love of hers, bestowed on him, should be speaken of. And if ever any age had cause to prize and keep in Remembrance the words and sayings, great deliverances and spiritual battles, and mighty and noble acts of God, wrought by the finger of his power, sure this age hath cause to be diligent in gathering up and keeping in Remembrance the mighty works of wonder, which our God hath wrought in our Day.... And among these babes, who thus came to receive the knowledge of the mysteries of the Kingdom of God, by the working of his divine power was this noble child, James Parnel, who was a vessel of honour

164

indeed, and mighty in the power and spirit of Immanuel, breaking down and laying desolate many mighty and strong holds, and towers of defence, in the which the old Deceiver had fortified himself and his children. Much might be spoken of this man, and a large Testimony doth live in my heart to his blessed life, and to the power and wisdom that abounded in him, but I do not intend at this time to write much about him, but to give the reader a brief account of my certain knowledge, which I had of him, and his life, and labors, and end.

As to his country and manner of life, and how he was about the age of fifteen or sixteen years brought to the knowledge of God, and to the working of his power in him, and how he obeyed the same in many travails and trials, until he came to about eighteen years of age; all this, I say, it being spoken to in another place, and before my particular acquaintance with him, I shall pass over, and only speak of things within the compass of my own knowledge.

When he was about eighteen years of age, the Lord (who had heard the cry of his own seed) put it into the heart of this young man to come into Essex, and to preach the word of life, and to proclaim the Acceptable Year of the Lord there, where it might indeed well have been said, Behold, the fields are white unto harvest; for, very many were there in that county, who were both weary and heavy laden with their sins, and were as weary with running to and fro, to seek a way out of them. . . . His coming was in the fore-end of the year 1655. Where he preached the gospel in many parts of that county, as Felsted, Stebben, Witham, Coxal, Halsted, and many other places, where many hungry souls had gladly received the Word of God, and it being mixed with faith in the hearts of them who heard it, it became effectual to the saving the souls of many. And after he had passed up and down many parts of that County, and planted divers good meetings, and confirmed them that had believed; he at length, about the middle of the summer, the same year, came to Colchester, upon the seventh day of the week, and on the day following preached the Gospel unto many thousands of people, first in his lodging; then in a steeple-house there, after the sermon; then in a great meeting, appointed on purpose; and after that disputed with the Town-Lecturer and another priest in the French-School, all in one day. In all which the wisdom, power and patience of Christ appeared very gloriously, to the convincing of my self and many more, who were witnesses of that day's work. So he spent that week in preaching, praying, exhorting and admonishing, turning the minds of all sorts of professors to the light of Jesus, which did search their hearts, and show their thoughts, that they might believe therein, and so might become Children of the Light; and many did believe, and found it so; and others were hardened and rebelled against the appearance of Truth, and became enemies, with whom he disputed daily in great soundness, and in the evidence and demonstration of the Spirit, by which also many were reached, and convinced of the Truth, and the mouths of gainsayers stopped. Which made many gnash their teeth on him; and some undertook to club out the priests and professors arguments by beating this dear lamb with fists and staves, who took all patiently; as particularly, one who struck him with a great staff as he came out of one of the steeple-houses, called Nicholas, and said,

"There, take that for Jesus Christ's sake"—to which he returned this answer, "Friend, I do receive it for Jesus Christ's sake." And many other intolerable affronts were offered him, in all which his Spirit was not seen to be raised in heat or anger; but was a pattern of patience and meekness. And having laboured in that great town about ten days, it lay upon him to go back to Cogshall (to a meeting holden as a fast, of which read more in that part of his writings, called, The Fruits of a Fast) from whence he was committed to Colchester Castle, and from thence had up to Chelmsford Assizes in irons, and again thither re-committed, where he remained until he offered up his life for his testimony. He lived in that castle about ten or eleven months, in great self-denial and carefulness, being truly watchful over the flock of God both in Essex and in Cambridgeshire, Huntingtonshire and the Isle of Ely, and elsewhere, where he had travailed, and turned many to God, and wrote many blessed and heavenly Epistles. Those books and papers, which could be found, are here composed for the view of those who desire to taste the first fruits of this tender plant; who in the days of his youth laid down his life for his blessed testimony: Many things he suffered in that prison, which is other where in this book to be found. And as he lay in prison, he laboured for the building up of them that were convinced; and he saw the desire of his soul concerning many, in whom he saw the seed which he had sown multiply and grow, to his refreshment. And at last, having passed through many trials and exercises, both inward and outward and fulfilled his testimony in patience, courage and faithfulness, and been a comfort to us who had believed, he at length laid down his head in rest and peace, stretching forth himself, saying, Here I die innocently:[21] And after his departure he was buried in the Castle yard, where other prisoners use to be buried, because the cruel jailer would not deliver his body without fees. And though he be, as to the outward, taken away, his life doth remain, and his testimony doth yet live in the hearts of many, and will live through generations to come; and happy and blessed are and shall all they be, who are partakers thereof, and are faithful therein, they shall be also partakers of that crown immortal with which he is crowned.

Stephen Crisp

[21] He died as a result of falling from a little cell in the dungeon wall, called "the hole," reached by a rope which in his state of weakness and exposure he failed to hold.

4. Francis Howgill: *The Inheritance of Jacob* (1655-66)

The first Quaker tracts presenting autobiography do so in a setting where personal experience is a witness and authentication of a message. Richard Farnworth's *Heart Opened* (1654) is specially in disproof of the need of parish ministry, and Hubberthorne's *True Testimony* (cf. p. 159) is also a prisoner's defense, but most of these "Confessions" are moving appeals to accept the Quaker Light. A good sample is Howgill's *Inheritance*, which saw a Dutch edition in 1660 and was reprinted in his *Works* (*The Dawnings of the Gospel Day*, 1676) after his death in perhaps the longest imprisonment any Friend suffered, with the exception of Dewsbury's at Warwick.

Francis Howgill may also represent in his life-story the leaders of the first decade of Quakerism, those who had been through the Puritan progression from parish church to Puritan parish to Independent to Baptist to Separatist. Through his boyhood experiences can be heard the voices of Puritan pastors trying to counsel a guilt-burdened boy. In due course he became a leader of the Westmorland Separatists and, after Firbank, of the sixty Quaker preachers. His wisdom and maturity were balanced by Burrough's quick mind and preaching ability, just as John Camm's was by John Audland, similarly a generation younger than his partner. It is striking that even while leaders of the Separatists each of these men had to go through bitter months of inner struggle before coming to "the new man" within them as Friends, and yet none seems ever again to have had to face such self-judgment.

THE INHERITANCE OF JACOB
DISCOVERED, AFTER HIS RETURN
OUT OF EGYPT

And the leading of the Lord to the Land of Promise declared, and some information of the way.

Or a word of exhortation to all professors in England, Scotland and Ireland, and to all the world where this will come, where the common salvation is declared, in which the saints believed, and deceit discovered and made manifest. Also a few words of exhortation to the Rulers of England and Ireland. *London: Printed for Giles Calvert at the Black Spreadeagle at the West End of Pauls, 1656.*[22]

[22] On Giles Calvert and his address, cf. p. 94.

Awake, O Zion, who hath long sitten in the dust in sorrow and bitterness, and hath been covered with ashes, and none hath had compassion upon thee; [omitting 13 lines of apocalyptic imagery about the Beast and the Whore] the time of thy deliverance has come, and the years of thy captivity are up. Arise, O Virgin, who art not defiled, who could not join with the daughter of Babylon in her whoredoms. Therefore they have mocked thee, and wagged their heads at thee, and have said in their hearts, "Who shall deliver thee?" Arise, shine forth, put on thy beautiful garments. Behold, thy king comes in his glory, who will adorn thee and crown thee with a royal diadem, in the sight of thine enemies who have reproached thee; and thy reproach will be taken away; for thy seed will be as the stars in multitude. They who have spoiled thee will be spoiled, and they who have destroyed thee shall be destroyed; for the King is coming out of his tent. Yea he has lifted up his standard against all that have spoiled thee; the destroyer has come up against Babylon. . . . [omitting six more lines of thunder] Rejoice for evermore all that love his appearance and who have waited for him; he has come to take vengeance upon his and your adversaries, for he has a sacrifice in Babylon to perform; to cut off all her children, who have despised thee, O Zion. [The mighty are summoned to trial.]

Awake, O arm of the Lord, and put on strength as in the days of old, to redeem thine own inheritance which hath long been by the heathen laid waste, and hath been trampled upon by the uncircumcised. . . . [omitting a paragraph of paraphrase from Deutero-Isaiah]

But, Oh Lord, thou seest how thy own seed lieth scattered, and ravenous beasts make a prey on it, and the devourers swallow it up. Therefore thou hast appeared in thy love and power for thine own name's sake, and will not suffer thy seed to be trodden on any longer by the prince of darkness, nor his children whom he hath begotten in his own image.

Arise, shine forth, thou everlasting covenant of light and peace, by which and in which all our fathers believed, and so obtained a good report, and were redeemed out of captivity to serve the Lord forever with one heart and mind, and worshipped in one spirit, in which faith they laid hold upon the perfect righteousness of Christ made manifest in them. . . . [The lamb has come to take his kingdom from the Beast.]

Wherefore all honest-hearted, in and under all forms of professions, who have traveled and are weary, and all you who have kindled a fire, and have warmed yourselves at the sparks thereof and yet still you lie in sorrow; O all ye that have panted and thirsted after righteousness, who have wearied yourselves in seeking among the dead graves and tombs for a savior, but have found no rest . . . [grave metaphors] for your sakes who are weary, and have found none to direct your way, a few lines I am moved in compassion to write to you. And if you will not receive it, you will not believe if one should rise from the dead. For I have obtained mercy through his free grace, from Christ, who is risen from the dead, and saw no corruption; by which grace I am saved from sin, and cleansed from unrighteousness, after long and sore labor and travail,[23] under Pharaoh the oppressor, from under whose dominion I am brought to worship the living God in spirit and truth, in his temple, where he dwells in righteousness forever.

And for the simples' sake (who have erred for lack of true knowledge, as I did in times past) I shall declare unto you a little in short of my travels in Egypt and, where darkness is so thick that if you wait diligently to see yourselves, you will feel it also.

From twelve years old I set my heart to know the God which the world professed and which I had read of in the Scripture, which Abraham, Noah, Moses, and the prophets, and the rest of the fathers worshipped. And I did fall into the strictest worship that was in that part wherein I lived; and often I desired to be alone, and attended much to reading and meditation. And then, as I was sober, and serious alone, I began to see "that all the sports and pastimes, and such as youth naturally delights in, were vanity, and lasted but for a moment." And while I was in folly and wantonness, doing of them, the nature which was run into transgression had pleasure in them, but as soon as I was come from among them I was judged in myself for what I had done, and this often made me weep. Then I resolved in my will, that I would never do so again, and for some time did restrain from the common practice of those in which I had walked. But as soon as I came among those things again, I acted those things again which before I did see to be vanity. But long before that I was checked for many things. And so I walked, often condemned in myself, when I was serious, and had no peace and then not knowing what to do, in much sorrow when I was alone. I had a desire to be alone, where I might not hear nor see any folly acted, and I did not go to the former exercises, although something in me hankered after it; but when I yielded not to it I was glad, and had peace. Then I began to oppose my fellows, with whom I had walked in wantonness; and then they began to revile me, and hate me, and scorn me; yet not withstanding I mattered not. Then I read much, and I prayed often, three or four times a day; but I knew not where God was, but in my imagination I imagined a God at a distance, and so went on.

Then I began to grow in knowledge without (which is sensual) and then I was puffed up, for the world admired me. But still, I was condemned for vain words and actions, and the root of iniquity grew in me. And then I followed a

23 Early Friends spelled "travail" and "travel" interchangeably.

more strict course, and often went five or six miles to hear some more excellent Means[24] (as they called it) and so did get more words: but still I was the same, nay, worse, for knowledge puffed me up. Then along to about fifteen years of age, I posted up and down after the most excellent sermons (so called) and so became acquainted with all the eminent Christians (so called) in the region where I lived. And I was despised by my parents, and by the world made a wonder, and great reproach came on me; but still, I saw they knew nothing, and it was no matter. And much sorrow fell upon me for four or five years; and when I was turned within, I was judged for all my iniquity formerly, and still my heart was shown to me, that it was corrupt. But as I kept within to the light in my conscience, I was restrained from many actions which I had a will to do, and in the instant when I have been doing any unrighteousness in actions or words, in many things I was often stopped. When I saw that I did it not, a great joy arose in me. And when I had done anything forwardly and rashly, I was judged. But this the teachers said was a natural conscience that kept from sin, and did restrain it, and they said, that he who had but restraining grace, (as they called it); he was but a tame devil.[25] And so I listened to their imagination, and so slighted the light as too low a thing, that was "but common grace that did preserve out of gross evils," but "the saints had a peculiar faith and grace;" and so I listened to them, and still I was convinced of sin; and they told how "the saints did believe in Christ, and so sin was not imputed, but his righteousness was accounted to them," and so I must seek him in the Means, [such] as prayer and receiving the sacrament, as they called it; and [they] judged me a worthy Communicant;[26] and in great fear I was that I should eat [the sacrament] unworthily. And none could tell me what the body of Christ was; insomuch that one time I read all the scripture that spoke of Christ's suffering. And they said, I must believe he suffered for me; and I believed all that they called faith, yet I could not see how he died for me, and had taken away my sin: for the witness in my conscience told me, I was a servant of sin, while I committed it. And they told me, I must not omit that ordinance [of Communion] for thereby strength was confirmed, and faith added. Insomuch on the one hand they pressed it as a duty, and on the other hand I saw that the scripture said "he who eats unworthily eats damnation to himself," I was in fear, notwithstanding none could accuse me without; yet then, afterward a great fear fell

24 "Means of Grace," usually sacraments, were the Puritan name also for prayer, preaching, and scripture reading, by which God might choose to reach even his elect.

25 Despite modern anti-Puritans, the Puritan gospel was opposed to legalism and self-righteousness, and attacked negative morality.

26 Communicant, i.e., a confirmed church member receiving Communion suitably.

on me, and I thought I had sinned against the Holy Ghost, and great trouble fell on me.[27]

Then they said, I had not come prepared; and yet I had all the preparation that they had spoken of; but still they were all physicians of no value.

Then I fasted and prayed, and walked mournfully in sorrow, and thought none was like me, tempted on every hand. So I ran to this man and the other, and they made promises to me, but it was only words. The witness of Christ showed me that the root of iniquity stood, and the body of sin whole. Notwithstanding, I was kept by a secret power from gross evils. But still sorrow compassed me about, and I questioned all that ever I had, which they said was grace, repentance and faith.

And then I told them there was guilt in me; and they said, "sin was taken away by Christ, but the guilt should still remain while I lived," and so brought me the saints' conditions, who were in the warfare, to confirm it. I said to myself, this was a miserable salvation . . . surely this is not the ministry of Christ, and so I ceased long by fits, and did not mind them, but kept still at home, and in desert places, solitary in weeping; and everything that I had done was laid before me. My every thought was judged, and I was tender, and my heart broken, and when I could sorrow most I had most peace, for something spoke within me from the Lord, but I knew him not then. They said that it was heresy to look for the word of the Lord to be spoken now in these days, but only the letter. So I regarded it not much, yet often I was made to do many righteous things by the immediate power and word of God, and then peace and joy sprung up in me, and promises were spoken, that he would teach me himself, and be my God. And often I did obey contrary to my will, and denied my will; but they told me "this was legal [=legalistic], to obey out of fear, and that was slavery, but there was an evangelical obedience" (as they called it). So I got above the fear, and yet acted the former things, which they called ordinances, and they said, that was son-like obedience, and Christ had done all.

Then there appeared more beauty in them called Independents, and I loved them, and so joined them. And I purchased books with all the money that I could get, and walked with and owned them as more separate from the world, and they pressed separation. But at last I saw it was but in words, that they would do things, and choose officers and members of themselves, and so they made themselves an Image, and fell down to it, yet there was some tenderness

---

[27] The "Sin against the Holy Ghost" is described (Matt. 12:31) as the only one unforgivable. Hence many Puritans (cf. Bunyan's *Grace Abounding*) were tormented to despair by fear that they had committed it. Puritan pastors (cf. William Perkins, *Cases of Conscience*, in *Works* [1597], I, 538-39) had to reassure them that those sensitive to sin could not commit this.

in them at first, but the doctrine was the same with the world's words without, of others' conditions.

They whom they called anabaptists appeared to have more glory and walked more according to the scripture, observing things written without. And I went among them, and there was something I loved about them. But after they denied all but such that came into their way as "out of the fellowship of the saints and doctrine of Christ," I saw the ground was the same, and their doctrine out of the life, with the rest of the teachers of the world, and they had separated themselves, and made another likeness. But still all said, the letter [of scripture] was the word and rule, and Christ at a distance without, had done all; and some of them holding freewill, others opposing, and all in [their own] will.

But still I loved them that walked honestly among all these; but though I had seen and owned all that I had heard; [omitting a long clause on fixed worship as an idol] after all this no peace nor no guide did I find. And then the doctrine of free grace (as they called it), some preached that all sin was done away, past, present and to come, and so preached salvation to the first nature, and to the serpent that bore rule, only believing this, and all is finished. To this I listened a little, and so lost my condition within. But still wherever I went, this was spoken in me, "his servant you are to whom you give obedience," and so I being overcome by sin, I had no justification witnessed in me, but condemnation.

Then some preached Christ within, but they themselves were without. [They] had but words; and yet they said, "all must be within" (unto which my heart did cleave) and spoke of redemption and justification, and all within, and of God appearing in Man, and overcoming the power of the devil. Then that in my conscience bore witness that it must be so, and I was exceedingly pressed to wait to find it so, and something breathed after the living God; and a true love I had for all who walked honestly in what profession soever. And I hated reviling one another, and that they should smite one another, and persecute one another. And with the sufferer I always took part. But still I saw, though they spoke of all things within, and of a power to come, that they enjoyed not what they spoke, for the same fruits were brought forth till at last I saw none walked as the ministers of Christ, nor none that pretended to the ministry had any such gift, neither pastor, nor teacher, nor any such members as were in the apostles' time. . . . [omitting a short paragraph on false ministers]

So at last there was something revealed in me, that the Lord would teach his people himself. And so I waited, and many things opened in me of a time at hand. And sometimes I would have heard a priest, but when I heard him, I was moved by the Lord, and his word in me spoke to oppose. And often as a fire I burned, and a trembling fell on me. Yet I feared reproach, and so denied the Lord's motion. And it was revealed in me to wait, and I should know his counsel. And the word of the Lord was in me: the time was at hand when the dead should hear the voice of the son of God; and it burned in me as fire, that the day was near. . . . Still my mind ran out, and out of fear into carelessness, for the cross of Christ I knew not; and yet I say I was wiser than my teachers I met with in that generation. (I do not glory in it, for condemnation is passed on it all forever.) Yet still I had, as my mind was turned to the light, pure openings and prophesies to come, and a belief that I should see the day, and should bear witness to his name. And so when things opened so fast, the wisdom of the flesh caught them; and so I went up and down, preaching against all the ministry; and also ran out with that which was revealed to myself, and preached up and down the countryside of the fulness that was in the old bottle, and so was wondered after, and admired by many, who had waded up and down as I had, and we fed one another with words, and healed one another in deceit: and all laid down in sorrow when the Day of the Lord was made manifest; for I was overthrown, and the foundation swept away, and all my righteousness and unrighteousness was all judged and weighted and all was found too light. . . .

And immediately, as soon as I heard one [i.e., Fox] declare, (one whose name is not known to the world, but written in the Lamb's Book of Life forever, in eternal record forever) as soon as I heard him declare that the Light of Christ in man was the way to Christ, I believed the eternal word of truth, and that of God in my conscience sealed to it. And so not only I, but many hundred more,[28] who thirsted after the Lord, but were betrayed by the wisdom of the serpent; we were all seen to be off the foundation, and all mouths were stopped in the dust. We all stood as condemned in our selves, and [we] all saw our nakedness, and were all ashamed, though our glory was great in the world's eye, but all was vanity.

And then after all this, I was ignorant as to what the first principle of true religion was. But as I turned my mind within to the Light of Jesus Christ . . . I saw it was the true and faithful witness of Christ Jesus. My eyes were opened, and all the things that I had ever done were brought to remembrance and the ark of the testament was opened, and there was thunder and lightning and great hail. And then the trumpet of the Lord was sounded, and then nothing but war and rumor of war, and the dreadful power of the Lord fell on me: plague, and pestilence, and famine, and earthquake, and fear and terror, for the sights that I saw with my eyes: and that which I heard with my ears, sorrow and pain. And in the morning I wished it had been evening, and in the evening I wished it had been morning and I had no rest, but trouble on every

28 This refers to the great separatist meeting at Firbank where Fox spoke in 1653.

side. And all that ever I had done was judged and condemned, all things were accursed; whether I did eat, or drink, or restrain, I was accursed. Then the lion suffered hunger, and the seals were opened, and seven thunders uttered their voices. My eyes were dim with crying, my flesh did fail of fatness, my bones were dried and my sinews shrunk. I became a proverb to all. . . . [omitting a dozen sentences from Psalms of lamentation]

I became a perfect fool, and knew nothing, as a man distracted; all was overturned, and I suffered loss of all. In all that I ever did, I saw it was in the accursed nature. And then something in me cried: "Just and true is his judgment!" My mouth was stopped, I dared not make mention of his name, I knew not God. And as I bore the indignation of the Lord, something rejoiced, the serpent's head began to be bruised, and the witnesses which were slain were raised. [another eight sentences of biblical woe and flaming judgment] And as I did give up all to the judgment, the captive came forth out of prison and rejoiced, and my heart was filled with joy. I came to see him whom I had pierced, and my heart was broken, and the blood of the prophets I saw slain, and a great lamentation. Then I saw the cross of Christ, and stood in it, and the enmity slain on it. And the new man was made. And so peace came to be made; and so eternal life was brought in through death and judgment. And then the perfect gift I received, which was given from God, and the holy law of God was revealed unto me, and was written in my heart. And his fear and his word (which did kill) now makes alive; and so it pleased the Father to reveal his Son in me through death; and so I came to witness cleansing by his blood which is eternal, and to glorify him forever; and am a minister of that word of eternal life which endures forever . . . and have rest and peace in doing the will of God, and enter in the true rest, and lie down in the fold with the lambs of God. . . .

These few things have I written for your sakes, who walk in darkness, that you may see where you are; and also you high cedars, who trust in the arm of flesh, that you may cease your boasting, and come down from the pinnacle where you are exalted. For the same must come upon you, if ever the Lord you know in truth and righteousness, even through the death of things, in the curse of all knowledge and wisdom is from below. Yea through the death of death that rules in you, which must be slain on the cross of Christ Jesus, if ever you come to true peace, and witness eternal salvation. . . . [omitting a paragraph on imaginers of the false Christ who approves the fashions of the world]

Therefore take warning, for it is not your good words, without the life of godliness, nor your swelling speeches, that are accepted with God; for he accepts nothing except that which is of himself, and by him wrought in the creature by his own will and power. And this destroys the carnal will, power and righteousness. And this work, which he works of himself, and by his power, and in his covenant, is perfect, and is accepted of God. Therefore, it is no longer the creature, but Christ, who is all in his saints. And so he brings all that follow him out of his works of condemnation (which are acted in the disobedient nature) . . . and leads all that believe and follow him in the living works of righteousness brought by him through faith, and is accepted and well pleasing to God. And here, all boasting is excluded, for all is of him, and from him; that works both the will and the deed; and here the Lord is admired in all his works and his works praise him.[29]

Wherefore all honest hearted, who travel [=travail] and are weary, and have found no rest for your souls, I say unto you, arise and come away. Lie not groveling in the earth like moles [digging for God in old dry wells]. Look upward, mind that which draws you from the earth. The covenant of life is made manifest! Glory to him in the highest! . . . Self must be denied, and that you must deny if you will receive of him, that he may be all, and you nothing. He gives freely, and his gift is perfect and pure, without spot, stain, or mixture. All who receive his gift, come by it to be presented perfect to the Father. . . . [omitting paragraph on preaching to the blind and spirits in prison]

Therefore, I say to you who look after righteousness, come hither who are weary, and I will show you where you may have true everlasting rest, which he has shed abroad in my heart by his free grace and everlasting love made manifest, after a long and a dark night, in which I passed without a guide, and so fell into the pit, and stumbled, and then sorrow and trouble compassed me about on every side, as an armed man. But now hath he shed abroad his grace in my heart, which saves me from sin, and leads out of the works of condemnation into his habitation, where no unclean thing can enter. And this grace has separated me from sin, and has constrained me to deny myself, and follow him through the death of the cross, and through the denial of all, both country and nation, kindred, and tongues, and people, and from wife and children and houses and lands, to publish his name abroad contrary to my own will, and to make known to you the riches of his grace, which all who wait in the light of Christ Jesus will come to see. . . . [omitting paragraph on finding Christ within]

Now, therefore, every one who thirsts, come to Christ Jesus, who is near to you; and wait to know his word in you, which is in the heart . . . as you wait diligently, and keep your minds to it. And this which shows you sin and evil. is in you, and makes manifest all that you have acted contrary to it; yea, even all that ever you have done, and will search your hearts, and is the eye that sees the deceit in all its transforming in you, and it will let you see. It has often checked and called, but you have not answered its call, and so have chosen your own way, and so have gone from the way, which is the light of

---

[29] This was the Quaker answer to the Puritans' charge that Quakers were self-righteous (cf. p. 281).

Christ in you. And so you run into the broad way; and that which desired after God hath not been nourished and fed, but hath been famished and another hath been fed, which now is for the slaughter. But now as you return home to within, to the true Light of Jesus, which is that one thing, which leads all men that own it, and to be guided by it, you shall have true rest and peace.

Now friends, there is something in man which must receive Christ, something of his own (learn what it is) which he comes to, and he cannot be joined to or with anything but that which is pure and undefiled. The pure in heart see God, and not the mortal mind, that despises his glory. [omitting six sentences on the blessing of Jacob and his call out of Egypt] Is this thing nothing to you, all you that pass by, to slight the love of the Father, in sending his Son [as] a Light to you? And him you despise; and as the Pharisees could not own him, they put the time far off, and so do you, and you cannot own that of him in you. You cannot be led by it, and so you follow strangers, and still are complaining, and put redemption [off] to another world. And so Satan has deceived you in looking abroad, and therefore, that which is at home is of no price to you. . . . [digression on the nature of the Serpent in the Self] For he takes none into union with himself, but those who follow him, and do what he commands, and are his fruit and offspring. And therefore, O foolish and unwise, how long will you feed on a dream that you are saved, when your rebellion is open to your own sight? To that of God in your consciences I speak.

All, therefore, that see the darkness that you live in, return home, that which is low mind, the meek spirit; and be not forward nor rash, but stand still in quietness and meekness, that the still voice you may hear, which till you come down within, you cannot hear. . . . So be low and still, if you will hear his voice, and wait to hear that speak that separates between the precious and the vile, now that which you must wait in is near you, yes, in you. The eye that sees, and the ear that hears that is of the Lord. . . . Now that which reveals the pure spiritual God must be in you pure and spiritual, for none knows the things of God; but by the Spirit of God. . . . [omitting sentences on the natural ear and the mortal eye] And so loving it, the good you will come to see from God will lead you out of sin and will sanctify you. The acceptable year you will see, and the day of vengeance. And this is he whom the Father has given for a Covenant: to bring man out of the alienation to himself again, and to reconcile man to himself, even by the blood of the Cross. He who is the Light is the Covenant, and he who is the Covenant is the Light, for they are one in him. And this covenant of peace is tendered to you who are far off . . . and so in the covenant of life abide, and you will see he is near you. He is the peace maker, the gift of God, which presents you perfect

176

in himself to the Father. This gift is free, and offered freely to all who will receive it; and yet you cannot receive the gift in your own wills, but through the denial of your own will. For the light is contrary to the will, and so you will see the will of the earthly man and God's will [as being] contrary. As you receive the will of God, you deny your own wills, and so do the will of another, and another guides you and leads you, and this is God's work alone. It is not of yourselves, but brought by Christ in his own way and truth. And so the covenant of God comes to be established to the Seed, and the foundation stands sure. His promise is fulfilled in you, as you come to witness the Seed which is one, in whom the promise is fulfilled.

And friends, you must wait to have judgment set up within you, and this is he who is the judge and the light of the world.

Wait to see the law set up within . . . and the rebellious nature yoked [earthquakes and thunder]. Wait in patience for the judgment, and let the Lord's work have its perfect operation in you; and so as you turn to him who has smitten and wounded you; he will bind up and heal. And give up all to the great slaughter of the Lord, to the Cross. . . . And as the earth comes to be plowed up, the seed which is sown comes up; and, the rocks broken, the water gushes out. You so will see that some promises will arise in you to the Seed which is coming up out of the grave, and so the love of God will appear in you, and you will be stayed, and see hope in the midst of calamity.

Then take heed that the serpent gets not that which is to the babe, and so the carnal come to be exalted. But as you wait, you will see the subtlety of the enemy . . . [and find help by the old Law of Moses] and your minds being turned to the Lord. As you own the gift which Christ has given you, that is, repentance, you will see to life, and then you will see something arising and shine in you. Opening your hearts, and there will be a breathing after the Lord and his righteousness, and standing in obedience in the cross. [The parables will be opened.] Your hearts will be broken, and water will gush out of the rock, and so love will increase in you, who abide faithful in your measure. The good and perfect gift of God will be made manifest in you, and the hope on which the soul comes to be anchored, will come to be witnessed. Hope purifies the heart. [The perfect law of liberty gives liberty to the Seed.]

And as you come to be redeemed from under the bondage of sin, and come above the bonds of death, and the pure principle lives in you, there will be a delight in you to do the will of the father, who has redeemed you from sin and its law to righteousness and its law, . . . [revealed as men obey it]. It leads to true peace, and will reveal in you the immortal Seed, which came not by the will of man, but is contrary, and revealed out of man's will. . . . This is the son of God, who leads out of time; and this is he whom the father revealed in

177

Paul. This is he of whom I am a witness, in whom I have redemption by the blood of the Cross. He is my sanctification, justification and wisdom. . . . [two paragraphs showing the kingdom of God is within]

And now a few words to you who would thrust yourselves into the kingdom, and would be called Christ's disciples, and Church members, who are gathered into confederacies, and make a likeness to yourselves, and are now professing the saints' conditions in words. How did you come to climb up so high in words, when as you are what you were before, if not worse? Think it not a hard saying, for it is so among many of you; and in the light (which is pure) you are weighed. When one comes to try you, your language betrays you, that you are not what you profess; for when you are tried by the saints practices, and life that was in them, and the enjoyment they had with God, you are found so far from being any such, that you even oppose the faith they believed in. As some of your pastors said openly to my face in the hearing of two hundred people, "all the saints died sinners" . . . and others of you say you believe that all the grace the saints enjoy is imperfect, yes, even faith is imperfect. Others say that all the righteousness that was wrought in them by faith was imperfect. Still others say, while the light of Christ Jesus condemned them, yet Christ justified them, and yet that which was wrought in them there was failings in it. You have imagined a faith and righteousness of your own, and such a Christ to talk of, and a redemption, so you may live in lusts, and be people pleasers and in the customs and fashions of the world, and covetousness, and plead for sin. You put perfect righteousness to another world; and thus the devil has deceived you. . . . That is such a faith as never was professed by any of the saints, whose words you profess. They had received faith, the gift of God, the least measure of which was perfect. . . . [They] became one with the Judge, and reconciled to him and his throne, and to the Lamb by him who is the mediator, who has made peace between them and the father. So they were justified in the sight of God; and this witness they had in them, that they pleased God, and were accepted by God. And this righteousness was wrought in them, and is now the same which is wrought in the saints, by him who is their light and life. This was the righteousness of faith. . . . [a long paragraph on the righteousness of the saints as wrought by Christ]

And therefore all you professors, who have built high towers and castles in your imaginations, and have told of reformation these many years, but you have nothing but a hand writing to establish your building on, and all your reformation has been but the washing of cups, and pulling down one thing, and set up another beggarly elementary Image; [you] do not witness the better hope brought in, nor the time of reformation, nor cannot abide that

178

any should declare it to you, nor believe it, nor hear it. [Your highest achievement is imperfect.]

Oh, when will you be weary of feeding on the wind, and of husks among swine, and on that which dies of itself? And when will you inquire after the living God, who is power? How long have you talked of his power to come? Many years. You are still as far off, if not further, than you were before. You have told of the glory of the Lord to be revealed, and of his law being written in the heart, and of God teaching his people himself, and of his spirit being poured out on his sons and daughters; and you cannot see that you have obtained nothing. And you have prayed, and what have you obtained? Nothing! For you have asked amiss [like the Pharisees]. When these things are witnessed in the life, which you have talked on so long, you cannot own them that do declare it. And when the power of God is declared to you, what it is, and where it is to be waited for, you cannot own it. This is too low for you; and unless the Lord will come in your way, the way that you prescribe to him, you will not look on him. [God reveals himself not to the fallen but to his Seed in man.]

How long have you talked of the Spirit, and worshipped in spirit? And yet indeed deny its leading and teaching, and live in the oldness of the letter, and crying up and setting up things that are carnal, visible and elementary, and washing is not known from sin, nor cleansing; and so you may see what operation your spirit you have talked on has, when you are still what you were.

Now the spirit of God is operative, and works a change in the ground, and translates all that follow and hearken to it into its own nature. [The gospel is glad tidings.] Now none can witness gladness of soul where there is guilt, which (you all affirm) is in every Christian, while in this world, and so you might see, that it's not the true Christ nor the everlasting Gospel you preach, but this you cannot bear. Yet you say, he has taken away your sin; how much is sin taken away? If you say, "all", how comes the guilt and trouble that is in you? ... For the Light is just, which is one with God, and when this condemns you, there is no God that will justify you. But you use to say, 'It's all done in Christ." I ask, "Where, if it be not taken away?" And unless you have the witness of it in you, your faith is vain. [The witness is Christ.] I say, there is no guilt where sin is taken away and crucified, but peace and rest in the holy God, who is unchangeable.

[Woe against the nation, and its parish teachers and rulers.]

[The Puritan rulers of Ireland under Henry Cromwell sent a warrant to arrest Quaker preachers. Howgill's warning to these rulers covers three solid pages.] Cork in Ireland, the 8th of the 11th Month, 1655.

179

5. *The Journal of John Banks* (1712)

With Banks's *Journal* we move from the autobiographical tract to the full-volume life. The array of testimonies and Penn's epistle preceding the narrative make clear that this book, like the collected works of Parnell, Burrough, and Howgill (cf. pp. 153, 164, and 167), was intended mainly for Quaker readers. Indeed by 1712 it was meant to remind them of earlier Friends' zeal. Banks himself no longer needs to tell his story to authenticate his message for outsiders, as had earlier Friends, Ranters, and Baptists like Bunyan.[30] Yet the heart of his narrative is still his convincement. The whole is only 140 pages, and over half of this is letters home. One suspects that when he wrote in 1696, Fox's *Journal* printed two years before had seemed to set a standard for including all available papers and travels; it encouraged his later editors to do likewise, even for a man who had in print only four short epistles. Banks's *Journal* and papers evidently appeared in two printings in 1712 (we print what seems the prior one) and has reappeared only in the *Friends Library* anthology. The printer, J. Sowle, dominated Quaker printing at the turn of the eighteenth century as much as Calvert and Simmons had in the first decade and still used Quaker terminology (Gracious-Street for Grace-Church, etc.).

John Banks also stands over against Howgill as a representative of the rank and file of Friends convinced in 1654-55 in the English Northwest. He had little background as a Puritan or in any other congregation and had indeed led the equivalent of parish worship (by reading the liturgy, prayers, and printed "homily" sermons sent from London). His father was a farmer but not a freeholder. His schooling stopped with grammar school. He seems to have gone through no long pilgrimages of agonized guilt before the coming of the Quaker message. Though his convincement was slow and painful like most other Friends', he shows thereafter few signs of self-doubt. Rather he has an openness, simplicity, and often a sense of wonder as to how he has been led.

A Journal of the Life,
Labours, Travels, and Sufferings (In and for the Gospel) of that Ancient
Servant and Faithful Minister of Jesus Christ John Banks. . . .

[30] Cf. Ivan Dean Ebner, "Seventeenth-Century British Autobiography: the Impact of Religious Commitment"; Ph.D. dissertation for Stanford, January, 1965).

[Heb. 11:2, 4]
(London, J. Sowle, in White-Hart-Court in Gracious-Street, 1712)

[John Banks's own writings are prefaced by a six-page letter to the "Friendly Reader" by William Penn and eight testimonies (23 pages) concerning John Banks by John Whiting; Pardshaw Meeting, Cumberland; John Bousted; Christopher Story; Somerset Quarterly Meeting; Glastonbury and Street Monthly Meeting (where Banks died); John's second wife Hannah Banks; and his son, daughters, and their husbands. There is also an Index and Table of Contents.]

The way and manner of my education, and convincement, and how I came to receive the knowledge of God, and of his blessed Truth; and of the travail of my soul under judgment; and how I came through the same, to obtain mercy at the Lord's hand, for sin and transgression; and how in his time, I came to be called forth into the ministry; and of my travels and exercises in that work and service; together with my imprisonments, and sufferings; also an abstract of letters writ to my wife, children and servants, and my wife's to me, with several papers and Epistles to Friends.

John Banks

Of My Education

I came of honest parents; my father's name was William and my mother's name was Emme; I was their only child, born in Sunderland, in [margin: 1638] the Parish of [2] Isell, in the County of Cumberland. And my father having no real estate of his own, took land to farm, and by trade was a fel-monger and glover.

Who in some years after removed to within the compass of Pardshaw Meeting; where they both received the Truth, sometime after me; and lived and died in it, according to their measures; to which Meeting I belonged above forty years.

And though my parents had not much of this world's riches, yet according to their ability, and the manner of the country, they brought me up well, and in good order, and were careful to restrain me from such evils as children and youth are apt to run into, and especially my dear mother, being a zealous woman. And their care therein for my good, and discharging of their duty, had a good effect with it as to me, (and so will it have, it's hoped, on all who perform their duty as they ought to their children in time; if not, they will, it's feared, be found guilty in the day of their accounts).

I was put to school, when I was seven years of age, and kept there until I was fourteen; in which time, I learned well both English and Latin and could write well. And when I was fourteen years of age, my father took me from school, and put me to teach school one year, at Dissington; and after that, got me to teach school at Mosser Chapel (near Pardshaw), where I read the Scriptures also to people that came there on the First Day of the week, an Homily as it is called, and sung Psalms, [3] and prayed; but I had no liking to the practice. But my father, with other people, through my entering into reasoning with them, overcame me.

For which service, my wages from the people, was to be twelvepence every house of them that came there to hear me, by the year, (and a fleece of wool) and my table free, besides twelvepence a quarter for every scholar, being twenty-four. This chapel is called a "chapel of ease"; the Parish Steeple-House being some miles off.[31] To which chapel, amongst the rest of the people that were indifferent where they did go for worship, came one John Fletcher, a great scholar,[32] but a drunken sottish man. And he called me aside one day and said I did read very well, of a youth, but I did not pray in form, as others used to do. And so he said he would teach me how to pray, and send it me in a letter. And did.

And when it came, I went forth of the chapel and read it; and when I had done, I was convinced of the evil thereof (at the same time) by the Light of the Lord Jesus which immediately opened in me, according to the words of the Apostle Paul, when he said concerning the Gospel he had to preach, he "had it not from man, neither was he taught it, but by the revelation of Jesus Christ." In answer to which, it rose in me: "But thou hast this prayer from man, and art taught it by man and one of the worst of many." So the dread of the Lord fell upon me, with which I was so struck, to my very heart, that I said in myself, "I shall never pray on this wise." And it opened in me, "Go to [4] the meeting of the people, in scorn called *Quakers,* for they are the people of God." And so I did the next First Day after; which was at Pardshaw.[33]

And this being before the end of the year, that I was to receive wages of the people for such service as I did, I could take none of them, being convinced of the evil thereof; nor never read any more at the chapel.

---

31 The parishes of the Northwest were often ten miles by five. For the sake of outlying villages far from the parish church, "chapels of ease" were often opened (these later often gave John Wesley, too, a place for preaching, so that Methodist churches in England today are still called chapels). Yet there was only one pastor per parish or sometimes for several parishes.

32 On John Fletcher, Cambridge-trained pastor at Dissington, cf. Mathews, *Calamy Revised.*

33 Friends' Meetings at Pardshaw, Cockermouth, Bolton, Isell, and Cald-beck had been begun late in 1653, though Fox did not come there until the following year. Cf. *FPT,* pp. 30-75. Most of these Meetings were held at first in the open air in the summer and broken up into house meetings for the winter months. Fox, Rawlinson, and Widders were active preachers here.

And then I being sixteen years of age and four months, in the 10th month, 1654, it pleased the Lord, and that effectually, to reach to my heart and conscience, by his great power, and pure living Spirit, in the blessed appearance, manifestation, and revelation thereof, in and through Jesus Christ, whereby I received the knowledge of God and the way of his blessed truth, by myself alone in the field, before I ever heard anyone called a Quaker preach, and before I was at any of their meetings. But the First Day that I went to one, which was at Pardshaw, as aforesaid, the Lord's Power in the meeting, so seized upon me, that I was made to cry out in the bitterness of my soul, in a true sight and sense of my sins, that appeared exceeding sinful; and the same day at evening, as I was going to a meeting of God's people, even those people scornfully called Quakers, by the way, I was smitten to the ground with the weight of God's judgment for sin and iniquity, that fell heavy upon me; and I was taken up by two Friends.[34]

And, Oh! the godly sorrow that did take hold of me, and seized upon me that night in the meeting; so that I thought in myself, everyone's [5] conditions was better than mine. So a Friend (as he told me some time after) being touched with a sense of my condition, (and did greatly pity me) was made willing to read a paper in the meeting (there being but a very few words spoken) which was suitable to my condition, that it helped me a little, and gave me some ease in my spirit; I being very much bowed down and perplexed, my sins being set in order before me. And the time that I had spent in the wildness and wantonness, out of the fear of God, in vanity, sport and pastime, came into my view and remembrance (the Book of my Conscience being opened). For I was by nature wild and wanton; though there was good desires stirring in me many times, and something that judged me and reproved me, and often strove with me to restrain me from evil. But not being sensible what it was, got over it; like those that make merry over the witness of God, even the witness and testimony of his pure Holy Spirit, in and through Jesus Christ his Son, made known and manifest God's great love to the sons and daughters of men; which was that, whereby the Lord many times did strive with me; until at last he prevailed upon me.

So that I may truly say, as a true and faithful witness for God, and the sufficiency of his power and quickening Spirit, (amongst many more) I did not only come to be convinced by the living appearance of the Lord Jesus of the evil and vanity, sin and wickedness that the world lies in (and that I was so much a partaker thereof); neither did [6] I satisfy myself that I was reached unto by the power of God. But by taking true heed thereunto,

[34] Physical seizures of this kind were fairly common among early Friends, along with the more usual quaking. Cf. the case of Jane Withers cited in Nayler's *Discovery of the Man of Sin* (1656), p. 45, and John Gilpin's seizures (*The Quakers Shaken*, 1653).

through watchfulness and fear, I came by one little after another to be sensible of the work thereof in my heart and soul, in order to subdue and bring down, tame and subject the wild nature in me, and to wash, purge, and cleanse me inwardly from sin and corruption; for that end, that I might be changed and converted. But before I came to witness that work effected, oh the days and nights of godly sorrow and spiritual pain for many months and some years that I travelled through! So that the exercise I was under did bear so hard, both upon my body and mind, that I was made to leave off the practice I was in, which was teaching of school (as aforesaid), which although good and lawful, yet not agreeable to me then in my condition, and did betake myself to learn my father's trade (with something of husbandry); which I did follow with all diligence, and lived with my parents, who in some time after me came to receive the Truth, which was great rejoicing to my soul.

And as I travailed in and under the ministration of condemnation, and true judgment for sin and transgression, great was the warfare and combats that I had with the Enemy of my soul, who through his subtility did what in him lay, to betray me from the simplicity of the Truth, that was begotten in me; and to persuade me to despair of my condition, as though there was no mercy for me. Though in some small measure, I knew the Lord had [7] showed mercy to me, which he mixed with judgment (upon the account of my sins past). So that sometimes, through that little experience that I had gained (in the travail of my soul) through faith that was begotten in my heart, I had so much strength, as to withstand the Enemy of my soul and his subtle reasonings, and could say, "What evil have I done, since I received the Truth?" And having nothing whereof to accuse myself, only some little things through childishness which I knew the Lord as a tender father had passed by, so through faith in the power of God and shining of his glorious light in my heart, I overcame the wicked one (the enemy of my soul), through a diligent waiting in the light and keeping close unto the power of God, in waiting upon him in silence among his people, in which exercise my soul delighted.

And Oh! the days and nights of comfort and divine consolation we were made partakers of in those days together (and the faithful and true in heart to God still are). And in the same inward sense, and feeling of the Lord's power and presence with us, we enjoyed one another, and were near and dear one unto another. But it was through various trials and deep exercises, with fear and trembling, that on this wise we were made partakers. Blessed and happy are they that know what Truth has cost them and hold it in righteousness. I say, through waiting diligently in the Light, and keeping close unto the power of [8] God (that is therein received), I came to experience the work thereof in my inward parts, in order to work my freedom from bondage and redemption from captivity. So that I felt by degrees the work of God to go on and prosper in me, and so gained ground more and more against the enemy of my soul, through faith in the power of God, without which is no victory obtained.

Now the way of my prosperity in the Truth and work of God, I always found was by being faithful unto the Lord, in what he in the Light manifested, though but in little and small things, which unfaithfulness in, is the loss and hurt of many in their growth and prosperity in the Truth.

And after that I had passed through great tribulation, in weeping and mourning in woods and solitary places, alone, where I often desired to be; after much exercise on this wise, I came to more settlement, and weightiness in my spirit; and peace in measure began to spring in my soul where trouble and sorrow in warfare had been. Then at some times, I would be ready to think within myself, that I should not meet with such combats and besetments again, by the Enemy of my soul, as I had met with and passed through. But notwithstanding all this (and much more than I see it my way to make mention of); the more I grew in experience in the dealings of the Lord with me, by the work of his power, so much the more I found, to the grief of my soul, did the enemy thereof transform himself; that when he could not prevail by [9] his former shapes and presentations, he in his subtlety could invent new ones. So that I came clearly to see, there was no safety for me to sit down there, satisfied with what I had passed through or the victory I had already obtained, but to travel on still, in faith and patience, and watch diligently, in the pure Light of Jesus Christ, where the true power is still received. For after many inward deliverances and strength and victory through faith that was given me, and I had experienced the Lord many times, according to the greatness of his wisdom, [he] made me sensible of my own weakness, in thinking within myself, as I have said, that there was no strength to stand nor place of safety for me to abide, but in his own power and arm of strength. So that under a true sense thereof, oh! how was I humbled, bowed, and laid low.

Wherefore I took up a godly resolution in his fear, "I'll rely upon the sufficiency of thy power, O Lord, for ever." So that about six years after I had received the Truth, by believing therein, being made sensible of the work thereof in my heart and soul, through great exercise and godly sorrow, I came to be settled in the power of God, and made weighty in my spirit thereby. So that I had some openings in and by the power and Spirit of Truth, in an inward and silent waiting upon the Lord, and not only openings and revelations, as did tend to minister comfort and satisfaction unto my own soul and spirit, in a renewed experience of the dealings of the Lord with me; but the Lord opened my mouth with a testimony [10] in the fresh springs of life that I was to give forth unto his travailing children and people. Oh! then a great combat I had through reasoning: I was but a child, and others were more fit and able to speak than I. But the Lord by his power wrought me into a willingness, and with fear and trembling I spoke in our blessed meetings.

And upon a time, as I was sitting in silence waiting upon the Lord, in a meeting of Friends, upon Pardshaw-Crag, a weighty exercise fell upon my spirit; and it opened in me, that I must go to the Steeple-House at Cockermouth, which was hard for me to give up to. But the Lord by his power, made me to shake and tremble, and by it I was made willing to go. But when I had given up to go, I would have known what I might do there; which was the cause that for a little time I was shut up within myself, and was in some measure darkened. So that I cried unto the Lord, that if it was his will that I must go, I would give up thereunto; and being made sensible it was, I did go, and went in the faith and quietness of my mind and spirit. And as I was going, it appeared to me, as if the priest had been before me; and it opened in me: [that I should say] "If thou be a minister of Christ, stand to prove thy practice; and if it be the same the Apostles and ministers of Christ was and is in doctrine and practice, I'll own thee; but if not I am sent of God this day to testify against thee." And so soon as I entered the place, where the hireling priest, George Larcom,[35] was preaching, he cried out: "There [11] is one come into the church like a madman, with his hat on his head. Churchwardens, put him out!" For he could not preach after I came into the steeple-house. And so they put me forth, as he bid them. (It was in Cromwell's time, and it was not long after, until the government changed, and he himself was turned out of the place.) And after some time that I was put forth, I was moved of the Lord, to go in again, and had strength given me to stay until the priest had done. But Oh! it was burdensome, confused stuff, for me to bear the hearing of. And then, with the words aforesaid I opened my mouth, in the dread of God's power; which made the hireling fly with all the haste he could, out at a contrary door than he used to do. And the people were in a great uproar, some to beat me, and some to save me from being beat. But when they had haled me out of the house, I was opened and enabled, by the power of God, to declare the Truth amongst the people, to manifest that Deceiver they followed. And having obeyed the requirings of the Lord, I came away in sweet peace, and spiritual comfort in my heart and soul.

And at a certain time, I being at a meeting of Friends, upon the Howhill, near Caldbeck in Cumberland,[36] whereunto came George Fletcher of

---

35 On George Larkham, Puritan pastor of Cockermouth, cf. *FPT,* p. 35. Cockermouth, like Sedbergh and the Kendal-Preston-Patrick area, was an island of Puritan influence and even of Separatism in the largely Anglican or indifferent Northwest. At the height of the Quaker awakening the Cockermouth pastors complained that their churches had emptied.

36 On the Caldbeck Meeting, cf. *FPT,* pp. 47-50.

Hutton-Hall, a Justice of the Peace[37] (so called), who came into the meeting rude and unmannerly, riding among Friends, they sitting upon the ground, and trod with his horse's feet upon a woman's gown that was big with child, a woman of note and well bred; (Oh inhumane!) and I was moved of the Lord to kneel [12] down to prayer, at the head of his horse. And as a wicked persecutor of God's People, as he always was, he struck me bitterly over my head and face with his horse-whip. But when he saw he could not move me, he called to his man (being near by) to take me away, who came in great fury, and took me by the hair of my head, and drew me down the hill. But I got upon my feet, and said to his master, "Dost thou pretend to be a Justice of Peace, and breaks the peace, and disturbs, persecutes and abuse God's peaceable people, and sets on thy servant so to do?" He said, we should know he was a Justice of Peace, before he had done with us; could no place serve us to meet in, but under his nose, (though it was at a great distance from his dwelling, upon the Common).[38] And this said Fletcher committed me and three more to the common jail at Carlisle; it being in that time when that Act was in force, "£ 5 [for the] first offence; £ 10 the second; and third: banishment."[39] And by his warrant, caused one cow and a horse, worth £ 6/10 s. to be distrained of my father, (for I did live with him) for my fine of £ 5; it being the first offence (so adjudged by him), and kept me in prison some weeks too. George Martin, a wicked hard-hearted man, being Jailer, put us in the common Jail, several days and nights, without either bread or water, because we could not answer nor satisfy his covetous desire, in giving of him 8 pence a meal for our meat. So he threatened when he put us in the common jail, he would see how long we could live there without meat; and did suffer none [to be brought] that he could hinder, neither [13] would he suffer any of our Friends to bring us any bedding, not so much as a little straw; so that we had no place to lie on, but the prison window, upon the cold stones; the wall being thick, there was room for one at a time. And when he saw he could not prevail, notwithstanding his cruelty, he removed us from the common jail, into a room in his own house, where he had several Friends prisoners for non-payment of tithes, at the suit of the said George Fletcher.

[37] On George Fletcher of Hutton Hall, the persecuting justice, see *CJ*, II, 409.

[38] By medieval tradition, the Commons were lands (usually pasture or moor) belonging to the whole village (or at least all tenants and freeholders) in common; hence the furor when rich landowners "enclosed" them for private sheep runs. They were thus legal places for public meetings.

[39] Banks is quoting the "Quaker Act" of 1662, which also included provisions about oaths. The otherwise similar Conventicle Act of 1664, aimed at all Puritans, was not yet in force. Under it several hundred Friends were sentenced to banishment, though few were actually transported abroad.

Now this jailer, George Martin, was often cruel, wicked, and abusive in his behavior to Friends: a hard-hearted man. But in a few years, he was rewarded according to his doings; for he himself was cast into prison for debt, and so ended his days.

And when the Quarter-Sessions began, which was in about two weeks after our commitment, at Carlisle (where we were called, spoken to, and examined, by one Philip Musgrave[40] of the said city, called a Justice, an old persecutor), [he said], under a great pretence of love to us, that if we would but conform and come to the church, they would show us all the favor they could. And when any one of us would willingly have answered his questions, or proposals, he would say, we must be silent; except we would conform, etc., for we might not preach there. But [he] would mockingly and hatefully say, "When you are banished to beyond the seas, then you may preach there." One of us replied: We were not afraid to be banished to beyond the seas, for we did believe, and had good cause so to do, that the Lord our God (whom we [14] did worship and serve) who by his great power had preserved us all along until now, on this side of the sea, would also preserve us on the other side, as we stood faithful in our testimony for him.

So we were set at liberty that session, goods being taken for all our fines. Only the Sheriff for the County, Wilfrid Lawson of Isell-Hall, being there, said to the jailer, "If they will not pay fees, put them into the common jail again; and keep them there until they rot." So the jailer did put us in the common jail again, because we could not pay him fees; where a bedlam-man,[41] and four with him for theft: and two [were] notorious thieves, called Redhead and Wadelad; two "moss-troopers" for stealing of cattle; and one woman for murdering of her own child. Now several of the relations and acquaintance of these were suffered to come to see them, after the sessions was over, who gave them so much drink that they were basely drunk most of them; and the prison being a very close nasty place, they did so abuse themselves and us, with doing all their necessaries so undecently, that it was enough almost to stifle some of us. So on the morrow, we let the jailer know how we were abused, whereupon he bid the turn-key bring us to the room where we were before, he scorned to keep us there: we were honest men, setting our religion aside. One of us answered, "If the tree be good, the fruit cannot be evil." So in a little time after we had been in his house, he gave us our liberty, without paying of fees. This was in the 5th month, 1663.

[40] On Sir Philip Musgrave, the notorious Royalist persecutor of Friends, see *CJ*, II, 392-93; BSP, p. 34, etc.

[41] Those committed as insane were named after "Bedlam," the Bethlehem hospital in London.

[15-17] [Here follow letters from Carlisle prison to his parents and to Friends.]

And in some time after, I had drawings in my spirit, to visit some neighbouring counties, as Westmorland, Lancashire, and some part of [18] Yorkshire; and that several times, before the Lord sent me forth into other countries [=counties]. So when I was clear of those counties, I returned home to my parents, and lived with them about a year more.

And then, upon the 26th day of the 6th month, 1664, I took a Friend by name Anne Littledale to wife, in a Public Meeting of God's People (in scorn called Quakers) in a Friend's house, in Pardshaw-Town, before many witnesses; as having freedom and liberty in the Lord so to do; which as a blessing and mercy I received from his hand, with many more, wherefore I am still bound in duty to give him the praise, and to return him the honour and glory, who lives for ever.

And about four years after I was married, the Lord called me forth to travel in the work of the ministry; and I was made truly willing, to leave and forsake all, in answer to his requirings. And I was to go into the south and west of England. Yea, I was made truly willing to leave my dear wife and sweet child, though near and dear unto me, and so went forth, in the power and Spirit of the Lord Jesus, and our Friend John Wilkinson and I traveled together in the Lord's work and service (this was Cumberland John Wilkinson).[42] We took our journey in the 2nd month, 1668, and we traveled into Yorkshire, and visited many meetings in diverse places, where we had good service for the Lord and his Truth.

A letter to my wife, upon my journey towards the west and south of England: [19]

Dear Wife,

Thou art dear and near to me, together with our little one, in the nearness of that pure spirit and power, by which the Lord has nearly joined us together, as one heart and mind; from a sense of whose pure love, felt to abound in my heart, I dearly salute thee, and let thee know that I am very well at present, both in body and spirit; for which I can do no less than bless and praise the holy name and great power of the Lord forever, who has so far preserved me in my journey, in true peace, satisfaction, and comfort in my

42 Distinguishing him from the John Wilkinson of Westmorland who led the Wilkinson-Story Separatists against Quaker unification and Fox's leadership in 1670-77. Cf. p. 512.

soul. Whereby it is confirmed to me, that I am in my place, and that work and service I have to perform is for the Lord, and the furtherance of his blessed Truth. Blessed be that day and time that ever I was made sensible of the same; or that the Lord should count me worthy to do any service for him.

Wherefore my dear, be encouraged to trust in the Lord more and more, and put your confidence in him in all things; who is alone able to do whatsoever he pleaseth, and seemeth good in his sight; for he can make all things work together for good to them that truly love and fear him, and is concerned for the prosperity of his blessed truth; though we must expect to meet with various exercises in the way, to come to be made partakers thereof.

[20] Remember my love and due respect to my parents, and let them know that I am well in every way; and to friends without respect of persons, as they inquire of me.

The desire of many people here is after the Lord, and they flock to our meetings like doves to the windows, when they hear of anyone who has the way of truth to declare. We have had a meeting every day this week, and will have one tomorrow, if the Lord will.

Your dear and loving husband, according to my measure of the truth received.

John Banks

Written near Bradford in
Yorkshire, the 14th of
the 3rd Month, 1668.

From Yorkshire we travelled into Nottinghamshire, Leicestershire and Warwickshire, where we had many blessed meetings: and whence I wrote the following letter to my wife. . . .

[21] From Warwickshire we travelled into Gloucestershire, and so to Bristol. . . . [letters to and from Anne Banks]

[27] hence we traveled westward through part of Devonshire . . . and so up to London . . . [letters to his wife and to his apprentice] again to Bristol. . . .

[32] The length of this journey was 1268 miles.

Now Friends, I do not intend nor desire to make a great volume, or enlarge, to give an account to the full of every particular of my journeys, over sea and land, in England, Scotland, and Ireland; but in as much brevity as I can, what may be material, and of most service, that the remembrance of my labors, travels, imprisonments and sufferings, may not be lost, but be kept on record, for the good of ages to come, amongst the rest of my brethren: [33] though but little, to what some have suffered, passed through, and undergone.

190

And now, to begin from the year 1668: From year to year, and time after time, I have traveled and gone over sea, betwixt England, Scotland, and Ireland, twelve times; and that often not without great difficulty, and danger of life, at sea, by many tempestuous storms; yet never at any time was I above two nights together at sea; insomuch, that after some times that I had taken shipping at White-Haven, the sea-men would be very desirous who should have me in their vessel, saying I was the happiest man that ever they carried over sea, for they got well along still when they had me, though sometimes in and through great tempests. And that God over all may have the praise of his own works, and the faithful [may be] encouraged to rely upon the sufficiency of his own power for ever, is the intent of my writing.

And with reverence, humility, and godly fear, I hope I may say that my labours and travels in three nations have been such, in preaching the everlasting Gospel in the demonstration of the Spirit . . . [that, without boasting] I have been made instrumental, to turn many unto righteousness, a considerable number of which are yet alive to witness unto the truth of what I say; even in eight Meetings in my native Country in Cumberland. . . . [34] [Though I went through much hardship] yet through the strength and ability of the power of God, was well kept and preserved in and through all, having faith therein.

And with all diligence, it's well known, when I was at home, I labored with my hands, with honest endeavors in lawful employments, for the maintenance of my family.

And about the beginning of the year 1670, which was the first time that I went for Ireland, and our ancient Friend, John Tiffin,[43] having drawings thither also, we took shipping at White-Haven. . . . [and landed at Carrick-fargus, in the North of that nation; for the North was most before us. And after we had visited Meetings thoroughly, and were well satisfied of the Truth of our service, we visited Friends along to Dublin and thereabout. And having had good and refreshing times with Friends in that city and elsewhere, and being clear, we returned home to our own country.]

But it was not long until the Lord required it of me to go to Ireland again. And in the third month, 1671, I was made willing to go, in obedience to the requirings of the Lord. And his power and presence was with me. And my desire was to be at the Half-Years Meeting at Dublin, which began the Fifth Day of the week, that I went to White-Haven the Third Day before, with an intent to take shipping there; and my dear wife, and several Friends, did go along with me. But the wind that day was quite contrary; so that my wife and Friends would have persuaded me to go home again (being 10 miles) because the wind was not like to serve. But I told them: I could not then, I might rely

43 On John Tiffin, the Cumberland Quaker, see BSP, p. 302; *FPT*, p. 38.

upon him that had power to command the [35] winds and seas, even the Lord alone. And so they went home, and I went that evening to a vessel that was ready to go, and I told the owner that I was willing to go with him to Dublin, and I desired some of his men, that if the wind was fair ere the morning, that they would call me at such a house.

They answered "Yea" with all their heart; but did I think the wind would serve so soon, that was so contrary? I said, "It was possible with the Lord, that it might." For I had faith in the thing, according to what was revealed unto me.

So in the morning, about the dawning of the day, being the Fourth Day morning, one came calling aloud to me, to make haste and come soon, the wind was fair, and the ship was near ready to sail. And a brave ready passage we had; so that according to my soul's desire, I came into the Meeting aforesaid, the Fifth Day, within half an hour after it was set, and a glorious heavenly meeting it was, where many faithful brethren from all parts of the nation were come; and the Lord's power was over all, and several living testimonies given, to show forth the greatness and sufficiency thereof. Wherefore we had cause of rejoicing, in the prosperity of the Lord's work, and our concern therein, and our unity, and brotherly fellowship one with another.

And the next day in the evening, as I was waiting upon the Lord, a great weight came upon my spirit; under which exercise I did patiently abide, until it opened in me in the motion of life, that I was to go southward, to a place called Wicklow (though I knew it not then, being 24 miles south from Dublin) where no Meeting of Friends before that time had been, that I could hear of, only one or two friendly people in it. . . . [Here follow three other letters to his wife from Ireland, and the account of his imprisonment at Wicklow.] [50]

And after that I was clear of that nation at that time, in about two years after the Lord required it of me to go and visit Ireland again, and coming to Wicklow, I went to the jailers to see Friends in prison, and to have a Meeting in the town. When the jailer saw me, he said, "Oh! Mr. Banks (as he called me) are you home again, I think you need not to have come any more, for you did your business the last time you were here, for I think all the town of Wicklow will be Quakers."

"But notwithstanding what is done," I said, "it is my business to come to see how the Lord's work prospers, for the work is his, we are no more than instruments in his hand, which he is pleased to make use of; and more than that, thou hast got a deal of my Friends in prison (I must needs visit them), being fourteen."

And the next time I came to visit this nation, I came to this place again, which was about two years more, the priest of Wicklow was dead, the governor gone for England, and no soldiers there, Truth still prospering, and

Friends' Meetings settled and established by the power of God in peace and quiet, and Friends well preserved, in and through their sufferings. Which makes me to say there is [51] none like unto the true and living God, who has wrought and is working wonders in the earth and is bringing strange and mighty acts to pass.

And when I had traveled most of the nation through (in visiting of Friends and people) being in the north, in that part called the "Scots Country",[44] I coming up to Antrim, and eight Friends more, with an intent to have a meeting at our Friend James Greenwood's house; when we came there, there was a constable with his staff, and a company of people with him. And he stood at the Friend's door, and said he had an order from the Lord Mazereen that we should not meet there. I bid him produce his order, and we would give him an answer. He holding out his staff said that was his order, and we should not meet there, meet where we would. I answered, "Keep to thy word, we shall be content to meet in the King's Street", being a market town, and Friends and many people being come together, my mouth being opened in a testimony for the Lord, and in love to the souls of the people, in turning their minds to the teachings of God in themselves.

The Constable with his staff came in a rage and fury, being a Presbyterian, to pull me out of the meeting; and I said to him in the authority of God's power, "Art thou not ashamed to manifest thyself a liar before so many people? Didst thou not say we should meet where we would, except in our Friend's house?" So he was smitten, and could do no more himself, but he went among the people, and got a butcher, a man picked for his purpose, to pull me away. And he came in a most rigid manner, and took me by one arm, and haled me down the street a little way; and there came a Friend out of the meeting, and said to him, "Cease from persecuting the innocent, lest the judgment of God fall upon thee." Which did immediately [52] seize upon him, and his hands were loosed from me, that he had no power to pull me any further, and there he stood trembling by me (I being declaring the Truth still), and he went home and took his bed, and never got from under the judgment till he died. . . . And in a little time I saw it my place to be silent, and our Friend George Grigson had his mouth opened . . . [and the Lord's] glorious power and heavenly presence in a most glorious manner did appear, and was livingly manifested in the meeting, and many were convinced, and several came clearly forth, to own and receive the Truth in the love of it.

And in the time of our Meeting, there was such a sudden storm of wind and rain, for the time it did continue, that I very seldom ever saw the like; for the water with the dirt ran with a stream amongst us, so that all or most of us

---

[44] The Scots-Irish of Ulster, planted by Queen Elizabeth, have been at odds with the Catholic Irish ever since; they produced few Quakers.

were wet to the skin. The storm of wind and rain was a true figure of their raging persecuting spirit; and when it was over, the sun did break forth, and shined very clear, so that it was a brave sunshine day, a true figure of the victory the Truth obtained through the power thereof.

This year going to London to the Yearly Meeting, I wrote the following letters to my wife. . . . [one letter from and seven to Anne Banks, including one from his next Irish journey, and a letter to his three children]

[65] And when my Friend John Watson[45] and I had traveled through the nation of Ireland, visiting Friends therein, and being much comforted and refreshed, together with them, in Truth's prosperity, being clear thereof, a concern came upon us to visit Friends in Scotland. And we sailed in a half decked boat from Dannaughadee in Ireland, and landed at Portpatrick in Scotland. And from Portpatrick, we traveled seventy miles in cold, frost and snow, in the 10th month, before we came where any Friends were, which was at Douglas; but the evening before we came there, the night came on, when we were upon a mountain, where no way was to be seen, for there was much snow and ice, so that we could not ride. And being much wearied with going on foot, and leading our horses, we lost our way. But at last Providence so ordered it, that we found a house, and two men came forth, and willingly set us into our way; so that we got to a Friend's house late at night at Douglas, whose name was William Michael. And we had a meeting there next day; and though there were but few Friends belonging to that place, we were sweetly refreshed and comforted together, in the enjoyment of the Lord's presence; whereby it is evident, with him there is no respect of persons, time, place nor number.

And from Douglas we traveled to Hamilton, and so to Drumboy, Badcow, Linlithgow, and Edinburgh, where we visited Friends, and other people, and had good service for the Lord; and so to Prestonpans, Leith, and Edinburgh again. . . .

[66] About this time, [1677] a pain struck into my shoulder, which gradually fell down into my arm and hand, so that the use thereof I was wholly deprived of; and not only so, but my pain greatly increased both day and night. And for three months I could neither put my clothes on nor off myself, and my arm and hand began to wither, so that I did seek to some physicians for cure, but no cure could I get by any of them; until at last, as I was asleep upon my bed in the night time, I saw in a vision, that I was with dear George Fox; and I thought I said unto him, "George, my faith is such that if thou seest it thy way to lay thy hand upon my shoulder, my arm and hand shall be whole throughout." Which remained with me after I awaked, two days and nights, that the thing was a true vision and that I must go to

45 On John Watson, see BBQ, pp. 372-73. He "went naked for a sign" in Carlisle in 1674.

Daybreak at Kendal: looking southwest from Underbarrow toward Swarth-moor (*from photograph by Hugh Barbour*)

G.F., until at last, through much exercise of mind, as a near and great trial of my faith, I was made willing to go to him; he being then at Swarthmoor, in Lancashire, where there was a meeting of Friends, being on the first day of the week. And some time after the meeting, I called him aside into the Hall, and gave him a relation of my concern as aforesaid, showing him my arm and hand; and in a little time, we walking together silent, he turned about, and looked upon me, lifting up his hand, and laid it upon my shoulder, and said, "The Lord strengthen thee both within, and without." And so we parted; and I went to Thomas Lower's[46] of Marsh-Grange that night; and when I was sat

46 Thomas Lower, the Cornishman who married Margaret Fell's daughter Mary, owning land near her ancestral home, was the secretary to whom Fox dictated most of his *Journal* manuscripts during and after their joint imprisonment at Worcester in 1674. His mother, wife of Humphrey Lower, may have been aunt to Edward Billing.

down to supper in his house, immediately, before I was aware, my hand was lifted up to do its office, which it could not for so long as aforesaid; [67] which struck me into a great admiration; and my heart was broken into true tenderness before the Lord; and the next day I went home, with my hand and arm restored to its former use and strength, without any pain. And the next time that G.F. and I met, he readily said, "John, thou mended, thou mended;" I answered, "yes, very well, in a little time." "Well," said he, "give God the glory", to whom I was and still am bound in duty so to do, (for that and all other his mercies and favours) who hath all power in his own hand, and can thereby bring to pass whatsoever seems good in his eyes; who by the same sits and prepares instruments, and makes use thereof as pleaseth him; who is alone worthy of all praise, honour and glory, both now, and for evermore. Amen.

[The next years saw other journeys to the South of England and letters to Anne Banks and to his daughter Sarah, who became a servant in London. In 1684 he was imprisoned for nearly seven years for refusal to pay tithes, again by Justice George Fletcher. Most of the rest of the *Journal* (pp. 95-123) consists of letters and public messages of warning written from Carlisle jail, and of accounts of his experiences there. In 1691, while John visited Meetings in London, Anne Banks died. From his last Irish trip (1694) came letters to his two younger children, and his personal account concludes with his settlement in Somerset in 1696.[47] Later letters and the account of his second marriage and last years were added by John Whiting, who also edited his public epistles that follow, most of them not previously in print.]

6. Stephen Crisp's *Journal* (1694)

Crisp's *Journal* was first printed in 1694, two years after his death, as the first part of his collected works (*A Memorable Account of the Christian Experiences, Gospel Labours, Travels and Sufferings of . . . Stephen Crisp*, printed by T. Sowle "near the Meeting-House in White-Hart Court in Grace-Church-Street"). The manuscript had been written four years earlier, before Fox's *Journal* was in print; he may have known of Fox's manuscripts, however, as well as of Bunyan's *Grace Abounding*: in 1691 he wrote a *Short History of a Long Travel from Babylon to Bethel* in allegorical form as a Quaker parallel to *Pilgrim's Progress.* Though

[47] The Meetinghouse at Street, Somerset, where Banks lived his last two decades, was so low that beams had to be carved out for the tall Banks to stand as he spoke in the Meeting. Cf. BSP, p. 367.

196

only sixty pages long, Crisp's *Journal* is careful narrative (diary notes and itineraries also survive, e.g., for his 1669 trip to the West of England).[48] It has no intruded letters or papers, but covers his whole life; we present mainly the first third, on his convincement.

Even as remembered thirty-five years later, Crisp's experiences are like those of Hubberthorne and Howgill in their passion for righteousness and burden of adolescent guilt. His repeated concern for power over corruptions, and sense "that it was not in my power to keep myself out of 'sin' " (p. 6), echo Augustine's experience. In his sensitivity about self-deceit, for instance in men's ability to use even repentance as a trick to restore self-esteem, Crisp stands out above other Quaker writers. Yet Dewsbury's, Farnworth's, Burrough's, Ambrose Rigge's and many other Friends' narratives have similar pictures of periods of struggle. Crisp is clearer than most about the renewed inner conflict over each new call to travel and about the role of the Meeting in guiding those who felt led. Crisp's first journey, through the North of England to Scotland in late autumn of 1659, about which he felt such doubts, was nevertheless important for Quakerism. These were, as he notes, the months in which the Puritan Commonwealth was collapsing (cf. p. 408); and the Cromwellian garrisons themselves were plotting to bring back the monarchy. Crisp's support for the little Meetings in those times of despair, and again in another visit the next year, must have been crucial to them. Indeed by February, 1661, when Crisp was arrested at Durham, he was known as "the leader of them in that county."[49] His *Journal* never mentions the death of his two children in the Plague of 1665, nor two later imprisonments. (His answers to the Deputy Lieutenant of Durham at his trial also survive.)

A JOURNAL OF THE LIFE
OF STEPHEN CRISP

Giving an Account of his Convincement,
Travels, Labours and Sufferings,
in, and for the Truth

O all ye saints and all ye inhabitants of the earth, let the name of Jehovah be famous among you; for there is no God like unto him; and let his mercies

[48] Cf. Caroline Fell-Smith, *Steven Crisp and His Correspondents* (1892), pp. xxx-xxxii.

[49] Dr. John Barwick to John Nicholas; letter quoted in Fell-Smith, p. xxiv, and in full in *ESP*, p. 128.

and judgements be remembered and recorded from generation to generation; for infinite is his goodness, and his loving kindness unspeakable. . . . [Psalm 77 quoted] [2] And in the sweet remembrance of his manifold innumerable mercies, I am even overcome. For my whole life hath been as a continued series of mercy and goodness, and all my days hath he been my upholder; when I knew him not he was nigh unto me; yea, when I rebelled against him, he ceased not to be gracious; his covenant stood with his seed Christ: and for his sake he spared me. . . . [thanks for his mercy]

And surely the Lord hath had an eye of tender compassion upon me; from the day that he formed me . . . for so soon as I can remember, and so soon as I was capable of understanding, he made me to understand that which consented not to any evil, but stood in my soul as a witness against all evil, and manifested that I should not lie, nor steal, [3] nor be stubborn, nor be disobedient, but should behave myself in meekness and quietness, and set truth before me, as that which was better than falsehood. This same witness even in the days of my childhood ministered peace and boldness unto me, when I hearkened to the counsel of it; but there was a contrary nature and seed in me that was of this world, and not of God; which inclined unto evil, and unto the way and manner of this evil world, as most of all suiting the carnal mind; and an eye began to open in me that saw what was acceptable with man, rather than what was well pleasing to God.

And that eye being daily ministered unto by the various objects and examples of vanity, a delight sprung up in that which was evil, and my senses became exercised with vanity, by which the pure seed became oppressed and grieved from day to day, and began to cry out against me; and condemnation began to be stirred up in me, and fear entered where before no fear was, and the pure innocence was lost; and then having at any time done or spoken any evil, then the light (or pure principle) in me would manifest it to me, and show me that I ought not so to have done. And I felt condemnation, which how to escape I knew not; but then the evil spirit that led to transgress would always stand ready to help in this need, and sometimes stirred up the subtlety in me to plead a reason for what I had done, or a provocation, or a good intent, or else to deny or at least to mitigate the evil of my deed, and so to stop the mouth of the witness of God, and to see if I could escape the condemnation of the witness of God, and [4] procure my own peace. But, alas, this was a miserable help, for the light would often shine through all this and quell my reasonings; and showed me, when I was but a child, that in the pure reason that is from God, there is no reason for any evil, let provocations, temptations or examples be what they can or will; and so was I often stripped naked from all my reasoning and coverings. And then I learned another way to get ease from the judgement, and that when I was very young, about seven or eight years old, I would use when judgement overtook me for evil, to yield

198

STEPHEN CRISP

that it was so; and therefore [I] thought, I must do something to please God again, and so hereupon I learned to pray, and to weep in secret, and to covenant with God for more watchfulness, and so then I thought for a season I was as one unburthened from my weight. Yet this best state was accompanied with many doubtings and questionings, whether my evils were blotted out or no [since temptation returned].... But this I knew, that I wanted power to answer the requirings of that in me, which witnesseth against evil in me, and this I lamented day and night. And when I was about nine or ten years old, I sought the power of God with great diligence and earnestness, with strong cries and tears; and if I had had the whole world I would have given it, to have known how to obtain [5] power over my corruptions. And when I saw the carelessness of other children, and their profaneness, and that they did not (that I could discern) think of God, nor were not in trouble, though they were far more wicked than I in their speech and actions; "Ah Lord!", thought I, "what will become of these? seeing so heavy hand is upon me, I can find neither peace nor assurance of thy love."

Then the enemy would tempt me to rest and be quiet, in that it was better with me than with others, and my reason wrought strongly to make up a peace to myself herein. But the pure witness followed me and left me not, but pursued me night and day, and broke my peace faster than I could make it up, for my mind was in my own works. . . .

Sometimes I heard men dispute, "that God sees no sin in his people"; then I said, "surely I am none of them; for he marketh all my transgressions." Otherwise, men talked of an Election, and a reprobation of persons before time; and that I considered diligently, and thought, if that were so, and I could but get so many signs and marks of an elect soul and might bring me to quiet, then I would keep it; and not be so tossed as I had been. Then I grew a very diligent hearer and regarder of the best ministers, as they were reputed; and went with as much diligence and cheerfulness to reading and to hearing sermons as other children [6] went to their play and sportings. And when I heard any one treat upon that point of Election, and how a man might know if they were elect, and would in their dark wisdom lay down signs of a true believer and signs of an elect soul, then would I try myself in their measure and weigh myself in their balance, and so gather up a little peace to myself, finding such things in me as they spoke of for signs, as a desire against sin, a loathing myself for sin, a love to them that were counted the best people, a longing to be rid of sin, etc. . . . And when I had gotten a little peace and quietness, and thought to hold it, alas, it would soon be shattered and broken, and when God's pure witness arose in me that I must be weighed in the true balance, oh then I found I was much too light; and anguish would again kindle in me, and a cry was in me, "Oh whither shall I go? and what shall I do? that I might come to a settled state, before I go hence and be seen

199

no more." And in this woeful condition the thoughts of death would bring a dread over soul and body; and trembling and horror was often upon me, fearing that I was set apart for a vessel of wrath forever and must bear the fiery indignation of God forever. And oh, that word "forever" would often be terrible to me, but how to prevent it I knew not; for now I began to perceive my own insufficiency and my want of God's power, and that it was not in my own power to keep myself out of sin, and the wages of it was death, so that I was in a great strait, sometimes thinking I had better give over [7] seeking, and sometimes thinking, if I perish I had better perish seeking, and here the good got the upper hand for a season, and I became a diligent seeker, and prayer, and mourner, and would often find out the most secret fields and unusual places, there to pour out my complaints to the Lord.

When I was but about twelve years old, my general and constant cry was after the power by which I might overcome corruptions, and although I heard the teachers of those times daily saying none could live without sin and the doctrine of perfection held as a dangerous error, yet that did not abate my cry. . . . For I remembered the words of Christ, "He that committeth sin, is the servant of sin," and that I knew was I. And in this iron furnace I toiled and laboured, and none knew my sorrows and griefs, which at times were almost intolerable, that I wished I had never been born, or that my end might be like the beasts of the field, for I counted them happy, for they had no such bitter combat here as I had, nor should not endure that hereafter that I feared I must endure after all. For I did see my misery, but I saw no way to escape. Then I thought I had best not keep my misery so close, but disclose it to some that [8] maybe might help me; but well might I say miserable comforters I found them all to be; for then they would bid me apply the promises by faith, and suck comfort out of the scriptures; and tell me of the apostle's state in the 7th of the Romans mentioned, and tell me it was so with him, and yet he was a servant of Jesus Christ. And such-like deceitful daubings as they had daubed themselves with, in like manner dealt they with me; not considering how the apostle called that "a wretched and an unde-livered state," as I might well do mine [groping in darkness]. . . . And as for the priests and professors of those times, the most of them would boast of experiences, and of the seal, and of assurances of the love of God, and what comfort they enjoyed by thinking or meditating of the suffering of Christ for their sins, etc. "Alas," thought I, "I could think of these things as well as you, but my wound still remains fresh, and I see that I am as one of the crucifiers while I live in sin, for which he died." And my soul longed after some other kind of knowledge of Him than that which was to be attained by reading, for I see that the worst as well as the best could attain to that. . . . [no help there]

Then I began to be somewhat more loosened in my mind from the priests (though I left [9] them not wholly), but now began to find out the meetings of those then called separatists, and to hear their gifted men so called, whose doctrine, I took notice, favoured more of zeal and fervency than most of the priests' did, neither did I see them so covetous to make a gain of preaching, not yet being come to see how they coveted greatness and applause of men, but I was often affected with their preachings. But still the former bond was upon me, and they yet strengthened it: to wit, that if I were not elected, I could not be saved; and how I might know, no man could tell me to my satisfaction. So the fear of this would often dash my comfort, and then I began to take notice of the loose walking of such separatists, yea, even of the teachers among them how that they were not yet redeemed from foolish jesting, from idle words, from anger and passion, and sometimes it broke out brother against brother, and so ran out to parties, and to breaches and schisms, and rending their churches, which they often both built and pulled down with their own hands. . . . [and wavered in doctrines]

Then I began when I was about seventeen or eighteen years of age to seek yet further; and hearing of a people that held forth "The Death of Christ for all Men," I went to hear them, and after some time I came to see that there was more light, and clearer [10] understanding of new scriptures among them than among the former. So I began to be conversant with them and frequent in their meetings. . . . So this ministered comfort a while; and I set myself to believe, and to get faith in Christ, and to reckon myself a believer, and found it a hard work, even too hard for me, though I cried aloud many times to have my unbelief helped. Yet when I saw sin prevail over me, "Alas!" said I, "where is that faith that purifies the heart, and giveth victory, mine is not such." [Growing in strength and desires, his conscience became even sharper, and he turned to reading philosophy.] [11] And I, poor man, knew not what to do, as to religion; I saw diverse . . . [but] I could see none of them hold forth that which I wanted, either in their life or doctrine, (to wit) power over corruptions, without which I knew religion would be in vain, and not answer the end for which I should take it up. So I desisted taking up any form, and kept in the wild field of this world, and wandered up and down, sometimes to one sort of people, sometimes to another, taking a sharp inspection into their lives and doctrines; though I confess, I left my own garden undressed, until many noisome weeds overgrew, and so that I began to lose my tenderness of conscience which I had had, and began to take pleasure in the company of the wicked, and in many things to become like them, and came to be captivated more than [12] ever with mirth and jollity. And oft [I] would sing when I had cause to howl and mourn, and fell to gaming and pastime, and presumed upon the mercy of God, and had a secret belief, that God would one day manifest his power and bring me out of this state; and therefore had often a dread upon me of running so far into wickedness as some others did,

and was kept from many gross evils that my companions ran into [thanks to God's goodness].... And often would I be arguing and conferring with them that were counted experienced Christians, how peace and assurance might be attained. Some would say by reading and applying promises, but that way I had tried so often and so long that it took now but little with me, for I saw I was in another state than that unto which the promises were made. Others said the only way [13] was to be obedient to the commands and ordinances of Jesus Christ, and to be comfortable to the primitive saints, in walking in church-order and Communion, where every one had the strength of many, and all the church bound to watch over every member. To these counsellors I hearkened, and was willing to do any thing, to find the power, and reproach should not keep me back, so I took up that ordinance (as they called it) of water baptism, expecting then to have found power more than before. And my will wrought strongly to bridle and keep down that airy part and sinful nature, and for a season strove to uphold and maintain myself to be in a better state than before; though the virtue that should sanctify and wash me I did not feel, my mind being abroad; and the reasons that kept me were not the operation of the pure love of God in my heart and his grace prevailing in me to teach me, but rather an eye to the reputation of my religion, and that I might not seem to have run and acted all in vain. But these reasons held but for a season, before the temptation grew too strong for my will, and the devil entered his own ground and prevailed upon me and led me captive into sin and evil, and drew me into vain company and vain sports and delights and pastimes again as before, so that I sufficiently saw I wanted what I wanted before, and had grasped but at a shadow.... [It had not been Christ's true baptism of purifying fire.] [14] And I testified unto the elders, so called of the church, that God would shortly overturn all our worships and religions, which stood in outward and carnal things, and would make known some way a top of them all that should stand forever. When they enquired what that way should be, I confessed I knew not, but waited to see what it might be.⁵⁰ [50]
And about those days many exercised themselves in talking and discoursing of a people called Quakers, after whom I listened. But though I hearkened with great diligence, I could hear no good report of them, but much harm and many false and wicked lies were cast upon them. Only this I took notice of, that they suffered cruel mockings and grievous sufferings patiently. Now I did expect that when the way of God was made manifest it would be hated and persecuted; yet I thought that should not at all deter or affright me from owning of it, and walking in it, if once I knew it. But forasmuch as I heard they held "perfection in this life," that was a thing the old wisdom of the serpent could not reach nor join with, but I reasoned against it strongly, in

---

⁵⁰ [50] This describes the doctrinal position of the seekers of this period.

that dark fallen wisdom in which many are still fighting for sin. . . . [15] In this same fallen wisdom did I reason divers ways, too many now to name, against the truth. . . . But a messenger of this truth I had not seen, but longed much to see one, wishing night and day that our parts might be visited by them, as I had heard others were. And at last the Lord sent his faithful servant and messenger of his everlasting gospel, James Parnell, to our town of Colchester, about the fourth month, 1655,[51] and in the 27th year of my age, who came in the name and power of the most high God, in which he turned many to righteousness, both there and in other countries [=counties] before, of whom some remain, and many are fallen asleep. When I saw this man, being but a youth, and knew not the power nor spirit that was in him, I thought to withstand him, and began to query and seek discourse with him. But I quickly came to feel the spirit of sound judgement was in him, and the witness of God arose in me and testified to his judgement and signified I must own it, it being just and true. And I the same day and hour testified that all our rods of profession would be lost or devoured by his rod, alluding to that of Moses and [16] the magicians of Egypt; which is and shall certainly come to pass. So that day I went to a meeting, and heard him declare the everlasting gospel, in the name and authority of the Lord, which I could not with all my wisdom and knowledge withstand, but was constrained to own and confess unto the truth. And here at the very first of my convincement did the enemy of my soul make trial to slay me; and that after this manner: that seeing my wisdom and reason was overcome by the truth, I could not therewith withstand it, therefore I received the truth, and held it in the same part with which I withstood it, and defended it with the same wisdom by which I resisted it, and so was yet a stranger to the cross that was to crucify me; and was at liberty in the discoursative spirit, to lay out my wits and parts for the truth. But I soon felt my sacrifice (though I offered the best my earth would afford) was not accepted, but something else was still called for; and a cry was in me which called to judgement. . . . [great struggle to understand]

So in this state I continued a month or two, but [17] then a swift sword was drawn against that wisdom and comprehending mind, and a strong hand gave the stroke, and I was hewn down like a tall cedar, that at once comes down to the ground.

But then, oh the woe, misery and calamity that opened upon me! Yea, even the gates of hell and destruction stood open, and I saw myself nigh falling thereinto, my hope and faith, and all fled from me, I had no prop left me to rest upon. The tongue that was as a river, was now like a dry desert; the eye that would, or at least desired to see everything, was now so blind, that I

---

51 This personal witness completes the story that Crisp himself tells in his testimony to Parnell (cf. p. 163).

could see nothing certainly, but my present undone and miserable state. Oh, then I cried out in bitterness of my soul, "what hath all my profession profited me? I am poor and blind and naked, who thought I had been rich and well adorned" [symbols of judgment]. . . . Oh, how doleful was my nights, and sorrowful was my days! My delights withered even in wife and children, and in all things; and the glory of the whole world passed away like a scroll that is burnt with fire; and I saw nothing left in the whole world to give me any comfort. My sun lost her light, and my moon was darkened, and the stars of my course were fallen, that I knew no more how to direct my way, but was as one forsaken in a howling desert in the darkest night; and when I saw what God had done (for I believed it was His doing) I was ready to cry, "I am forsaken forever, and never was sorrow [18] like mine, my wound is incurable, and my sickness none can heal." Alas! My tongue nor pen cannot express the sorrows of those days in which I sat me down in silence, fear and astonishment, and was encompassed with sorrow and darkness; and I knew none to make my moan unto. . . . [no hope of joy] So after long travel, strong cries, and many bitter tears and groans, I found a little hope springing in me, that the Lord in his own time would bring forth his Seed, even his elect Seed, the seed of his covenant, to rule in me; and this was given me at a time when a sense of my own unworthiness had so overwhelmed me in sorrow and anguish, that I thought myself unworthy of any of the creatures; forasmuch as I was out of the covenant of God, and hereupon was tempted to deny myself of them. Then did the hope of the resurrection of the just spring in me, and I was taught to wait on God, and to eat and drink in fear and watchfulness, showing forth the Lord's death till he should come to be raised to live and reign in me.[52] So then I waited as one that had hope that God would be gracious to me; yet something in me would fain have known the time how long it should be, but a faithful cry was in me, which called that to death. And upon a time, being weary of my own thoughts in the Meeting of God's People, I thought none was like me, and it was but in vain to sit [19] there with such a wandering mind as mine was, while, though I laboured to stay it, yet could not as I would. At length, I thought to go forth; and as I was going, the Lord thundered through me, saying, "That which is weary must die". So I turned to my seat and waited in the belief of God, for the death of that part which was weary of the work of God; and yet more diligent in seeking death, that I might be baptized for the dead; and that I might know how to put off the old man with his deeds and words, and imaginations, his fashions and customs, his friendship and wisdom, and all that appertained to him. And the cross of Christ was laid upon me, and I bore

[52] Here Crisp uses sacramental language for his sharing Christ's death by inner crucifixion.

it. And as I came willingly to take it up, I found it to be to me, that thing which I had fought from my childhood, even the power of God; for by it I was crucified to the world, and it to me, which nothing else could ever do. But oh, how glad was my soul when I had found the way to slay my soul's enemies; oh, the secret joy that was in me in the midst of all my conflicts and combats, I had this confidence, if I take but up the cross, I shall obtain victory, for that's the power of God through faith to salvation, and as I have found it so in some things, so I shall do in all in due time. Then the reproach of the gospel became joyous to me; though in those days it was very cruel and grievous to flesh and blood, yet I despised it, and that for the joy that was now set before me, of which I had some hope I should in time be made a partaker, if I abode faithful. And that was my great care night and day, to keep so low and out of the workings of my own will, that I might discern [20] the mind of God, and do it, though in never so great a cross to my own. Yet the Enemy of my soul followed me close and very secretly, and taking notice how willing I was to obey the Lord, he strove to get up into the seat of God, and to move as an angel of light, to betray me, and to lead me into something that was like the service of God. And many sore conflicts did I meet withal before I was able in all things to distinguish between the workings of the true spirit and power, from that which was but [the old self] transformed. But forasmuch as I had now surely tasted of the love and goodness of God, I trusted in him, and committed the keeping of my soul unto him in singleness of heart [Ps. 104:35]. . . .

So the more I came to feel and perceive the love of God, and his goodness to flow forth upon me, the more was I humbled and bowed in my mind to serve him, and to serve the least of his people among whom I walked. And as the word of wisdom began to spring in me, and the knowledge of God grew so, I became as a counsellor of them that were tempted in like manner as I had been; yet being kept so low that I waited to receive counsel daily from God, and from those that were over me in the Lord and in Christ. . . . [growth of the Meeting] [21] Being called of God and his people to take the care of the poor, and to relieve their necessities as I did see occasion, I did it faithfully for diverse years, with diligence and much tenderness, exhorting and reproving any that were slothful, and encouraging them that were diligent, putting a difference according to the wisdom given me of God, and still minding my own state and condition, and seeking the honor that comes of God only. And a cry was in me to keep on my spiritual armour, for all enemies were not yet put under my feet, so I kept my watch, not knowing well where the enemy might appear. . . .

About the year 1659, I often felt the aboundings of the love of God in my heart, and a cry to stand given up to his will, (which I thought I was, not knowing or foreseeing what the Lord was intended to do with me): but his eye lay further than mine. This love and tenderness and bowels of compassion wrought so in me that it extended even to all men on the whole face of the earth. . . . And upon a time, as I was waiting upon the Lord, his word arose in me, and commanded me to forsake [22] and part with my dear wife and children, father and mother, and to go and bear witness to his name in Scotland, to that high professing nation. But when that came to pass I found all enemies were not slain indeed; for the strivings, strugglings, reasonings and disputings against the command of God that I then met withal cannot be told or numbered. Oh! how I would have pleaded my own inability, the care of my family, my service in that particular Meeting, and many more things, and all that I might have been excused from this one thing which was come upon me, that I thought not of, or looked not for. But after many reasonings, days and weeks by myself, I thought it best to speak of it to some of the faithful elders and ministers of this everlasting gospel; not knowing but they might discourage me, and something there was that hoped it. But contrarily they encouraged me, and laid it upon me to be faithful. So then I gave up, and acquainted my dear wife therewith, which began me a new exercise, the enemy working in her strongly to stop me. But in much patience was I kept, and in quietness, and went and visited Friends' Meetings about Essex and part of Suffolk, chiefly to see them, and to take my leave of them, and in some meetings the Lord would open my mouth in a few words to the refreshing of Friends, but I rather choose silence, when I might so. The winter drew nigh, and something would have deferred it till next summer. But the Lord showed me it must not be my time, but his time. Then I would have gone by sea, but the Lord withstood me, and showed me it must not be my way, but his way; [24] and if I would be obedient he would be with me, and prosper my journey, otherwise his hand would strike me. So I gave up all, and with pretty much cheerfulness, at last I obeyed, and about the end of the seventh month I went forth, and visited the churches of Christ.

As I went along in Lincolnshire and Yorkshire, I quickly perceived the Lord was with me more than at other times, and my journey became joyful; and the more in that though I were but weak, poor and low, yet God gave me acceptance among the elders of his people, and in every place my testimony was owned. . . . So I got into Scotland in the ninth month, that year, and traveled to and fro that winter on foot with cheerfulness. Many straits and difficulties attended me (which I forbear to mention) it being the time of the motion of the English and Scottish armies, upon which came the revolution of government, and the bringing back King Charles the Second into England. Well, about the 11th or 12th month I returned and travelled into the west to Westmorland, part of Lancashire, and so up to the southward, and in about five or six months' time was by the good hand of God brought home to my wife and children and relations, in all my journey being sweetly accompanied

206

with the presence of the Lord, and his power often filled my earthen vessel and made my cup to overflow: "Praises forever be to his Name," saith my soul.

[23] [53] And in all my journey I lacked not anything that was good for me but as it was my care in singleness to serve the Lord, so was the tender care of the Lord over me, and he supplied me with whatever was needful in my journey. Yet all along a secret hope did live in me, that when the present journey should be accomplished, I should be freed from this service, and have liberty to return to my calling and family, but contrarily it proved; for when I had been at home a few days, it lay upon me to go up to London, to visit the brethren and church of God there. So I went in great fear and dread of God into that city; and having continued there a few days, departed northward again at the commandment of the Lord, and found my ways prosperous wherever I went. And great encouragement did I daily receive from the Lord, who blessed my labour of love, that, besides the peace and joy I felt in myself, I saw the effect of my labour and travail of my soul in divers places made manifest, by divers being turned from darkness to light, and from serving the devil's power unto the power of God. But still trials attended me and a prison became my portion, nigh two hundred miles from home,[54] and great and grievous threatenings were breathed out against me, and the same spirit which wrought in the persecutors, both in their cruelty and subtlety, strove to work in me also.

But I cried to the Lord, and he helped me, and my faith failed me not, and I fulfilled my service and testimony; and at length was delivered, and several thousands more, by a public proclamation from the king, and then returned to my own house, [25] after about eight months' absence. . . . [Next journeys, to preserve unity]

[26] And about the year '63, I was moved to cross the seas, and to visit the Seed of God in the Low Countries, which I did with cheerfulness; and though in an unknown land, and with an unknown speech, yet by an interpreter sometimes, and sometimes in my own tongue, I declared the truth to the refreshing of many, and to the bringing back some from error, and having accomplished that visit, I returned in peace to England. . . . [journey of 1667 to northern England] [28] And after a year or two years' travel thus in England, the Lord laid yet more of the weight and care of the affairs of his people in the Low Countries upon me, and I found drawing towards them. And in the year '69, I went over and visited the Meetings, obtained diverse new Meetings, and they set up a Man's Meeting among them, to see to the good ordering and governing of the affairs relating to truth, and Friends. And

---

53 In the 1694 edition the numbers for pp. 23 and 24 have been switched.
54 His arrest in Durham; cf. *ESP*, p. 128.

this time did it please the Lord to open my understanding abundantly, that I began to declare in their own tongue the things that God had committed unto me to minister, and several received the everlasting gospel, and were brought to feel the power of God, by which they are saved from the world, and the polluted ways therein. Then being travelling in those provinces of Holland, Friesland, and Groningen, etc., I was moved to pass into Germany, to which I gave up in the fourth month that same year, and by the way met with many perils and dangers, by reason of the horrible darkness, popery, cruelty and superstitions of those lands and dominions through which I travelled; so that sometimes it was as if my life were in my hands, to offer up for my testimony. But the Lord preserved me, and brought me upon the 14th day of that month to Griesham near Worms, where I found divers who had received the everlasting truth, and had stood in a testimony for God about ten years, in great sufferings and tribulations, who received me as a servant of God; and my testimony was as a dew upon the tender grass unto them. I had five good Meetings among them, and divers heard the truth, and several were reached and convinced, and Friends established in the faith. It was also just in an hour of temptation and time of trial that the Lord had cast me there; for the prince of that land, called the Pfalzgraf, had imposed a fine upon them for their Meetings. . . . So I went to Heidelberg, to the prince of that land,[55] and had a good opportunity with him, and laid before him the danger of his proceeding on in persecution. . . . [In 1669 he made a trip to Cornwall and back with Samuel Cater; then with Peter Hendricks a journey from Holland through Hamburg to Fredrikstadt in Denmark, and back via Emden. He made much the same circuit in 1673; but in 1677, due to failing health, he could visit only Holland and Friesland, as he did each of the next three years and in 1683. Crisp's second wife Gertrude was Dutch.]

7. *The History of the Life of Thomas Ellwood* (1714)

Unlike Hubberthorne, Banks, and Howgill, but like Crisp, Thomas Ellwood was from the South of England, and well educated (having been briefly at Oxford). Unlike Crisp, Ellwood was

[55] Karl Ludwig, a Wittelsbach and not of the same family as Elizabeth, Princess Palatine, aunt of the later English King George I of Hanover, and abbess of a sort of Protestant nunnery at Herwerden near Münster. Her family had lost the Palatinate and Bohemia to the Catholics in the disastrous opening months of the Thirty Years War. She was a friend of Penn and Barclay and corresponded with Crisp.

also from the country gentry; so indeed were the Fells, Gervase Benson, and Anthony Pearson in the Northwest, but none of these became Quaker writers except Margaret Fell. Ellwood's *Life* shows an ease of style and vigor of narrative that made it for a century the best loved of all Quaker journals after Fox's.

The first hundred pages of Ellwood's *Life* concern his entry into Quakerism despite the opposition of his father, and the ridicule he faced for wearing his hat before friends. This section, though it avoids biblical tags and stereotyped phrases, parallels journals like Banks's, and has moreover been presented in Jessamyn West's tasteful *Quaker Reader*.[56] It is mainly important for introducing us to a key circle of Quaker gentry: Isaac and Mary Penington, Mary's daughter Gulielma Springett, and her eventual husband William Penn. From this section we get vignettes of other Friends: in a farmhouse called the Grove, Ellwood met Nayler and Burrough in 1659.

> As for Edward Burrough, he was a brisk young man, of a ready tongue (and might have been, for ought I then knew, a scholar), which made me the less to admire his way of reasoning. But what dropped from James Nayler had the greater force upon me, because he looked like a plain simple country-man, having the appearance of an husbandman or a shepherd (p. 50).

Later, in defiance of his father, Ellwood went back to the Peningtons again. He had been going through his time of darkness and struggle and had admitted in public to being a Quaker.

> It being fifteen long miles thither, the ways bad, and my nag but small, it was in the afternoon that I got thither. . . . I hastened in, and knowing the rooms, went directly to the little parlor, where I found a few Friends sitting together in silence, and I sat down among them, well satisfied, though without words. When the meeting was ended, and those of the company who were strangers withdrawn, I addressed myself to Isaac Penington and his wife, who received me courteously. But not knowing what exercise I had been in, and yet was under, nor having heard anything of me, since I had been there before in another garb, were not forward at first to lay sudden hands on me, which I observed and did not dislike. But as they came to see a change in me, not in habit only, but in gesture, speech and carriage, and which was more in countenance also (for the . . . gravity upon my face) they were exceeding kind and tender towards me.

56 Viking, 1962, pp. 142-62.

We present here, somewhat abridged, Ellwood's account of the persecutions under the Quaker and Conventicle Acts, both as a record of experiences and as the most compelling narrative writing from early Quakerism.

[105] While I was then in London, I went to a little Meeting of Friends, which was then held in the house of one Humphry Bache a goldsmith, at the sign of the snail in Tower Street. It was then a very troublesome time, not from the government, but from the rabble of boys and rude people, who upon the turn of the times (at the return of the King) took liberty to be very abusive. . . .

[107] [Later in the year] I wrote to my friend Thomas Loe, to acquaint him, that I had procured a place for a Meeting, and would invite company to it; if he would fix the time, and give me some ground to hope, that he would be at it.

This letter of mine, instead of being delivered according to its direction, was seized, and carried (as I was told) to the lord Falkland, who was then called Lord-Lieutenant of that county.

The occasion of this stopping of letters at that time, was that mad prank, of those infatuated Fifth-monarch-men, who from their meeting house in Coleman Street, London, breaking forth in arms, (under the command of [108] their chieftain Venner) made an insurrection in the city; on pretence of setting up the kingdom of Jesus; who (it is said) they expected would come down from heaven, to be their leader. So little understood they the nature of his kingdom; though he himself had declared it was not of this world.

The King, a little before his arrival in England, had, by his declaration from Breda, given assurance of liberty to tender consciences; and that no man should be disquieted, or called in question for differences of opinion in matters of religion, who do not disturb the peace of the kingdom. Upon this assurance dissenters of all sorts relied, and held themselves secure. But now, by this frantic action of a few hot-brained men, the king was, by some, held discharged from his royal word and promise, in his foregoing declaration publicly given. And hereupon letters were intercepted and broken open; for discovery of suspected plots, and designs against the government. And not only dissenters' meetings, of all sorts, without distinction, were disturbed; but very many were imprisoned, in most parts, throughout the nation; and great search there was, in all countries [=counties], for suspected persons, who, if not found at meetings, were fetched in from their own houses. . . . [Ellwood was therefore imprisoned at Oxford.]

[133] After this imprisonment was over, I went sometimes to Isaac

Penington's house at Chalfont, to visit that family, and the Friends there-abouts. There was then a Meeting, for the most part, twice a week in his house. . . .

[137] The nation had been in a ferment, ever since that mad action of the frantic fifth monarchy men; and was not yet settled: but storms, like thunder showers, flew here and there by coast; so that we could not promise ourselves any safety, or quiet in our Meetings. And though they had escaped distur-bance for some little time before: yet so it fell out, that a party of horse were appointed to come, and break up the Meeting that day; though we knew nothing of it, till we heard, and saw them.

The Meeting was scarce fully gathered when they came. But we that were in the family, and many others were settled in it, in great peace and stillness; when on a sudden, the prancing of the horses gave notice that lightning was at hand.

We all sat still in our places, except my companion, John Ovy, who sat next to me. But he being of a profession that approved Peter's advice to his Lord, to save himself, soon took the alarm: and with the nimbleness of a stripling, cutting a caper over the form that stood before him, ran quickly out at a private door (which he had before observed) which led through the parlor into the gardens, and from thence into an orchard: where he hid himself, in a place so obscure, and withal so convenient for his intelligence by observation [138] of what passed; that no one of the family could scarce have found a likelier.

By that time he was got into his burrow, came the soldiers in; being a party of the county troop, commanded by Matthew Archdale of Wycombe. He behaved himself civilly, and said, he was commanded to break up the Meeting, and carry the men before a justice of the peace: but he said he would not take all; and thereupon began to pick and choose, chiefly as his eye guided him, for I suppose he knew very few.

He took Isaac Penington, and his brother, George Whitehead, and the friend of Colchester, and me, with three or four more of the county, who belonged to that Meeting.

The justice carried himself civilly to us all; courteously to Isaac Penington, as being a gentleman of his neighborhood: and there was nothing charged against us, but that we were met together without word or deed. Yet this being contrary to a late proclamation (given forth upon the rising of the fifth monarchy men) whereby all dissenters' meetings were forbidden, the justice could do no less than take notice of us.

[139] Wherefore he examined all of us (whom he did not personally know) asking our names, and the places of our respective habitations. But when he had them, and considered from what distant parts of the nation we came; he was amazed. For G. Whitehead was of Westmorland in the North of

England; the grocer was of Essex; I was of Oxfordshire; and W. Penington was of London.

Hereupon he told us, that our case looked ill, and he was sorry for it: for how (said he) can it be imagined that so many could jump altogether at one time and place, from such remote quarters and parts of the kingdom; if it was not by combination and appointment.

He was answered, that we were so far from coming thither by agreement, or appointment; that none of us knew of the others coming, and for the most of us, we had never seen one another before: and that therefore he might impute it to chance, or, if he pleased, to providence.

He urged upon us, that an insurrection had been lately made by armed men, who pretended to be more religious than others; that that insurrection had been plotted and contrived in their meeting house, where they assembled under color of worshipping God; that in their meeting house issued forth in arms, and killed many: so that the government could not be safe, unless such meetings were suppressed. [After two nights Ellwood was released.]

[153] I mentioned before, that when I was a boy, I had made some good progress in learning; and lost it all again before I came to be a man: Nor was I rightly sensible of my loss therein, until I came among the Quakers. But then I saw my loss, and lamented it; This I had formerly complained of to my especial Friend Isaac Penington; but now more earnestly: which put him upon considering, [154] and contriving a means for my assistance.

He had an intimate acquaintance with Dr. Paget, a physician of note in London; and he with John Milton, a gentleman of great note for learning, throughout the learned world, for the accurate pieces he had written, on various subjects and occasions.

This person, having filled a public station, in the former times; lived now a private and retired life in London: and having wholly lost his sight, kept always a man to read to him; which usually was the son of some gentleman of his acquaintance, whom, in kindness, he took to improve in his learning. . . .

[156] I went therefore and took myself a lodging as near to his house (which was then in Jewen Street) as conveniently as I could: and from thenceforward went every day in the afternoon (except on the first days of the week) and sitting by him in his dining room, read to him in such books in the Latin tongue, as he pleased to hear me read.

At my first sitting to read to him, observing that I used the English pronounciation, he told me, if I would have the benefit of the Latin tongue (not only to read and understand Latin authors, but to converse with foreigners, either abroad or at home), I must learn the foreign pronunciation. To this I consenting, he instructed me how to sound the vowels.

[158] But, as if learning had been a forbidden fruit to me, scarce was I

212

well settled in my [159] work, before I met with another diversion, which turned me quite out of my work.

For a sudden storm arising, from I know not what surmise of a plot, and thereby danger to the government; and the Meetings of dissenters (such I mean as could be found, which perhaps were not many besides the Quakers) were broken up throughout the city: and the prisons mostly filled with our Friends.

I was that morning (which was the 26th day of the 8th month, 1662) at the Meeting at the Bull-and-Mouth by Aldersgate; when on a sudden, a party of soldiers (of the trained bands of the city) rushed in, with noise and clamor: being led by one who was called Major Rosewell, an apothecary (if I misremember not) and at that time under the ill name of a papist.

As soon as he was come within the room, having a file or two of musketeers at his heels; he commanded his men to present their muskets at us: which they did; with intent (I suppose) to strike a terror into the people. Then he made a proclamation that all who were not Quakers might depart if they would. . . .

[160] The soldiers came so early, that the Meeting was not fully gathered when they came; and when the mixed company were gone out, we were so few, and sat so thin in that large room, that they might take a clear view of us all, and single us out, as they pleased.

He that commanded the party, gave us first a general charge to come out of the room. But we, who came thither at God's requirings, to worship Him (Acts 5:29) stirred not; but kept our places. Whereupon he sent some of his soldiers among us, with command to drag, or drive us out: which they did roughly enough. . . .

[161] He led us up Martins, and so turned down to Newgate, where I expected he would have lodged us. But to my disappointment, he went on through Newgate, and turning through the Old Bailey, he brought us to Fleet Street. I was then wholly at a loss to conjecture whither he would lead us, unless it were to Whitehall [162] (for I knew nothing then of Old Bridewell). But on a sudden he gave a short turn, and brought us before the gate of that prison, where knocking, the wicket was forthwith opened and the master, with his porter, ready to receive us. . . .

As soon as I was in, the porter pointing with his finger, directed me to a fair pair of stairs on the further side of a large court, and bid me to go up those stairs and go on till I could go no further.

Accordingly I went up the stairs. The first flight, whereof, brought me to a fair chapel, on my left hand, which I could look into through the iron gates, but could not have gone into if I would.

[163] I knew that was not the place for me. Wherefore, following my

213

direction and the winding of the stairs, I went up a story higher. . . . Observing a door on the further side, I went to it and opened it with the intention of going in. I quickly drew back, being almost affrighted at the dismalness of the place. For besides that the walls, quite round, were laid all over from top to bottom in black, there stood in the middle of it a great whipping post, which was all the furniture it had. . . .

Looking earnestly, I spied on the opposite side a door which giving me hopes of a further progress, I adventured to step hastily to it and opened it.

This let me into one of the fairest rooms that (so far as I remember) I was ever in. And no wonder, for though it was now put to this mean use, it had, for many ages past, been the royal seat or palace of [164] . . . King Henry the Eighth, who . . . kept his court in this house and had this (as the people in the house reported) for his dining room, by which name it went.

This room in length (for I lived long enough in it to have time to measure it) was threescore feet and breadth proportionable to it. In it, on the front side were very large bay windows in which stood a large table. It had other very large tables in it with benches around and at that time the floor was covered with rushes against some solemn festival which (I heard) it was bespoken for. . . .

An excellent order, even in those early days, was practised among the Friends of that city, by which there were certain Friends . . . appointed to have the oversight of the prisons . . . to take care of all Friends, the poor especially, that should be committed thither.

[166] This prison of Bridewell was under the care of two honest, grave, discreet and motherly women whose names were Anne Merrick (afterwards Vivers) and Anne Travers, both widows.

They, so soon as they understood that there were Friends brought into that prison, provided some hot victuals, meat, and broth (for the weather was cold) and ordering their servants to bring it them with bread, cheese and beer, came themselves also with it. And having placed it on a table gave notice to us that it was provided for all those that had not others to provide for them or were not able to provide for themselves. And there wanted not among us a competent number of such guests.

[167] Although the sight and smell of hot food was sufficiently enticing to my empty stomach (for I had eaten little that morning and was hungry), yet considering the terms of the invitation, I questioned whether I was included in it. After some reasonings at length concluded, that while I had tenpence in my pocket, I should be but an injurious intruder to that mess which was provided for such as perhaps had not two pence in theirs.

Having come to this resolution, I withdrew as far from the table as I could and sat down in a quiet retirement of the mind till the repast was over, which was not long for there were hands enough at it to make light work of it.

214

When evening came, the porter came up the back stairs and opening the door told us if we desired to have anything that was to be had in the house, he would bring it us for there was in the house a chandler's shop at which beer, bread, butter, cheese, eggs and bacon might be had for money. Upon which many went to him and spake for what of these things they had a mind to, giving him money to pay for them.

[168] Among the rest went I and (intending to spin out my ten pence as far as I could) desired him to bring me a penny loaf only. When he returned we all resorted to him to receive our several provisions which he delivered. When he came to me he told me he could not get a penny loaf but he had brought me two half-penny loaves.

Some of the company had been so confident as to send for a pound of candles that we might not sit all night in the dark and having lighted divers of them and placed them in several parts of that large room, we kept walking to keep us warm.

After I had warmed myself pretty thoroughly and the evening was pretty far spent, I bethought myself of a lodging and casting my eye on the table which stood in the bay window, the frame whereof looked, I thought, somewhat like a bedstead. Wherefore willing to make sure of that, I gathered up a good armful of the rushes, wherewith the floor was covered, and spreading them under [169] that table, crept in upon them in my clothes, and keeping on my hat, laid my head upon one end of the table's frame instead of a bolster.

My example was followed by the rest who, gathering up rushes as I had done, made themselves beds in other parts of the room and so to rest we went.

Next day, all those who had families or belonged to families had bedding of one sort or another brought in, which they disposed at the ends and sides of the room, leaving the middle void to walk in.

But I, who had nobody to look after me, kept my rushy pallet under the table for four nights altogether, in which time I did not put off my clothes.

In this time, divers of our company . . . [170] were released. Among these, one William Mucklow who lay in a hammock. He, having observed that I only was unprovided of lodging came very courteously to me and kindly offered me the use of his hammock while I should continue a prisoner. This was a providential accommodation to me which I received thankfully, both from the Lord and from him and from thenceforth I thought I lay as well as I ever had done in my life. . . .

*   *   *   *   *

[173] And now the chief thing I wanted was employment, which scarce any wanted but myself, for the rest of the company were generally tradesmen

215

of such trades as could set themselves on work. Of these divers were tailors, some masters, some journeymen; and with these I most inclined to settle. But because I was too much a novice in their art to be trusted with their work, lest I should spoil the garment, I got work from a hosier in Cheapside, which was to make night waistcoats of red and yellow flannel for women and children. And with this, I entered myself among the tailors, sitting crosslegged as they did, and so spent those leisure hours with innocency and pleasure, which want of business would have made tedious. And indeed, that was, in a manner, the only advantage I had by it; for my master (though a very wealthy man and [174] one who professed not only friendship but particular kindness to me) dealt, I thought, but hardly with me. For (though he knew not what I had to subsist by) he never offered me a penny for my work till I had done working for him and went (after I was released) to pay him a visit. . . .

About this time (while we were prisoners in our fair chamber), a friend was brought in and put among us, who had been sent thither by [Mayor] Richard Brown to beat hemp, whose case was thus.

He was a very poor man who lived by mending shoes. On a seventh-day night late, a car-man (or some such laboring man) brought him a pair of shoes to mend desiring him to mend them that night that he might have them in the morning, for he had no others to wear. The poor man sat up at work upon them till after midnight and then finding he could not finish them, he went [175] to bed intending to do the rest in the morning.

Accordingly he got up betimes, and though he wrought as privately as he could in his chamber, that he might avoid giving offense to any, yet could he not do it so privately but that an ill-natured neighbor perceived it and went and informed against him for working on the Sunday. Whereupon he was had before Richard Brown who committed him to Bridewell for a certain time, to be kept at hard labor in beating hemp, which is labor hard enough.

It so fell out that at the same time were committed thither (for cause I do not now remember) two lusty young men who were called Baptists, to be kept also at the same labor.

The Friend was a poor little man of a low condition and mean appearance; whereas these two Baptists were topping blades that looked high and spake big. They scorned to beat hemp and made a pish at the whipping post. But when they had once felt the smart of it they soon cried, "Peccavi" and submitting to the punishment, set their tender hands to the beetles.

The Friend, on the other hand, acting upon a principle, as knowing he had done no evil for which he should undergo that punishment, refused to work. For refusing was cruelly whipped, which he bore with wonderful constancy and resolution of mind.

[176] The manner of whipping there is: to strip the party to the skin from the waist upwards and having fastened him to the whipping post (so that he can neither resist nor shun the strokes), to lash the naked body with long but

216

slender twigs of holly which will bend almost like thongs and lap around the body, and these having little knots upon them, tear the skin and flesh and give extreme pain.

With these rods they tormented the Friend most barbarously and the more, for that, having mastered the two braving Baptists they disdained to be mastered by this poor Quaker. Yet were they fain at last to yield when they saw their utmost severity could not make him yield. And then, not willing to be troubled longer with him, they turned him up among us.

Yet when we inquired of him how it was with him and he had given us a brief account of both his cause and usage, it came in my mind, that I had in my box (which I had sent for from my lodging to keep some few books and other necessaries in) a little galley-pot with Lucatellu's Balsam in it. . . .

Then melting some of the balsam, I, with a feather anointed all the sores and putting a softer [177] cloth between his skin and his shirt, helped him on with his clothes again. This dressing gave him much ease and I continued it till he was well. And because he was a very poor man, we took him into our mess, contriving that there should always be enough for him as well as for ourselves. Thus he lived with us until the time he committed for was expired and then he was released.

We were still continued prisoners by an arbitrary power, not being committed by the civil authority nor having seen the face of any civil magistrate from the day we were thrust in here by soldiers (which was the 26th day of the eighth month) to the 19th day of the tenth month following.

On that day we were taken to the sessions at the Old Bailey. But not being called there, we were brought back to Bridewell and continued there until the 29th of the same month and then we were carried to the sessions again.

I expected that I should be called first because my name was first taken down. It proved otherwise, so that I was one of the last that was called which gave me the advantage of hearing the pleas of the other prisoners and discovering the temper of the court.

The prisoners complained of the illegality of their imprisonment and desired to know what they had lain so long in prison for. The court regarded nothing of that and did not stick to [178] tell them so. For, said the Recorder to them, "If you think you have been wrongfully imprisoned, you have your remedy at law and may take it if you think it worth your while." "The court," said he, "may send for any man out of the street and tender him the oath; so we take no notice how you came hither but finding you here, we tender you the Oath of Allegiance which if you refuse to take, we shall commit you and at length Praemunire[57] you." Accordingly, as every one refused it, he was set aside and another called.

---

57 *Praemunire* ("to warn") was a thirteenth-century act against treason and papal power, requiring an oath of sole loyalty to the king. Because its

By this I saw it was in vain for me to insist upon false imprisonment or ask the cause of my commitment. I had before furnished myself with some authorities and maxims of law on the subject, to have pleaded, if room had been given, and I had the book (out of which I took them) in my bosom, for the weather being cold I wore a gown girt about the middle and had put the book within it. But now I resolved to waive all that and insist upon another plea which just then came into my mind.

As soon, therefore, as I was called, I stepped nimbly to the bar and stood upon the stepping (that I might the better both hear and be heard) and laying my hands upon the bar, stood ready, expecting what they would say to me.

I suppose they took me for a confident young man for they looked very earnestly upon me and we faced each other without words for awhile. At length the Recorder (who was called [179] Sir John Howell) asked me if I would take the oath of allegiance.

To which I answered, "I conceive this court hath not the power to tender that oath to me in the condition wherein I stand."

This so unexpected plea seemed to startle them so that they looked one upon another. "What? Doth he demur to the jurisdiction of the court?" And thereupon the recorder asked me, "Do you then demur to the jurisdiction of the court?" "Not absolutely," answered I, "but conditionally with respect to my present condition and the circumstances I am now under." "Why, what is your present condition?" said the Recorder. "A prisoner," I replied. . . .

"But," said the Recorder, "will you take the oath if you be set free?"

[180] Thus we fenced a good while till I was both weary of such trifling and doubted also, lest some of the bystanders should suspect I would take it if I was set at liberty. Wherefore when the recorder put it upon me again; I told him plainly, "No". I thought they ought not to tender it me till I had been set at liberty. Yet if I was set at liberty I could not take that, nor any other oath, because my lord and master, Christ Jesus, had expressly commanded his disciples "not to swear at all." As His command was enough to me, so this confession of mine was enough to them. "Take him away" they said. Away I was taken and thrust into the bail dock to my other friends who had been called before me. As soon as the rest of our company were called and had refused to swear we were all committed to Newgate and thrust into the common side.

When we came there we found that side of the prison very full of Friends who were prisoners there before (as indeed were, at that time, all the other parts of that prison, and most of the other prisons about the town) and our

penalties included indefinite imprisonment and confiscation of the condemned, it was a favorite weapon of judges against Quakers under the Restoration, since a Quaker, for whatever reason he might have been arrested, could be expected to refuse all oaths. Not all justices were so unjust.

addition caused a great throng on that side. [181] Notwithstanding which, we were kindly welcomed by our Friends whom we found there and entertained by them as well as their condition would admit, until we could get in our own accommodations and provide for ourselves.

We had the liberty of the hall and the liberty of some other rooms over that hall to walk or work in during the day. But in the night we all lodged in one room which was large and round having in the middle of it a great pillar of oaken timber which bore up the chapel that is over it.

To this pillar we fastened our hammocks at the one end and to the opposite wall on the other end. Quite round the room and in three degrees or three stories high, one over the other so that they who lay in the upper and middle row of hammocks were obliged to go to bed first because they were to climb up to the higher by getting into the lower. Under the lower rank of hammocks by the wall sides were laid beds upon the floor in which the sick and such weak persons as could not get into the hammocks lay. And indeed, though the room was large and pretty airy, yet the breath and steam that came from so many bodies of different ages, conditions and constitutions packed up so close together was enough to cause sickness amongst us and [182] I believe did so. For there were many sick and some very weak, though we were not long there, yet in that time one of our fellow prisoners, who lay in one of those pallet beds, died.

This caused some bustle in the house. The body of the deceased, being laid out and put into a coffin, was carried down and set in the room called the lodge so that the coroner might inquire into the cause and manner of his death. The manner of their doing it is thus: as soon as the coroner has come, the turnkeys run out into the street under the gate and seize upon every man that passes by till they have got enough to make up the coroner's inquest. And so resolute these rude fellows are that if any man resists or disputes it with them they drag him in by main force, not regarding what condition he is of. Nay, I have been told they will not stick to stop a coach and pluck the men out of it.

It so happened that at this time they lighted on an ancient man, a grave citizen, who was trudging through the gate in great haste, and him they laid hold on, telling him he must come in and serve upon the coroner's inquest. He pleaded hard, begged, and besought them to let him go, assuring them he was going on very urgent business and that the stopping him would be greatly to his prejudice. But they were deaf to all entreaties and hurried him in, the poor man chafing without remedy.

When they had got their complement and were shut in together, the rest of them said to [183] this ancient man. "Come, father, you are the oldest man among us. You shall be our foreman." When the coroner had sworn them on the jury, the coffin was uncovered that they might look upon the body. But

219

the old man, disturbed in his mind, at the interruption they had given him, had grown somewhat fretful upon it. He said to them, "To what purpose do you show us a dead body here? You would not have us think, sure, that this man died in this room? How then shall we be able to judge how this man came by his death unless we see the place wherein he died and wherein he hath been kept prisoner before he died? How know we, but that the incommodiousness of this place wherein he was kept may have occasioned his death? Therefore, show us the place wherein this man died," said he.

This much displeased the keepers and they began to banter the old man, thinking to have beaten him off it. But, he stood up tightly to them. "Come, come," said he, "though you have made a fool of me in bringing me in hither, ye shall not find a child of me, now I am here. Mistake not yourselves. I understand my place and your duty and I require you to conduct me and my brethren to the place where this man died. Refuse it at your peril."

They now wished they had let the old man go about his business rather than by troubling him, have brought this trouble on themselves. But when they saw he persisted in his resolution and was peremptory, the coroner told them they must show him the place.

[184] It was in the evening when they began this work and by this time it had grown to be bedtime with us. We had taken down our hammocks (which in the day were hung up by the walls) and had made them ready to go into and were undressing ourselves in readiness to go into them. When on a sudden we heard a great noise of tongues and of tramplings of feet coming up towards us. And by and by one of the turnkeys, opening our door, said, "Hold, hold. Don't undress yourselves; here's the coroner's inquest coming to see you."

As soon as they had come to the door (for within the door there was scarce room for them to come), the foreman who led them, lifted up his hand and said, "Lord bless me, what a sight is here! I did not think there had been so much cruelty in the hearts of Englishmen to use Englishmen in this manner. We need not now question," said he to the rest of the jury, "how this man came by his death. We may rather wonder that they are not all dead; for this place is enough to breed an infection among them. Well," added he, "if it please God to lengthen my life till tomorrow, I will find means to let the King know how his subjects are dealt with," added he.

[191] These are some of the common evils which make the common side of Newgate, in measure, a type of hell on earth. But there was, at that time, something of another nature, more particular and accidental which was very offensive to me.

When we came first to Newgate, there lay (in a little by-place like a closet, near the room where we lodged) the quartered bodies of three men who had been executed some days before for a real or pretended plot which was the ground, or at least pretext, for that storm in the city which had caused this imprisonment. The names of these three men were Philips, Tongue and Gibs. The reason why their quarters lay so long was: the relations were all that while petitioning to have leave to bury them; which at length with much ado was obtained for the quarters, but not for the heads which were ordered to be set up in some parts of the city.

[192] Which as it had rendered my confinement there by much more ill ease, so it made our removal from there to Bridewell, even in that respect, the more welcome. Whither we go now.

For having (as I hinted before) made up our packs and taken our leave of our Friends whom we were to leave behind; we took up our bundles on our shoulders and walked, two and two abreast, Old Bailey into Fleet Street and so to old Bridewell. It being about the middle of the afternoon and the street pretty full of people, both the shopkeepers at their doors and passengers in the way, should stop us and ask us what we were and whither we were going. When we told them we were prisoners going from one prison to another (from Newgate to Bridewell). "What," they said, "without a keeper?" "No," said we, "for our word, which we have given, is our keeper." Some thereupon would advise us not to go to prison, but to go home. But we told them we could not do so; we could suffer for our testimony but could not fly from it. I do not remember we had any abuse offered us, but were generally pitied by the people.

[At this point Ellwood inserts the poem *Speculum Seculi* (cf. p. 437).]

[215] After we were come back from Newgate I had a desire to go thither again and to visit my friends who were prisoners there; more especially my dear friend (and father in Christ) Edward Burrough, who was then a prisoner with many Friends more in that part of Newgate which was then called Justice Hall. Whereupon the porter, coming in my way, I asked him to let me go out for an hour or two to see some friends of mine that evening. . . .

[216] Thereupon, away walked I to Newgate where having spent the evening among friends I returned in good time.

Under this easy restraint we lay till the court sat at the old Bailey again. Then, whether it was that the heat of the storm was somewhat abated or by what other means Providence wrought it, I know not, we were called to the bar and without further question, discharged. . . .

[220] But, alas, not many days (not to say weeks) had I been there ere we were almost overwhelmed with sorrow for the unexpected loss of Edward Burrough who was justly very dear to us all. [Ellwood was arrested at a funeral and spent some months in Aylesbury jail.]

[246] But now being released and returned home I soon made a visit to Milton [at Chalfont] to welcome him into the county.

After some common discourses had passed between us, he called for a manuscript of his which being brought, he delivered to me, bidding me take it home with me and read it at my leisure, and when I had done so return it to him with my judgement thereupon.

When I came home and had set myself to read it, I found it was that excellent poem which he entitled, *Paradise Lost.* After I had, with the best attention, read it through, I made him another visit and returned him his book with due acknowledgment of the favor he had done me in communicating it to me. He asked me how I liked it and what I thought of it which I modestly but freely told him and after some further discourse about it, I pleasantly said to him, "Thou hast said much here of paradise lost, but what of paradise found"? He made [247] me no answer but sat some time in a muse and broke off that discourse and fell upon another subject. After the sickness was over and the city well cleaned and had become safely habitable again, he returned thither. And when afterwards, I went to wait on him there (London), he showed me his second poem called, "Paradise Regained". In a pleasant tone he said to me, "This is owing to you, for you put it into my head by the question you put to me at Chalfont which before I had not thought of."

[253] Some time after was that memorable Meeting appointed to be held at London; through a divine opening, in the motion of life, in that eminent servant and prophet of God, [254] George Fox; for the restoring and bringing in again those who had gone out from Truth and the Holy Unity of Friends therein by the means and ministry of John Perrot.

This man came pretty early amongst Friends and early, too, took upon him the ministerial office; and being though little in person yet great in opinion of himself, nothing less would serve him than to go and convert the Pope. In order whereunto, he (having a better man than himself, John Luff to accompany him) travelled to Rome where they had not been long ere they were taken up and clapped into prison. Luff (as I remember) was put in the Inquisition and Perrot in their Bedlam or hospital for madmen. . . .

He was released and came back to England. And the report of his great sufferings there (far greater in report than in reality), joined with a singular show of sanctity . . . [255] made way for the more ready propagation of that peculiar error of his, of keeping on the hat in time of prayer as well public as private unless they had an immediate motion at that time to put it off. . . . I amongst the many who were caught in that snare. . . .

[256] But when that solemn Meeting was appointed at London for a travel in spirit on behalf of those who had thus gone out that they might rightly return and be sensibly received into the unity of the body again, my spirit rejoiced. . . .

Thus in the motion of life were the healing waters stirred and many through the virtuous power thereof restored to soundness and indeed not many lost. And though most of these who had returned were such as with myself had before renounced the error and forsaken the practice, yet did we sensibly find that forsaking without confessing (in case of public scandal) was not sufficient; but that an open acknowledgement (of open offenses) as well as forsaking them was necessary to the obtaining of complete remission.

[257] Not long after this, G.F. was moved of the Lord to travel through the countries, from county to county, to advise and encourage Friends to set up Monthly and Quarterly Meetings for the better ordering the affairs of the Church, in taking care of the poor, and exercising a true gospel-discipline for a due dealing with any that might walk disorderly under our name and to see that such as should marry among us did act fairly and clearly in that respect. [The next section concerns his marriage to Mary Ellis.] At length as I was sitting all alone, waiting upon the Lord for counsel and guidance in (in itself) to me so important an affair, I felt a word . . . which said, "Go and prevail." . . . which was a great surprise to her for she had been taken in an apprehension (as others also had done) that mine eye had been fixed . . . nearer home [on Gulielma, daughter of Mary Penington]. . . . [283] It soon became a stormy time. The clouds had been long gathering and threatened a tempest. The Parliament had sat some time before and hatched that unaccountable law which was called the [Second] Conventicle Act; if that may be allowed to be called a law by whomsoever made it, which was directly contrary to the fundamental laws of England, to common justice, equity and right reason as this manifestly was. . . .

By that act the informers, who swear for their own advantage as being thereby entitled to a third part of the fines, were many times concealed, driving on an underhand private trade. . . .

[284] This unlawful, unjust, unequal, unreasonable and unrighteous law took place in almost all places and was vigorously prosecuted against the Meetings of dissenters in general, though the brunt of the storm fell most sharply on the people called Quakers. Not that it seemed to be more particularly levelled at them but that they stood more fair, steady and open as a butt to receive all the [285] shot that came, while some others found means and freedom to retire to coverts for shelter.

No sooner had the bishops obtained this law for suppressing all other meetings but their own, but some of the clergy of most ranks and some others too who were over-much bigotted to that party, bestirred themselves with might and main. . . . Yet it took not alike in all places, but some were forwarder in the work than others, according as the agents intended to be chiefly employed therein, had been disposed thereunto. . . .

[310] Scarce was the beforementioned storm of outward persecution from the government blown over when Satan raised another storm of another kind against us on this occasion. The foregoing storm of persecution as it lasted

long so in many parts of the nation, and particularly at London, it fell very sharp and violent especially on the Quakers. For they having no refuge but God alone to fly unto, could not dodge and shift to avoid the suffering as others of other denominations could and in their worldly wisdom and policy did alter their meetings with respect to both place and time and forebearing to meet when forbidden or kept out of their meetinghouses. So that of the several sorts of dissenters, the Quakers only, held up a public testimony as a standard or ensign of religion by keeping the Meeting duly and fully at the accustomed times and places so long as they were suffered to enjoy the use of their meetinghouses. When they were shut up and Friends kept out of them by force, [311] they assembled in the streets as near to their meetinghouses as they could.

This bold and truly Christian behavior in the Quakers disturbed and not a little displeased the persecutors who, fretting, complained that the stubborn Quakers break their strength and bore off the blow from those other dissenters whom, as they most feared, so they principally aimed at. For indeed the Quakers they rather despised than feared as a people from whose both peaceable principles and practices they held themselves secure from danger, whereas having suffering severely and that lately too, by and under the other dissenters, they thought they had just cause to be apprehensive of danger from them and good reason to suppress them.

On the other hand, the more ingenious amongst other dissenters, of each denomination, sensible of the ease they enjoyed by our bold and steady suffering (which abated the heat of the persecutors and blunted the edge of the sword, before it came to them), frankly acknowledged the benefit received; calling us the bulwark that kept off the force of the stroke from them and praying that we might be preserved and enabled to break the strength of the enemy. Nor could some of them forbear, those especially who were called Baptists, to express their kind and favourable opinion of us, and of the principles we professed which emboldened us to go through that, which but to hear of was a terror to them. . . .

8. Isaac Penington's Pilgrimage and Letters of Counsel (1650 and 1681)

Isaac Penington may be called the most experienced mystic among early Friends. His wife Mary, widow of a sensitive Puritan colonel and country gentleman, Sir William Springett, was his intellectual and spiritual equal, though her own religious experiences, told in a manuscript for her granddaughter, were not printed until 1821.[58] She and Isaac had five children, besides their half-sister Gulielma Springett, who as a teen-ager won Ellwood's heart but married William Penn. Isaac Penington, however, was already a mystic before he married or became a Friend. Though, or perhaps because, his father and namesake was a Puritan alderman and in 1642-43 mayor of London, young Penington was already disillusioned with Puritan political hopes before the crisis years 1648-50 and had turned toward radical selflessness and inwardness. He began to publish little treatises, printed by Calvert and others, some on politics but mostly on inward rebirth and self-denial (none of these was included by Ellwood in Penington's *Works* in 1681). As we turn to the last of five that he wrote in the opening six months of 1650, we must ask how their ideas are related to his later Quakerism.

Penington's Puritanism, like early Quakerism, accepted the Puritan doctrine of man at its depth. The total surrender of self-will, he said in his earliest writing (*The Touchstone or Tryall of Faith*, 1648), is the only true redemption. This theme of the rebel will in man runs through until Penington's latest letters (cf. p. 240). In 1649 he re-applied a catch phrase used to justify the king's execution as he wrote on *The Great and Sole Troubler of the Times . . . or a Glimpse of the Heart of Man.* Yet he found in the Ranters, with their total surrender to what they took to be the Spirit within them and disregard for social approval or morality, the roots of a new spiritual openness. He disliked the Ranters' deeds and boasting but feared to put new human norms to judge them, in place of the old: "This I have felt, power enough to batter to confound me in everything, but no power to build anything or so much as to fix me in a state of confusion."[59] Evidently he had been through similar experiences of "broken-

---

[58] Cf. *Events in the Life of Mary Penington* (1910); no life of Penington seems to have been written since the *Memoirs of the Life of Isaac Penington* by Joseph Gurney Bevan (1830, but often reprinted) other than as part of Maria Webb's *Penns and Peningtons* (1867); L. V. Hodgkins, *Gulielma, Wife of William Penn* (1947); and articles such as Ruth L. Armsby's thesis "The Quaker View of the State, Its Nature, Powers and Limitations, with special reference to Isaac Penington" (Univ. of Birmingham, 1932) and Andrew Brink, "The Quietism of Isaac Penington" in *JFHS*, LI (1965-67), 30-53. Robert J. Leach's *Inward Journey of Isaac Penington* (Pendle Hill History Studies No. 6, 1943) consists of devotional excerpts from Penington's *Works* (1761 edition).

[59] *Severall Fresh Inward Openings* (1650), p. 29; quoted by Brink, p. 48.

ness" and wrestled with the seeming injustice of God. He had discovered in a special way, like Jung and Kierkegaard, the grace of God by which a man feels divinely led to dare to break taboos. In 1650, Penington's mysticism, like Eckhart's, was leading him to a God beyond good and evil. By 1653 he began to reaffirm that immorality was the leading of self, not of the Spirit; but as he came into contact and then into fellowship with Friends in London, Bedfordshire, and Buckinghamshire, he began to find a positive way beyond both self-will and openness. He had to find anew that the Spirit led to righteousness and spoke through a fellowship; he was turning back from full mysticism into full Quakerism. His earlier mysticism had been self-conscious but as light in touch as that of Erasmus; yet it spoke of much suffering.

Light or Darknesse, Displaying or Hiding itself, as it pleaseth, and from or to whom it pleaseth, Arraigning, Judging, Condemning, both the Shame and Glory of the Creature . . .
   and severall other Inward openings, Through Isaac Penington (Junior), Esq.
                Jer. 4:23-26
London, Printed by John Macock, 1650.

READER, Behold . . . and thou shalt see a strange sight: one who hath been deeply affected with Wisdom, true wisdom, heavenly wisdom, spiritual wisdom, inward wisdom, and vehemently pursuing it from the womb, . . . at length wholly stripped of all his riches in this kind. . . .

Never was I perfectly at enmity with anything but folly. It was not simply sin that I was at variance with, but the foolishness of sin. I knew well enough that God and the Creature had an hand in the same act, even in every act of sin; I could bear with it in God because he knew how to do it *wisely*; but I could not bear with it in the Creature, because it did it so foolishly. That which made God so lovely in my eye was chiefly his wisdom. . . .

[A-3] But now, I have been so tossed and tumbled, melted and new-molded, that I am changed into that which I thought it utterly impossible for me ever to be. I am at peace, if not in love, with folly. I begin to prefer folly at my very heart above wisdom. I am half persuaded that there is a more sweet, quiet and full enjoyment of one's self in a state of folly, than in a state of wisdom, besides its being a nearer, readier, and easier passage to somewhat else. I confess, I am not yet so far subdued and changed, as to be content to take up a state of folly to perpetuity, but only for a season to lie down in it, to obtain a little ease and respite, and to have the visage and remembrance of that wisdom perfectly blotted out, which did formerly so ravish and enchant

226

me. In this state of Folly, I find a new state of things springing up in me. . . . They are strangely formed in me. . . . [A-4] As for me, I have nothing to do with them, but to let them have their course in me, and through me, which I am now at length become very free into; indeed in the present state wherein I am, I am altogether unable to stop them in it. . . . I begin to yield up myself somewhat freely into the hands of this unknown potter, to mold me into what he himself has a mind. I am weary of, and much weaned from, my own will and desires, even those which were most pure, most spiritual, and now begin to lisp to this hidden Power which I know not, yet feel working in me. Thy will, thy unknown will, thy undesired will (by any but thyself) be done. . . . Let not me nor any else be what we would, but [A-5] what thy will pleaseth to have us; and fulfill thy whole will and counsel upon us, without giving us the least account of it, until thou pleasest. If thou wilt lead us into folly, sin, death, hell, anything, everything, do what thou wilt, carry us whither thou wilt. Let our will wholly die in us, that it may never avoid anything more, nor choose anything more in any kind, but as thy will chooseth for us.

Ye cannot but be offended at this kind of voice, O ye wise men, who know groundedly and from principles of light and wisdom, how to frame your desires and requests. . . . I have nothing to say to persuade or invite thee to cast thine eye, or bestow any pains on, or give any regard to that which follows. . . . This Light, this Darkness, (be it what it will) is of a deeper kind than thine is (this must be blotted out before this can be written) and thine eye cannot discern it. This is of a new stamp, of a new nature, of a new edition, and lies open only to the judgment of the new eye. . . .

[A-6] This is an angry age, and men can hardly bear anything though they are thoroughly crossed in it, for the less they can bear, the more is laid upon them; yet methinks the wise should be able to bear. . . . Therefore have no regard to me, but use thine own freedom in thinking, speaking, judging. It is only in regard to thyself that I [A-7] should advise thee to be sober and silent, concerning that which thou canst not yet reach; which counsel, if thou canst receive, it may be for thine ease and advantage, which when thou comest to feel what belongs to true torment and loss, thou wilt then know how to prize. . . .

[He then includes a sermon "To All Sorts of People," with its own preface:]

[3] I am made so weak, by continual different exercises upon my spirit, (which I find powerfully destroying and blotting out in me, whatever I have been, or have desired to be, and molding and forming me to somewhat else, which I neither expected nor desired . . .) that I am become altogether unable to resist it, otherwise it is likely at this time I should not have troubled thee.

One word more: there was a passage in [my] book, last set forth, which I hear hath administered offence to divers. The passage was about "pure sporting with sin," which they think cannot be. I will not say that I spake that upon a deeper ground, than man usually speaks upon; yet this I cannot but say, it is my interest, and I must stickle for it, though not with men, yet in my own spirit. Some questioned with me, whether I meant the act of sin? I confess my eye or thoughts was little upon the act, but upon the inward nature of it, which must not remain in perpetual enmity, but at last be owned as an excellent servant to him, by whom and for whom all things were made, out of whom they come, and into whom they return, according to his own will and guidance. And sin could never had done him that service that it has, if it had not had that nature that it has. And sin must have its due from the righteous judge, who will as well be glorified in being just unto sin, as in showing his wisdom and power in conquering it.

In a word: to the creature, in the present state of the creature, under the present law of the creature, according to the [4] judgment of the eye of the creature, everything is unlovely; and he that sees them not to be so, falls short of the perfection of the creaturely eye. But come deeper, beyond this state, beneath this law: look with a true eye, and there you shall find all this unloveliness pass away, and an excellency appear, that the creature could never so much as imagine or dream of. And now come back with this eye into the present state of all things, and behold them through the true glass, and you shall see them all new here also, and very far differing from what you did or could take them to be in your creaturely apprehension.

[The sermon itself is on the text Job 9:22: "He destroyeth the perfect and the wicked."]

[7] He that bringeth both the perfect and the wicked upon the stage may turn either of them off from the stage when he will. There is no more to hinder him from destroying the perfect than there is to hinder him from destroying the wicked. They are both equally his. They are both at his dispose. They are one and the same under several representations, and he has appointed them both to one and the same end, which is destruction. This I will stand to, overthrow if you can: "he destroyeth the perfect and the wicked."

"Perfect and wicked:" perfect are such as are upright under that administration under which they are set, who in their state and motions suit with the law of it. God has a law for every thing he brings forth in this state of weakness. He that suits with the law of his administration . . . is perfect; he who deviates wholly from it is wicked. Adam has his law of forbearing the forbidden fruit; the Jews theirs of circumcision, keeping the Passover, etc. Christians theirs likewise, of faith, love, spiritual obedience, spiritual worship, a sweet, meek, humble, heavenly conversation, etc. Now so far as each of these did answer their peculiar law, they came towards that perfection, towards that righteousness, which they were appointed to. . . .

[8] Now nothing doth so much discover his sovereignty as his falling upon the righteous, upon the perfect. Ye think to secure yourselves by his faithfulness, his Word, his promises, to which he must be faithful; and will ye not have him faithful to his sovereignty? He is Lord of all, and has the dispose of all, and let him make never so many deeds of gifts . . . still he has the power of life and death in his own hands. . . .

Reason 2: Because all dispensations are but for a season, they are not everlasting. Therefore eternity delights to swallow them up. Perfect and wicked are both of the same lump, only differently clothed to act their several parts, which when they have done, their [9] clothes must be taken off, and they turned back into the lump again. There is nothing durable but *the eternal state of things*. Now therefore hath God treasured up destructions for all dispensations, because it is suitable to all dispensations. It is as fit for the King to be stripped of his gorgeous apparel when the play is done, as the beggar of his rags. This is but a momentary righteousness or perfection, a momentary wickedness or imperfection, according to the law of the present dispensation. And the righteousness, the wickedness, the law of the dispensation, the dispensation itself, all must pass into the dust again. When they have lived out their transitory life, and acted their several parts, they must return to death. . . .

Besides, the righteous have a double advantage: one in their present life; another in their ensuing death.

In their present life, they both enjoy themselves and their God, in such a way as the wicked cannot, nor are in any wise capable of, [10] in their present state and practice of wickedness.

And in their ensuing death they have another advantage, it being a more immediate step to somewhat further than the death of the wicked can be: (I speak not of the shadow of death, but of that which is death indeed, the dying of the spirit in and to its present state).

Therefore there is no ground, why the righteous should be discouraged in pursuing righteousness, nor why the wicked should please himself in abounding in wickedness, though ground sufficient for both to bear of either, and to long after somewhat more perfect. . . . Nor are the wicked so much to be blamed as they think: (they have their parts to act, and they are fitted to their parts). This dispensation will have its end, and then you will find no such great difference between you and them as you thought there was. Destruction will make an end of their wickedness, yea and it will make an end of your righteousness also, and then ye will become both one lump of clay, without either good or evil. . . .

[11] We were all made by him who is the great potter or former of all things . . . till it hath quite confounded and brought us to a perfect loss in all our own hopes, desires, and apprehensions; yea, till at last it hath quite swallowed us up in itself: Where, when we are dead, buried, and cease to be, know, or desire any more, that Life may at length spring up in us, which till then we are incapable of any distinct desiring or possessing. And the passage to this, though it be very dreadful to the flesh, being even through the Gates of Hell, death and destruction, yet it is in no small measure joyful to the eye of that Spirit which discerns it to be but a passage, and a necessary passage too. And what brave royal heart would refuse to join issue with this request? O let all shadowy perfections, all perfections that come in and by administrations, die and pass away, be swallowed up by a death, by a destruction, more powerful than themselves; that so way may be made for the discovery of true and complete perfection, that it [12] may come forth to swallow up both destruction and all that it hath destroyed, for ever; and to bring forth itself and everything again in its primitive glory, that they may return to that beauty wherein they were, before they were stained by that vanity, misery and vexation whereunto all things are at present subjected.

In the depth of his mystical language is also a nihilism or love for death that shows a terrible weariness of soul. This is largely gone from his autobiographical statements after he joined Friends in 1656-58. Penington left no journal, but Ellwood printed several manuscript fragments as part of the testimony section of his collected works and noted others scattered through the works themselves. The most beloved of these, the most quoted of all Penington's writings, seems to include his mystical experience, yet stresses mainly its ethical inadequacy.

ISAAC PENINGTON'S
ACCOUNT OF HIS SPIRITUAL TRAVEL
from Thomas Ellwood's Testimony prefacing the 1681 edition
of Penington's *Works.*

To the world and the affairs of it he was very much a stranger, but deeply experienced in the things of God. For his affection being set on things above, his conversation was in heaven, and his life hid with Christ in God. He was but a pilgrim on the earth, and is now gone home. In his family, he . . . to his wife was a most affectionate husband, to his children, a loving and tender father, to his servants a mild and gentle master, to his friends a firm and fast

230

friend, to the poor compassionate and open-handed, and to all courteous and kind. Very zealous he was for the truth, unwearied in promoting it, bold and undaunted in the defense of it, faithful in his testimony to it, patient and cheerful in his suffering for it. A right good and pious man indeed was he, one that truly feared God and warily eschewed evil. . . .

The account he gives of his spiritual travel is as follows:

A true and faithful relation (in brief) concerning myself, in reference to my spiritual travels, and the Lord's dealings with me. I say true and faithful, because it is of the Truth, and not given forth in my own will, but in the Lord's will, and requirings of me at this time, for his service. The relation is as follows:

I have been a man of sorrow and affliction from my childhood, feeling the want of the Lord and mourning after him, separated by him from the love, nature and spirit of this world, and turned in spirit towards him, almost ever since I could remember.

In this sense of my lost estate, I sought after the Lord, I read scriptures, I watched over mine own heart, I cried unto the Lord for what I felt the want of, I blessed His Name in what he mercifully did for me, and bestowed on me, etc. Whatever I read in the scriptures, as the way of God to my understanding, I gave myself to the faithful practice of, being contented to meet with all the reproach, opposition and several kinds of sufferings, which [4th p.] it pleased the Lord to measure out to me therein. And I cannot but say, that the Lord was good unto me, did visit me, did help me, did teach me, did testify his acceptance of me many times, to the refreshing and joy of my heart before Him.

But my soul was not satisfied with what I met with, nor indeed could be, there being further quickenings and pressings in my spirit, after a more full, certain and satisfactory knowledge; even after the sense, sight and enjoyment of God, as was testified in the scriptures to have been felt and enjoyed in the former times. For I saw plainly, that there was a stop of the streams, and a great falling short of the power, life and glory which they partook of. We had not so the spirit, nor were so in the faith, nor did so walk and live in God, as they did. They were come to Mount Sion and the heavenly Jerusalem, etc. which we had hardly so much as the literal knowledge or apprehension what they were. So that I saw the whole course of religion among us, was (for the most part) but a talk to what that they felt, enjoyed, possessed and lived in.

This sense made me sick at heart indeed, and set me upon deep crying to God, close searching the scriptures, and waiting on God, that I might receive the pure sense and understanding of them, from and in the Light, and by the help of his Spirit. (And what the Lord did bestow on me in that state, with thankfulness I remember before him at this very day. For he was then my

231

God, and a pitier and a watcher over me; though he had not pleased then to direct me, how to stay my mind upon him and abide with him.) And then I was led (indeed I was led, I did not run of myself) into a way of separation from the worship of the world, into a gathered society. For this both the scripture and the spirit of God in me gave testimony unto; and what we then met with, and what leadings and help we then felt, there is a remembrance and testimony in my heart to this day. But there was somewhat wanting, and we mistook our way. For whereas we should have pressed forward into the spirit and power, we ran too much outward into letter and form. And though the Lord in many things helped us, yet therein he was against us, and brought darkness, confusion and scattering upon us. I was surely broken and darkened, and in this darkened state, sometimes lay still for a long season, secretly mourning and crying out to the Lord night and day; sometimes I ran about, hearkening after what might appear or break forth in others, but never met with anything, whereto there was the least answer in my heart, save in one people, who had a touch of truth. But I never expressed so much to any of them, nor indeed felt them at all able to reach my condition.

At last, after all my distresses, wanderings and sore travels, I met with some writings of this people called *Quakers*, which I cast a slight eye upon and disdained, as falling very short of that wisdom, light, life, and power, which I had been longing for and searching after. I had likewise (some pretty distance of time after this) opportunity of meeting with some of them, and divers of them were by the Lord moved (I know it to be so since) to come to me. As I remember, at the very first they reached to the life of God in me, which life answered their voice, and caused a great love in me to spring to them. But still in my reasonings with them, and disputes alone (in my mind) concerning them, I was very far off from owning them, as so knowing the Lord, or so appearing in his life and power as my condition needed, [5th p.] and as my soul waited for. Yea, the more I conversed with them, the more I seemed in my understanding and reason to get over them, and to trample them under my feet, as a poor, weak, silly, contemptible generation, who had some smatterings of truth in them, and some honest desires towards God, but very far off from the clear and full understanding of his way and will. And this was the effect almost of every discourse with them. They still reached my heart, and I felt them in the secrets of my soul, which caused the love in me always to continue, yea sometimes to increase towards them. But daily my understanding got more and more over them, and therein I daily more and more despised them.

After a long time I was invited to hear one of them (as I had been often, they in tender love pitying me, and feeling my want of that, which they possessed) and there was an answer in my heart, and I went in fear and trembling, with desires to the most High, who was over all and knew all, that

232

I might not receive anything for truth, which was not of him, nor withstand anything which was of him, but might bow before the appearance of the Lord my God, and none other. And indeed, when I came, I felt the presence and power of the most High among them, and words of truth, from the spirit of truth, reaching to my heart and conscience, opening my state as in the presence of the Lord. Yea I did not only feel words and demonstrations from without, but I felt the dead quickened, the seed raised, insomuch as my heart (in the certainty of light and clearness of true sense) said, "This is he, this is he, there is no other; this is he whom I have waited for and sought after from my childhood, who was always near me, and had often begotten life in my heart, but I knew him not distinctly, nor how to receive him or dwell with him." And then in this sense (in the melting and breakings of my spirit) was I given up to the Lord, to become his, both in waiting for the further revealing of his seed in me, and to serve him in the life and power of his seed.

Now what I met with after this, in my travels [=travails], in my waiting, in my spiritual exercises, is not to be uttered; only in general I may say this, I met with the very strength of hell. The cruel oppressor roared upon me, and made me feel the bitterness of his captivity, while he had any power. Yea the Lord was far from my help, and from the voice of my roaring. I also met with deep subtleties and devices to entangle me in that wisdom, which seems able to make wise in the things of God, but indeed is foolishness and a snare to the soul, bringing it back into captivity, where the Enemy's gins prevail. And what I met with outwardly from my own dear father, from my kindred, from my servants, from the people and powers of the world, for no other cause but fearing my God, worshipping him as he has required of me, and bowing to his Seed (which is his Son) who is to be worshipped by men and angels for evermore, the Lord my God knows, before whom my heart and ways are; who preserved me in love to them, in the midst of all I suffered from them, and does still so preserve me, blessed be his pure and holy Name.

But some may desire to know, what I have at last met with. I answer, I have met with the Seed. Understand that word, and thou will be satisfied, and enquire no further. I have met with my God, I have met with my Saviour; and he has not been present with me without his salvation, but I have felt the healings drop upon my soul from under his wings. I have met with the true knowledge, the knowledge of life, the living knowledge, the knowledge [6th p.] which is life, and this has had the true virtue in it, which my soul has rejoiced in, in the presence of the Lord. I have met with the Seed's father and in the Seed I have felt him my father. There I have read his nature, his love, his compassions, his tenderness, which have melted, overcome and changed my heart before him. I have met with the Seed's faith, which has done and does that, which the faith of man can never do. I have met with the true birth, with the birth which is heir of the kingdom, and inherits the kingdom. I

233

have met with the true spirit of prayer and supplication, wherein the Lord is prevailed with, and which draws from him whatever the condition needs, the soul always looking up to him in the will, and in the time and way which is acceptable with him. What shall I say? I have met with the true peace, the true righteousness, the true holiness, the true rest of the soul, the everlasting habitation, which the redeemed dwell in. And I know all these to be true, in him that is true, and am capable of no doubt, dispute or reasoning in my mind about them; it abiding there, where it has received the full assurance and satisfaction. And also I know very well and distinctly in spirit, where the doubts and disputes are, and where the certainty and full assurance is, and in the tender mercy of the Lord am preserved out of the one, and in the other.

Now (the Lord knows) these things I do not utter in a boasting way, but would rather be speaking of my nothingness, my emptiness, my weakness, my manifold infirmities, which I feel more than ever. The Lord has broken the man's part in me, and I am a worm and no man before him. I have no strength to do any good or service for him, nay I cannot watch over or preserve myself. I feel daily that I keep not alive my own soul, but am weaker before men, yea weaker in my spirit (as in myself) than ever I have been. But I cannot but utter to the praise of my God, that I feel his arm stretched out for me; and my weakness (which I feel in myself) is not my loss, but advantage before him. And these things I write, as having no end at all therein of my own, but felt it this morning required of me, and so in submission and subjection to my God, have I given up to do it, leaving the success and service of it with him.

Aylesbury, 15th of 3rd month, 1667.
I.P.

Penington's Letters

In his secluded life at Chalfont, interspersed with five imprisonments, mainly at Aylesbury jail, Penington saw his vocation within the Quaker movement to be as a writer. He presented mainly theological expositions and rebuttals, and many of these works are clear and at times moving. The collections of his works, first (1681) in folio, have been reprinted in two- and four-volume editions in England and America (London, 1761, 1784; Sherwood, N. Y., 1861-63). Yet their sober, heavy tone makes them unsought today. By contrast his personal letters to those in spiritual crisis have become his best-loved writings. John Kendall found a collection of these at Colchester, which he printed in 1796; and after these reached London John Barclay added many others, which were then included in his "Select Series" volume of Penington's writings (1837) and the 1862-63 edition of the *Works*. The follow-ing selection, drawing on both these editions, shows Penington, out of a background richer and more complex, guiding anew Friends who must go through the same process of self-knowledge and struggle that has been traced in Hubberthorne and other Friends; so that our cycle is complete.

[John Kendall, 1796 edition, p. 16] To a couple that were upon marrying.

Dear Friends,

It is a great and weighty thing that ye are about, and ye have need of the Lord's leading and counsel therein, that it may be done in the unity of his life, that so Friends in truth may feel it to be of God and find satisfaction therein.

Friends, the affectionate part will be forward in things of this nature, unless it be yoked down: and it will persuade the mind to judge such things to be right and of the Lord when indeed they are not so. Now if it be not of the Lord, but the affectionate part, friends cannot have unity with it, nor will it prove a blessing to you; but you will find it an hurt to your conditions and a load upon your spirits afterwards, and the fruits and effects of it will not be good but evil and then, perhaps, ye will wish that ye had waited more singly and earnestly upon the Lord, in relation to the thing, and that ye had taken more time and consulted more with friends, before there had been any engagements and affections. The Lord by his providence hath given you a little time of respite. O retire unto him and abase yourselves before him, and pray to him to counsel you, by his good spirit, for your good, that if it be not of the Lord, the power (waited upon by you) may loosen your affections in this respect. But if it be of the Lord, and be orderly brought before Friends, and their counsel and advice sought in the fear of the Lord, they will have unity with it and with gladness express their unity, which may be a strength unto you against the tempter afterwards.

This is in true love to you and in singleness of heart, the Lord knoweth.

From your friend in the truth,

I.P.

4th of 3rd Month, 1668

[John Kendall, 1796 edition, pp. 25-29]

Dear Friend,

Since I last saw thee, there have been many deep and serious thoughts on my heart concerning thee, and a sense of thy state as before the Lord, and

235

breathings of heart for thee. I am sensible that the Spirit of the Lord is striving with thee, and in some measure opening thy heart towards him and his Truth; and I am sensible withal that there is much striving against him and many strongholds of wisdom and reasonings in thee which must be broken down before Truth can spring up in thy heart and exercise its power in thee and have full command in thee.

Now this morning when I awakened, there were three things sprang up in me, which my heart did singly and earnestly desire for thee. One was that thou mightest be led by God's holy Spirit into the new and living covenant, where Christ is revealed and the soul united to him as its Lord and King in a bond of indissoluble union. Another was that thou mightest daily be taught of God and learn of him in this holy, new, pure, and everlasting covenant. The third was that thou mightest be true and faithful to God, to obey and follow him, in whatever he teaches and requires of thee.

If thou wert but in this state, thou wouldest find sweetness and rest, peace and power, and the righteousness of our Lord Jesus Christ, and life eternal, revealed in thy own heart; and with joy draw water out of the wells of salvation.

Now if thou come to witness Christ's appearance in spirit, and wilt become a disciple unto him, there are three things thou must apply thy heart to learn of him, which indeed are the sum of the gospel, or of what is taught in and by the gospel. The first is to fear God: this is the beginning of the true heavenly wisdom, and this is the perfection and the end of wisdom also; for the true wisdom not only brings into the fear, but it builds up in the fear. . . . [three sentences on the fear of God]

[26] The second is (which depends upon and flows from the former) to give glory to God, in discerning his life and power and the virtue of his Spirit and his grace, working all in thee, and so still ascribing the glory to him of all thou art, dost or canst do. . . . And they that are here feel their own poverty and nothingness, as in themselves; and that their way to become strong in Christ is first to become weak in themselves; and so when they are strong in him, he who is their strength is glorified and admired, and self is of no reputation or value forever and ever; for that is cleaved to which brought self down; and that power and spirit being cleaved to, it still keeps it down.

The third is that thou learn to worship God in spirit and truth. Oh, this worship is precious indeed; and this is the only sort of worship which God seeketh and regardeth among the many various kinds of worshippers which appear at this day. This worship was declared by Christ and taught his disciples, but it has been in great measure departed from; and though many have sought after it, yet none could ever find it. . . . [dangers in false worship]

[27] Now that thou mayest come into this state and learn all these lessons

of the Lord in the new covenant, there is one thing indispensably necessary for thee, which is to know the hour of God's judgment in thy own heart, and to lie under the judgment of the Lord, bearing it till he finish it and bring it forth unto victory. For this is the way whereby he purges and redeems the soul, to wit, by the spirit of judgment and burning. Thou must therefore wait for and come to feel the spirit of the Lord near thee, discovering sin to thee and revealing judgment against it and executing his righteous judgment upon the evil nature in thee, that he may raise up that good and tender plant of righteousness (out of the dry and barren ground), which his mercy is to.

Friend, mind the words which now spring in my heart to thee (for now my heart is open to thee in the true love and pure sense which is of God), which are these. If thou come to know God's Spirit and to receive it and to feel it work in thee and its pure light shine from the fountain and spring of life, thou wilt have a quicker sense and discerning therefrom, than can arise either from words written, or from thoughts; that is, the Lord will show thee the way whereof thou doubtest, quicker than a thought can arise in thee; and the Lord will show thee evil in a pure sense of the new nature, quicker than thou canst think or consider of anything. And indeed this is needful, for sin lodges in the evil nature inwardly and works not so much by a known law set up in the mind, as by a secret nature; and if [28] it be not resisted and withstood by another nature, it can never be overcome. . . . [the inner judgment]

Perhaps these words at present may be hard unto thee; but if thou come to wait on God's holy Spirit and to the feeling of his appearance in thy heart and learn of him to know what is good and what is evil in thy words, ways, worship, yea, and in thy very heart and thoughts, and also choose the good and refuse the evil; they will grow easier and easier and plainer and plainer daily, as thou comest into the sense and experience of the things which they mention; and thou wilt find Christ inwardly revealed in spirit. . . . [and as inner Word]

The Lord so guide thee, manifest himself to thee, help thee, and lead thee by his holy spirit and power, as that thou mayest come undeniably to experience and to be satisfied by him about these things. And mind not so much to know, as to be obedient and subjected to the Lord (both in thy heart and in thy conversation also) in the least things that he makes manifest. If the Lord would show thee but this one thing, that to use Thee and Thou to a particular person is proper language [29] and scripture language, and that to say You is improper and arose from pride and nourisheth pride, and so is of the world and not of the Father; and so bow thy spirit to him in this one thing, thou little thinkest what a work it would make within thee, and how strongly the spirit of darkness would fight against thy subjections thereto. . . . [The Lord lead thee.]

This is from one who wandered long in the vast, howling wilderness, wayless from the Shepherd and Bishop of the soul, and was sorely afflicted, tossed with tempests, and not comforted; but at length it pleased the Lord in tender mercy to visit me, and by his own outstretched arm, to gather me into his own fold; where I have met with the holy mount of God and his city, the heavenly Jerusalem and the spirits of the just men and God, the judge of all that ever ariseth or can arise in the heart and Christ, the mediator, and the new covenant, wherein and whereby he mediates. . . . [said not to boast, but to help]

[30] The Lord give thee the sense and favour of these things, that thou mayest thereby be kindled to wait on the Lord, to be led into light of the living, that thou mayest live and walk with him therein, who is, and dwells, and walks with his, in the light. O, house of Jacob, come ye, let us walk in the light of the Lord, and let us come up to Sion, the holy hill of God, and to the gospel Jerusalem, that there he may teach us of his ways, and we may there learn of him to walk [31] in his paths; for there is the place of wisdom and true understanding, which none know but those that are taught of God.

This is in true friendship and tender love to thy soul,
from its friend in truth and sincerity.
26th of 8th month, 1670   I.P.

[John Barclay, 1828 edition, as Letter XLVII, pp. 157-59; *Works*, 1861 edition, III, 552-53] To Abraham Grimsden.

Friend,

Thou hast made some profession of truth, and at times come amongst us; but whether thou hast been changed thereby and been faithful to the Lord in what has been made manifest to thee, belongs unto thee diligently to inquire. There is no safe dallying with truth. He that puts his hand to the plow must not look back at anything of this world, but take up the cross and follow Christ in the single-hearted obedience, hating father, mother, goods, land, wife, yea, all for his sake; or he is not worthy of him. The good hand of the Lord is with his people, and he blesseth them both inwardly and outwardly; and they that seek the kingdom of heaven and the righteousness thereof, in the first place, have other things also added; but they that neglect the kingdom and are unfaithful to truth, seeking the world before it, the hand of the Lord goes forth against them, and they many times miss of that also of the world, which they seek and labor for.

[158] Truth is honorable. Oh take heed of bringing a reproach upon it by pretending to it and yet not being of it, in the pure sense and obedience, which it begets and brings forth in the hearts and lives of the faithful. But if any be careless and unfaithful to what they are convinced of, and so, for the

238

present, bring a reproach upon God's truth, which is altogether innocent thereof, the Lord, in his due time, will wipe off that reproach from his truth and people; but the sorrow and burden will light upon themselves, which will be very bitter and heavy to them in the day that the Lord shall visit them with his righteous judgments.

Oh, consider rightly and truly. It had been better for thee, thou hadst never known truth, nor been directed to the principle and path of righteousness, than, after direction thereto, to turn from the holy commandments and deny obedience to the righteous One. The Lord give thee true sense and repentance, if it be his holy pleasure, and raise thee out of this world's spirit, to live to him in his own pure Spirit. It is easy to profess and make a show of truth, but hard to come into it. It is very hard to the earthly mind to part with that which must be parted with for it, before the soul can come to possess and enjoy it. Profession of truth, without the life and power, is but a slippery [159] place, which men can easily slide from; nay, indeed, if men be not in the life and power, they can hardly be kept from that which will stain their profession. The Lord, who searcheth the heart, knows how it is with thee. Oh, consider thy ways, and fear before him, and take heed of taking his name in vain, for he will not hold such guiltless:

I am in this, faithful and friendly to thy soul, desiring its eternal welfare, and that it may not forever perish from the presence and power of the Lord.

I.P.

[John Barclay edition, pp. 172-173; also *Works*, 1861 edition (N. Y.) and 1863 edition (Philadelphia)]

O Dear Friend:

The eternal love of my father is to thee, and because he loves thee and would entirely enjoy thee, therefore doth he so grievously batter and break down that which stands in the way. What he is doing towards thee, thou canst not know now, but thou shalt know hereafter. Only be still and wait for the springing up of hope in the seasons the Father sees necessary, that thou mayst not faint under his hand, but be supported by his secret power until his work is finished. The great thing necessary for thee at present to know is the drawings of his Spirit, that thou mayst not ignorantly withstand or neglect them, and protract the day of thy redemption.

Oh! look not after great things; small breathings, small desires, after the Lord, if true and pure, are sweet beginnings of life. Take heed of despising "the day of small things," by looking after some great visitation, proportionable to thy distress, according to thy eye. Nay, thou must become a child, thou must lose thy [173] own will quite by degrees. Thou must wait for life to be measured out by the Father and be content with what proportion, and at what time, he shall please to measure.

Oh! be little, be little; and then thou wilt be content with little. And if thou feel now and then a check or a secret smiting—in *that* is the Father's love; be not over-wise or over-eager in thy own willing, running, and desiring, and thou mayst feel it so and by degrees come to the knowledge of thy Guide, who will lead thee, step by step, in the path of life and teach thee to follow and in his own season, powerfully judge that which cannot or will not follow. Be still, and wait for light and strength and desire not to know or comprehend, but to be known and comprehended in the love and life which seeks out, gathers, and preserves the lost sheep.

I remain thy dear friend and a well-wisher to thy soul, in the love of my Father.

I.P.

[John Barclay, 1828 edition, pp. 229-30; also in *Works*, 1861 edition, III, 530] To Sarah Elgar.

The child which the Lord hath taken from thee was his own. He hath done thee no wrong, in calling it from thee. Take heed of murmuring, take heed of discontent, take heed of any grief, but what truth allows thee. Thou hast yet one child left. The Lord may call for that too, if he please; or he may continue and bless it to thee. Oh, mind a right frame of spirit towards the Lord in this thy great affliction! If thou mind God's truth in thy heart and wait to feel the seasoning thereof, that will bring thee into and preserve thee in a right frame of spirit. The Lord will not condemn thy love and tenderness to thy child or thy tender remembrance of him; but still, in it be subject to the Lord and let his will and disposal be bowed unto by thee, and not the will of thy nature set above it. Retire out of the natural, into the spiritual, where thou mayest feel [230] the Lord thy portion; so that now, in the needful time, thou mayest day by day receive and enjoy satisfaction therein. Oh, wait to feel the Lord making thy heart what he would have it to be in this thy deep and sore affliction!

I.P.

Nunnington, Sixth Month, 1679

Now let the world see how thou prizest Truth, and what Truth can do for thee. Feed on it; do not feed on thy affliction; and the life of Truth will arise in thee, and raise thee up over it, to the honour of the name of the Lord, and to the comfort of thy own soul.

[John Barclay, 1828 edition, pp. 290-92, Letter LXXXVI] To Richard Roberts.

R.R.

Thou didst acquaint me, that Timothy Fly, the Anabaptist teacher, did charge me with denying Christ's humanity, and also the blood of Christ, which was shed at Golgotha, [291] without the gates of Jerusalem, and that I own no other Christ but what is within men.

Sure I am, that neither T. Fly, nor any other man did ever hear me deny, that Christ, according to the flesh, was born of the Virgin Mary, or that that was his blood which was shed without the gates of Jerusalem. And the Lord, who knoweth my heart, knoweth that such a thing never was in my heart; nay, I do greatly value that flesh and blood of our Lord Jesus Christ and witness forgiveness of sins and redemption through it. Yet, if I should say I do not know nor partake of his flesh and blood in the mystery also, I should not be a faithful witness for the Lord. For, there is the soul's food which gives life to the soul, even the living bread and the living water. For, there is living bread and living water; and the flesh and blood in the mystery, on which the soul feeds, is not inferior in nature and virtue to the bread and water. There is a knowing Christ after the flesh, and there is a knowing him after the Spirit, and a feeding on his Spirit and life; and this doth not destroy his appearing in flesh or the blessed ends thereof, but confirm and fulfill them.

The owning of Christ being inwardly in his saints, doth not deny his appearing outwardly [292] in the body prepared; unless T.F. can maintain this, that the same Christ that appeared outwardly cannot appear inwardly. "Know ye not your own selves, how that Jesus Christ is in you, except ye be reprobates?" 2. Cor. xiii.5. "And if Christ be in you, the body is dead because of sin, etc." Rom. viii.10. "Christ in you, the hope of glory." Col. i.27. "Behold, I stand at the door and knock; if any man hear my voice and open the door, I will come in to him." Rev. iii.20. "I will come again," saith Christ; "ye are now in pain, as a woman in travail, full of sorrow for the loss of my outward bodily presence; but I will come to you again in Spirit," John, xvi. and he that "dwelleth with you, shall be in you," John xiv.17. And then when the Bridegroom is inwardly and spiritually in you and with you, "your heart shall rejoice, and your joy no man taketh from you." John, xvi.22. And so, the apostles and primitive Christians did "rejoice, with joy unspeakable, and full of glory," I Peter, i.8, because of the spiritual appearance and presence of the Bridegroom. And yet there is no other bridegroom, who now appears in Spirit, or spiritually in the hearts of his, than he that once appeared in the prepared body, and did his Father's will therein.

I.P.

241

PART C:

Truth Defended

Introduction

At his examination for blasphemy in 1652, James Nayler declared, "If I cannot witness Christ nearer than Jerusalem, I shall have no benefits by him; but I own no other Christ but that who witnessed a good confession before Pontius Pilate; which Christ I witness in me now."[1]

Nayler's statement illustrates a central theme in Quaker theology: the unity of subjective and objective Christian experience. In numerous theological pamphlets the Quakers stated the theme as it related to the person and work of Christ, revelation, and holiness. For the Friends the world was metaphysically and historically Christ-centered. Although Geoffrey Nuttall thinks the Quakers lacked "a sense of the Christian watershed in history,"[2] it would appear more accurate to acknowledge their heightened awareness of Christ presently leading his church. Naive as their indictment of other and past forms of Christendom may have been, they were certainly not gnostic. They believed Christ had come to teach his people himself, as George Fox said. To the early Friends such a statement would not admit to qualitative equivalences. It stated their belief about who was doing what in the world process. To their critics who deprecated the historicity of Christ, the Quakers reiterated their conviction that Jesus Christ of Nazareth was the Light whom they proclaimed.

[1] Cf. p. 261.

[2] *The Holy Spirit in Puritan Faith and Experience* (Oxford: Basil Blackwell, 1946), p. 159.

Because of the immediacy of Christ's presence as Light to judge and lead, and of the Spirit as power, Friends' witness to their faith was more often spoken than written, and as we have seen, proclaimed rather than analyzed. Clear theological statements came first as replies to challenges, either at trials (cf. p. 260), or, as verbal debate was continued, in tracts (cf. p. 263). Intellectually, the Puritan pastors were often well aware where the issues lay, but Friends like Nayler and Penington were equally alert and able to show the basic consistency of Quaker preaching and practice with scripture and Christian orthodoxy, as well as to refute specific false charges.

In setting their position clearly, several early Friends felt led to summarize Quaker theological teachings, not as new, but as differing from accepted practice, for instance regarding sacraments. A paper by Edward Burrough, *A Declaration to All the World of Our Faith* (1658), is a sample of a large body of such doctrinal writings by early Friends. Francis Howgill's *Invisible Things of God* (1659) and *The Glory of the True Church Discovered* (1662, see esp. ch. II on "The Entering in of the Apostacy"); James Nayler's *Love to the Lost* (1656) and *Milk for Babes* (1661); and many of Penington's longer tracts, such as *The Way of Life and Death* (1658) and *The Scattered Sheep Sought* (1659), belong to this form. In addition to clarifying and defending Quaker teachings, a strong witness to personal experience is present and seems to grow within these tracts, reaching a climax in Penington's *Naked Truth* (1674) and Robert Barclay's *Apology* (1678). Barclay also tried to summarize the Quaker message in its doctrinal essentials in his *Theses Theologicae* and in its rootage in scripture in his *Catechism.*

Fox wrote doctrinal tracts and debates at all stages of his work, and his longest work, *The Great Mistery* (1659), is a compendium of replies to Puritan theological challengers. A compact statement testifying to Quaker orthodoxy, George Fox's *Letter to the Governor of Barbados,* is one of the best-known epistles, for it was carried within the Books of Discipline of the Quaker Yearly Meetings, especially during the nineteenth century. The doctrinal writings of George Fox were gathered together in 1706 under the title *Gospel Truth Demonstrated, in a Collection of Doctrinal Books, Given Forth by that Faithful Minister of Jesus Christ, George Fox, Containing Principles Essential to Christianity and Salvation, Held among the People Called Quakers.* It forms three volumes of the collected works (1831). Although these writings

246

lacked the organization found in Robert Barclay's more widely used *Apology*, they convey the same basic Christian doctrines.

Quakers did not put any theological proposition ahead of the noetic experience of which they spoke; but it is unfair to presume that public relations or desire for conventionality on the part of these Quakers shaped their use of religious language. It might be said that Friends somewhat impatiently restated the essentials of the Christian flame that fired up England in their day of spiritual visitation.

The Quaker view of revelation is bolder than that of most other seventeenth-century Puritans, as Nuttall has so ably documented. Does the Holy Spirit speak apart from the scriptures? Or is he only the illuminer of its truth? These issues had been argued ever since John Calvin, and the Quaker theologians and their Puritan opponents continued the debate. Indeed, the issue has become a kind of classic Quaker-Baptist controversy.[3] At times it seems the debate between the Quakers and Richard Baxter only sharpened pens for polemic. But the debate did force the Quakers to determine the line between certainty and conceit. After all the smoke of verbal battle had settled, the basic issue is that stated by Robert Barclay, who declared, "When the matter is sifted to the bottom it resolves in tradition or revelation."[4]

The Quakers understood revelation as the source from which the scriptures truly came in testimony about the works of God. In this sense scripture is tradition at its truest level. But they were confident that the one who inspired the scriptures could teach and apply scriptural truths immediately to the individual. They believed the Holy Spirit enabled men to drink at that stream from which biblical truth flowed.

In 1650 George Fox was imprisoned at the Derby House of Correction for six months for saying he was sanctified. He and others were charged with blasphemy and accused of claiming to be "upright as Christ." These early Quakers cited scriptures that called them to be saints, and witnessed to their generation that the scriptures had been fulfilled in their lives. For them the call to holiness was not some deliberate overstatement aimed at nudging

[3] A truce appears in the contemporary writings of Bernard Ramm, a Baptist theologian. See his *Special Revelation and the Word of God* (Grand Rapids: Eerdmans, 1961).

[4] Robert Barclay, *Concerning the Possibility and Necessity of Immediate Inward Revelation* (2nd edn., 1703), "Advertisement to the Reader."

reluctant disciples, nor an interim ethic in which man could live situationally as he waited for tomorrow's millennial kingdom. The Quakers claimed Paul's call for victory over that "body of sin."

George Fox wrote, "Justification and sanctification are one, not two things really distinct in their nature, but really one; for Christ 'is he that sanctifies and justifies' " (*Works*, 1831, III, 487). Elsewhere Fox wrote that it cost Christ "his blood to purchase man out of this state he is in, in the fall, and bring him up to the state man was in before he fell."[5] Robert Newton Flew[6] writes that the "chief distinction of the Quaker doctrine of perfection was that its centre was in the Cross of Christ."

Theologically, the Protestant movement had "protested" cheap sanctification whereby the counsels of perfection were relegated to the monastic few whose concrete vows of poverty, chastity, and obedience gave public deference to gospel discipline while salving the private consciences of the many whose sin accounts were handled by the sacerdotal enterprise system.

In protesting the abuse of sanctification, Protestants had reacted to the opposite, antinomian extreme, against such "works righteousness." At least, so thought the Quakers who protested what Bonhoeffer in our century labeled "cheap grace." These fiery preachers within the seventeenth-century Camp of the Lord accused the Puritans of "pleading for sin" or "preaching up sin to the grave." They spotted hypocrisy in a purely forensic view of the atonement wherein the sinner used Christ as tax-shelter to avoid the need for meeting divine demands. Of the Ranters, William Penn observed wryly, "but that they might sin more freely, at his cost."[7]

To Friends, the Roman provision of purgatory and the neo-Calvinist provision of moment-of-death cleansing from carnality appeared equally unworthy of the efficacious character of Christ's atoning death. The doctrinal writings reflect the Quaker restatement of sanctification (by which the atonement brought actual righteousness in men), just as their journals describe the inward struggles for and joyous affirmation of the purging baptism with the Holy Spirit through which they became indeed new creatures

5 *Works*, V, 270-71; cf. VI, 436ff.

6 *The Idea of Perfection in Christian Theology* (London: Oxford Univ. Press, 1934), p. 291.

7 George Fox, *Journal* (Philadelphia, 1838), I, viii.

in Christ and witnessed his righteousness fulfilled in their daily lives. For the early Quakers Christ's death and resurrection make life in the kingdom possible now. In their age of throbbing hope neither psychological explanation nor cultural fatigue provided rationalization for sins. And if their exuberance bordered on spiritual pride at times, such was the price they paid for emphasizing a neglected aspect of the Christian faith. At its best the Quaker experience focused on Christ becoming the center of human personality; at its worst it exhibited a self-righteous legalism without the saving grace of public confession.

There is pathos in Baxter's plea to a young man drawn to Quakerism, "Your teacher has spent twenty, if not a hundred hours, in such meditations where you have spent one."[8] The Quakers did not measure baptism of the Holy Spirit by the hourglass, however, any more than they did the length of sermons.

Following the Civil War in the United States during the late nineteenth century, Methodist revivalism helped to awaken Quakers from quietistic complacency and stamped a portion of the movement with Methodist theological formulae and procedures. In the eighteenth century the influence had been the other way, as Dean Freiday points out.[9] There are important differences between Quaker and Methodist formulations of the doctrine of perfection. These differences arise because Wesley started from the Calvinist presumption of the personal infusion of holiness at the moment of death, working backward from that point to suggest a kind of earlier sainthood. The Quakers assumed that the Pentecostal experiences of spirit-baptism as found in the Book of Acts with its emphasis on both power and purity constitute the norm for salvation.[10]

In the seventeenth-century struggle over how Truth could be known and have authoritative certainty, the Quakers closed upon neither reason nor sense perception. Nor did they choose Immanuel Kant's form of the *synthetic apriori*. Without God's revelation both reason and sense perception to them seemed mere notions,

8 *Quakers' Catechism*, cf. p. 267.

9 *Barclay's Apology in Modern English*, ed. Dean Freiday (xxxiv), private publication, Elberon, New Jersey, 1967. Freiday indicates that Wesley was familiar with Barclay's *Apology*, borrowing from it as well as other Quaker writings (sometimes without acknowledgment).

10 Arthur Roberts, "Holiness and Christian Renewal," *Quaker Religious Thought*, Vol. IX, No. 1 (Spring, 1967).

ideas "about" rather than "of." With direct revelation both reason and sense seemed to confirm the existential intuition of God. God compels beyond empirical probability or logical conclusion.

Not all Quakers utilized the same philosophical systems. The movement's ablest theologian, Robert Barclay, was essentially a Cartesian dualist whose beginning point, however, was immediate revelation rather than the indubitable "I think; therefore, I am." Barclay argued that God sets the terms by which men can know him, and that such terms are conformable to reason and are faithfully witnessed through scripture. Rationalizing tendencies in the eighteenth century made of Barclay's *Apology* a handbook of quietism, however, with its negation of the senses and a resulting diminution of effort analogous to hyper-Calvinistic forms of earlier rationalism that discouraged evangelism—an impasse broken by Jonathan Edwards, who in Lockean fashion proclaimed that God uses outward means.

Both George Fox and Samuel Fisher could better be classified as spiritual phenomenalists. Theirs is the cosmic Christ projected upon a providential unfolding of history rather than upon a Teilhardian evolution. The Anglican bishop, George Berkeley, developed a spiritual idealism that systematized the theological vision of men such as Fox and Fisher whereby both the imprinting of God in "real things" and the re-presenting of images constitute divine-human communication.

It is too bad Fisher is so long-winded. Despite his deplorable syntax, he articulates a Quaker existential, Anselmic approach to God, beyond second-hand knowledge or hearsay evidence. In the entertwining nexus of scriptural authority, rational understanding, and direct illumination, sources and tests of truth were not always easily sorted out among the early Quakers. But the "leap of faith" that the Quakers took was an act of commitment beyond deductively drawn reason or probability conjecture.

To early Quakers doctrine was not unimportant but rather subordinate. They did not impinge qualitative eternality upon materialistic temporality. With Christ as the center of the universe, the Lord of history and the Savior of mankind, they hung on to Bible and spirit, inward and outward experience of Christ, heaven both now and in the future, grace and triumph, authority and freedom. It was a creative synthesis, but difficult to maintain, as later history demonstrated.

1. *Saul's Errand to Damascus* (1653): The Trial of Fox and Nayler

In compactness and intensity the first careful theological debate was also the Quakers' best. It represents three stages: the trial of Fox at Lancaster Assizes, October, 1652; the trial of Nayler at Appleby the next January; and the flurry of written documents that followed. At the first trial, according to Fox,[11] there were forty "priests" present in addition to the three justices (West and Fell being sympathetic); at Appleby Higginson himself was present. Foiled at Lancaster, the Puritans meanwhile drew up a petition to Cromwell. When, therefore, the Friends got hold of a copy of the petition from the Lancashire pastors and rushed *Saul's Errand* into print, they beat out their Puritan opponents in reaching the forum of Puritan public opinion in the London area (the petition was hence never published). Higginson's tract (see p. 63) then tried to recoup by covering more widely all aspects of the Quaker threat: he seems to have succeeded, to judge by how often other Puritans cited him. Already in this exchange the Quakers and Puritans had seen most of the key issues, and identified clearly what their opponents said about them.

[George Fox and James Nayler]
SAUL'S ERRAND TO DAMASCUS:

With his packet of letters from the high-priests against the Disciples of the Lord; or a faithful transcript of a petition contrived by some persons in Lancashire, who call themselves ministers of the Gospel, breathing out threatnings and slaughters against a peaceable and godly people there by them nick-named Quakers. Together with the defence of the persons thereby traduced against the slanderous and false suggestions of that petition, and other untruths charged upon them. Published to no other end, but to draw out the bowels of tender compassion from all that love the poor despised servants of Jesus Christ, who have been the scorn of carnal men in all ages.

Mat. 5.10.11.12. [quoted in full]

London, printed for Giles Calvert, at the black Spread-Eagle, at the West-end of Pauls, 1654.[12]

11 From his endorsement on the reverse side of a copy in his own handwriting of the questions and answers given here on p. 253; see *CJ*, pp. 68-70 (with illustration) and 413.

12 This tract is usually ascribed to Fox and Nayler as authors, since the main sections are theirs, but the title-page and epistles to the Puritan peti-

To all that love the Lord Jesus Christ.

Dear Hearts,

You love the Lord Jesus Christ, and not him alone, but Christ with all his train. . . .

To the contrivers and subscribers of the petition.

Dear Hearts,

Is this a time to chide, and be angry, and pick quarrels? and (if you must needs do so) can you find no other objects of your indignation, but the *Lord's* Disciples; but peaceable, holy, humble, self-denying men? Is not the work of the ministry to preach the Gospel? Is not the sword of the magistrate appointed to the punishment of evil doers, and to the praise of them that do well? Are you incumbent in your duties? Are you laying out your talents to the end they were given you, or are you mistaken in the thing? When did you proclaim war against drunkards, swearers, common blasphemers, enemies to the Lord and his people? Have you none of those among you? . . .

To the Christian reader.

These are to let thee know, that the only wise God at this time hath so by his providence ordered it, in the north parts of Lancashire, that many precious Christians (and so for many years accounted, before the nickname Quakers was heard of) have, for some time past, forborne to concorporate in parochial assemblies, wherein they profess themselves to have gained little of the knowledge of Jesus Christ. And it is, and hath been put upon their hearts to meet often (and on the Lord's day constantly) at convenient places, to seek the Lord their Redeemer, and to speak of such things (tending to mutual edification) as the good Spirit of the Lord shall teach them; demeaning themselves without any offence given to any that truly fear the Lord.

But true it is, that some men and interests of those parts do take great offence at them and their Christian and peaceable exercises; some because they have witnessed against pride and luxuriant fulness, have therefore come armed . . . into their assemblies in time of their Christian performances, and have taken him whom the Lord at that instant had moved to speak to the rest, and others of their assembly (after they had haled and beaten them) and carried them bound hand and feet into the open fields, in the cold of the night, and there left them to the hazard of their lives, . . . pious, peaceable

tioners, the Christian Reader, etc. are not Fox's style or vocabulary; the first epistle may be by Nayler; the second I would more easily attribute to a London Friend, perhaps one of the Dring brothers. On Calvert, see p. 90.

252

men, who desire nothing more than to glorify their God in their generation, and are and have been more faithful to the interest of God's people in the nation, than any of the contrivers of the petition. . . .[13]

However, Reader, we need not fear; we hope the Lord will never suffer that monster persecution again to enter within the gates of England's White-Hall. . . .

[p. 10] *More Objections Against George Fox*[14]
charged upon him by the contrivers of the aforesaid petition; and answered by him, as followeth.

(*Objection) 1*: That he did affirm that he had the Divinity essential[ly] in him.

Answer: For the word *essential*[*ly*], it is an expression of their own: but that the saints are "the temples of God" (II Cor. 6:1), and God doth "dwell in them" (Eph. 4:6), that [I witness and] the Scripture do[th] witness. And if God dwell in them, then the Divinity dwells in them. And the Scripture saith "Ye shall be partakers of the Divine nature" (II Pet. 1:4), and this I witness; but where this is not, they cannot witness it.

(*Objection 2*): That both Baptism and the Lord's Supper are unlawful.

Answer: As for that word *unlawful*, it was not spoken by me: but the (Baptism) [sprinkling] of infants I deny and there is no Scripture that speaks of a sacrament. But that Baptism that is in(to) Christ, with "one Spirit into one body," that I confess according to Scripture; and the Lord's Supper I confess; and (that) the bread the saints break is the body of Christ. And that cup that they drink is the blood of Christ, this I witness (Gal. 3:27; John 6:53-58; II Cor. 10:16).

(*Objection 3*): He did dissuade men from reading the Scriptures, telling them that it was carnal.

Answer: For dissuading men from reading the Scriptures, (that) [it] is false, for they were given to be read as they are, but not to make a trade upon:

13 The pastors, squires, and justices of the Northwest, despite Cromwell's screening, were often Royalists who had opposed Parliament in the first Civil War, or at best Presbyterian conservatives who had opposed it in the second. Quakers were often former Cromwellians and radical Puritans, and even those like Banks who had never left home were locally called "roundheads."

14 Fox's own manuscript of this dialogue is in the Spence MSS, and seems to have been the basis for this tract and, through a less accurate copy (with covering notes by Nayler and Thomas Lawson), for that printed almost simultaneously by Aldam and the York Castle prisoners as *A Brief Discovery of the Three-fold Estate of Antichrist* (1653). [Passages here in brackets are only in the MS version.] (Parenthesis items are not in the MS.)

[but] the letter is carnal and killeth: but that which gave it forth is spiritual, eternal, and giveth life: and this I witness. [II Cor. *3*:6]

(*Objection 4*): That he was equal with God.

Answer: That was not so spoken: but that "He that sanctifieth, and they that are sanctified, are of one" (Heb. 2:1), and the saints are [11] all [of] one in the Father and the Son, of his flesh and of his bone, this the Scripture doth witness: And "Ye are sons of God;" and the Father and the Son (are) [is] one; (and "they that are joined to the Lord are one Spirit, and they that are joined to an harlot are one flesh.") Eph. *5*:30. [Heb. *2*:11]

(*Objection 5*): That God taught deceit.

Answer: That is false, and (was) never [was so] spoken by me; (God is pure).

(*Objection 6*): That the Scriptures (are) [was] Antichrist.

Answer: That is false, but that they which profess the Scriptures, and live not in the life and power of them, as they did that gave them forth, that I witness to be Antichrist.

(*Objection 7*): That he was the judge of the world.

Answer: (that) "the saints shall judge the world," the Scripture [doth] witness (it); whereof I am one, and I witness the Scripture fulfilled. I Cor. *6*:2, 3.

(*Objection 8*): That he was as upright as Christ.

Answer: Those were not so spoken by me; but that "as he is, so are we in this present world" (I John 4:17): That the saints are made "the righteousness of God" (I Cor. 5:21): That "the saints are one in the Father and the Son," that "we shall be like him" (I John 3:2), and that all teaching which is given forth by Christ, is to bring the saints to perfection, even "to the measure of the stature of the fulness of Christ:" This the Scripture doth witness [and I do witness to be fulfilled. John *4*:17, Ephes. *4*:1-13] (Where Christ dwells. must not he speak in his temple?).

---

[12] *Queries Propounded to George Fox*
by some of the contrivers of the
petition, and by him answered.

Query: Whether there be one individual God distinguished into the Father, Son, and Holy Ghost, or not:

Answer: Herein thou wouldst know, whether God be individual, yes or no, which is but a busy mind; for hadst thou the witness in thyself thou wouldst know that he is; but the heathen know not God, and all that know him not, are heathen living in the wicked imaginations of their own hearts, and that is thy condition: For "God is a spirit," and "none know him but the Son, and he to whom the Son is revealed:" [John *4*:24, Matt. *11*:27] the Son and the

Word is one. "He that hath ears to hear let him hear, what the Spirit saith," [Rev. 2:7] for thou, natural man, thou knowest not the things of God.[15]

Query: Whether a believer be justified by Christ's righteousness imputed, yea, or no?

Answer: "He that believeth is born of God;" and he that is born of God, is justified by Christ alone without imputation.

Question: Whether he that believeth that Christ hath taken away his sin, is clean without sin in this life, as Christ himself, or not?

Answer: He that believeth is born of God, and "he that is born of God sins not, neither can he sin, because his seed remaineth in him"; "as he is, so are we in this present evil world." [I John 3:9-10, 5:19]

Question: Whether a believer be without all sin in this life, or not?

Answer: Christ being made manifest, is made manifest to take away sin, and "in him is no sin at all; he that abideth in him, sins not; he that sins is of the Devil; and hath not seen him, [13] neither known him, herein are the children of God made manifest, and the children of the Devil." [I John 3:5-8] All you that read these queries, read these things in yourselves, whether ye be the children of God, or the children of the Devil; and whether ye understand what ye write, yes or no.

Question: Whether his works as well as his person, be perfectly holy and good or no?

Answer: "A good tree cannot bring forth evil fruit; and if the root be holy, the branches will be holy also;" and "every one that doth righteousness is righteous, even as he is righteous." But as for that person, it is a busy mind in thee that ask'st thou know'st not what; for "God is no respecter of persons:" he that respecteth persons commits sin, and, he that commits sin, transgresseth the law.

Question: Whether saints in this life, without any addition hereafter, are perfectly just, perfectly holy, completely glorious in this life, and are not capable of any addition after death, in the least degree but only of manifestation?[16]

Answer: If that thou know'st what a saint is, thou wouldest know a saint's life, for they passed through death to life; but thou art yet alive to sin, and dead to righteousness; seeing it be not so; but he that is dead to sin is alive to righteousness: and lives in God, and God in him. "The Lord is our righteousness," and he saith, "Be ye holy as I am holy:" for "without holiness no man shall see the Lord." "Be not deceived, God will not be mocked." Thou

---

15 This kind of sudden turn from theological to personal argument was typical of early Friends (see Nayler's answers to Baxter), who proclaimed and preached first, and based all theology on experience.

16 Calvin's position had been that Christians are only fully sanctified in the next life.

hypocrite, dissemble not with him: he that is perfectly holy is perfectly just: where this is revealed, there needs no addition; for "the man of God is perfect."

Question: Whether the two sacraments, Baptism and the breaking of bread ought necessarily to continue in the Church, or not?

Answer: Thou askest thou know'st not what, concerning two sacraments which there is no Scripture for. Thou askest a question, which is an addition to the Scripture; and thou that dost add, the plagues of God are added to thee. Who come into the true Church, are "baptized with one spirit into one body," [Ephes. *4*:5] but as for sprinkling infants; there's no Scripture for it: I deny it; [14] in the true Church of God there is no talk of such carnal things. Thou sot, the bread which the saints break, is of the body of Christ; he is "the bread of life." The Church is not the steeplehouse, but the Church is in God, and those that eat the bread of life, live forever: the Church is in God, and the bread of life is there, and it shall continue forever.

Question: Whether Christ in the flesh be a figure or not: and if a figure, how and in what?

Answer: Christ is the substance of all figures; and his flesh is a figure; for everyone passeth through the same way as he did, who comes to know Christ in the flesh: "there must be a suffering with him, before there be a rejoicing with him." Christ is an example to all to walk after; and if thou knew'st what an example is, thou wouldst know what a figure is, to come up to the same fulness.

Question: Whether there be any heaven or hell for the Elect or Reprobate after death, [or only] in man in this life, or not?

Answer: There is no knowledge of heaven or hell; but through death "the wicked shall be turned into hell, and all them that forget God," there to be tormented; there is a hell, thou shalt find it. Heaven is God's throne; and heavenly notions within shall be shaken: for God is pure, and nothing that is unclean shall stand before him: and he hath said he will dwell in man.

Question: Whether the ministration of the ministry by man is to continue till the end, or not?

Answer: The ministration of the world is the ministry of man, and doth not lead to an end, but keeps in time, and that must have an end; for it is not of God. The ministry of God is to draw people up to himself; but that is "not of man, nor by man nor according to man;" for Paul was "made a minister according to the will of God," [Gal. *1*:1, 4] who had not received it of man, neither was it taught him of man, and was a minister of the Spirit. But the ministers of the world receive their learning at Oxford and Cambridge, and are taught of men, and speak a divination of their own brain, which is conjuring; and bewitch the people with those things which are carnal: [such]

256

as to sprinkle infants, and [15] tell them of a sacrament which there is no Scripture for; and saying they are the ministers of Christ, [while they] act those things which he forbids, [such] as to "have the chiefest place in the assemblies, the uppermost room at feasts, the greetings in markets, and to be called of men masters," [Matt. 25:6, 10] and "with pretence make long prayers," which Christ forbids, and profess and say they are the ministers of Christ: wherein they show themselves to be Antichrist. And see if thou[17] do not uphold these Antichrists, and say they are the ministers of Christ.

Question: Whether the written Word, I mean the Scriptures, be the power of God unto salvation to everyone that believes, or not?

Answer: The written Word is not the power of God, nor the Scriptures are not the salvation; but he that doth believe hath the life of them. Who is born of God, shall never die; as it is written, he that believeth is born of God, and he that is born of God hath the witness in himself, that God is the cause of man's salvation, and not the Scripture nor the letter.

James Nayler's Answer, and declaration, touching some things charged upon him, by the men aforesaid:

Having heard of divers untruths cast upon me, by some of the priests in their high places, though I stand only to the Lord in respect of my self; yet lest any that love the truth, should be led on by these false reports to speak evil of those things they know not; I shall lay open the truth, as it is revealed in me, touching those things whereof I have been falsely accused.

First, concerning Jesus Christ, that he is the eternal word of God, "by [16] whom all things were made," and are upholden; which was before all time, but manifested to the world in time, for the recovery of lost man: which "Word became flesh, and dwelt amongst" the saints (John 1:2, 3, 4, 5, 14), who is "the same, yesterday, today, and forever;" who did and doth dwell in the saints; who suffered, and rose again, and ascended into Heaven, and is set at the right hand of God, to whom "all power is given in heaven and in earth," who fills all places: is the light of the world, but known to none but to those that receive and follow him, and those he leads up to God, out of all the ways, works and worships of the world, by his pure light in them, whereby he reveals the man of sin; and by his power casts him out. And so prepares the bodies of the saints a fit temple for the pure God to dwell in: with whom dwells no unclean thing: and thus he reconciles God and man:

17 Here the Quaker writer turns to the reader, whose personal surrender is asked for.

and the image of God which is in purity and holiness, is renewed: and the image of Satan, which is all sin and uncleanness, is defaced: and none can witness redemption, further than Christ is thus revealed in them, to set them free from sin: which Christ I witness to be revealed in me in measure (Gal. 1:16; II Cor. 13:5; Col. 1:27).

2. Concerning the Scriptures, that they are a true declaration of that word which was in them that spoke them forth, and are of no private interpretation, but were given forth to be read and fulfilled in the saints, as they were given forth by the Holy Ghost, without adding or diminishing; and were not given forth for men to make a trade on to get money by: but as they are they are profitable "for doctrine, for reproofs, for correction, for instruction in righteousness, that the man of God may be perfect, thoroughly furnished unto every good work" (II Tim. 3:17). But they who trade in the letter, and are ignorant of the mystery, deny all perfection: and none can rightly understand the Scriptures, but they who read them with the same spirit that gave them forth; for "the natural man understands not the things of God, for they are spiritually discerned" (I Cor. 2:15).

3. Concerning Baptism: the true baptism is that of the spirit, "with the Holy Ghost, and with fire:" Baptized by one spirit into one body: not "the washing away the filth of the flesh, but [17] the answer of a good conscience towards God by the resurrection of Jesus Christ;" without which no other baptism can save us, they being but figures or shadows; but this baptism of Christ is the substance, whereby we are baptized into his death, and "those that are baptized into Christ have put on Christ" (Gal. 3:27).

4. Concerning the Lord's Supper. The true supper of the Lord is the spiritual eating and drinking of the flesh and blood of Christ spiritually; which the spiritual man only eateth, and is thereby nourished up into eternal life: without which eating there can be no life in creature, profess what you will; and all who eat of this bread, and drink of this cup have real communion in Christ the head, and also one with another, as members; and are of one heart, and one mind, a complete body in Christ. Now the world who takes only the outward figures, and are not brought in "discerning of the Lord's body, eat and drink damnation to themselves, become guilty of the body and blood of Christ" (I Cor. 11:27, 28, 29); and calls this a communion, but lives in envy, strife, and debate, fighting, and going to law one with another, for earthly things.

5. Concerning the Resurrection: That all shall arise to give an account and receive at the last day according to their works, whether good or evil. These bodies that are dust shall turn to dust, "but God shall give a body as pleaseth him; that which is sown in corruption, shall be raised in incorruption; it is sown a natural body, it is raised a spiritual body; and as we have borne the image

258

of the earthly, so we shall bear the image of the heavenly" but "flesh and blood cannot inherit the Kingdom of Heaven; neither doth corruption inherit incorruption; for we must be changed" (I Cor. 15:8, 42, 43, 44, 20). But they who cannot witness the first Resurrection within themselves, know nothing of the second, but by hearsay; and therefore, say some of your teachers that Christ is in Heaven with a carnal body. Now that Christ who is the first fruits, should be in Heaven with a carnal body, and the saints with a spiritual body, is not proportionable.

6. *Concerning magistracy*: It is an ordinance of God, ordained for the punishment of evil doers, and an encouragement for them that do well; where justice and righteousness is the [18] head, and ruleth out partiality, that land is kept in peace; and those that judge for the Lord I honour as my own life, not with a flattering honour, putting off the hat and bowing of the knee, which is the honor of the world, "having men's persons in admiration because of advantage" (Jude 16) for self-ends; but from my heart for conscience sake, as to the power which is of God. Though the prophets were often sent by the Lord, to pronounce judgement against unjust men who had the power committed to them and did not judge for God, but for self-ends, yet they never attempted any violence against them, but used all means to persuade them to "love mercy, do justice, and walk humbly with God" (Mic. 6:8), that they might be established, and the wrath of God turned from them; For those that be of God, cannot rejoice in the sufferings of any but would have all to turn and find mercy.

7. *Concerning the ministry*: The true ministers of Jesus Christ have always been, and are still, such as come not by the will of man, but by the will of God, neither are they fitted for the work by anything of man, but by God alone: for the true ministry is the gift of Jesus Christ, and needs no addition of human help and learning; but as the work is spiritual, and of the Lord, so they are spiritually fitted only by the Lord, and therefore he chose herdsmen, fishermen, and plowmen, and such like; and as he gave them an immediate call, without the leave of man: so he fitted them immediately without the help of man. And as they "received" the gift freely, so they were to "give freely" (Matt. 10:8). And whenever they found any of the false ministry, that taught for hire, cried out against them, and pronounced woes against them, [19] and showed them that they lay in iniquity, because they thought that the gift of God could be bought and sold for money (Acts 8:20). . . . [eight more biblical examples omitted, but cf. p. 360]

[omitting a section on "the persecutions of James Nayler by the priests of Westmorland"]

[29] *The Examination of James Nayler, upon an Indictment of Blasphemy, at the Sessions at Appleby, in January, 1652.*

Justice Pearson. Put off your hats.

James. I do it not in contempt of authority: for I honor the power as it is of God, without respect of persons, it being forbidden in Scripture. He that respects men's persons, commits sin, and is convinced of the law as a transgressor.

Just. Pearson. That is meant of respecting persons in judgment.

James. If I see one in goodly apparel, and a gold ring, and see one in poor and vile raiment, and say to him in fine apparel, sit thou in a higher place than the poor, I am partial, and judged of evil thoughts.

Col. Briggs.[18] If thou wert in the Parliament house, wouldst thou keep it on?

James. If God should keep me in the same mind I am in now I should.

Col. Briggs. I knew thou wouldst contemn authority.

Jam. I speak in the presence of God. I do not contemn authority, but I am subject to the power, as it is of God for conscience sake.

Just. Pears. Now authority commands thee to put off thy hat, what sayest thou to it?

Jam. Where God commands one thing, and man another, I am to obey God rather than man.

Col. Benson. See whether the law command it, or your own wills. [The indictment was read, wherein James was indicted for saying that Christ was in him, and that there was but one word of God.]

Col. Briggs. Where wast thou born?

Jam. At Ardishaw, two miles from Wakefield.

Col. Briggs. How long livedst thou there?

Jam. Until I was married, then I went unto Wakefield parish.

Col. Briggs. What profession wast thou of?

Jam. A husbandman.

Col. Briggs. Wast thou a soldier?

Jam. Yea; I was a soldier betwixt eight and nine years.

Col. Briggs. Wast thou not at Burford among the Levelers?[19]

Jam. I was never there.

---

18 Nothing seems to be recorded in Quaker sources regarding this Col. Briggs. Justice Pearson was Anthony Pearson of Durham, later, though not permanently, a Friend.

19 In May, 1649, after the execution of King Charles I failed to lead to the radical forms for which they had petitioned, Levellers persuaded some Cromwellian regiments to a mutiny against the "Rump" Parliament, which Crom-

Col. Briggs. I charge thee by the Lord that thou tell me whether thou wast or not?

Jam. I was then in the North, and was never taxed for any mutiny, or any other thing, while I served the Parliament.

Col. Briggs. What was the cause of thy coming into these parts?

[Here Nayler tells of his call while plowing and his second sudden call to leave home, which Higginson reported; cf. p. 68.]

[31] Just. Pears. What difference then between the ministers and you?

Jam. The ministers affirm Christ to be in heaven with a carnal body, but I with a spiritual body.

Just. Pears. Which of the ministers say Christ is in heaven with a carnal body?

Jam. The minister so called of Kirkby Steven.

(Priest Higginson stood up, and affirmed it again openly before all the Court.)

Quest. Was Christ man or no?

Jam. Yea, he was, and took upon him the seed of Abraham, and was real flesh and bone; but is a matter not known to the carnal man; for he is begotten of the immortal seed, and those that know him, know him to be spiritual; for it was the Word that became flesh, and dwelt amongst us: and if he had not been spiritual, he had not wrought my redemption.

Just. Pears. Is Christ in thee as man?

Jam. Christ filleth all places, and is not divided. Separate God and man, and he is no more Christ.

Just. Pears. If we stand to dispute these things, we should have the ministers.

[32] Col. Briggs. Wast thou not of a Kirk about Sawrby?

Jam. I was a member of an independent church at [Mansfield] Woodkirk.

Col. Briggs. Wast thou not excommunicated for thy blasphemous opinions?

Jam. I know not what they have done since I came forth; but before I was not to my knowledge. . . .

Col. Briggs. Didst not thou write a paper, wherein was mentioned, that if thou thinkest to be saved by that Christ which died at Jerusalem, thou art deceived?

Jam. If I cannot witness Christ nearer than Jerusalem, I shall have no benefit by him: but I own no other Christ but that who witnessed a good confession before Pontius Pilate; which Christ I witness in me now. . . .

[33] Just. Pears. To the Word: What sayest thou to the Scriptures? are they the Word of God?

well suppressed at Burford. To many radical Puritans this was the betrayal of their revolution (despite Cromwell's later efforts to satisfy them by the nominated "Parliament of Saints"). Nayler can here deny being a "bolshevik."

Jam. They are a true declaration of the word that was in them who spoke them forth.

Higginson. Is there not a written Word?

Jam. Where readest thou in the Scriptures of a written Word? The word is spiritual, not seen with carnal eyes: but as for the Scriptures they are true, and I witness them true, in measure fulfilled in me, as far as I am grown up. . . .

[The tract closes with John Lawson's answers to charges against him.]

2. The *Quakers' Catechism* Debate: Round 1, Richard Baxter versus Nayler (1655)

The "Saul's Errand" tract debate and the Lancaster and Appleby trials preceding it had focused on Quaker claims to be indwelt by Christ's Spirit and infallibly guided by it: *Saul's Errand,* Aldam's *Discovery,* and Higginson's *Irreligion* (cf. pp. 358, 64) were followed by lesser blasts. But new debates arose constantly, usually after face-to-face exchanges had been standoffs. Debate tracts bulk as over half of Quaker published writings throughout the half-century, and we cannot do justice to them or even list them. Key opponents were involved: Roger Williams, John Bunyan, and John Tombes among the Baptists, Danson the Presbyterian and Owen the Independent, John Toldervy the Ranter and Lodowick Muggleton the Seeker. On the Quaker side, Fox, Nayler, Burrough, Penington, Penn, and Samuel Fisher each published nearly a thousand pages of such material, and dozens of other men were involved. After 1670, an increasing portion of these were repetitious debates with ex-Quakers: John Pennyman, William Rogers, Francis Bugg, and last and most prominently the Scot, George Keith (cf. p. 559). These last, though often beginning in internal debates on Quaker discipline and organization (cf. p. 514), often attacked Quaker Christology.

We present the debate focusing around Richard Baxter and the issues of pride and self-righteousness that lie close to the heart of both Puritan and Quaker experience. Richard Baxter, the great Puritan pastor of Kidderminster, was less known then than later as the great interpreter of Puritan ethics in practice, as his huge *Christian Directory* did not appear until 1673. But he already "occupied a unique place in the religious life of his time," both because of his devotional *Saints' Everlasting Rest* and six to eight

262

sermon books already published (altogether there are 280 books or editions of his works by 1700). Above all he was the greatest advocate of an all-inclusive pastoral care through a Puritan parish system. To fight sectarianism he tried being a Cromwellian chaplain. He founded the Worcestershire Association for parish pastors in 1653 and drew up its petition to Parliament to adopt this as a national pattern. He was thus a natural target for roving Quaker preachers, and five are mentioned in Baxter's tract. They spoke in various Worcestershire churches, but missed Baxter in his own, failed to draw him into a public debate, and evidently sent him the written challenges that he here answers. When later he did meet the Quaker doctor Edward Bourne at home, Baxter was courteous.

It is not clear whether anyone beyond Baxter's tract itself drew Nayler into the debate, since when it came out Nayler was in London and Thomas Goodaire and Richard Farnworth spent most of 1655, after their exchanges with Baxter, in Worcester and Danbury jails. Nayler's tract was not reprinted in his collected works, and hence is rare. It is nevertheless typical of his best theological thinking, despite the tragic failure of either Baxter or Nayler to understand each other's strengths. Baxter had long seen the lack of love and humility in all Separatists, as they rejected all other men as Christians. Yet his responses as a pastor, which will seem familiar to any minister today, also show his unconscious arrogance about his calling as a teacher and scholar. Nayler, who saw Baxter as a dramatic contrast to Quaker understandings of ministry, does not see or answer Baxter's objections to the spirit of Quakerism, though theologically the men were well matched. As Barclay also realized, the key point Friends needed to make, in answer to the probing attack against self-righteousness by Puritans and the whole tradition of Paul, Augustine, and the Reformation, was that the perfect righteousness that Friends said God demanded was possible not as a human achievement or acts of merit, but only as the Spirit of God acted through men, and by God's power, not man's.

THE QUAKERS' CATECHISM
or
THE QUAKERS QUESTIONED

Their questions answered and both published,
for the sake of those of them who have not

yet sinned unto death, and of those undergrounded
novices that are most in danger of their
seduction.

By Richard Baxter. London. Printed by A.M.
at the Anchor and Bible in Paul's Church-
yard, and Francis Tyton at the Three Daggers
in Fleetstreet, 1655.

To the reader.

Reader, I suppose thou wilt marvel that I trouble myself with so wild a generation as the people called Quakers are, or that I trouble thee with a few hasty lines which I wrote on such an occasion. I'll truly tell thee the cause of both. They sent me several papers, one of them containing the queries which I answer, and others of them almost nothing but a bundle of filthy railing words ("Thou serpent, thou liar, thou deceiver, thou child of the Devil, thou cursed hypocrite, thou dumb dog"), with much more of the like. They chose out one day when it pleased God to confine me to my chamber by sickness, to come into our assembly,[20] and after morning sermon to fall a-questioning the preacher, my assistant. Because he avoided public disputing with them at that season, as not taking it for a profitable spending of the Lord's Day, they call him "the hireling that flieth," it seems referring to John *10*:12, and so confessing themselves to be the wolves. I find that they do so challenge, and brag, and triumph, if we say nothing to them, and that too many simple people expect that we should answer them, that (after an unprofitable verbal discourse with an unreasonable railing fellow,) I resolved to send them this brief answer to their questions. And because they abhor syllogisms and disputings, I was fain to deal further with them in their own questioning way. I had before offered to come and answer all their queries in their assembly, if they would consent that I might do it without disturbance; but instead of permitting that, they denied it, and sent me a letter of reviling, calling me, over and over, serpent and hypocrite, and the like names, and commanding me in the name of the most high God to answer their questions in writing, that they might print them with their reply. So that if I say nothing, they will insult; if I write to them, they will print it. Being, therefore, so far called to speak, I chose rather to print my own papers, how mean soever, than let them do it.

Two objections, I foresee, will be raised against me. One is that the persons

---

[20] Goodaire and Farnworth did not mean to miss Baxter, and report disappointment that they did so.

are so contemptible and the errors so gross, that it's a needless work to strive against them; to which I say, let sad experience witness whether it be needless, when they so much multiply, and so many where they come are presently infected. The salvation of the poorest Christian is so far from being contemptible that it is worth much more than our greatest diligence. 2: It will be said, it is but the churches of the Separatists and Anabaptists that are emptied by these seducers, and it's best even let them alone to keep their own flocks, and secure their churches, or if they fall off, it may show others the tendency of their ways, and so prevent their turning aside, to which I answer: 1. Though the stream of apostates be such as were first Anabaptists or [A-4] Separatists, yet here and there one of the young, unsettled sort do fall into that stream, who were not before of them, but perhaps inclining to them, and so do some few who had no religiousness. 2. I had far rather that men continued Separatists and Anabaptists than turned Quakers or plain apostates, and therefore would do all that I can to hinder such an emptying of their churches as tends to the more certain filling of hell. It's better to stop them in a condition where we may have some hope of their salvation, than to let them run into certain perdition. I did therefore take it to be my duty when these poor neighbors, who had before been Anabaptists, Separatists, and some Seekers, had turned Quakers, to offer them a verbal answer to all their vain questions, that I might have had so much opportunity to undeceive them. When they refused that, and said they would not be drawn into a serpent's snare, I thought best to send them my answer in writing, committing it to some of their neighbors, that they might desire leave to read it in their assembly. And when I heard that they would not grant that either, for all their insulting adjuring of us to answer them, but talk of printing something against me, I chose rather to tell the world of these passages between us, than leave them to their reports, especially hearing how they increase in London and other parts, and that the ignorant have need of some plain information to prevent their apostasy and perdition in this temptation.

April 20, 1655   R.B.

To the Separatists and Anabaptists in England.

Though God's mind is most plainly revealed to us in his written word, yet are his providences also teaching, and it is the duty of his servants to read and study them. . . . I am not of their mind who make light of the strange providences in our military affairs and changes of state, though I think every carnal admirer of them does not understand them, but it's a matter of very sad consideration that many of those same men who seem so much to magnify these do no more observe, understand, and lay to heart the more remarkable providence of our heavy spiritual judgements. . . . [B-1] The hand of God is apparently gone out against your ways of Separation and Anabaptism. It is your duty to observe it. You may see you do but prepare too many for a further progress—Seekers, Ranters, Familists, and now Quakers, and too many professed infidels, spring up from among you, as if this were your journey's end, and the perfection of your revolt. . . . I have heard yet from the several parts of the land but of very few who have drunk in this venom of the Ranters or Quakers, but such as have first been of your opinions, and gone out[21] at that door. The rest are but here and there a young person who was not noted for any great matter of religiousness, or only liked it and inclined to your ways. One of the queries which they have put to me is what express scripture I have for infant baptism, which I must show without consequences, or else confess myself a false prophet. And another tends to prove us no true churches. The Quakers, then, are Separatists and Antipedobaptists,[22] though more.

[B-2] And it is very remarkable that it is a pretence of our impurity and of a greater purity with you that is pleaded by those who first turn over to you, and that this height of all impieties should be the usual issue of a way pretended to be exact and clean. Doubtless it is none of God's mind by this to discourage any from purity and true reformation, but to show his detestation of that spiritual pride which makes men have too high thoughts of themselves, and too much to condemn others, and to desire to be further separated from them than God in the day of grace doth allow of. . . . In one word, it is most evident that spiritual pride turns most men from us to you, and that this is the very sin that undoes such a multitude. . . .

[B-3] I beseech you take this plain admonition in good part from a desirer of your recovery and salvation.

Richard Baxter

An answer
to a young unsettled friend, who, before[-hand] inclining
strongly to Anabaptistry, at last fell in with the Quakers,
and desired my thoughts of them and their ways, which seemed
agreeable to the scriptures.

21 I.e., the Baptists and Separatists had pulled out of the parish churches, and thus were open to Quaker ideas.

22 Antipedobaptist: rejecting child baptism, either for the sake of adult immersion (Baptists) or for none (the Friends). Both groups rejected outward rituals for the unconverted, whereas inclusive-membership churches regard their role as bringing men *into* grace.

I marvel why you took it for so great a work of grace to convert you from profaneness, and now will take it for a greater work to convert you to it again, or to much worse. Was it not the same ordinances that you despised before conversion, which you now much more despise? Was it not the same ministers that then you scorned whom you now reproach with far greater bitterness? . . . Dare you cast out the holy worship of Christ as false worship, and seek to draw people into the contempt of it? Dare you damn those churches and millions of saints that Christ has bought with his precious blood? Dare you seek to draw men to hate their teachers, whom Christ has set over them? . . . [B-4] You know you are a young man, and have had little opportunity to be acquainted with the Word of God, in comparison of what your teacher has had. If you presume that you are so much more beloved of God than he, that God will reveal that to you without seeking and study, which upon the greatest diligence he will not reveal to him; what can this conceit proceed from but pride? God commands study and meditating day and night in his laws. Your teacher has spent twenty, if not a hundred, hours in such meditation where you have spent one; he has spent twenty if not a hundred hours in prayer to God for his spirit of truth and grace, where you have spent one. His prayers are as earnest as yours, his office is to teach. Therefore God is, as it were, more engaged to be his teacher, and to make known his truth to him, than to you. Is it not then apparent pride for you to be confident that you are so much wiser than he, and that you are so much more lovely in God's eyes. . . ?

And for the Quakers, you are blind if you see not their horrible pride. You'll perhaps think it strange that pride should be the very master-sin in them that go in so poor a garb, and cry out against pride as zealously as they do, and go up and down the world, as if they were sent from heaven to persuade men to wear no lace, or cuffs, or points, [C-1] and who damn so many ministers for being called masters. But, alas, do you not know that pride of inward qualifications, commonly called spiritual pride, is the most killing and abominable? The better the thing is that you are proud of, the worse is your pride. Oh, what a brave thing does it seem in these men's eyes, that they should seem to be possessed with such an excellent spirit as can trample upon worldly glory, and can boisterously condemn all who are not of their own sect, and who can despise dignities, and be equal with the greatest. Yea, that only they should have this admirable spirit, and all others are the children of the Devil, and under their feet. . . .

1. They affirm themselves to be perfect without sin, yea, some of them say they are Christ and God. And is it possible that any man in this life, that is not mad with spiritual pride, can indeed believe that he has no sin? What? That he transgresses no law? That he loves God in the highest degree that he is bound to do? That he never has a thought or word that is sinful, nor

sinfully loses one minute of his time? Yea, and this when in the eyes and ears of the wisest, they foam out their own shame, as the raging sea casts out the dirt. The Devil himself has either less pride or less ignorance, than to think himself to be perfect without sin. If they have no sin, what need they pray, "forgive us our sins," or what further need have they of the blood of Christ, or his intercession, to procure them any further forgiveness? If you can see no pride in this, I fear you are blinded with them to destruction.

2. And is it not apparent pride in them to set up themselves so far above all the people of God on earth? Yea, to vilify the most holy and eminent servants of God, and condemn all the churches in the world, as if heaven were made for them alone.

3. And yet more unmatchable pride and impious infidelity is it, to damn all the church and people of God for this 1600 years at least. . . . And is not that man either an infidel and enemy to Christ, or stark mad with pride, who can believe that Christ had no church till now, and that all the ministers of the gospel for 1600 years were the ministers of the Devil (as they say of us who tread in their steps) and that all the Christians of that 1600 years are damned (as now they dare denounce against those who succeed them) and that God made the world, and Christ died for it, with a purpose to save none but a few Quakers whom the world never knew till a few years ago, or at least a few heretics who were their predecessors of old. . . . [Fourth, they rail in the language of Satan.]

[C-2] To your question what I think of these men, I will tell you what I think and am past all doubt of: Young raw professors who have more zeal than knowledge, . . . if they are once brought to be wise enough in their own eyes and to despise their teachers, then they are like a man who has lost his way in a dark night, or who has lost his guide in an unknown wilderness. . . . The Papists and the Devil know this well enough, and therefore their first endeavor is to unsettle these people . . . by bringing the ministers into contempt with them. For if they could once accomplish this fully, and separate the people from their pastors, and so assault the people alone, or with weak and unlearned teachers only, they might then easily bear down all before them. . . .

[C-3] If you ask me how I know that it is Papists who thus seduce them, I answer: 1. Because they do the Papists' work, and maintain their cause, as far as yet they dare venture to bring it forth. I could tell you of abundance of Popery that the Quakers and Behmenists[23] maintain, as that the Pope is not Antichrist (which is at least to their advantage whether Popery or not) and

---

[23] The followers of Jacob Boehme, the seventeenth-century German cobbler and mystic, who also attacked externalism in religion. Cf. Rufus Jones, *Spiritual Reformers of the 16th and 17th Centuries*, pp. 2, 8, 234, etc.

268

the disgracing and secret undermining [of] the sufficiency of the scripture, the decrying of the ministry, the unchurching of our churches, the slighting of justification by imputed righteousness, and drawing men to the admiration of their inherent righteousness, and of their works; the crying up the light within us, and the sufficiency of common revelation, the setting up the strength of man's free will, the asserting the necessity of a judge of controversy above scripture (which they are content should be the spirit of revelation awhile, till they can boldlier exchange that for the Pope), the extolling of monastical community and virginity, and alienation from worldly employments; the doctrine of perfection without sin in this life, with many more of the like nature. All this the Papists have taught the Quakers.... If you say not, then who think you should reveal all this Popery to the Quakers—not the spirit of God, for he is not the author of Popery or any falsehood. If it were the devil, then it seems that Popery and the Quakers' faith are hatched by the prince of darkness. And whether it were friars or devils or both that make Quakers, it's not worth the while to dispute, as long as we know that it is Popery that they hold, and the Devil befriendeth it. [At this point Baxter quotes in full a deposition of George Cowlishaw of Bristol that a former schoolmate, an Irishman named Coppinger, had trained in Rome as a friar and recognized two chief London Quakers as fellow-Franciscans.]

[D-1] The Lord open your eyes, and humble your heart, and acquaint you with your great darkness and imperfections, and with the sufficiency of Holy Scriptures, and the necessity of his order and ministry, and the need that you have of those guides whom you despise, and the obedience and submission that you owe them, and the excellency of the churches' unity, and the mischief of all divisions and heresies, and recover you from their snares.

Your true friend,
Richard Baxter

[1] An answer to the Quakers' Queries

Miserable creatures:

Before the last I wrote to you, I had received three several papers with the names of three several persons of you inscribed, *viz.* one Jane Hicks, one Thomas Chaundler, and Edward Neway.... Since that time I have received two more, one subscribed by Richard Farnworth and Thomas Goodaire, and another without any subscribed name....

[4] Your first query is "What's the first principle of the pure religion," to which I answer: 1. That God is, and next, that he is a rewarder of them who diligently seek him (Heb. *11*:6). 2. Do you ask this as learners? No, that you renounce. Or as teachers? Why then do you not show your commission to teach? ...

Your second query is whether they are a church of Christ who beat and persecute them who witness forth the truth in his name, etc. Answer: Doubtless it's possible for a true church to be guilty of injuries. But you have as little cause to put this question as the Turk has. What would you answer if a Jew or a Turk or a witch should put this question: "Is it a true church that persecutes them that witness the truth?"[24] ... Go to some of your gossips, the friars or other Papists, and ask them this question: whether it is a true church [5] which set up the Spanish Inquisition? and caused the French Massacre?[25] ...

Your third question is about infant baptism. Of that I have already written a whole book, which in modesty you should peruse, before you call to me for more. Have you soberly read what I have written already? If not, to what purpose should I write more to you of the same subject? ...

Your fourth, fifth, sixth, seventh, eighth, and ninth queries are all about tithes, the substance of which I had answered long ago to some of your leading brethren, in a book called *The Worcestershire Petition Defended*,[26] to which book I refer, to spare the labour of speaking one thing twice; and modesty should have taught you to take notice of that which I have done already, before you call for the same things again. Only let me now add these queries also to you:

Qu. 1. Whether you have read any of those books that were written long ago, to prove that tithes are still of divine right? If you have not, were it not well beseeming a tender [6] conscience to hear all that can be said, before men adventure to rail against that which they do not understand?

Qu. 2. Whether there is not sufficient scripture to warrant a man to dedicate part of his lands to God, for the service of his church, and promoting of his worship? Yes, whether they did not, in the primitive times, so dedicate all, selling it, and laying down the price at the apostles' feet?

Qu. 3. Is it not lawful to take and use that which is so dedicated? And if the

24 Quakers advocated toleration for non-Christians; but Baxter is here using, just as clearly as Friends often did, the kind of appeal to personal experience and faith that excludes the opponent from the possibility of a reply.

25 The Spanish Inquisition, and the St. Bartholomew's Day massacre of Protestants throughout France in 1572, had become standard examples of Catholic intolerance as a result of John Foxe's *Book of Martyrs*. The forcible reconversion to Catholicism of France, Poland, and Austria and the attempt in Holland made the threat all too real to Englishmen.

26 *The Worcestershire Petition to the Parliament Defended* (1653) supported his *Humble Petition of Many Thousands in ... Worcestershire* (1652), which predated the formal Association of Puritans and was also signed by many key laymen; see G. F. Nuttall, *Richard Baxter* (1965).

apostles and first church officers might take all, may not we take the tenths, when they are thus devoted?

Qu. 4. If our ancestors, many an age ago, have given the tenths to the church for the ministry, are not those sacrilegious church-robbers who should now take them away? . . .

Qu. 5. If one who bears the bag prove a Judas and thief, whether are all the apostles therefore thieves, or all the churches and pastors greedy dogs? . . .

Qu. 6. Whether I, or other ministers, do ask the people so much for preaching as the Quakers receive themselves? Do you not receive meat and drink, to sustain your lives? But we ask not meat or drink of any, nor anything else, that is theirs. The tithes are none of theirs, nor ever was, nor their fathers' before them; but they bought or took leases of their lands, with the condition of paying the tenths as none of their own. . . .

Qu. 7. If the supreme rulers of the Commonwealth may lay an excise or tax on the nation, and pay soldiers with [7] one part of it, what forbids but that they may pay ministers of the gospel with the other part?

Qu. 8. Where does any scripture forbid paying or taking tithes?

And where you ask us so often whether the apostles took the tenths, I tell you again they took more, that is men sold all and laid down the money at their feet. It's true that then the poor also were maintained out of it, and if you will show a commission to examine us, we will give you an account how far we maintain the poor out of our mere tenth part. In the mean time it's unreasonable that you demand, that we should "so maintain them as to suffer no beggars." For if all that a minister has will not maintain twenty poor people if he gives it them all, how should he then maintain a hundred with it?

Your tenth query is whether Christ enlightens every one who comes into the world, to which I answer, yes, he does so. All that come into the world of nature, he enlightens with the light of nature, so called because that it is a knowledge gotten by the "book of the Creatures" and natural means, without supernatural revelation, though it is of grace also as it is freely given after a forfeiture. And all who come into the world of grace he enlightens with the light of supernatural revelation. . . .

[8] I lately saw another paper of your queries which you have dispersed in other places, which speaks almost only of this inward light, in which I perceived: That you falsely intimate that we deny the necessity of an inward light, whereas we maintain that the external light of the Word alone is not sufficient without the inward light of the spirit. [But] you there intimate to us a supposed sufficiency of the inward light that every man in the world has. [Do] you mean it is sufficient to leave men without excuse (that we maintain, as well as you), or is every man's light sufficient to his salvation? If so, was it sufficient before Christ preached the gospel and sent his apostles? Or is it now sufficient to all who have never heard the gospel? If so, is not the

271

gospel a vain and needless thing? If the world has sufficient light, what need they your teaching, or discourse, or conviction? If all have sufficient light within them, what need there any converting grace? . . . If all men have sufficient light within them, why you got up into the judgment seat and pronounced me so often to be in darkness, and to be void of the light, and to have none of the Spirit. If all have it, why may not I have it? . . .

[9] Your eleventh query is whether we have seen God's face. Answer: 1. By the eye of reason I have seen that there is a God, and that he is infinite, incomprehensible, most great and most good, etc. 2. The same I have seen more clearly by the eyes of faith. 3. But I never saw God by the eye of flesh, for none can so see God and live, nor has any man seen God at any time, saving the only begotten son, who is in the bosom of his father, he has declared him. 4. Nor have I seen him in glory intuitively, or as the glorified in heaven do. If you say you have seen more, I shall not be very forward to believe you, till I see better fruits of it. I also therefore demand of you whether he who has seen God does not abhor himself (as Job did) in dust and ashes? And whether the true knowledge of God does not ever abase the soul, and make a man very mean in his own eyes? And then is it likely that ever those men had the true knowledge of God, who make it their business to exalt themselves as having the Spirit, and being perfect without sin, and to revile and be-dung other men with their reproaches. . . ? If ever you come to the last saving sight of God, it will mightily change the proud strain of your spirits, and make you abhor the thoughts of your present evil ways.

Your twelfth query is whether we have the same infallible spirit as the holy men of God had, who spoke forth the scriptures. Answer: Why must you know this? Are all dogs and serpents with you who have not that infallible spirit? But we hear the croakings of your Papist guides in that word "infallible;" that's the pillar of their kingdom, and the master-point of their new religion, that their church is infallible. [10] But I will answer you and your masters together in a word. 1. The prophets and apostles had infallible inspirations of new matters of divine verity, not before revealed, because they were to be God's penmen and messengers of such new revelations; I have none such that I know of. 2. The prophets and apostles were guided infallibly in the manner as well as the matter, so that every word that they wrote to the churches was infallibly true. I have no such infallibility, nor your grandfather the Pope neither. . . . But if by infallibility, you should mean the clearness and subjective certainty, as distinct from the objective and bare truth of our conceptions, of that certainty men have different degrees. All true Christians are certain of their fundamentals, yet sometime with some doubting, so that they may find cause to say with the apostles, "Lord, increase our faith," or, "We believe, help thou our unbelief." . . .

Your thirteenth question is "what is Hell's mouth that the wicked go in at, etc." I answer You are liker to know, ere long, than I.

Your fourteenth query is whether the Bible is the word of God, and Matthew, Mark, Luke, and John are the gospel, and whether there were any gospel before them, and whether they are the light? To which I answer, 1. Only Jesus Christ is the co-essential, co-eternal Word of the father. 2. But the holy Scriptures are the temporal expressed word, that is, the signs of God's mind to men, so that Christ and the Scriptures are not called the Word in the same sense, no more than is the word of a man's mind and the word of his mouth or pen. This signifying word was preached before it was written, and then was the gospel, but it was written after it was so preached at first, that it might be a standing rule, and might be kept entire and sure to the church to the world's end. For the bare memories of men would not have kept them for us with such certainty as they have been kept in scripture and delivered unto us. This word therefore is the light, but not as Christ is the Light, or as the Spirit is the Light, for there are many lights that must concur to give us light. [12] So God in Christ is the sun, man's reason is the eye, the gospel or word of God is the external light flowing to us from the sun. The Spirit closes these two together, even the gospel and our reason, and by its powerful work in that closure, breeds a special illumination in the soul, which the word alone could not produce.

I shall add some queries to you: Do you believe the scriptures to be true or not? If you do, then you must believe what they say of themselves; but they call themselves the word of God. (Mark 7:13; Rom. 10:8; II Cor. 2:17; II Cor. 4:2; I Thes. 4:5; I Pet. 1:25.)

Your fifteenth query is whether we own revelations or no. Answer: I own all divine revelations, and disown all diabolical ones, so far as I know them. I own all those blessed revelations contained in the holy Scriptures, for they were infallibly sealed by multitudes of uncontrolled miracles and a spirit of holiness. I believe that the scriptures or laws of Christ being finished and sealed, we must hold these till the coming of Christ (I Tim. 6:13, 14), and that these are able to make men wise to salvation without any more additions, and therefore no more is to be expected. But yet I believe: 1. That God has not [13] tied himself from revealing particular matters in subserviency to scripture extraordinarily, as divers murders have been revealed, and the like matters of fact. 2. And I believe that all true Christians have the illuminating, sanctifying spirit of Christ to help them to know all the meaning of the scripture which is of flat necessity to salvation. . . .

Your sixteenth question is about singing David's psalms, to which I say: . . . If all scripture is written for our use and learning, why may we not speak to God in the words of David's psalms as well as any other scripture?

Your seventeenth question is "what's the soul of man which the ministers of the gospel are to watch for, as they who must give an account to God, and what is it that captivates the soul." The soul is that spiritual substance which causes by its lower power your life, growth, and nourishment, by its next power your feeling, and by its highest power (proper to man of all inferior creatures), your reasoning, intellective knowledge and rational willing and affections, which together with the body constitutes the whole man. . . .

[Baxter responds with questions about the care of souls and says Friends' souls are captive to sin.]

[15] Your eighteenth question is what is the flaming sword that keeps the tree of life, and what the cherubims. Answer: . . . It shall suffice me to know that the flaming sword is God's terrible restraint, and the cherubims are angelical executioners of his will. Wisdom has two gates, the gate of grace and the gate of glory. These things are seen by faith now, and by intuitive intellection in the life to come.

Your nineteenth question is whether they who stand praying in the synagogues or idols' temples, and love greetings in the markets, and bind heavy burdens on the people, and are called of men "master," be not out of Christ's doctrine. Answer: [16] I had rather have a lower room at a feast than a higher, and ordinarily rather none than either. I use not the chief seats in synagogues. I sit in the midst of the assembly; and, so I may conveniently be heard when I am to speak, I care not where I stand. Greetings in the market-place when did I desire? Or to be called Rabbi? But I pray you mark that . . . it is not being called Rabbi or master that Christ intends, but a proud desire of and love of those titles. As a man may accept of the highest room for order, who loves it not in pride, so may he accept of the title of master from those who owe him respect, though he loves it not in pride.

Besides, Christ forbids the name of master no further than he forbids the name of father: verse 9, "call no man your father upon earth," and yet do you not know how often the word "father" is owned in scripture, and children "commanded to love and obey their fathers," and honour them. [Baxter spends four pages analyzing the use of "Master" and "Teacher" in the scriptures, and their Greek and Hebrew meanings.]

[20] [Thomas Goodaire] charged me also to be empty of the Spirit because I studied, and told me he did not study, no, not in speaking what to say. I the less marvel at his nonsense. But I pray God forgive me that I study no more. Do you think we cannot talk without study as well as you, and I hope a little better? And when the lazy fit overtakes ministers, they are ready to preach without study as well as you do. Solomon knew, and I know to my sorrow, that much study is a weariness to the flesh, and might I but plough

274

and dig, I should yet hope to live in some competent health, who now spend my days in continual pain and languishing.

Your twentieth question is, did ever the Lord of heaven and earth, [21] or Jesus Christ bid thee, or any of you, "Go, and preach to a people," or was any of the apostles or ministers of Christ made minister by the will of man? Answer: The Lord called his first apostles by his own voice, and appointed them to call others, and to establish an order for the succeeding of others in that office of the ministry to the end of the world (Mat. *28*:21), . . . that they who should ever after be called might not expect a voice from heaven to their ears, but might be called in Christ's appointed way. And in this way I have been called by Christ. The signs of his call are: 1. My competent qualifications. 2. My thirst after the good of souls and the buildings of that house of God. 3. The ordination of authorized church officers. 4. The call and consent of the people of Christ, over whom he has set me. 5. And afterwards the success of my labours. 6. And some daily assistance of the Spirit in these labours. 7. And some testimony of the Spirit to my conscience of God's acceptance. These seven set together are my evidence of mission, show you the like if you can.

Your twenty-first question is whether had any ministers of Christ an hourglass to preach by, or took a text, and raised doctrines, reasons, uses, motives, or a carnal bell to call people together by. Answer: . . . [22] Scripture is God's laws, and is sufficient rule for doctrines, and worship itself, but was never intended to name to you every circumstance that is lawful about that worship. Has scripture told you at what place you shall meet, or at what hour? . . . These circumstances are purposely left by Christ to the determination of human prudence, as occasions shall require. . . .

But, I pray you, if an hourglass is unlawful, tell us whether a clock is lawful, or a dial, or a watch? Or whether it is lawful to observe by the sun how the time passes? And why is one more unlawful than another?

[23] The twenty-second question is this, whether are not they who seek for the fleece, and make a prey upon the people, and are hirelings, be not false prophets.

Answer: Read but Mal. *2* and *3* without spectacles, and then judge.

Your twenty-third query is whether do you own trembling and quaking, [24] which the scripture witnesseth? Answer: I own the fear of the Lord, which is the beginning of wisdom, and think him blessed who fears always, and that he who hardeneth his heart shall fall into mischief. But I think that the great quaking that was in the army of the Philistines was no virtue or blessing to them, nor any sign of God among them (I Sam. *14*:15). And I think that "perfect love casts out fear," and that those shakings and quakings . . . come not from the humble sense of sin or judgement, or the like, but in violent motions of the body affectedly.

Your twenty-fourth and last question is "whether do you say you shall be free from the body of sin while you are on the earth, and whether shall any be perfect, yea or nay."

Answer: I believe that all true converts are free from the dominion of sin, but not from the remnants of it, and that our grace is of a perfect kind, as a small candle is of a perfect kind of fire, which yet will not enlighten all the town or house, nor scatter away all the darkness as the sun will do. I believe also that in the instant of death, when we part with the flesh, we part with all the remnants of sin. And for the doctrine of personal sinless perfection here. . . . I think that it is a part of the Papists' dung which they have taught you to feed upon. Christ's kingdom is an hospital, he has no subjects in it but diseased ones. The Father's kingdom before had perfect subjects, and so shall it have again, when Christ has perfected us. For when he has [25] perfected us by healing all our diseases and subduing all our enemies, even the last enemy, death (at the resurrection), then will he give up the kingdom to the Father. But now, "in many things we offend all" (Jam. 3:2), and there is no man on earth who does good and sins not. And if we say we have no sin, we deceive ourselves, and the truth is not in us, therefore the truth is not in you Quakers.

I conclude my answer with this question to you: If you think you are perfect, without sin, whether do you also think that you are already in heaven or perfect glory? For what can keep the soul from the perfect enjoyment of God, but sin? And to enjoy God perfectly is to be glorified perfectly. But I forgot that your brethren think heaven and hell is only within men. Perhaps you look for no more heaven than you have.

Having been at this labor at your command, to answer your queries, may I not in reason expect that you should answer some of mine, which I do but request and not command?

1. Are they not the very same ministers which you rail at, and which all the drunkards, swearers, whoremongers, [26] and sensual wretches in the country do hate and rail at as well as you? Are you not then on their side and possessed with the same spirit?[27] Would not all the covetous, malignant, ungodly enemies of piety have tithes down as well as you?

2. Whether it be not the same spirit which moves in you and in the Papists? When the Papists say that we are no true ministers, our congregations are no true churches, who own us as their pastors, . . . so say the Quakers. . . . [The other queries will be taken up as Nayler quotes and answers them.]

---

[27] This is the same argument Friends used in asking toleration. Those who oppose evil ought to be good, and their critics must be evil.

[JAMES NAYLER]
AN ANSWER TO A BOOK CALLED

THE QUAKERS' CATECHISM.

Put out by
RICHARD BAXTER

Wherein the slanderer is searched, his questions
answered, and his deceit discovered, whereby the
simple have been deceived: and the Popery
proved in his own bosom, which he would
cast upon the Quakers.

Published for the sake of all who desire to come out of
Babylon, to the foundation of the true Prophets and
Apostles, where Christ Jesus is the Light and Cor-
nerstone; where God is building a habitation
of righteousness and everlasting Peace;
where the Children of Light do rest.

Also some queries for the discovering the false
grounds of the literal priesthood of these days,
in the last times of Antichrist.

London, printed in the year 1655.

[3] To thee, Richard Baxter:

Who hast bent thy tongue against the innocent, casting out thy envious slanders against the Lamb, who is appeared against the oppression and deceit of all sorts of people? . . . Is this the end of all thy profession, that thou art become a bloody persecutor? . . . and what are we, that thou art set against a poor despised people? . . . Truly this will not be for your peace; He against whom you are risen will break you to pieces, [p. 4] whatever become of our persons. And thou wilt see the day, Rich. Baxter, when thy deeds will come to remembrance, and thy slanders set in order. But remember now thou art warned, while thou hast time.

Though striving for masterhood and vain jangling I abhor, yet for the truth's sake, and the seed that is scattered, I cannot be silent; . . .

In what thou writes "To the Reader," in thy book, thou says thou supposes he will marvel thou troubles thyself with so wild a generation as the people called Quakers are, or that thou writes these few hasty lines on such an occasion. But thou sayest thou wilt tell the cause, which is that they have sent to thee five several papers: one of them with these queries which thou answers, and others of them almost nothing but a bundle of filthy railing

277

words, as "Serpent," "Liar," "Deceiver," Child of the Devil," "cursed Hypocrite," "dumb Dog."

I say every rational man may well marvel that these words should be so hastily by thee called filthy railing words, . . . seeing there is not one of these words but by the Spirit of Jesus Christ they have been used, to such who are in that nature to whom they belong. The same Spirit can do no other but use the same words, without respect of persons, wherever any is found in that practice. Hadst thou said we had been railers, the sin had not been so great; but to say those words given forth by the holy Ghost, as is plain in Scripture, are filthy railing words: here thou calls the Spirit filthy and unclean.

[5] Thou says further, they chose a day to come into your assembly, and fell a-questioning the preacher, thine assistant, and because he avoided disputing with them and fled, therefore they called him the hireling that fleeth, and so confessed themselves to be wolves. . . . But though the hireling did flee, doth this prove them wolves, or did they then confess themselves to be wolves? But though they missed thee then, did not they meet with thee at Worcester, even in the high place where thou wast preaching, and there demanded of thee how the ministers of Christ and the ministers of Antichrist might be known? But could get nothing from thee, more than from thine assistant, unless such words as these—"people regard him not"—and words stirring up the people to hale them out; which being readily executed by thy hearers, prevented the hirelings fleeing. But Tho. Goodaire, staying till thou had done, and then speaking to thee and the people, all the satisfaction he got was that he was haled to prison; yea twice hath he been imprisoned by thy ministry. . . .

[6] And whereas thou would make people believe that we would not suffer you to come to our meeting; did not Richard Farnworth in one letter charge thee and Priest Osland to come to a meeting which was appointed at Chadwitch, in answer to your own letters? Which meeting was appointed and kept, and many people of several judgements came into the meeting with expectations, but neither thou nor Priest Osland appeared, though you had sent your boasting letters for a challenge about the same. . . .

Thou confesses our publishing things hath put thee upon printing; and are they to be blamed for charging thee to answer their questions in writing, who would neither come to their meeting nor suffer them to speak at thine, but sent them to prison? . . .

[7] Two objections, thou says that thou sees, will be raised against thee: one is that the persons are so contemptible, and the errors so gross, that it is a needless work to strive against them. To which thou answers that our multiplying where we come, and the salvation of poor Christians, makes the necessity.

To which I say: what generation thou art of, who holds the persons of any

278

contemptible, is easily judged by any who have that spirit which respects no man's person. . . . And for our multiplying, that must increase to thy torment . . . for God is multiplying his seed as the stars of heaven. The Lamb hath set up his standard, whereat all the beasts of the field rage; yet he will take the victory. And for thy salvation thou tells on, what dost thou intend to save them from, who art preaching up sin as long as they live?

And again thou says, "It's but the Churches of the Separatists and Anabaptists, that are emptied by these seducers, and it's best to let them alone to keep their own flocks."

I say, some of your Churches are so emptied that you have few left to hear you but profane persons, swearers, oppressors, drunkards, and fighters, such as beat in your synagogue, and these are become your prime hearers.

[p. 9] As to thy paper to the Separatists and Anabaptists: . . . all that know anything of the fear of God knows that most of those people have separated from you parish teachers upon this account, (to wit) your infidelity and impiety. . . .

But it seems thou hast lost some of thine also, as well as the Anabaptists; and thou prints a letter, thou says, thou sent to one of them to reclaim him, under pretence that he desired thy thoughts of us and thy evil thoughts thou returns him in this letter.

And thou says he was a young and unsettled one, yet tells how much pains he had taken in duty, and how much zeal he had professed for God, and that he by so great a work of grace was converted from profaneness, etc. . . . And thou goes on to show him that he must needs be fallen from grace, because he is fallen from your Ministry. . . .

[p. 10] Thou further goes on and tells him whence this error comes, even from hellish pride; and to prove this, thou tells him: where we have spent one hour, thou hast spent an hundred in study and meditation, and prays to God for his Spirit of truth and grace, and that thy prayers is as earnest as ours, and thy life is much more holy and heavenly than ours. And therefore God is, as it were, more engaged to thee, to make known his truth to thee, than to us; and is not this apparent pride for us to be so confident, that we are wise and beloved in the eyes of God, and that we run about with the shells on our head, etc., in comparison of thee.

I say, the hellish pride thou hast plainly discovered, where it is. But whose righteousness is all this by which thou hast thus engaged God to thee, who art but yet praying for the Spirit of truth and grace? We know God freely gives a measure [p. 11] of his Spirit to every one of us, freely to profit withal; and improving that to his praise, we receive more freely. And we are so far from engagement of God by all we do, that we find ourselves unprofitable servants; but this thou knowest not with thy vain light words. . . . And thou

279

says pride is the master sin of the Quakers, and thou proves it, because that we go in a poor garb, and cry out against pride, as if we were sent from Heaven to persuade men to wear no lace, cuffs or points, and to damn so many ministers for being called Master; but, says thou, spiritual pride is the most killing, and so goes on railing against us for these things, calling that spirit in scorn, "an excellent spirit," that can trample on all worldly glory. I say, "Blasphemer, thou shalt know when thou hast finished thy rage, that thou hast spoken against the holy Spirit of God, sent from Heaven, which both in Christ and his Apostles did persuade against and condemn such things. . . .

And thou sets down four particulars, wherein thou wilt prove our language of Hell, and the Devil speaking by our mouths. The first is: they affirm themselves perfect without sin; and this thou says is impossible, and they are mad that believe it. I say, that we affirm self-perfection is but thy lying slander, or that we say we are Christ or God, as thou says we do. But that we witness perfection from sin, so far as we have received Christ, we own it as God's commands and gift, the end of Christ's coming, and of giving forth his ministry; as these Scriptures may witness: *Matth.* 5:48; *James 1*:17, *John 3*:8; *Eph.* 4:11, 12, 13, . . . Neither doth perfection exclude praying and the blood of Christ, for in his blood and [p. 12] prayer it is wrought, and we kept.

Thy second thing is: that we set up ourselves above all the people of God on earth, that we vilify the most holy and eminent servants of God, and condemn all the churches of the world. To which I shall say no more but this: that these are three of thy lies racked up together, lest thou should fall.

Thy third thing is: that we damn all the people of God for 1600 years at least. I say, this may well be matter of offence to thee, to deny all thy generation since the Pope to this day; therefore thou calls it unmatchable pride. But for those whom you have tortured, martyred and burned, whipped and imprisoned, to this day, who suffered for conscience sake, following the Lamb—in their measure them we own, and with them we suffer. Though thou say God had never such a people on earth of these men's ways, yet was this the Church of Christ, whereof he was the head, and is the head. And there it was visible, and there it is to all who are not blind: And if these be the few heretics (thou tells on) that thou says were our predecessors of old, I say we cannot but own these in their measure, though we go under the name of heretics with them, by the same generation.

Thy fourth thing is: that which thou calls our proud, scornful, railing language. . . . I say, the language of Christ we use to thee, who art found in the work of Satan; therefore thou canst not bear it. . . . And thus thou proves it, saying, "What if Christ called Judas a Devil, is it therefore lawful to call Peter so?" I say, yea, if Peter be found in the Devil's work (Matth. *16*:23): much more thou and thy generation, who none of you yet come so far as

Peter, who denied all to follow Christ. But you will have all you can get, though you deny Christ and all his rules for the getting of it: As thou goes on still pleading for thy masterhood, saying . . . that it is not the title, but the lording over men's faith that is for [p. 13] bidden. All those that know anything of the Faith of Christ sees you to be guilty of both, but will give you neither.

Thou tells thy thoughts of us, says thou: "it was the main advantage that the Reformers had for the ruin of the Papal Kingdom, to persuade men that the Pope was Antichrist: and to disgrace the Popish Clergy;" and, says thou, "they would attempt the destruction of our Church by the same means." I say, "why not?" "Why may not that which lops off some of your branches, now the time is come, cut up the whole root?" And whereas thou says that the Papists have begotten this present sect of Quakers, I say the Devil is not divided against himself. . . . And thou says, we have here and there a Papist, lurking to be the chief speaker among us. I say . . . if thou know such among us and do not produce it, then art thou deceitful to the trust of the Nation. But if thou know none, then art thou a false accuser; . . . adding lies, saying that we say the Pope is not Antichrist, that we undermine the Scriptures, decry . . . justification by imputed righteousness . . . set up strength of man's free will, the exalting of Monastical Community and Virginity, and alienation from worldly employment. All this, says thou, the Papists hath taught the Quakers. . . . Instead, thou hast proved the Devil thy head and father; for we confess the Pope to be Antichrist, and all you Popish Clergy of his lineage, and with the Scriptures we so prove it; which Scriptures we own, with the true ministry and churches, justification by Christ's righteousness, freely put and given to us; whereby our own righteousness we deny, and set up the Light within us.

[He ties up Catholic with Presbyterian persecution and then goes on to Baxter's answers to the original Quakers' questions.]

[p. 17] Our first query is: what's the first principle of pure Religion? Thy answer is that God is; and next, that he is a rewarder of them that diligently seek him; and thou queries the ground of our asking.

I say the ground of our asking is: that the folly of such teachers as know not God and his way may be made manifest, as it is by thy answer; for the knowledge of what God is is the substance, ground and end of all pure Religion. If thou had answered this query to the satisfaction of any honest desires, then thou must have confessed to the Light that God hath given in Christ Jesus, to lead out of darkness. . . .

Second query: whether they are a Church of Christ that beat and persecute them that witness for the truth in his name? And to this thou answered that it's possible for a true Church to be guilty of injuries; but to cover thy guilt in

281

this, thou would rank us amongst Turks and witches, wherein thou shows how thou would order these injuries done to us, if it were in thy power....

[p. 18] Third query, thou says, is about Infants' Baptism: and not being able to prove thy practice herein, either by command or example, thou shuffles it off with telling of a book, and ... infolds a lie in it, saying the Anabaptists are our founders.

And 5th, 6th, 7th, 8th and 9th queries, thou says, are all about tithes, but ... instead of answering six of ours, thou starts ten of thy own.

Thy first is: whether we have read any of those books that proves that tithes are still of divine right. I say, by no other divinity than the Pope's authority, canst thou ... prove tithes to Christ's Ministers to be by divine right; prove it by the Book of Scripture.

Thy 2nd and 3rd queries is whether the Scripture doth warrant a man to dedicate part of his lands to God for the service of his Church....

I say, suppose that be granted, that a man may freely give his own to God; must the hireling therefore take men's goods against their wills, to maintain such a ministry and worship as God never set up? ...

[p. 20] Thy 6th is, whether you ask so much of people as Quakers do. Thou shameless man, whom do we ask anything on? We abhor thy beggarly practice herein, and are fed freely....

The sum of thy 8th query: if the rulers may lay excise or taxes, why not a settled maintenance for you? I say, because the one is allowed on in the Scripture; but the Magistrate was never to force a maintenance for the ministry, neither under law nor Gospel.... But God ever took care of them that are his.... Nay, it's you that knows him not, therefore dare not trust him, but envies such as do....

[The Quakers'] Tenth query: whether Christ enlightens every one that cometh into the world. And thy answer is: all that come into the world of nature, he enlightens with the light of nature, and this thou says is [p. 21] begotten by the "book of the creature." And all that comes into the world of grace, he enlightens with the light of supernatural revelation. I say: ... Thou blind guide, doth any light lead into the world of grace, as thou calls it, but the light of Christ, and is that begotten by the creatures' book? ... Thou adds a heap of queries: 1. Whether this light be sufficient to leave men without excuse; or is it sufficient to salvation? I say, both to condemn such as love their evil deeds, and to lead to life all that follow it, John 3:19 and 8:12. 2. Was it sufficient before Christ preached the Gospel, or is it now sufficient to all that never heard the Gospel? If so, is not the Gospel needless? I say, all that believed in him to come, has sufficiently of his light to guide them in what God then required. But when he was come, then the Gospel was preached to every creature under Heaven, then all was called to repent, and wait for the Kingdom of God, which was at hand within them, which they did not know who denied the light; yet the light being come into the world, was their condemnation. Thus the Gospel is not a needless thing but the power of God to salvation to all that receive it: for as many as received the light, to them he gave power to become the Sons of God; to the rest it is condemnation. Third query: if the world have sufficient light, what need they your teaching? I say, to exhort them to that light, to wait and abide in it.

[2nd 21: misnumbered] Our 11th query: whether thou hast seen God's face? And to this thou utters a deal of confusion, saying that by the eye of reason, thou hast seen God to be infinite, incomprehensible, and saith, none hath seen God; and then asks a query: whether he that hath seen God do abhor himself as Job did, and says, is it likely that ever those men had the true knowledge of God, who exalt themselves as having the Spirit, and being perfect men without sin?

I say, art not thou ashamed of thy folly, who would persuade people that having the Spirit and being without sin could keep [a man] from seeing God. Thou blind, for can any come to know God but by the Spirit? And where wilt thou have this Spirit if not within? (*Rom. 8*:9) Can he be any of Christ's who hath not his Spirit, or can any unclean thing stand before God, or come in his sight? But if any witness this Spirit, and sanctification by it, thy filthy mind calls it pride.

Twelfth query: whether you have the same infallible Spirit as the holy men of God had, who spoke forth the Scripture? And instead of answering plainly . . . [22] thou says the Prophets and Apostles were guided infallibly in the manner and matter, so that what they writ to the Church was true; but thou hast no such infallibility. I say, if thou had such a Spirit, your pulpits would have more truth, and thy book not so full of lies as it is; . . . for the Spirit of God is but one, and who hath it hath an infallible guide in matter and manner, if he keep to it. And he that is not guided by this, hath the spirit of Satan; and I know that so far as any are led by the Spirit, it guides into all truth if it be not erred from.

But says thou, I shall never like such pretenders to the Spirit. I know thou dost not; for that guide leads out of thy kingdom. Says thou, all true Christians are certain of their fundamentals, yet with doubting: Here thou hast declared thy damned foundation. But true Christians know a foundation without doubting. And thou falls to comparing us with the Pope, and would make us like him; I say, were it not we cry down his worship, means, and authority that remains in you, we should not have so much of your malice. Are not you his dear children, as like as may be? Have you so soon forgot who begot you into your parsonages and masterships, and ordained you. . . .

[p. 24] Query 13: What is hell's mouth that the wicked go in at? And to this thou says it sufficeth thee to know that hell is a state of endless misery, where such as we shall everlastingly bear God's wrath. I say, that's thy desire to know? But were thou not blind, thou wouldst know it is for liars, slanderers, the Man of Sin and his disciples, who plead for his kingdom.

Query 14: whether the Bible be the Word of God, and *Matthew, Mark, Luke* and *John* the Gospel? And whether there were any Gospel before them? And whether they be the Light? To this thou gives not answer . . . and tells of a different sense betwixt Christ, the Scriptures. And thou says it was written that it might be a standing rule, and kept entire, and sure, to the world's end. But . . . scarce two of you can agree about it, what is the meaning of it, and how many copies is there of it? Which of them is the standing rule? [p. 25] And so imagines that Christ, the Spirit, and the Word are not one, nor enlightens all alike. Says thou, man's reason is the eye, and the Gospel is external, and the Spirit closeth these two together, and so breedeth a spiritual illumination, which the word alone could not procure; whereas the Scriptures witness the Word, by which alone all externals were made, and the Word for reconciling again and making new.[28]

And thou asks some queries: first, whether we believe the Scriptures be true. I say yea; then says thou, they call themselves the word of God, and thou brings some Scriptures to prove it, but not one that says the letter is the word; . . . and to prove the Bible to be the Word, brings "The word is in the heart"; but no wonder thou be blind, who says man's reason is the eye.

Query 15: whether you own revelations or no. And to this thou says, thou owns all divine revelations and disowns all diabolical ones . . . but the revelations thou own is what is written. . . . Yet says thou, these are able to make men wise to salvation, without any further additions, and when thou hast done, says they must have the Spirit of Christ to help them. But thou might do well to show thy opinion, whether the spirit can make wise to salvation without them.

[26] Query 16 is about singing David's Psalms: and for answer to this thou sends us a book of Cotton and Ford, but when thou and thy hearers sings David's words, saying you "have no scornful eye," you "have roared all the day long," your "bones hath quaked," you "have made your bed to swim with tears," no liar shall dwell in your house, etc., are not a nest of liars all found lying together? . . .

Query 17: what is the soul of man, etc.? And thou says it's the cause of our life. I say thou knows not him who is the cause of our life, no more than thou dost the soul. . . .

[27] Fourth query: thou says if the present pastors be not true ministers, tell you who are, and where you may find them, and where they have been

---

28 A compact summary of the difference: Puritans said the Spirit brings scripture to men, Quakers that scripture brings men to the Spirit.

from Christ till now? I say those are true ministers and ever was, who wandered to and fro, having no certain dwelling place, of whom the world was not worthy; who ever bore witness against the false Prophets that bear rule by their means, and the priests that preached for hire. . . . Who would have believed that you, who have had so many millions of pounds for teaching people to forsake sin, . . . now if any declare that he hath forsaken it and is set free, you preach it down as the most dangerous error that ever was; and cry out to drunkards, swearers, thieves, murderers, and whoremongers, "come not near [Quakers] lest you be deceived;" and now [you] get up more money for preaching up sin while the world stands, than you took for preaching it down. Yet if we tell you you are bringing people into covenant with the Devil for term of life, you say we rail on you. Ask any that ever believes your teaching, if they believe that Christ is able to redeem them from committing sin in this world; "nay none can be free here". . . .

But say you, this persecution of ours is not as theirs was; they persecuted Christ and such as he sent, but these are wanderers and vagabonds, and disturbs our peace and worships, etc. But the light is come, your mists will not hide you. . . . Where had ever ministers of Christ hand in persecuting any upon any account whatsoever? Prove your practice herein.

[29] Query 18: what is the Flaming Sword that keeps the Tree of Life, and the Cherubims? This thou answers with calling it a foolish question, for thou that never saw the Flaming Sword and Cherubims, never came near the Tree of Life; but as I said before, feeds upon death, thy own cursed carnal knowledge, which God hath forbidden.

Query 19: whether they that stand praying in the synagogues or idols' temples, and love greetings in markets, and bind heavy burdens on the people, and are called of men masters, be not out of Christ's Doctrine? Thou goes on, and where thou cannot deny but thou art in the steps of the PHARISEES, yet says thou, I do not love it; they loved it to be called master, etc., but I do not. Well, thou says in words thou loves it not, but come to thy practice. . . .

[p. 31] It's no hard thing with you to take Paul's words, who wandered up and down in hunger and nakedness, coveted no man's money, nor gold, nor apparel, and was chargeable to none, nor took ought against the will of the owner, etc. (*2 Cor. 11*:27), and with two or three consequences and meanings from your original [sermon text], you will make it prove you four or five hundred [pounds] a year, and a great house to live in. And this you will not have by favor but force, and yet they are thieves that denies to give you their goods when you ask it. . . .

[p. 32] Nor is he void of the fear of God, who denies thee to be a faithful minister of Christ who ministers against the command of Christ, saying a minister of Christ is called Master, and that to deny your Greek and Hebrew is to deny Christ, as though a natural language was Christ. And thou calls some sacred languages, thou idolater. Is not every language natural to them who are bred in them? . . .

Query 20: did ever the Lord of Heaven and Earth, or Jesus Christ [p. 33] bid thee or any of you go and preach to a people? Or was any of the Apostles or ministers of Christ made ministers by the will of man? To this thou answers after the old way, and begins another story, telling the Lord called the Apostles by his own voice, and left them to call one another to the end of the world. . . . All the parish teachers, both in this nation and many more, have had their ordination and holy order, since the Pope's time, he says, from Peter. . . . But thou proceeds to deny any to expect a call from Heaven.

Query 21: whether had any ministers of Christ an hourglass to preach by, or took a text, and raised doctrine, uses, reasons, motives [in a sermon] or a carnal bell to call people together by. Prove these things by plain Scripture, or else be silent and never profess yourselves to be ministers of Christ more. . . . Thou will not be tried by thy own "standing rule," but says these [customs] are purposely left by Christ, to be determined of human [p. 34] providence. What providence is that which is human providence, to which your worship of God is left? Is his worship human, and your tithes divine? They who worship in truth have the Spirit of Truth to guide them into all truth in his whole worship. Can you therefore set an hour to begin and end for hundreds of years, by a glass, or by a clock either, and not limit the Spirit?

[p. 35] Query 22: whether are not they that . . . seek for their gain from their quarter, and seek for the fleece, and make a prey on the people, and are hirelings, be not false Prophets: yea or nay? And are not such to be cried out against, now as they was then? This being thy own condition, thou art so wise as to let it alone without an answer. . . . Thou bids us read *Malachi*; so we have, and in the second chapter, first and last, and the rest of the chapter: [there] we find thy generation, and thy practice, and your end coming on apace.

Query 23: whether do you own trembling and quaking which the Scriptures witness? And this thou looks upon to be a curse, or a Papist trick, or motion of the Deceiver, etc. All the holy men of God that ever did declare the way how they came to see God, came through [trembling] as the Scriptures can witness in *Moses, David, Daniel,* the Prophets and Apostles. But, says thou, perfect love casts out fear. What now! Art thou talking of perfection?

Last query: whether do you say you shall be free from the body of sin while you are on the earth, and whether shall any be perfect: yea or nay? And to this thou says, thou believes that in the instant of death when you part with the flesh, you part with all the remnants of sin. I say you must part with your sin when you are dead and can sin no more if you would. . . . But that this covenant of hell and death should be for any less than term of life, that's against your faith which you have preached and live in, and against your covenant, too. Yet if we do but say that you are ministers of the Devil and such as uphold his kingdom of sin, while people live and the world stands, you cannot bear it, though we do but declare thy own confession. [p. 36] And for the saints owning perfection, read *Eph. 4*:12, 13; *Col. 1*:28; *Phil. 3*:15; *I Thess. 3*:10 and *5*:2; *Psalms 18*:32 and *101*:2; *Heb. 10*:14; *I Cor. 2*:6; *James 1*:4; *II Cor. 7*:1, with many more places, too many to set down here, which all declare their belief in perfection, and thee a false witness. O thou blasphemer! Dare thou speak thus of the perfection of God, which he gives to all that wait upon him, and hunger after his righteousness? . . . Thou blind guide, had the first man Adam power to defile in this world, and hath not the second Adam power to cleanse to the uttermost, in this world what is defiled, all that come to him? The last enemy (says thou) is death, which shall then be overcome at the last resurrection; a large time art thou taking for sin and death to reign, till all men be dead. . . . [p. 37] Thou runs to that one place which all thy father's children use to plead: *I John* 1. "If we say we have no sin, we deceive ourselves, and the truth is not in us;" therefore, says thou, the truth is not in you Quakers. I say John was there showing to little children that there could be none free from sin further than they was in Christ, not in self, nor while anything of self remained.

Thou proceeds to ask more queries, and thou desires me to speak truly to the point in question. I say, so I shall in plainness, passing by words to no purpose.

And first thou says, "Are not they the very same ministers you rail at, which all the drunkards, swearers, whoremongers, and sensual wretches in the country do hate and rail at? . . .

[p. 38] Answer: I say: railing we deny, and speak the truth against those we find out of the doctrine of Christ, who are one with drunkards and swearers, whoremongers, and sensual wretches . . . who fight for such a ministry with clubs, and stones, and stocks. . . .

Thy second query is made up of a bundle of lies, which I shall return thee again from whence they came; as first: that we seduce the people from true teaching; 2. that we condemn the Scriptures; 3. that we prefer some translation or language before another; 4. that we maintain free-will before conversion; 5. or deny it to be only the fruit of the Spirit in the Elect; 6. that we hold forth any for the fulfilling the commands of God, but Christ only in them that believe; 7. that we make our perfection only in casting off worldly callings, relations, names or any other thing, but in Christ himself; 8. or that thou hast anything under our hands that says so; 9. that we place our righteousness in our own works; 10. that we deny the imputed righteousness of Christ; 11. that we (instead of preaching the righteousness of Christ) call out for our own formal righteousness; 12. that our righteousness consists in any outward thing or places; 13. that we say no man may call master or mistress any further than Christ forbids it, to the Devil's pride in proud men as Pharisees, hirelings or the like; 14. that our righteousness lies in forbidding those things; 15. that we are ignorant of Christ's righteousness; 16. that we take the most satanical lies and slanders to be our righteousness; 17. that the Papists and we conspire together. These seventeen devilish lies hast thou laid upon us, yet if we so call them the father of them is offended. [p. 39] And as for the Papists denying your ministry, or confessing the sufficiency of the light of Christ, or witnessing freedom from sin in him: . . . I say, shall we deny the truth because they profess it? Or the light of Christ and his redemption because they profess it in words? I say nay, nor doth this prove us of the same spirit with them, for it is the fruits that manifests the Spirit and not words; and by that we deny both the Papists and you. . . .

[p. 44] Query 5: "Are not the ministers whom these men despise of the same calling [and] practice as those were that suffered death in the flames of Queen Mary's days: such as Bradford, Hooper, Latimer, Ridley, Cranmer, Saunders, Philpot, and the rest?[29] Were not these called masters, did they not preach in pulpits and take tithes or money for preaching as their due maintenance, and the other things that the Quakers accuse us for? And do not these men justify the bloody opposers of them and condemn God's saints afresh?"

Answer: I say it was for denying of that which was the Popish way of worship, according to their measure of light, that these men then suffered, and being faithful to that measure they were accepted, though the fullness of the light was not then come. But this is no ground to uphold the rest of their Popish inventions contrary to Gospel worship and if they thus fared, who did but witness against some branches, what may we expect, who holds forth that light which strikes at the root? Therefore we think it not strange to see your rage greater. . . .

[p. 55, misnumbered] Query 15: was that light in Paul which persuaded him that he ought to do many things against the name of Jesus sufficient to convert him to the faith of Jesus? . . . Or had Cornelius sufficient light within him before Peter preached unto him? Or had all the world sufficient light within them, before Christ sent abroad his Apostles to preach the Gospel unto them? Or did Christ send them a needless light by his Apostles? . . .

Answer: I say Christ hath enlightened everyone that comes into the world, yet is the light in darkness, though darkness comprehends it not. Therefore Peter was sent to Cornelius, Ananias to Paul, and the Apostles to the world, not to give them eyes, but to open the blind eyes, and to turn them from darkness to the light, as is plain. Christ and the Apostles came into the world

[29] These were the great Protestant martyrs under Mary Tudor, 1653-58.

288

for that purpose, though Christ was the light before the world was; yet came into the world to open the eyes. . . .

[p. 45] Query 17: Is it not a most sottish trick of you to go up and down prating and commanding, and yet refuse to show your commission from God, and to call ministers to show theirs and refuse to show your own, but say it is invisible within you?

[p. 46] Answer: Our call and commission is invisible as to you, as ever it was to the world, yet herein is it showed that we are found in the same practice and suffering that all the saints of God ever was, for declaring against the false worships.

Query 19: Is not that man an infidel and a scorner of Christ that dare say he came into the world and shed his blood to gather only a few raging Quakers in England 1652 years after his incarnation? If Christ have no subjects but these, he is a poor king. . . .

Answer: The nearest comparison as I find in Scripture whereby to show what a church Christ had, since the mystery of iniquity and Popish priesthood and parish masters was set up in the falling away, may be compared to his church [in Israel] from the time that the hirelings and false prophets begun amongst the Jews to preach for hire, and bear rule by their means, etc., even till Christ's coming in the flesh; which church was sometimes visible but in a few despised prophets. . . .

[p. 47] And the kingdom of Christ hath been poor according to thy judgement, yet hath these been his subjects; nor hath he been without a body. Yet is he not come to save a few raging Quakers only, but with ten thousand of his saints is he come to be avenged of that bloody generation.

[Nayler concludes his tract with thirteen more questions of his own, mostly issues already raised in his replies to Baxter.]

3. George Fox's *Great Mistery of the Great Whore Unfolded* (1659)

Baxter's *Worcestershire Petition Defended* had already inspired in 1653 two Quaker countertracts, Aldam's *Brief Discovery* and Benjamin Nicholson's *Truth's Defence*, but Baxter seems not to have known or replied to these directly. *Quakers' Catechism*, though in a sense already a second round of debates with Baxter, was a new beginning due to the Quakers' visits. Its only direct reply, other than Nayler's, came in a 420-page folio volume Fox put out in 1659, during the year of political chaos; probably during his months of illness and retirement at Thomas and Ann Curtis' home at Reading, he assembled several dozen anti-Quaker tracts by all the great Puritans of the day, and answered the lot. A scholar might have been driven by the challenge to work out a systematic Quaker theology answering all objections, but Fox's method was the same as in all earlier Quaker debate tracts, to rebut each separately, phrase by phrase. In the same volume, then, but at widely scattered points, he tackled the Worcestershire Petition, the *Quakers' Catechism*, and Baxter's *Second Sheet for the Ministry* of 1657. The second of these sections follows.

From:

THE GREAT MISTERY OF THE GREAT WHORE UNFOLDED.
George Fox; London, printed for Thomas Simmonds
at the Bull and Mouth near Aldersgate, 1659.

[27] *Richard Baxter's Book called The Quakers' Catechism*

> *His principles follows, and his works, which are to the fire to be condemned. And as for his lies and railings, and brawlings and revilings, we turn them back to himself, which for them, the greatest will be his own sorrow.*

Pr. He saith in a letter at the beginning of his book, to a friend: "To say that any is perfect, and without sin, is the Devil speaking in man. . . ."

Ans. Contrary to the language of the apostle and Christ, who bid them be perfect, and the apostle spoke wisdom among them "that are perfect," and said, "they were made free from sin." And it is the Devil speaking in man that speaks for sin, while men are upon earth, and speaks. . . .

Pr. He saith, "Christ does not condemn men for being called of men Master, and it is not the title, . . ."

Ans. Contrary to Christ's words, who saith, "be you not of men called Master, for you have a master in heaven, even Christ, and you are all brethren." And thus he tramples upon the commands, and makes the commands of Christ of no effect, which is one of the marks that Christ gives to the multitudes to know the hypocrites by, and so does not only deny Christ's commands, but teaches men to break them. So crucifies Christ, and says they are his ministers, but that's the Antichrist that abides not in his doctrine, as in II John.

Pr. And he saith, "People are tossed up and down like a bundle of feathers, and novices. . . ."

290

Ans. How should they be otherwise than be tossed up and down by you, when you deny perfection, of being perfect, and call it the voice of the Devil speaking, that speaks of perfection, and overcoming sin? ... All the perfection is in Christ the second Adam, the covenant of God, out of sin and transgression, and so "who are in Christ are new creatures," and "old things pass away, and all things become new." ...

Pr. He saith, "a true church is guilty of injury. ..."

Ans. Contrary to the scriptures, where the apostle saith the church is the pillar and ground of truth, without spot or wrinkle or blemish, or any such thing.

Pr. He saith, "God has commanded a sufficient maintenance in general for ministers, and left it to human prudence to judge what is sufficient. ..."

Ans. By this he hath left the Spirit, to judge, and the wisdom of God which acts by his commands; and so runs into earthly human prudence. Therefore is there so much oppression for tithes and maintenance for ministers, and so much making havoc, and prisoning and persecuting for the same, and the power denied which the apostles had to [28] eat and to drink, which Christ gave them. ...

Pr. He saith, "all who come into the world are lighted with the light of nature."

Ans. For so he calls the Light, which John calls the "true light (which is Christ) that lights every man that comes into the world;" so [he] is ignorant of John's doctrines, and the scriptures, a man not fit to teach, but is gotten up by an usurped authority, and is not able to divide the word aright, but with the scriptures thou art corrected, and the Light that lights every man that comes into the world, the natural lights were made by it, the sun and moon, and so forth. And men that are born blind are enlightened with that Light which was before the sun was, before all things were made, "which came a light into the world to lighten every man, that all men through it might believe." Now all men may see how all men are mad against John, Christ, and the apostles' doctrine, that bore witness to the true Light, and Christ bid believe in it.

Pr. He talks of, and preacheth up, an external word.

Ans. Which the Scripture speaks nothing of, nor the prophets, nor Christ, but saith, "the word that lives, abides, and endures forever;" and [it speaks] of the scriptures of truth that cannot be broken; and of God's words, and Christ's words, and that is not external, this is not agreeable to sound words that cannot be condemned, but that is like his doctrine that knows not the eternal. But the ministers of Christ did not tell people of an external word, but an eternal word; but you being made by the will of man, speak to the people of an external.

Pr. He saith, he "hath not seen God in glory, nor any man. ..."

291

Ans. We do believe thee; and the priests have not seen him, but the saints saw him, and Job saw him, and Isaiah saw him the Lord of hosts, and Stephen saw him, and Abraham saw his glory, and the apostle saw him, "and beheld his glory, the glory of God." . . .

Pr. He saith, "The word infallible is the pillar of the Popish kingdom, and the master-point of new religion. . . ."

Ans. . . . Contrary to the apostle, who had many infallible proofs of the Spirit of Jesus Christ, and they who have not are none of his, and who have the Spirit of Christ, have that which is infallible, and lets them see infallible proofs, as thou mayst read in Scripture. And who have the Spirit of God, have that which is infallible. And the religion which is out of the infallibility, and out of the Spirit of God, is vain, and there is thine, and the Pope's, as your fruits have declared. . . .

Pr. And thou says, "Thou hast no such revelation as the apostles had as thou knowest of, and the apostles were brought to speak infallibly to the church by an infallible spirit. . . ."

Ans. We do believe you, for you are the false spirit, you and the Pope that went forth from the apostles into the world, that Christ said should come, that inwardly ravened from the spirit, and went forth from the apostles, and only have had the sheep's clothing, and so are the spirits which the apostles bid the saints try (which went forth into the world) that had the true Spirit, the record, the Spirit of God. And they that have found the record, the Spirit of God tries all your spirits, and finds you fallible, . . .

[29] Pr. He says, "The holy scriptures are the temporal word, etc."

Ans. Now see if this be not an undervaluing the Scriptures of truth, and the words of God and Christ, and the prophets and apostles, which cannot be broken: he calls it a temporal word, which the scripture teacheth no such doctrine, but thy lying spirit.

Pr. He saith, "The gospel or Word is the external light flowing out unto us from the son. . . ."

Ans. Contrary to the scripture, which saith, "the gospel is the power of God unto salvation to every one who believes," so not temporal, not a temporal light. And the light which cometh from the Son of God, that lighteth every man that cometh into the world, that is not temporal, thou that saith so art in the delusion.

Pr. He says, "The Scriptures are able to make men wise unto salvation without any more additions, and there is no more to be expected. . . ."

Ans. Contrary to the Scripture itself, and to the apostle's doctrine, who saith, "through the faith they are able to make wise to salvation." So there is an addition which the apostles adds and all the saints and true believers, which is the faith which thou art reprobated from, and so no minister of Christ, in the un-victory, so in the world's lusts.

Pr. He says, "The soul of man is a spiritual substance. . . ."

292

Ans. Now consider what a condition these called ministers are in: They say that which is a spiritual substance is not infinite in itself, but a creature, that which came out from the Creator, and is in the hand of the Creator, which brings it up, and to the Creator again, that is infinite itself, which the hand goes against him who does evil, in which hand the soul is, which is immortal and infinite; which hand is infinite; [that] which brings it up to God is infinite.

Pr. He saith, "Do not they blasphemously make Christ an idol, who call our temples idols' temples?"

Ans. Christ's body was and is the temple of God, who ended all outward temples made with hands, and so that is no idol, but others are idols, held up by you and the Pope, Jews and Gentiles, who prison the seed of God in yourselves. And Stephen was stoned to death for denying the Temple, and for witnessing the substance: so have you almost stoned many to death for denying your idols' temples.

Pr. He calls that "most ignorant and sottish dealing to own Christ's commands that bids 'be not called of men Master.' " (See p. 18.)

Ans. And thus he shows his ignorance and sottishness, and doth not read "Mr. Paul," "Mr. Peter," and they transgress the doctrine of Christ.

Pr. He saith, "All the ministers since the days of the apostles were to be ordained and called, which the apostles were not. . . ."

Ans. Does not the apostle speak of them who usurped the authority? Yes, we say that all of you and the Pope since the days of the apostles are called by men, and made by men, who are the false spirit that went forth into the world, . . . And as no prophecy of scripture came by the will of man, therefore all as do get the Scripture in their own wills out of the Holy Ghost, are made by man, such are out of unity with God, with Scriptures, with one another. . . .

[30] Pr. He saith, "The scripture is God's law, and a sufficient rule for doctrine and worship itself. . . ."

Ans. Now many may have the scriptures, and if they have not the Spirit that gave them forth, they do not worship God in the Spirit. And they who have the scriptures and do not do the will of Christ, they know not his doctrine. And the law is light.

Pr. He saith, "But I must tell you, that our bells are not carnal; if they were, they would scarce sound so well, or last so long. . . ."

Ans. And if they are not carnal, then they are spiritual, and in that all the world will judge thee, that they are things seen, and so they are temporal and carnal.

And whereas thou speakst of "baptizing your bell?" Have not many bells in England been baptized? And was not the Pope the first author of it? And we do say that they are carnal and not spiritual, let them never sound so well, and last never so long, though in many towns you have made them to tune psalms, yet we cannot say that these are spiritual that can tune psalms, neither dare we, but do judge them who do say they are so.

Pr. He saith, "To say a man is freed from the body of sin while on earth is part of the Papists' dung which they have taught you to feed upon. . . ."

Ans. Contrary to the scriptures and the apostle's words, who saith, "they were made free from sin," which was before you or the Papists were. And contrary to John, who bids them "try the spirits," he saith, "he who is born of God does not commit sin, neither can he, because the seed of God remains in him," I John.

Pr. Again he saith, "Christ's kingdom is a hospital, and has no subjects in it but diseased ones."

Ans. We read of no such thing in Scripture, that Christ's kingdom is a hospital, and his subjects are diseased ones. But they who follow the Lamb, in their mouth is no guile, nor spot, nor fault before the throne of God, and are the elect which God lays no sin to; and they are the faithful, and called, and chosen that overcome the world, and his kingdom stands in power, and in righteousness, and joy in the Holy Ghost, and is not a "hospital," nor his subjects diseased ones, for he heals them, and converts them, and washes them. The diseased, or such as come unto Christ to be healed, them who come to him he heals them of what infirmity soever it be, and cures them and clothes them in the right mind. Therefore thou art corrected, and worthy of correction, and all the diseased ones are in your kingdom, physicians of no value.

Pr. "What can keep the soul from the enjoyment of God but sin. . .?"

Ans. It is the unbelief in Christ, the Light, and the offering, and in his blood that keeps from the enjoyment of God, who is the way to God, which the Light lets see that.

4. The Controversy with Baxter: Later Rounds (1657-60)

Even before Fox had written *The Great Mistery*, Baxter had opened a new round of the tract debate. As Burrough notes, he did not reply to Nayler's questions in *Answer to Baxter*,[30] but took a new initiative in *One Sheet Against the Quakers*. His ideas were not so new, nor were those of Burrough and William Storer

[30] Smith lists *An Answer to the Quakers' Queries* in 1655, but Wing knows no surviving copies and it is probably just one of the five editions of *Quakers' Catechism* which appeared in 1655-57, of which Smith lists but three.

294

in countertracts. Baxter's next response was *One Sheet for the Ministry*, followed in the same year (1657) by *A Second Sheet*, to which George Whitehead replied. Baxter and Tombes wrote *True Old Light* in 1660 and Samuel Fisher wrote two Quaker answers; and so on. If space permitted, it might be more edifying to reproduce here parts of John Bunyan's tract debate with Burrough, John Faldo's with Penn, or Fisher's with Owen and Danson; instead we close this tract-debate material with excerpts from Baxter and Burrough in 1657, to show how debates and tracts were a challenge like anti-Quaker laws, against which almost any Quaker might feel personally called to throw himself.

ONE SHEET AGAINST THE QUAKERS

Richard Baxter
London, 1657

[1] ... The man that will stand safe, and look on the folly and misery of all these sects, with prudence to his own advantage, must be a sincere Catholic Christian, saved from infidelity and impiety, having [2] one God, one Mediator between God and man, one Holy Spirit; being a member of that one catholic Church, which is not confined to the sect of Papists, or the sect of Anabaptists, or any sect, but containeth all the true Christians in the world, though some parts of it be reformed and pure, and others more deformed and corrupt; having one catholic rule, the Word of God; and a catholic love to all Christians in the world, with a care and desire of their welfare, proportionable to their several degrees of loveliness. Being myself a member of this catholic Church encourageth me the more boldly to do my part in defending the cause of God, against the assaults of all these deluded ones, and particularly the Quakers. I shall here give ... those reasons ... that move me to conceive, that no Christian or reasonable man, should be a Quaker, or approve of or excuse their way.

Reason 1. The Quakers (with the Seekers) deny and revile the Church and ministers of Christ, and yet cannot tell us of any church or ministry which is indeed the right. ... I dare not be of so narrow a catholic Church as the [3] Papal is, much less as the Quakers or any upstart sect. I profess myself a member of a far wider catholic Church than all of them set together, in which I hope to live and die. ...

[7] Reason 8. The Quakers' way is too cruel and uncharitable to be the way of God. They damn the most humble, holy, faithful servants of God; to whom God has promised salvation. All the ministers and Churches of Christ that adhere to the ministry, they pronounce them, children of the devil. ...

Yea they must venture into the Throne of God, and ordinarily take on them to know men's hearts, to judge them hypocrites. Those that dwell and walk with God, and have lain longer at his feet in prayers and tears, than any of them, and walk in uprightness in the midst of a malicious world, and spend themselves in the work of God; even these must be damned at a word by a boy or wench that's but a Quaker, as confidently as if God had bid them speak it.

Reason 9. After all their sins, they most impudently pretend to a [8] sinless perfection. They are not content that we allow of a perfection in kind, which is our sincerity, or a perfection of parts, which is our integrity, or a perfection of eminency or high degree. All these we do allow of; and we desire an absolute sinless perfection, and confess it is our commanded duty. But they maintain that many of them are without sin altogether. So that by this you may see that the Quakers suppose themselves to have no need of Christ, and so the word and truth is not in them. They dare say, it seems, to God or to the Redeemer, "we will not be beholden to Thee for the pardon of any more sin, or for the blood of Christ to that end." . . .

Reason 11. Their doctrines are self-contradictory, and therefore they cannot be of God. . . . [9] They will revile the ministers as blind guides, and tell their people they are all in darkness, and the way to damnation? And yet all have sufficient light within them? If all, why not the ministers, and their people? Are not they man?

Reason 13. The doctrine and practice of the Quakers is contrary to the experience and holy nature of the saints. They have found a renewing light and life, by this scripture and ministry which the Quakers make so light of. They tell our people, that our ministry does no good, and none are the better for it; which the experience of many thousand does confute, who can say as the man in John 9:25, "One thing I know, that whereas I was blind, now I see." . . . They cannot be so barbarously ungrateful, and so rebellious.

Reason 14. The Quakers . . . are so notoriously proud. . . .

[10] Reason 15. They plainly discover a persecuting spirit. For what man can reason think but that they run up and down the world to bring the ministry into hatred. . . . They that so damn our godly hearers, would not they persecute them also? I confess I make no doubt of it, but if they had power, many of them would do more than silence the ministry, even persecute them to death as their ancestors have done.

[11] Reason 19. They are already in divisions among themselves, as few as they are! As the contention between Nayler and his followers, and Fox and his followers, and others of them show. [Five more reasons are given.]
Sept. 5, 1657

MANY STRONG REASONS CONFOUNDED,
Which would hinder any reasonable man from being A QUAKER:
And Offences taken out of the way. But particularly
Four and twenty arguments

Overturned and confuted; Put forth and sent into the world by Richard Baxter. . . .

And this is for the satisfaction of honest people by a friend, E. B. [Burrough]

London, printed for Thomas Simmons at the Bull and Mouth near Aldersgate, 1657

[4] First . . . it had been more honest for him to have made a sufficient reply to have defended his former works, and cleared himself of his former lies . . . charged against him; . . . For that book which he often mentions and boasts of, called, *The Quakers' Catechism*, was sufficiently answered, and his folly laid open by a friend to the truth, in a book called, *An Answer to the Quakers' Catechism*; to which book he never equally replied to this day.

1. His first reason which he brings forth against the Quakers is, "That they deny and revile the churches and ministers of Christ;" . . .

Answer: . . . The church of Christ we own, and are of it, which are gathered out of the world through the preaching of the Gospel, and separated from the world and all its works and ways which are evil, and are joined to Christ the head, in the Spirit, and one to another as members of Christ. . . .

[8] 8. His eighth reason, "The Quakers' way is too cruel and uncharitable to be the way of God. They damn," he said, "the most humble, holy, faithful servants of God, to whom God has promised life, etc."

Answer: This is not the least of his lies: our way is Christ, and is neither cruel nor uncharitable, but pure, and holy, and zealous against all sin, and cannot bear and suffer iniquity, but reproves it. Neither do we damn any, but warns all to repent. . . .

9. His ninth reason; saith he, "After all their sins they most impudently pretend to a sinless perfection, etc."

Answer: . . . Many of us do witness that Christ has done away our sins, and in him we are complete through faith, in which we are perfect without sin, and it is not of ourselves. And that perfection we exhort all to press after. . . .

[12] 13. He saith, "They have found a renewed light and life by the Scriptures and ministry which the Quakers make so light of, etc."

To this I answer: As for the people's sakes of England, I wish his words were true, and that they had indeed found a renewing light and life by this ministry; . . . and though he said, "The experiences of many thousands doth confute this," yet say I, the experiences of ten thousand times so many more shall confirm it.

[13] 15. His fifteenth reason. Saith he, "They plainly discover a persecuting spirit. Why (saith he) what men can in reason think but that they run up and down the world to bring ministry into hatred, etc."

To this I answer, little of this doth appear that our spirits are persecuting spirits, for we pray for our enemies, and do forgive them that doth evil entreat us, and renders to no man evil for evil. For if we had sought vengeance, or prosecuted the good laws of England against those that had wronged and robbed us, and unjustly caused us to be put in prison, many might have deeply suffered by true justice before this day, if we had not forgiven our enemies, and blessed them that hated us. . . .

5. Edward Burrough's *Declaration to All the World of Our Faith* (1657)

The attempts to make systematic statements of Quaker faith, like the debate tracts, were meant mainly to clear Friends from charges of heresy. There was little attempt to interpret new doctrine or even to convince the non-Quakers to enter the movement. In later stages, Friends' doctrinal tracts can be divided into those purely defensive (and often rigidly traditional in their language), and the tracts and longer works, such as Barclay's *Apology*, which were meant at least equally to teach younger Friends and those attracted to Quakerism. Nayler began the movement in this direction, with *Love to the Lost* (1656).

But in 1657 Nayler was in prison (see p. 36), and all Quakers in disgrace. Burrough was in London, and though we find no record of the immediate background of this tract, he was that year concerned not only to vindicate Friends, but to strengthen the shaken Quaker movement and to reconcile Fox and Nayler if possible. This statement is an early and interesting summary of Quaker ideas on Christ, but also on the state, and notably of the roles of "pure reason" and of liberty to reprove sin, within Quaker claims about freedom in religion.

A DECLARATION TO ALL THE WORLD
Of our Faith; and What we Believe.

And this is written that all people upon earth may know by whom, and how we are saved, and hopes for eternal life; and what we believe concerning God, Christ, and the Spirit; and of the things that are eternal, appertaining to all mankind to know and believe.

Concerning God, Christ, and the Spirit, thus we believe:

First, that there is only one God, who is a spirit; and his presence filleth heaven and earth; and he is eternal and everlasting, the creator and preserver of all things; and heaven and earth and all things therein by him were framed and brought forth; and all things remain unto this day by his power; and whatsoever he will in heaven and earth he brings to pass by his word and power. And we believe that this God only is, and ought to be feared, loved, obeyed and worshipped by all creatures; and no other thing besides him in heaven and earth. And we believe that his worship and obedience and fear and love is to be given in spirit, even in what his own spirit moveth and leadeth his People unto. And we believe his true worship required and accepted of him is not by the traditions of men in outward observances, or set days, or places; but [he] is worshipped only in spirit and truth, without respect of time, places or things; and that none can worship him in righteousness, but his children, who are born of his Spirit, and are led and guided thereby.

And we believe, that this God hath given his [2] Son Christ Jesus into the world, a free gift unto the whole world; and that every man that cometh into the world is lightened by him, that every man might believe and be saved. And we believe, that he is given into the world, and no nation, country or people excepted; but unto all mankind is he given of God, and hath lightened them and every man through[out] the world that believeth in and receiveth Christ, who is the wisdom and power of the Father, shall be saved with eternal Salvation; and every one that believeth not in him shall be damned, and shall possess everlasting misery. And we believe that salvation, justification and sanctification is only in him, and wrought by him and no other: for there is no other name given under heaven, but him alone, by which salvation is. And we believe all that receive him and believes in him are reconciled to God and are made alive to God, to live in him in all things, and doth receive the forgiveness of sins, and are set free from all unrighteousness and from the body of sin and death, and hath the witness of the Spirit in them. And the Spirit of the Father they have received, and it witnesseth in them of the

299

Father and of the Son, and of the things that belong unto their peace. And it is the earnest of the inheritance and the seal of the promise of eternal life, and by it are the deep things of God revealed to mankind, and by it the Father and the Son dwells in the saints, and by it have they fellowship one with another; and the Father, Son and Spirit are one. And this we faithfully believe.

Again, concerning Christ we believe that he is one with the Father, and was with him before the world was; and what the Father worketh it is by the Son; for he is the arm of God's salvation, and the very power and wisdom of the creator; and was, is, and is to come, without beginning or end. And we believe that all the prophets gave testimony of him, and that he was made manifest in Judea and Jerusalem, and did the work of the Father, and was persecuted of the Jews, and was crucified by his enemies; and that he was buried, and rose again, according to the Scriptures. And we believe [3] he is now ascended on high, and exalted at the right hand of the Father for evermore; and that he is glorified with the same glory that he had before the world was; and that even the same that came down from heaven, is ascended up to heaven, and the same that descended is he that ascended. And we believe even that he that was dead is alive, and lives for evermore; and that he cometh, and shall come again, to judge the whole world with righteousness, and all people with equity and shall give to every man according to his deeds, at the day of Judgment, when all shall arise to condemnation or justification; he that hath done good shall receive life, and he that hath done evil everlasting condemnation.

And we believe he is to be waited for in spirit, to be known after the Spirit, as he was before the world was; and that is the knowledge unto eternal life, which all that believe in him do receive. And he subdues death, and destroys him that hath the power of it; and restoreth from death to life, and quickeneth by his spirit all that the Father hath given him. And we believe such he justifieth and sanctifieth, and such are taught of him. But he condemns all that believe not, but continues in unbelief, and are not taught of him. And this we faithfully believe.

And we believe that unto all people upon the face of the whole earth, is a time and day of visitation given, that they may return and be saved by Christ Jesus, who is given of the Father to call the worst of men to repentance; and the most ungodly of sinners are convinced by him of their ungodly deeds, that they might believe, and be converted and saved. And we believe herein is the love of God manifested to all mankind; and that none are shut out by him before they were born into the world:[31] but unto all men is a Visitation

31 Quakers from the beginning rejected predestination; so, however, did the free or General Baptists from whom they sprang; and most other Separatists did also, since they addressed strong messages of repentance to any who would hear.

given, and they that do perish, it is because they do not believe in Christ; and destruction is of a man's self, but salvation is of God, through believing in his Son, who takes away sin, and reneweth into his own image, that they may become heirs with him. And we believe that there is a crown of eternal glory, and an inheritance of eternal life to be enjoyed [4] for evermore by all that believe, and are chosen of God; and that there is an everlasting misery and destruction to be possessed by all that believe not, but continue in the state of reprobation, and are not changed from the ways of sin and death, but walk after the ways of their own hearts' lusts, fulfilling the will of the flesh, in the evil of this world, and follow not Christ the Light of the world that they may be saved. And we believe upon all such the wrath of God abideth, and that they have no part in the inheritance of God.

And we believe that it is only he that is born again of the Spirit, and that walks after the Spirit, who is changed from death to life, and who is redeemed out of the world and all its ways. Such only must inherit the Kingdom of God, and they only have right thereunto, and none besides: even they that are washed and cleansed from all unrighteousness by the blood of Jesus by which their sins are remitted. For his blood cleanseth from all unrighteousness and sin all they that walk in the Light, which Christ Jesus hath lightened the world withal.

And we believe that the saints upon earth may receive forgiveness of sins, and may be perfectly freed from the body of sin and death, and in Christ may be perfect and without sin, and may have victory over all temptations by faith in Christ Jesus. And we believe every saint that is called of God ought to press after perfection, and to overcome the Devil and all his temptations upon earth; and we believe, they that wait for it shall obtain it, and shall be presented without sin in the Image of the Father. And such walks not after the flesh but after the Spirit, and are in covenant with God, and their sins are blotted out and remembered no more; for they cease to commit sin, being born of the seed of God.

And we believe, the gospel of Christ is the power of God unto salvation, and that it ought to be preached freely unto all people, and Christ to be held forth unto all mankind, by the ministry sent of him. And we believe this ministry is received by the gift of the Holy Ghost; and all they that receive it are lawfully called to the ministry; and they may preach the Gospel [5] of Christ freely, as they have received it freely: And this ministry is not of man, but of God, and is made powerful to the converting of sinners, and to the bringing of people to God, and to the knowledge of his ways. And we do not believe, that any man is a minister of Christ, without the gift of the Holy Ghost, or that the Gospel can be received by natural learning or education. And we believe such as preach for hire and hath hire for preaching are not the lawful called ministers of the Gospel of Christ; such as are proud and high-minded and covetous men who do not profit the people at all; such as have run and never were sent of Christ, who calleth by his Spirit into the work of the ministry. And as every one hath received the gift of that, his Spirit, so he may administer to others.

Concerning rulers and governors we believe that there ought to be rulers and governors in every nation, city, country and town. And they ought to be such men as fear God and hate every evil way; who will judge for God and not for man; and will judge righteously, equally and justly; and will give true and sound judgment unto all men, without bribery, or respect of persons; not regarding the rich above the poor, but being a praise unto all that do well and a terror to all evil-doers whatsoever; having knowledge in the pure Law of God and themselves continually exercised therein. And we believe that every law of man ought to be grounded upon the Law of God, pure reason and equity being the foundation thereof, that God's witness in every man may answer to it. And the law ought to be known unto all people, before transgression be charged or punished in any man. And we believe that every transgression ought to be punished according to its nature; and that the punishment exceed not the greatness of the transgression, neither ought any transgressor to escape unpunished. Neither ought any upon false suspicion or jealousies, to be caused to suffer without the testimony of true men or the confession of the [accused] party. And we believe that the executors of the law ought to be just men, and not given to pride, drunkenness, or any [6] other evil whatsoever; and ought to be chosen every year or otherwise, by the consent of the people; and that no man be stopped of his free choice. And we believe that all governors and rulers ought to be accountable to the people, and to the next proceeding rulers, for all their actions, which may be enquir'd into upon occasion; and that the chiefest of the rulers be subject under the law and punishable by it if they be transgressors, as well as the poorest of the people. And thus true judgment and justice will be brought forth in the earth, and all that do well will have praise, and live in rest and peace; and all evil-doers whatsoever may stand in awe, and be afraid of God and just men and the execution of good laws.

Concerning religion, we believe that it is only the spirit of the Lord that makes men truly religious; and that no man ought to be compelled to or from any exercise or practice in religion, by any outward law or power; but every man ought to be left free, as the Lord shall persuade his own mind, in doing or leaving undone this or the other practice in religion; and every man, of what profession in religion soever, ought to be protected in peace, provided himself be a man of peace, not seeking the wrong of any man's person or estate.

And we believe that to oppose false opinions and unsound doctrines and principles, seeking to convince them that oppose themselves, by exhortation or sharp reproof, by word or writing, ought not to be counted a breach of the peace; or to strive about the things of the Kingdom of God, by men of contrary minds or judgments, this ought not to be punishable by the magistrates and their laws. For we believe, the outward laws and powers of the earth are only to preserve men's persons and estates, and not to preserve men in opinions; neither ought the law of the nation to be laid upon men's consciences, to bind them to or from such a judgment or practice in religion. And we believe that Christ is and ought only to be Lord and exerciser of men's consciences; and his Spirit only must lead into all truth.

[7] And we believe that obedience and subjection in the Lord belongs to superiors, and that subjects ought to obey in the Lord those that have rule over them; and that children ought to obey their parents, and wives their husbands, and servants their masters, in all things which are according to God, which stands in the exercise of a pure conscience towards God. But where rulers, parents or masters, or any other, command or require subjection in any thing which is contrary to God, or not according to him, to such causes all people are free, and ought to obey God rather than man. And we believe, that herein God will justify them, being guided and led by his Spirit in all that which is good, and out of all that which is evil.

Again, we believe concerning Election and Reprobation, that there is a state of Election and a state of Reprobation, a state chosen of God and a state rejected of God, and that all man kind are in one of these states. All that are elected, are elected in Christ. And all that are out of him are in the state reprobate, bringing forth fruits of death and darkness, being a child of wrath and disobedience in the alienation and separation from God, in the transgression, unreconcil'd to God, the enmity ruling in the heart, being in the fall, and not restored to God again, but ignorant of his power and of his wisdom, having the understanding darkened, that they cannot see nor perceive the things that are eternal. And in this condition his best works are sin; and whatsoever he doth, he cannot be accepted of God, for he is dead to God and alive to all evil, bringing forth all his works out of that ground which is cursed. This is the condition of all mankind upon the face of the earth in the first Adam, and this is the state of reprobation; and all that abide herein are rejected of God, and shall never inherit eternal life, but go into perdition. Yet have all such a day of Visitation, that they may return out of the state of reprobation; but hating knowledge and despising the love of God they continue in the state reprobate, and the Wrath of God abides upon them. But they that are chosen of God, are delivered from wrath; [8] for they believe in the Light, and becomes children of the Light, and are renewed in mind and heart, and receiveth the Love of the Father, and becometh planted into Christ the second Adam, and are chosen in him to bring forth fruit unto the Father. And all their fruit springeth from that ground which is blessed; for they are led by the Spirit of the Father. And such are in the state of Election, who is made heirs with Christ of the everlasting inheritance that never fades away. And this we faithfully believe, that mercy is not showed to the reprobate, nor judgment to them that are chosen of God.

And this is to go abroad in the world, that all people may understand what we believe, and what we have received of God; and they that believe this, and walk therein, by the Spirit of the Father shall be saved; but they that believe not, but are disobedient to the truth, shall be condemned, because they do not believe. Much more might be written, but in short, this is given forth, by one that hath believed and received the knowledge of those things from God. A friend unto all people,

Edward Burrough

London, printed for Thomas Simmons at the Bull and Mouth near Aldersgate, 1657.

6. Samuel Fisher's *Apokrypta Apokalypta* on Eschatology (1661)

In form this tract seems to revert to the debate-pattern that predominated in early Quaker theological writing. Actually, however, Fisher has here used a set of unpublished, essentially anonymous questions as a springboard from which to leap into an area where Quakers were often challenged and their answers usually fragmentary or illogical: the soul and the afterlife. Quakers liked to insist that heaven and hell were spiritual "states" men could know in the present life, and the Day of Judgment an event some had already passed through. These ideas had somehow to be squared not only with Christian traditions but with the Quakers' own expectation of final judgment upon the unrepentant. (Fisher's answer is nevertheless a "realized eschatology" where the afterlife will continue, not reverse, present experience.) Quakers also had never neatly wedded the usual Greek-Christian ideas about an immortal soul with their own discoveries of the necessary death of self-will and "the old man" in inner rebirth. Friends were also used to language from Genesis 3 about "the Seed of the Serpent" and "the Seed of the Woman" as reinterpreted by Paul to refer to the heirs of the first Adam and of Christ the "second Adam." Fisher did as much as the mixture of metaphors allowed to tie all this together, with assistance from the Greeks' and "Early Church Fathers' " division of man into the three elements of body, soul, and spirit. His identification of spirit with the new

304

Seed of Christ, buried until a man's spirit-rebirth set it free, was new. So also, among Friends, was his effort to identify the soul with a man's will, able to identify itself with either God or the Devil (some Friends, including Fox, seem to suggest that the "natural" soul of men, unless taken up into the Seed, perished literally at death). Fisher thereby also began to help Friends around the biggest weakness in early Quaker thought, the assumption that a man's will or character was inherently an obstacle to his obedience to the Light: it must be "crucified" and totally supplanted by the indwelling Spirit of Christ the Seed. This attitude led to passivity and quietism in the long run and meantime to an assumption (both fruitful and risky) that Christian character could never be seen or known as an independent reality but only as a process of constant self-denial and obedience. Fisher's way forward was not followed for two centuries, and even now Friends find it hard to deal in words with the heights and depths of Christian personality.

Samuel Fisher shows himself here, as in all his writings, as the most scholarly and loquacious of early Friends. (His *Rusticus ad Academicos* runs to 450 folio pages.) His Oxford Master's degree shows itself in his constant use of Greek and Latin (mostly omitted in this abridgement). Yet he did see theological issues more clearly, subtly, and shrewdly than any other Quaker contemporary.

APOKRYPTA APOKALYPTA

Velata *Quaedam* Revelata

Some Certain Hidden, or Veiled Spiritual Verities Revealed. Upon Occasion of Various Very Prying, and Critical Queries

	God,	
	The Devil, &	Body
Concerning	Man, as to his	Soul, and
	Heaven,	Spirit.
	Hell,	
	Judgement, &c.	
	George Fox,	
Propounded to	John Perrot,[32]	
	Samuel Fisher.	

32 John Perrot, just back from the papal prison in Rome, had not yet broken with Fox and more group-oriented Quakers and here emerges as a prominent London Friend for a brief interval.

And after that (with a complaint for want of, and stricter urgency for an answer) re-propounded to Edward Burrough.

By two persons, choosing to notify themselves to us no other way than by these two unwonted (if not self-assumed) titles, viz. Livinus Theodorus, and Sabina Neriah.[33] Which truths (as there inspired by the spirit of God) are here expired in love to the souls of men.

From out of a hole in the gate-house[34] at Westminster through an earthen vessel there imprisoned for the testimony of Jesus, known among men by the name of SAMUEL FISHER.

LONDON, Printed for Robert Wilson, 1661[35]

[omitting the Letter to the Reader]

Some Certain, Hidden, or Veiled Spiritual Verities
Revealed, &c.

Friends, . . .
Livinus Theodorus, and Sabina Neriah.

I have seen your thirteen queries propounded to G.F., J.P., and myself, or either of us, together with your (seeming sympathetical) preface to them, . . .
[2] I well know, that in the power and spirit of God, truth may be unfolded both much more, and to many more also, that are of open and honest hearts, in one hour by word of mouth, than it can by the writing of many days, to men who have . . . more desire merely to know, than mind to do what good is already known.

[4] And as for your owning or disowning of us to any such, as before you shall oppose us, it's little to us, if ye own us to be of the truth, unless ye come together with us into union with it; for we know (whether ye confess to, or deny us) that we are of God, & that the world lieth in that wickedness that cuts off from him; and that we are *angeloi aletheias,* such as hold forth that infallible everlasting truth of God, which hath very amply revealed to us of its secrets. . . .

[5] Query 1. What is God really in himself, without any definition? And in

---

[33] Modern scholars have been no more successful than Fisher in identifying the anonymous questioners: they may have belonged to a group like the Muggletonians who held essentially Old Testament ideas of death and resurrection.

[34] Fisher died of plague four years later, apparently still as a prisoner.

[35] On Robert Wilson, Giles Calvert's brother-in-law and briefly successor as printer, see p. 390.

what did he dwell, and manifest himself before the foundation of the Heavens and the Earth was laid?

Answer 1. God, as he is really in himself, is beyond all definition of ours at all, . . . but, if speaking by way of such description as those have made of him, who have seen and known him, . . . I answer, God, (whatever more he is, that's nothing to us) . . . is really in himself, whatever he hath at any time, in and by his Son, revealed himself to be, in and to his holy prophets, and children; and whatever they in all ages (as moved by him so to do) have declared him to be, whether by word of mouth or Scripture. And so whatever ye there read, God is, that God is really, indeed, and in truth, (viz.) a spirit, light, love, that one, omnipotent, all-sufficient, spiritual, substantial, living, everlasting, infinite subsistence, which hath his own being of himself, and gives being, life, breath and all things unto all, in whom we, and all mankind, who are his offspring, both live, move, and have our being.

Howbeit, there is not in every man, no not in all those that read of him there, and can speak of him what they there read, the true knowledge of him so, . . . For they only truly know him to be this or that, who witness him truly to be this or that to and within themselves. And those [6] know him not, . . . that prate this and that of him like [mag]pies and parrots, which may be taught . . . yet come not to find and feel him so to be . . . in his own Light, by which he draws nigh to, and is not far from every one of us. By which [Light] . . . in some measure, though not the same measure, he manifests something of himself in every conscience; . . . and to such as love him and keep his Commandments given out in the same, he manifests himself in such wise as he will not do to the world. Yea, in such wise that they can experimentally say . . . that God is, and that he is true, good, merciful, faithful, just, righteous in taking vengeance; that he is a judge, a protector, a saviour, a redeemer. . . . [7] Whereas therefore ye query, What God really is in himself? As God saith of himself, I am that I am; so say I, *Deus est id quod est*: God is what he is: And if ye, who by your asking of us, profess yourselves to be yet ignorant of him, . . . would know him in any measure, as he is really in himself; my counsel to you is, to stand still in his own counsel, namely, his Light in your own consciences, that in that you may be led forth into his life and likeness, even into the image of his Son, the light of the world, the righteous, pure, meek, innocent, gentle, loving, peaceable, inoffensive, merciful, compassionate, tender, patient Lamb of God, that takes away the sin of it, who is the express image of the Father. . . . Wait for his appearing in his own spirit and power to restore his own image in your hearts; that as he appeareth, ye may appear with him in his glory, which is fulness of grace and truth, being transformed into his image from glory to glory, by the operation of his Holy Spirit, that as he appeareth, ye may be like him, and so see him as he is. . . .

307

[8] Query 2. Whether is there a manifestation of God in everything that hath a life, motion and being, in this outward creation? And whether is a creature to expect ever to know God under any other dispensation or administration, further than by the manifestation of the Spirit of God in him, . . .

Answer 2. This second query stands in two parts, to the first of which I answer, Yes, as 'tis said, *Deo plena sunt omnia: Est Deus in nobis, agitante calescimus ipso. . . .*[36]

To the second, I answer, Nay; there is no other way, dispensation, or administration, in, or under which a creature is to expect to know God, further than by the manifestation of [9] the spirit of God in him; for it is written, Rom. *1*. 19. whatever is to be known of God, is manifest in men, for God doth show it in them.

Query 3. Whether are the Spirit of God, the spirit of man, and the spirit of the Devil, three different spirits?

Answer 3. Yea, the Spirit of God, the spirit of the Devil, and the spirit of man, are three distinct spirits.

Query 4. Whether be they essentially impregnated in man? If so, when, and after what manner were the said spirits infused into him?

Answer 4. In this query there is a fallacy, called, *A bene divisis ad male conjuncta*: i.e. A question asked of many things together, which (in some sense at least) may be truly affirmed of some of them, but cannot be affirmed of them all: I answer therefore, they are not all three (as your query seems to intimate) essentially impregnated in man; neither are they all three *de esse homini*; for first, as to the Spirit of God, a man may remain a man, i.e. A man of the Earth (as to his essentials) when the Spirit of God which was once given him, is (as David prayed it might not be from himself) no less than totally taken from him; therefore God's Spirit is not essentially impregnated in man. And as to the spirit of the Devil, man was (*quod esse*) truly and formally man, before the spirit of the Devil did prevail to enter him, and will be so again, when that unclean spirit is again ejected and cast out of him. . . .

[10] Query 5. What is the spirit of man in itself? Is it natural, yea or nay? Is it mortal or immortal? And whether hath it a being different from the body (when expired)? If so, how, and where, clearly demonstrate.

Query 6. Whether is there a soul in man distinct from the said spirit? If yea, what is it? and where is its present situation in man? (plainly manifest it distinguishable) And whether (after the decease of a man) it hath a being apart from the body? If yes, where? and whether in that state it be sensible

---

36 All things are full of God, God is in us, we grow warm by his own moving (from Ovid's *Fasti*, VI:5). I owe this reference to Professor Stephen Heiny.

308

either of consolation and happiness, or torment and sorrow? And after what manner shall it enjoy the one, or have the other inflicted upon it?

Query 7. Whether is it possible for the soul of man to live without a body? If not, into what body doth it betake itself? Or how is it propagated to eternity?

Query 8. What is its properties and operations? And what were them souls spoken of in the Revelation, which John said he saw crying under the altar? And what is that altar? And where did he see it to be? And whether had them souls bodies? If yes, what bodies were they?

[11] Answer. As to this fifth query, wherein you are busy, high-flown, clambering [=clamoring?], and ever-curious in querying. What the spirit of man is, and whether natural, mortal, or immortal? And whether it hath a being when the body is expired? If so, how, and where, &c. With which fifth query, not only the latter part of the fourth, but also the whole sixth, seventh and eighth (wherein ye are as critically inquisitive, running out into various quirks, quiddities, and quomodities about the soul, as *Quae? Quid? Ubi? Qualis? Quando? Quibus auxiliis? Cur?* Under which forms of querying, one pragmatical spirit may ask more questions than many wise men may find either while, or will, or good ground to reply to) are so far co-incident, that one cannot be well clearly answered without the rest, I say thus, both unto it, and to the rest, *Viz.*

That man (as God at first made him) was a creature consist[ing] of these three, namely, body, soul, and spirit; each of which the Apostle prays on the behalf of them (as in the saints) that they might be kept blameless to the coming of our Lord Jesus (I Thess. 5:23). Each of which, though concurrent with the rest, to the complete making up of that one *compositum*, or creature called man (as God at first made him) are yet distinct in themselves, and separable the one from the other.

First, as for the outward earthly body, which was framed of the dust, of the outer earth, into which dust, (as into its first principle) it must once return: that is but the earthly tabernacle, in which the soul, (which is in truth more the man, than it is) dwells, and hath its place of residence, and situation for a time.

As for the soul, . . . [12] as to its having a being, apart from the body, after the decease of the body, or of the man, so far as to his outer body, I affirm it hath; and though in your dark minds, ye doubt the possibility of its being without a body, and therefore feign a certain transmigration of it of necessity into some other body, when it comes to pass out of its own; yet I deny that as a mere Pythagorean dream. It's not necessary that it must betake itself into some other body, when it departs from its own, in order to its propagation to eternity; for it is immortal as to any utter annihilation (however, it may die by sin from God, who is the truest life thereof, and so cease to be such a living soul, as at first he made it) and because immortal, therefore in its nature eternal, i.e. never ceasing to have some being or other, either good or evil to all eternity. . . .

And since ye ask: if so, where? I answer: . . . [13] If by where? ye intend (as by the following words ye seem to do) in what state, namely a state of bliss, or a state of torture; that may fall out . . . according to that condition of distance and alienation, or of nearness and conjunction, that it stood in, to either God's spirit, or the Devil's, at the time of its departure from the body.

And whereas it's queried, Whether in that state of separation from the body, it can be sensible either of consolations and happiness, or torment and sorrow? I answer, Yes, Why not? (it being a spirit) as well as other spirits, *viz.* the Devils, who were most afraid of going into their torment. . . .

Thirdly: as to the spirit of man, which is the best, highest, and most noble of the three aforesaid, which concurs to the constituting of man in his primitive perfection, it is that breath of life, which God breathed into his soul after he had formed him (as to his body) of the dust of the earth, whereby he came to be a living soul; a soul that did partake of something of God's own life; whereby it did live in his sight. This is that living principle of the divine nature, which man did before his degeneration, and shall again after his regeneration, partake of. In respect [14] of which, he was, and shall be again (as he takes heed to come into union with it, and thereby to recover to his first estate) called the Son of God, as Adam was before he fell; and in respect of which he is said (principally) to be made after God's own image, and to be the very image and glory of God; this is that incorruptible, immortal Seed of God, which whoever comes to witness himself brought forth into the likeness of, is said to be born of God, to be of God, to be the child of God, that doth righteousness. . . .

This is that noble, royal, righteous, holy Seed, which while man was at first born, made, created and planted after the nature and image of, he was said to be planted a noble vine; wholly a right seed, till by being alienated, separated, and estranged from it into his earthly part, he became a degenerate plant of a strange vine unto the Lord, a seed of evil-doers, that are never more to be renowned, unless they come again to be born of this holy Seed, which is *anothen*, from above. . . . [15] This spirit of man is the very principle of spiritual life to his soul, as the soul is the principle of natural life to his body; whereby as that becomes a living body through the union of it with the soul; so the soul respectively becomes a living soul, through its union with the said spirit. These three are the three principles, after which the man is respectively, and differently denominated, sometimes after the one, sometimes after the other, . . .

[16] And as to your asking concerning the spirit of man, whether it be natural or no? I answer, That it is natural, i.e. pertaining to the very nature of

that man which God first created, and of the man of God which to that primitive nature is restored.[37] For howbeit it is of the divine nature, and so supernatural, as in reference to man in the fall, who is of the Devil's marring, yet to the constitution of such a man as God at first made after his own image, and glory, to partake of his own divine nature, it is natural: And though it is as natural to man *in statu corrupto*, to sin, and break the law of God, as for a natural brute beast to drink in water, yet to that man, who is God's image and glory, by participation of the divine nature, it is as natural as it was to Christ, whose meat and drink it was to do God's will. . . .

[17] And whereas ye query, whether the said spirit of man is mortal or immortal? I answer, it is immortal, and neither mortal nor corruptible, but that immortal and incorruptible Seed of God, even something of that living Word, which is said to be made flesh, and to dwell in the saints, that is said to be ingrafted or put into man's heart, whereby he being begotten into the will of God, is said to be born of God, and the Son of God; which principle, or innate word, being received with meekness, saves that soul from sin, and so from the second death, as it stands in union and conjunction with it. . . .

And whereas ye ask, Whether this spirit of man hath a being distinct from the body, when expired; and if so, how and where?

I answer, It hath a being distinct, not only from the body, when deceased; but from the soul also when expired. . . .

[18] And howbeit, the body and soul both may perish, as they separate from this spirit, yet it lives and abides forever, together with all that doth the will of God made manifest in it. This is that in respect of which, man regenerated by it, is man indeed. . . . This is that spirit of man that goeth upwards, and draweth the soul upwards toward God, from whom it is breathed into man; when the spirit of the beast, of brutish man goeth downward to the earth from whence it came, and draws downwards, even to the chambers of death, and the depths of Hell. . . . Eccles. 12. . . . [19] That soul which the body dies from, while they both lived together in sin, dies both from it, and from God that gave it, forever; and is left naked, and divested both of its own body, and its own spirit also, and lies in separation not only from both these, but also from God and his good Spirit, tormented among all evil spirits forever.

Query 9. What, and where is that Heaven in which it's said God doth dwell? Is it above the firmament, or must a creature wait to know it manifest in him, and not otherwise?

Answer 9. Heaven is the highest place in either outward and local, or inward

---

[37] I.e., man in the state of the first Adam before the Fall. Most Friends, like Barclay, preferred to distinguish the "natural" state of fallen man from the state of grace.

311

and spiritual salvation, . . . The Heaven in which it's said God dwells, is neither only above the firmament, nor only under the firmament, but both above it, and below it, and even everywhere; where he manifests himself in his love and mercy, goodness, grace and glory: And as he dwells in no place, so as to be anywhere (circumscriptively) included, so in every place, he is so, as to be nowhere at all excluded. . . . The Apostles' dwelling (*politeuma*) was in Heaven, Phil. *3*, only whilst they were bodily here on earth. Therefore, Heaven is as well under, as above the firmament; yea, it is in very deed in his people's [20] hearts, in every humble, broken and contrite spirit.

And whereas ye ask, Whether a creature must wait to know it in himself only, and not otherwise? I say, not so neither; for Heaven shall be manifest, and known not only inwardly in their hearts, who wait for it; but outwardly also, to such as wait not for it within themselves (as Lazarus' bosom was to the rich man's sight afar off) so far only as shall tend to the aggravation of their anguish, who shall see themselves shut out everlasting from sharing in it. To conclude, the Heaven, which is God's throne, God's house, God's tabernacle, . . . is not only that high place, locally situated above the skies, but that high and holy place also, of a low and humble heart, and a broken and contrite spirit, that trembles at his word; there he delights to manifest himself, who is the high and lofty one, who inhabiteth eternity, and to make his abode, even in them who are meek and lowly, . . . who are to have dominion over the wicked in that morning that is appearing. . . .

[21] Query 10. What is Hell? and where is it? Is it a certain local place? or that, which through the creature's disobedience, is manifested in him; and that there is no other?

Answer 10. Hell is the Valley of Jehoshaphat, i.e. of the Lord's judgment (as the word is in English) where with fire, and his sword he pleadeth with all flesh, where he easeth himself of his adversaries, and maketh his indignation known to his enemies, whither the Lord comes like a whirlwind, to render his anger with fury, and his rebukes with flames of fire; where the worm that eats in the entrails of the wicked never dies, and the fire is never to be quenched; . . . This is that Valley of Jehoshaphat, to which . . . all the heathen must be awakened and summoned to come up to account out of the dark cells of their own deceitful and desperately wicked hearts, even to that Light, which is the least of seeds, and lies lowest under the lust of the world. . . . This is as a burning within, kindled under all men's fleshly glory, of which (meanwhile not denying it to be also a certain local place, as ye speak) we [22] affirm that it is within the conscience of every malefactor or impenitent rebel against the light, where the wrath of God is manifested against sin, and on the creature for its disobedience. . . .

Query 11. What is it in man that must be made sensible of the joy of the one, through obedience, or the torment of the other through disobedience, since what God hath loved, he loves to the end, and the earth must return to the earth, and the spirit to him that gave it.

Answer 11. The soul of man is that in man, which when once departed from its body, which it's the life of, and also from its aforesaid spirit, which is its life, must be made sensible of the consolations through obedience, or of the tribulation through disobedience. . . .

[23] Query 12. What is that city that hath no need of the light of the sun, nor the moon to shine in it, &c.? And where is its situation? And what is that honor and glory, which the kings of the [24] earth must bring into it? And in what manner must they perform it? Also, how, and when shall they that are saved, be made inhabitants of it?

Answer 12. What need ye query this of us, if either ye heeded the Light in you, which manifests all things in their proper seasons, to such as wait in it; or if ye had well heeded that very Scripture either, out of which your query seems to be fetched, and founded? Where ye may as well read what that city is that hath no need of the sun to shine in it, as that it hath at all no need thereof, where it's evidenced to be those saints of God that follow the Lamb, who is their light, the new Jerusalem which is above, the mother of all the free-born children of God, which is as a bride adorned for her husband, with whom the tabernacle of the Lord is, and with whom he dwells. And as for the situation of it, is it not expressly said (as in the vision it was seen) that it comes down from God out of Heaven? therefore 'tis a state here on earth. . . . [25] And whereas ye ask, When shall those that be saved be made the inhabitants of it? I answer, So soon as ever they are saved from the sin, which is that alone that slays the soul, and separates it from its part and portion there. . . .

Query 13. What are the chains in which the angels (who kept not their first estate) are reserved under darkness unto the judgement of the great day? And where is the place of their confinement? And what is the great day, and the judgement? We pray you plainly demonstrate.

Answer 13. The chains which the angels who kept not their first estate, are reserved in, are the same under which men, who kept not their first estate, are also reserved under darkness, unto the judgement of the great day, and that is the darkness itself, into which they are both gone forth from the light, . . . [26] in the deceitful counsels of their own hearts, in their own corruptions, under the bondage of which the whole creation groans, and travels [=travails] in pain together to be delivered. . . .

And as for the great day, and the judgement thereof, it is the Light of the Lord (for the light he called day, and the darkness he called night) and the judgement that the said Light layeth to the line, . . . reveals from God nothing but vengeance, tribulation, wrath, and anguish, perplexity and disappointment, woe, cursing, and vexation of spirit on every evil spirit, and on every

313

soul of man that is found in evil-doing; the eternal judgement of which day of the Lord, is over . . . all man's glory and pomp, which Hell now opens her mouth wide to receive and over everyone, and everything that is high and lifted up. . . .

7. Robert Barclay's *Catechism and Confession of Faith* (1673)

After studying under the Catholics at the Scots College in France and under the Presbyterians at Aberdeen, Robert Barclay could match Samuel Fisher as the theologically best trained of early Friends; only Barclay the Scot usually wrote first in Latin and afterward in English, like most seventeenth-century scholars. Barclay was, like Penn, a country squire, convinced of Quakerism young but only after the Restoration, and thus early called into persecution and the needs to lead and publicly defend the movement. Both men wrote voluminously, were prominent in Yearly Meetings in the 1670's and '80's, and traveled to visit Friends and sympathizers in Holland and Germany. Barclay was named governor of East Jersey just as Penn was opening Pennsylvania, and organized shiploads of settlers (though never coming himself). Yet while Penn was ever more involved in political affairs, Barclay preferred to contribute as a systematic writer. His *Apology* (1675-78), while never a rival to Calvin's and Aquinas' great syntheses of thought and doctrine, became virtually the official statement of Quaker beliefs for outsiders, and among Friends was treasured also for its warmth of personal witness about worship and inwardly led ministry. Too long to include in this collection, and too vital to abridge, the *Apology*, like Fox's *Journal*, deserves to stand alone.

The *Catechism and Confession of Faith*, while admittedly only a fifth the length, ran the *Apology* a close second throughout Quaker history in popularity (Smith knew of twenty-seven *Catechism* reprintings in English and five in other languages, versus thirty-four and thirteen of the *Apology*). The *Catechism* is nevertheless rarely quoted, being in fact mainly a chain of biblical quotations supporting Quaker beliefs. It is somewhat of a tour de force, and moreover the passages are chosen sensitively and with care to match the spirit as well as the ideas of Quakerism. Yet clearly it is hard to say what weight it carries outside those

Christian communities for which the Bible is already the prime authority. Barclay himself was also clearly trying to parallel and parry the *Westminster Confession* and *Catechism*. Notes for this book, written in 1672, were found by D. Elton Trueblood and Hans Buchinger in the Latin portion of Barclay's unpublished Notebook (see Trueblood, *Robert Barclay* [1968], p. 263). In our reprinting of the *Catechism* the page-marks [in square brackets] and the identification of biblical passages are taken from the fourth edition, 1701 (except for those preceded by =), but are run into the text. Relatively unimportant or repetitive quotations have been replaced by their identification (also in square brackets), but none ignored. The *Confession of Faith,* on the other hand, sufficiently duplicates the *Catechism* in thought and outline that it is here omitted entirely.

A CATECHISM
AND CONFESSION OF FAITH

Approved of, and Agreed unto by the General Assembly of the Patriarchs, Prophets, and Apostles, Christ himself being Chief Speaker in and among them, which containeth a true and faithful account of the Principles and Doctrines which are most surely believed by the Churches of Christ in Great Britain and Ireland, who are reproachfully call'd by the name of Quakers, etc.

[no publisher or place given]

[1673]

Chap. I
Of God, and the True and Saving Knowledge of Him

Quest. Seeing it is a thing unquestioned by all sorts of Christians, that the height of happiness consists in coming to know and enjoy eternal life, what is it in the sense and judgment of Christ?

A. This is Life Eternal, that they might know thee the only true God, and Jesus Christ whom thou hast sent. (John *17*:3)

Q. How does God reveal this knowledge?

A. For God, who commanded the light to shine out of darkness, has shined in our hearts, to give the light of the knowledge of the glory of God, in the face of Jesus Christ. (II Cor. *4*:6.)

Q. How many gods are there?

A. One God. [Eph. 4:9; I Cor. 8:4, 6.]

[2] *Q*. What is God?

A. God is a spirit. (John *4*:24.)

315

Q. Among all the blessed, glorious and divine excellencies of God, which are ascribed and given to him in the scriptures, what is that which is most needful for us to take notice of, as being the message which the apostles recorded in special manner to declare of him now under the gospel?

A. This then is the message which we have heard of him, and declare unto you, that God is light, and in him is no darkness at all. (I John *1*:5.)

Q. What are they that bear record in heaven?

A. [I John 5:7.]

Q. How comes any man to know God the Father according to Christ's words?

A. All things are delivered to me of my Father; and no man knows who the Son is, but the Father; and who the Father is, but the Son, and he to whom the Son will reveal him. (Luke *10*:22; Mat. *11*:27.) Jesus says to him, I am the way, the truth and the life; no man comes to the Father but by me. (John *14*:6.)

Q. By whom, and after what manner does the Son reveal this knowledge?

[3] *A.* But as it is written: eye has not seen, nor ear heard; neither have entered into the heart of man, the things which God has prepared for them that love him. But God has revealed them unto us by his Spirit; for the Spirit searches all things—yea, the deep things of God. For what man knows the things of a man, save the spirit of a man, which is in him? Even so the things of God knows no man, but the Spirit of God. Now, we have received not the spirit of the world, but the Spirit which is of God, that we might know the things that are freely given to us of God. (I Cor. *2*:9, 10, 11, 12.) [Also John 14:26.]

Chap. II
Of the Rule and Guide of Christians
and of the Scriptures

Q. Seeing it is by the Spirit that Christ reveals the knowledge of God in things spiritual, is it by the Spirit that we must be led under the gospel?

[4] *A.* [Rom. 8:9.]

For, as many as are led by the Spirit of God, they are the sons of God. (*8*:14.)

Q. Is it an inward principle, then, that is to be the guide and rule of Christians?

A. But the anointing, which ye have received of him, abideth in you; and you need not that any man teach you, but as the same anointing teaches you of all things and is truth and is no lie; and even as it has taught you, you shall abide in him. (I John *2*:27.) But as touching brotherly love, you need not that I write unto you; for you yourselves are taught of God to love one another. (I Thess. *4*:9.)

Q. I perceive by this, that it is by an inward anointing and rule that

Christians are to be taught. Is this the very tenor of the New Covenant-Dispensation?

A. [Heb. 8:10, 11 = Jer. 31:33, 34 and John 6:45 = Isa. 54:13.]

[5] *Q*. Did Christ then promise, that the spirit should both abide with his disciples and be in them?

A. And I will pray the father, and he shall give you another comforter, that he may abide with you forever, even the spirit of truth, whom the world cannot receive, because it sees him not, neither knows him. But ye know him; for he dwells with you and shall be in you. (John *14*:16)

Q. For what end were the Scriptures written?

A. For whatsoever things were written aforetime were written for our learning that we through patience and comfort of the Scriptures might have hope. (Rom. *15*:4)

Q. For what are they profitable?

A. Thou hast known the Holy Scriptures, which are able to make thee wise unto salvation through faith which is in Christ Jesus. All Scripture is given by inspiration of God and is profitable for doctrine, for reproof, for correction, for instruction in righteousness, that the man of God may be perfect, [6] thoroughly furnished unto all good works. (II Tim. *3*:15, 17)

Q. Wherein consists the excellency of the scriptures?

A. Knowing this first, that no prophecy of the scriptures is of any private interpretation, for the prophecy came not in old time by the will of man; but holy men of God spoke as they were moved by the Holy Ghost. (II Pet. *1*:20, 21)

Q. The scriptures are then to be regarded, because they came from the spirit and they also testify that not they but the spirit is to lead into all truth. In what respect does Christ command to search them?

A. Search the scripture, for in them you think you have eternal life, and they are they which testify of me. (John *5*:39)

Q. I perceive there was a generation of old that greatly exalted the scriptures and yet would not believe nor come to be guided by that the scriptures directed to. How does Christ speak such?

A. [John 5:45, 47.]

[7] *Q*. What ought then such to be accounted of, notwithstanding of their pretences of being ruled by the scriptures?

A. [II Pet. 3:16.]

Chap. III

Of Jesus Christ being manifest in the flesh;
the Life and End of it.

Q. What are the scriptures which do most observably prophesy of Christ's appearance?

A. [Deut. 18:15; Isa. 7:14.]

Q. Was not Jesus Christ in being before he appeared in the flesh? What clear scriptures prove this, against such as erroneously assert the contrary?

[8] *A*. But thou Bethlehem Ephratah, though thou be little among the thousands of Judah, yet out of thee shall he come forth unto me, that is to be ruler in Israel, whose goings forth have been from of old, from everlasting. (Mic. *5*:2). In the beginning was the word, and the word was with God, and the word was God. The same was in the beginning with God; all things were made by him, and without him was not anything made that was made. (John *1*:1, 3). Jesus said unto them, "Verily, verily, I say unto you, before Abraham was, I am." (John *8*:58). And now, O Father, glorify thou me with thine own self, with the glory which I had with thee before the world was. (John *17*:5). And to make all men see what is the fellowship of the mystery, which from the beginning of the world has been hid in God, who created all things by Jesus Christ. (Eph. *3*:9) [Also Col. 1:16; Heb. 1:2.]

[9] *Q*. These are very clear, that even the world was created by Christ. But what scriptures prove the divinity of Christ against such as falsely deny the same?

A. (John *1*:1.) Whose are the fathers, and of whom as concerning the flesh Christ came, who is over all, God blessed forever, Amen. (Rom. *9*:5). Who being in the form of God, thought it not robbery to be equal with God. (Phil. *2*:6) [Also I John 5:20.]

Q. What are the glorious names the scripture gives unto Jesus Christ, the eternal son of God?

A. And his name shall be called, Wonderful, Counsellor, the Mighty God, the Everlasting Father, the Prince of Peace (Isa. *9*:6); who is the image of the invisible God, the first born of every creature (Col. *1*:15); [10] who being the brightness of his glory, and express image of his person (or more properly, according to the Greek, "of his substance"). (Heb. *1*:3) [Also Rev. 19:13.]

Q. After what manner was the birth of Christ?

A. Now the birth of Jesus Christ was on this wise: when as his mother Mary was espoused to Joseph (before they came together) she was found with child of the Holy Ghost. (Matt. *1*:18) [Also Luke 1:30-35.]

[11] *Q*. Was Jesus Christ, who was born of the Virgin Mary and supposed to be the son of Joseph, a true and real man?

A. Forasmuch as the children are partakers of flesh and blood, he also himself took part of the same, that through death he might destroy him that had the power of death, that is, the devil. For verily he took not on him the nature of angels, but he took on him the seed of Abraham. Wherefore in all things it behooved him to be made like unto his brethren, that he might be a merciful and faithful high priest. (Heb. *2*:14, 16, 17). For we have not an high priest which cannot be touched with the feeling of our infirmities, but

318

was in all points tempted as we are, yet without sin. (Heb. *4*:15). And the gift by grace, which is by one man, Jesus Christ, has abounded unto many. (Rom. *5*:15) [Also I Cor. 15:20, 21.]

Q. After what manner does the scripture assert the conjunction and unity of the eternal Son of God, in and with the man, Christ Jesus?

[12] *A*. And the word was made flesh and dwelt among us (and we beheld his glory, the glory as of the only begotten of the Father) full of grace and truth. (John *1*:14). For he whom God has sent, speaks the words of God; for God gives not the spirit by measure unto him. (John *3*:34). How God anointed Jesus of Nazareth with the Holy Ghost and with power, who went about doing good and healing all that were oppressed of the devil; for God was with him. (Acts *10*:38). For it pleased the Father that in him should all fullness dwell. (Col. *1*:19) [Also Col. 2:9; 2:3.]

Q. For what end did Christ appear in the world?

A. For what the law could not do in that it was weak through the flesh, God, sending his Son in the likeness of sinful flesh and for sin, condemned sin in the flesh. (Rom. *8*:3) [Also I John 3:4, 5.]

[13] *Q*. Was Jesus Christ really crucified and raised again?

A. For I delivered unto you first of all that which I also received, how that Christ died for our sins, according to the scriptures. And that he was buried and that he rose again the third day, according to the scriptures. (I Cor. *15*:34)

Q. What end do the scriptures ascribe unto the coming, death, and sufferings of Christ?

A. For mine eyes have seen thy salvation, which thou hast prepared before the face of all people, a light to lighten the gentiles and the glory of thy people Israel. (Luke *2*:30, 32). Whom God has set forth to be a propitiation through faith in his blood, to declare his righteousness for the remission of sins that are past, through the forbearance of God. (Rom. *3*:25). And walk in love as Christ also has loved us and has given himself for us, an offering and a sacrifice to God for a sweet smelling savour. (Eph. *5*:2) [Also Col. 1:20, 21.] [14] Neither by the blood of goats and calves, but by his blood, he entered in once into the holy place, having obtained eternal redemption for us. How much more shall the blood of Christ, who through the Eternal Spirit offered himself without spot to God, purge your consciences from dead works to serve the living God? (Heb. *9*:12, 14) [Also I Pet. 3:18.] Hereby perceive we the love of God because he laid down his life for us. (I John *3*:16) [Also Heb. 9:15.]

Q. Is Christ then the mediator?

A. For there is one God and one mediator between God and man, the man Christ Jesus who gave himself a [15] ransom for all to be testified in due time. (I Tim. *2*:5)

Q. Was not Christ the mediator until he appeared and was crucified in the flesh?

A. He is the lamb that was slain from the foundation of the world. (Rev. *5*:12; *13*:8)

Q. Is it needful then to believe that the saints of old did partake of Christ as then present with and nourishing them?

A. [I Cor. 10:1, 2, 3, 4.]

Q. But whereas most of these scriptures before mentioned do hold forth that the death and sufferings of Christ were appointed for the destroying, removing and remitting of sin: did he so do it while he was outwardly upon earth as not to leave anything for himself to do in us, for us to do in and by his strength?

A. For even hereunto were ye called because Christ also suffered for us, leaving us an example that you should follow his steps. (I Pet. *2*:21) [Also Col. 1:23, 24 and II Cor. 4:10, 11.] [16] And that he died for all that they which live should not henceforth live unto themselves but unto him that died for them and also rose again. (II Cor. *5*:15). That I may know him and the power of his resurrection and the fellowship of his sufferings being made conformable to his death. (Phil. *3*:10).

Chap. IV
Of the New Birth, the Inward Appearance
of Christ in Spirit, and the Unity of the Saints with him.

Q. Does Christ promise then to come again to his disciples?

A. I will not leave you comfortless; I will come unto you. (John *14*:18)

[17] *Q*. Was this only a special promise to these disciples? Or is it not the common privilege of the saints?

A. [Isa. 57:15 and II Cor. 6:16.] Behold I stand at the door and knock. If any man hear my voice and open the door, I will come in to him and sup with him and he with me. (Rev. *3*:20).

Q. Does the apostle Paul speak of the Son of God's being revealed in him?

A. But when it pleased God, who separated me from my mother's womb and called me by his grace to reveal his son in me that I might preach him among the heathen. (Gal. *1*:15, 16)

Q. Is it needful then to know Christ within?

A. Examine yourselves whether you be in the faith; prove your own selves. Know you not your own selves how that Jesus Christ is in you except you be reprobates. (II Cor. *13*:5)

Q. Was the apostle earnest that his inward birth of Christ should be brought forth in any?

320

[18] *A*. My little children of whom I travail in birth again until Christ be formed in you. (Gal. *4*:19)

Q. What says the same apostle of the necessity of this inward knowledge of Christ and of the new creature beyond the outward?

A. [II Cor. 5:16, 17.] But you have not so learned Christ if so be that you have heard him and have been taught by him as the truth is in Jesus. That you put off concerning the former conversation, the old man, which is corrupt, according to the deceitful lusts; and be renewed in the spirit of your mind; and that you put on the new man which after God is created in righteousness and true holiness. (Eph. *4*:21-24.)

Q. Is this Christ within the mystery of God and hope of glory which the apostle preached?

A. To whom God would make known what is the riches of the glory [19] of this mystery among the gentiles; which is Christ in you the hope of glory whom we preach. (Col. *1*:27, 28.)

Q. Does the apostle anywhere else press the putting on of this new birth?

A. [Rom. 13:14.]

Q. Does he write to any of the saints as having put off the old and put on the new man?

A. [Gal. 3:27.] Seeing that you have put off the old man with his deeds and have put on the new man which is renewed in knowledge after the image of him that created him. (Col. *3*:9, 10.)

Q. What speaks Christ himself of the necessity of this new birth?

A. Jesus answered and said unto him, "Verily, verily, I say unto thee, except a man be born again, he cannot see the kingdom of God. (John *3*:3)

Q. Of what seed comes this birth?

A. Being born again not of corruptible seed but of incorruptible, by the word of God which lives and abides forever. (I Pet. *1*:23.)

[20] *Q*. What does the apostle Paul witness of himself concerning this new life?

A. I am crucified with Christ; nevertheless I live—yet, not I, but Christ lives in me. (Gal. *2*:20.)

Q. What is the preaching of the cross of Christ?

A. For the preaching of the cross is to them that perish, foolishness; but unto us that are saved it is the power of God. (I Cor. *1*:18)

Q. What effect had this cross in the apostle? And how much prefers he the new creature to all outward and visible ordinances and observances?

A. But God forbid that I should Glory, save in the cross of our Lord Jesus Christ, by whom the world is crucified unto me and I unto the world: For in Jesus Christ neither circumcision avails any thing, nor uncircumcision, but a new creature. (Gal. *6*:14, 15.)

Q. What speaks Christ of the unity of the saints with him?

A. [John 14:20; 15:4, 5; and 17:21, 23.]

[21] *Q*. What says the apostle Paul to this purpose?

A. For both he that sanctifies and they that are sanctified are all of one, for which cause he is not ashamed to call them brethren. (Heb. *2*:11.)

Q. What says the apostle Peter?

A. [II Pet. 1:4.]

[22] Chap. V.

Concerning the Light Wherewith Jesus Christ Has Enlightened Every Man; The Universality and Sufficiency of God's Grace to All the World, Made Manifest Therein.

Q. Wherein consists the love of God towards fallen and lost man?

A. For God so loved the world that he gave his only begotten son that whosoever believes in him should not perish but have everlasting life. (John *3*:16) [Also I John 4:9.]

Q. What is intended here by the world? All and every man, or only a few?

A. But we see Jesus, who was made a little lower than the angels for the suffering of death, crowned with glory and honour, that he by the grace of God should taste death for every man. (Heb. *2*:9) [Also I John 2:1, 2.]

[23] *Q*. Methinks the apostle John is very plain there in mentioning the whole world which must be not only the saints but all others, seeing he distinguishes the world from himself and all the saints to whom he then wrote. What says Paul elsewhere in this matter?

A. [Col. 1:27, 28.] For this is good and acceptable in the sight of God our saviour who will have all men be saved and to come to the knowledge of the truth; who gave himself a ransom for all, to be testified in due time. (I Tim. *2*:1, 2, 4, 6.)

Q. What is the apostle Peter's testimony in this?

A. The Lord is not slack concerning his promise (as some men count slackness) [24] but is long-suffering to us-ward, not willing that any should perish but that all should come to repentance. (II Pet. *3*:9)

Q. Are there any more scripture passages that prove this thing?

A. [Ezek. 33:11; Ps. 145:8, 9; II Cor. 5:19.]

Q. Seeing then by these scriptures it appears that the love of God is held out to all, that all might have been or may be saved by Christ; What is to be judged of those who assert that God nor Christ never purpose love nor salvation to a great part of mankind and that the coming and sufferings of Christ never were intended nor could be useful to their justification but will and must be effectual for their condemnation even according to God's purpose, who from their very infancy to their grave, withheld from them all means of salvation? What says the scripture to such?

[25] *A*. For God sent not his Son into the world to condemn the world but that the world through him might be saved. (John *3*:17) [Also John 12:46, 47.]

Q. From what scripture, then, come these men to wrest an opinion so contrary to truth?

A. [Rom. 9:11, 12, 13, on God's hatred of Esau.]

Q. . . . Does not the scripture mention any other cause of God's hating Esau than merely his decree? What says the same apostle elsewhere?

[26] *A*. Lest there be any fornicator or profane person, as Esau, who for one morsel of meat sold his birth-right; for ye know how that afterward when he would have inherited the blessing he was rejected. (Heb. *12*:16, 17)

Q. But seeing that such allege that it is because of Adam's sin that many, even children, are damned, does not the scripture aver that the death of Christ was as large to heal as Adam's sin could be to condemn?

A. [Rom. 5:15, 18.]

Q. That proves abundantly that Christ's death is of sufficient extent to make up any hurt Adam's sin brought upon mankind. What is then the cause of condemnation?

A. He that believes on him is not condemned; but he that believes not is condemned already because he has not believed in the name of the only begotten son of God. (John *3*:18) [Also II Thess. 2:10, 11, 12, on love of the Truth.]

[27] *Q*. . . . Is the gospel or glad tidings of this salvation brought nigh unto all by which they are put into a capacity of receiving the grace and being saved by it?

A. If you continue in the faith grounded and settled and be not moved away from the hope of the gospel which you have heard and which was preached to every creature which is under heaven, whereof I, Paul, am made a minister. (Col. *1*:23.)

Q. What is the gospel?

A. I am not ashamed of the gospel; for it is the power of God unto salvation to every one that believes. (Rom. *1*:16.)

Q. Is the gospel hid?

A. If our gospel be hid, it is hid to them that are lost, in whom the God [28] of this world has blinded the minds of them which believe not, lest the light of the glorious gospel of Christ should shine unto them. (II Cor. *4*:34.)

Q. Is the light then come into the world? And are not men condemned because they love it not, and not because it is hidden from them?

A. And this is the condemnation: that light is come into the world, and men love darkness rather than light. (John *3*:19.)

Q. Why do they so?

A. Because their deeds are evil. (John *3*:19.)

Q. Is every man enlightened by this light?

A. He was not that light, but was sent to bear witness of that light. That was the true light, which enlightens every man that comes into the world. (John *1*:8, 9.)

Q. Does this light discover all things?

A. All things that are reproved are made manifest by the light; for whatsoever does make manifest is light. (Eph. *5*:13.)

Q. Do evil men preach up this light or mind it?

A. Every one that does evil, hates the light, neither comes to the light, lest his deeds should be reproved. (John *3*:20) They are of those that rebel against the light. (Job *24*:13.)

[29] *Q.* Do good men love it and follow it?

A. He that does truth, comes to the light that his deeds may be made manifest that they are wrought in God. (John *3*:21.)

Q. What benefit does redound to such as love the light and walk in it?

A. [I John 1:7.]

Q. Does Christ command to take heed to the light?

A. While you have the light, believe in the light, that you may be the children of the light. (John *12*:36)

Q. Were the apostles commanded to turn people to the light?

A. [Acts 26:17, 18.]

Q. Does this light abide with every man all his lifetime, in order to save, or only during the day of his visitation?

[30] *A.* Yet a little while is the light with you; walk while you have the light lest darkness come upon you. (John *12*:35) [Also Heb. 4:7.]

Q. How can it be proved that there is a day, wherein people may know things concerning their peace, which afterwards may be hid from them?

A. And when [Jesus] was come near, he beheld the city and wept over it, saying, "If thou hadst known, even thou, at least in this thy day, the things which belong unto thy peace? But now they are hid from thine eyes." (Luke *19*:41, 42.)

Q. Is there any further scripture-proof of the Lord's willingness to gather a people who would not and therefore were condemned?

A. O Jerusalem, Jerusalem! thou that killest the prophets and stonest them which are sent unto thee, how often would I have gathered thy children together, even as a hen gathers her chickens under her wings; and you would not? (Mat. *23*:37; Luke *13*:34.) [Also Matt. 18:32, 33, 34.] [31] Then Paul and Barnabas waxed bold and said: "it was necessary that the word of God should first have been spoken to you; but seeing you put it from you and judge yourselves unworthy of everlasting life, lo we turn to the gentiles." (Acts *13*:46) [Also Prov. 1:24, 25, 26 and Jer. 18:9, 10.]

Q. Does God's spirit strive then for a season and afterwards forbear?

A. And the Lord said, "My spirit shall not always strive with man." (Gen. 6:3)

[32] *Q.* May it then be resisted?

A. You stiff-necked and uncircumcised in heart and ears, you do always resist the holy ghost; as your fathers did, so do you. (Acts 7:51) [Also Rom. 1:18.]

Q. Has God manifested to man, that which may be known of himself?

A. That which may be known of God is manifest in them, for God has showed it unto them. (Rom. *1*:19)

Q. Is then this Light or Seed sown in the hearts of evil men?

A. And he spoke many things to them in parables. Behold, a sower went forth to sow. And when he sowed, some seeds fell by the wayside, etc. Some fell among stony places, etc. and some fell among thorns, etc. (Mat. *13*:3-7)

Q. Are these places where the seed is said to have fallen understood of the hearts of men?

A. [Matt. 13:18, 19.]

[33] *Q.* Is this Seed small in its first appearance?

A. The kingdom of heaven is like to a grain of mustard seed. . . . (Mat. *13*:31, 32)

Q. Forasmuch as many understand not this, under the notion and appellation of Light or Seed, it being quite another dialect than the common, (though I must needs confess, it is the very language of the scriptures), is a saving manifestation of the Spirit given unto all?

A. The manifestation of the Spirit is given to every man to profit withal. (I Cor. *12*:7)

Q. Surely, if it be to profit withal, it must be in order to save; for if it were not useful, yea, sufficient to save, what profit could it be of? But in regard some speak of a grace that is common, and of a grace that is saving, is there such a grace that is saving, is there such a grace common unto all as brings salvation?

A. The Grace of God that brings salvation has appeared to all men. (Tit. *2*:11)

Q. That which brings salvation must needs be saving. What does that grace teach us?

A. Teaching us, that denying ungodliness, and worldly lusts, we should live soberly, righteously and godly in this present world. (Tit. *2*:11)

[34] *Q.* Certainly that which teaches both righteousness and godliness must be sufficient; for therein consists the whole duty of man. What says the apostle elsewhere of this instructor?

A. And now, brethren, I commend you to God and to the Word of his grace which is able to build you up and to give you an inheritance among all those that are sanctified. (Acts *20*:32.)

Q. What is the word of God?

A. The word of God is quick and powerful and sharper than any two-edged sword, piercing even to the dividing asunder of soul and spirit and of the joints and marrow, and is a discerner of the thoughts and intents of the heart. Neither is there any creature that is not manifest in his sight, but all things are naked and open to the eyes of him with whom we have to do. (Heb. *4*:12, 13)

Q. Ought we to take heed to this word?

A. We have also a more sure word of prophecy, whereunto you do well that you take heed, as unto a light that shines in a dark place until the day dawn and the day-star arise in your heart. (II Pet. *1*:19)

Q. I perceive the scriptures are very clear, both concerning the universality and sufficiency of this Light, Seed, grace and [35] Word of God; but is this Word nigh or afar off, inward or outward?

A. [Rom. 10:6, 7, 8.]

Q. . . . Is there any scripture speaks of the Light's being inward?

A. God who commanded the light to shine out of darkness has shined in our hearts to give the light of the knowledge of the glory of God in the face of Jesus Christ. But we have this treasure in earthen vessels, that the excellency of the power may be of God and not of us. (II Cor. *4*:6, 7.)

Q. But seeing it is also called the seed of the kingdom, is the kingdom of God also within?

A. The kingdom of God comes not with observation; neither shall they say, "Lo here, or Lo there"; for behold the kingdom of God is within you. (Luke *17*:20, 21.)

[36] Chap. VI
Concerning Faith, Justification, and Works.

Q. What is Faith?

A. Faith is the substance of things hoped for and the evidence of things not seen. (Heb. *11*:1.)

Q. Is Faith of absolute necessity?

A. Without faith it is impossible to please him; for he that comes to God must believe that he is and that he is a rewarder of them that diligently seek him. (Heb. *11*:6.)

Q. Are we justified by faith?

A. [Gal. 3:24.] Wherefore the law was our school-master to bring us unto Christ that we might be justified by faith.

Q. What is the nature of this faith that availeth to justification?

A. For in Jesus Christ neither circumcision availeth anything, nor uncircumcision, but faith which works by love. (Gal. *5*:6)

326

Q. Are works then necessary to justification as well as faith?

A. But wilt thou know, O vain man, that faith without works is dead? . . . (James *2*:20-24)

[37] *Q.* If then both be equally required in justification, what are these works which the apostle excludes so much?

A. By the deeds of the Law there shall no flesh be justified in his sight. (Rom. *3*:30)

Q. But though we be not justified by the deeds of the Law, is not this to exclude boasting that the grace of God may be exalted?

A. For by grace are you saved through faith and that not of yourselves; it is the gift of God; not of works, lest any man should boast, for we are his workmanship created in Christ Jesus unto good works. (Eph. *2*:8-10.)

Q. Are even the works which are performed by grace excluded? Are we never said to be saved or justified by them?

A. [Tit. 3:5-7.]

[38] *Q.* I perceive, then, that to be justified by grace is to be justified or saved by regeneration, which cannot exclude the works wrought by grace and by the Spirit. How does the apostle add in the next verse for the maintaining this against these that cavil about the Law?

A. [Tit. *3*:8, 9.]

Q. Does the apostle Paul, that is so much against justification by the works of the Law, speak anywhere else of being justified by the Spirit?

A. But you are washed, but you are sanctified, but you are justified in the name of the Lord Jesus and by the Spirit of our God. (I Cor. *6*:11)

[39] *Q.* But since the law gives not power nor ability to obey and so falls short of justification, is there no power under the gospel, by which the righteousness of the Law comes to be fulfilled inwardly?

A. For what the Law could not do in that it was weak through the flesh, God sending his own son in the likeness of sinful flesh, and for sin, condemned sin in the flesh, that the righteousness of the law might be fulfilled in us, who walk not after the flesh, but after the spirit. (Rom. *8*:3, 4.)

Q. Seeing then there is Power in the spirit, is not works through it a condition upon which life is purposed under the new covenant?

A. For if you live after the flesh, you shall die; but if you, through the spirit, do mortify the deeds of the body, you shall live. (Rom. *8*:13)

Q. Do not the apostles, then, frequently propose life to people upon condition of repentance and other works?

A. Repent you therefore and be converted, that your sins may be blotted out. (Acts *3*:19) [Also Rom. 8:17 and II Tim. 2:11, 12, 21.] [40] Remember therefore from whence thou art fallen and repent and do the first works; or else I will come unto thee quickly and remove thy candlestick out of his place except thou repent. (Rev. *2*:5.)

Q. It appears clearly by these passages that the apostle excludes only our righteousness, . . . as being necessary to justification and not such works as the law of the spirit of life leads to and are not so much ours as Christ in us. Are not such good works rewarded though they require no absolute merit as being the fruits of free grace; yet does not God judge according to them and may they not be said to have a reward?

A. [Ezek. 18:5, 6, 7, 8, 9.] [41] For the son of man shall come in the glory of his father with his angels and then he shall reward every man according to his works. (Mat. *16*:27) [Also Acts 10:34, 35.] The righteous judgment of God, who will render to every man according to his deeds, to them who by patient continuance in well-doing seek for glory and honor and immortality, eternal life. . . . But glory, honor and peace to every man that worketh [42] good, to the Jew first and also to the gentile. (Rom. *2*:5-10). For we must all appear before the judgment-seat of Christ, that everyone may receive the things done in his body, according to that he hath done, whether it be good or bad. (II Cor. *5*:10) [Also II Thess. 1:5; James 1:25; Heb. 10:35; I Pet. 1:17; and Rev. 22:12, 14.]

[43] *Q*. It should seem that the purpose of God, in sending his son the Lord Jesus Christ, was not simply to save man by an imputative righteousness altogether without them; but also by the washing of regeneration, or an inward righteousness. What says the scripture further of this?

A. And thou shalt call his name Jesus, for he shall save his people from their sins. (Mat. *1*:21). Looking for that blessed hope and the glorious appearing of the great God and our saviour Jesus Christ, who gave himself for us, that he might redeem us from all iniquity and purify unto himself a peculiar people, zealous of good works. (Tit. *2*:13, 14)

Chap. VII
Concerning Perfection, or Freedom from Sin.

Q. I perceive then by all these scriptures afore-mentioned, that Christ as well as he has purchased pardon for our sins, has also obtained power by which we may even here be cleansed from the filth of them. May we expect then in this life to be freed from the dominion of sin?

[44] *A*. For sin shall not have dominion over you. (Rom. *6*:14)

Q. For what reason?

A. For you are not under the law but under grace. (Rom. *6*:14)

Q. How comes the apostle then to cry out and complain of sin, saying, "Who shall deliver me from the body of this death?" Does he speak that as a condition always permanent to him and other saints, or only that which he had passed through? What says he afterwards?

A. There is therefore now no condemnation to them which are in Christ

328

Jesus, who walk not after the flesh, but after the spirit. For the law of the spirit of life in Christ Jesus has made me free from the law of sin and death. . . . (Rom. *8*:1, 2, 35-39)

[45] *Q*. What saith that apostle then unto such, who taking occasion from his words, should plead for continuance in sin for term of life and think to be saved by the imputative righteousness of Christ, as being under grace?

A. What shall we say then? Shall we continue in sin that grace may abound? God forbid. What then? Shall we sin because we are not under the law but under grace? (Rom. *6*:1, 2.)

Q. Is not the apostle then so far from supposing that condition of being always under sin to be his own constant condition or that of all the saints, that he even supposed many of the then church of Rome, to whom he wrote, to be free of it? How bespeaks he them as in relation to this matter?

A. How shall we that are dead in sin, live any longer therein? . . . [46] Let not sin therefore reign in your mortal body that you should obey it in the lusts thereof. Neither yield you your members as instruments of unrighteousness unto sin; but yield yourselves unto God, as those that are alive from the dead; and your members as instruments of righteousness unto God. Know you not that to whom you yield yourselves servants to obey, his servants you are to whom you obey whether of sin unto death or of obedience unto righteousness? But God be thanked that you were the servants of sin; but you have obeyed from the heart that form of doctrine which was delivered unto you. Being then made free from sin, you became the servants of righteousness. . . . [47] For the wages of sin is death; but the gift of God is eternal life through Jesus Christ our Lord. (Rom. *6*:2-7, 11-13, 16-23)

Q. It would appear then that God requires of us to be perfect?

A. Be you therefore perfect even as your Father which is in heaven is perfect. (Mat. *5*:48)

Q. Is it then possible to keep the commandments?

A. My yoke is easy and my burden is light. (Mat. *11*:30) For this is the law of God that we keep his commandments, and his commandments are not grievous. (I John *5*:3)

Q. Is it necessary then for salvation to keep the commandments?

A. [Rev. 22:14.]

[48] *Q*. Do you understand by this perfection that any have so kept the commandments as never to have sinned?

A. If we say that we have not sinned, we make him a liar; and his word is not in us. (I John *1*:10)

Q. . . . May they notwithstanding thereof come to know forgiveness for the guilt but also cleansing from the filth?

A. If we say we have no sin, we deceive ourselves, and the truth is not in

329

us. If we confess our sins, he is faithful and just to forgive us our sins and to cleanse us from all unrighteousness. (I John *1*:8)

Q. That scripture seems to be very plain, being compared with the other before mentioned. But because some are apt to mistake and wrest the words of that apostle, what says he elsewhere? Did he judge any could know God or be true Christians who kept not the commandments?

A. My little children, these things write I unto you, that you sin not; and [49] if any man sin, we have an advocate with the father, Jesus Christ the righteous. And hereby do we know that we know him if we keep his commandments. (I John *2*:1, 3) [Also I John 2:4-6; 3:2-10.]

[50] *Q.* It is very plain by these passages that the apostles were far of another mind than those that plead for sin during term of life; and much against the deceit of those who will esteem themselves good Christians while they live in their sins?

A. Not every one that says unto me, "Lord, Lord," shall enter into the kingdom of heaven; but he that does the will of my Father which is in heaven. Therefore, whosoever hears these sayings of mine and does them, I will liken him to a wise man which built his house upon a rock. (Mat. 7:21, 24). If you know these things, happy are you if you do them. (John *13*:17.)

Q. What says the apostle Paul further concerning the needfulness of this thing?

A. Circumcision is nothing, and uncircumcision is nothing; but the keeping of the commandments of God. (I Cor. 7:19)

[51] *Q.* Was not this according to the apostle Paul's judgment the very intention of Christ to have his church and children to be pure and without spot?

A. According as he has chosen us in him before the foundation of the world that we should be holy and without blame before him in love. (Eph. *1*:4) [Also Eph. 5:25, 26, 27.]

Q. Does not Paul press the same thing further besides the other passages above mentioned?

A. Having therefore these promises, dearly beloved, let us cleanse ourselves from all filthiness of the flesh and spirit, perfecting holiness in the fear of God. (II Cor. 7:1) [Also 13:11.] Labouring fervently for you in prayers that you may stand perfect and complete in all the will of God. (Gal. *4*:12) [Also I Thess. 3:13 and 5:23.]

[52] *Q.* Is not this then the very end for which God appointed teachers in his church?

A. And he gave some [to be] apostles; and some prophets; and some, evangelists; and some, pastors and teachers; for the perfecting of the saints, for the work of the ministry, for the edifying of the body of Christ. Till we all come in the unity of the faith and of the knowledge of the Son of God, unto a perfect man, unto the measure of the stature of the fulness of Christ. (Eph. *4*:11-13.)

Q. Seeing this is so much pressed by the holy men, does . . . the Scripture (which cannot lie) give none of the saints this testimony as being free from sin at some times, and so not always and daily sinning, as is supposed?

A. Noah was a just man and perfect in his generations; and Noah walked with God. (Gen. *6*:9) And the Lord said unto Satan, hast thou considered my servant Job that there is none like him in the earth, a perfect and an upright man, one that fears God and eschews evil. (Job *1*:8) [Also Luke 1:1, 2.]

Q. That proves sufficiently as to particular persons. But what does the scripture intimate of this nature, even of considerable numbers?

A. [Eph. 2:4-6.] But you are come unto Mount Sion, and unto the city of the living God, the heavenly Jerusalem, and to an innumerable company of angels, to the general assembly and church of the first-born, which are written in heaven, to God, the judge of all, and to the spirits of just men made perfect. . . . (Heb. *12*:22, 23) [Also Rev. 14:1, 4.]

[54] Chap. VIII
Concerning Perseverance and Falling from Grace.[38]

Q. Is it enough for a believer to be sure that he has once received true grace? Or is there any further certainty requisite?

A. Wherefore the rather, brethren, give diligence to make your calling and election sure; for if you do these things, you shall never fall. (II Pet. *1*:10)

Q. May one that has received true grace have ground to fear or suppose he can fall?

A. But I keep under my body, and bring it into subjection; lest that by any means, when I have preached to [55] others, I myself should become a castaway. (I Cor. *9*:27)

Q. That greatly contradicts the doctrine of such as say, "once in grace, ever in grace." But does the apostle Paul express this only out of an humble esteem of himself? Or does he judge or suppose the like of other saints?

A. Take heed, brethren, lest there be in any of you an evil heart of unbelief in departing from the living God. But exhort one another daily, while it is called today; lest any of you be hardened through the deceitfulness of sin. (Heb. *3*:12, 13). Let us labor therefore to enter into that rest, lest any man

---

38 Whereas perfection as a human possibility and challenge was a characteristic Quaker teaching, Friends rejected the Puritans' alternative sources of confidence, notably the perseverance of the Elect in grace; for Friends rejected the doctrine of predestination that guaranteed salvation to those who had experiences of conversion (unless later events proved it a false conversion) and excluded all others.

fall after the same example of unbelief. (Heb. *4*:11) [Also 6:4, 5, 6 and 12:15.]

[56] *Q*. Doth he speak this only by supposition, or does he assert it not only possible, but certain?

A. For the time will come, when they will not endure sound doctrine; but after their own lusts shall they heap to themselves teachers, having itching ears. And they shall turn away their ears from the truth, and shall be turned unto fables. (II Tim. *4*:3, 4)

Q. Does the apostle even judge it necessary to guard such a one as his beloved son, Timothy, against this hazard?

A. This charge I commit unto thee, son Timothy, according to the prophecies which went before on thee, that thou by them mightest war a good warfare, holding faith in a good conscience; which some having put away, concerning faith have made shipwreck.[39] (I Tim. *1*:18, 19) [Also 6:10 and II Tim. 2:17, 18.]

[57] *Q*. Does the apostle anywhere express his fears of this, as a thing that may happen to any number of people, who once truly received the faith of Christ?

A. [Rom. 11:20; I Tim. 4:1 and 3:5.]

Q. What is the apostle Peter's mind; does he judge that such as have known the right way may forsake it?

A. Cursed children which have forsaken the right way and are gone astray, . . . [58] For if after they have escaped the pollutions of the world, through the knowledge of the Lord and Saviour Jesus Christ, they are again entangled therein, and overcome, the latter end is worse with them than the beginning. . . . (II Pet. *2*:14-18, 20-22)

Q. Gives he any cautions to them that stand, as supposing they may also fall?

A. You therefore, beloved, seeing you know these things before, beware, lest you also being led away with the error of the wicked, fall from your own stedfastness. (II Pet. *3*:17)

Q. May a man be truly a branch in Christ, or a real member of this body and afterwards be cut off?

A. If any man abide not in me, he is cast forth as a branch and is withered. (John *15*:6)

[59] *Q*. May a righteous man then depart from his righteousness?

A. But when the righteous man turneth away from his righteousness, and committeth iniquity and dieth in them; for his iniquity that he has done, shall he die. (Ezek. *18*:26; [cf. 33:13])

---

[39] Barclay quotes the King James Version rather than the usual Quaker phrase "made shipwreck of Conscience."

Q. May a believer come to such a condition in this life, from which he cannot fall away?

A. Him that overcometh will I make a pillar in the temple of God, and he shall go no more out; and I will write upon him the name of the city of my God, which is New Jerusalem, which cometh down out of heaven from my God; and will write upon him my new name. (Rev. *3*:12)

Q. May such an one come to be assured that he is in this condition?

A. For I am persuaded that neither death nor life, nor angels, nor principalities nor powers, nor things present nor things to come, nor height nor depth, nor any other creature shall be able to separate us from the love of God which is in Christ Jesus our Lord. (Rom. *8*:38, 39)

[60] Chap. IX

Concerning the Church and Ministry.

Q. What is the Church?

A. . . . the house of God, which is the church of the living God, the pillar and ground of truth. (I Tim. *3*:15)

Q. Who is the head of the church?

A. [Col. 1:13.] And he is the head of the body, the church, from which all the body by joints and bands, having nourishment ministered, and knit together, increaseth with the increase of God. (Col. *2*:19)

Q. What kind of persons make the Church?

A. Them that are sanctified in Christ Jesus. (I Cor. *1*:2). And the Lord added to the church daily such as should be saved. (Acts *2*:47)

[61] *Q.* Hath not Christ appointed officers in the church, for the work of the ministry?

A. Wherefore he saith, when he ascended upon high, he led captivity captive and gave gifts unto men. And he gave some [to be] apostles; and some prophets; and some, evangelists; and some, pastors and teachers; . . . (Eph. *4*:8, 11, 12)

Q. What kind of men should such as are teachers and overseers of the church be?

A. [I Tim. 3:2-7; Tit. 1:7-9.]

[62] *Q.* What is incumbent upon such to do?

A. Take heed therefore to yourselves and to all the flock over which the Holy Ghost has made you overseers, to feed the church of God. (Acts *20*:28) [Also I Pet. 5:1-3.]

Q. Though they be not to lord over the flock, yet is there not a respect due to them in their place?

A. Let the elders that rule well be counted worthy of double honour, [63] especially they who labour in the word and doctrine. (I Tim. *5*:17)

Q. Albeit then, among true Christians, everyone that believeth is to have the witness in himself, being persuaded in himself by the spirit; yet is there not also a real subjection to be to one another in the Lord?

A. [I Cor. 14:32 and Heb. 13:17.] And we beseech you, brethren, to know them which labor among you and are over you in the Lord, and admonish you; and to esteem them very highly in love, for their work's sake. (I Thes. 5:12, 13). Likewise, ye younger, submit yourselves unto the elder; yea, all of you be subject one to another, and be clothed with humility; for God resisteth the proud and giveth grace unto the humble. (I Pet. 5:5)

Q. How ought true teachers to minister in the church?

A. As every man hath received the gift, even so minister the same one to another, as good stewards of the manifold [64] grace of God. If any speak, let him speak as the oracles of God. If any man minister, let him do it as of the ability which God giveth; that God in all things may be glorified through Jesus Christ. (I Pet. 4:10, 11)

Q. I perceive then that every true minister of the church of Christ is to minister of the gift and grace of God, which he hath received. But some are of the judgment that natural wisdom or parts and humane learning are the qualifications which are of absolute necessity for a minister; but grace they judge not to be so absolutely necessary but that one may be a minister without it. What saith the scripture in this case?

A. A bishop must be sober, just, holy, temperate. (Tit. *1*:7, 8)

Q. Methinks it is impossible for a man to be blameless, just, holy, sober and temperate, without the grace of God. So that if these qualifications be absolutely necessary, then surely that without which a man cannot be so qualified must be necessary also. But what saith the scripture as to the necessity of natural wisdom and humane learning?

A. Where is the wise? Where is the scribe? Where is the disputer of this world? Hath not God made foolish [65] the wisdom of this world? For after . . . the world by wisdom knew not God, it pleased God by the foolishness of preaching to save them that believe. (I Cor. *1*:20, 21)

Q. It seems then the preachings of the true ministers are not gathered together by wisdom and learning. It hath been supposed that a man must be greatly skilled in learning to make a good sermon. What is the apostle's judgment in the case?

A. For Christ sent me not to baptize but to preach the gospel; not with wisdom of words, lest the cross of Christ should be made of none effect. (I Cor. *1*:17). And I was with you in weakness and in fear and in much trembling; and my speech and my preaching was not with enticing words of man's wisdom, but in demonstration of the spirit and of power, that your faith should not stand in the wisdom of men but in the power of God. (I Cor. 2:3, 4, 5)

334

Q. I perceive the apostle lays far more stress upon the demonstration and power of the Spirit in a preacher than upon humane literature. Ought ministers then to preach as the spirit teaches them?

A. Also we speak not in words which man's wisdom teacheth but which the Holy Ghost teacheth. (I Cor. 2:13) [66] And they were all filled with the Holy Ghost and began to speak as the spirit gave them utterance. (Acts 2:4)

Q. Is it Christ then that speaketh in and through his ministers?

A. For it is not you that speak but the spirit of your father which speaketh in you. (Mat. *10*:20) [Also Mark 12:11; Luke 12:12; and II Cor. 13:3.]

Q. What is the apostle's mind of that human learning which some cry up so much and think so needful in a minister?

A. Beware lest any man spoil you through philosophy and vain deceit after the tradition of men, after the rudiments of the world, and not after Christ. (Col. 2:8) [Also I Tim. 6:20.]

Q. Though true ministers speak not by the natural wisdom of man; yet is their testimony altogether void of wisdom?

A. Howbeit, we speak wisdom [67] among them that are perfect; yet not the wisdom of this world nor of the princes of this world that come to nought. (I Cor. 2:6 [and 7])

Q. What is the reason that man by his natural wisdom is not capable to minister in the things of God?

A. For what man knoweth the things of a man save the spirit of a man which is in him? Even so the things of God knoweth no man but the Spirit of God. But the natural man receiveth not the things of the Spirit of God; for they are foolishness unto him; neither can he know them because they are spiritually discerned. (I Cor. 2:11, 14)

Q. These scriptures do sufficiently hold forth that the true call to the ministry is from God; that which maketh a true minister is the gift and grace of God; that the true and effectual preaching of a faithful minister is such as is from the inward teaching and leading of the Spirit of God. But what say the scriptures, touching the maintenance of ministers?

A. Let him that is taught in the word, communicate unto him that teacheth in all good things. (Gal. 6:6). [68] If we have sown unto you spiritual things, is it a great matter if we shall reap your carnal things? If others be partakers of this power over you, are not we rather? Nevertheless, we have not used this power, but suffer all things, lest we should hinder the gospel of Christ. . . . (I Cor. 9:11-14) [Also I Tim. 5:18.]

Q. I perceive by these scriptures that there lieth an obligation upon the saints to help with outward things such as truly minister unto them spiritual; but this seems to be voluntary. Ought not therefore true ministers to preach whether they be sure of this or not? What says the apostle of himself in this case? And what advises he others?

A. But I have used none of these things; neither have I written those things that it should be so done unto me; for it were better for me to die [69] than that any man should make my glorying void. For though I preach the Gospel, I have nothing to glory of; for necessity is laid upon me; yea, woe is unto me if I preach not the Gospel. . . . What is my reward then? Verily, that when I preach the Gospel, I make the Gospel of Christ without charge, that I abuse not my power in the Gospel. (I Cor. *9*:15, 16, 17, 18) [Also Acts 20:33-35.]

Q. It is observable that the apostle everywhere makes special mention among the qualifications of teachers, that they be not given to filthy lucre. What ought we then to think of those teachers as will not preach without hire? Yea, that will by violence take from those who receive no spirituals from them? Are they like to be the ministers [70] of Christ? Or what else saith the scripture of such?

A. Yes, they are greedy dogs which can never have enough; and they are shepherds that cannot understand; they all look to their own way, every one for his gain from his quarter. (Isa. *56*:11) [Also Ezek. 34:2, 3, 8.] Thus says the Lord, concerning the prophets that make my people err, that bite with their teeth, and cry peace; and he that puts not into their mouths, they even prepare war against him. . . . (Micah *3*:5, 11)

[71] *Q*. These are plain testimonies from the prophets: Are there none such from the apostles?

A. Perverse disputings of men of corrupt minds, and destitute of the truth, supposing that gain is godliness; from such withdraw thyself. But godliness with contentment is great gain. For we brought nothing into the world, and it is certain we can carry nothing out. And having food and raiment, let us therewith be content. But they that will be rich fall into temptation and a snare, and into many foolish and hurtful lusts, which drown men in destruction and perdition. For the love of money is the root of all evil; which while some coveted after, they have erred from the faith and pierced themselves through with many sorrows. (I Tim. *6*:5-10) [Also II Tim. 3:2; Tit. 1:10, 11; II Pet. 2:13, 14, 15, and Jude 11:16.]

[73] *Q*. Ought there to be any order in the church of God?

A. Let all things be done decently and in order. (I Cor. *14*:40)

Q. What good order is prescribed in the church concerning preachers? Is it fit that only one or two speak, or many more, if moved thereto?

A. If anything be revealed to another that sits by, let the first hold his peace. For you may all prophesy one by one, that all may learn, and all may be comforted. And the spirits of the prophets are subject to the prophets. For God is not the author of confusion, but of peace, as in all the churches of the saints. (I Cor. *14*:30-33)

Q. Is there any promise that daughters as well as sons shall prophesy under the gospel?

A. And it shall come to pass afterwards that I will pour out of my spirit upon all flesh and your sons and your daughters shall prophesy, your old [74] men shall dream dreams, your young men shall see visions. (Joel *2*:28)

Q. Is that promise fulfilled, and to be fulfilled?

A. [Acts 2:16-17.]

Q. Is there any such instance of old in the scriptures?

A. And the same man had four daughters, virgins, which did prophesy. (Acts *21*:9)

Q. But may all women speak; or are any commanded to keep silence in the church?

A. Let your women keep silence in the church; for it is not permitted unto them to speak; but they are commanded to be under obedience, as also says the law. And if they will learn anything, let them ask their husbands at home; for it is a shame for women to speak in the church. (I Cor. *14*:34, 45) [Also I Tim. 2:11, 12.]

[75] *Q*. ...Hath this no limitation? Doth not the same apostle give directions, how women that speak should behave themselves in the church?

A. Every man praying or prophesying, having his head covered, dishonours his head. But every woman that prays or prophesies with her head uncovered, dishonors her head; for that is even all one as if she were shaven. (I Cor. *11*:4, 5)

Chap. X
Concerning Worship

Q. What is the worship that is acceptable to God?

A. But the hour cometh, and now is, when the true worshippers shall worship the Father in spirit and in truth; for the Father seeketh such to worship him. God is a Spirit, and they that worship him, must worship him in spirit and in truth. (John *4*:23, 24)

[76] *Q*. Seeing prayer is a part of worship, when ought we to pray?

A. And he spake a parable unto them to this end, that men ought always to pray, and not to faint. (Luke *18*:1). Pray without ceasing. (I Thes. *5*:17)

Q. Hath God no respect to the manner of calling upon him?

A. For there is no difference between the Jew and the Greek; for the same Lord over all, is rich unto all that call upon him. (Rom. *10*:12)

Q. Doth God hear the prayers of all that call upon him?

A. The Lord is nigh unto all them that call upon him, to all that call upon him in truth. (Psalm *145*:18) [Also Prov. 15:29; John 9:31; and I John 5:14.]

[77] *Q*. After what manner doth the apostle declare he will pray?

A. What is it then, I will pray with the spirit, and I will pray with the

337

understanding also: I will sing with the Spirit, and I will sing with the understanding also. (I Cor. *14*:15)

Q. Must we then pray always in the spirit?

A. Praying always, with all prayer, and supplication in the spirit, and watching thereunto with all perseverance, and supplication for all saints. (Eph. *6*:18)

Q. Since we are commanded to pray always in it, can we do it of our own selves without the help thereof?

A. Likewise the Spirit also helpeth our infirmities, for we know not what we should pray for as we ought. But the Spirit itself maketh intercession for us, with groanings which cannot be uttered. . . . (Rom. *8*:26-27)

Q. I perceive that without the leadings and help of the Spirit, prayers are altogether unprofitable. May not a man truly utter those things that are spiritual without the Spirit's assistance?

[78] *A*. Wherefore I give you to understand that no man speaking by the Spirit of God calleth Jesus accursed, and that no man can say that Jesus is the Lord but by the Holy Ghost (I Cor. *12*:3).

Q. This is strange; it seems the Spirit is much more necessary than many called Christians suppose it to be, some of which can scarce give a good account whether they have it or want it. But if a man speak things true upon the matter, are they not true as from him, [even] if spoken without the Spirit?

A. And though they say, "the Lord liveth," surely they swear falsely (Jere. *5*:2).

Q. Is it apparent from all these Scriptures that the true worship of God is in the Spirit; and as it is not limited to a certain place, neither to any certain time, what shall we think of them that plead for the observation of certain days?

A. [Gal. 4:9-11.] Let no man therefore judge you in meat or drink, or in respect of an holy day, or of the New Moon or of the Sabbath [79] Day, which are a shadow of things to come; but the body is of Christ (Col. *2*:17).

Q. Seeing it is so, may not some Christians as lawfully esteem all days alike, as others may esteem some days above another? What rule giveth the Apostle in this case?

A. One man esteemeth one day above another, another esteemeth every day alike. Let every man be fully persuaded in his own Mind. . . (Rom. *14*:5-6).

Q. But is it not convenient and necessary that there be a day set apart to meet and worship God in? Did not the Apostles and primitive Christians use to meet upon the first day of the week, to make their Collections and to worship?

A. [I Cor. 16:1, 2.]

338

[80] Chap. XI
Concerning Baptism, and Bread and Wine

Q. How many Baptisms are there?

A. One Lord, one Faith, and one Baptism. (Eph. *4*:5)

Q. What is the Baptism?

A. The like figure, whereunto even Baptism doth now save us, (not the putting away the filth of the flesh, but the answer of a good conscience towards God). . . (I Pet. *3*:21 [and 22]).

Q. What saith John the Baptist of Christ's Baptism? How distinguisheth he it from his?

A. I indeed baptize you with water unto repentance; but he that cometh after me, is mightier than I, whose shoes I am not worthy to bear, he shall baptize you with the Holy Ghost, and with fire. (Mat. *3*:11)

Q. Doth not Christ so distinguish it also?

[81] *A.* And being assembled together with them, commanded them, that they should not depart from Jerusalem, but wait for the promise of the Father, which, saith he, ye have heard of me. For John truly baptized with water, but ye shall be baptized with the Holy Ghost, not many days hence. (Acts *1*:4, 5)

Q. Doth not the Apostle Peter also observe this?

A. [Acts 11:15, 16.]

Q. Then it seems John's Baptism must pass away, that Christ's may take place; because John must decrease, that Christ may increase.

A. [John 3:39.]

Q. I perceive then, many may be sprinkled with, and dipped and baptized in water, and yet not truly baptized with the Baptism of Christ: What are the real effects in such as are truly baptized with the Baptism of Christ?

A. Know ye not, that so many of us as were baptized into Jesus Christ, [82] were baptized into his death? Therefore we are buried with him by Baptism into death, that like as Christ was raised up from the dead by the glory of the Father, even so we also should walk in newness of life. (Rom. *6*:3-4) [Also Gal. 3:12 and Col. 2:12.]

Q. I perceive there was a Baptism of water, which was John's Baptism, and is therefore by John himself contra-distinguished from Christ's. Was there not likewise something of the like nature appointed by Christ to his Disciples, of eating bread, and drinking wine, in remembrance of him?

A. For I have received of the Lord, that which also I delivered unto you, that the Lord Jesus, the same night in which he was betrayed, took bread; and when he had given thanks, he brake it, and said, Take, eat; this is my body which is broken for you; this do in remembrance of me. After the same manner also he took the cup, when he had supped, saying, This cup is the

339

new Testament in my blood; [83] this do ye, as oft as ye drink it, in remembrance of me. (I Cor. *11*:23-25)

Q. How long was this to continue?

A. For as often as ye eat this bread, and drink this cup, ye do shew the Lord's death till he come. (I Cor. *11*:26)

Q. Did Christ promise to come again to his Disciples?

A. I will not leave you comfortless; I will come to you. Jesus answered and said unto him, If a man love me, he will keep my words, and my Father will love him, and we will come unto him, and make our abode with him. (John *14*:18-23)

Q. Was this an inward Coming?

A. At that day ye shall know that I am in my Father, and you in me, and I in you. (John *14*:20)

Q. But it would seem, this was even practiced by the Church of Corinth, after Christ was come inwardly: Was it so, that there were certain appointments positively commanded, yea, and zealously and conscientiously practiced by the saints of old, which were not of perpetual continuance, nor yet now needful to be practiced in the Church?

A. If then your Lord and Master have washed your feet, ye ought also to wash one another's feet. For I have given you an example, that you should do as I have done to you. (John *13*:14, 15) [Also Acts 15:28, 29.] [84] Is any man sick among you? let him call for the elders of the Church, and let them pray over him, anointing him with oil in the name of the Lord.[40] (James *5*:14)

Q. These commands are no less positive than the other; yea, some of them are asserted as the very sense of the Holy Ghost, as no less necessary than abstaining from fornication, and yet the generality of Protestants have laid them aside, as not of perpetual continuance: But what other scriptures are there, to show that it is not necessary [for] that of bread and wine to continue?

A. For the Kingdom of God is not meat or drink; but righteousness and peace and joy in the Holy Ghost. (Rom. *14*:17) [Also Col. 2:16, 20-22.]

[85] *Q*. These scriptures are very plain, and say as much for the abolishing of this, as to any necessity, as ought can be alleged for the former. But what is the bread then, wherewith the saints are to be nourished?

A. Then Jesus said unto them, Verily, verily, I say unto you, Moses gave you not that bread from Heaven, but my Father giveth you the true bread from Heaven. For the bread of God is he which cometh down from Heaven, and giveth life unto the world. Then said they unto him, Lord, evermore give

---

[40] This text was used by Roman Catholics to justify the "last rites" of Extreme Unction. But Barclay is arguing with Protestants.

us this bread. And Jesus said unto them, I am the bread of life; he that cometh to me, shall never hunger; and he that believeth on me shall never thirst. . . . (John 6:32-35 [and 48-58])

[86] Chap. XII
Concerning the Life of a Christian, in General,
What and How it Ought to be in this World.

Q. What is true religion?

A. Pure religion and undefiled is this,—to visit the fatherless and the widows in their affliction and [87] to keep himself unspotted from the world. (James 1:27)

Q. What is required of Man?

A. He hath shewed thee, O man, what is good; and what doth the Lord require of thee, but to do justly, and to love mercy, and to walk humbly with thy God? (Micah 6:8)

But to this man will I look, even to him that is poor, and of a contrite spirit, and trembleth at my word. (Isa. 66:2)

Q. Doth God then require people to be Quakers, to tremble at his word? Was there any such among the saints of old?

A. Then were assembled unto me every one that trembled at the words of the God of Israel. (Ezra 9:4) [Also 10:3.]

Q. It seems Ezra loved well, and had a high esteem of Quakers, since he would have their counsel followed: Do any other of the prophets point out Quakers, or Tremblers, as God's people?

A. Hear the word of the Lord, ye that tremble at his word: Your brethren that hated you, that cast you out [88] for my name's sake, said, let the Lord be glorified; but he shall appear to your joy, and they shall be ashamed. (Isa. 66:5) [Also Jer. 33:9.]

Q. The Prophets promised good things there to Quakers: What becometh of those that tremble not, and are not such?

A. Hear now this, O foolish people! and without understanding, which have eyes, and see not; which have ears, and hear not: Fear ye not me, saith the Lord; will ye not tremble at my presence? &c. (Jer. 5:21, 22)

Q. Are then all God's children Quakers? and are we commanded to quake or tremble in order to our salvation, both under the law, and now under the Gospel?

A. [Ps. 2:11; Dan. 6:26.] Work out your own salvation with fear and trembling. (Phil. 2:12)

[89] Q. What be the chief Commandments?

A. Thou shalt love the Lord thy God with all thy heart, and with all thy soul, and with all thy mind. This is the first and great Commandment, and the

341

second is like unto it. Thou shalt love thy neighbor as thyself. On these two Commandments hang all the law and the Prophets. (Mat. 22:37-40)

Q. What ought a Christian to seek after in the first place?

A. Seek ye first the Kingdom of God and his righteousness, and all these things shall be added unto you. (Mat. 6:33)

Q. How ought Christians to behave themselves in this world?

A. But this I say, Brethren, the time is short: It remaineth, that both they that have wives, be as tho' they had none; and they that weep, as tho' they wept not; and they that rejoice, as tho' they rejoiced not; and they that buy, as tho' they possessed not; and they that use this world, as not abusing it; for the fashion of this world passeth away. (II Cor. 7:29, 30, 31)

Q. What saith the Apostle Paul further, as that which is fit for Christian men and women to be found in?

A. I will therefore, that men pray every where, lifting up holy hands [90] without wrath and doubting. In like manner also, that women adorn themselves in modest apparel, with shamefacedness and sobriety; not with broidered hair, or gold, or pearls or costly array; but (which becometh women professing godliness) with good works. (I Tim. 2:8, 9, 10)

Q. I observe the Apostle is much against the vanity and superfluity of clothes among Christians; what saith Peter to this?

A. [I Pet. 3:3, 4.]

Q. The Apostle is very plain there: But what saith the scripture, as to respect of persons among Christians?

A. My Brethren, have not the faith of our Lord Jesus Christ, the Lord of Glory, with respect of persons. For if there come unto your assembly a man with a gold ring, in goodly apparel; and there come in also a poor man, in vile raiment; and ye have respect to him that weareth the gay clothing, and say unto him, sit thou here in a good place; and say to the poor, stand thou [91] there, or sit here under my foot-stool: are ye not then partial in yourselves; . . . ye have despised the poor. Do not rich men oppress you, and draw you before the judgment-seats? Do they not blaspheme that worthy name by the which ye are called? . . . (James 2:1-9)

Q. Tho' that be indeed sufficient to reprove the different ranks among Christians, upon the account of riches or birth; yet is there not a relative respect among Christians, as betwixt master and servant: What admonition gives the Apostle in this case?

A. [Eph. 6:5-9.]

[92] Servants, obey in all things your masters according to the flesh, not with eyeservice, as men-pleasers, but in singleness of heart, fearing God. And whatsoever ye do, do it heartily, as to the Lord, and not unto men; . . . (Col. 3:22-25) [Also 4:13; I Tim. 6:1, 2; and Tit. 2:9-10.]

[93] Servants, be subject to your masters with all fear, not only to the

good and gentle, but also the froward: For this is thankworthy, if a man for conscience toward God endure grief, suffering wrongfully: For what glory is it, if when ye be buffeted for your faults, ye shall take it patiently? But if when ye do well, and suffer for it, ye take it patiently; this is acceptable with God, . . . because Christ also suffered for us, . . . (I Pet. 2:18-21)

Q. What good admonitions give the Scripture, as to the relation betwixt parents and children?

A. Children, obey your parents in the Lord, . . . that [94] it may be well with thee, and thou mayest live long on the earth. And ye fathers, provoke not your children to wrath; but bring them up in the nurture and admonition of the Lord. (Eph. 6:1-4)

Q. What between husbands and wives?

A. Wives, submit yourselves unto your own husbands, as unto the Lord. For the husband is the head of the wife, even as Christ is the head of the Church; and he is the Savior of the body. Therefore as the Church is subject unto Christ, so let the wives be to their own husbands in every thing. Husbands, love your wives, even as Christ also loved the Church, and gave himself for it. . . . (Eph. 5:22-25) [Also 28, 31, 33 and Col. 3:19.]

[95] Likewise, ye wives, be in subjection unto your own husbands; that if any obey not the Word, they also may without the Word be won by the conversation of the wives, while they behold your chaste conversation coupled with fear. Likewise ye husbands, dwell with them according to knowledge, giving honour unto the wife, as unto the weaker vessel, and as being heirs together of the grace of life, that your prayers be not hindered. (I Pet. 3:1, 3, 7)

Q. What is the armor of a true Christian; and wherewith ought he to wrestle?

A. [Eph. 6:11-17.]

[96] *Q.* What are Christian's weapons, and for what end?

A. For tho' we walk in the flesh, we do not war after the flesh; for the weapons of our warfare are not carnal, but mighty through God, to the pulling down of strong holds, casting down imaginations, and every high thing, that exalteth itself against the knowledge of God, and bringing into captivity every thought to the obedience of Christ. (II Cor. 10:3, 4, 5)

Q. Ought strife and envy to be among Christians?

A. [James 3:13-18.]

[97] *Q.* Ought wars to be among Christians? From whence proceed they?

A. From whence come wars and fighting amongst you? Come they not hence, even of your lusts, that war in your members? Ye lust, and have not; ye kill, and desire to have, and cannot obtain; ye fight and war, yet ye have not, because ye ask not. (James 4:1, 2)

Q. What saith Christ even of defensive war?

343

A. But I say unto you, that ye resist not evil; but whosoever shall smite thee on thy right cheek, turn to him the other also. (Mat. *5*:39) [Also Luke 6:27-29.]

[98] *Q.* What saith the Apostles?

A. Recompence to no man evil for evil. (Rom. *12*:17) [Also I Pet. 3:9 and I Thess. 5:15.]

Q. It was lawful of old to swear; and an oath for confirmation was to them an end of all strife: Is it not lawful for Christians also to swear?

A. Again, ye have heard that it hath been said by them of old time, thou shalt not forswear thyself, but shalt perform unto the Lord thine oaths. But I say unto you, swear not at all; neither by Heaven, for it is God's throne; nor by the earth, for it is his footstool; neither by Jerusalem, for it is the city of the great King: Neither shalt thou swear by thy head, because thou canst not make one hair white or black. But let your communication be yea, yea; nay, nay; for whatsoever is more than these, cometh of evil. (Mat. *5*:33-37)

[99] But above all things, my brethren, swear not; neither by heaven, neither by the earth, neither by any other oath; but let your yea be yea, and your nay, nay; lest ye fall into condemnation. (James *5*:12)

Q. Is it fit for Christians or believers to receive carnal and worldly honor one from another?

A. How can ye believe, which receive honor one of another, and seek not the honor that cometh from God only? (John *5*:44)

Q. Doth God allow us to give flattering titles to men?

A. . . . For I know not to give flattering titles; in so doing my Maker would soon take me away. (Job *32*:[21], 22)

Q. What should we say to such as quarrel with us for speaking proper sound words, as *thou* to one, *you* to many; which is Christ's and the saints' language in the Scripture?

A. [I Tim. *6*:3, 4.]

[100] Hold fast the form of sound words, which thou hast heard of me, in faith and love, which is in Christ Jesus. (II Tim. *1*:13)

Q. What is the great Commandment given by Christ to his Disciples, as that which even declareth them to be such, and is also pressed by his Apostles?

A. A new Commandment I give unto you, that you love one another; as I have loved you, that you also love one another. By this shall all men know that ye are my Disciples, if ye have love one to another. (John *13*:34, 35) [Also 15:12, 17; Eph. 5:1, 2; and I John 4:20, 21.]

[101] *Q.* Is humility very needful to Christians? What like must we be ere we can enter the Kingdom?

A. And Jesus said, Verily, I say unto you, except ye be converted, and become as little children, ye shall not enter the Kingdom of heaven. . . . (Mat. *18*:3, [4])

Q. Ought Christians to lord over one another? what rule giveth Christ in this case?

A. But Jesus called them unto him and said, Ye know that the princes of the Gentiles exercise dominion over them; and they that are great, exercise authority upon them. But it shall not be so among you; but whosoever will be great among you, let him be your minister. And whosoever will be chief among you, let him be your servant. Even as the son of man came not to be ministered unto, but to minister, and to give his life a ransom for many. (Mat. *20*:25-28)

Q. How then are Christians in this world?

A. Behold, I send you forth as sheep in the midst of wolves; be ye therefore [102] wise as serpents, and harmless as doves. (Mat. *10*:16) [Also Luke 10:3.]

Go your ways; behold, I send you forth as lambs among wolves.

Q. Are we then to expect affliction and persecution here?

A. And ye shall be hated of all men for my name's sake; but he that endureth to the end shall be saved. (Mat. *10*:22 or Mark *13*:23) [Also Luke 21:17.]

If the world hate you, ye know that it hated me before it hated you; if ye were of the world, the world would love his own; but I have chosen you out of the world, therefore the world hateth you. (John *15*:18, 19)

These things have I spoken unto you, that in me ye might have peace. In the world ye shall have tribulation; but be of good cheer, I have overcome the world. (John *16*:33) [Also II Tim. 3:12.]

Q. Ought we then to fear persecution?

A. Fear not them which kill the body, but are not able to kill the soul; but rather fear him who is able to destroy both soul and body in Hell. (Mat. *10*:28) [Also Luke 12:4, 5.]

[103] *Q.* What advantage is it to them that suffer persecution cheerfully, and hazard to them that shun it?

A. [Matt. 5:10.] [Also I Pet. 3:14.]

Whosoever shall confess me before men, him will I confess also before my Father which is in Heaven. But whosoever shall deny me before men, him will I also deny before my Father which is in Heaven. He that loveth father or mother more than me, is not worthy of me. And he that taketh not his cross, and followeth after me, is not worthy of me. He that findeth his life shall lose it, and he that loseth his life for my sake, shall find it. (Mat. *10*:32, 33, 37-39) [Also Luke 12:8-9.] [104] Then said Jesus unto his Disciples, If any man will come after me, let him deny himself, and take up his cross, and follow me. For whosoever will save his life, shall lose it; and whosoever will lose his life for my sake shall find it. (Mat. *16*:24, 25) [Also II Tim. 2:12; Luke 14:26; 9:23-24; Mark 8:34, 35.]

[105] *Q.* There is nothing more certain, according to these Scriptures, than that Christians must suffer persecution in this world, even in their persons and estates; but shall they not also suffer in their good names, in being accounted with blasphemers, heretics and deceivers?

A. The Disciple is not above his master, nor the Servant above his Lord. It is enough for the Disciple, that he be as his Master, and the Servant as his Lord: If they have called the master of the house Beelzebub; how much more shall they call them of his household? (Mat. *16* [*10*]:24-25) [Also Matt. 5:11; Acts 6:11, 12 and 17:6.]

[106] But this I confess unto thee, that after the way which they call heresy, so worship I the God of my fathers; believing all things which are written in the law and the Prophets. (Acts *24*:14) [Also I Cor. 4:13.]

By honour and dishonour, by evil report and good report, as deceivers, and yet true. (II Cor. *6*:8)

Q. It is easily apparent from what is mentioned, that Christians are to expect persecution and tribulation; and that they are always the sheep, and never the wolves; the persecuted, and never the persecutors; the afflicted, and not the afflicters; the reproached, and not the reproachers; Is it not fit then that Christians be so far from persecuting others, that they ought to pray for their persecutors? Is this Christ's command?

A. But I say unto you, love your enemies; bless them that curse you, do good to them that hate you, and pray for them which despitefully use you and persecute you. (Mat. *5*:44)

[107] *Q.* Was this Christ's own practice?

A. Then said Jesus, Father, forgive them, for they know not what they do, &c. (Luke *23*:34)

Q. Is Christ herein to be our example?

A. [I Pet. 2:21-23.]

Q. Is there an instance of any saint in Scripture who followed his example herein?

A. And [Stephen] kneeled down, and cried with a loud voice, Lord, lay not this sin to their charge, &c. (Acts 7:60)

Q. It appears by all these Scriptures, that Christianity consisteth in the exercise of fear and trembling, humility, patience, and self-denial: What ought we then to think of such who place much of their religion in abstaining from marriage, and certain meats; worshipping of angels, and other such acts of voluntary humility?

A. Now the Spirit speaketh expressly, that in the latter times some shall depart from the faith, giving heed to seducing spirits, and doctrines of [108] devils; speaking lies in hypocrisy; having their conscience seared as with a hot iron, forbidding to marry, and commanding to abstain from meats, which

God hath created to be received with thanksgiving of them which believe and know the truth. (I Tim. *4*:1, 2, 3)[41] [Also Col. 2:18.]

Chap. XIII
Concerning Magistracy

Q. What is the duty of a magistrate?

A. The God of Israel said, the Rock of Israel spake to me: He that ruleth over men must be just, ruling in the fear of God. (II Sam. *23*:3)

Q. What do the Scriptures speak of the duty of such as are under authority?

A. Let every soul be subject to the higher powers; for there is no power but of God. The powers that be, are ordained of God. Whosoever therefore resists the power resists the ordinance of God; and they that resist [109], shall receive to themselves damnation. For rulers are not a terror to good works, but to the evil. Wilt thou then not be afraid of the power? Do that which is good, and thou shalt have praise of the same; for he is the minister of God to thee for good. But if thou do that which is evil, be afraid; for he beareth not the sword in vain: For he is the minister of God, a revenger to execute wrath upon him that doth evil. Wherefore ye must needs be subject, not only for wrath, but also for conscience-sake. (Rom. *13*:1-5) [Also I Pet. 2:13-15.]

Q. Ought tribute to be paid to them?

A. For, for this cause pay we tribute also, for they are God's ministers, attending continually upon this very thing. Render to all their dues: tribute to whom tribute is due, custom to whom custom, fear to whom fear, honour to whom honour. (Rom. *13*:6, 7) [Also Matt. 22:21.]

[110] *Q*. Are we obliged to obey magistrates in such things as we are persuaded in our minds are contrary to the commands of Christ?

A. And they called them, and commanded them not to speak at all, nor teach in the name of Jesus. But Peter and John answered and said unto them, Whether it be right in the sight of God, to hearken unto you more than unto God, judge ye. For we cannot but speak the things which we have seen and heard. (Acts *4*:18-20) [Also 5:27-29.]

Q. What ought to be magistrates' behaviour in such cases, according to the counsel of the wise Gamaliel?

[111] *A*. Then stood there up one in the Council, a Pharisee, named Gamaliel, a doctor of law, had in reputation among all the people, and commanded to put the Apostles forth a little space, and said unto them, Ye

---

[41] It is not clear whether Barclay has in mind the Muggletonians or the Catholics.

347

men of Israel, take heed to yourselves what ye intend to do, as touching these men, and now I say unto you, Refrain from these men, and let them alone; for if this counsel, or this work, be of men, it will come to nought: But if it be of God, ye cannot overthrow it, lest haply ye be found even to fight against God. (Acts 5:34, 35, 38, 39)

Q. What command giveth Christ to his people under the Gospel, in relation to this matter? How doth he hold forth their duty under the parable of the tares?

A. [Matt. 13:27-29.]

Q. Doth he explain these tares as the wicked, whom the Godly must not take [112] upon them to cut off, lest thro' mistake they hurt the good; but leave it to God, to do it by his angels?

A. [Matt. 13:38-41.]

Chap. XIV
Concerning the Resurrection

Q. What saith the Scripture of the resurrection of the dead?

A. And have hope towards God, which they themselves also allow, that there shall be a resurrection of the dead, both of the just and unjust. (Acts *24*:15)

Q. To what different end shall the good be raised from the bad; and how are they thereunto reserved?

[113] *A*. Marvel not at this, for the hour is coming, in the which all that are in the graves shall hear his voice, and shall come forth; they that have done good, unto the resurrection of life; and they that have done evil, unto the resurrection of damnation. (John 5:28, 29) [Also II Pet. 3:7.]

Q. What must be answered to such as ask, How the dead are raised, and with what body?

A. . . . All flesh is not the same flesh; but there is one kind of flesh of men, another flesh of beasts, another of fishes, and another of birds. There are also celestial bodies, and bodies terrestrial; but the glory of the celestial is one, and the glory of the terrestrial is another. . . . [114] So also is the resurrection of the dead. It is sown in corruption, it is raised in incorruption: It is sown in dishonour, it is raised in glory: It is sown in weakness, it is raised in power: It is sown a natural body, it is raised a spiritual body. There is a natural body, and there is a spiritual body. (I Cor. *15*:36-44)

Q. The Apostle seems to be very positive, that it is not the natural body, which we now have, that shall rise; but a spiritual body.

A. Now this I say, Brethren, that flesh and blood cannot inherit the Kingdom of God; neither doth corruption inherit incorruption. Behold I shew you a mystery: we shall not all sleep, but we shall all be changed in a

348

moment, in the twinkling of an eye, at the last trump; for the trumpet shall sound, and the dead shall be raised incorruptible, and we shall be changed. . . . Then shall be brought to pass [115] the saying that is written, Death is swallowed up in victory; O Death, where is thy sting? O Grave, where is thy victory? (I Cor. *15*:50-55)

[Chapters XV and XVI are Barclay's Confession of Faith in twenty-three articles together with a short introduction. Chapter XVII is a short exposition with, and appeal to, all other "Professors" [of Christianity]. Chapter XVIII examines the scripture texts used by the Westminster Assembly.]

PART D:

Quaker Life as Testimony

Introduction

Quaker ethics has commended Friends to many at a distance and even drawn many men to join the movement. Quakers have a reputation for positive action and service, not simply for moral purity. On many issues such as rejection of slavery and of cruelty to the insane, Friends pioneered in directions followed by all Western nations. Being trusted by both sides, Quakers have sometimes been able to mediate or make peace in wartime or civil chaos.

Careful study may be needed to convince earnest, eager folk that modern Friends are not always heroic and that early Quaker behavior arose from a radical experience of Christ and the Spirit rather than from humanitarianism. The specific "testimonies" or ethical norms among early Friends arose directly from their total inner surrender of pride and self-will to Christ's Light. They were indeed often practiced in public for the sake of witness, even as shock tactics, to bring other men to the same inward revolution. The refusal of "hat-honor" even to those who took off their hats to Quakers was a case in point.

A cultural and even a regional influence worked, indeed, in shaping some of the testimonies. A shepherd in a moorland home kept his hat on among equals; a gentleman did not. Similarly, Friends said "thee and thou," not to exalt the poor, but to humble the rich and the gentry, who normally (as still in France and Germany) said "thee and thou" only to children and servants. Yet it was normal for farmers and craftsmen, especially in the North and West of England where Quakerism began, to say "thee and thou" with equals; this was not so in southeastern England or

353

in court society.[1] Some Quaker customs were prepared by radical Puritan practices and outlooks; for instance, to consider the names of St. Paul's Church-Yard or of Christ-mas as popery, and January and Thursday as relics of paganism. Many Baptists, too, said "Paul's-Yard," 10th Month[2] and Fifth-Day, and refused to celebrate December 25th as unbiblical. Nevertheless all these customs, and the more obvious ones of clothing and honesty, were part of a single whole, the rejection of all that fed human "lordship" and self-gratification, whether in the Quaker himself or in his hearers. Each testimony was part of the proclamation and appeal, acted as well as spoken.

When an ethical tract focused on a single issue, therefore, this may only have reflected the particular situation of the addressee or of the Quaker writer (cf. p. 359). Other ethical tracts covered the whole battle front and are virtually proclamation tracts (cf. p. 363). Nevertheless certain Quaker testimonies brought Friends so frequently afoul of the law that careful pleading was needed. What may thus be called a *defense tract* sought to show the common basis between Friends' practice and their opponents'. Some even linked Quaker actions to the purpose of the law itself, for instance as to oaths. Quakers refused to swear, partly in fear of manipulating God to support human credibility, partly because oaths were closely linked to profanity and to new calls for allegiance to new and changing governments, and partly from rejecting the assumption that only special safeguards would ensure men's honesty. Thus the Quakers claimed to be fulfilling the true purpose of laws requiring oaths when they offered to suffer the same penalties for any untrue statements that the law imposed for perjury.[3] Against the Puritans, Friends hoped to use the same kind of argument in refusing "Tithes," i.e., taxes for support of parish churches, since

[1] Cf. Hugh Barbour, *The Quakers in Puritan England* (New Haven: Yale Univ. Press, 1964), pp. 164-66. Even the American "Quakerisms" such as "thee is" are rooted in regional dialect backgrounds.

[2] Quakers and all Englishmen used until the following century the old Julian calendar whereby the year began on March 25, and September was the seventh month. In this volume dates in January-March are therefore given by both styles: 1660/61, etc.

[3] Friends also regularly invoked the very explicit biblical bans on swearing: Matthew 5:33-37 and James 5:12. These had been used by Anabaptists and some English Baptists to support their own similar stand. They provide one of the few cases where Friends took over simultaneously from pre-Quaker groups both a strong testimony and the arguments supporting it.

354

the Puritans, too, had rejected the imposing upon them of Anglican liturgies, priests, and vestments contrary to scripture and their consciences (here, Puritans' consciences and biblical interpretations yielded no more than did Friends', however).

Tracts for toleration thus raised the same problem of finding a common basis with their opponents. The Quakers' passionate appeals presented the basic evil as the persecutors' efforts to restrain the Word of God in his saints. Friends never questioned the Quakers' divine call to condemn and interrupt the worship of others and their duty to "disturb the peace" of their hearers, since such peace rests only on self-will (cf. p. 367). Friends' arguments never assumed that any anchoring-point for arguments could outrank the direct command of God to themselves. As a basis for common consent to toleration between faiths, this may seem naive. Tracts on toleration had a rich intellectual heritage before Quakerism arose, notably among the English Baptists and Independents, and in the rationalist and humanist tradition of Erasmus, which was shaped into Natural Law theory by Grotius and into rationalistic Puritanism by John Milton.[4] Friends, however, always began from God's authority, rather than from nature, reason, or human rights. Only after 1675 did William Penn begin identifying Truth with all men's conscience directly, and both with natural rights and common human interests.

Friends, then, added to toleration literature no new set of arguments for religious equality. Instead they gave new insights into the meaning of persecution. They saw that the persecutor's anger often reflected his own half-unconscious guilt projected against the Quaker who brought it into the Light. Violence in general was a sign of men's resistance to Truth, rather than a weapon against evil.

Quiet tracts showing why men persecute, like Penington's (p. 371), may seldom have reached the persecutor's eyes. Fox's presentation of the same challenge (cf. p. 383), like a modern psychiatrist's trick of presenting his patient's anger as confirmation that his diagnosis was right, no doubt only increased that anger. A later generation of Englishmen could learn from these arguments, and meanwhile the rain of toleration tracts may have made the climate

---

[4] Cf. W. K. Jordan, *Development of Religious Toleration in England* (Cambridge, Mass.: Harvard Univ. Press, 1932-40); Michael Freund, *Die Idee der Toleranz in England der grossen Revolution* (Halle, 1927); Johannes Kuhn, *Toleranz und Offenbarung* (Leipzig, 1923).

George Fox before Justice Middleton (*from lithograph by Robert Spence; used by permission*)

of opinion slightly milder. Their main achievement, though, was indirect. The toleration tracts allowed Friends to root both their public peace testimony and their own appeal against persecution in the deepest soil of their own thought and experience. The Spirit *could* never move men to violence or persecution, they said, not only out of self-consistency, but because to do so would be inherently contrary to the real conquest of evil, which was the heart of the Spirit's work on earth.

In relation to war, the Quaker peace testimony was mainly visible after 1659. In some of Cromwell's garrison regiments, Quaker converts were sacked for insubordination before they had occasion to refuse to kill (there were dramatic cases of the latter,

such as Thomas Lurting's on an English warship, in later years).
But the peace testimony of Friends let them show in the short run
that they were a "peaceable people" despite all the fears and
violence of Charles II's Parliaments. In the long run it prepared
them to handle creatively the problems of peace-keeping and
toleration when they needed to govern Pennsylvania.

Friends' *political tracts* were in the early years much rarer than
their encounters with rulers. Such meetings were usually concerned with the ruler's "spiritual state," or else with his persecutions or with the interconnections of both of these. Even a
politicized ex-soldier and ex-Leveller like George Fox "the Younger"[5] saw in all the complex events of 1650-60 nothing but the
divine judgment upon successive governments that had refused the
Quaker Light (cf. p. 393). The crisis-year of 1659, however, did
lead three or four Friends to put onto paper their political ideals
in detail (cf. p. 408). The results were an interesting blend of the
legal and electoral reforms urged by the populists and "Levellers"
with Quaker testimonies about oaths, churches, and freedom of
both worship and preaching. For the moment these blueprints
were inevitably ignored, but they bore fruit later in the constitution of West Jersey and Pennsylvania; these also blended liberal
ideas of human rights and natural law, English traditions of self-
government, with Quaker concern for spiritual freedom and nonviolence.

In form and style it is hard to diagram overall changes in Quaker
ethical tracts during our fifty-year period. Prophetic presentations
aimed at overall convincement became rarer after the persecutions
of the 1660's began. Toleration tracts and defense tracts of particular Quaker testimonies became the special work of individuals like
Burrough, Penn, and Penington, in proportion to their having time
to write them. Ethical writings for circulation among Friends
themselves became commoner but also more thorough and practical, especially on economic issues. These were at first more commonly manuscript epistles than tracts and will be taken up in Part
E. These, unlike the defense and toleration tracts, remained fully
rooted in Quaker religious experience.

In William Penn's moral maxims, the *Fruits of Solitude* and the
more Quakerly *No Cross, No Crown*, these streams come close to
merging again, and Quaker Light, general Christian commitment,

---

[5] He was not related to the famous Fox, and was "younger" in Quakerism
not in age.

and common human wisdom out of even classic Greek and Roman writers reinforce each other. The proverb-style and sober mood here were far from early Quakers' prophetic proclamations; yet the message of surrender of self-will continues. When Penn took part in English politics, this merging of outlooks was carried still further. His campaign tract for the election to Parliament of Whigs, with their policy of toleration (cf. p. 441), used conscience as a basic human norm of Truth, regardless of whether a man opened his conscience to the Quaker Light for the overcoming of self-will. Indeed Penn identifies common sense and common advantage with natural law and both of these with conscience.

Penn's argumentation, then, varying from sentence to sentence and in emphasis from tract to tract, has moved far from the fully Spirit-centered claims for freedom and authority in early Quaker tracts. Penn prepared the way for the splitting of Quaker concerns between basic testimonies still resting on the Spirit's command and Quaker tradition, and the issues of reform in which Quakers worked on increasingly secular grounds with all England. This double vision characterized eighteenth-century Quakerism and to some extent Friends ever since, except insofar as conscience has been accepted as the ultimate word in both realms. Yet Penn's reformism kept within the Quaker tradition, even if in a weakened form, the early Quaker sense that the world and history were the arena of God's working, not simply the inner life of a sect. Just as inner experience and world history merged again in the slavery concern of John Woolman, so again in many later periods their reunion, often by a renewed awareness that the Light within is the Spirit of Christ the Lord of men, has been the source of new life among Friends.

1. Thomas Aldam: *False Prophets and False Teachers* (1652-53)

This may have been the earliest Quaker writing to appear in print;[6] it is appropriate that it should center on the professional ministry and Friends' condemnation of the parish churches and

6 Its only possible rivals are Richard Farnworth's *Discovery of Truth and Falsehood* and five of his other tracts written the same winter and probably printed later in spring or summer. Its place of publication is unknown, but

the compulsory tithes by which they were supported. Aldam and his brothers-in-law John and Thomas Killam were evidently leaders of a separatist congregation at Warmsworth that was the first after Fox's home group at Mansfield to accept his leadership. Aldam went with Fox to the other South Yorkshire separatist groups where Nayler and Dewsbury were won, and may have introduced them. All these men had accepted judgment by the "Inner Light" before meeting Fox. On Fox's next visit to Warmsworth, in the winter of 1651-52, Aldam was arrested, though Fox as a stranger was not. Had he not spent the next two years as a prisoner in York Castle, Aldam might have become along with Fox the leader of early Quakerism. The co-signers of the tract had apparently been leading the Quaker "Awakening" around Malton in northeastern Yorkshire, and, except for Elizabeth Hooton, were former members of Yorkshire separatist groups (about Pears see p. 387 and Index). Jane Holmes reacted over-intensely to the imprisonment and was severely "eldered" by Aldam, and later by Dewsbury and Farnworth when they visited the prisoners.

FALSE PROPHETS AND FALSE TEACHERS DESCRIBED 1652.

All the holy men of God, they spoke forth freely and when any spoke for hire, it was a filthy and a horrible thing; and the Lord did abhor it and sent forth his true prophets to cry out against them. (Isaiah 55:1, 2, 3). Isaiah spoke freely and he was sent to cry out against them that did not speak forth freely without hire. (Isaiah 56:10, 11, 12). His watchmen, saith he, "are blind and cannot see, they are dumb dogs, yea greedy dogs, that can never have enough, every one looks for his gain from his quarter;" they did so then, and do they not so now. Everyone looks for his gain from his quarter where he is and for great means; those that have eyes to see, may see, and the Lord abhors it. Jeremiah spoke freely and was sent to cry out against them that did it for hire (Jer. 5): "A horrible and a filthy thing is committed in the land, the prophets prophesy false things, and the priests bear rule by their means, the people love to have it so." It was so then, but is it not so now, do not the priests bear rule by their means over you, and do not you love to have it so? O foolish people that have eyes to see and cannot see, ears to hear and

the border of the title-page is a design used on other tracts printed by Giles Calvert of London, who also printed the other tracts of Aldam and Farnworth that year. For the opening of this fruitful contact, via Benjamin Nicholson, Samuel Buttivant, and Amor Stoddart, see p. 473.

cannot hear, hearts and cannot understand; but what will you do in the end, saith the Lord. All people, see if you hold not up this filthy thing, which God sent his true prophets to cry against? Ezekiel he spoke freely and spoke against them that spoke for the fleece, see Chap. *34.* See if your shepherds do not teach for the fleece. But saith the Lord, I will take them out of their hands; they shall no longer be meat for them, neither shall they feed themselves any more of the flock, but saith the Lord, [2] I will take them out of their hands, and I will feed them myself and be their teachers. Now the Lord is coming to teach all his freely; and there is no teacher like him, and they that are taught of the Lord deny all teaching without. If you would be taught of the Lord, cease from your hirelings. Micah spoke freely and was sent to cry against them that did not, (Chapter 3), saith he: "the prophets divine for money, and the priests preach for hire, and they lean upon the Lord and say, is not the Lord among us;" they did see then, but they do not see now, but saith the Lord: "they ran but I did not send them; therefore they shall not profit this people at all," (See Jeremiah *23*). The Lord will not have his gifts to be bought and sold; they are worse than Simon Magus, for he would have bought the Spirit, but these buy and sell the letter for carnal ends and acts as in stage plays for money. But the Lord abhors it; therefore hold it not up. . . . Try your priests, and let the Scriptures be fulfilled; see if they will not go to law with you; and if they do, you shall see that they were never taught of Christ, for he saith, "if any man sue thee at the law and take away thy coat, let him have thy cloak also." Now if they were sent of Christ, they would abide in his doctrine, "for he that abideth not in the doctrine of Christ is a devil." And Christ when he sent forth his, "he bade them take neither bag nor scrip, but saith he, freely ye have received, freely give." And if they were taught of him, they would obey him and keep his sayings; but those that buy their wares, they must either set them forth at a great rate, or else lose by them; and then they would lose their mastery which they have got by their learning and their means. All the teachers of the world they are masters by their learning and their benefits. But those that were taught of Jesus [3] Christ, they were not so, (see Mat. *22*). But he taught them to deny it, and they abode in his doctrine. You do not read in all the holy scriptures that any of the holy men of God were Cambridge or Oxford scholars or university men or called masters, but on the contrary they were plain men and laboured with their hands and taught freely as they had received it freely from the Lord. Read the Scriptures, and you may see what sort of men they were which taught the people: Abel, he was a shepherd, (Gen. *4*:2), Jacob, a keeper of sheep, (Gen. *30*:31), Moses, a shepherd, (Exod. *3*:1), Elisha, a plowman, (I Kings *19*:19, 20), Amos, a herdsman, (Amos *7*:14), Paul, a tentmaker, (Acts *18*:3), Simon and Andrew were fishermen, (Mark *2*:14). They were not wise and learned men, as the scribes and Pharisees were, which Christ cried woe against. . . . [4] Now Christ is come to set free from those heavy burdens and to ease the people of them; his ministry is free and not burdensome. Those that are sent of him are not so. They are got into a seat above the scribes and Pharisees; they sat but in Moses' seat pretending to do justice, but they did not as they said; so the professed ministers are got up into the seat of Christ to take off oppression. But they are oppressors, for the ministry of Christ "is to feed the hungry and to clothe the naked and let the oppressed go free," and to throw down those abominations which the Lord hath sent his true prophets to cry out against, as pride and covetousness, drunkenness, lying and swearing, and oppression. But it is held up and contended for by them, for they are the kings of pride in towns where they are; and their wives go in their hoods, veils and rings, which are odious to the Lord, and poor people are burdened by them. . . . [5] See what Paul speaketh in II Tim. 3:1, 2, 3, 4, 5, he then seeing false teachers going forth; but he gave a description how they might be known. Of this sort are they, saith he, "Proud, covetous, false lovers, boasters, heady, highminded, railers, false accusers, incontinent, fierce, despisers of those which are good, lovers of pleasures more than lovers of God, having a form of godliness, but denying the power thereof; from such turn away." First look at the trees, and then at the fruits, and see if this sort of men be not now and hath been a long time. "But the Lord is risen in the hearts of the people and hath opened their eyes that were blind and causes them to see clearly and bids them let their light shine forth to others that sit in darkness." But he is coming to take away the veil that is spread over all nations; and then shall they see clearly. But those that have eyes may see that this sort of men preach now, and that for hire, which is contrary to the doctrine of Christ. . . . The ministers of Christ were what they spoke; they walked answerable to their ministry, that it might not be burdensome. They walked as examples to others. Can a proud man leave off from pride, he may speak against it; but if he speak against it and live in it, he is an hypocrite. . . . [6] The ministers of Jesus Christ were examples for others to walk by, see Titus 1: "They were blameless, as the stewards of God, not self-willed, not soon angry, not given to wine, no strikers, not given to filthy lucre." Where is your example among all your professed ministers? They were lovers of hospitality, they were lovers of good men, they were holy, they were just, they were temperate. Where is your example? They were what they spoke. Paul laboured night and day, that he might not make the gospel of Christ burdensome, for, saith he, "yourselves know how ye ought to follow us, for we behaved not ourselves disorderly among you, neither did we eat any bread for nought, but wrought with labour and travail night and day, that we might not be chargeable to any, but to make ourselves examples unto them that follow us"; where is your example? See I Thess. *1*:5. For, saith he, "we use not flattering words," as ye know; he called them to witness it, neither a cloak of covetousness. . . . [7] He that saith he is in Christ ought to walk as he walked. Did ever he preach for money, or did he give forth command for his to take hire; how dare any of you hirelings say you are sent of Christ? Did he say one thing and do another? Was he not what he spoke in all things? Were not his ministers examples for others to walk by? And he exhorted others to mind their conversation, saith Paul, "Be ye followers of me as dear children, even as I am a follower of Christ." And Christ saith, "Learn of me, for I am meek and lowly of heart." Now those that were his true ministers they followed his example, and they exhorted others to follow them. And he that is taught of Christ now abideth in his doctrine, but he that abideth not in the doctrine of Christ is a devil; and he that saith he is in Christ ought to walk as he walked in all holy conversation. Then you that profess yourselves to be his ministers and to be sent forth from him, where did you receive a commission of him to be taskmasters? Or to take hire, or to be proud or covetous, or to live in pleasures, or to live in hypocrisy, to say that you are not? They that were sent forth by him were sent freely and to undo the heavy burdens and to be examples for others to walk by. Where did you receive your mastery? Christ saith, "let him that is greatest among you be your servant, and Christ is the same yesterday, today, and forever." Where did Christ make use of outward means to back him; but he denied it and was persecuted by it, where did he envy and hate and oppress any? Walk according to him if you be sent of him, and do not persecute and hate and envy, and go to law, for neither he nor his did. And if you be sent of him make proof [8] of your ministry, as they did that he sent forth and cause not the gospel of Christ to be burdensome and blamed by you. The true ministers gave no occasion of offence in anything, that their ministry should not be blamed. . . . Woe to the idol shepherds, woe unto them, for they have gone in the way of Cain and have run greedily after the error of Balaam for reward, who perished in the gainsaying, and so shall they, except they repent.

Thomas Aldam.
Elizabeth Hooton.
William Pears.
Benjamin Nicholson.
Jane Holmes and
Mary Fisher.

Prisoners of the Lord at
York Castle. 1652.

2. Edward Burrough's *Message of Instruction to Rulers* (1657)

A large part of Burrough's voluminous works were written as warning or exhortation to Cromwell, and particularly to his increasingly conservative generals and Parliaments, though in the late 1650's he also wrote much in defense or exposition of Quaker teaching (cf. pp. 297 and 298). Though not the best known of his works then or since, the "Message for Instruction" is the clearest statement of Quaker defense on the charges for which the Friends were repeatedly imprisoned. At first reading it may seem outrageous to claim that since God led them, everything that Friends did was good and legal. This is the theocratic claim of Friends, that when they were led by the Spirit they were above the law; and indeed that only men led by the Spirit should rule and execute laws. It may also trouble modern Friends that Burrough so eagerly concedes the law's right to punish wicked men. Yet, once one sets aside the "special pleading" for Quakers and one's own shock at Friends' suspicion of merely representative government, Burrough's tract is a challenge to re-examine the basis of all law and of all conscientious claims for exemption from it.

A
MESSAGE
FOR
INSTRUCTION,
TO
ALL THE RULERS, JUDGES AND MAGISTRATES, TO WHOM
THE LAW IS COMMITTED:

Showing what Just Government is, and how far the Magistrate's Power reacheth, and what the Sword of Justice is to cut down, and what it is to defend.

Whereby they may learn, and be directed to discern betwixt the Guiltless, and the Guilty; and betwixt a Matter of Wilful Wrong by Evil-Doers, which they are to punish, and a Matter of Conscience, by men that fear God, which they are to be a Praise unto, and not a Terror; and in particular, divers Causes are discover'd, which are prov'd to be Matters of Conscience, and not of Wilful Wrong; though many therefore are unjustly persecuted and afflicted as Evil-Doers.

363

With an Exposition of some parts of the Law; for the Edification of such, as desire to judge Righteously between Man and Man, who would discern of different Causes; and justifie the Righteous, and Condemn the Evil-Do-er. 1657.

Concerning government and magistracy, this I have to say:

It is an ordinance of God, ordain'd of him for the preserving of peace among men; for the punishing and suppressing of evil-doers, and for the praise of them that do well; that men's persons and estates may be preserv'd from the violence and wrong-dealing of evil men: And for this end government was ordained of God, to be set up in the Earth, by the institution of the Lord; that righteousness should go free, and the wicked be bound and limited.

Now such as handle the Law, and the executors thereof, who are ordain'd of God to judge and govern the people, ought to be just men, fearing God, and walking in his law, and hating and denying every false way; that people may receive examples of righteousness, and holy and lawful walking, from their conversations. And they that are set to govern the people, ought to have the spirit of true and sound judgment, to try into the root of all causes, whereby they may be able to discern of different causes, and to give just judgment in all things; and such will judge by equal measure for God, and not for man, but without respect of persons; and such will be a terror to transgressors, and will strengthen and encourage them that do well. . . . And all ought to receive just judgment from just men by the just law; for the law is a defence about all the righteous, to defend and preserve them; in peace and freedom, from all their enemies, who are to be limited by the law, as I have said: And they that are reconciled to God, whose consciences are exercised towards God in all things, they are not under the law, nor the law hath no power over them; for the law is fulfilled in them by Christ, who teacheth them in all things to walk without offence towards God and all men, in truth and in righteousness to God, and all men; and such the law of man is to defend, and not to judge them; to justify them, and not to condemn them. . . . And they seek not the wrong of any man's person or estate, but seeks the good of all, forgiving their enemies, and praying for them, and seek not vengeance upon their adversaries, but they bear all things patiently; and such are the servants of God, and not transgressors of his law, nor the just laws of man; and if such do suffer by a law, that law is unjust, and so is that magistrate that executes that law; and that suffering is not for evil-doing, but for a good conscience sake; and the innocent can rejoice in such suffering, but the executioners thereof shall howl and weep. . . .

And therefore all magistrates are to weigh, and be considerate in all these things, and so to act and judge among men, as they may give a good account unto God, and all men; and when a cause is brought before them to give judgment of, or any accus'd unto them, that they should execute the law upon, they should by the spirit of the Lord first try into the ground and nature of such matters, to know whether it be a wilful and supposed wrong or injury done between man and man, or it be of ignorance, or want of better knowledge, or such like, or whether it be a matter of conscience, or about religion, or the worship of God, whereupon the controversie dependeth. . . . But if it be a matter of conscience about religion, or the worship of God, then the magistrates, with their law, ought not to meddle therein, or to judge of such matters; for these things, concerning the things that are spiritual, are out of their jurisdiction, and not in their power to judge of. . . .

And now as concerning this one thing, which is, oppression in the nation, brought forth through the unjust and false execution of the laws, whereby many tender consciences are afflicted, and not for any wrong or evil-doing, but for the exercise of a pure conscience. Whereas many for a pure conscience sake do deny and cannot pay any thing to maintain a steeple-house, or place of worship, which the people of the world do worship in, and where they commit idolatry; neither can they, for conscience sake, pay any thing to uphold such worship, and such a ministry and ministers, which are not of Christ, nor ever were sent of him, but of Antichrist, and such by which the people are led in blindness and error, as manifestly doth appear through the whole land: And yet the magistrates, some of them being as blind and ignorant as the people, do compel many people by their writs, and orders and judgments, to maintain a priest and steeple-house, which for conscience sake they deny to maintain; and yet by authority from the magistrates are the innocent men's goods spoil'd by distress, and great oppression exercis'd upon many poor people, to maintain and uphold the ministry and worship of this generation. . . . Neither is there any reason or equity in this matter, that any should be forc'd and compell'd by injustice and oppression, to uphold a house of worship, which others worship in, and not they; and they knowing that worship to be abomination to the Lord also, and not the true worship of the true God. And there is no justice nor religion in it, that any should be caused by force to uphold a house, for other people to commit and practice idolatry in. If the house were for any good purpose, or honest practice, as for poor or impotent people to dwell in, or such like, who had not houses of their own, because of their poverty; then that were a deed of charity to uphold it, and the people of God would not deny it, but could freely give their money to such a use or end. But because it is not to such a use . . . they rather suffer the spoiling of their goods, and affliction upon their bodies, than to pay their money for such a use or end; and herein the magistrates do great injustice in the sight of God, and his saints, and contrary to reason, and a good conscience, in causing innocent men's goods to be spoiled by cruelty, to uphold a place of idolatrous worship, contrary to men's tender consciences.

And the unjustness of these things cries for vengeance upon the ungodly rulers and people, who cause the just and upright to groan by oppression. . . . And because of these things is the wrath of God kindled, and shall not be quench'd, till it hath consumed the wicked from off the face of the earth; that the just God may be feared, and his people enjoy their freedom and liberty in the practice of the pure religion, and the exercise of their pure consciences; and this will the Lord bring forth in his appointed time, according to his promise, that his people may rejoice in him over all their oppressors and cruel task-masters, which do unjustly oppress the seed of God.

And as concerning the maintaining of ministers, it is the same in nature, and as unjust and unequal, as upholding of worshipping-houses; for though many, out of a good conscience, do deny to maintain a professed minister, by paying to him so much, or such a sum; yet they do not hereby wrong him wilfully, contrary to right, in breaking any contract or covenant, formerly made with him by themselves, or predecessors; nor they do not withhold from him anything, which properly belongs to him as debt. . . . What though it was formerly done, such a sum paid, and such a gift freely given by our ancestors, in the time of ignorance and darkness; that practice of theirs then doth not bind any now to do the same, seeing no record can appear, that they bound themselves and their heirs for ever so to do; and now hath the clear light of the gospel sprung forth, and the light of the day hath discovered all the works of ignorance; and though the man that claims such a gift, or hire, as debt to him, because of his labour, let them pay him for whom he doth labour, and who do partake of his ministry and labour, and let others be free, who for conscience sake cannot do it. . . . This makes the thing a matter of conscience to many, that for no better use, nor to no other end they should pay their money (which cannot be justly claimed, as a just debt, but as a gift at most) to the upholding of such men, and such practices, which are not according, but contrary to God, in labour, life, and practice; and to uphold and maintain a man as a minister of Christ, which is not so. . . . Now if their money was to maintain a man that's poor, or if that man had not of his own sufficiently to preserve his wife and children from want, then it were a work of charity to give something, if it were every year, or oftener, to maintain him and his family; and the people of God would not refuse to give something for this end; no man should compel them, nor have cause to spoil their goods for it. But as he professeth himself a minister of Christ, and a labourer in the gospel, but is not so, but lives in pride, and the vanities of this world; upon such an account they cannot maintain him, nor give him any thing at all, with a safe conscience. . . . And the people of the Lord do claim this as their privilege, belonging to them by the just laws of God and men, to worship God in spirit and in truth, and to uphold and maintain that worship only, without being compelled by force to maintain any other whatsoever, and they claim

366

as right unto them to maintain what ministers, and uphold what ministry, as they know is sent of God, by which people are profited, and which they have received the knowledge of God through, by his spirit, and to be free to maintain how and as the Lord leads them unto, without being forced by any law, or unequal authority, to maintain the false prophets and hirelings, and deceivers, who live in pride and excess. . . .

Again there is another suffering great and grievous which is unjustly laid upon the people of God, which suffering is not for Evil-doing, but for a good conscience sake, as is manifest; as because many are moved of the Lord by his Spirit to go into the steeple-houses, and meeting-places, or other places to reprove sin, and among people, or to exhort them unto good, and to follow Christ, and to deny the wickedness of this world, or such like, as they are moved, some are moved to reprove a hireling teacher, who deceives the people, and walks in the steps of the false prophets, and lives in pride and vanity and evil, contrary to the doctrine and practice of Christ and the Apostles. And this practice of the servants of the Lord in reproving evil, and exhorting to good, is called a disturbance of the peace, and an unlawful practice, and such like; it is falsely judged by unjust men, who know not the spirit of the Lord, nor the moving thereof. And because of this, many innocent men are caused deeply to suffer, contrary to a good conscience; and some are sent to the house of correction, there suffering cruel things from hard-hearted men; and some are put in the stocks, and whipped, and others fined, and cast into prison; and such like sufferings are unjustly imposed upon them, and not for evil-doing, as I have said. For though they reprove sin in teachers, or in people, or exhort them to good, whether in steeple-houses, markets, or other places; yet they do not hereby wrong any man's person or estate. Neither is this any matter of wilful wrong, or to such an intent, neither doth it disturb the peace, nor is any unlawful practice; but only out of a good conscience to God and man is it done. And it is a matter of conscience to the servants of the Lord to do so, and they cannot leave it undone, lest they would transgress the law of God in their own consciences; because they are commanded of God so to do, that people may be instructed in the right way to God, and be converted out of every false way. And this is the very end of their work, and their intent in doing it; and they ought not in justice to suffer for it. For it is according to the law of God, and in reason and in a good conscience, and the Lord justifies them in it. Then that law and judgment must needs be corrupt and unjust, which condemns the people and servants of the Lord, as for evil-doers, for obeying the commands of God, and for the exercise of their pure consciences, and no man's person or estate being wronged, or injured, but only sin and wickedness reproved, and exhorted from. And hereby thus is the law perverted, and true judgment turned backward, and the guiltless is condemned guilty.

Also many of the Servants of the Lord do deeply suffer, and is deeply afflicted by injustice, for the exercise of a good conscience in other things, as because they cannot put off their hats and bow in respect to men's persons, according to the vain customs of the heathen; and because they cannot swear upon a book, by kissing it, and laying the hand upon it, according to the idolatrous form, and for such like causes, because many cannot fulfil the lusts and wills of men, that live in pride and evil ways, in these and other things, therefore are the people of God put to great sufferings, though they deny not the honour due to all men in the Lord, without bowing the hat, nor to affirm the truth in every cause, in faithfulness without an oath. Now to keep on the hat, which is a cover for the head, to keep from cold or heat, for health's sake, before any man whatsoever, though never so great or noble, is not any wrong or injury to the man's person or estate before whom it is done, but only the high mind and the proud nature, and that which is exalted above the fear of God, which would be Lord over his fellow creatures, that same is offended and troubled, which bears not the image of God, but of the devil. And the children of the Lord cannot do it, nor give honour to him, nor be subject, and pleasing to that man, who is of that spirit and of that nature which is not of God, but exalted in pride, and vain-glory above the fear of God, and against him, and would be worshipped, and had in honour and reverenced of his fellow-creatures, who hath not so much riches in this world as he, nor is so proud in apparel as he; and because of that he looks to be bowed unto with hat or knee, and is offended if he be not, and then in his pride he rages and is vexed, and seeks revenge against such as cannot honour him, and respect him in his pride and vain-glory; but as I said this is not done as a matter of wrong unto any, though the hat be not bowed or put off, but it is a matter of conscience unto the people of God, and for a good conscience sake they do deny, and may not give obedience, and honour, and respect, out of the fear of God, to proud flesh, and to men which is not in the fear of God, which expects reverence out of the Lord, and they know it is nothing else that is offended but proud flesh, and an exalted mind, and a man that fears not God, neither walks in his ways.

And likewise though many deny to swear at all, though not to testify the truth; yet they do not wilfully wrong hereby to any man's person or estate, but it is a matter of conscience unto them, and with a good conscience they cannot swear, but do deny it upon all conditions, because Christ hath commanded not to swear at all, and the Apostle doth exhort, above all things, not to swear; and therefore it is a matter of conscience unto many, and not a matter of purposed wrong towards any man. And though here it may be objected: but for want of an oath, a just man may lose his just cause; because judgment depends upon witness by oath: to that I answer, that is because, the law is not according to Christ, by which the judgment comes, but is unjustly grounded upon the breach of Christ's command, viz. swearing; and whether ought the man to be blamed or condemned as a transgressor, who keeps Christ's command, and cannot swear at all upon any terms, or whether that law ought not to be corrected and regulated to be according to the law of Christ, and all that which is contrary in the execution thereof to be condemned and removed, that a just man's witness may be given and taken upon occasion, without an oath. . . . That law and authority must needs be unjust which oppresseth, or punisheth the exercise of a good conscience, as for evil doing; and this shows the blindness and ignorance of men in authority to whom the law is committed who discerns not, neither makes a difference betwixt things done in the fear of God, and in the exercise of a good conscience towards him, and things done out of an evil mind to evil intents, purposely and wilfully to do wrong and injury to men's persons and estates; for all magistrates ought to learn this, and to distinguish, that their power and authority may justify the one, and condemn the other, that in the nations, that all the upright and well-doers may rejoice, and live in rest and peace, and all the workers of iniquity, and such as do evil may be afraid, and fear to offend just men, and just laws; and thus would the name of the Lord be great in the earth among men; and such a government renowned for ever, and such magistrates would be a praise to generations after them, and a blessed example to ages to come.

But now some may say, and object: how shall this be known? and who can tell and discern of such causes, and who it is that do their works, out of the exercise of a good conscience, and who do their deeds out of an evil mind, and to an evil intent, and so is wrong dealing, and worthy of punishment: this is a doubtful cause may some say, and difficult to be known and understood. But to this I answer, and say, to all such as have the spirit of the Father, and are led thereby, and in their judgment guided therewith, this is an easy thing to discern, and an easy matter to know and find out; and such as cannot discern and distinguish in such matters, have not the spirit of God, nor the spirit of true and sound judgment; neither is indeed ordained of God, nor fit to judge the people, nor the honour of a ruler and judge belongs not to such a one who cannot find out a matter, nor know and judge between the precious and the vile, how to justify the one, and how to condemn the other. . . . If the work be done by a man, out of a good conscience, and as a matter of conscience, then he doth it in the fear of God, and in the cross to his own will, and in meekness and tenderness of heart, not seeking himself in what he doth, but is willing to suffer for the truth's sake, and for what he doth, and will not resist evil, or the false judgments of men, but patiently, and quietly bears all things, for the Lord's sake; and in all what he doth or suffers, he gives the glory to the Lord, who works his works in him, and gives him strength and patience willing to suffer for them. . . .

Wherefore, all ye rulers, and ye that are set to judge the people, be now awakened to just judgment, and to a sound discerning, and put on the spirit of true judgment, even the Spirit of the Lord, that you may receive it, to be taught in all things, how to walk with God, that you may answer his call, and the end of your authority, in judging justly all sorts of men, rendering to every man according to his deeds; even condemnation and judgment to evil-doers, and a praise and defence to all that do well. And this is written in love to you all, showing you how to put a difference betwixt the precious and the vile; between the just and unjust, that you may be the more happy, if this you observe; not leaving your names a reproach, and a scorn to after ages, which is the effect which doth follow all such as pervert justice, and turns true judgment backward, with misery and destruction upon themselves and posterity for evermore.

A True and Faithful Exposition of some part of the Laws of ENGLAND:

You have a late act for the taking up, and punishing of idle, loose and dissolute persons; such as are vagrants, and wandering rogues, vagabonds and sturdy beggars: Now this law is good, if it be duly and justly executed upon such as are truly guilty herein; and it is right that sturdy beggars, and rogues, and idle and disorderly persons, should be taken up from wandering, and set on work in some good employment in the creation, which may maintain themselves, and prevent them from worse things: But now you must take heed of judging any to be such, who are not really so; for, many of the servants of the Lord now, as it was in generations past, are moved to leave their own country, and dwellings, and relations; and go abroad in the nations, to preach the Gospel of Christ, and to bear witness of his name in the world; to the turning of people from the ways of sin and death, to the way of righteousness and truth; and it may be such cannot give you an account, or sufficient cause of their travelling abroad (so as to satisfy you).

Also you have another late act for the observation of the Lord's Day, wherein is inserted, that none shall wilfully, maliciously, or of purpose disturb, or disquiet the public preacher, or to make any public disturbance in the congregation. Now the Law is good, and it is right that all such be punished, who do maliciously, wilfully, or of an evil purpose disturb or disquiet any man, or people, to the danger of breach of public peace; and let all such be punished according to their desert: but yet you must take heed in this cause; for many of the servants of the Lord are, and may be moved by the power of the Lord to come into a congregation, or an assembly of people to declare against sin and iniquity, and the ways of wickedness. . . .

370

Also it is inserted in the same act against many evil things, as drinking in taverns, inns, ale-houses, strong-water-houses, or to tipple unnecessarily, or any other house, & C. and also against travelling, and walking on that (Sabbath) day vainly and prophanely, & C. Now the law is good, that evil exercise be prevented, and prophaneness in every respect on that day, and on every day, and that such be punished that are found in any evil exercise whatsoever. But yet you must take heed that none of the innocent suffer hereby; for many of the people of God may, and do travel on that day to meet together to worship God, and to wait upon him, to find his presence, and to receive of his refreshments to their souls; but this cannot be judged an evil practise, or prophane travelling, or breach of the Sabbath; . . .

I am a real friend to the common-wealth, and a lover of justice and true judgment, and fully affected towards just government, and wish well to magistrates.

(The 9th Month, 1657) E.B.

The last two long tracts Edward Burrough wrote, *Anti-Christ's Government* and *The Case of Free Liberty of Conscience* (both 1661), return to the issues of toleration. They represent his most careful and mature thought and deserve reprinting also some day. They begin with the same central theocratic emphasis: "you intrench on God's sovereignty, and usurp his authority, in exercising lordship over the conscience, in and over which Christ is only king" (*Case,* p. 4) but go on to spell out both the spiritual and the political consequences of making men hypocrites in religion, quote Jeremy Taylor and biblical precedents, and begin to raise the issues of harmony in a multi-church society.

3. Isaac Penington: *Concerning Persecution* (Robert Wilson, 1661)

Penington's earnest and voluminous theological tracts are as clear as any early Friend's; but except at times when he appeals to his own experience, as in *Naked Truth,* they lack the warmth and vitality of his pastoral letters. His tract on persecution is also in a quiet vein, but shows his ability to express well the insight of many Friends, notably Fox and Nayler (cf. pp. 146, 107), that persecution is a reaction in anger, and that this anger is not only the effort of man's self-will and pride to reject the Light of the judging Spirit, but also a sign that the Spirit has been at work. From this flowed the later Quaker message that all forms of violence are the devil's distractions from the crucial inner struggle against evil.

CONCERNING PERSECUTION

Which is
The Afflicting or Punishing that which is Good under the Pretence
of its being Evil.

Given forth to this nation, that at length the true bottom and foundation of a lasting peace and settlement may be espied, the spirits of the governors and people fixed thereon, and that dangerous rock of persecution (whereon both the powers and people of this nation have so often split) carefully avoided by all. . . . by *Isaac Penington* the younger

London, Printed for Robert Wilson, in *Martins le Grand,* 1661.

Preface [4]

That which is to redeem the world out of misery is the power of the Gospel: and precious is the peace which comes thereby, after the work of the spiritual sword (with the trouble thereof) is finished. O how blessed would the principle and power of life make the world, might it but have its free course therein: O how happy is that man, who bears the condemnation because of sin, follows the guidance of the living God, and who waits for the day of his salvation! O the sweet inward peace of spirit which is enjoyed after the storm and after the judgment of that which is to be judged and destroyed! And that which makes our person happy, the same must make nations happy. There is no true settlement or abiding security, but in the settled and abiding principle. God is arisen to shake the earth, and it can settle no more upon the old foundations: yea, the same God hath shriveled up the old Heavens, and they can no more be stretched forth again. "Behold, I make all things new," saith the Lord in the days of the Gospel, when he stretcheth forth the arm of his power. And who is he who shall venture to establish the old Heavens and the old Earth, which the Lord God is removing and causing to pass away, and abolish the new Heavens and the new Earth, which the Lord God hath created and formed and is establishing? O that men

372

knew the place of wisdom, that they might be wise and not fight against their creator, from whom their strength comes, and against whom their strength cannot prevail. O that men could see how industrious they are to keep up misery, and to keep out of happiness. The eye of man (in the fallen and corrupt state) cannot see aright: and mis-seeing, how can he choose but mis-aim and mis-act? And mis-aiming and mis-acting, how can he attain his end? But the Lord's counsel shall stand, and he will fulfill all his pleasure in every heart and throughout the Earth. Happy is he who is weaned from himself, and begotten in the light of life which is incorruptible, he shall stand and be blessed, when all flesh falls before the breath of the Lord and becomes miserable: and the fall of all the fleshly will, wisdom and strength hasten apace; happy is he who is delivered from them before the day of their ruin, which is nearer than man is aware of, or can believe. . . .

[5] *1. What or Who it is that is Persecuted.*

The persecuted in all ages is that "which is born after God's spirit," [6] Gal. 4.29. He that is new-created in Christ Jesus, who is formed in the image and by the spirit of God (which is contrary to the image and spirit of the world) and who follows Christ in the leadings and teachings of his spirit (which is out of and contrary to the course, fashions, ways and customs of the world). This is the man that is persecuted in all ages, he that is of another spirit and principle than the world and so cannot be as the world is (being made otherwise by God) nor walk as the world walks, nor worship as the world worships, being taught and required of God to do otherwise. This is the man who is afflicted, reproached, hated, hunted, persecuted. And so the Apostle lays it down, not only as a thing to be in his age, but in after ages also, 2 Tim. 3:12. "Yea and all that will live godly in Christ Jesus, shall suffer persecution." Men may talk of Christ, profess Christ, worship Christ according to the way that is set up in nations, and avoid persecution; but come under the new principle, come into his life, live Godly in Him, become really subject unto the power and direction of his spirit: then there is no longer avoiding of persecution. That which comes into the life of Christ, comes presently into a proportion of suffering from that which is contrary to his life. . . .

2. What or who it is that persecuteth or is the persecutor.

The persecutor, in all ages, is that which is after the flesh. The spirit and principle in man which is from beneath, puts the men in whom it is upon persecuting the other principle and the persons in whom it appears: or more plainly thus: That which is of the world, that which loves the world and the present state thereof; that which lies in the darkness, is in unity with it, loveth it, and the corrupt ways thereof; that hates the Light, and persecuteth the children of the Light, who are witnesses against and reprovers of the darkness, *John 3*:20. . . . [7]

3. The nature of persecution, or what it is to persecute.

Persecution is the opposition of the flesh against the spirit. The fretting or dashing of the earthly spirit, or spirit of man corrupted, against that which is born of God; the fighting of the unregenerate and unrenewed spirit in man, against the spirit of man renewed by the regenerating power of the spirit of God; the fighting, the opposing of this spirit against the other, is persecution. Whatever any man does in his own will, according to his own wisdom, and after the inclination of his own heart, against another who desires to fear the Lord, (who waits on him for the counsel and guidance of his spirit, that he might obey and worship him aright) is persecution. The principle of God teaches to fear the Lord not according to the fear which is taught by the precepts of men, but according to the fear which God puts into the heart; it teaches likewise to worship the Lord, not according as man invents and thinks good to prescribe, but as the Lord instructs and requires; it teacheth likewise not to conform to the world, but to deny it, and come out of it: Now the hating, opposing, and punishing of that which is thus taught, because of these teachings and its obedience thereto, this is persecution. The rising of the heart against such, is persecution in the heart. The reproaching, scoffing at or speaking evil of such, is persecution with the tongue. (So Gal. *4*:29, 30). . . . The smiting, fining, imprisoning, of such, etc. in relation to anything that they do from this principle, is persecution with the hand, [8] or lifting up of the power either of a particular person, or of a magistrate against such.

4. The grounds of persecution, or what are the things that cause the one spirit and principle to persecute, and the other to be persecuted.

1. The enmity of the birth of the flesh against the birth of the spirit: . . . that which walks and worships in the will and according to the inventions of man's wisdom, and in shadows and fleshly forms pleasing to the flesh, cannot endure that which worships in spirit and truth.

2. The contrariety of that which is born of God and drawn out of the world, to that which is of the flesh (or of corrupt man) and left in the world, this is that which incenseth, and draweth forth the enmity in the corrupt principle. . . . John *17*:16, 14. They are of another spirit, of another image, of another make, of another heart, of another desire, of another manner of carriage and demeanor, of another principle, and have other ends in all they do, than the world: And their whole course and conversation (being in the light and in the love, and in true purity of mind) reproves the world, which

lies in the darkness and in the enmity, and walks in the wickedness. And how can the world bear this, in the midst of all their height, glory, and greatness, to be continually reproved by a poor and contemptible generation, as God's choice in the world have for the generality of them always been, even looked upon by the world as the offscouring thereof, as not fit to be suffered to have a being in it, but rather as deserving to be scoured from it?

The Light, whereof the children of the Light are born, and [9] which they hold forth (or rather, which God holds forth by them) condemns the world. The evenness, sweetness, and straightness of their conversation and practices condemns the unevenness, crookedness and perverseness of the spirit of the world. The integrity, seriousness and spirituality of their worship (with the living power and presence of God, appearing among them) condemns the deadness, formality and hypocrisy of the worships of the world, who draw nigh to God with their lips, when it is manifest that their hearts are far from Him, being ensnared and captivated with vanities and self-interests and love of the world and earthly things. Indeed the whole course and manifestation of the Light and power of God in them is a continual upbraiding of the principle and ways of darkness in the men of the world. And how can the men of the world forbear making an unrighteous war, even a war of persecution against that which invades their territories and makes war with them in righteousness? Can darkness choose but fight to save its own dominions? It must put out the Light or it cannot save its own, but will be losing ground daily.

3. Because of the children of the Light leaving and coming out of the world. They were once of the world, as well as others. Of the same nature, of the same spirit, of the same corrupt will, of the same corrupt wisdom, walking in their way, worshipping according to their worships, approving and observing their customs, fashions and vanities. But when the spirit of Christ called them out of the world, and created in them that which could hear his voice and was willing to follow him, then they left all these and stood witnesses (in God's spirit which called, and in that life which was begotten in them, and in the fear, love and power of that God who quickened them) against all these. And this angers the world, in that they were once of them, but left them. Had they stayed in the world, and been still of the world, the world would have loved them. . . . [10]

5. The Ways and Means of Persecution.

The ways and means of persecution are very many. Who can want instruments to afflict the innocent and helpless, who can neither resist the evil which is offered them, nor harm that which offers it? I shall only here mention three general heads, to which many particulars may be referred.

1. One great way of persecution is by making use of laws already made, either according to their proper tendency to that end and purpose, or by

bending them aside from their proper intent, to reach those whom they have a mind to afflict and persecute. Thus the Jews, when they had a mind to have Christ put to death, told Pilate, "We have a Law, and by our Law he ought to die," *John 19*:7.

2. Another way is by making new laws fit for their purpose, whereby they may catch, ensnare and suppress that which is contrary to their spirit and principle, and which will not bow thereto. ... Thus *Dan. 6*:7, 8. ... Thus have articles been framed, and statutes made here in England, (as in King Henry VIII and in Queen Mary's days) which have been great engines of persecution. And thus have there been some late laws made in New England to the same effect, though better might have [11] justly been expected from them. And this is not only a certain way, but a very plausible way likewise, whereby the persecutor hides himself from the imputation of persecution and appears as a just executor of the law; and so represents him, who is upright before God and innocent in the sight of God, as an offender and breaker of the law, and so justly punishable. ...

3. A third way of persecution is by the hand of violence, without either law, or so much as pretence to law. Thus the persecuting spirit, when it hath power in its hand, and is out of fear, smiteth (with the open fist of wickedness) that which is an enemy to, and stands a witness against its wickedness.

6. The Ends of Persecution, or what the Persecuting Spirit aims at in its Persecuting, and would fain attain thereby.

1. The main end of persecution is to bring the children of Light, (who have left the evil, darkness and corruption of the world) back to the world again. ... There is a great fight between the spirit of God and the spirit of the world, in the two seeds; the spirit of God striving to bring the spirit of the world [12] under, and the spirit of the world striving to bring the spirit of God under. This is well known in the heart, where the new birth is witnessed. O what striving there is by the powers of darkness, with all manner of secret temptations and forcible oppositions (so far as the Lord permits) to bring the heart (which the Lord hath begun to redeem and in some measure set free from them) under their power again! And the same that stirs up the darkness in the heart against the seed and birth of Light there, the same stirs up the darkness in other men against it also. The Lord knows what bitter fights we have had with the enemy in our own hearts, before we could leave our principles, paths and practices of darkness, how hard it hath been to us to deny the world and come out of it: and yet when the Lord hath conquered and subjected the darkness in our own hearts in any measure, then we meet with a new fight abroad in the world, the same principle and power in them

376

fighting against us, as did at first in ourselves (and still is, so far as any of it is left in any of us) to bring us back under darkness again, even from the Light and leadings of the Spirit, and from single obedience thereto: for it is the aim and endeavor of the same spirit in others. And if they could but bring us back from our God into the world again, they would be at peace with us as well as with other men, and love and cherish us as they do the rest of the world.

2. A second end of persecution in the spirit that persecuteth is to keep the children of the Light from gaining further ground. The kingdom of God and his truth is of a growing, spreading nature. It is like leaven, like salt, like the light of the morning; its nature is to leaven, to season, to overspread and gather mankind from the evil, from the darkness, from the corruption, from the death and destruction. Now the spirit of the world, and that spirit which ruleth the world is loathe to lose ground; and therefore hunts and seeks to destroy the vessels wherein the Light appeareth, and from whom it shineth forth, and to make them appear as odious as they may, that they may keep all their own territories and dominions [13] in a perfect detestation of them and distance from them. Thus though the people of God have still been an innocent people, and simple as to the subtlety and deceit of the Serpent, and weak and foolish in compare with the wise and strong ones in the worldly nature and spirit: yet they are still represented as most dangerous, most subtle and pernicious, as shrewd deceivers, witches, Jesuits, etc., yea, anything that is hateful and hated.

3. A third end of persecution is to afflict, grieve, vex, disturb and torment those whose principles and practices are displeasing to them. . . .

7. The Colour, or Pretence which men put upon their Persecutions of that which is Good.

Persecution is so hateful (and hath such a blackness of spirit in it) that it cannot endure to appear in its own colour. Where is the man that would appear to persecute that which is good in men, or men because of their goodness? Therefore all persecutors, though they still persecute that which is good and those which are good, yet they still represent and charge them as evil, that they might thereby hide the badness and unjustness of their persecutions from their own eyes, and from the eyes of others. . . . [14]

8. The Blessedness of the Persecuted

The disciple of Christ, who is persecuted for conscience sake, who suffers from men and their laws for the uprightness of his heart towards, and for his obedience unto Christ, that man is precious in the eye of Christ and hath his blessing with Him: yea, the more men disesteem and hate him upon this account, the greater is his blessedness. . . . [15] *Matth.* 5:11, 12. He is blessed in several respects.

1. That man is in that spirit and in that way which God hath chosen, and so he is in a happy state and condition at present. He is in the path of life, in the way of peace, under the leadings of God's spirit. . . .

2. The recompence which God will give to them in the world to come who cleave to him and his truth, for all the persecutions which they endure in this world for his truth's sake, is exceeding great. "Great is your reward in Heaven." *Mat.* 5:14. . . .

3. The reward is great in this world also. There is a hundred fold recompence to be reaped in his life. The peace of God in the conscience, the presence of God, the life of God, the virtue of God, the glory of the spirit of God (which accompanieth, resteth with, and abideth on the heart which is faithful, and waiteth upon God for patience, meekness, innocency and strength to carry through the sufferings) may well be valued at above a hundred fold income and recompence, for all the hardships and tribulations which are undergone for his name-sake. "If ye be reproached for the Name of Christ, happy are ye; for the spirit of glory and of God rests upon you." I *Pet.* 4:14.

9. The grievous misery of the Persecutors.

It is a miserable thing to be deceived about that which is good, to put good for evil, light for darkness, sweet for bitter and so (under a mistake at least) become a persecutor of good. All good is of God, and he that is against good is against God; and it is a dreadful thing for the creature to set himself in battle against his creator, and to engage the power and wrath of the omnipotent one against him, though while the eye is shut, it doth not appear to men, either that they are against God, or that their danger is so great thereby, as indeed it is. The children of God are as the apple of His eye: Who can touch them, and He not be deeply sensible? yea, and they are most dear to God in that, for which the world most persecutes them. And therefore their danger and misery must needs be great, which may further appear in these three respects.

1. In respect of the weight of wrath, which their persecutions of others here will bring upon themselves in the world to come. . . . [17]

2. The hand of God doth often overtake them in this world, and the Lord doth many times curse their very blessing to them, insomuch as they cannot enjoy this world with that sweetness and content they might. . . .

3. By all their persecutions and afflictions they shall but increase and cause to grow, that which they strive to suppress. This is misery indeed. . . . [18] O ye sons of men be wise, do not contend with the Lord; be not bewitched by

the cup of fornications, from the pure spiritual worship of the living God, into man's inventions, which the Lord's soul loathes; nor do not strive to hold any back from the Lord, whom the Lord draws after him: but consider his power, wait to know his work in the world, and do not intrench upon his dominions, but be thankful for and content with your own. . . .

Therefore, O magistrates of this nation, do not make use [19] of the sword to suppress the plants of God, but to cut down that which manifestly is not of God. Look abroad throughout this nation, behold how much evil there is to grieve and provoke the Lord, and to divert good from the nation, and to bring wrath upon it and the government thereof, strike at that in righteousness and true judgment, and with mercy to creatures, souls and bodies: but that which certainly is of God, meddle not with; and that which may be of God, for ought ye know, be circumspect in meddling with, lest ye engage God against you. It were better to let many tares grow, than pluck up one ear of corn. . . . The chief cause of this misery (from whence it principally ariseth) is men's meddling with those things which God hath reserved for himself. . . . [20]

10. The way and means to avoid Persecution.

1. By a true awe and fear of God in the heart. The fear of God teacheth to depart from iniquity, and to seek the crucifying and bringing under of the worldly spirit in a man's self, and to wait daily to have God's will revealed, and likewise to be made obedient thereunto. Now he that is in this temper of spirit, will hardly be drawn to persecute another. . . . [21]

2. By meekness of spirit. The Gospel makes meek, tender, gentle, peaceable, fills with love and sweetness of spirit, teacheth to love, to forgive, to pray for and bless enemies: and how shall this man persecute? Can a Lamb persecute? Can a dove persecute? Indeed a wolf in sheep's clothing may raven and devour, but a true sheep cannot. As the power of the Gospel is known, the devouring and persecuting nature is destroyed: and that being taken away, persecution soon comes to an end.

3. By a sober and patient consideration of their cause whom they persecute, and what is in themselves which causes them to persecute them. . . .

4. By a righteous frame of spirit, which is willing to do by another, as he would be done to in the like case. Persecution ariseth from unrighteousness and selfishness; righteousness and true equity would soon end it. If no man would make another man's conscience bow by force who would not have his own so bowed, persecution would soon cease. . . . [22]

5. By taking heed and watching against the corrupt and carnal principle, with the reasonings, self-ends and interests thereof, and hearkening to the principle of God, which teacheth and speaketh right reason. . . .

11. And lastly consider the fruits and effects of persecution, which are very many. . . .

1. In a great degree it hindereth the growth of the present good in every age and generation. . . . [23]

2. It wholly tends toward hindering the shooting up of any further seeds of good, which God hath to sow in the earth. . . . [24]

Object. But will not this undermine magistracy, and interrupt its punishing of evil-doers, if they should be thus tender and considerate? For what man cannot pretend conscience for what he does? And if the magistrate should hearken to every pretence of conscience, the laws would soon be silent, government at a stand, and everyone do what they list, bringing all manner of licentiousness and disobedience to authority, under a pretence of conscience.

Answ.

1. Conscience is of God; and tenderness and consciousness towards him is necessary to the receiving of his pure fear, and towards the springing up and growth of all good in the heart. The seed of good is tender: and if it be not received into tender and well-prepared earth (but into thorny, stony or highway ground) it cannot grow. And it cannot reasonably be supposed, to be the intent of God in appointing governments, that ever their laws or authority should hurt that tenderness of consciousness, wherein his seeds of good are sown.

2. It is true, the corrupt nature of man, which is selfish and seeketh covers for evil, may also seek this cover to hide iniquity under, and may pretend conscience when there is no matter of conscience at all, but self-will and self-ends at bottom.

3. Notwithstanding this, God would not have the true conscientiousness and tenderness in any of His crushed; nor can it be done by any person, authority or law, without provoking God on the one hand, or without injury to such who are so dealt with: *viz.* who are punished by man for the exercise of that conscientiousness which is of God, and which he requireth and is pleasing to Him. [25]

4. It were far better in itself, safer for governors, more agreeable to equity and righteous government, and more pleasing to God and good men . . . to spare many evil men, than to punish one good man: For mercy and sparing (even of offenders) is natural to that which is good, but severity and punishments are unnatural, and but for necessity's sake. . . .

5. As government came from God: so the righteous execution of it depends on God. . . . And will not the Lord assist that magistrate, who in his fear waits on him, and is not willing to spare the evil and afraid to hurt the good? . . .

4. Quaker Appeals to Rulers: Elizabeth Hooton[7] to Noah Bullock at Derby (SMS 2:43; 1651)

Sometime during the twelve months Fox spent in Derby jail in 1650-51,[8] he was joined by Elizabeth Hooton, at whose home at Skegby near Mansfield a separatist group had shared an emotional upsurge of "the power" that first clearly distinguished Quakerism as a movement and Fox as a leader. Her letter of remonstrance to "Noah Bullock of Derby in the town," and headed "this was sent to the mayor [?][9] of Derby from Good-[wife] Hutton," was much later endorsed by Fox "to the mayor of Derby from Elizabeth Hooton, 1650," though the date and Bullock's rank are actually unsure.[10] At the time, however, Fox seems to have made a careful and (for him) unusually fair copy[11] over his own signature,[12] which he later endorsed as his own letter to the mayor. Thus her letter ranks with Fox's own Derby prison fragments[13] as the oldest surviving Quaker documents.

O friend, you are a magistrate in place to do justice, but in prisoning of my body you have done contrary to justice according to your own law. O take heed of pleasing men more than God; for so did the scribes and pharisees [who] sought the praise of men more than God. I was a stranger & ye took me not in; I was in prison & ye visited me not. O friend, your envy is not against me

[7] For biography of Elizabeth Hooton, see Index.

[8] Cf. p. 33 and Fox, *Journal* (1911), I, 2-14; *Short Journal,* p. 4, etc. Fox endorsed her letter and his own as 1650, but he was certainly still in prison the following summer, when he refused a captaincy in the Parliamentary army. Elizabeth Hooton's imprisonment is dated 1651 by Emily Manners, *Elizabeth Hooton* (1914), p. 6, following Besse (I, 137). She had reproved a priest.

[9] So E. Manners, H. J. Cadbury (*Swarthmore Documents in America*), p. 11, etc.: reading "meir," it can also be read "the men of Derby."

[10] On Bullock as magistrate but not mayor, cf. Manners, p. 78.

[11] Etting, *Early Quaker Papers,* p. 26. Fox follows the corrected wording in her version (see below), and makes uncharacteristically few corrections himself.

[12] It is a gay reversal of later roles to imagine Fox as amanuensis for another Friend, and shows his respect for her. Yet his version is signed, not in her name, but faintly by "iorg foxe," and may have been sent independently (though in either case it is hard to explain the "engrossment" remaining in Fox's hands).

[13] Cf. p. 55 and *Annual Catalogue,* pp. 31-32.

but against the power of the truth.[14] I had no envy to you but love. O take heed of oppression, for the Day of the Lord is coming, that shall burn as an oven, and all the proud & all that doth wickedly shall be as stubble, & the day that cometh shall burn them,[15] saith the Lord of Hosts; it shall neither leave root nor branch.[16] O friend, if the love of God was in you, you would love the truth & hear the truth spoken & not prison unjustly. The love of God beareth & suffereth & envyeth no man. If the love of God had broken your heart,[17] you would show mercy; but you do show forth what ruleth you. Every tree doth shew forth his fruit; you do show forth your selves openly, for drunkenness, swearing, pride & vanity ruleth from the teacher to the people & this set up. O friend, mercy & true judgment & justice is cried in your streets. O take heed of the woes: woe be to the crown of pride; woe be unto them that drinketh in bowls,[18] & the poor is ready to perish.[19] O remember Lazarus & Dives:[20] & Dives that man fared deliciously every day, & the other a beggar. O friend, mind these things, for they are near you: see that you be not the man. Would you have me put in jail, which have not transgressed your law nor misbehaved myself? Consider, is this the good old way that you was taught?[21]

Elizabeth Hutton.

5. Direct Appeals by Quakers to Magistrates: Camm and Howgill Visit Cromwell (1654)

(ARBMS No. 20: John Camm [and Francis Howgill] to Margaret Fell, March 1653/54; cf. *JFHS,* XXVIII [1931], 54-55; BBQ, p. 156, etc.). This seems to have been the first of several

14 Fox wrote "the power of truth which I had . . . ," missing the sense.

15 Fox wrote "born them them up," apparently in carelessness.

16 This reference to Malachi 4:1 would also remind the Puritan magistrates of the "Root and Branch Bill" by which Parliament had abolished the bishops in 1641.

17 Fox has "hearts."

18 Fox corrects the quotation to "drink wine in bowls" (Amos 6:6, which concludes, "but are not grieved over the ruin of Joseph").

19 Elizabeth Hooton first wrote "ready to starve"; Fox has only this, her corrected version.

20 Luke 16:19-31; Elizabeth Hooton has a crossed-out word (now illegible) at this point.

21 Fox has "taught with."

O frend you ar a magastrat in pla to do iued tb but impri[soneme]
my body you have don contrar toineses according to your ow[n law] o
tase head of pleasing men mor then god for so did y scribes and [phari]
sought y preaes of men mar then god i was a stranger & ye took
not in i was in prison & ye [uis]ied me not o frend your ener is [not]
ag aigest me but agenest y power of truth wich i had no enm[ie]
you but love o tase head of oppreshion for y day of y lord is com
y that shall born as a oven and all ye proud o all [that] doth wick[ly]
shall be as stoubel o the day that cometh shall [burne] born
them them up seath y lord of ostes it shall nether leave
root nor branch o frend if the love of god was in you you
would love y truth o heare y trth speson o not prison
[m]eeth the love of god beareth o sufferith o envieth no man if y love of
god had broken your hartes you [would] shew mercy but you do shew
in forth what ruleth you every tree doth shew forth it fruit
you do shew forth your selues to oppulse for dronknes swaring
prid uanair ruleth from the thearer to y people o thus see we
o frend mercy o true iudgemen o inesties is writh in your [street]
os oppreshion un mersefulle o cruelte o hatred o [envie] o
pleasures o wontonnes suc neb o y power is not reegard in
your streats o tase head of the woes wo be to the crouen of
prid wo be un to them that drinketh wine in boelles o ye [that]
is redy to vearesh or mear the [poore] o divers o divers y now [her]
ed sixteobly every day o the other a begger of rind mind this thing[h]
[fo]r ye are ner you see that you be not the men would you hear
[m]e but in bale wich have not traues grases your low [nadir]
be hased my selef consider is this the good onele[s] wey take
you woo tought with
[illegible] co y mare at darke

visits in which Oliver Cromwell took time for careful talks with Quaker leaders, including later Anthony Pearson and Fox himself. In his sympathy for all radical Puritans, Cromwell clearly appreciated the integrity of Friends. On several occasions he ordered their release from local jails; but in regard to their interruption of the worship services of other congregations, and to their insistence that he abolish the national parish system, Cromwell was always firm. It is an irony of history that his tolerant spirit was not accepted by Friends, who could be satisfied only by the complete and agonized submission to Christ's Light through which they had gone and by the worship to which this led. Pearson visited Cromwell in July, 1654 (SMS 3:34=*EQL* No. 70), and spoke "enough to have broken his heart, but in his pride and loftiness and wit cast it (off)." Yet on his next visit in November, Cromwell stood hatless before Pearson. Fox's famous visit came in March, 1655. Several members of the Protector's household became Friends.

Dear Mother in the eternal Truth of God:

Our dear and tender love in the fountain of love is dearly presented unto thee and the church in thy house. After long waiting in great fear lest we should not have spoken unto the great man, O.P., yet the twelfth day after we came into London the Lord made way, that we came unto him into his chamber, where there was none but himself and his two men. It was about six o'clock at night. We had most part of an hour time with him, where we delivered thy letter into his own hand; and he seemed to receive it thankfully. He is plausible in his words, and said thou were a good woman; he had heard much of thee; but he is too wise in comprehension and too high in notion to receive Truth in plainness and demonstration of the Spirit. He gathered the substance of all words we spake unto him, and judged them in his reason; and what he could comprehend out of them, so he took them, and went about to question whether they were the word of the Lord or not, by his carnal reason. But he argues strongly for the priests, and for the popish law to uphold them, and pleads for every man's liberty and none to disturb another; and so he would keep up himself, by getting or keeping favor with all. And so sin must be upholden by a law. He is full of subtlety, and can stand on everyone. It was told us he used to wear rich apparel, but he had a gray rough coat on, was not worth three shillings a yard: when we came to him he had heard we were plain men, and he condescended unto us. He offered us money, or anything we needed, but we denied to take anything from him; so he desired us to leave him: he was tired with business, and we should come to him within a day or two. So we shall discharge our consciences to him in the sight of God, and leave it upon his conscience whether he will hear or forbear. We have little fellowship in the city. The pure simplicity is lost; all have eaten of the tree of knowledge, and so is puffed up in knowledge and stumbles at the Cross. Nay, they have not so much heard of a Cross, but lust and pride and all manner of filthyness, such as cannot be declared. O, the rich and boundless love of God unto us, the people of the North, who hath separated us from the pollutions of it, and hath gathered us together into the unity of the Spirit. O, prize that love for evermore.

After we had waited about five days, we were moved to write a letter unto him, and made use of Captain Howard to get it to him, or else we should not have gotten admittance to him. But really, he is in great danger to be lost; for he hath got the form of Truth but fights against the power of Truth. For he holds that all the worships of this nation is the worship of God. But the blind cannot judge of Truth. I shall say no more; but our love in the Lord Jesus Christ salutes all. Farewell. We do think to stay a week in the city. There is some that is convinced of the Truth,[22] some few simple hearts, and for their sakes we shall stay some few days. We are well and want nothing; so we rest thine in the unity.

Francis Howgill

March the 27th, 1654. John Camm

6. A Quaker Petition: "To the Parliament of this Commonwealth," printed and bound within Nayler's and Fox's tract, *Several Petitions Answered* (London: Calvert, 1653), of which it forms pp. 61-64

The use of group petitions to rulers came naturally to Friends from the beginning, for they lived in the age of the great Leveller petitions to Parliament of 1649. The role of the Lancashire Puritans' petition as a background to *Saul's Errand to Damascus* has been shown (p. 263), and this first large-scale Quaker petition dates from the same winter months of 1652-53 as that tract and those first printed, from Aldam and Nicholson in York Castle (p.

---

22 See above, p. 82, and p. 473 below. Captain Howard may have been Charles Howard of Naworth, who though an heir of the Norfolk Howards and Cumberland Dacres was captain of the Protector's body-guard and a member of the Parliament of Saints for Cumberland, and later was made Deputy Major-General for Cumberland and Westmorland—certainly no Quaker. Cf. *DNB*.

359). That winter was one of political ferment, when Cromwell began to lay plans for dissolving the "Rump" of the Long Parliament of Saints and to rule the nation permanently through a Council of State. A major push here came from a series of meetings of the Puritan army officers in London, which included letters to the Council and to the regimental rank and file, January 28, 1652/53 (cf. S. R. Gardiner, *History of the Commonwealth and Protectorate,* II, 233). These asked for new and frequent Parliaments, reform of the law, and liberty of conscience. Within two weeks Benjamin Nicholson had seen one and replied from York Castle jail in *Some Returns to a Letter which came from the General Meeting of Officers. . . . Also, A Blast from the Lord or a Warning to England* (dated Feb. 8, 1652/53 but printed about April, 1653, by Calvert in London). He called on them to obey the Lord promptly and fully, to limit Parliament to the godly, and to protect Quaker worship and itinerant preachers, since "the Lord alone shall be the teacher and sole ruler of his people" (p. 7).

The Westmorland Friends' petition is still addressed to the Rump Parliament and to Cromwell in his title of General (he was only formally proclaimed Protector in Dec., 1653). From the reference to the Appleby Assizes of January, 1652/53, we can date it within the next two months.

To the Parliament of this Commonwealth, and the General and Major General[23] of the Army

A Declaration of the present condition of several inhabitants in Westmorland, and some part in Lancashire, whose names are subscribed, who have been faithful to the Parliament, and serviceable in their places to this Commonwealth, to the hazard of their lives, liberties and Estates.

Declareth:

That the Lord hath made known himself and manifested his love to us, in letting us see the deadness and emptiness of all the outward ministry of the world, and hath according to his own promise led us forth of the barren wilderness of outward carnal worships, and is himself become our teacher, and hath made us willing to wait alone upon him for teaching: by the power and virtue of which, we deny all the teaching which stands in the will of man

---

[23] Presumably John Lambert, leader and spokesman of the radical Puritan officers.

whatsoever. And so meeting together to wait upon the Lord's unlimited power, exhorting and building up one another in our most holy faith, according to the practice of all the Saints before us, not only spending the First Day of the week in such exercises, but several other days and nights, as the Lord gives us opportunity, to the great refreshment of our souls, and uniting of our hearts to the Lord and one to another, to his everlasting praise and glory; and having occasion to praise the Lord for that freedom which the Parliament doth allow us; For which the priests much maligns us, and stirs up the ignorant people in their Public Assemblies, to execute their rigor upon us, fomenting lies, and accusing us to the magistrates falsely, causing some to be indicted, some imprisoned, and some bound over for no just cause at all; and hath done all that in them lies to deprive us of that Liberty which their Parliament hath afforded. As may appear by several orders made at a late Sessions at Appleby in Westmorland, wherein they ordered that we shall not meet together in the night time, which hath been the practice of the saints in former ages, and hath been our practice because there are many servants and young laboring people which cannot come on the day, which comes at night because we would not give an occasion of offence. Wherein we do witness that while we did meet together on the night to sport and spend the time in vanity we were not meddled withal; but now we do testify against all such practices, who lives now in the same nature hates us. But justice which cuts down filthiness and gives way for truth to rise, we own. But there are several got into Commission of the Peace, formerly Malignants,[24] and some that have been actually in arms against the Parliament, contrary to the Act of Parliament, and are utter enemies to the Truth; as doth appear not only here but likewise in Yorkshire, where there hath been ten of our brethren and sisters kept in prison in York Castle, some of them the most part of a whole year, and since the last assizes were kept in close prison, until one of them died, and so continued in close prison until it pleased the Lord to move the hearts of some to procure them more liberty.[25]

[24] The "malignants," or Royalists, were especially strong in the Appleby region, and in the Northwest of England generally, and many took part in revolts or plots against the Commonwealth; these included the conservative Puritan pastors after 1646, and the gentry (except for Fell and West) who served as J.P.'s.

[25] William Sykes, of Knottingly, imprisoned for nonpayment of tithes, died in York Castle, October 26, 1652 (Besse, II, 90) among the Quaker prisoners; so, about 1654, died William Pears, and thus they can claim along with Parnell (p. 160) the title of being the first Quaker martyrs. As the release of the York prisoners by Cromwell was later than this petition, the easing of confinement may have been the work of Major-General Harrison, who visited them in July, 1652 (SMS 1:373=*EQL* No. 4).

And whereas we are a people accused to deny magistracy, it is not so; for justice we own in our souls, which cuts down corruption, which keeps the soul in death. For "let every soul be subject to the higher power; for all power is of God" (Rom. *13*:1), and that we set up, own, and honor, for conscience sake, and all men in the Lord.

Likewise our dear brother James Nayler lies in prison in Appleby, who served the Parliament under the command of Major General Lambert between eight and nine years, as we believe some of the Army can witness. All that we desire is, that books may be printed, whereby the Truth may be manifested; and if we transgress or offend, we are willing to suffer.

This Petition was signed by Three hundred and twenty-nine of the inhabitants of Lancashire and part of Westmorland.

7. Theocratic Perspectives on Contemporary History: *A Noble Salutation . . . Unto Charles Stuart* by George Fox "the Younger" (1660)

A quarter-century was to pass before Friends would have the chance, in New Jersey and Pennsylvania, to put into practice theocratic ideas about the rule of the saints, such as those in Burrough's toleration tracts. But Friends' petitions and replies to petitions show that at no time were they out of touch with political affairs. Nicholson's tract, and Billing's which is to follow, included concrete agenda for Parliamentary action; yet, as Puritan groups ran, Friends were chary with blueprints. Until a ruler might be fully convinced as a Quaker, most petitions and letters were appeals on single issues, unlike the proclamation tracts addressed to rulers. These latter, therefore, with their stated or implied doctrines of government and history, are our best picture of Quaker ideas about the state.

Appropriately, the best political tracts before Penn's were those of an old Cromwellian soldier, who may have been a "Leveller" politically, but was certainly sympathetic with the "Fifth Monarchist" attitude toward the rights of even a minority of saints to rule in God's name. He had been won for Quakerism in Suffolk in 1655, i.e., he was younger in faith than the famous George Fox and apparently unrelated to his namesake. Already in 1659, when the radical army leaders thrust aside both Parliament and Richard Cromwell, the Suffolk Puritan Fox wrote to encourage their rule through the "Committee of Public Safety"; his tract was called: *A few plain words to be considered by those of the Army, or others, who would have a Parliament that is chosen by the voices of the People, to govern the three Nations; wherein is shewed unto them, according to the Scriptures of Truth, that a Parliament so chosen are not like to Govern for God, and the good of his People.* On the one hand, Fox's tract answered the argument "that it is England's Birth-right, that the People should choose their Lawmakers," by noting that "many thousands of men in England have been wronged of . . . their Birth-right: for such as are not freemen of some Corporations, or have not free land of their own, are not permitted to choose Parliament men, though they be far more honest and understanding men than many that . . . have . . . free land worth forty shillings by the year." But, more basically, "a Parliament that is chosen by most voices, are not like to act for God" under any circumstances, because the "soberest and honestest men" are always "over-voted by the wild disaffected people, who sometimes have been stirred up by their priests."

The "Noble Salutation," like Burrough's *Trumpet of the Lord,* sees God's hand beneath all events of Commonwealth history and warns even the king that therefore only those who grant toleration to the saints will prosper.

A
NOBLE SALUTATION
AND A FAITHFUL
GREETING
UNTO THEE
CHARLES STUART,
Who art now
PROCLAIMED KING
OF
England, Scotland, France,[26] *& Ireland.*

From the Counsel and Nobility of the Royal Seed, the Lion of the Tribe of Judah, the Everlasting King of Righteousness, who Reigneth in

George Fox the younger

[26] The claim of English kings upon the throne of France dated from Becket's King Henry III in the late twelfth century and was never taken seriously after Joan of Arc's day in the fifteenth.

389

A Copy of this was Delivered in Writing by Richard Hubberthorne[27] into the King's Hand at Whitehall, the 4th day of the 4th Month, 1660. And this may be of Service to any of those called Royalists (or others) if they in Moderation will Read it, and for that Cause it is upon me to send it abroad in Print.

LONDON

Printed for S.D. and are to sold by Robert Wilson,[28] at his Shop at the Sign of the Black-spread Eagle and Wind Mill in Martins Le Grand; 1660.

The Heads (or Particulars) *Viz.*

Several wholesome sound exhortations (and weighty things opened) unto thee, O King.

II. Concerning the overturning of thy father and those that took his part, and the cause and manner of it; and how the instruments employed in the work were acted, and how they corrupted themselves, for which cause God forsook them, and gave them up to work their own destruction.

III. Concerning thy coming so far into power again, and those that took part with thy father and thee, who were conquered; and the cause of it, and how the things hath been wrought, which being truly considered, it may stop all fleshly glorying.

IV. Concerning the great danger thou art in, in thy coming in, and in thy place, and the reasons why it is so, plainly demonstrated.

V. Concerning religion and the spirit of persecution, and how and from whom it sprang, and by whom it hath been practiced, and what means the Apostles used to bring into the truth, and to preserve in it, and how they walked towards those that would not receive the truth, and towards those that turned from the truth.

VI. Concerning what government and governors the people of the Lord (called Quakers) stand for, and what they stand against; that so thou mayest see that it is not names that we stand for or against; but that which is righteous we are for, and that which is unrighteous we are against.

VII. How we resolve in the strength of the Lord to stand for that which is righteous, and against that which is unrighteous.

[27] On Hubberthorne and his visit to the king, see pp. 89, 147. On June 4, 1660, Charles II had been back in London less than a week, but the promise of toleration in his Declaration of Breda had been well known for two months.

[28] Giles Calvert fell into disgrace at the Restoration; Robert Wilson and later his wife continued to print Quaker books, using Calvert's sign of "the black spread-eagle." S. D. was presumably Simon Dring.

VIII. Concerning a government and governors, wherein something may be seen to be good, and something bad; what we resolve in the Lord to do in such a case, declared.

IX. Concerning plotting, or using a carnal weapon, and from whom we expect deliverance, and what we are confident God will bring to pass in his time.

X. Concerning revenge and what may follow if it be sought and what if not, and what the Lord intends to bring upon this Nation, and for what cause he will do it if speedily repentance be not come unto; and how we have suffered, and are freely given up to the Will of God. And some tender desires concerning the people of this Nation and thee, expressed.

[p. 3] 1. Several wholesome sound exhortations, etc. . . .

The God of heaven hath put into my heart to write unto thee, and in tender love both to thy soul and body, to lay before thee several things, whereby thou may come to see and consider how the mighty hand and justice of the invisible God hath been in these overturnings and changes, which have happened in these Nations of late years. Therefore consider these things: the mighty God, the everlasting father, he is the King of Kings, and the Lord of Lords, and the whole earth is his and the fullness thereof, and he rules over the kingdoms of men and gives them unto whomsoever he pleases. Yea, he pulls down one and sets up another, and there is no overturning or changing in kingdoms, but it is either by his commission or permission; and the Lord does not do anything, neither suffers he anything to be done, unto persons or kingdoms without a cause (though he may do whatsoever he pleases) and who shall call him to an account? Yet all his doings are righteous, and his ways are just and equal altogether; and it is for the unrighteousness sometimes of a king or kings, and sometimes of a people, and other times of both, that the Lord does break, or suffer a Nation or Nations to be broken; and when he determines to break a people or to change governments (or to suffer such things to be done) in vain do men strive to preserve or uphold them. And the Lord may and does make whomsoever he pleases his instruments, for to do his determined work; and when they have done his work, then he may do whatsoever he [p. 4] pleases with them. And many times his instruments, when they begin his determined work, appear very contemptible unto many. Yet, such speak foolishly and without understanding who say that such instruments are too weak and cannot prevail, seeing all power is in the hand of God, who can give wisdom and strength and courage unto whomsoever he pleases. . . . Now such things as these, O king, come oft to pass, and none of them without a cause; and they that are truly wise learn further and get understanding through all these things; therefore is true wisdom better than strength, and a right understanding is better than an earthly crown. Therefore, O king, wait to feel the noble principle of wisdom, which God has inspired thee withal; for there is a measure of it in thee, though it has been hid, and that measure is the light, which Christ the Wisdom of God has enlightened thee withal, which light in thee is that which never h'ad fellowship with darkness in thee, or its deeds, nor concord with the Devil or his works; but makes manifest and reproves all such things: which light, being received in the love of it, and believed and waited in, man becomes a child of it, and so it gives him a good understanding and opens an eye in him, whereby he comes to see the hand and workings and appearance of the invisible God. [p. 5] . . . .

Secondly, Concerning the overturning of thy father, etc.

Concerning thy father and those that took his part, there was an eminent hand of God in breaking them down and bringing them under; and God did it not without a cause; for the iniquity in them provoked the holy God to anger, and the height and pride of their spirits grieved and pressed the Spirit of the just God. And after he had a long time borne with them and warned them with his Eternal Light in their consciences, yet they repented not, but still grieved his good Spirit by many provocations, and waxed higher and higher against him in disobedience. His anger then was kindled against them, and his indignation waxed hot; and he arose in the fiery spirit of his jealousy, to ease himself of his adversaries and avenge himself of his enemies; and because the living, wise, eternal God (who made all the nations of the earth of one blood, and is no respecter of persons) saw that those that took part with thy father were generally (according to outward appearance) accounted the wisest, richest, noblest and stoutest men, and that they did glory in their wisdom, riches, nobility, stoutness and strength, and vaunted themselves over them that were made of the same blood. He (the living God) did then appear in contemptible instruments (as to outward appearance), as tradesmen, ploughmen, servants and the like, with some others, which I know thy father's party made a mock at, and even scorned them as it were, and thought it too low and too base a thing to engage war against such a contemptible people. Yet in such, I say, did the Lord appear to carry on that work which he had [p. 6] determined, even to bring down the loftiness of Man and to stain the pride and glory of flesh, and that thy father's party might have come to see that they were but men, made of the same earth and blood that others were. And the Lord God appeared mightily in those his instruments, giving them wisdom, courage, and strength to manage a war against a far more mighty and wise people, as to outward appearance, than themselves, and they prevailed daily against their enemies. And the affections of the people run forth and inclined towards them. And God struck thy father's party with dauntedness of spirit and turned their wisdom backwards and prospered them not in the field, but sometimes caused them to flee before their enemies, and other times gave them into their hands; and yet they repented not, neither did they humble themselves before the Lord, but fretted and strove, and some blasphemed and cursed even for madness to see how they were defeated. Yet they strove in vain, for God was against them, and they grew weaker and weaker, until they were even wholly subdued and brought under their enemies and given into their hands for a prey; that so they durst not scarce act or speak anything against their enemies. And thus the Lord stained the glory and pride of that people which took part with thy father and thee, by a low and contemptible means, as to outward appearance. Though I do verily believe that those in whom God did appear against thy father, thyself, and those that took that part, did act several things against you, beyond their commission they had from God; yet he did permit them. And in several of them who did engage against thy father and his party, there was once a tender, honest, good principle. in the day when they were low; and there was true desires in some of them after a just liberty, both as appertaining to conscience and in things betwixt man and man; and they were truly sensible of many oppressions which were in the Nation, both in matters of religion and in the laws and customs of the land; and they cried unto God when they were low and vowed unto him (and engaged unto man) that if he would deliver their enemies into their hands, that then they would remove all [p. 7] oppression and make the people of these nations a free people, and that they should have their just rights and liberties, both as men and as Christians. Now after thou hadst also striven against them (with a perfidious people, to wit, the Scots) and ye were defeated, the Lord gave their enemies so into their hands, that they had as much outward power in these three nations as they could desire; and they also became a dread and a terror to some nations about them. And they had power and opportunity to have removed all oppression out of the Land. But alas, covetousness and self-seeking lusts sprang up in most of them, and leavened them; and when they had rest and fullness, they forgot the Lord, who had raised them from a low degree; and they forgot the oppression of their brethren also, and regarded not to pay their vows to God and man. But after a time the chief of them got into thy father's houses and lands, and into thine, and into some of those that took your parts, and others they sold, and so thereby became great in the earth. And then their lusts increased, and they grew wanton against the Lord also, and boasted themselves over those whom they had conquered; and some of them began to creep into those places and things themselves, which they had cried out against in others, and so built and set up the same thing in and among themselves which they had thrown down and destroyed in another;

393

only in deceit and hypocrisy, they got other names for them. Then several of the Army that were amongst them, when they saw their deceit and wickedness and that they did not intend the thing which they did pretend, durst not for conscience sake continue any longer amongst them; but left them several years ago and declared against them. And others since, that feared the Lord, were turned out by them; so that in a short time many of them became greater oppressors and persecutors than those whom they had conquered, and so provoked the Lord to anger. Then the Lord raised up many prophets and servants, and sent them amongst those who had acted thus treacherously; and some also wrote unto them, and laid their abomination plainly before them, and showed them wherein they had erred, and exhorted them to [p. 8] repentance; and plainly showed unto them what the Lord required at their hands; and sometimes were made to reprove them sharply and plainly, and prophesied unto them, that the Lord would confound and break them to pieces one against another, and suffer them to be destroyed if they repented not speedily. But they would not hearken, but grew stiff-necked against the Lord and his people and suffered many of them to be oppressed, their goods spoiled, and some of them to be imprisoned unto death in their names. And thus they rebelled against the Lord more and more, and boasted of their strength and wisdom and valour; and so forgot how that it was the Lord that raised them up from a low degree and gave them power over their enemies. And thus they wrought grievous provocations in his sight, so that then the anger of the Lord was kindled against them; and as they forsook him, so he forsook them; and at length he gave them up to the counsels of their own hearts, because they had rejected his counsel. And then they began to divide and split amongst themselves and to betray one another for self-ends; and their courage began to fail, and faintness and deadness of spirit seized upon them; and having plunged themselves so far into covetousness and lusts, the cloud of error grew so thick upon them that they could not see the cause that they once were so zealous for. And then confusion fell upon them, and they groped like blind men and knew not at what they stumbled; neither knew they for whom, nor for what to stand; but sometimes cried up and engaged for one thing, and shortly after cried against it and threw it down again; and some of them cried for one thing, and other brought forth another thing; and so like Babel's builders (whom God determined to scatter) they acted; and their eye being blinded, they wrought their own destruction. And few of them saw it, until it was come upon them; and them that did were as men amazed, and knew not how to help themselves. And thus the just hand of the Lord came upon an hypocritical, deceitful, professing people, who in words have made a great professing that they knew God, but in works they have denied him; and therefore hath the Lord [p. 9] taken away their strength for the present, and turned their wisdom backwards, and stained their glory, that they also might come to see what they were, and what the Lord did for them, and what they are fallen from, that so happily some of them may come to find repentance and to be humbled under the mighty hand of God, and the Lord may heal their backslidings and may raise up his own eternal witness in them (the Tabernacle of David) which hath been fallen down.

3. Concerning thy coming so far into power again, etc.

Now, observe the hand of the Lord in thy coming so far into power again, and those who took part with thy father and thee. First, consider the cause of it (in the fear of the Lord), and thou wilt find that it is because they unto whom God gave such power over you were not faithful unto God, as hath been said before, but grieved the Spirit of the Lord with their hypocrisy from day to day, talking for liberty, but behold they brought forth oppression, and so became worse than you that went before them, who did not profess so much for liberty in words. And this I know, that if they had been faithful unto the Lord, thou and those called thy friends could not have come over them thus as ye have done. Therefore let no man deceive thee by persuading thee that these things are thus brought to pass because the kingdom was thy own proper right, and because it was withheld from thee contrary to all right, or because that those called Royalists are much more righteous than those who are now fallen under thee. For I plainly declare unto thee, that this kingdom and all the kingdoms of the earth are properly the Lord's, and that he may and does give them unto whomsoever he pleases; and whensoever he please, he may take them away again and give them unto others, and when he does thus, it is not contrary to right. And this know, that it was the just hand of God in taking away the kingdom from thy father and thee, and giving it unto others; and that also it is now the just hand of the Lord to take it again from them and bring them under thee; though I shall not say, but that some of them went beyond their commission against thy father, when they were brought as a rod over you, and well will it be for thee if thou becom'st not guilty of the same transgression now thou art brought over them. And [p. 10] this consider: that those who are called thy friends, who were conquered, have humbled themselves but little under the hand of the Lord, but are still found to be in great transgressions. And also consider the manner how this thing hath been wrought, and carried on, concerning the bringing in of thee again; that so there may be no fleshly boasting, for the thing is plainly discerned by them whose eye is single, and I shall declare it unto thee, Mark; the Army[29] having acted so deceitfully, the lusts and gain of the world

---

[29] This may refer to the overthrow of the "Rump" of the "Long Parliament" in 1653 (cf. p. 19), but may also describe the political chaos of 1659, as the following sentences clearly do; Lambert and the officers were key figures at both times.

blinded their eye, and they having so far provoked the Lord, until his decree was sealed against them, and he had determined that they should be broken. After this they split among themselves and turned from one thing to another and knew not where to rest, and the Lord suffered some to rise up from among themselves to deceive the rest; and so they through dissimulation (in professing to stand for those who had so eminently stood against thy father and thee) got power to weaken and turn out those that were really against thee, as disturbers of the Good Old Cause (as they termed it),[30] and so by little and little strengthened those that stood for thee. And thus the deceived blind men provided a rod for themselves, and so by little and little wrought themselves under it; and it is just upon them, for the rod is for the fool's back. So let this be considered, that this was not carried on by the stoutness of those that stood for thee, nor yet by a visible plain down-right dealing, but rather through the hidden mystery of deceit, which was suffered to work against those whom God had determined should be broken, that so, by the same way whereby they had deceived others, which was, by pretending to stand for that which they did not intend, I say, even by the same way, they in the end should be deceived themselves.[31] So let none glory in what is done concerning this thing, as if it were done by their valour or wisdom, though I can truly say, the hand of the Lord hath permitted these things, and that for the causes before mentioned, and he will be glorified in all these overturnings.

4. Concerning the great danger thou art in, in thy coming in, etc.

And also, consider the danger that thou art in, in thy coming in as king of these nations, for it is exceedingly great as things stand, and this hath been much upon me to lay before thee. And it is in tender love both to thy soul and body; for I plainly see [p. 11] that if thou should come in upon the account of the people called Presbyterians,[32] if thou should not satisfy the ungodly covetousness of their priests, there is several of them would be ready to serve thee as they did thy father if they were permitted. And if thou do come in upon the account of those people called old Royalists, truly, though

---

[30] George Monk and the Cromwellian garrison in Scotland did not announce their support for the Restoration of King Charles until they had marched south and shattered the support for General Lambert and the radical Puritans.

[31] Lambert and Vane had claimed to plan abolition of the parish church system but had delayed acting upon this, despite prodding by Quaker "prophets"; they in turn were deceived by Monk.

[32] In 1660, the Presbyterians supported Monk in hopes of a broad-bottomed national Church that would include themselves and exclude the Baptists and Quakers. They, too, were in for a shock when "High Anglicans" took charge in 1661.

I do believe they would abhor such a thing as to sell thee; yet the iniquity of many of them is so great, and there is so much swearing, lusts and vanity amongst them, that except they repent, they are not like long to prosper, but the hand of the Lord will assuredly break them also. And furthermore consider, there are a deceitful people in these nations, for there are many thousands that now appear highly for thee in words, that if they could see a likelihood of a change, they would appear as much or more against thee. Therefore consider thy standing and be not high-minded, but fear and take heed lest thou falls. And never go about to engage the people unto thee by oaths, lest thou cause many to forswear themselves.[33] For truly this people, a great part of them are a perfidious people, as they have manifested themselves, who one while have sworn for a King and Parliament, and shortly after they have sworn against a King, single person or House of Lords, and shortly after they have sworn or engaged for a single person again and called one another Lords;[34] and a little while after have turned against that government and cried up a Parliament again; and now the same people are generally crying up a King again. And truly those rulers who have imposed so many several engagements upon the people, they have done exceeding evilly therein. And how abominably have these dirty, deceitful, covetous priests acted in all these changes? Oh, it is hard to utter their deceit, who one while have prayed for a King and Parliament, and when they saw the King was likely to fall and that he was no ways likely to maintain them, then they turned against him and prayed only for the Parliament, and asserted their authority, and cursed them that would not go out to help against the mighty. And shortly after, when Oliver Cromwell had turned out the Parliament and set up himself, then they cried up (and prayed for) him, and many of them began to assert his authority to be just; and when he died, many of these priests began to address themselves to his son, and [p. 12] fawned upon him, that he might provide for their god, which is their belly. And they appeared to be sorrowful for his father's death, and blasphemously termed him the light of their eyes and the breath of their nostrils; and they told Richard that God had left him to carry on that glorious work which his father had begun. And some of these priests compared Oliver to be like unto Moses and Richard to be like unto Joshua, who should carry them into the promised land. But surely these blind priests are yet in Egypt, the land of darkness, and there are like to die except they

[33] Oaths of allegiance, always a key issue for Friends, became crucial in 1661, when they became automatically guilty of treason under the oaths of praemunire and under the special "Quaker Act."

[34] Oliver Cromwell, the "single person" given royal power under the Instrument of Government of 1653, eventually restored in 1657 the House of Lords, or rather a new, nominated Upper House to replace that abolished in 1649. It, too, passed in 1659.

repent. And surely those that made Oliver chancellor of one of their universities, they hoped he should have continued longer in his place than he did; but it is manifest that they are such as the prophet said, night should come upon them, and they should have no vision. And how soon did some of them turn for a Parliament again, when the Army turned out Richard? And when George Booth made a rising,[35] and they thought there would be a turn, then some of them cried out against the Parliament, and began to curse such as would not go out against them; and when George Booth was taken, then many of them began to petition to the Parliament, and to excuse themselves, that they had no hand in that rising. And now they are generally crying up and praying for thee, and all this is for their bellies; therefore if thou wilt believe them and trust to their prayers, thou art worthy to be deceived by them. And all that will uphold them in that state they are in and compel others to maintain them, they are not like to prosper. . . . Yet, this I testify in the Lord, that such ministers as the Scriptures of Truth own, I own; and such a maintenance as Christ allowed his ministers to take. Therefore now, O king, be wise and cleave unto the Lord with thy whole heart, and he will teach thee to love thy enemies and to do unto all men as thou wouldst they should [p. 13] do unto thee; and also it will reach the witness of God in all people, and thou wouldst become honorable in their hearts, and hereby they would be engaged and drawn unto thee more than by oaths or force of arms. But if thou wilt not hear and do the thing that is just and right in the sight of the Lord, then will the Lord appear against thee; and when thou hast filled up thy measure, thou shalt be assuredly broken, and then shalt thou know that God hath spoken unto me. And if thou dost not speedily seek to stop this abounding ungodliness which shows in this nation (and which hath much increased since there was a likelihood of thy being brought in), verily an evident hand of God shall come upon thee, which thou shalt not in any ways be able to escape. Therefore consider it speedily, for verily the mighty God is greatly displeased, by reason of the great wasting and spoil that is made of his creatures, in a way of rejoicing and triumphing concerning thee; . . . and they go stammering and staggering because of drunkenness; and sober people that fear the Lord can scarce pass in the streets without being scoffed at, threatened, or having violence done unto them, by those that appear for thee, who bitterly will curse, and wish that which they call the pox and plague upon us; and the next words cry out and say, "God save King Charles." . . .

And also, when we have been peaceably met together to wait on the Lord

---

[35] Conservative Puritan pastors made peace with each new government. In quickly mastering George Booth's Royalist rising of 1659, Lambert had seemed to have made the army's radical Puritan position secure after Richard Cromwell fell.

and to hear and declare the everlasting truth, we have been abused, and part of our houses and windows broken, and some of us knocked down and torn, as though they would have pulled us limb from limb, and our blood drawn, knocking us down without respect had to age or sex; and this they say thou wilt bear them out in, and they expect an order they say shortly from thee, either to banish or hang us all. And in thy name, was I commanded and fetched out of a meeting at Harwich upon the first day of this week and haled to prison without being examined, [p. 14] and without a mittimus; and this was because I was made in the dread and power of the living God, to cry aloud against the cursing and the rudeness which I then heard and beheld amongst the people in the streets. And I was made to utter these words and say, "Woe, woe unto the rulers and teachers of this nation, who suffer such ungodliness as this and do not seek to suppress it"; and for this was I put in prison. O king, for these things will the Lord God visit, and if thou seek not to stop them, thou wilt feel God's hand for it. Verily, I declare unto them, in the fear of the Lord, I never heard of nor beheld so great profaneness as I have done within these few weeks past. Oh, it is hard to utter how much wine and strong drink hath been devoured in waste, by people's drinking of healths unto thee:[36] some upon their knees, and some otherwise; even until some have been so drunk, they could neither speak or go right. And what abundance of wood hath been wasted and devoured in making of great bonfires (as they call them) which they have done, as they say, to rejoice because of thy coming; . . . and such noises have been heard of late in cities and towns, as scarce ever have been the like, by shooting off of guns both great and small, and by ringing of bells, and by people's singing and laughing and shouting like riotous mad men, and the streets in several places strewn with flowers, and the like. And this is done in rejoicing concerning thee, and what abundance hath been devoured in feasting and banqueting and abominable rejoicings? And also, consider in what great need poor people are of such creatures as have been thus devoured, and consider what can be the end of all these things. Now the Lord is my witness, when I have seen and felt this ungodliness, a tender pity hath arose in me towards thee, because I have beheld the danger that thou art in, which is exceeding great. Let no man deceive thee by persuading thee that thou art in a safe condition, because the outward strength of the nation appears to be at thy command. For consider this: Oliver Cromwell and his party had as much of that strength (or more once) as thou hast now; and those called thy party were fallen as much under them, as they are now under [p. 15] thine. And yet consider how their strength was taken from them, and how it vanished away like smoke. Yea, the

---

[36] King Charles had a sense of humor and would have enjoyed reading this. Poor Fox had none.

Lord is righteous and powerful, and if he speaks but the word, it must be fulfilled; and truly, God is highly provoked. Therefore take heed what thou dost.

5. Concerning religion and the spirit of persecution, etc.

And as concerning religion, I exhort and warn thee in the name and fear of the Lord, to take heed that thou bind not the consciences of any, and that thou suffer no other means to be used about religion but what the apostles used. For all this killing and imprisoning and persecuting about religion, the Lord abhors it; yea, the Papists' killing and imprisoning and persecuting of the Protestants, and the Protestants' killing and imprisoning and persecuting of the Papists and others about a form of religion: these things are of the Devil, the destroyer in them both, and not of Christ, who came not to destroy men's lives but to save them. And consider: Cain was the first murderer about religion, who slew righteous Abel, and Cain was for it a vagabond.[37] And the vagabond Jews persecuted Christ and the saints; and the saints, since Christ suffered without the gate by and for sinners, used no persecution about religion, but Christ said that inwardly ravening wolves should come. . . . So mark: these antichrists killed those that held the testimony of Jesus, which is the spirit of prophecy. And here the whore (adulterated from God) got up, and she drank the blood of the saints and martyrs of Jesus, and the kings of the earth committed fornication with her and drank her cup: and she sat upon nations, kindreds, tongues, and people. So all this imprisoning, and killing, and whipping, and stocking, and stoning, and mangling [p. 16] of the creatures about religion is practiced among the heathens and the antichrists, the apostatized Christians who are gone out from Christ and the apostles' spirit and doctrines. For they wrestled not with flesh and blood, but with principalities and powers and spiritual wickedness in high places. So they fought against spiritual wickedness and not against creatures, and the weapons of their warfare were not carnal but spiritual. They used no imprisoning, stocking, whipping, stoning, hanging, burning, banishing, or mangling of the creatures to persuade or turn them to their religion; neither did they use any other force to turn people to the pure religion, than that which proceeded from the invisible power of God's eternal Spirit in them, which struck at the spiritual wickednesses and the evil thoughts and imaginations which were exalted in people above the knowledge of Christ. And so they sought to bring the wickedness into captivity, and not the creatures; but to bring them into liberty, by turning them from darkness

---

[37] Cain, Balaam, Pharaoh and Antichrist appear regularly in Quaker anti-persecution tracts.

to light, and from Satan's power unto the Power of God. And them that had known the truth and turned from it and became heretics, after the first and second admonition (if they would not hear) they rejected, knowing that such were condemned in themselves. But they did not give order to kill such. . . . They did not persecute any, nor use any outward force with any about religion, neither did they give any command for such a thing. And to preserve in the truth such as were come to it, they used patience, meekness, long-suffering, and sound doctrine; and kept them and commended them unto the ingrafted word (which was nigh in their hearts and in their mouths), the which was able to save their souls. And did not threaten to persecute them if [p. 17] they did turn out of the truth. Therefore, they that persecute about religion are not for Christ, but antichrists; that is, against Christ. So take heed that thou dost not set up persecution about religion upon any pretence whatsoever, nor tolerate it. For the Lord God hath brought forth a people in these nations, and he will bring forth more, that cannot nor may not bow unto any other thing in their worship, than unto the name of Jesus, whose name is called the Word of God. And if thou oppressest this people, the Lord will assuredly take away thy power and avenge their cause; for he careth for them. And verily, we have not another to trust in than the name of the Lord, and we know that he will not suffer anything to come upon us, but what shall work for his Glory and our good. But these things are spoken unto thee, that thou might'st fear the Lord, and might'st not pull judgement upon thy own head.

6. Concerning what government and governors the people of the Lord (called Quakers) stand for, and what they stand against, etc.

This I declare in the truth and presence of the Lord (and I know there are many thousands in these nations that are of the same mind with me): that it is not for the name that may be put upon a government, that we either stand for or against: but it is a righteous government which we stand for and earnestly desire after, both in things appertaining to God and man. And we, for ourselves, desire no greater liberty, either in things religious or in things civil betwixt man and man, than we desire all others might enjoy. And if such a government as this be set up, then if he that is chief, in taking care and seeing that justice may be done to all, without respect of persons, if he be called a King, a Judge, a Protector or a General, we shall not be against either or any of the names. Or if the care and trust be laid upon more, if they be called by the name of a Parliament, or a Council, or a Committee, or King and Parliament, or any, we are content and shall willingly submit unto righteousness from them, or any of them, as our duty. And it is that which is unrighteous [p. 18] (which is called a government, wherein oppression, partiality, and cruelty is exercised, either in things relating unto conscience in matter of worship, or in things civil betwixt man and man) that we stand against. And if such a thing be set up and called a Government, and if the chief in it be called a King, or a Judge, or a Protector, or a General, or a Parliament, or a Council, or a Committee, or King and Parliament, we cannot stand for any of the names nor submit unto the unjust things commanded by them, any other ways than through a patient suffering under it. And this according to the strength of the Lord, we shall be willing to do.

7. How we resolve in the strength of the Lord to stand for that which is righteous, and against that which is unrighteous, etc.

The way how we shall stand for the righteous government and governors is by yielding all due lawful obedience unto them and their commands; and by laboring in the Power of the Lord to bring down and to keep under the evil lust in people, which is the cause of all wars and rebellions and transgressions. Also, the manner how we shall stand, through the power of the Lord, against that which is unrighteous (though it be called a government, and against unrighteous governors) is by bearing our testimony against them in the power of the Lord; and by yielding no other obedience to them than in submitting patiently to suffer and endure whatsoever punishment the Lord shall suffer them to lay upon us. And this shall turn against them daily and weaken them and bring shame upon them. For persecution is to them that persecute us a token of perdition, but unto us salvation, and that from the Lord.

8. Concerning a government and governors, wherein there may something seen to be good and something bad, etc. . . . [19]

Whatsoever is good in either, we shall be ready through the Lord's strength to submit unto, and own, and we shall labor to preserve and cherish that. And as the Lord shall move us, we shall be willing to show the governors in plainness, what is wrong in them, and in the government. And if they refuse to hear us, and afflict us, we shall in patience yield our bodies, to suffer under that which is bad in either. However, we shall discountenance it, and labor through the power of the Lord in a Spiritual warfare to destroy it, that so it may further appear that we are not against Magistracy but for it (it being God's ordinance), and that we are only against that in magistrates and people which would and which doth defile and pollute the place of Magistracy.

9. Concerning plotting, or using a carnal weapon; and from whom we expect deliverance, etc.

And, I further testify in the Lord that I do not intend, neither have I any such thought in my heart, either to plot for or against thee, or any other upon the earth; for I do not expect deliverance by a carnal sword, and yet I know deliverance shall come, with or without the help of man; and in vain have been, and shall be, all the strivings, compellings, and murderings about religion, church, and worship. . . . And into the belief of this, I know that the Lord that gathered several thousands into the same mind with me, that are called by the name of Quakers. And we could desire, if it were the will of God, even that all men were of the same mind. And these that are otherwise minded, we shall leave them unto the Lord, to do what he pleaseth with them. And we are freely given up unto the will of God, and we have committed our cause unto him, and he shall bring it to pass, that so it may plainly be made manifest, [p. 20] that we are a people saved by our God, from whom we expect deliverance. And he hath made us willing to wait until he bring it to pass. And this we are confident of, that the everlasting Gospel, which is the power of God, shall again be preached unto all nations, kindreds, tongues and people; and that the whore of Babylon, the beast and his horns, and his names which have prevailed against the bodies of the holy people in the night of apostasy, shall cease to prevail against the saints. And then shall the saints of the most High possess the Kingdom. And we do believe that God will overturn and overturn, until he hath brought to pass the thing that he hath decreed, which is to establish righteousness in the earth: and then shall there be judges as at the first, and councillors as at the beginning, and kings shall become nursing fathers, and queens shall become nursing mothers, and the kingdoms of the world shall become the kingdoms of the Lord and of his Christ. And hereof we have an assurance in the Spirit of truth, and yet, we never expect to know Christ after the flesh to reign, but he shall reign over all the earth, whose kingdom is an everlasting kingdom, and all powers shall serve and obey him, who is King of Saints.

10. Concerning revenge, and what may follow if it be sought, and what if not, etc.

Take heed of seeking revenge. O let not the enemy of thy soul, within or without, get thee into blood. Vengeance is the Lord's and he will repay it. Therefore wherein thy enemies went beyond their commission against thy father, or any that took his part, leave that unto the Lord, who will reward every one in righteousness, according to their deeds done in their bodies. And consider how far Christ was from seeking or desiring revenge, when they murdered him as concerning the flesh, who said, "Father, forgive them, for they know not what they do." Oh, mind that spirit, and consider he was greater than thy father, and he was free from all transgression. . . . [p. 21] And many of thy enemies, and also of those that are called thy friends, might be converted unto God, and so ye might be united in true love one unto another, and this were better than conquering by force. . . . But if thou resolvest to avenge thyself and those called thy friends which have suffered, it will raise up the desperate aggravating part in man, and so the thing may kindle again the murdering spirit. And the Lord may suffer it to break forth into blood, which if it should, it may be the saddest time that ever thou yet sawest. For this I know, and do steadfastly believe: that after God hath tried his people, he will assuredly bring an overflowing scourge upon this nation, and many shall fall and perish by an evident hand and judgement of the Lord, except they repent speedily. . . . And he hath sent many of his servants and prophets to warn this nation and others; and many thousands have believed us, and are gathered into peace with us, notwithstanding they see a great judgement to come upon the earth. And though many have believed us, yet alas, the far greater part hath either beaten, or imprisoned, or [p. 22] scoffed at, or slighted and rejected us, and the testimony which we hold. . . . Therefore, seeing people will neither hear the prophets of the Lord, nor regard the Light of his Son in their consciences, the Lord will leave striving with such a people, and bring sudden destruction upon them, and deliver his chosen. . . . So, we are given up to the will of the Lord, and do patiently wait for his mighty appearance to deliver us, who have long been a suffering people, who have suffered both by Parliaments, Army, Protectors, and by those called thy friends also. Yea, we have suffered and been most cruelly treated, even by rulers, priests and people, professors and profane, because we could not join unto the evil in either, but have been made to reprove them for it, and to exhort them unto that which is good; and so we must yet do, so long as we find the Lord requiring it at our hands. . . .

And now, O king, as thou expects the blessing and presence of the Lord with thee in thy government, fear and dread his presence, by standing in awe of his living witness, the Light, which he hath placed in thy conscience, to guide and direct thee in all thy ways, that his wrath may be turned away from thee. [p. 23] But if it should prove so, I shall have peace, for I am clear of thy blood, inasmuch as in plainness I have let thee see how things have been, and how they may or shall be, and wherein thy danger stands, and how that righteousness only establisheth the throne. . . .

Given forth in Harwich jail in Essex, the 16th day of the third month called May, 1660.

Where I suffer for the testimony of Jesus, through the envy of the Devil, who is the false accuser of the brethren.

8. George Fox's Statements on the Peace Testimony (1660)

Fox's answer as a young man in Derby jail, when offered a commission in Cromwell's army, had been that he "knew from whence all wars did arise, even from the lust, according to James (4:1), and that I lived in the virtue of that life and power that took away the occasion of all wars."[38] To this statement Fox had little to add for a decade except reiterating his use of spiritual, not carnal weapons (cf. I Cor. 10:4). The crisis of the Commonwealth in 1659, and the need in 1660 to present evidence to the king and his Parliament that Friends planned no revolts, led to two new types of statements.

To Friends themselves Fox wrote "to take heed to keep out of the powers of the earth that runs into wars and fightings," arguing that those who fight, like persecutors, "have turned against the just and disobeyed the just in their own particulars" (i.e., hearts), so that "he who goes to help amongst them is [gone out] from the just in himself, in the mud and unstayed state."[39] Fox's most formal statement (Epistle No. 177) showed that Friends could pay taxes and keep the peace while refusing weapons. His fullest interpretation is printed here from SMS 7:47 (it has been placed at 1660 in Bicent [*Journal*, I, 448-50], but the original is undated, and the style suggests Fox's last years).

To the king and government Fox and other Friends made various statements, the most formal of which was presented personally by Margaret Fell to the king, April 22, 1660, and had been countersigned by Fox, Hubberthorne, Fisher, Stoddart, Caton, Roberts, John Stubbs, Ellis Hookes, and five others;[40] it explained all the Quaker "testimonies" that seemed antisocial. Another, printed for broadcast through the streets in January, 1661/62, was reprinted in 1684 and often since. It made the crucial point that, although Friends must obey the Spirit in each new moment, Christ's Spirit itself was consistent:

> That Spirit of Christ by which we are guided is not changeable, so as once to command us from a thing as evil, and again to move unto it; and we do certainly know and so testify to the world, that the Spirit of Christ,

38 *Journal* (1694), p. 46; manuscript source missing.

39 SMS 2:103; cf. *Journal* (Nickalls, p. 358). The original is in Fox's hand.

40 Cf. Margaret Fell, *A Brief Collection (Works)* (London, 1710), pp. 202-10.

which leads us into all Truth, will never move us to fight and war against any man with outward weapons.[41]

We include here in full a shorter letter in his own hand from Fox to the king, from the Haverford collection:[42]

George Fox to the King

We can speak the truth as it is in Jesus; and "God is our record and witness," and "verily, verily," which is as much as to say amen, amen, or truly, truly; and a testimony by the mouth of two or three witnesses every word is established according to Christ and the Apostle's doctrine, who commands us that we should not swear at all; which we cannot without going into sin and condemnation according to Christ's and the Apostle's doctrine, Matthew the fifth and James the fifth.

And the just law, we know, the higher power which God hath ordained, which was added because of transgressions: thrones for the punishment of evil doers which are for perjurious persons, menslayers, and injurious persons; which law is good in its place and a praise for them that do well; which was not made for the righteous. And therefore there must be a difference put between the precious and the vile.

And all plots, murders, and tumultuous meetings against the king or any of his subjects we do deny, who owns no meeting but what is peaceable and to worship God.

George Fox's Paper to Friends to Keep Out of Wars and Fights (SMS 7:47)

All friends everywhere, keep out of plots and bustlings and the arm of flesh; for all that is among Adam's sons in the fall, where they are destroying men's lives like dogs and beasts and swine, goring, rending and biting one another, and destroying one another, and wrestling with flesh and blood. From whence rises wars but from the lust and killing? And all this is in Adam in the fall out of Adam that never fell, in whom there is peace and life. And ye are called to peace, therefore follow it. And Christ is that Peace, and Adam is in the fall. For all that pretends to fight for Christ, they are deceived, for his kingdom is not of this world; therefore his servants doth not fight. Therefore fighters are not of Christ's kingdom, and are without Christ's

---

41 *Journal* (1694), p. 234.

42 Cf. Henry J. Cadbury, *Swarthmore Documents in America* (London, 1940), No. 17, p. 47.

kingdom, for his kingdom stands in peace and righteousness. And so fighters are in the lust, and all that would destroy men's lives are not of Christ's mind, who comes to save men's lives. Christ's kingdom is not of this world, it is peaceable; and all that be in strifes are not of his kingdom, and all such as pretends to fight for the Gospel (the Gospel is the power of God, before the devil or fall of man was), which are ignorant of the Gospel, and all that talk of fighting for Sion, are in darkness; for Sion needs no such helpers. And all such as profess themselves to be ministers of Christ and Christians, and go beat down the whore with outward carnal weapons, the flesh and the whore are got up in themselves in a blind zeal. That which beats down the whore, which got up by the inward ravening from the spirit of God, the beating down of the whore must be by the inward rising of the sword of the spirit within. All such as pretend Christ Jesus and confesseth him and runs into carnal weapons, wrestling with flesh and blood, throws away the spiritual; (they) that would be wrestlers with flesh and blood, they throw away Christ's doctrine, and flesh is got up in them, and they are weary of their sufferings; and such as would revenge themselves be out of Christ's doctrine; and such as would be stricken on the one cheek, and would not turn the other be out of Christ's doctrine, and such as do not love one another and love enemies be out of Christ's doctrine. And therefore you that be heirs of the blessings of God, which was before the curse and the fall was, come to inherit your portions. And you that be heirs with the Gospel of peace before the devil was, live in the Gospel of peace.

Let your conversation preach to all men and your innocent lives, that they which speak evil of you and beholding your Godly conversation may glorify your father which is in heaven. And all friends everywhere this I charge you, which is the word of the Lord God unto you all, live in peace, in Christ the way of peace, and in which seek the peace of all men and no man's hurt. And therefore live in the peaceable life, doing good to all men, and seeking the good and welfare of all men.

G. F.

Let this go among friends everywhere.

9. Edward Billing's *Mite of Affection* (1659): A Political Platform

Until 1659, Quaker appeals to rulers usually moved directly from asking for toleration (with attacks on the tithe-paid ministry) to demanding the personal submission of the ruler to the Spirit. Proclamation of impending divine judgment and rule on earth was often included. That approach reflected Friends' actual relationship to Oliver Cromwell: mutual respect, plus deadlock over the parish pastors and over Cromwell's refusal to become a Quaker. In 1659, Oliver was dead, his son Richard had been forced to resign, and two groups of radical Puritans, those under Lambert in the army and those under Haselrig and Vane in the "Rump" of the Long Parliament, were sparring for control and groping for policies. It is natural that the first Quakers to propose a careful platform of political policies did so as radical Puritans writing to radical Puritans.[43]

Edward Billing seems to have come from a family of Cornish gentry. He was probably the cousin of Loveday Billing Hambly, the "mother" of Cornish Quakerism, and of Philadelphia Billing Wortevale; he possibly attended Oxford; and he was certainly a Cornet (=2nd Lieut.) in Cromwell's garrison in Scotland when Fox convinced him there in 1657 and reconciled him to his estranged and extravagant (Scottish?) wife Lillias.[44] Billing may have been discharged by General Monk soon afterward, presumably for Quakerly disregard of ranks, titles, salutes, and military obedience. By the next year Billing was in London, one of the weighty Friends signing a document appealing for the release of Quakers then in prison.[45] During the next six years he wrote six other tracts besides the *Mite of Affection,* all to the Parliament, his "late fellow-souldiers," or his Quaker fellow-prisoners. He spent most of the winter of 1660-61 in Gatehouse Prison, was again under the Council of State's eye the next year, and in 1670 had all his goods distrained for Conventicle Act fines. He had become a brewer, and these fines, plus his wife's expensive tastes, drove him to bankruptcy.

At this point an ingenious scheme was cooked up to pay off his

[43] The year Billing wrote saw also Fox's own *To the Parliament . . . 59 Particulars*, and George Bishop's *Honest, Upright, Faithful and Plain Dealing*; in 1660 came Thomas Lawson's *Appeal to the Parliament concerning the Poor*, the only careful Quaker study of the Poor Law before Bellers. Bishop, too, had been a Puritan politician, and Lawson a Cambridge-educated Puritan.

[44] For data on Billing see two articles by L. Violet Holdsworth and John L. Nickalls, in Howard H. Brinton, ed., *Children of Light* (1938), pp. 85-133, where Violet Holdsworth speculates on the transfer of the aunt's name to Penn's city. The family name is variously spelled Byllynge, Byllings, Bylyng, etc., and Edwin Bronner suggests an original form of Boulanger from France; but it is clear that the contemporaries pronounced and often spelled it Billing. Several other Edward Billings appear in English records of those years.

[45] Cf. *ESP*, pp. 39-45.

debts, mainly to Quakers (though he had also to make formal apology so as to clear Friends of complicity in his bankruptcy). William Penn, Gawen Lawrie of London, and Nicholas Lucas of Hertford, as trustees for his affairs, were soon involved, and may have been from the start. The plan involved buying the then totally undeveloped territory of West Jersey (roughly southwest of a line from Delaware Water-gap to Little Egg Harbor) from Sir John Berkeley (Lord Stratton), whom both Billing and Penn knew well, and who had never developed the land grant given him by King Charles. Billing's thousand-pound payment to Berkeley was in fact put up by another Friend, John Fenwick, who later tried, in conflict with Penn's intentions and perhaps their agreement, to procure repayment, not in cash but in a one-tenth share of the Jersey land, on which he set up a sort of independent "Duchy of Grand Fenwick" at Salem. This later merged with the main West Jersey colony centered at Burlington. In any case Billing's trustees kept the land title, and by selling off farms and townships to Quaker emigrants paid off Billing's debts for the time being.[46]

Billing and Penn, however, had become emotionally involved in colonization. The end result was Pennsylvania, including Penn's famous *Frame of Government* for it. Friends had always believed that Christ's Spirit would rule the earth, not merely suffer there. But the change of outlook from their proclamation of judgment to the administration of new settlements was dramatic. Friends in England felt wary about Quakers emigrating to escape persecution (the Anglican government was in some ways more wholeheartedly pleased to see them go). In any case West Jersey in the 1670's, followed in the next decade by the Quaker projects in East Jersey and Pennsylvania, involved Friends both in selling and publicizing virgin lands, and more crucially in drawing up charters and constitutions to govern new communities. The key document here, which owes more to Billing than to Penn, was the "Concessions and Agreements of the Proprietors, Freeholders and Inhabitants of the Province of West-New-Jersey," drawn up in the summer of 1676 and signed by all the settlers the following March. For two decades it was disputed whether or not the king and Berkeley had intended to grant the right to set up a government; but Billing

---

[46] For West Jersey, see John E. Pomfret, *The Province of West New Jersey, 1609-1702* (Princeton, 1956); Hugh Barbour, "From the Lamb's War to the Quaker Magistrate" in *Quaker History*, Vol. LV, No. 1 (1966). Later, Barclay, Arent Sonnemans Lawrie and Rudyard became involved in the colony of East Jersey.

meant to create one. In the process, his brain-storming of 1659 was translated into one of the earliest written constitutions ever put into practice.

Billing's tract, like Penn in his own colony or Friends arguing for toleration, needed to begin from basic principles that others besides Friends could accept. This was a basic shift in the theocratic, "Lamb's War" perspective toward the state. Yet the way had been prepared by radical Puritans of the 1640's. The same mixture of appeals to Christ's authority, to nature and natural rights, to national interests, and to English liberties in Magna Carta and common law, which emerged in Penn's writings, also had appeared in the first Puritan justification of Parliament against the king in 1641 and in the writings of William Walwyn, John Lilburne, and the army radicals in 1647-53. In Penn's case the "Whig" flavor, liberal but cautious and "bourgeois," moved at times to outright paternalism (see below, p. 441). But the army radicals, speaking through their agents or "agitators" at the Putney debates of 1647 and in a series of tracts, had been so radical as to alarm Cromwell. It is usual to call these Puritan army radicals the Levellers, partly due to their plea for universal suffrage and their attacks on ministers' tithes and trade monopolies. It is necessary to distinguish the Levellers from the purely Bible- and God-centered "Fifth-Monarchy" theocrats like Feake and Harrison. These wanted Saints' Rule, not manhood suffrage. It was to these latter that early Friends like George Fox "the Younger" came closest. Yet Lilburne the Leveller and most of his followers were not only intensely religious; they found God's presence most keenly in their moments of martyrdom or of political vision. Lilburne, after despairing of political campaigning, ended as a Quaker himself. Thus we must assume that Billing and even Penn had been raised knowing ideas and tracts from the Levellers. Our notes on Billing's *Mite of Affection* will compare it not only with the West Jersey "Concessions and Agreements" but with the major Leveller tracts:[47] *The Case of the Armie* (1647); "The Earnest Petition of many Freeborn People," surviving in *A Declaration of Some Proceedings of Lt. Col. John Lilburne* (Feb., 1647/48); *A Humble Petition* (Sept., 1648); and *The Agreement of the Free People* from March, 1649, after Charles I's execution. Billing's tract appeared in

---

[47] See Godfrey Davis and William Haller, eds., *The Leveller Tracts, 1647-1653* (New York: Columbia Univ. Press, 1944).

print late in 1659 (Thomason picked up his copy Oct. 28), just as the Council of State, led by the army "Grandees," was once more driving the "Rump Parliament" from power. Billing thus avoids discussing some key issues: the ultimacy of Parliamentary power and details of suffrage, quorum rules, etc., to which he returned in the Jersey constitution. Other issues crucial to the earlier Levellers (such as Land Tax rather than Excise) could be minimized in 1659. At times Billing's tract seems outrageously partisan; the authority of the Spirit speaking through the Quaker preacher of judgment is in the end left supreme. Billing's tract would probably have had little influence even had Parliament still sat to pass such laws. In fact, of course, George Monk's army marched south from Scotland two months later (Jan. 1, 1660/61) to restore the king (cf. George Fox the "Younger," p. 388). Only in Jersey could these ideals still apply.

A MITE OF AFFECTION
Manifested in 31. Proposals
Offered to all the Sober and Free-born People
within this Common-wealth

Tending and tendered unto them for a
Settlement in this the day and hour
of the World's Distraction
and Confusion

Yet a little while, and the light is with ye; but the Night
cometh shortly, wherein no man can work.

London
Printed for Giles Calvert, at the Black-Spread-Eagle at the
West end of Pauls, 1659.

1. First, that the magistrate have no coercive power whatsoever, in matters of religion, faith, or worship; but that all persons within the dominions of this commonwealth, professing faith in Christ Jesus, shall have full and free liberty of the exercise of his or their consciences, in matters of faith towards God, to all intents without any restriction whatsoever, though of different persuasions as aforesaid; and that none be secluded from peaceably inhabiting within the dominions of this Commonwealth, who believe in the eternal and ever-living God. And that no person shall upon any pretence whatsoever be

imprisoned or undergo any manner of punishment for the exercise of their conscience toward God. And that all such as are so imprisoned be forthwith released, and freely set at liberty; And that no person or persons whatsoever, within this commonwealth, be forced or constrained by any law made, or to be made, by any power, pretence or pretences whatsoever, to uphold, or pay towards the maintenance of any minister, public or private preacher, in any kind whatsoever; but that everyone be left to his own liberty therein, to do as seemeth him good, and not to be forced to pay to any person whom he neither hires, hears, nor sets at work; knowing this to be equal in the sight of God and just men.[48]

2. Secondly, that none be compelled to swear, or take an oath against their conscience, it being contrary to the express command of Christ, who saith, swear not at all. But that the same punishment be inflicted on him that shall speak falsely,[49] cozen, cheat or bear false witness in any case whatsoever, as if he swore falsely; proportioning his punishment that shall do so, as he thought to have punished the other by his false testimony and witness; which is equal, the law being for the lawless and disobedient.

3. That no person or persons within the dominions of this Commonwealth (who are not subservient to a foreign state) nor have forfeited their liberty by delinquency, or having a hand in any of the late plots or rebellions against the Commonwealth, be secluded from any public trust or place of trust, either in Parliament, Council, Army, or other judicatures, or place of trust whatsoever within the dominions of this Commonwealth.[50]

4. Fourthly, that no person or persons whatsoever, who have persecuted any for their conscience, or committed any to prison for their conscience, shall be capable of electing or being elected into any place of trust within the dominions of this commonwealth, till a further manifestation be given of his

---

[48] This cluster of issues—toleration, tithes, and parish ministry—was most intensely debated throughout the Commonwealth, and notably by the "Parliament of Saints" of 1653, not only by Friends. See *Case of the Army* (hereafter *CA*), p. 19; *Declaration of Proceedings (DP)*, p. 32; *Humble Petition (HP)*, points No. 4, No. 16, No. 25, etc.; *Agreement of the People (AP)*, points No. XX, No. XXIII, and No. XXIV. See also West Jersey "Concessions and Agreements" (WJ), section No. XVI, and the "Great Law" of Pennsylvania.

[49] Oaths already bothered the Levellers (*CA*, p. 19) and were specifically not required in West Jersey (No. XX) and the Pennsylvania Fundamental Laws. In England itself the issue sent many Friends to prison until the Affirmation Acts of 1696 and 1722 provided alternatives, first for some Friends, and finally even for the "dissatisfied." Cf. BSP, ch. VII.

[50] Universal suffrage is implied here, and explicitly claimed in *DP*, p. 32; and the provision for forty acres of land for every freeman settling in West Jersey (WJ, No. III) guaranteed the same there.

or their good affection towards the people of God and equal and just liberty of every individual person, though of different persuasions, within the dominions of this Commonwealth.[51]

5. Fifthly, that no person or persons whatsoever be tried for life, limb, liberty or estate, but by a jury of twelve men of the neighborhood, or others who shall well know each other, reserving the right of just exception against any judge, juryman or witness, if any justly can be made; and that no person or persons whatsoever, now residing or happening to be within the dominions of this commonwealth, shall be condemned to death, or adjudged to pay any mulct, fine, or undergo any penalty or corporal punishment, or suffer any prejudice whatsoever, but by known and lawful witnesses, being produced face to face, or by witnesses as aforesaid; the which is according to the declaration of the holy men of God recorded in the Scripture of Truth.[52]

6. Sixthly, that all servile tenures or copyholds within this commonwealth, being the badge or yoke of the conquest, be thoroughly considered, and made consistent with the wellbeing of a firm commonwealth, due regard being had to every man's just propriety.[53]

7. Seventhly, that no person whatsoever within this commonwealth, nor the dominions thereof, be put to death for theft, but be forced to labor with their own hands, till such time that he or she so offending the just law of God and man hath restored to the party wronged two-, three-, or fourfold or otherwise fold for their theft, till satisfaction be made to the person wronged as aforesaid. But he that spills man's blood, by man let his blood be spilt.[54]

8. That the whole law and all proceedings in law whatsoever within this commonwealth be forthwith removed into each county, wapentake, hundred or town (commonly called parishes); and that all unrighteous patents given forth by the late kings, and others who have called themselves rulers of this Commonwealth, be forthwith called in, repealed, and made void. And that there be one and the same just laws holding, and tenure made, and given forth to all the people residing within this Commonwealth. And to the end that they may be truly known to every individual person, let the law be printed, that every one may know that law which he is to be subject to, to the intent

[51] This unique proposal nevertheless has parallels in WJ, No. 14 and No. 33.

[52] Jury trial and confrontation with accusing witnesses were asked, together or separately, by *HP*, No. 7, *AP*, No. XXV, and other Leveller tracts, and enacted in WJ, No. XVII.

[53] Copyhold or customary feudal tenure seemed oppressive to yeomen; yet in fact it often protected their rights better than a rent system with no controls. *CA*, p. 19, makes the same plea, arguing like Justice Coke that the Normans in conquering England in 1066 had removed older English liberties.

[54] The ban on death penalties for theft was enacted in WJ, No. XXVIII.

that no man may be condemned by a law he neither knows, nor ever heard of, nor understands; neither indeed can he, when as it lies in the breast of other men. And further, that so much of that law may be read to every person (called or summoned before any judicature), as concerns the person or persons so summoned, as aforesaid.

9. That Courts of Record be firmly settled in each county within this commonwealth, with honest judges, empowered finally to hear and determine of all causes that shall arise within each county respectively within this commonwealth, it being for the benefit and good of the faithful denizens within this Commonwealth.[55]

And likewise, that all manners of bonds, bills, obligations, leases, deeds, bequeathments, assignments, deeds of gift, donations, wills and testaments, contracts, bargains, and sales of lands, tenements, seizing and seizures, mortgages, pledges, pawns, or other dispositions and transactions whatsoever, from five pounds downwards to five shillings, if the party or parties borrowing and lending, contracting, leasing and selling, or any otherwise bargaining, as is aforesaid, or can be said, shall desire the same, to twenty thousand pounds and upwards, without limitation,[56] be recorded in each county; that is to say, in the Court be erected: and is hereby declared fit to be erected; to wit, one in the shire town of each county, hundred, riding, wapentake. And also that two persons be appointed, to be forthwith in each parish throughout the Commonwealth, freely chosen of the same inhabitants, to take, receive and keep for the present, and at the present making of any bargain, entering into articles, contract, or other dispositions whatsoever; or anything for the firm holding inviolably of all things relating to *mine* and *thine*, (made, and to be made) and forthwith (that is to say, within forty-eight hours); to have and see the same recorded in the county, hundred, riding, or wapentake Court, as aforesaid. . . . [Deeds to be recorded within 48 hours and to be binding meanwhile.]

And that any party or parties whatsoever, that shall buy, lend, sell, convey, pawn, pledge, mortgage, or otherwise dispose, contract, give, bequeath, or appoint to be given or disposed of, or exchange house for house, land for land, or any otherwise contract or transact for any thing or things relating to this world and the well-being of mankind, and durable beyond all peradventure, and without contradiction, continuing, and possessing or disposing of

[55] Next to the church, reforms of law most preoccupied the "Levellers" and "Parliament of Saints." Cf. *AP*, pp. 15, 18, 19. The issue of patents, i.e., monopolies, whether by Charles I or by Cromwell, also aroused intense feelings against both special courts in London, and against exclusive rights in trade.

[56] Billing here shows himself the businessman, as also in enacting WJ, No. XXIV.

the same: if the parties on both sides shall desire it, be delivered, received and recorded as aforesaid; that so every person or persons may be secured and defended in any and every outward thing, except by his or their own and wilful neglect. For the binding laws are for the lawless, but the good man's word is as binding to him as the law; and those that shall take each other's word in any of the matters relating to this world have free liberty so to do. But a provision shall be made to preserve and secure every individual person within this Commonwealth from being by cunning and deceitful men ensnared, oppressed, defrauded, cozened, or cheated in any case whatsoever, as aforesaid.

10. Tenthly, that every person within this commonwealth have full and free liberty if he please to plead his own cause in any Court, in any matter of difference whatsoever that shall or may happen to be between party or parties within the dominions of this commonwealth.[57]

11. Eleventh, that in cases of any differences whatsoever arising between party and parties within this commonwealth: The first appeal and trial of the same be in the same parish where the trespass is done and controversy happeneth to arise,[58] and that the manner of this first trial be by a jury of twelve honest men of the same parish, without respect of persons or esteem of any man's outward quality. And that one of those persons who are elected by the parishioners to receive and record writings in the hundred and wapentake Courts, as is said in the ninth Article, be by a lot drawn (as is hereafter expressed) and enabled to give judgement in any difference arising in the said parish, (life and limb, and other personal liberties excepted, which are to be referred to the County Court only). And if the persons so adjudged shall any or either of them dislike of the judgement given or verdict of the twelve men or two thirds of them without which judgement shall not be given, I say if any dislike be then and in that case, he, she, either or any of them shall have free liberty to appeal to the wappentake, riding or hundred Court where all the justices within the said hundred or wappentake are to be four times in the year, where and at which place and time the party or parties grieved may appeal the second time and there be reheard, and the matter or matters fully and absolutely determined by those Justices of the Peace. Always provided that the verdict of the jury and judgement of the first judge thereupon be by the plaintiff or his appointment fairly written and to the

---

[57] Freedom to plead without a lawyer, in view of high legal fees and Quakers' familiarity with laws, was often a sharper issue for Friends than for Levellers. . . . Cf. WJ, No. XXII.

[58] The localization of jury trials, especially for civil cases, was a standing dream of radical Puritans, who knew how often only rich landowners could afford to carry cases to the London courts; cf. CA, p. 19; also WJ, No. XXII.

justices aforesaid presented; and that, after the whole matter shall be by all parties concerned fully related, and by the justices (being all together) sufficiently debated, each having heard another's judgement herein and thereof. Then lots be given by an unconcerned person to all the aforesaid justices, in one of which lots shall be written these words, (*viz.*) *thou at this time and in this case art to give final judgement.* And if the plaintiff or plaintiffs, any or either of them shall be found in the fault, then the judge to whom the lot is given shall award him or them to pay all the defendent or defendents' charges [or other damages in case of false judgment].

12. Twelfth, that all the justices within the whole county meet twice in the year at the county town, and there to sit upon, and try, acquit, dismember or put to death all who shall be guilty of and deserve the same, and make an absolute jail delivery.[59]

The manner of which shall be (to wit) after witnesses, jury and the prisoner being fully heard and by all the justices orderly debated, then lots be drawn or given to all the said justices in three of which lots shall be written these words (to wit). You, or any two, or all three of you, shall give final judgement concerning the prisoner now before you and in your sight, and remember ye judge not for man only, but for God the father of mercy, judgement, and justice.

13. Thirteenth, that all felons, that is to say, murderers and the like, be committed to the county gaol, and no other (unless upon necessity), but however that no trial be proceeded unto till such time he or they be translated, carried, or transported to the county gaol.[60]

14. Fourteenth, that there be an equal uniting of the places commonly called parishes, towns and villages, and that ten parishes so equally united, consisting of a hundred families or upwards, make a Hundred,[61] and that the people within each such Hundred may every year elect and freely choose one

---

[59] The key issue here was prompt trial in major cases. Cf. *AP*, No. XVII; WJ, No. XIX.

[60] Friends had too often been thrown in with felons in town and local jails. County jails could provide separate rooms for different types of offenders.

[61] This proposal links to No. 27, and proposes a sort of Constitutional Convention such as the nominated "Parliament of Saints" was meant to be. The grouping of ten parishes into each Hundred (an old Saxon name, as was Wapentake, for an area smaller than a county) was meant to ensure proportional representation (see WJ, No. XXXII). The inequality of Parliamentary voting districts nevertheless increased until the "rotten boroughs" of the eighteenth century were often "pocket buroughs" of single landowners. The fantastic proposal to fine persecutors who ran for office and all who voted for them was never enacted.

or two persons to be their representative or representatives in Parliament, there to branch forth the proposals now proposed and to make other good laws and statutes, as need from time to time shall require; but still let it be remembered that no persecutor of any for conscience's sake do elect or be elected for the first election, who shall sit but twelve months and be dissolved. I say let such who have persecuted ignorantly or through zeal or maliciously willingly submit and see what those who have not persecuted any for conscience will bring forth.

And that every person that shall suffer himself to be elected, and stand to be elected, and accept of the same, being not within the qualifications mentioned in the 3rd and 4th Article, and thereupon shall presume to enter in and sit within the walls of the house of Parliament, shall forfeit to the Commonwealth a considerable sum of money and shall be forthwith secured till such time he make payment of the same, and that the person and persons who shall give his or their voice for electing any such person who is not qualified as is expressed in the article aforesaid shall also forfeit, pay or be secured, till he or they so offending, five pounds.

15. Fifteenth, that any officer, either military or civil, or other public minister of state whatsoever, being employed in or by, from or under this commonwealth or any the dominions thereof, that shall be found to cozen, cheat or defraud this nation or nations thereunto belonging, shall be compelled to restore fourfold; and forthwith be dismissed of his employment as a robber of his country and forever made incapable of bearing any manner of office or place of trust within the dominions of this commonwealth.[62]

16. That any person whatsoever that shall be put to death for any matter or cause whatsoever shall not forfeit to the commonwealth, or any other person or persons whatsoever residing within the same, one penny of his estate real or personal; but it shall go to his or their relations, as if no fault had been committed.

17. That the unrighteous prison commonly called the King's or upper Bench, and all other illegal prisons be forthwith made void; and that all men who have estates may so far as their estates will reach forthwith be forced to pay their just debts, and that such who have or will satisfy their creditors so far as they are able be forthwith set at liberty.

18. That all unrighteous, cruel and exacting jailers, notwithstanding they have a patent for the same, they may have satisfaction for any such patent and forthwith be removed, and others put into their places, fearing God and hating covetousness. And that henceforth no patent may be sold, settled, or given to any person or persons whatsoever for term of life, but upon his or

---

[62] Cf. *DP*, p. 30; this law, too, presupposes a police power like Cromwell's to enforce it.

their good behaviour.[63] And that all gaols, bridewells, and other houses of correction, or prisons, or places of restraint whatsoever within the dominions of this Commonwealth may be repaired, made strong, warm and decent, that so all dungeons, vaults, little-eases or other nasty holes within the said prisons respectively, may be filled up or at least never more to be used to the abusing the creature, the handy-work of God, the creator; that so all persons whatsoever may have decent prisons and all other necessaries fit for man or woman though he or she be to die for the fault for which they are imprisoned.

19. That there be wholesome provision made that so there be no man, woman nor child suffered to beg or want within the dominions of this Commonwealth. But let such men, women, and children that are able to work be forced so to do, and that such as through age or nonage are not able may be christianlike provided for.[64]

20. That all images and places of idolatry and things which are without and are visibly seen of men, belonging to the Commonwealth, which are the nourishment and upholding of popery and popish orders, be forthwith removed and abolished.[65]

21. That all card and dice makers, gaming houses, music houses, dice and card-players whatsoever, and all and every profane pastime and heathenish customs be forthwith forbidden by a law throughout the dominions of this Commonwealth, and that a sufficient penalty be laid upon the offenders and breakers of the said law.[66]

22. That no person within this Commonwealth who hath served an apprenticeship or by his own industry hath attained to knowledge and hath wherewith to set or put himself in a capacity to provide for himself and family may be prohibited from so endeavouring within any the dominions of this Commonwealth, notwithstanding any pretended charter or charters whatsoever.[67]

[63] Friends were experienced regarding jailors and jails, and pioneers in their reform; cf. WJ, No. XXII. The nearest Leveller equivalent is *DP*, p. 30, on court fees.

[64] As the Elizabethan Poor Law, based on local parishes, broke down, many Puritans tried to restore it, as did even Charles I. Cf. *HP*, No. 13, Thomas Lawson's tract, and the writings of Peter Cornelius, preparing the way for Bellers.

[65] Who but a Friend or a Fifth Monarchist would hope for such a law?

[66] This catalogue of the vices all Puritans hated underlay their attacks on Charles I's *Book of Sports*, but under Cromwell they were too busy to legislate about them.

[67] Monopolies, whether by individuals or guilds and "Companies," were hated by other merchants. See *CA*, pp. 15, 18; *DP*, p. 31; *HP*, No. 10; *AP*, No. XVIII.

23. That all weights, sizes and measures whatsoever be made equal, of one length, breadth, depth, circumference, weight and bigness, within the dominions of this Commonwealth.[68]

24. That the estates that are or shall be at any time forfeited to this commonwealth be sequestered and the revenue thereof brought into a public treasury for the speedy relief of the widows of soldiers, maimed soldiers, fatherless and friendless children of such who have adhered to and served this Commonwealth, or otherwise suffered in the late wars; and that the overplus, if any be, may go towards the payment of the debts of the public, and that all the debts and loans whatsoever for which any person hath the public engagement of the nation or any obligation consonant thereunto be forthwith satisfied.[69]

25. That, in order to the defraying of the public charge of the commonwealth, all persons be equally assessed proportionably according to their estates real and personal, always provided that any person or persons within this commonwealth who shall pay his or their tax towards the defraying of the public charge shall not be secluded according to their several abilities and capacities from having interest, command or employment, and to be a member, officer, superior or inferior in and of the Army, Navy, Parliament, Council or other place of public trust whatsoever within the dominions of this commonwealth, notwithstanding he or they be of different persuasions or differently denoted as to their religion, provided they be such who have not persecuted any for their conscience, nor forfeited their right by plots, rebellion or otherwise against this commonwealth.[70]

26. That any person or persons who have been by the late single person,[71] for his or their consciences, and without the breach of any just law ejected or unrighteously secluded from any place of trust, military or civil whatsoever, within the dominions of this Commonwealth be (at least) forthwith restored to his or their places respectively.

27. That the government of this Commonwealth and the dominions thereof be by annual Parliaments. And until such time that the wappentakes and hundreds can be settled and equally divided, in the meantime, let each persuasion or sect forthwith choose out from among themselves 20 or 30 persons, respect being had to the qualifications expressed in the 3. and 4.

---

[68] The Levellers ignored this issue, but Friends were concerned for cheating in daily markets.

[69] Here Billing speaks as the ex-soldier. This is the dominant complaint in *CA* (1, 16, 19).

[70] Here the Levellers' hatred of excise taxes motivated Billing's alternative.

[71] The "single person" was Oliver Cromwell. Billing hereby aligns himself with the "republican" "Rump Parliament" against the army "Grandees."

Article, to meet and confer together in order to an election of representatives to sit in Parliament.[72] And that all who shall so be elected may pass the examination and trial of the persons before appointed, and that the persons of the diverse persuasions before mentioned do not sit and continue above three months, that so there may be a speedy and effectual settlement of this Commonwealth in these high and scarcely to be paralleled overturnings and distractions.

28. That any person residing within this commonwealth (to wit) within England, Ireland and Scotland, have free leave to port, transport, transmit or any otherwise to exchange, traffic and trade betwixt port and port, haven and haven, or any other usual landing place whatsoever, backward and forward, within any or either of the three nations, as to him or them shall meet, without paying for any such goods whatsoever so transported backward or forward as foreign, and let the three nations in this matter be equally alike, that so the long talked on Commonwealth may no longer continue to be a particular wealth. And that the three nations be justly united, that God the Father of mercy and justice (whose righteous soul is grieved with oppression) may take delight to dwell in the midst of us.

29. That the first Parliament agree upon such fundamental laws for the durable settlement of this commonwealth, that it shall be exclusion for any person that shall be afterwards elected and sit as a member of Parliament to move the alteration of the same; wherefore let the first qualifications be good, that none hereafter but good men may be admitted.[73]

30. That no person whatsoever hold or possess any manner of civil employment belonging to the public longer than one year, without being elected or appointed anew and giving a complete account for his last year's trust to such as shall by the people's representatives in Parliament be appointed to examine and receive the same, that so every man may taste of subjection as well as rule, and that any person in public trust who shall be found in any ways to defraud the commonwealth shall be forthwith dismissed of his employment as a public thief and likewise be forced to restore fourfold, and forever made incapable of being admitted into any public place of trust either military or civil whatsoever.[74]

[72] Annual Parliaments, though first demanded for protection against the Monarchy, became by 1659 also a slogan of men hoping to curb Parliament. Cf. *HP*, No. 2 (for biennial sessions); *AP*, No. VIII (annual Parliaments, a watchword of later Levellers).

[73] Billing wrote this into WJ, No. XIII. Penn, too, tried to build in a clause forbidding altering the Pennsylvania Fundamental Laws, but with less severe penalties.

[74] Cf. WJ, No. XXXII. Levellers had some equivalent suggestions, especially as to the army.

31. That any person who shall commit any sin by trespassing or otherwise doing violence to any, and call that his or their liberty or conscience shall be punished as an evildoer; always provided (and it is hereby intended) that no man or woman be ensnared in anything, which the just law of God written in the heart shall lead unto, but have free liberty to speak for or declare the truth according to the example of blessed Jesus and the holy men, in season and out of season, in any place, time or season whatsoever; and that none be hereby ensnared about anything which is false worship and false worshippers, their set days, times and places whatsoever.[75] And let him that keeps a day keep it to the Lord, but let none be forced to observe the precepts or traditions of men as to their set days, times, places and worships for which Christ nor his apostles have left no example, and he who worships the living God must do it in spirit and truth, and not by outward observations, neither is the holy One tied to any place, time or season whatsoever; and that people who in their vain imaginations think to limit or circumscribe the holy One to or from any place, time or season whatsoever fool themselves. For if the disciples be there, he will come in though the doors be shut (or secured by an outward law), and they gladly receive as also those who are not offended at him, though his visage be more marred than any man's, and his shape uncomely to the vulturous eye.

Postscript

And this we recommend to all the sober and free-born people of this commonwealth, as a testimony we bear to our country, and unto every individual person in it, this being an essay towards its speedy, firm and future settlement on such a basis as may fully answer the just and righteous principle of God in every man's conscience, unto which we leave it, and as it leads any to add to the furtherance of this (good intended) work, it will be acceptable to us, and unto all the upright hearted on the earth.

Wherefore let not this slip out of any of your minds as a tale that's told, but let every one mind the good work of his generation. And do not join with Moab, Amon, and Amalek, lest ye perish in this the day of the Lord.

THE END

[75] Once again Billing speaks purely as a Quaker.

10. "The Concessions and Agreements of West New Jersey" (MS: 1676)

The original copy of the "Concessions and Agreements" of West Jersey is treasured by the Council of Proprietors of West New Jersey (still surviving as a hereditary corporation) at Burlington, New Jersey. The only printed editions seem to be the Council's own pamphlet and that in W. A. Whitehead, et al., eds., *New Jersey Archives,* 1st Series (1880), I, 241ff. It is a remarkable document in foreshadowing Penn's policy toward Indians. But by 1674 Quakers had come to know Indians well in all the American colonies. See below, p. 495. Sections I-XII concern land settlement.

THE CHARTER OR FUNDAMENTAL LAWS, OF WEST-JERSEY AGREED UPON

Chapter XIII.

That the following Concessions are the Common Law, or Fundamental Rights, of the Province of West New-Jersey.

That the Common Law or Fundamental Rights and Privileges of West New-Jersey, are individually agreed upon by the Proprietors and Freeholders thereof, to be the Foundation of the Government, which is not to be altered by the legislative authority, or free assembly hereafter mentioned and constituted, but that the said legislative authority is constituted according to these Fundamentals, to make such laws as agree with, and maintain the said fundamentals, and to make no laws that in the least contradict, differ or vary from the said Fundamentals, under what pretence or allegation soever.

Chapter XIV.

But if it so happen that any person or persons of the said free assembly, shall therein designedly, willfully, and maliciously, move or excite any to move, any matter or any fundamentals of the said laws in the Constitution of the government of this Province, it being proved by seven honest and reputable persons, he or they shall be proceeded against as traitors to the said government.

Chapter XV.

That these Concessions, Law or Great Charter of Fundamentals, be recorded in every common Hall of Justice within this Province. . . .

Chapter XVI.

That no men, nor number of men upon earth, hath power or authority to rule over men's consciences in religious matters, therefore it is consented, agreed and ordained, that no person or persons whatsoever, called in question, or in the least punished or hurt, either in person, estate or privilege, for the sake of his opinion, judgment, faith or worship towards God in matters of religion. But that all and every such person, and persons, may from time to time, and at all times, freely and fully have, and enjoy his and their judgments, and the exercise of their consciences in matters of religious worship throughout all the said Province.

Chapter XVII.

That no proprietor, freeholder or inhabitant of the said Province of West New-Jersey, shall be deprived or condemned of life, limb, liberty, estate, property or any ways hurt in his or their privileges, freedoms or franchises, upon any account whatsoever, without a due trial, and judgment passed by twelve good and lawful men of his neighbourhood first had: And that in all causes to be tried, and in all trials, the person or persons arraigned may except against any of the said neighbourhood, without any reason rendered, (not exceeding thirty-five) and in case of any valid reason alleged, against every person nominated for that service.

Chapter XVIII.

And that no proprietor, freeholder, freedenison, or inhabitant in the said Province, shall be attached, arrested, or imprisoned, for or by reason of any debt, duty or other thing whatsoever (cases felonious, criminal and treasonable excepted) before he or she have personal summon, or summons, left at his or her last dwelling place, if in the said Province, by some legal authorized officer, constituted and appointed for that purpose, to appear in some Court of Judicature for the said Province, with a full and plain account of the cause or thing in demand. . . . And if he or they shall be condemned by legal trial and judgment, the penalty or penalties shall be paid and satisfied out of his or their real or personal estate so condemned, or cause the person or persons so condemned, to lie in execution till satisfaction of the debt and damages be made. Provided always, if such person or persons so condemned, shall pay and deliver such estate, goods, and chattels which he or any other person hath for his or their use, and shall solemnly declare and aver, that he or they have not any further estate, goods or chattels wheresoever, to satisfy the person or persons, (at whose suit, he or they are condemned) their respective judgments, and shall also bring and produce three other persons which shall in

423

such open Court, likewise solemnly declare and aver, that they believe in their consciences, such person and persons so condemned, have not wherewith further to pay the said condemnation or condemnations, he or they shall be thence forthwith discharged from their said imprisonment.

Chapter XIX.

That there shall be in every Court, three Justices or Commissioners, who shall sit with the twelve men of the neighbourhood, with them to hear all causes, and to assist the said twelve men of the neighbourhood in case of law; and that they the said Justices shall pronounce such judgment as they shall receive from, and be directed by the said twelve men, in whom only the judgment resides, and not otherwise. . . .

Chapter XX.

That in all matters and causes, civil and criminal, proof is to be made by the solemn and plain averment of at least two honest and reputable persons; and in case that any person or persons shall bear false witness, and bring in his or their evidence, contrary to the truth of the matter as shall be made plainly to appear, that then every such person or persons, shall in civil causes, suffer the penalty which would be due to the person or persons he or they bear witness against. And any person . . . in a criminal cause, shall be found to have borne false witness for fear, gain, malice or favour, . . . such person or persons, shall be first severely fined, and next that he or they shall forever be disabled from being admitted in evidence, or into any public office, employment, or service within this Province.

Chapter XXI.

That all and every person and persons whatsoever, who shall prosecute or prefer any indictment or information against others for any personal injuries, or matter criminal, or shall prosecute for any other criminal cause, (treason, murder, and felony only excepted) shall and may be master of his own process, and have full power to forgive and remit the person or persons offending against him or herself only, as well before as after judgment, and condemnation, and pardon and remit the sentence, fine and punishment of the person or persons offending, be it personal or other whatsoever.

Chapter XXII.

That the trials of all causes, civil and criminal, shall be heard and decided by the verdict or judgment of twelve honest men of the neighbourhood, only to be summoned and presented by the sheriff of that division, or propriety where the fact or trespass is committed; and that no person or persons shall be compelled to fee any attorney or councillor to plead his cause, but that all persons have free liberty to plead his own cause, if he please: And that no person nor persons imprisoned upon any account whatsoever within this Province, shall be obliged to pay any fees to the officer or officers of the said prison, either when committed or discharged.

Chapter XXIII.

That in all public Courts of Justice for trials of causes, civil or criminal, any person or persons, inhabitants of the said Province, may freely come into, and attend the said Courts, and hear and be present, at all or any such trials as shall be there had or passed, that Justice may not be done in a corner nor in any covert manner, being intended and resolved, by the help of the Lord, and by these our Concessions and Fundamentals, that all and every person and persons inhabiting the said Province, shall, as far as in us lies, be free from oppression and slavery.

Chapter XXIV.

[Registers of deeds, leaves, land-grants, etc. to be kept both in London and in West Jersey]

Chapter XXV.

That there may be a good understanding and friendly correspondence between the proprietors, freeholders, and inhabitants of the said Province, and the Indian natives thereof.

It is concluded and agreed, that if any of the Indian natives within the said Province, shall or may do any wrong or injury to any of the proprietors, freeholders, or inhabitants, in person, estate or otherways howsoever, upon notice thereof, or complaint made to the commissioners, or any two of them, they are to give notice to the sachem, or other chief person or persons, that hath authority over the said Indian native or natives, that justice may be done, and satisfaction made to the person or persons offended, according to law and equity, and the nature and quality of the offence and injury done or committed.

And also in case any of the proprietors, freeholders, or inhabitants shall any wise wrong, or injure any of the Indian natives there, in person, estate or otherwise, the commissioners are to take care upon complaint to them made, or any one of them, either by the Indian natives or others, that justice be done to the Indian natives, and plenary satisfaction made them according to the nature and quality of the offence and injury. And that in all trials wherein

425

any of the said Indian natives are concerned, the trial to be by six of the neighbourhood, and six of the said Indian natives.

Chapter XXVI.

It is agreed when any lands is to be taken up for settlements of towns, or otherways, before it be surveyed, the commissioners are to appoint some persons to go to the chief of the natives concerned to acquaint the natives of their intention, and to give the natives what present they shall agree up-on. . . .

Chapter XXVII.

[Men leaving the Province must post their names 3 weeks before (for creditors?).]

Chapter XXVIII.

That men may peaceably and quietly enjoy their estates:

It is agreed if any person or persons shall steal, rob, or take any goods or chattels from or belonging to any person or persons whatsoever, he is to make restitution two fold out of his or their estate. . . .

If any person or persons, shall willfully beat, hurt, wound, assault, or otherways abuse the person or persons of any man, woman, or child, they are to be punished according to the nature of the offence, which is to be determined by twelve men of the neighbourhood, appointed by the commissioners.

Chapter XXIX.

For securing estates of persons that die, and taking care of orphans. . . .

Chapter XXX.

In case when any person or persons kill or destroy themselves, or be killed by any other thing. . . .

The estate of such person or persons, is not to be forfeited. . . .

Chapter XXXI.

All such person or persons as shall be upon trial found guilty of murder, or treason, the sentence and way of execution thereof, is left to the General Assembly to determine as they in the wisdom of the Lord shall judge meet and expedient.

426

The General Assembly and their Power

Chapter XXXII.

That so soon as divisions or tribes, or other such like distinctions are made; that then the inhabitants, freeholders, and proprietors, resident upon the said Province, . . . do yearly and every year meet on the first day of October, or the eighth month, and choose one proprietor or freeholder for each respective propriety in the said Province, (the said Province being to be divided into one hundred proprieties) to be deputies: . . . which body of deputies, trustees or representatives, consisting of one hundred persons chosen as aforesaid, shall be the general, free and supreme assembly of the said Province for the year ensuing and no longer. . . .

Chapter XXXIII.

And to the end the respective members of the yearly assembly to be chosen may be regularly and impartially elected.

That no person or persons who shall give, bestow or promise directly or indirectly to the said parties electing, any meat, drink, money or money's worth, for procurement of their choice and consent, shall be capable of being elected a member of the said assembly, . . . or execute any other public office of trust within the said Province, for the space of seven years thence next ensuing. And also that all such elections as aforesaid, be not determined by the common and confused way of cries and voices, but by putting balls into balloting boxes. . . .

Chapter XXXIV.

To appoint their own times of meeting, and to adjourn their sessions from time to time, . . . shall be the full power of the General Assembly; and that the votes of two thirds of the said Quorum, shall be determinative in all cases whatsoever coming in question before them, consonant and conformable to these Concessions and Fundamentals.

Chapter XXXV.

That the persons chosen, do by indenture under hand and seal, covenant and oblige themselves to act nothing in that capacity but what shall tend to the fit service and behoof of those that send and employ them. . . .

Chapter XXXVI.

That in every General free Assembly, every respective member hath liberty of speech. . . . And that if any member of such Assembly shall require to have

427

the persons' names registered, according to their yea's and no's, that it be accordingly done. . . .

Chapter XXXVII.

And that the said Assembly do elect, constitute and appoint ten honest and able men, to be commissioners of state, for managing and carrying on the affairs of the said Province, according to the law therein established, during the adjournments and desolutions of the said General free Assembly, for the conservation and tranquility of the same.

Chapter XXXVIII.

That it shall be lawful for any person or persons during the session of any General free Assembly in that Province, to address, remonstrate or declare any suffering, danger or grievance, or to propose, tender or request any privilege, profit, or advantage to the said Province, they not exceeding the number of one hundred persons.

Chapter XXXIX.

To enact and make all such laws, acts and constitutions as shall be necessary for the well government of the said Province, (and them to repeal) provided that the same be, as near as may be conveniently, agreeable to the primitive, antient and Fundamental Laws of the nation of England. Provided also, that they be not against any of these our Concessions and Fundamentals before or hereafter mentioned.

Chapter XL.

By act as aforesaid, to constitute all courts, together with the limits, powers, and jurisdictions of the same (consonant to these Concessions) as also the several judges, . . . not exceeding one year or two at the most, with their respective salaries, fees and perquisites. . . . And that no person or persons whatsoever, inhabitants of the said Province, shall sustain or bear two offices in the said Province, at one and at the same time.

Chapter XLI.

That all the justices and constables be chosen by the people and all commissioners of the public seals, treasuries, and Chief Justices, Ambassadors, and collectors be chosen by the General Free Assembly.

428

Chapter XLII.

That the commissioners of the treasury of the said Province, bring in their account at the end of their year, unto the General Free Assembly. . . .

Chapter XLIII.

By act as aforesaid, to lay equal taxes and assessments, and equally to raise money or goods, upon all lands or persons, within the several proprieties, precincts, hundreds, tribes, or whatsoever other divisions shall hereafter be made and established in the said Province. . . .

Chapter XLIV.

By act as aforesaid, to subdivide the said Province into hundreds, proprieties, or such other divisions, and distinctions, as they shall think fit. . . .

In testimony and witness of our consent to and affirmation of these present laws, Concessions and Agreements. We the proprietors, freeholders, and inhabitants of the said Province of West New-Jersey, whose names are under written, have to the same voluntarily and freely set our hands, dated this third day of the month commonly called March, in the Year of our Lord one thousand six hundred and seventy six.

E. Bylynge
Richard Smith
Edward Nethorp
John Penford
Daniel Wills
Thomas Ollive
Thomas Rudyard
Gawen Laurie
William Penn
[and 139 others]

11. George Fox's *Warning to All the Merchants in London* (1658)

The early Friends may claim to have brought greater changes in economic practice with less new economic theory than any religious group since the Cistercian monks began to raise sheep. They pressed uncompromisingly the Puritan standards of honesty and established single-price selling in place of bargaining. They extended the Puritan protest against luxury and waste so as to insist that all products serve actual need, not popular demand. They also transformed the old medieval tradition that a parish community cares for its own poor, which Queen Elizabeth had tried to re-establish by a national "Poor-Law" placing all beggars and vagabonds under charge of local Justices of the Peace. Friends had known the cruelty of such Justices to wandering strangers and their indifference to quiet poverty: they took responsibility on the one hand within the Meeting community for all Friends in need. They also, like many radical Puritans, tried to revive national concern for houses and work for the poor. Thomas Lawson's *Appeal Concerning the Poor* (1660) was the most concrete Quaker proposal before John Bellers, whose ideas, however, owed quite as much to the wider scope of Fox's tracts.

Fox's *Warning to All the Merchants* is representative of many sermons and proclamations he made in marketplaces and before the Justices who sat to fix food prices. He is scathing against the open deceit of bargainers. He also, like William Penn in several early tracts, sees the luxury of the rich as the wasted food and clothing that might have helped the poor. Fox's doctrine of "the creation," the physical world as essentially good raw material to be used by the Spirit for men's true needs, underlies all Quaker economic thought. Finally, Fox's proposals for homes where the poor might work with dignity, while always the ideal for any "poor-house," led to Bellers' proposal for a "College of Industry," a cooperative vocational school.

This tract is typical of Fox's dictation too, in its endless repetitions (mostly deleted), formless grammar, and ethical impact.

A
WARNING
to all the
MERCHANTS IN LONDON
and SUCH as BUY and SELL
with an Advisement to them to lay aside their superfluity
and with it to nourish the POOR
by G. F.:
London,
printed for Thomas Simmons at the Bull and Mouth near Aldersgate, 1658.

430

A warning to all the Merchants in London . . .

for them to keep to yea and nay to all people in their common occasions, for whatsoever is more than these, cometh of evil; and to take heed of . . . cozening, and cheating, and defrauding one another, and dissembling one with another; and to take heed of deceitful merchandise in all their buying and selling, and in all their exchanges; . . . for as a swift witness is the Lord come to plead with you, and against you that use deceitfulness in your merchandise, and use it in your buying and selling, and "Sir," and bow the hat, and scrape the foot, and make the curtsy, and "master," and "mistress," in your service, and forsooth, this is your vain custom; and ask many times the worth, double of the thing to some people. And under this compliment-ing way, and in it, lies the deceit and over-reach, and lurks to cozen and cheat, telling a falsehood, a flattery; so by fair speaking and flattering words, oft times the simple is deceived: Therefore this is a charge from the living God to you all, be true, be faithful to God, be just, be innocent, and ask no more for the thing than you would have: Be at a word, "so say and so do." When you ask more than you will have, or almost double, and say you will not take it except you have so much, and then send your boys after them, and so take [2] it, you are not here at "so say, and so do;" and here are you judged with the law of liberty to be out of it, far off the life of Chris-tians. . . .

And again ye merchants, great men, and rich men, what a dishonor is it to you to go in your gold and silver, and gold chains about your necks, and your costly attire; and your poor blind women and children and cripples crying and making a noise up and down your streets; a dishonor to your city; showing that you are not under the Law, nor under the Gospel. For under the Law [of Moses] they had tithes and tenths to feed all the fatherless and strangers, for tithes was for that work and end. For how can you go up and down in your superfluity, and abound in your riches, and see the poor, blind, and cripples go about your streets? Which, of all other, the blind should be taken care of; therefore let these things be minded and considered, and fear God, and do that which may be an honor to you, and Christianity, and your city. And in all your shops, and warehouses, and exchanges, keep to your words, and "so say, and so do," and you may not cozen and cheat one another, nor no people. For this city hath a name and a bad report of deceitful merchandise, which deceives the country people that deals with you: O therefore blot it out, and do so no more, but judge one another in these things, and be a good savor, and commend yourselves to the innocent and simple, that a child may come among you and not be wronged; and that will be pleasing to God that you do righteously, and to the just God, that you do justly. And then to the righteous just God you will be a good savor, and to the country people. . . . [Page 3 largely repeats page 1.] For truth is risen that will keep out all deceit; therefore be sober, and take it patiently, and live in it, for truth will make you free; therefore if you will be made free by truth, give over your deceitful merchandise, and give over your many words, and keep to yea and nay; . . .

[p. 4] Therefore take in the blind, halt and lame, and obey the things that Christ commands you, ye that call him Lord; take in the blind and the cripples that cries up and down your streets, and feast them when you make your feasts; for the rich feast the rich, and not the poor that cannot feast them again. And see now if you will take up the cross of Christ, and obey his command; then you will become like unto them, when you obey Christ's command. . . . All the while your poor and blind and lame cripples and women and children are crying up and down your streets and steeplehouse doors and alleys and corners, after you that call yourselves Christians; and yet they are Christians as well as you, and so members of the same body; so you may say, be clothed, be filled, be warmed, and be such a people the Apostle speaks of, yet let them be crying up and down the streets not provided for. So this is to hang gold on the back and let the leg go bare. For all are members of one body, the poor as well as the rich. . . . There was not a beggar in Israel among them.[76] Now judge yourselves, and see how short you come of them in life and practice, which say you are Christians, and profess the Gospel.

These things are a grief to many sober people in the city, to see that magistrates hath no more feeling of these things, and yet so much profession of religion, and preaching among them, and so much riches that men never knew want of. And thereby many comes to be hardened. . . . They might think if it were but to keep the honor of their city, they would not let above all [5] things, blind men and cripples and lame people and poor fatherless children make a noise up and down the streets, and steeplehouse doors. But out of their abundance they would lay a little aside, and have a place provided that all the poor, blind, lame cripples should be put into, and nurses set over them, and looked to, cherished, and seen unto that they do not want. And thus them that could work, to work. And this would be a good savor of the city, and of the magistrates, aldermen, and merchants of the city, and to the sober people, and to the Lord God, that there should not be seen a beggar walk up and down the streets, but that there might be a place where they might be maintained with a little out of their superfluity. Yea, before there should be such a noise with the poor, the blind, the lame, and the fatherless, every one lay by a little of their abundance, and spare some off of their backs in gold and silver lace, or their chains and rings. For who

---

76 This phrase, recurring in tracts by Thomas Lawson and many radical Puritans, echoes the spirit of Deuteronomy 15 and Leviticus 19.

considereth not the cry of the poor, but turneth his ear from them, them their Maker will not regard. And all who do not visit the fatherless, and the poor, and the sick, and feed the hungry, and clothe the naked, and are of a profession of religion and makes a talk of Christ's words and the prophets and Moses, such are in the wisdom below, which is earthly, sensual, and devilish, not preservers of the creation, not in the wisdom that is from above, which is gentle, easy to be entreated, by which the creation is to be preserved, by which it must be ordered again to the glory of God. You [are] going in your gold and silver, yea in your very shoes laced, and the poor want bread, want stockings and shoes; and you [have] your many dishes change of dishes, and that you call novelties, and the poor cannot get bread. Spare one of your dishes, and let it be carried to the place for the poor, and do not let them come begging for it neither, but let them have a place where they may be kept, and that will be for your honor and renown. For consider what abundance of riches is in this city and what good you might do with it, or how soon you may be taken [6] from it or it from you, by fire or sea; and yet for all this ye will not consider your poor brethren which are made of the same blood and mold, to dwell upon the face of the earth. . . . Come to the pure religion, which is to visit the fatherless, to visit the sick, and relieve the hungry, and clothe the naked, that brings you to practice and to do the will of God. And give over your living in words, and your hearts afar off, surfeiting in riches, iniquity, and deceit; but come to honesty and plain dealing, and mercifulness and take heed of pride, and loftiness, and wanton-ness, and haughtiness, and walk humbly before the Lord, that you may come to the life the saints was in, the prophets, Christ, and the Apostles were in.

For the mighty day of the Lord is coming, wherein every one of you must give account of his deeds done in the body, and every man's work must be tried by fire, and every man's works shall be brought to the light, and manifest by it. So your day is not past; while you have time, prize it.

G. F.

THE END

12. Fox's *Line of Righteousness* (1661): Quaker Life as Testimony

Fox's letter to Friends about economic ethics seems at first glance little different from his warning to non-Quaker merchants: many of the same phrases recur, with the same repetitive formlessness. Yet where the tract to the merchants moved from prophetic appeal to specific reforms for the sake of the poor, the *Line of Righteousness*, reprinted at least twice for use among Friends, presents briefly the idea of Quaker life as testimony, indeed as "a Terror" to those who know in their hearts they act dishonestly. If a Friend can "act Truth," he will witness to the Seed buried in each man. Thus lives will preach. Thus it is just Friends' most positive testimonies or moral stands (as distinct from negative refusal of tithes and war) that most clearly show Quaker ethics as a whole fabric, centered on Truth, and inseparable from the proclamation of repentance. Quaker social ethics was never a mere sum of particular concerns and protests; always it was part of a totally opened life. Yet just in this letter of 1661, with its consciousness of the Quaker community as distinct from the world in its standards, can be found the beginning of the turn from Quakerism as a missionary movement to the Society of Friends as a "peculiar people."

THE LINE OF RIGHTEOUSNESS AND JUSTICE STRETCHED FORTH OVER ALL MERCHANTS, &c.

and an exhortation unto all Friends and people whatsoever, who are merchants, tradesmen, husbandmen, or sea-men, who deal in merchandise, trade in buying and selling by sea or land, or deal in husbandry, that ye all do that which is just, equal and righteous in the sight of God and man, one to another, and to all men; and that ye use just weights and just measures, and speak and do that which is true, just and right in all things; that so your conversations, lives, practices and tongues may preach to all people and answer the good, just and righteous principle of God in them all. In which ye may be serviceable unto God, and to the creation in your generation, and a blessing both to God and man.

London, printed for Robert Wilson,[77] at the sign of the Black-spread-eagle and Windmill, in Martins Le Grand, 1661.

---

[3] All Friends everywhere, live in the Seed of God, which is the righteousness itself, and inherits the wisdom, and is the wisdom itself; with which wisdom ye may order, rule and govern all things which be under your hands (which God hath given you), to his glory. Govern and order with his wisdom

---

[77] Robert Wilson was Giles Calvert's brother-in-law, and continued his press for about a year after Calvert was arrested and banned from printing by the Restoration regime. Then he too was silenced.

all the creatures that ye have under you, and all exchangings, merchandizing, husbandry. Do what ye do in the wisdom of God, and with it, which is pure from above and gentle, and easy to be entreated. With this wisdom (which is not earthly, sensual, nor devilish) you do good unto all, and hurt no one, nor yourselves; for it is pure, and preserves pure.

So this is the word of the Lord God to you all: Keep all in the power of God over all the unrighteous world; which power of God was before it was; in which power of God you will be preserved in justice, in truth, in equal balance, and weights and measures; in the truth, uprightness and honesty to all people.... "Do rightly," that is the word of the Lord God to you all, whether ye be tradesmen, of what calling or profession, or sort soever, or husbandmen: "Do rightly, justly, truly, holily, equally" to all people, in all things; and that is according to that of God in every man, and the witness of God, and wisdom of God, and the life of God in yourselves; and there you are serviceable in your generation, labouring in the thing that is good, which doth not spoil, nor destroy, nor waste the creation upon the lusts.

And all merchants whatsoever, sea-men, and traffickers by sea or land, this is the word of the Lord God to you all: Do justly, speak truly to all people whatsoever: then are ye a dread and a terror to the unjust. Wrong no man, over-reach no man (if it may be never so much to your advantage) but be plain, righteous and holy; in this are you serviceable to your own [4] nation and others.... "Live in the life of Truth, and let the Truth speak in all things and righteousness..." [which gives victory over the powers of evil and death]. The power and life of God that goes over the power of death,... hath the blessing and the increase of the heavenly riches; and that shall not want the creatures, nor any good thing from them the Lord will not withhold. So be careful to do good in all things to all people whatsoever: in the fear of God serve him, and be diligent, and not stubborn in anything, but pliable in the power of God, that keeps you over all the powers of unrighteousness.... Then will your words, lives, and conversations preach and manifest, that ye serve God in the new life, and that ye have put off the old man and his deeds, which are unrighteous.... But live and reign in the righteous life and power of God, and wisdom (that presseth all the other down) to answer the good and just principle in all people; and that will win people to deal with you: "Doing Truth to all, without respect to persons"; to high or low whatsoever, young or old, rich or poor: and so here your lives and words will preach wherever ye come.

[5] All husbandmen and dealers about husbandry whatsoever, cattle or ground, to you all this is the word of the Lord God: ... [Deny yourselves and live by the Cross.]

In all husbandry, speak Truth, act Truth, doing justly and uprightly in all your actions, in all your practices, in all your words, in all your dealings, buyings, sellings, changings and commerce with people, let Truth be the head, and practice it: And in all your words let Truth be spoken: This brings righteousness forth, and deceit to the judgment-bar. Wrong no man, nor covet, nor cheat, nor oppress, nor defraud any man, in any case. . . .

So speak the Truth, whether merchants or tradesmen: and all sorts of people whatsoever in all your occasions, and in all your tradings, dealings and doings, speak the Truth, act in the Truth, and walk in the Truth; and this brings righteousness forth; for it answereth the witness of God in everyone, which lets everyone see all the deeds and actions they have done amiss, and words which they have spoken amiss: So the witness of God within them ariseth a swift witness against them, for their words which they have spoken amiss, and for their actions which they have done amiss, and brings them to the [6] judgment-bar, and to condemnation. . . .

So ye all Friends of what calling soever, that dwell in the power of God, and feel the power of God, and light of Christ Jesus: Dwell in that, act in that. . . . So let your lives preach, let your light shine, that your works may be seen, that your father may be glorified; that your fruits may be unto holiness; and that your end may be everlasting life. Dwell in the power of the Lord God, and light and life, with which ye may feel and see before the unrighteousness was. . . . [a paragraph on being good or bad examples]

[7] And all of what trade or calling soever, keep out of debts; owe to no man anything but love. Go not beyond your estates, lest you bring yourselves to trouble, and cumber, and a snare; keep low and down in all things ye act. For a man that would be great, and goes beyond his estate, lifts himself up, runs into debt, and lives highly of other men's means; he is a waster of other men, and a destroyer. He is not serviceable to the creation, but a destroyer of the creation and creatures, and cumbreth himself and troubleth others, and is lifted up, who would appear to be somebody; but being from the honest, the just and good, falls into the shame. Therefore dwell everyone of you, under your own vine (that know redemption from the earth) and seek not to be great, but in that, and dwell in the Truth, justice, righteousness and holiness; and there is the blessing enlarged.

And no one (of what calling soever) run into debt, usury and exaction; for many people have been wronged thereby. . . . [repeating the previous paragraph] Live in the life, and in the Seed, the power and righteousness that is everlasting, . . . in which ye come to live the life which is well-pleasing to God; a life which shall stand when the world is ended. And in this life, power and wisdom of God, that is endless, you are a terror to all that be in the wisdom below; you are a terror to all that be in the unrighteous actions and words: And you are a terror to all that be in the unjust and unequal doings, and all the defrauders, cozeners, cheaters, over-reachers, liars and wrong-dealers. In the power of God and his life [8] in which ye have justice, ye have

Truth, ye have equity, ye have righteousness; and it cometh to be to you as natural; your words, your lives, your conversations, your presence, and your practices, both judge and preach. . . . You reach and answer the good and just principle of God in everyone; and it you will make at the last to confess you, though they may go on in the contrary for a time. . . .

The wicked and unrighteous owe envy and hatred, and with that they pay their debt. But the righteous, just and harmless, who owe nothing to any man but love; with that they pay their debt. But drunkards, adulterers, swearers, rioters, who eat and drink and rise up to play, and live in pleasures wantonly upon the earth, fighters, quarrellers, envious, malicious, unjust, unrighteous; all such actions and practices, judge out of the power of God, and out of his kingdom.

13. Thomas Ellwood's *Speculum Saeculi* (1667): The Quaker as Poet

John Milton returned from Italy as a young poet determined to devote his muse to God; with an interlude of unhappy marriage and happy service to Cromwell's government, he returned to this call in his blindness. Milton's secretary Ellwood caught the vision; but genius is not contagious. Yet our "mute inglorious Milton" is one of the few Friends who tried poetry. A number of testimonies, notably two to Howgill (*Dawnings of the Gospel-Day*, pp. c2-6), are cast in verse; but Quaker intensity did not lend itself to the formality of poetry or music in the Baroque age.

SPECULUM SECULI
OR A
LOOKING-GLASS
FOR THE
TIMES

Why should my modest Muse forbidden be
To speak of that which but too many see?
Why should she, by conniving, seem t'uphold
Men's wickedness, and thereby make them bold
Still to persist in't? Why should she be shy
To call them beasts, who want humanity?

Why should she any longer silence keep
And lie secure, as one that's fast asleep? . . .
[42 lines omitted]

[179] *Words are too shallow to express the rage,*
The fury, madness of this frantic age.
Numbers fall short to reckon up the crimes,
Which are the recreations of these times.
Was Sodom ever guilty of a sin,
Which England is not now involved in?
By custom, drunkenness so common's grown
That most men count it a small sin, or none.
Ranting and roaring they affirm to be
The true characters of gentility.
Swearing and cursing is so much in fashion
That 'tis esteem'd a badge of reputation.
What dreadful oaths! What direful execrations
On others! On themselves what imprecations
They tumble out, like roaring claps of thunder,
As if they meant to rend the clouds asunder!
Mockers do so abound in every place
That rare it is to meet a sober face.
Ambition, boasting, vanity and pride
(With numbers numberless of sins beside)
Are grown, thro' use, so common that men call
Them peccadilloes, small, or none at all.
[180] *But Oh! the luxury and great excess*
Which by this wanton age is used in dress!
What pains do men and women take alas!
To make themselves for arrant bedlams pass!
The fool's pied coat, which all wise men detest,
Is grown a garment now in great request.
More colours in one waistcoat now they wear
Than in the rainbow ever did appear:
As if they were ambitious to put on
All colors that they cast their eyes upon,
Thereby outstripping the chameleon quite,
Which cannot change itself to red or white.
Each man, like Proteus, his shape doth change,
To whatsoever seemeth new or strange,
And he that in a modest garb is drest,
Is made the laughing-stock of all the rest.
Nor are they with their baubles satisfied,

438

But sex-distinctions too are laid aside.
The women wear the trousers and the vest,
While men in muffs, fans, petticoats are drest.
Some women (Oh! the shame!) like rampant rigs,
Ride flaunting in their powder'd perriwigs.
[181] *Astride they sit (and not ashamed neither)*
Dressed up like men, in jacket, cap and feather.
All things to lust and wantonness are fitted.
Nothing that tends to vanity omitted.
To give a touch on every antic fashion
Which hath been worn of late within this nation
Might fill a volume, which would tire, no doubt,
The reader's patience, if not wear it out.

Come now, ye ranting gallants of the times,
Who nothing have to boast of but your crimes;
Ye Satan's Hectors, who disdain to swear
An oath beneath God: damn me, if he dare, . . .
               [omitting 8 lines]
[182] *Unless unto the highest strain ye swell,*
And wish the Devil make you bed in Hell,
This know, the long provoked God is come,
From whom you must receive that dreadful doom;
Depart, ye cursed, and forever dwell,
Where beds of torment are prepar'd, in Hell. . . .
               [omitting 20 lines]
[183] *A sort of men have overrun this nation,*
Who are a burden to the whole creation.
Men shall I call them, or the viper's brood?
Lovers of evil, haters of all good.
These, swell'd with envy, in a great despite
To Christ, with fist of wickedness do smite
(Not their own fellow-servants; for they are
The Devil's slaves, by him bor'd thro' the ear,
But) God's ambassadors, whom he hath sent
To warn them of their sins, and cry, Repent;
Or to denounce his judgments against those,
That set themselves his message to oppose.
These persecute the innocent, and say,
"When they are gone, 'twill be a merry day."
[184] *These grind the poor; the needy these oppress;*
Widows devour; tread on the fatherless.

Far from themselves they put the evil day,
Remove impending judgments far away;
And yet in vain they strive t'escape the stroke
Of that just God whom boldly they provoke.
For they afflict his people, slay his sheep,
Beat those whom he appointed hath to keep
And feed his tender lambs; rend, tear, devour,
Suppress God's worship to their utmost pow'r. . . .
[omitting 20 lines]
This is that sin, that sin which cries aloud;
Louder than all the rest, the guilt of blood,
Which is the strongest cord the Devil hath
To draw down on mankind God's heavy wrath.
Weeping I sigh, and sighing weep to see
The rod, which God prepared hath for thee,
O England, who dost evilly intreat
His messengers, and dost his prophets beat.

Ah, England, ah, poor England, I bewail
Thy sad estate. O that I might prevail
In my desires for thee! Then shouldst thou be
As full of joy, as now of misery.
For then should plenty in thy fields be found,
And all thy garners should with grain abound.
Then peace, long-lasting peace should in thee dwell;
For God would all thine enemies repel;
And he himself would take delight in thee,
So thou the glory of the world would'st be. . . .
[omitting 28 lines]
Be warned then, ye rulers, and let all
Of whatsoever rank, both great and small,
Tremble before the Lord, and cease to rage
Against our God's peculiar heritage.
[188] *For, of a truth, his long-provoked hand*
Is stretched out in judgment o'er this land;
And ye must feel it; for he hath decreed,
To vindicate his long-oppressed seed.
And in his fury, he will vengeance take
In our behalf, who suffer for his sake.
Then shall ye know, that he, who sits on high,
Regards us as the apple of his eye.

440

14. William Penn's *One Project for the Good of England* (1679)

This is not Penn's greatest work, though it fairly represents his style. Certainly his *Rise and Progress of the . . . Quakers, No Cross No Crown,* and *Fruits of Solitude*, often reprinted, have also been most read. The account of his trial with William Mead in *The People's Ancient and Just Liberties* is more dramatic, and Penn's constitution-making for Pennsylvania in the long run more influential. Full and fair treatment for Penn, as Fox, must rest upon past and future volumes.[78]

The tract selected here pursues farther than any other a path that Penn blazed for Friends, the appeal to non-Quakers on nonreligious grounds. This way opened, as was noted already, in relation to toleration, where Friends hoped to reach the consciences even of those they could not convert. But conscience, though always for Friends more relative than the voice of God that might speak through it, was also religious in Quaker eyes. Indeed, Penn tended to absolutize it more than had early Friends, as he talked less about the Light or Christ within men. But in a political crisis Penn went beyond religious appeals even to men's consciences: using the traditions of natural law, English loyalty, and economic interest that had been used by the Levellers, and in a more casual and inconsistent way by Billing, Penn uses secular arguments. In the process he prepares the way for a separation of religious and secular, of church and state, like that which Roger Williams and many Separatists intended. But Penn, at least in Pennsylvania, did not intend such a breach, still hoping that liberty of conscience and morality would form a basic center in which Friends and non-Quakers would meet. In the end, despite periods of quietism and social withdrawal, Friends have taken the way of Penn and not that of Williams. Without much intellectual clarity they have tried not to separate their religious life and worship from their involvement in politics and social reform.

---

[78] The central parts of the works named and a half-dozen others are reprinted in Frederick Tolles and E. G. Alderfer, eds., *The Witness of William Penn* (1957), and old editions of his collected works are widely available, though the "Penn papers project," based at the Historical Society of Pennsylvania, hopes to print a more complete and scholarly edition. Many good biographies by Edward Beatty, William I. Hull, Catherine Owens Pears, and C. E. Vulliamy overlap studies by Edwin Bronner, Gary Nash, and many others on Penn's dealings with Pennsylvania.

441

From a basis of ethical concern they have approached their daily work without cutting it off from inner leading by Christ's Spirit, but also without creating a "rule of saints" or even a totalitarian sect community.

Penn's *Project for the Good of England* reflects a situation where Penn faced all these ambiguities. The previous year he had testified before Parliament and won from them a substitute for the oath of allegiance to king and protestantism that Quakers might have accepted, only to see it die when Parliament was dissolved. In the ensuing election he risked his own and Quakers' reputation to campaign for Algernon Sidney and the Whig policy of toleration for Protestants—and lost. The same year the witch-hunt against Jesuit plots to Catholicize England, begun by Titus Oates, had uncovered genuine plots; Penn as friend of the secretly Catholic king and his brother had to make doubly clear that he was no "front man" for Jesuits when he advocated toleration of worship. The Parliament, and Penn's plea, died once again. The Toleration Act of 1689 did not solve the issue of oaths, and indeed Penn's solution, as revived in milder form in 1696, still seemed to many Friends to change words more than realities as to oaths. Yet Penn had recognized Friends' desire to affirm loyalty to government and nation, and in many English and American crises since then ways have been found to show this.

ONE PROJECT FOR THE GOOD OF ENGLAND:
That Is, Our Civil Union is Our Civil Safety.
Humbly Dedicated to the Great Council, The Parliament
of England.
[No publisher or date named: 1679]

Religion, as it is the noblest end of man's life, so it were the best bond of human society, provided men did not err in the meaning of that excellent word. Scripture interprets it to be loving God above all, and our neighbors as ourselves; but practice teacheth us that too many merely resolve it into opinion and form. And this is the reason of that mischief and uncertainty that attend government. No sooner one opinion prevails upon another, (though all hold the text to be sacred) but human society is shaken, and the civil government must receive and suffer a revolution; insomuch that when we consider the fury and unnaturalness of some people for religion, (which shows they have none that's true, religion making men most natural as well as

442

divine) we have reason to bewail the misunderstanding as well as mis-living of that venerable word.

But since 'tis so hard to disabuse men of their wrong apprehensions of religion, and the true nature and life of it, and consequently as yet too early in the day to fix such a religion upon which mankind will readily agree as a common basis for civil society, we must recur to some lower but true principle for the present, and I think there will be no difficulty of succeeding.

'Tis this, That civil interest is the foundation and end of civil government, and where it is not maintained entire, the government must needs decline. The word "interest" has a good and bad acceptance: When it is taken in an ill sense, it signifies a pursuit of advantage without regard to truth or justice; which I mean not. The good signification of the word, and which I mean, is a legal endeavor to keep rights, or augment honest profits, whether it be in a private person or a society. By "government," I understand a just and equal constitution, where might is not right, but laws rule, and not the wills or power of men, for that were plain tyranny. . . .

Having thus explained the terms of the principle I have laid down, I repeat it, viz., That civil interest is the foundation and end of civil government, and prove it thus: The good of the whole is the rise and end of government; but the good of the whole must needs be the interest of the whole, and consequently the interest of the whole is the reason and end of government. None can stumble at the word good, for every man may easily and safely interpret that to himself, since he must needs believe, 'tis good for him to be preserved in an undisturbed possession of his civil rights, according to the free and just laws of the land, and the construction he makes for himself will serve his neighbor, and so the whole society.

But as the good of the people is properly the civil interest of the people, and that, the reason and end of government, so is the maintenance of that civil interest entire, the preservation of government. For where people are sure of their own, and are protected from violence or injury, they cheerfully yield their obedience, and pay their contribution to the support of that government. But on the contrary, where men are insecure of their civil rights, nay, where they are daily violated, and themselves in danger of ruin, and that for no sin committed against the nature of civil interest, (to preserve which, government was instituted) we ought to suppose their affections will flag, that they will grow dead-hearted, and that what they pay or do may go against the grain: And to say true, such unkindness is ready to tempt them to believe they should not of right contribute to the maintenance of such governments as yield them no security or civil protection. Which unhappy flaw in the civil interest, proves an untoward crack in the government; men not being cordially devoted to the prosperity of that government that is exercised in their destruction. . . . Wherefore, wise governments have ever taken care to preserve their people, as knowing they do thereby preserve their own interest, and that how numerous their people, so large their interest. For not only Solomon has told us, that "the honour of a prince is in the multitude of his people," but experience teaches, that plenty of people is the riches and strength of a wise and good government; as that is where vice is corrected and virtue encouraged, and all taken in and secured in civils, that have the same civil interest with the government.

But as the good and interest of the whole is the rise and end of government, so must it suppose that the whole (which takes in all parties) concurs in seeking the good of the government; for the reason of the government will not suffer it to protect those that are enemies to its constitution and safety; for so it would admit of something dangerous to the society, for the security of which government was at first instituted.

It will follow that those that own another temporal power superior to the government they properly belong to make themselves subjects not of the government they are born under, but to that authority which they avow to be superior to the government of their own country, and consequently men of another interest. . . .[79]

The principle thus far lies general, I will now bring it to our own case:

England is a country populous and Protestant, and though under some dissents within itself, yet the civil interest is the same, and in some sense the religious too. For, first, all English Protestants, whether conformists or nonconformists, agree in this, that they only owe allegiance and subjection unto the civil government of England, and offer any security in their power to give, of their Truth in this matter. And in the next place, they do not only consequently disclaim the Pope's supremacy, and all adhesion to foreign authority under any pretence, but therewith deny and oppose the Romish religion, as it stands degenerated from Scripture, and the first and purest ages of the Church; which makes up a great negative union. . . .

[Two more paragraphs against papal authority]

The civil interest of English Protestants being thus the same, and their religious interest too, so far as concerns a negative to the usurpation and error of Rome; I do humbly ask, if it be the interest of the government to expose those to misery that have no other civil interest than that of the government? . . . One would think 'twere reasonable that they should not suffer by Protestants, who if Popery have a day are likely to suffer with them, and that upon the same principles. Experience tells us that the wisest architects lay their foundations broad and strong, and raise their squares and structure by

[79] As is clear below, he is referring to papal authority as supreme for Catholics.

the most exact rules of art, that the fabric may be secure against the violence of storms; but if people must be destroyed by those of the same interest, truly that interest will stand but totteringly, and every breath of opposition will be ready to shake it.

'Twas the inconfutable answer Christ made to the blasphemers of that power by which he wrought miracles: "A kingdom divided against itself cannot stand." What he said then, let me on another occasion say now, an interest divided against itself must fall.

I know some men will take fire at this, and by crying "The Church, the Church," hope to silence all arguments of this nature; but they must excuse me, if I pay no manner of regard to their zeal, and hold their devotion both ignorant and dangerous at this time. It is not the way to fill the Church, to destroy the people. . . .

The meaning of it is to debilitate the Protestant cause in general, by exciting the Church of England to destroy all other Protestant interests in these kingdoms, that so nothing may remain for Popery to conflict with but the few zealous abettors of that Church.

For 'tis government she aims at, to have the reins of power in her hand, to give law and the scepter.

To do this she must either have a greater interest than the Protestants that are now in possession, or else divide their interest, and so weaken them by themselves, and make them instruments to her ends. That her own force is inconsiderable is clear: She has nothing within doors to give her hope but the discord of Protestants. . . .

[Two further paragraphs showing Catholic gains by Protestant discord]

This being the case, I would take leave to ask the zealous gentlemen of the English Church, "If conformity to the fashion of their worship be dearer to them than England's interest and the cause of Protestancy?" If their love to Church-government be greater than to the Church and her religion, and to their country and her laws? Or better able of themselves to secure Protestancy and our civil interest against the attempts of Rome, than in conjunction with the civil interest of all Protestant dissenters?

Being brought to this pinch, I conceive they must . . . hasten to break those bonds that are laid upon dissenters of truly tender and (by experience) of peaceable consciences; and by law establish the free exercise of their worship to almighty God, that the fears, jealousies, disaffection and distraction, that now affect the one common interest of Protestants, may be removed. . . .

The civil government is greatly concerned to discountenance such bigotry; for it thins the people, lessens trade, creates jealousies, and endangers the peace and wealth of the whole. . . .

I ask, if more custom comes not to the King, and more trade to the kingdom, by encouraging the labour and traffic of an Episcopalian, Presbyterian, Independent, Quaker and Anabaptist, than by an Episcopalian only? If this be true, why should the rest be rendered incapable of trade, yea, of living? What schism or heresy is there in the labor and commerce of the Anabaptist, Quaker, Independent and Presbyterian, more than in the labor and traffic of the Episcopalian?

I beseech you give me leave, is there ever a Church-man in England, that in distress would refuse the courtesy of one of these "dissenters?" If one of them should happen to fall into a pond or ditch, would he deny to be helped out by a dissenter's hand? Is it to be supposed he would in such a pickle be stomachful, and choose to lie there, and be smothered or drowned, rather than owe aid to the good will of a poor "fanatic?" Or if his house were on fire, may we think that he would have it rather burnt to the ground than acknowledge its preservation to a "nonconformist?" Would not the act be orthodox, whatever were the man? No, no; Self will always be true to its interest, let superstition mutter what it will.

But since the industry, rents and taxes of the dissenters are as current as their neighbors', who loses by such narrowness more than England, than the government and the magistracy? For till it be the interest of the farmer to destroy his flock, to starve the horse he rides, and the cow that gives him milk, it cannot be the interest of England to let a great part of her sober and useful inhabitants be destroyed about things that concern another world. And 'tis to be hoped that the wisdom and charity of our governors will better guide them both to their own real interest and their people's preservation, which are inseparable; so that they may not starve them for religion, that are as willing, as able, to work for the good of King and country.

I beseech you, let nature speak: . . .

All the productions of nature are by love, and shall religion propagate by force? If we consider the poor hen, she will teach us humanity. Nature does not only learn her to hatch, but to be tender over her feeble chickens, that they may not be a prey to the kite. All the seeds and plants that grow for the use and nourishment of man, are produced by the kind and warm influences of the sun. Nothing but kindness keeps up human race: Men and women don't get children in spite, but affection. 'Tis wonderful to think by what friendly and gentle ways nature produces, and matures the creatures of the world; and that religion should teach us to be froward and cruel is lamentable: This were to make her the enemy instead of the restorer of nature. But I think, we may without offence say, that since true religion gives men greater mildness and goodness than they had before, that religion which teaches them less, must needs be false. What shall we say then, but that even nature is a truer guide to peace, and better informs us to preserve civil interest, than false religion, and consequently, that we ought to be true to the natural and just

446

principles of society, and not suffer one of them to be violated for humor or opinion. . . .

We know, that in all plantations [i.e. colonies] the wisdom of planters is well aware of this; and let us but consider that the same ways that plant countries must be kept to for preserving the plantation, else 'twill quickly be depopulated.

That country which is false to its first principles of government, and mistakes or divides its common and popular interest, must unavoidably decay. And let me say that had there been this freedom granted eighteen years ago, Protestancy had been too potent for the enemies of it. . . . Witness the careful government of Holland, where the preservation of their civil interest from fraction hath secured them against the growth of Popery, though it be almost tolerated by them. So powerful are the effects of an united civil interest in government.

But there is a two-fold mistake that I think fit to remove. First, that the difference betwixt Protestants and their dissenters is generally managed, as if it were civil. . . .

They neither acknowledge nor submit to any other authority. They hold the one common civil head, and not only acquiesce in the distribution of justice by law, but embrace it as the best part of their patrimony. So that the difference between Protestants and their dissenters is purely religious, and mostly about Church-government, and some forms of worship, apprehended to be not so pure and Apostolical as could be desired, and here it is, that tenderness should be exercised. . . . But as to the second, [between papists and Protestants] in reality the difference is not so much religious as civil. Not but that there is a vast contrariety in doctrine and worship too; but this barely should not be the cause of our so great distance, and that provision the laws make against them; but rather that fundamental inconsistency they carry with them to the security of the English government and Constitution unto which they belong, by acknowledging a foreign jurisdiction in these kingdoms. So that drawing into question and danger the constitution and government, there seems a discharge upon the civil government from any further care of their protection. . . .

To come then to our point, shall English men by English men, and Protestants by Protestants, be free or oppressed? This is, whether shall we receive as Englishmen and Protestants those that have no other civil interest than that which is purely English, and who sincerely profess and embrace the same protestation, for which the ancient Reformers were styled Protestants, or for the sake of humour or base ends disown them and expose them and their families to utter misery?

I would hope better of our great church-men's charity and prudence; but if they should be so unhappy as to keep to their old measures, and still play the gawdy, but empty, name of Church against the civil interest and religion of the nation, they will show themselves deserted of God, and then how long it will be, before they will be seen and left of all sober men, let them judge. For to speak freely, after all this light that is now in the world, no ignorance can excuse such zeal.

Could some Church-men but see the irreparable mischiefs that will attend them (if sincere to their present profession) unless prevented by a modest and Christian condescension to dissenting Protestant Christians, they would never suffer themselves to be misguided by stiff and rigid principles at this time of day.

If Christianity, that most meek and self-denying religion, cannot prevail upon them, methinks the power of interest, and that self-interest too, should have some success, for in those cases they use not to be obstinate.

But I expect it should be told me, "That this is the way to ruin the Church, and let in an anarchy in religion. . . . I am glad to obviate this, before I leave you, seeing the contrary is most true; for it leaves the Church and Church-men as they are, with this distinction, that whereas now conformity is coercive, which is Popish, it will be then persuasive, which is Christian. And there may be some hopes, when the parsons, destitute of the magistrate's sword, shall of necessity enforce their religion by good doctrine and holy living; nor ought they to murmur, for that which satisfied Christ and his Apostles should satisfy them: His kingdom is not of this world, therefore they should not fight for him, if they would be his servants and the children of his kingdom; Christ, and not civil force, is the rock his church is built upon. Nor indeed has anything so tarnished the cause of Protestancy as the professors of it betaking themselves to worldly arms to propagate their religion. David could not wear Saul's armour, and true Protestants cannot use Popish weapons, imposition and persecution. In short: 'Tis the very interest of the Church of England to preserve the civil interest entire, or else Popery will endanger all; but that cannot be unless all of that civil interest be preserved; therefore Protestant dissenters should be indulged.

But some will say, There is a difference even among dissenters: some will give a security to the civil government by taking the oaths; others will not, and be it through tenderness, how do we know, but Papists will shroud themselves under the wings of such dissenters, and so in tolerating Protestant dissenters to fortify Protestancy, in reality, Popery will be hereby sheltered incognito.

I answer, first, that such oaths are little or no security to any government, and though they may give some allay to the jealousy of governors, they never had the effect desired. For neither in private cases, nor yet in public transactions have men adhered to their oaths, but their interest. He that is a knave, was never made honest by an oath: Nor is it an oath, but honesty that keeps honest men such. Read story and consult our modern times, tell me what government stood the firmer or longer for them? Men may take them for their own advantage, or to avoid loss and punishment: but the question is, what real benefit or security comes thereby to the government? It is certain they have often ensnared a good man, but never caught one knave yet. . . .

Our common interest, and the laws of the land *duly* executed: These are the security of our government.

For example, a man swears he will not plot, yet plots; pray what security is this oath to the government? But though 'tis evident that this be no security, that law which hangs him for plotting is an unquestionable one. So that 'tis not for wise governors, by swearing men to the government to think to secure it; but all having agreed to the laws, by which they are to be governed, let any man break them at his peril. Wherefore good laws, and a just execution of them, and not oaths, are the natural and real security of a government.[80]

But next, though some may scruple the oaths, those very persons will very cheerfully promise their allegiance on the same penalties, and subscribe any renunciation of Pope and foreign authority, which the art of man can pen; nor would it be hard for you to believe they should subscribe what they have always lived.[81]

To that part of the objection, which mentions the danger of Papists' concealing themselves under the character of Protestant dissenters, [they] will swallow the oaths too; for the declaration flatly denies the religion, but the oaths only the Pope's supremacy, which even some of themselves pretend to reject. Therefore those that can sincerely subscribe the declaration cannot be Papists.

If it be yet objected that Papists may have dispensations to take the oaths, or pardons when they have taken them; these last six months prove as much; there is no fence against this flail. At this rate they may as well be Protestants, as Protestant-dissenters; ministers or bishops in churches as speakers or preachers in meeting-houses. This objection only shows the weakness of both oaths and declaration for the purpose intended, and not that they can hide themselves more under one people than another. . . .

[Dissenters] not taking the oaths proves plainly they have no dispensations nor hopes of absolution, and therefore no Papists: shall they then lie under

80 He did not here raise the question of conscientious objection to laws voted by a majority. In 1682, in his Frame of Government for Pennsylvania, though still defining good government in terms of good laws, if "the people are a party to those laws," he was willing to regard good men as more basic than good laws; this was Penn's ethics-centered equivalent of theocracy.

81 Quakers were always willing to suffer the penalties of perjury for any falsehood.

the severities intended against Papists, who have none of their dispensations or absolutions to deliver them from them? This is (with submission but in plain terms) to make the case of the kingdom worse; for it destroys those who are not guilty and whom, I believe, you would not destroy.

Having brought the matter to this, I shall offer you a new test.

The New Test

I, A. B., do solemnly and in good conscience, in the sight of God and men, acknowledge and declare that King Charles the Second is lawful king of this realm, and all the dominions thereunto belonging. And that neither the Pope nor See of Rome, nor any else by their authority have right in any case to depose the king, or dispose of his kingdom, or upon any score whatever to absolve his subjects of their obedience, or to give leave to any of them to plot or conspire the hurt of the king's person, his state or people; and that all such pretences and power are false, pernicious and damnable.

And I do farther sincerely profess, and in good conscience declare, that I do not believe that the Pope is Christ's vicar, or Peter's lawful successor, or that he or the See of Rome, severally or jointly, are the rule of faith or judge of controversy, or that they can absolve sins. Nor do I believe there is a purgatory after death; or that saints should be prayed to, or images in any sense be worshipped. Nor do I believe there is any transubstantiation in the Lord's Supper, or elements of bread and wine, at or after the consecration thereof by any person whatsoever. But I do firmly believe that the present communion of the Roman Catholic Church is both superstitious and idolatrous. And all this I do acknowledge, intend, profess and declare without any equivocation, or reserve, or other sense, than the plain and usual signification of these words, according to the real intention of the law-makers, and the common acceptance of all true Protestants.

This is the test I offer; large in matter, because comprehensive of oaths and test too, yet brief in words. [He suggests ways of getting all citizens to uphold this declaration.]

But as in case of such hypocrisy, a severe penalty should be inflicted, so pray let provision be made that if any person so subscribing should be afterwards called by the name of Jesuit or Papist, without very good proof, it should be deemed and punished in the open sessions, for a slander and breach of peace, yet so, as that the penalty may be remitted at the request of the abused party. . . .

I shall conclude with this request, first, to almighty God, that he would please to make us truly and deeply sensible to his present mercies to us, and to reform our hearts and lives to improve them thankfully. And, secondly, to you, that we may be loving, humble and diligent, one to, and for another; for as from such amendments we may dare promise great and sudden felicity to England, so if looseness in life, and bitterness in religion be not speedily reprehended and reformed, and the common civil interest maintained entire, God will, I justly fear, repent he has begun to do us good, adjourn the Day of our Deliverance to that of our repentance and moderation, and overcast these happy dawnings of his favour, by a thick and dismal cloud of confusion and misery: Which God avert!

These things that I have written are no wild guesses, or maybe's, but the disease and cure, the danger and safety of England; in treating of which, that God that made the world knows, I have not gratified any private spleen or interest (for I am sorry at the occasion) but singly and conscientiously intended his honor, and the lasting good of England, to which all personal and party considerations ought never to submit.

Your own faithful and most affectionate
Philanglus.

15. John Bellers' *Proposals for Raising a College of Industry* (1696)

Bellers' attitudes toward the upper-class estate owners and the poor may seem close to Max Weber's stereotype of Protestantism—hardly the "veritable phenomenon in the history of political economy" that Karl Marx considered him. He did concede more to merchants' values and popular viewpoints than even did Penn. Most of his writings were "reformist," aiming at convincing the maximum number of men with a limited platform of reforms: wider voting rights (like the old Levellers); a Parliament of Europe (like Henri IV, and incidentally Penn); improvements in medicine and in prisons; the first clear plea against capital punishment. If he concedes so much to human greed and weakness in his repeated argumentation, one can almost hear him do so in response to Friends who call him an optimist who has forgotten basic Quaker teachings about the perversion of the "natural" man.

Bellers' schemes were always too good to work, but not fantastic. He wrote from his own experience with Quaker work programs for the poor, as himself a rich merchant turned country squire. His "College of Industry" proposal, as he admitted, merely revived and refined the best ideals of the medieval work-houses and guilds. He started raising money for such a "college"; one was built at Clerkenwell after his death (closer in practice to a children's and old-folks' home), which later became the elite Saffron Waldron Boarding School. Robert Owen had limited success with such a commune as Bellers wanted, and the similar kibbutzim of Israel have prospered. But what is significant from the standpoint of Quaker history is that Bellers was left by Friends to carry out his plan as a private voluntary proposal. Penn's politics, and even his colonies, were programs in which inherently only a few could share; surprisingly many did, even though other Friends were opposed to Penn's worldliness. Bellers presented his schemes to Yearly and Quarterly Meetings and got neither formal backing nor disownment, but his plan "is left to him to do with as he sees meet."[82] With Bellers the era of Quaker volunteer service begins. Hence we reprint mainly the sections that show to whom he appealed and on what grounds.

PROPOSALS FOR RAISING
A COLLEGE OF INDUSTRY
Of All Useful Trades and Husbandry,
With Profit for the Rich, a Plentiful Living for the Poor,
And,
A Good Education for Youth.
Which will be Advantage to the Government, by the Increase
of the People, and their Riches.
By John Bellers.
MOTTO: Industry brings Plenty
[II Thess. 3:10]
London, Printed and Sold by T. Sowle, in White-Hart-Court in
Gracious-Street.
1696.

To the LORDS and COMMONS. Assembled in Parliament

The cries and miseries of some, and idleness and lewdness of others of the poor, and the charge the nation is at for them being great, hath encouraged me to present you with some proposals of embodying the poor so together,

---

[82] 2nd Day's Morning Meeting minute for 26/6/1695, quoted by A. Ruth Fry, *John Bellers, 1654-1725* (London, 1935), p. 7. This volume reprints most of Bellers' tracts with a biographical introduction.

that thereby they may be made of equal value to money (by their raising a plentiful supply of all conveniencies of life). And by this example the parish rates, and many commons, may be most profitably employed. . . .

John Bellers.

To the Thinking and Public-Spirited.

Christianity mends, but mars no man's good nature; it binding us to love our neighbor, and that love, to desire our country's prosperity. And from that love do I meditate the public good, and publish these proposals I think tends to it: Believing there is many who would be glad to see the poor reformed in manners, and better provided for to live that will be willing to contribute their assistance with money, and advice towards it, when opportunity shall be offered them. . . .

Such as are willing to set forward this undertaking, may enter their subscriptions with Edward Skeat, at William Reynolds's, Goldsmith, at the Cup and Star near Fleet-Bridge in Fleet-Street; or Herbert Springet, Attorney, in George-Yard in Lombardstreet, London.

[1] The INTRODUCTION.

It's the interest of the rich to take care of the poor, and their education, by which they will take care of their own heirs: For as kingdoms and nations are subject to revolutions and changes much more (and nothing commoner than) for private families to do so; and who knows how soon it may be his own lot, or his posterity's, to fall poor? Is there any poor now, that some of their ancestors have not been rich? Or any rich now, that some of their ancestors have not been poor? . . .

There is three things I aim at: first, profit for the rich, (which will be life to the rest.). Secondly, a plentiful living for the poor, without difficulty. Thirdly, a good education for youth, that may tend to prepare their souls into the nature of the good ground.

[2] However prevalent arguments of charity may be to some, when profit is joined with it, it will raise most money, provide for most people, hold longest, and do most good: For what sap is to a tree, that profit is to all business, by increasing and keeping it alive; so employing the poor, excels the barren keeping them; in the first, the increase of the poor is no burthen, (but advantage) because their conveniencies increase with them; but in the latter, there is no strength or relief but what they have from others, who possibly may sometimes think they have little enough for themselves.

As a good and plentiful living, must be the poor's encouragement; so their increase, the advantage of the rich; without them, they cannot be rich; for if one had a hundred thousand acres of land, and as many pounds in money, and as many cattle, without a laborer, what would the rich man be but a laborer? And as the laborers make men rich, so the more laborers, there will be, the more rich men (where there is land to employ and provide for them). Therefore I think it the interest of the rich to encourage the honest laborers marrying at full age; but by the want of it, it seems to me the world is out of frame, and not understanding its own interest; the labor of the poor being the mines of the rich.

For is it not strange to consider how industrious the world is, to raise corn and cattle, which only serves men, and how negligent of (or rather careful to hinder) the increase of men, who are a thousand times better than beasts, being to serve God? Do not men greatly reproach their maker, as if he had chosen the uselessest part of the creation to serve him, whilst men think them the least worth their while to raise? . . .

[3] This College-fellowship will make labor, and not money, the standard to value all necessaries by. And though money hath its conveniencies, in the common way of living, it being a pledge among men for want of credit; yet not without its mischiefs; and call'd by our Saviour, The Mammon of Unrighteousness; . . .

[4] Tho it's not so natural for the old and rich to live with a common stock, yet more natural with the young and poor, witness the several hospitals of England and Holland: Old people are like earthen vessels, not so easily to be new moulded, yet children are more like clay out of the pit, and easy to take any form they are put into.

The variety of tempers, and the idle expectations of some of the first workmen, may make the undertaking difficult; and therefore the more excellent will be the accomplishment: And if the poor at first prove brittle, let the rich keep patience; seven or fourteen years may bring up young ones that life will be more natural to: And if the attaining such a method, would be a blessing to the people, certainly it's worth more than a little labor to accomplish it. When by the good rules thereof may be removed, in great measure, the prophaneness of swearing, drunkenness, etc. with the idleness and penury of many in the nation. . . . And it's as much more charity to put the poor in a way to live by honest labor, than to maintain them idle; as it would be to set a man's broken leg, that he might go himself, rather than always to carry him.

[5] *A Specimen showing how the rich may gain, the poor maintain themselves, and children be educated, by being incorporated as a College of all sorts of useful trades, that shall work one for another, without other relief: Suppose three hundred in a college, to work the usual time or task as abroad, and what any doth more, to be paid for it, to encourage industry.*

Two hundred of all trades I suppose sufficient to find necessaries for three

454

hundred, and therefore what manufacture the other hundred make, will be profit for the founders.

2 A Governor and Deputy	2 Linen and	1 Hatter
2 Shoemakers	2 Woollen Weavers	1 Capper
3 Tailors	4 Cooks	2 Carpenter and Joiner
1 Baker	4 Gardeners	2 Bricklayer and Laborer
1 Brewer	1 Tanner	1 Cooper
1 Butcher	1 Feltmonger	2 Smiths
1 Upholsterer	2 Flax-Dresser and Thread-Maker	1 Pin-Maker
1 Barber	1 Tallow-Chandler	1 Needle-Maker
1 Physician	1 Soap-Maker	2 Butler and Store-Keeper
		44

Women and Girls.

2 Governess and Deputy	6 Nurses	4 House-Cleaners
6 Bed-Makers	6 Washers	6 Seamsters to make and mend Clothes
5 Knitters or Weavers of Stockings	20 Linen and	
	20 Woolen Spinners and	
2 Spinners and Carders for Stockings	Carders	
	5 Dairy-Maids	82

A Farm of £500 per an.

2 A Steward and his Wife	3 Plowboys	3 Hinds for Cattle
3 Plowmen	4 Taskers	6 Hedgers and Laborers
	3 Shepherds	24

> 44 Tradesmen, etc.
> 82 Women and Girls.
> 24 Men and Boys upon the Farm
> 10 Men's Work at £15 each, is £150 a year, for Fuel, Iron, etc.
> 5 Men's Work at £15 each, is £75 a year for House-Rent
> 35 Men's Work at £15 each, is £525 a year, for Rent of a Farm for Meat, Drink, etc.
> ___
> 200
> 100 People's Labor, if but £10 each, is £1000 per annum Profit, but if we value them at £15 each, is £1500 Profit.
> ___
> 300

I do not suppose the computation is exact to a man, for as some trades useful are not set down, so there is some of them set down, who are able to provide for two or three times that number. But if it should require 220 people to provide necessaries for 300, it will pay the undertakers well enough.

[7] And that this computation is not much out of the way, of 200 providing all necessaries for 300, it may appear.

First, from a view of the nation, where I suppose not above two thirds, if one half of the nation, are useful workers; and yet all have a living.

Secondly, from the many advantages [7] the college will have over others, for there will be saved,

1. Shop-keepers

2. All Useless Trades
3. Lawsuits
4. Bad Debts
5. Dear Bargains
6. Loss of Time for want of Work.
7. Many Women and Children's Work.
8. Beggars. . . .

And all their Servants and Dependents.

[8] All the mechanicks will be ready at harvest, to help in with it, in a quarter of the time others do it, which when wet, may be of great advantage; which change of work, as it will be acceptable to many, so for the health of such as are used to sitting much.

Proposals to the College Founders. . . .

I propose for every 300 persons the raising of

£10000   To buy an Estate in Land of £500 per annum
£2000   To Stock the Land, and
£3000   To prepare Necessaries to Set the Several Trades to Work.
£3000   For New-building or Repairing Old.
         In all 18000 pound.

By which means the trouble of raising money to pay rent, will be saved, and the founders may have the more goods from the college, if desired, and the undertaking will not be so apt to miscarry in its infancy.

. . . [9] Corrections to be rather abatements of food etc. than stripes; and such as deserve greater punishments, to be expell'd, or sent to a House of Correction, but not in the College, for two reasons; first, it will relish too much of Bridewell; secondly, their ill company and example will tend to corrupt the youth. . . .

Ninthly, because the whole success (under the Providence of God) will lie

456

in a right beginning, . . . therefore let the nation be looked through for the first workmen, if can find but three or four in a county (the rest may be prentices) of good lives and tempers. . . .

[10] Though the computation be but 300 in a College; there may be 3000, or more: And such a one may be at

Colchester, where are made Bayes and Perpetuanoes.

Taunton, for Searges,

Stroud, for Cloth,

Devonshire for Kersies, and other places for other goods.

As also at the sea-coast may be raised several Colleges, as nurseries to the most effectual and successfulest fishery. . . .

[12] Here people's children of estates may be boarded and educated in all useful learning, who seeing others work, at spare times, instead of playing, would be learning some trade, work not being more labor than play; and seeing others work, to imitate them would be as much diversion to the children as play, which would the more insure them to business, when grown up. . . .

An hundred pound a year in such a College, I suppose will maintain ten times as many people as £100 a year in alms-houses, or hospitals. . . .

Some of the Advantages the Poor Collegians will have.

1. From being poor, they will be made rich, by enjoying all things needful in health or sickness, single or married, wife and children; and if parents die, their children well educated, and preserved from misery, [13] and their marrying encourag'd, which is now generally discouraged.

2. As the world now lives, every man is under a double care, besides his bodily labor; first, to provide for himself and family: Secondly, to guard against the intrigues of his neighbour's over-reaching him, both in buying of, and selling to him; which in such a College will be reduced to this single point, of doing only an easy day's work; and then instead of everybody's endeavoring to get from him, everybody is working for him; and they will have more conveniencies in the College than out. . . .

[14] 6. The regular life in the College, with abatement of worldly cares, with an easy honest labor, and religious instructions, may make it a nursery, and school of virtue.

7. The poor thus in a College, will be a community something like the example of primitive Christianity, that lived in common, and the power that did attend it, bespeaks its excellency; but considering the constitution of mankind that have estates (but it's not so with the poor) it was none of the least miracles of that age, and so abated as other miracles did.

A Few Rules for Governing the College-Workmen.

1. All the colleges and hospitals of England and Holland, should be visited, to see what rules and orders they have for governing their societies, that may be useful in this college.

[15] 2. All sorts of tradesmen should be consulted, what is a common and reasonable day's work for a man, that the rules and laws of the College may be made according.

3. It should be called a College, rather than a Work-house, because a name more grateful; and besides, all sorts of useful learning may be taught there.

4. The members of the College may be distinguished in caps and clothes; as the Master-workmen from the prentices, and women from girls.

5. A certain number of the boys and girls should be appointed weekly to wait at table upon the men and women at meals, that as much as may be, the men and women may live better in the College than anywhere else. . . .

Of the Education of Children, and Teaching them Languages.

1. Though rules, as well as words, must be understood to make a complete scholar, yet considering words lies in the memory, and rules in the understanding, and that children have first memory before understanding; by that nature shows memory is to be first used; and that in [16] the learning of language, words should be first learned and afterwards rules to put them together; children first learning the words of their mother-tongue, and then sentences. . . .

And therefore I think vocabulary and dictionary is to be learnt before accidence and grammar; and children's reading and discoursing one to another, gives a deeper impression than reading to themselves, . . .

2. Four hours in a morning, and four in an afternoon, is too long to tie a child to his book; . . .

3. A rebellious temper must be subdued by correction, (for better be unlearned than ill-bred) but such will not make ingenious scholars; stripes weakening that presence of mind which is needful to a ready learning. Understanding [17] must rather be distilled, as children can take it, than drove into them; grief hurting the memory, and disordering the thoughts of most. Raise a child's love to what he should learn, by rewards and emulation; for beating them (only) to make them learn spoils their natural parts . . . by which some, that would make anything better than scholars, are made only mere scholars.

4. . . . Beyond Reading and Writing, a multitude of scholars is not so useful to the publick as some think. . . .

5. Though learning is useful, yet a virtuous, industrious education tends more to happiness here and hereafter; . . .

For at four or five years old, besides Reading, boys and girls might be taught to knit, spin, etc. and bigger boys turning, etc. and beginning young, they would make the best artists; . . .

[19] Several advantages:

1. There will be all sorts of employs and tools for every age and capacity to be employed with.

2. All languages (and learning) may be learned there, by having some of all nations (tradesmen) who may teach their mother-tongue to the youth, as they teach it their own children.

3. Men and children submit easier to rules and laws they see others submit to as well as themselves, than if they were alone; as children in a school, and soldiers in an army, are more regular, and in subjection, than when scattered asunder. . . .

6. There may be a library of books, a physick-garden, [20] for understanding of herbs, and a laboratory, for preparing of medicines. . . .

I believe the present idle hands of the poor of this nation, are able to raise provision and manufactures that would bring England as much treasure as the mines do Spain, . . . it being the multitude of people that makes land in Europe more valuable than land in America, or in Holland than Ireland; regular people (of all visible creatures) being the life and perfection of treasure, the strength of nations, and glory of princes.

[The remaining eight pages of the tract answer possible objections.]

PART E:

The True Church Restored

Introduction

William Penn and others referred to the Quaker renewal of the church as "primitive Christianity revived." Was this just so much rhetoric or did they make good their boast? The following documents enable us to describe behaviorally some of the organizational characteristics of the Quaker movement. The letters and epistles give us the flavor of the movement; they also remind us how extensively the printing press was used as a persuasion instrument within an essentially free church movement. Both procedures and issues are illustrated, moving from the funding of missionary activity to crisis resolution in the testing of corporate authority, especially in relationship to the cult of personality that developed around James Nayler. The earliest letters presented here show how Quaker leaders, in trying to help the publication and the morality of other Friends, began to exercise control over them.

The major work in this section, Robert Barclay's *The Anarchy of the Ranters,* provides a theoretical solution to the issue of individual versus corporate guidance in the setting of the conflicts over John Perrot's individualism and of the disowning of Wilkinson and Story and their followers; in the end it enhances the authority of the Friends group over any individual; but within the group it gave Fox and other pioneer Quaker leaders institutional rather than charismatic authority. Whatever may have been the Quaker deviations from current ecclesiastical practices, it is apparent that they sought to intensify the corporate nature of the church rather than to diminish it. As early as 1651 George Fox parted company with Rice Jones, a Baptist newly converted to the movement and then estranged from it. The Ranter movement of

463

which Jones became a part accepted the extremes of subjectivism that lost even the objectivity of Jesus Christ. Against this George Fox and Robert Barclay labored to establish a position of Spirit-led consensus based upon the model given in the thirteenth chapter of Acts. Their attempts at an authentic community of Christians, together led of the Holy Spirit, was tested by the various schismatic conflicts that presaged the development of church polity. After the relatively innocuous conflict with Rice Jones had come the episode of James Nayler's symbolic reenactment of the messianic march into Jerusalem, which led to his imprisonment and branding as a blasphemer.[1] The Nayler episode in 1656 was followed in the next decade by Perrot's resistance both to the principle of corporate authority and to a *de facto* apostolate, and by the Wilkinson-Story defections in the '70's. As leaders failed or died in jail, the organizational structures of Quaker groups had to be authorized to stand alone, and the Spirit-led leaders given a clear place *within* this authoritative Meeting.

The Quaker movement was organized into a connectional system of meetings with their area increasing inversely with the frequency of meeting. Only recently have Friends brought significant modification to Fox's system of Monthly, Quarterly, and Yearly Meetings established during the 1660's and 1670's. This development constituted an attempt realistically to express as a gospel order the awareness of the church among those who had been gathered to the Lord and brought into a worshipping fellowship through the evangelizing ministry of the Quaker preachers. The epistles and queries of the Yearly Meetings took increasingly mandatory form and became Books of Discipline. The movement that would be the church became a state in Pennsylvania; when Quakers gave up leadership of this state at the time of the French and Indian War they replaced efforts to establish a godly commonwealth by developing both the concern and machinery for colonizing, godly lobbying, and acts of benevolence.[2]

The restitutionist themes reflected in such phrases as "primitive

---

[1] See pp. 481-485.

[2] See Sidney V. James, *A People Among Peoples* (Cambridge: Harvard Univ. Press, 1963), for a study of eighteenth-century benevolence. See also Frederick Tolles, *Quakers in the Atlantic Culture* (New York: Macmillan, 1960); Edwin Bronner, *William Penn's Holy Experiment* (New York: Temple Univ. Publications distributed by Columbia Univ. Press, 1962); and Isaac Sharpless, *A Quaker Experiment in Government* (Philadelphia, 1902).

464

Christianity revived" or "the true church restored" were sounded to an audience of seekers looking for alternatives to the forms by which they had experienced the church. The seekers had resisted the arbitrary nature of Presbyterianism and Independency. One of the seekers, John Saltmarsh, remembered the gifts of the Spirit to the members at Corinth:

> Now in the time of *apostasy* of the churches, [he said] they find no such gifts, and so they dare not meddle with any outward administrations, dare not preach, baptize, or teach: they find in the churches nothing but *outward ceremony.* . . . They wait for a restoration of all things and a setting up of "Gospel Officers," "Gospel Churches," "Gospel Ordinances," according to the pattern in the New Testament. They wait for an apostle or some one with a visible glory and power able in the Spirit to give visible demonstration of being sent.[3]

Visible glory, power, and demonstration marked the Quaker renewal of the church, which to their eyes was surfacing out of the dark night of apostasy.

Although they rejected the liturgical abstractions, Friends were highly sacramental in expecting the flow of divine grace through human interchange in family, worship, and work. Oliver Cromwell espoused not a church but a godly Commonwealth, and Gerrard Winstanley, the "Digger," a more socialistic vision of the same. (To Winstanley, the earth is the "common treasury, and all men are equally brothers called to work in it.")[4] For Winstanley the inward bondage of the mind was the result of outward social bondage, whereas in the same year George Fox told the people of Ulverston that "He loves the *Light,* and brings his Works to the *Light,* and there is no occasion at all of stumbling."[5] To Fox the field of the heart contains the "hidden pearl."[6]

[3] Condensed from Saltmarsh's *Sparkles of Glory* (London, 1648), pp. 214-21, by Rufus M. Jones, *Studies in Mystical Religion* (London, 1923), pp. 455-56.

[4] *True Leveller* in *Standard Works,* ed. Sabine, p. 260.

[5] George Fox, *Journal* (ed. Nickalls), p. 143.

[6] *Gospel Truth Demonstrated, Works,* IV, 164-68. Compare Winstanley, *The Law of Freedom (Standard Works,* ed. Sabine, p. 520), with George Fox, *Journal,* p. 143. Winthrop Hudson, in "A Suppressed Chapter in Quaker History," contends that Winstanley was a true originator of the Quaker movement and that the Ellwood edition of Fox's *Journal* attempted to foster a myth of Fox as founder in order to avoid the embarrassment of

A study of the writings of George Fox enables one to discern the following characteristics of the church: it is a gospel fellowship, a gospel order, a holy community, and a fellowship of evangelism.[7] According to Fox, Christ's inward baptism brings into common experience "the spiritual fellowship, which is the true church fellowship, even the Church which is in God."[8] "The pillar and ground of truth" is Fox's common definition of the church metaphysically.[9] The words "fellowship," "church-fellowship," or "gospel fellowship" define the church for George Fox sociologically. It is Christ who makes possible the church, not the church that establishes Christ, in Fox's judgment. Members of the true church know one another through the mystery of the new birth and the leadership of Christ. Such is the gospel fellowship. "The world," said Fox, "would have a Christ, but not to rule over them."[10] Yet Friends also rejected a view like that of William Dell, a Puritan pastor turned seeker, that a true church is "wholly a spiritual and invisible society."[11] Emerson W. Shideler stated that this way "the church was not only the communion of saints in ideas, it was a communion of saints in fact for Fox."[12]

Friends, indeed, recognized that the bond of Christian fellowship applies beyond practical reach: for Isaac Penington the church is "a people gathered by the life and spirit of the Lord."[13] Yet in the appointment of Men's Meetings and Women's Meetings, and

Winstanley's social radicalism. (See Winthrop Hudson, "A Suppressed Chapter in Quaker History," *Journal of Religion,* XXIV [April, 1944], 110-14. See also Winthrop Hudson, "Gerrard Winstanley and the Early Quakers," *Church History,* XII [1943], 177-94.) In this latter article he asserts that the two men were "in complete agreement theologically and characterized by the same social sensitivity." Not so! Despite George Fox's intuitive sensitivity to the images out of the earth and his frequent pastoral allusions, the differences between the two men are striking and basic, nor has any personal connection between them, or between their followers, been demonstrated.

7 See Arthur Roberts' dissertation "George Fox's Concept of the Church," microfilmed, Boston University, 1954.

8 Epistle No. 372, *Works,* 206.

9 See, for example, Epistle No. 222, *Works,* VII, 228.

10 Epistle No. 2, *Works,* VII, 17.

11 William Dell, "The Way to True Peace and Unity in the True Church of Christ," *Sermons Series* (London, 1652), p. 157.

12 Emerson W. Shideler, "An Experiment in Spiritual Ecclesiology: The Quaker Concept of the Church," unpublished Ph.D. dissertation, Univ. of Chicago, microfilmed, 1948, p. 40.

13 Isaac Penington, *Works,* IV, 8ff.

the development of a body of elders in the Second Day Morning's Meeting of London, George Fox sought to see the church "settled according to the gospel order and the power of God."[14] In 1667 Fox records, "and the Lord opened to me—and let me see what I must do, and how I must order and establish the Men's and Women's Monthly and Quarterly Meetings in all the nation, and write to other nations, where I came not, to do the same."[15]

Whether the Lord intended for this structure to continue for three centuries may be debated. Recently a number of Quaker "Yearly Meetings" have developed new nomenclature and a different time rhythm. Previous to these recent changes from "Monthly Meetings" the only serious change in formal organization had been the abandonment of the separate men's and women's business Meetings in the nineteenth century and the development of a federative organization of many Yearly Meetings. Both from the example of George Fox and from the "Second Day Morning Meeting's" oversight over the spoken and written ministry of Friends, it is apparent that the Quaker movement aimed to recapitulate the apostolate of the early church not by direct copy but on the basis of the Holy Spirit endowing certain individuals with leadership in the church. The vituperative Francis Bugg declared that Fox was a Moses (actually, he was more like Paul) taking the place of Christ.[16] But Francis Howgill said of Fox, "This man speaks with authority."[17]

The leadership of the Quaker movement was shared, however, and was grounded upon a belief that Christ led his people himself and gave gifts in varying degrees throughout the church. With all due regard to an assessment of ego-needs in the controversies that arose within the Quaker movement, and because of it, over the matter of authority, the movement did intend to provide a structure by which the will of God could be known infallibly in the contemporary church, as it had earlier been known by the apostles and faithfully recorded in scripture. It was perhaps arrested evan-

14 The *Journal* (ed. Nickalls), p. 513. Cf. also p. 491.

15 Fox's *Journal* (ed. Nickalls), p. 511. Cf. Epistle No. 308, *Works*, VIII, 59.

16 Francis Bugg, *The Pilgrim's Progress, from Quakerism, to Christianity, etc.* (London, 1698), pp. 131ff. See Epistle No. 308, *Works*, VIII, 61 in which Fox details his sacrificial leadership on the model of Paul in II Corinthians 11.

17 *Journal* (ed. Nickalls), p. 107.

gelistic outreach, rather than theory, which left the Quaker movement with a network of local or regional meetings but no continuing apostolate.

The "General Assemblies of the Ministry at London, or Elsewhere"[18] were left by Fox to be the guardians of the gospel order, entrusted with the task of sending forth an authentic ministry and providing the proper discipline in the church. The settlement of Yearly Meetings as representative bodies took some ten years in the 1670's and '80's, first only as an adjunct to the yearly meeting of traveling ministers.

The "restored church" faced the world as a holy community, not as an institution. Holiness as a mark of the church was to be demonstrated devotionally through worship, ethically through the testimonies, and socially through the Christian community. The nature of early Quaker worship has been variously but often partially described. It was functional rather than ritualistic either on the basis of silence or speech.[19] The holy community constitutes the primary loyalty-group, transcending the nation or state as the embodiment of God's kingdom. The recording of births and marriages and deaths and the scrupulous attendance upon the discipline of offenders that developed during the next generations were efforts to enable Quakers really to be the people of God. Practical needs also defined the holy community of the church as those who were their moral and financial responsibility, rather than as all those who in any way looked for guidance from Christian families. The masters of families in Barbados were encouraged by George Fox to include "negroes and tawny Indians" in their instruction or to entrust the task to others on their behalf.[20] Yet, released from the closely knit bounds of persecution and withdrawn from conquest of the world by evangelism, the Quaker church became haunted by birthright membership. This hampered its aggressiveness in the world with which it had come to terms or at least to a truce.

The church had been considered by Friends a fellowship of evangelism. As Elton Trueblood has reiterated in our times,

18 Epistle No. 308, pp. 59ff.

19 See Arnold Lloyd, *Quaker Social History, 1669-1738* (London: Longmans, Green, 1950), pp. 121ff. He shows that among early Friends the silent or "retired" meetings were at first less common than those devoted mainly to preaching to the unconvinced, although based on devotional silence.

20 *Journal* (ed. Nickalls), p. 605.

Quakerism was a movement of ministers without laity. Burrough called it the "camp of the Lord." At its outset ecstatic revival led Fox and others who shared a sense of the leading of the Holy Spirit. In this sense it was a Baptist-type lay movement but with a worldwide vision that accented its apocalyptic flavor. Christ had come and was restoring his church in the latter days preparatory to the time when the kingdoms of this world should become the kingdom of God. The letter of George Taylor to Margaret Fox, included in this series, shows the development of the Kendal Fund that was to make such worldwide evangelizing possible. The recording of gifts in the ministry grew out of a concern for corporate guidance in the leadership of the Holy Spirit. Certificates of approval from particular Meetings helped avoid the scandal of "bad spirits."[21] Approval went up the ladder, as it were, from the local to the Yearly Meeting. A practice aimed at preventing wildfire, it resulted in censorship by conservative elders to the minimizing of prophetic function, and until the development of pastoral ministry in America in the nineteenth century with its system of regular financial support within an increasingly specialized economic order, it tended to make ministry possible only to the rich.[22]

1. The Sharing of Quaker Life through Letters (The Swarthmore Manuscripts)

The natural practice by which early Friends in their travels wrote letters to George Fox or Margaret Fell at Swarthmoor Hall seems to have been developed into a regular system for reporting and mutual help after the conference of leading Friends at Swan-

[21] George Fox, Epistle No. 264, *Works*, VII, 349.

[22] Cf. Barclay, *Apology*, Prop. X, sec. XXVIII. Note also the doggerel by Thomas Ellwood included in Braithwaite, *Second Period of Quakerism*, pp. 360-61.

> *May none beyond Seas go but who can spare*
> *Sufficient of their own the charge to bear?*
> *Must Christ be so confin'd he may not send*
> *Any but such as have Estates to spend?*
> *God bless us from such Doctrine and such Teachers*
> *As will admit of none but wealthy Preachers.*

469

nington over the New Year, 1654-55. Friends such as Alexander Parker thereafter also forwarded news of all other Quaker preachers in areas where they traveled. The accumulation of letters at Swarthmoor Hall was partially sorted and identified by Fox himself, during a stay there (perhaps in 1675-77); later most of them were brought to London, often after staying in family homes until the nineteenth century. From Devonshire House they were moved with the Friends' offices and library to Friends House on Euston Road, where they have become the most extensive raw material for writers on the rise of Quakerism.[23] The sharing of the responsibility of guidance, which formed the bridge from personal counsel to group discipline, can be found in an early letter:

James Nayler, Letter to Margaret Fell, 26 July [1653] from Gervase Benson's house near Sedbergh, Yorkshire (SMS 3:3=*EQL* No. 37)

Thou art sealed in my heart, my sister; thy care for the babes is pleasant, and in it thou prospers; in these parts I see it, where thou hast been pruning; the Lord God Almighty bless thee with the fresh rivers of the values [=valleys?]. Water the living plants, my life. I am going towards Bishopric.[24] The Prince of Darkness is up, here at Appleby, but hath not much power. The night before the Sessions, I was amongst the beasts, and see them raving in their beastly nature, foaming out their venom, but could not; therefore tormented. I had a meeting at Stricklandhead the latter Sessions-day, to add to it; and so

23 Microfilms of these "Swarthmore Manuscripts" (=SMS) are at the libraries of Earlham, Harvard, Haverford, and Swarthmore Colleges. From this collection A. R. Barclay drew most of the *Letters of Early Friends* he published in 1841. Other early Quaker letter-collections have also been printed, such as the Caton MSS, the *Letters to William Dewsbury* (ed. Henry Cadbury [London: FHS, 1948]), and most of the ARBMS collection published seriatim in *JFHS*, besides the older samplings of Penn's and Penington's letters. Though transcribed by Elizabeth Jermyn, most of the Swarthmore Letters, including those presented here, have never seen print. A careful chronological index with detailed cross-references on all people and places mentioned was prepared by Geoffrey Nuttall and duplicated by Friends House in 1952 under the name *Early Quaker Letters* (=*EQL*); it covers simply Volumes 1, 3, and 4 and the years up to 1660. Our debt to Nuttall here and in the biographical index will be evident.

24 The Bishop of Durham had been the feudal lord of all of County Durham, which early Friends hence knew as "Bishoprick."

passed [on]. Oh, our defence for ever; but the beasts are exceeding mad at the work.

As for Ellen Parr: I hear that she is come towards thee; inquire and send for her if she be not come to thee. Judge the death, but save the little thing which I have seen moving in her. Let her stay a while with thee, and show her the way of love, which is much lost in the heights. And as thou finds movings, inquire of [the progress of] Truth, and write out to the flock of God. In the meekness thou hast power; bring down under thy feet what is above thee. There all feed in safety, my blessed, beloved ones; farewell.

My dear love to Margaret,[25] and the rest of the family; you little ones, peace be amongst you.

From Gervis Benson's house, the 26th day.   J.N.

2. Moral Discipline: Thomas Aldam, Letter to Margaret Fell, October 30, 1654 (SMS 4:89=*EQL* No. 91) from York Castle

As in the letter preceding, a sensitive concern for the individual's growth here overshadows the desire to dissociate Friends from individuals' misdeeds and disgrace, which later played a more central role in Quaker discipline. Except for her imprisonment at York, nothing is recorded about Agnes Wilkinson. (John Wilkinson the future Quaker Separatist came from New Hutton, near Kendal, and may have been related.)

Dear sister M: FF:

My dear love in the eternal Truth of God doth thee salute in the eternal unity. In the unchangeable life, & love of God, in my measure of God, I am with thee, rejoicing to hear of thy steadfastness, boldness, and faithfulness for the eternal truth of God; and to trample upon all deceit, in the power of God; in whose power thou stands armed against the wiles of Satan within and without; who art grown up into the large wisdom of God; which doth comprehend the wisdom of the world. And in thee is the salt to savor the unsavory spirits, which talk of truth, but live in deceit; which are to be cast

25 Margaret Fell's oldest daughter Margaret, later married to John Rous, had already the previous summer gone with a sister to visit the Quaker prisoners at York (cf. SMS 1:73=*EQL* No. 4).

out from the Children of the Light; to be trodden upon, that the separation may be made betwixt the precious and the vile, and the Children of the Light [are] to meet in one judgment: to justify no act done contrary to the Light; but that all words which are unsavory may with the Light be judged; and all actions done in the dark in holes and corners be brought to the Light to be proved and tried by the Light, what is acted in the Light and what is acted contrary; that all things acted contrary to the Light may by the Light be cast out. And here is one, a Friend in the measure of God which she hath received, in which she walks and is kept in tenderness; which I have sent unto thy house from York, with Agnes Wilkinson, who hath acted contrary to the Light in filthiness, and is cast out with the Light with them who was partakers with her; as a letter will let thee understand, which Agnes is to deliver to thy own hand sealed with my own seal: T.A. She hath received command to give it to thy own hand; see the seal be not altered. Receive this friend Bessie Vallance into thy house. My brother G:ff: did write to me to send Agnes to her mother's house; she is cast out, though she owns the condemnation; kneeling upon her knees at York. She was sent back from my brother G.FF: to us after she was sent out of prison, and I had command to send her to her mother's house; and I was moved of the Lord, to send her by thee to give thee charge of her, and a watch be set over her, to keep her out from amongst Friends till Friends do receive her, and she in her condemnation walk. I desire thee, send a Friend with Bessie Vallance to her [i.e. Agnes] mother's house and let that Friend come back toward York again with her [Bessie]. She is a stranger in that country in traveling. Let any tender Friend accompany her back towards York again: And watch thou over that spirit in Agnes Wil [kinson]. She hath been made to own her condemnation divers times. But, dear heart, it is not yet right; for the seal and the will speaks, from the sense of the just in prison; and the will and seal breaks out in passion. And so the will gets ease, and the judgment ceases; and the mind turns from the sword. But a subtle appearance in the condemnation it is, to deceive the simple, that she into unity may be received. But keep her out; and see that she be set and kept to labor; that flesh may be brought down, and that which would be at ease in the flesh may be brought to judgment; and the Life raised up to reign over her will; which now doth her filthiness condemn, wherein she hath acted contrary to the Light; who is by the Light cast out and kept out, and is for the plagues and the sword: till the just be delivered out of bonds, which is in prison. Take heed of receiving her in amongst you hastily, lest you take a burden; of which I do you forewarn of. To thee I have cleared my conscience in the truth of God, to the Church in thy house. I have been twice (?) at Captain Bradford's house with my dear brother G:ff: who is a father of the faithful in heart; before whom no iniquity can stand, with whom is my life.

Farewell from York Castle the 30th of the 8th Month 1654. Thy dear brother: T: A.

3. Arranging for Publishing the Earliest Quaker Tracts: Thomas Aldam, Letter to Amor Stoddard, from York Castle, February 19, 1652/53[26] (ARBMS 15)

Dear friend Captain Stoddard, my dear and tender love in eternal truth salutes thee. The everlasting power of the Lord guide thee and keep thee faithful unto the Lord, rather to suffer persecution with the people of God than to choose the pleasures of this present world. O be valiant for the truth upon earth; be valiant in the Lord's work. Quench not the Spirit: seek not thy own things, but the things of Jesus Christ, and give up thy self wholly to be guided by him. Thou hast tasted largely of his love. Abide in the vine, and thou shalt bring forth much fruit. The eternal power of the Lord establish thy heart in righteousness, and guide thee with his wisdom; that the Lord may be glorified in thee; sounding forth his everlasting praises; to whom be all honor, praise and thanksgiving now and forever. Dear friend: I am with thee in the unity of the spirit of this divine love; in that which thirsteth after purity and righteousness; therein with thee have I unity; beware of hiding thy talent. There is a great charge lieth upon thee and all other that he hath made him self known to, that they be faithful in his work. It did much rejoice me to hear my Father's voice sounding forth through you; and in the demonstrance of the chief Officers of the Army;[27] therein hearing a general convincement upon your spirits, that you have been seeking your own things and not the things of Jesus Christ. Now that you are convinced, the Lord looks for obedience. It is not a bare Confession, but it is they which forsake, that shall have mercy. Dear friend, I do not look at thee, nor any, as to put my confidence in the arm of flesh; but my rejoicing is in that Christ hath made himself manifest in flesh in you; who is come to convince the world in you; of sin and of all unrighteousness; who is come to establish his own Kingdom in righteousness, and throw down the powers of Anti-Christ who hath stand in forms and shadows, and signs without; and throwing down the false

26 For the background of Aldam's imprisonment, see p. 359.

27 For the army officers' appeals to their men and to Cromwell's Council, see p. 386.

worships, to bring true freedom to all his sons and daughters, who worship him in spirit and in truth; for such are they whom he seeketh to worship him. Farewell, my dear friend in the eternal truth; and his everlasting power keep and guide you in the strait way of self denial. The cry of the poor oppressed commonwealth are great. The cry is: oppression, oppression; injustice, injustice. Corrupt men set up to judge of the ways of God, which never knew him; whose mouths are full of reproaches; hearking to lies. Justice cries for vengeance to be poured down upon the Man of Sin. Dear friend, I desire thee to send me *The Discovery of the False Temple & the True Temple;*[28] if it be printed, with the other of *The Priests of the World.*[29] Samuel Buttivant did write to my brother Benjamin,[30] that they would be printed bef. the 3rd day of February; and I desire thee to send them immediately as thou canst; they would be very serviceable here with us. I desire thee send me 200 hundreds of them or 300 as Samuel Buttivant doth declare in his letter would be printed. And send me word in thy letter what thou didst pay for the printing of them and I shall use some means to send the money. I shall send money up by the carrier which brings the books. Dear friend, do not fail me, and let me know in thy letter whether thou receives this my letter or not. My dear love in the Lord remembered to Samuel Buttivant. All my dear brethren and sisters, fellow-prisoners, salutes you,

from York Castle
the 19th of February 1652.

Thy dear friend in the everlasting truth, Tho: Aldam A prisoner of the Lord at York Castle.

4. The "Kendal Fund" for Aid to Quaker Preachers Traveling or Jailed: George Taylor, Letter to Margaret Fell, 26 February, 1654-55 from Kendal (SMS 1:214=*EQL* No. 126)

Funds were evidently contributed to support them and their families as soon as the "valiant sixty" Friends set out to preach through all England in the summer of 1654. These were evidently

---

[28] This is a section of *A Brief Discovery of the Threefold Estate of Antichrist,* by Aldam, Benjamin Nicholson, John Harwood, and Thomas Lawson (1653). Cf. p. 64.

[29] May refer to *False Prophets and False Teachers* (1652-53). Cf. p. 358.

[30] Benjamin Nicholson was still in prison with Aldam at York, where Buttivant had been briefly.

administered at first by Margaret Fell personally (cf. BBQ, pp. 135-37). Late in the year, about the same time as the Swannington conference, she wrote appealing for support in such aid to Friends over a wider area, and designating George Taylor and Thomas Willan of Kendal to be treasurers (see her *Works,* pp. 56-59). A large number of letters, now lost, were evidently written by traveling Friends to the treasurers of the fund, and their contents were summarized in newsletters sent to Margaret Fell along with their accounts (cf. *EQL).*

Dear elect and pretious sister: in the eternal, everlasting and unchangeable power and life of unity do we salute thee, and all the rest of the Church that are in thy house. We need not give thee an account of our friends in the South, only we have written to them of Norwich[31] thy mind concerning the money and shall send it the next week by the carrier. For them at Appleby [jail]:[32] they have no need at present. When any is, our care shall be to supply them. Agnes Ayrey and John Spooner are, as we are informed, married; it were well if it had been done in the Light; our spirits cannot relish it; only we leave it in silence for fear of giving offence; but it were well if less of that were practised amongst Friends.[33] It seems that Oliver Cromwell and his Council have put forth a Declaration that none shall disturb the priests, but if they do they shall be taken [as] disturbers of the civil peace, as he calls it. It was thus: "This day the 15° By his highness, A Proclamation Prohibiting the disturbing of ministers and other Christians in their Assemblies and meeting;" Giles Calvert's wife,[34] it seems, hath cast some aspersions of Anthony Pearson and of the truth as we hear. He may, it is like, go up and

31 Margaret Fell would have heard via Fox the reports of all those gathered at Swannington; "them of Norwich" refers to Richard Hubberthorne, George Whitehead, James Lancaster, and Christopher Atkinson in the jail there, where Atkinson later was disowned for "lewdness" with a woman.

32 Howgill and Nayler were by this time out of Appleby jail. "Them at Appleby" may be Christopher Taylor, Thomas Taylor, and Anne Ayrey (cf. SMS 1:14=BBQ, p. 141). John Spooner visited them there (cf. Besse, II, 8). The Spooners were married February 9, 1654/55, by a Westmorland Puritan pastor. See *JFHS,* X, 19.

33 At this stage, Friends still lacked their own marriage procedures, though Cromwell had legalized civil marriages in 1653, and a folk-ceremony of "handfast marriages" in the absence of a priest was used in the Northwest. The problem, however, led Fox to urge Friends to set up committees and procedures to oversee marriages. The earliest Quaker wedding may be that of Thomas Holme and Elizabeth Leavens in 1654.

34 Giles Calvert's wife was a Baptist (and unlike his sister, never a Friend), but published at his press when he was legally enjoined not to, at the Restoration. Pearson, squire and member of Parliament from County

clear them. The Protector as they call him hath ordered some new books to be taken from Giles and carried to Westminster but what or what quantity we yet know not. We sent word by this last post to know which books they were, or what they did in it; but for sure this: they were of our books; here is some cabbage seed Tho: Bewly sent thee. He hath been very active since thou sent that note into Cumberland; and Friends there have been very free in their general meetings, in "distributing to the necessity of the saints." We have received from them near seven pounds,

from Pardshaw meeting	[£.] 02	--	12 [s.]	--	03 [d.]
from Caldbeck meeting	02	--	03	--	10
from Wiggton meeting	00	--	12	--	08
from Penreith meeting	00	--	09	--	06
from Isell meeting	01	--	00	--	00
	06		18		05 [sic]

We shall give the notice of what we do receive from Friends in Westmorland and Lancashire shortly, though we have been a while at under, yet we are like to be masters now, but servants still to the least of the members of Christ: 26 of the 12th month [1654]

Tho: Willan, Geo: Taylor

5. Letters and Leadings to Co-ordinate a Quaker Mission: Edward Burrough, Letter to Margaret Fell, from Dublin,[35] September, 1655 (SMS 3:17=*EQL* No. 179)[36]

Durham, was the most prominent Quaker convinced up to this time but, perhaps as a result, began from 1654 to pull back and eventually rejoined the established church.

[35] This was the first major Quaker mission in Ireland, but William Edmondson, a north-of-England settler in Ulster, had taken Quakerism home with him from a visit to Lancashire in 1654, and in the same year there had been brief visits by Richard Cleaton (=Clayton) and James Lancaster, Miles Halhead and Miles Bateman, besides a long trip by Edmondson with John Tiffin preaching in Ulster. Burrough and Howgill had recently turned over their impressive gatherings in London to James Nayler, and both felt led independently to visit Ireland together. Their response there came mainly from Cromwell's Puritan garrisons—positive from the Baptists who had ranked high under Fleetwood, negative from the Protector's son Henry Cromwell when he became Governor-General.

[36] See a cutdown version of this in *LEF,* CIII; also BBQ, pp. 212-18.

With no control or authoritative controller, Friends learned to support each others' projected mission trips by promptness in writing and in personal conscientiousness to respond.

M.F.

My dearly and eternally beloved Sister, in whom my soul and life is refreshed, by the remembrance of thee, Oh thou daughter of God, and a mother in Israel, a nourisher of the father's babes and children, who are begotten by the everlasting word; thou art comely in thy beauty clothed with the sun, and the moon underneath thy feet. Thou art all glorious and fair; thy raiment is of needle work and thy art full of glory within, thou daughter to the great king,[37] by whom I am ravished with love which burneth in my breast. Thou art in thy life and glory to be above all things desired after. I who am of thee and doth in the measure behold thee, and partake with thee of thy life and glory and fullness do dearly salute thee, in the everlasting fountain of life at whom I do drink with thee, and art daily nourished, and everlasting refreshed. But, my dear, now I do suffer, and beareth a burden; it is very great. With heaviness of Spirit I write, yea and with my eyes full of tears, unto thee. For I am separated outwardly from my dear eternally everlastingly beloved brother ff: H:,[38] who was my right hand man in the war, before whom many a philistine hath fallen. Yea through blood and tears cold I have followed. And truly when I consider what the Lord hath done by us, my heart is rent and broken. Many glorious day we enjoyed and many pleasant hour we had together, in dividing the spoil of our enemy.[39] For our hand was always strong in battle; and our ensign was lifted up above our enemies, and even thousands have fallen on our right hand and our left. But according to the will of God we are now separated, he into the west of this nation, 100 or 6-score mile from Dublin, where I must stay a season for ought I do see. And truly under great suffering, for few here is which hungers after God, and blindness and deafness hath possessed all. Little Eliz: Fletcher:[40] is at present

37 See Revelation 12:1 and Psalm 45. Such ecstatic affection is found in most early Friends' letters, but came to be an embarrassment after Nayler's "Fall" in 1656, and was cut out by Ellwood and Whitehead from later printings of such letters, and by Fox even from some manuscripts.

38 Francis Howgill; see p. 85. See also *LEF,* CII and CV, for Howgill's description of these same events, and SMS 3:16 for Burrough's continuation of this narrative.

39 The parallel is David's grief at losing Jonathan (II Sam. 1:20-26).

40 Elizabeth Fletcher from Kendal (cf. ARBMS 118). This letter shows the interaction of personal leading and group planning. By January Elizabeth Smith had come to join Elizabeth Fletcher, both had gone on westward, and

here, but I know not how long she stays. Her dear love is to thee, and to all the flock of God. Truly I suffer for her, she being as it were alone, having no other woman with her, in this ruinous nation, where it is very bad traveling every way afoot, and also dangerous (but we are much above all that).[41] If it were the will of the Lord, that any women were moved to come over to her; ff: H: & I was speaking of Anne Wilson. Thou may write to her or to G: ff: of it as thou art moved; And truly we wait in patience under great suffering at present, hoping some true lads may be moved to come over, which might be serviceable in the work of the Lord here. I was glad that ff: H: had so good an opportunity of passing in his journey; he went with a Cornet,[42] and some others which was very loving to us, and came to meetings while they stayed in the city [of Cork]. To all the family and to ye dear flock of God thereaway salute us. Though his name be not here yet, his love is forever to you all. We have not had any letter from you in the north nor not from London, since we came. We have written to London, but have had no return; here is a post weekly, if the wind lie not wholly contrary.

O my dear, let thy prayers be to the everlasting father for us; that his dread may go along with us; over all. Our parting was a heavy burden upon us both; especially in this strange nation, but we saw it to be of God; and we bore the Cross of it. As thou canst at opportunity, write to us; it will make me glad. One face of a friend would rejoice my soul; gladly would I hear of G. ff: and J.N. and of the rest in the south where I know the work of the Lord is glorious, and though some do rejoice, yet truly at present, we are men of sorrows; but in the will of our heavenly father resting. I am thy dear Bro: E.B:

four English Friends and two Dubliners were in Dublin prison; and by March Burrough and Howgill had reunited and been arrested at Cork, tried at Dublin, and deported; but Richard Waller, Richard Roper, and Barbara Blaugdone had independently felt led to come from England to continue their work. Soon afterward came Thomas Loe who was to convince William Penn; also perhaps George Keith.

41 In his next letter, from Waterford, Burrough reported: "being moved, I passed from it [Dublin] to this place; for our service lies only in great towns, and cities, for generally the country is without inhabitant, except bands of murderers, and thieves, and robbers [i.e. Irish], which waits for their prey, and devours many, from which yet we are preserved."

42 This was possibly Edward Cook, cornet from Cromwell's own troop of horse, later disciplined for becoming a Friend.

6. The Mutual Confirmation of "Leadings" and the Discipline of Its Refusal: Barbara Blaugdone,[43] Letter to George Fox, October, 1656 (SMS 3:194=*EQL* No. 328)

The testing of a "moving of the Spirit" against the "sense of the Meeting" or the sensitivity of "weighty Friends" came early and vitally in the pilgrimage of John Banks (cf. p. 185), Stephen Crisp (cf. p. 206), and many other newly convinced Quakers. Fox and other leaders were slow to challenge any Friend's "leadings" where self-will and immorality were not involved. Yet it is clear that restraint was often needed upon wilder impulses credited to the Spirit. An early example of its effectiveness, and of Friends' dependence upon each other spiritually, can be read between the lines of this letter.

George: I had these words rose in me: "Wo be to that nation whose teachers are fools and princes are children,[44] that hew unto themselves broken cisterns that will hold no water; therefore everyone to your tents;[45] return into your own habitations, even to the Light which Christ Jesus hath enlightened you withal. For as ye take counsel of the mouth of the Lord, even so shall your work prosper." This rose in me the first day the Parliament sat; but I was then in prison, and I knew not whether that might be shown to me which was done by another to them in a steeple-house.[46] If it hath not been done, and

---

[43] Late in a long life, Barbara Blaugdone wrote and published *An Account of the Travels of B.B.* (1691). Convinced at Bristol by Camm and Audland in 1654, she promptly wrote an intense letter to Fox (SMS 1:155), which he seems wisely to have ignored. Soon after, she felt led to go to Dublin, arriving just in time to denounce the governor, Henry Cromwell, in God's name for deporting Burrough and Howgill. Whether Barbara's imprisonment, here mentioned, was at Cork, where she next went, or later at Marlborough or in Devonshire, is not clear (cf. *JFHS*, XLVIII [1956]; John M. Douglas, "Early Quakerism in Ireland"). But it is fairly sure that Fox did not encourage her to go to Jerusalem, and that the Friends she felt led to enlist did not feel led to go with her. There is no evidence that she felt sure enough of her call to Jerusalem to disregard such a discipline by group silence, and to go; but later she gave up the use of flesh, wine, and beer and joined "the war against Amalek" by preaching tours from Basingstoke to Biddeford and twice more in Ireland.

[44] She echoes Isaiah 3:2; does she have young Henry Cromwell in mind?

[45] Here Jeremiah 3:2 is combined with I Kings 12:16, and outward with inward events.

[46] Geoffrey Nuttall links this with a "sign" done at the door of Parliament by Samuel Fisher on September 17, 1656 (see his *Works*, pp. 1-4).

479

thou see the work be mine, I desire a line from thee the second or first post. Mary Belcher is nigh unto death, as she thinks, with an ague and fever. If I hear not from thee, I shall abide here till the understanding of those I writ to thee of be opened, that should go with me to Jerusalem; they have all been very sick, and have something lies on them. But one of them would fain come to thee.

Barbara Blagdone

Since that, I saw Christopher Burket, Sara Smitten and Margret Thomas should pass to Jerusalem; but the time I knew not, nor of those I writ to thee of before.

7. Direct Confrontation: George Fox, Letter to James Nayler, September, 1656 (SMS 3:195=*EQL* No. 317)

In the setting of the famous conflict between Fox and Nayler in Exeter jail, and the ensuing "fall" of Nayler into disgrace by his "Palm Sunday"-style ride into Bristol, we present two letters showing aspects of mutual discipline among Friends. See *JFHS* (1929), p. 13, and Nuttall's, Brailsford's, or Emilia Fogelklou Norlind's biographies of Nayler for the events in Bristol. Fox, just released after exhausting months in "Doomsdale" dungeon at Launceston, found Nayler with other Friends imprisoned at Exeter. Nayler was himself exhausted after his London mission but also fasting and surrounded with neurotic women disciples, whose criticisms Fox asked Nayler to restrain. Nayler's refusal led to a meeting where Nayler, at a prison window below ground, asked Fox outside to kiss him in reconciliation and was in turn refused. This letter dates[47] from the same week (cf. *EQL*), though it was dictated or survives in a copy.

James: thou hadst judged and written thy secret and false letters against him thou shouldest not; thou shouldest not deal so presumptiously against the

---

[47] Shortly after his arrest at Bristol Nayler had in his pocket the original of the slightly later SMS 3:193, a copy of which, in George Bishop's handwriting (cf. Cadbury, *Swarthmore Documents in America,* pp. 26-27), was later endorsed in Fox's hand: "To James Nayler in Exeter prison . . . this letter was found in James Nayler's pocket when he was taken, and it cleared Friends."

innocent and thereafter thou wouldest have kissed him when thou hadst done this. A innocency and justice is delivered from that and you all, and Truth, innocency and justice is set atop of you all; and this you must read and own.

And James, it will be harder for thee to get down thy rude company, than it was for thee to set them up (if ever thou come to know and own Christ), whose impudence doth speak and blaspheme the truth.

Martha Simmonds and Stranger and his wife is denied for their lies and slanders & so judged out with the Truth.

ff. G.

This is sent from G.ff to be given to J.N.

8. Disownment and Friends' Dissociation from Nayler's Disgrace: George Bishop, Letter to Margaret Fell, October 27, 1656, from Bristol (SMS 1:188=*EQL* No. 3)

George Bishop was always the politician; he was thus perhaps the first Friend to realize how the Puritan powers in England would feel about Nayler's "blasphemous" ride. He does not minimize in this letter, therefore, the aloofness of Bristol Friends from Nayler, for which Bishop may have been largely responsible. He had just come from some days with Fox at Reading, and knew and took Fox's position regarding Nayler. Bishop's desire to "clear the innocent," both in the eyes of the nation and of Friends like Margaret Fell, by "testifying against this spirit" which had produced "works of darkness," was to mark a turning point for Friends. Without intending an excommunication that would cut off offenders from the sources of grace (with the Spirit, who could do that?) or "hand them over to Satan," Friends for two hundred years would increasingly "disown" the acts, and (unless repentant) the actors, who disgraced Quaker Truth. George Bishop was also always the story-teller; thus his narrative is our fullest account of a dramatic episode.

M.F. Dear Sister

In the eternal truth, into which we are baptized according to our measures, do I salute thee, and thy children with thee, who are begotten by the immortal Seed, heirs of the inheritance which is incorruptible, and that fadeth not, through the riches of his grace, who is God overall blessed forever,

VERITABLE PORTRAIT

ET L'HISTOIRE DE IACQVES
NAYLOR, Chef des Trembleurs & pretendu
Meſſie, Auec ſon Arreſt de condamnation, pro-
noncé par le Parlement d'Angleterre.

Ce viſage peint en ce lieu
Se dit vn Prophete de Dieu;
Mais qui diroit à ce viſage
Qu'il eſt né pour mourir en cage;
Sans mentir ſeroit aujourd'huy
Vn meilleur Prophete que luy.

482

who hath visited us with the Dayspring from on high, and accepted us in the beloved, and keepeth us in this great hour of temptation and the powers of darkness which is come upon these parts. [half a line crossed out] For thou mayst understand, that on the 6th day of the last we[ek] between the 2nd and 3rd hour in the afternoon, J.N. and his company (being released at Exeter) came into this town with full purpose and resolution to set up their Image, and to break the truth in pieces, and to bruise and tread down and beguile and devour the tender plants of the Lord in this his Vineyard, as before was given forth, with which being overfilled and made drunk with the indignation of the Lord. They brought in J.N. on horseback, who rode with his hands before him. One rein of his bridle Mart[ha]: Simmonds led, and Han[nah] Stranger: the other. And some went on his sides and Hannah's husband went bare before him, and Doreas Erbury with a man of the Isle of Ely[48] rode after, and thus they led him, and thus he rode and through the town, the women singing as they went "holy, holy, holy: Hosannah." And so passed to the White Hart, a bad Inn,[49] where they lay when they brought him first to Bristol on the Fifth Month; multitudes following them (for the whole town was around) through the streets thither, and into their chamber, though it had rained very hard, before whom the women put off some of their upper-garments to dry them at the fire.

This noise soon brought the magistrates together; who sent for them all. And J.N.s pockets they searched, and found about him [illegible] and letters of these women to him, wherein they call him Jesus (and that his name was no longer James) the only begotten Son of God, the King of Israel, the Prince of Peace, with such like, by which the mystery of iniquity which worked (?) was brought forth, which we sought formerly to have covered, and judged down, but now was brought forth before the sun, and which the world desired, and the enemy sought after, come to pass. And with these were other letters taken, discerning and judging that spirit that was leading them and seeking to recover him, one that, G.F., which was written with my hand,[50] and sent to him from Reading when we were there together about the 12th instant (a copy of which I have enclosed thee) and two of thine, and one of

48 On Samuel Cater from Littleport, Ely, see p. 162.

49 Though Friends Dennis Hollister and Henry Row were part owners, the Innkeeper was no Quaker (cf. BBQ, pp. 252, 566).

50 Presumably the copy of SMS 1:193 reported in *Swarthmore Documents in America.*

James Nayler as blasphemer (*from a French tract, without date or author, in the Quaker Collection, Haverford College Library*)

Eliz. Smith's, which exceedingly served the truth as it was ordered by the wisdom of God, seeing this thing must come forth, to the saving of it and us all before the world clear and innocent of their defilements.

The women (as I hear) owned their papers, and sang before them as before and M. lightly took him by the hand, and said Hosanna; and to prison they sent them all, notwithstanding their pass from O.P., viz. J.N., M. and her husband, H. and her husband; the Isle of Ely man, and Dorc: Erb[ury].

Whilst they were before the magistrates our Meeting was: whither to its like they had come with the town after them had not the magistrates put them up: but with us in silence was the pure sense of the Lord very great. And the Lord went forth with his Power to preserve all his lambs and babes in one, and to break the powers of darkness, and to chain them down so that Friends are all kept and preserved; none are hurt, none go to visit them (as I can hear of) and whatever is of God raised and stirred up against this work of darkness; for that those who had a secret love to Truth and yet never appeared were manifest, and that of God in the whole town witnessed to us, and our innocency, even in our enemies, and begat in them a good savor, and much moderation, and a secret joy, (even in some persecutors, our own it was which was it) that we were clear. And whereas their highest rage might have been expected, the mighty power of the Lord chained down all, and doth chain down all. And the priests are cut short of their hopes of striking the truth, as one with these, and in much wisdom, and honor surrounds the truth, over all, the right raised, the wrong chained down. So that as the wisdom of the Lord hath ordered it, seeing this was to come forth, it is best that at first ["so far" crossed out] it should come out here, and in such a manner, before it had either scattered here, or defiled other parts. For now it is manifest, and a Testimony from the living presence of the Lord is gone and given against it in the hearts of all, and the letters of Friends saves the truth, and this work of Darkness is cut off, and confounded and all Friends in all parts preserved, whose simplicity is not now beguiled, but witnesseth against those works of Darkness. This is the Lord's doing, and it is marvellous in our eyes. Eternal living praises be unto him, out of whose mouth proceeds the Sword with two edges with which [paper torn] against his enemies and cuts short the expectation of the [paper torn] the destruction of Jerusalem. [page torn and some words blotted]

The next day J.N. was sent for before the magistrates, [some of] the priests being present, and G.F.'s letter was read to him sentence by sentence, and asked he was whether he would own it, some of which he did, and some he said was a lie, as that passage where it is said this is the word of the Lord God to Thee, and Martha Symonds who[?] is called your Mother, so he denied his Mother. But as to their other questions, they obtained nothing of advantage from him; for he was subtile, few in words, and low; of whose examination and of the papers I have endeavored to get copies, that so might have the certainty, which if I can procure, its like I may send copies [to] Thee, and of this thing as it proceeds. But to J.A. I have wrote more particularly who its like may inform Thee; and I see little against them they will make in the issues as to their lives which the priests breathe after.

This day M. was examined alone and I hear how she rambled [ranted?] into declaring how she spake first to J. and compassed him [?] how he was at Bristol before, with such like; which cleared the innocent the more who before this day saw and testified against this Spirit. And G.F. letters was read to her, she was very confident and boasted what her work should come, and threshed Farmer the priest exceedingly. But of these things I can little enlarge, Friends staying whilst this is wrote, and I am not so certain of particulars. The magistrates told James of our denying him, and so read your letters and examined him upon them and took notice that we judged him and were not one with him. So hath the Lord wrought all things in the behalf of his truth which stirs everywhere, and makes our Meetings precious, who in this sharp exercise are put to it (though young and tender) to thresh the power of Darkness. The Lord hath ordered it so to be by his mercy. I pray for us that we may be kept stedfast and unmoveable to the praise of his Grace, that his name may be by us honored who is the King immortal, God only wise blessed for ever.

Dearly beloved in the Lord, I had thy letter and was refreshed in spirit [?] I received thine by J. Wilkinson to J.N.[51] and because these things passed so I opened it, and saw it convenient not to deliver it lest it should be taken, and then thou (?) knows not what that might prove and private [?] I keep it, but to thee do give this notice.

As to the moneys sent, there is a note enclosed. My dear love is to M.F. and thy other children and to all Friends, and to thy Husband. My wife dearly salutes ye all. In my measures of the living [? paper torn] . I am

Bristoll, 27th 8th Month 1656   Thy Brother
                                            G. [paper torn]

The enclosed is given forth by G.F. for all the magistrates in these nations, a great part of which is layd on me. And as thou art free thou mayest take care that copies thereof be taken, and sent to the magistrates in Westmorland, Cumberland, Bishoprick, Northumberland, and Scotland, G.F. would have the English every one to have one if it [reaches?]

51 This letter, preserved among Margaret Fell's papers, is quoted almost in full in BBQ, pp. 249-50.

9. George Fox's *Epistles*

The most beloved and searching of all Fox's writings are probably his epistles to Friends, and modern interpreters such as Howard H. Brinton[52] have rightly used them as the key to Fox's thought. Yet they are also the central source for our understanding of Fox's relationship to the Quaker Meetings he gathered, for his understanding of ministry and worship, and for the growth of Quaker organizations. Aware of his role as a new apostle like Paul, he wrote formal epistles "to all Friends" or "to Friends" of a particular area (not always now identifiable); informal and truly personal notes, even to his family or later to his wife, are rare. The epistles selected here are from the edition assembled and printed by Ellwood in 1698, and the sequence-numbering is his. Manuscript sources, where known (many being now lost), and minor textual corrections are drawn from Henry Cadbury's *Annual Catalogue of Fox's Papers,* and from Cadbury's handwritten notes on his own copy of the *Epistles.*

No. 5. To His Parents (Cadbury 47K, Post MS); undated, but printed by Ellwood under 1652. Notice here, as throughout the early pages of Fox's *Journal,* his need to establish the authority of his own inner voice over against his father's judgment.

Dear Father and Mother in the flesh, but not to that birth which speaks to you, (for like to that which doth beget is that which is begotten), praises, praises be given to my heavenly Father, who hath begotten me again by the immortal word.

To that of God in you both I speak, and do beseech you both for the Lord's sake, to return within and wait to hear the voice of the Lord there; and waiting there, and keeping close to the Lord, a discerning will grow, that ye may distinguish the voice of the stranger, when ye hear it. Oh, be faithful, be faithful to the Lord in that ye know; for in the backslider the Lord hath no pleasure, neither shall their damnation slumber. Oh, be faithful! Look not back, nor be too forward, further than ye have attained; for ye have no time but this present time: Therefore prize your time for your soul's sake. And so, grow up in that which is pure, and keep to the Oneness; then shall my joy be full. So fare ye well! And the Lord God of power keep you in his power! To him be praises for evermore!   G.F.

[52] *Friends for 300 Years* (1952).

No. 10. To Friends, 1652 (Cadbury: John Rouse's Book=Mark-ey MS). A classic summary of the experience of the Light or Spirit as it works within men

Friends,

Whatever ye are addicted to, the tempter will come in that thing; and when he can trouble you, then he gets advantage over you, and then ye are gone. Stand still in that which is pure, after ye see yourselves; and then mercy comes in. After thou seest thy thoughts, and the temptations, do not think, but submit; and then power comes. Stand still in that which shows and discovers; and there doth strength immediately come: And stand still in the Light, and submit to it, and the other will be hushed and gone; and then content comes. And when temptations and troubles appear, sink down in that which is pure, and all will be hushed, and fly away. Your strength is to stand still, after ye see yourselves; whatsoever ye see yourselves addicted to, temptations, corruption, uncleanness, &c., then ye think ye shall never overcome. And earthly reason will tell you, what ye shall lose. Hearken not to that, but stand still in the Light, that shows them to you, and then strength comes from the Lord, and help, contrary to your expectation. Then ye grow up in peace, and no trouble shall you move. David fretted himself, when he looked out; but when he was still, no trouble could him move. When your thoughts are out, abroad, then troubles move you. But come to stay your minds upon that Spirit, which was before the letter: have ye learned to read the Scriptures aright? If ye do anything in your own wills, then ye tempt God; but stand still, in the power of God be obedient, which brings peace.   G.F.

No. 14. To Quaker Ministers, 1652 (Cadbury: E-14, 57K). This is the first place where separation is clearly made between the quiet Meetings of convinced Friends, and public preaching at "threshing meetings" for the unconvinced.

All Friends, that are grown up in the life and power of the Truth, see that when ye appoint your meetings in any open place, in the fields, on the moors, or on the mountains, that none appoint meetings in your own wills; for that lets in the wills of the world upon the life of Friends, and so ye come to suffer by the world. But at such meetings let the wisdom of God guide you, that some may be there to preserve the Truth from suffering by the world; that all burdens may be kept off and taken away: So will ye grow pure and strong. And when there are any meetings in unbroken places, ye that go to minister to the world, take not the whole meeting of Friends with you thither, to suffer with and by the world's spirit; but let Friends keep together, and wait in their own meeting-place: So will the life in the Truth be preserved, and grow. And let three, or four, or six, that are grown up and are strong in the Truth go to such unbroken places, and thresh the heathenish nature; and there is true service for the Lord: And to you all this is the counsel of the Lord! The Grace of God, the Father of our Lord Jesus Christ, be with your spirits! Amen.   G.F.

No. 16. To Friends, 1652 (Cadbury=E-16—copy in Salem County, New Jersey, Historical Society). Like Nayler, Fox identifies God's love with the judgment of men inwardly under the Light.

To all you, my dear Friends, who have tasted of the immediate, working power of the Lord, and do find an alteration in your minds, and do see, from whence your virtue doth come, and strength, that doth renew the inward man, and doth refresh you; which draws you in love to forsake the world, and that which hath form and beauty in it to the eye of the world; and hath turned your minds within, which see your houses foul, and corruptions strong, and the way narrow and straight, which leads to life eternal: To you all I say, Wait upon God in that which is pure. Though you see little, and know little, and have little, and see your emptiness, and see your nakedness, and barrenness, and unfruitfulness, and see the hardness of your hearts, and your own unworthiness; it is the Light, that discovers all this, and the love of God to you, and it is that which is immediate, but the dark understanding cannot comprehend it. So, wait upon God in that which is pure, in your measure, and stand still in it every one, to see your saviour, to make you free from that which the Light doth discover to you (to be evil.) For the voice of the bridegroom is heard in our land; and Christ is come amongst the prisoners, to visit them in the prison-houses; they have all hopes of release-ment and free pardon, and come out freely, for the debt is paid; wait for the manifestation of it, and he that comes out of prison shall reign.

So, meet together all ye, that fear the Lord God, and think upon his name, his mercies endure for ever; his mercies are in temptations and troubles, his mercies are in afflictions, in reproaches and in scorns. Therefore rejoice, ye simple ones, which love simplicity, and meet and wait together to receive strength and wisdom from the Lord God; and in departing from sin and evil, ye will be able to speak to the praise of the Lord: And meeting and waiting in his power, which ye have received, in it all to improve your measure, that God hath given you; for ye never improve your measure, so long as ye rely upon any visible thing without you; but when ye come alone to wait upon God, ye shall every one have a reward according to your deserts, and every one your penny, who are called into the vineyard to labour. Therefore be faithful to God, and mind that which is committed to you, as faithful servants, labouring in love; some threshing, and some ploughing, and some to keep the sheep: He that can receive this, let him: And all to watch over one another in the Spirit of God. So God Almighty bless, guide and prosper you unto his kingdom, where there is no tribulation. When your minds run into anythings outwardly, without the power, it covers and veils the pure in you.

No. 131. Formal Epistle to Friends (SMS 2:95). Most of this epistle is omitted. Here Fox warns against judgmental ministry among the "settled" Friends.

All Friends everywhere, take heed of printing anything more, than ye are required of the Lord God. And all Friends everywhere, take heed of wandering up and down about needless occasions, for there is danger of getting into the careless words, out of seriousness, weightiness and savouriness. And all Friends everywhere, take heed of wronging the world or any one in bargains, or over-reaching them; but dwell in the cool, sweet and holy power of the Lord God, and in righteousness, that it may run down amongst you; and that will keep you low. And all Friends everywhere, take heed of slothfulness and sleeping in your meetings; for in so doing ye will be bad examples to others, and hurt yourselves and them. And all take heed of going up and down to minister but as ye are moved of the Lord God, or to speak in meetings or any other places; for travelling to such is dangerous to lift them up, going amongst settled meetings that are settled. For there is difference betwixt Friends going into the world, and of coming among them, that are come to silent meetings, and to feed there; for that which may be seasonable to the world, may not be to them.

Let this be read in your meetings.

George Fox's address to Friends in the Ministry, given at John Crook's house, 31st March, 1657 (from *CJ*, I, 317-23). Here Fox shows the temporary nature of Quaker ministry, which opens direct contact between men and the Spirit and then steps aside.

Friends, take heed of destroying that which ye have begotten. . . . Though that be true and may be the pure Truth which [a man] speaks, yet if he doth not remain in that and live in that in the particular, but goes out, that same, that which he is gone out from cometh over him. . . . He cometh to an end and doth not remain.

And take heed of many words, but what reacheth to life, . . . that which reacheth to the life from the life received from God, that settles others in the life. . . . And so Friends must be kept in the life which is pure, and so with that they may answer the life of God in others which is pure. For if Friends do not live in the life which they speak of, [so] that they answer the Life in those that they speak to, the other part steps in. . . .

In all Meetings you come into, when they are set silent, they are many times in their own. Now a man, when he is come out of the world, he cometh out of the dirt; then he must not be rash. . . . Then he must come and feel his own spirit, how it is when he comes to them that sit silent; for if he be rash, then they will judge him, . . . for he may come in the heat of his spirit out of the world. . . .

Now there is a great danger too in traveling abroad in the world, except a man be moved of the Lord, by the power of the Lord, for then he keeping in the power is kept in his journey and in his work, and it will preserve him to answer the transgressed and keep above the transgressor. . . . For now though one may have openings when they are abroad to minister to others, but as for their own particular growth, [it] is to dwell in the life which doth open. So if any one have a moving to any place and have spoken what they were moved of the Lord, return to their habitation again, and live in the pure life of God and fear of the Lord. And so will ye in the life and the sober and seasoned Spirit be kept. . . .

So that which doth command all these spirits where heats and burnings come in, in that wait, which chains them down and cools. For there is no hasty rash brittle spirits, though they have prophecies, [that] have gone through.

. . . That which Friends do speak they must live in, and so may they look that others may come into that which they speak.

The power of the Lord God has been abused, and the worth of truth has not been minded; there has been a trampling on and marring with your feet; . . . but every one may be kept in the pure power and life of the Lord: then the water of life comes in: then he drinks and gives others to drink.

Now when any one shall be moved to go to speak in a steeple-house or a market, turn in that which moves, and be obedient to it. Now that which would not go must be kept down. . . . And take heed that the lavishing part do not get up.

Now it is a mighty thing to be in the work of the ministry of the Lord and to go forth in that, for it is not as customary preaching, but to bring people to the end of all preaching: for [after] your once speaking to people, then people come into the thing ye speak of. . . . Now if words be rashed out again unsavory, then they . . . may hurt again that which he has got up. . . . So walk in the love of God.

No. 248. An Exhortation to Set Up Women's Meetings (1666); almost identical to No. 296 (1673) (which sounds like the older of the two wordings, where they differ)

Friends, all to keep your Meetings in the power of the Lord God, that hath gathered you; and none to quench the Spirit, nor despise prophesying, and so keep up your testimony in public and private: Let not the mouths of babes and sucklings be stopped, nor the seed in male or female, but all be valiant for the Lord's Truth upon the earth. Concerning your Women's Meetings; encourage all the women of families, that are convinced, and minds virtue, and loves the Truth, and walk in it; that they may come up into God's service, that they may be serviceable in their generation, and in the creation, and come into the practice of the pure religion, which you have received from God, from above; that everyone may come to know their duty in it, and their service in the power and wisdom of God: For now the practical part is called for. For people must not be always talking and hearing, but they must come into obedience to the great power of the great God of heaven and earth.

And so, that none may stand idle out of the vineyard, and out of the service and out of their duty; for such will talk and tattle, and judge with evil thoughts of what they in the vineyard say and do: and therefore the power of God must call all, into their duty, into their service, into their places, into virtue and righteousness, and into the wisdom of God: For all that are out of their duty in their services, though they may have the knowledge of it, yet are not serviceable in the creation nor in their generation; and the power of God must go over, and is over all such; by which all must be acted, and in which true obedience is known.

And therefore train up your young women to know their duty in this thing, that they may be in their services and places; which they are to do in the power and wisdom of God; by which you are kept open to the Lord, to receive of his gifts and graces, and of his life, through which you are to minister one to another: And all keeping in it, then there is none to let (n)or stop its flowing(s); but through it you are all watered, as a garden of plants; by which you are nourished. And so, all be faithful and diligent in the Lord's business. And make all the sober women, professing Truth in the country about you, acquainted with this thing. And read this in your Monthly

Meetings, when you are gathered together. And when you have made the sober women acquainted, in the towns and countries, and have them together, then read this amongst them. So, no more but my love.   G.F.

No. 253. To Peter Hendrix, Cheesemonger, in the Fish Lane, in the three Leyden Cheeses at Amsterdam, 1667. Fox wanted to collect records of sufferings of Friends overseas, just as in England, and to organize aid to the victims. Here is also an early example of the use of disownment, as aimed at clearing the reputation of "Truth."

Dear Friends, in the everlasting power of the Lord God, I salute all the faithful and upright, among whom the Lord hath joy and delight; in which everlasting power of God have you your unity, fellowship, and dominion. And so Friends, all sufferings of Friends, of what sort soever, for conscience sake to Christ, in Holland, in Germany, in Zealand, in Gilderland, in the Palatinate, in Friesland, Swedeland, Switzerland and Hamburg, send an account for what they have suffered, and by whom; together with the examples that are fallen upon the persecutors; with their mittimusses and examinations, send all these to London, to Friends there; that if any ambassadors or agents, out of any of those places, come to London, Friends may make application to them; for there are some Friends, who are ordered for the same purpose, to take knowledge of such things. And likewise, if any Friends have come over into those parts of the world, and have not walked answerable to the Gospel of Truth, but have walked scandalously and disorderly, whether they have been such who have come over to minister, or sea-men, and factors, or merchants, or masters of ships, whereby the Lord God hath been dishonoured, and his holy name blasphemed; by which his people are called. And also all such who have not been faithful in their callings between man and man, but have been deceitful in their callings, and have been exactors, and have not been true to their word; by such doings they cause the holy name of the Lord God, and his righteous Truth, to be evil spoken of. That a list of all such may be gathered up, and sent over to London, to such who are to receive them; and that if they condemn those things and have given forth a paper of condemnation against them, if so, that we may have a copy of it also to take away the reproach of their transgressions from Friends. And let faithful Friends amongst you meet together to consider and take care about these things.   G.F.

And take heed of hurting any concerning marriages, if the thing be right (through any earthly reasoning) lest they do worse.

And so all be diligent for the Lord God and his Truth upon the earth, and

492

the inheritance of a life that hath no end, that you may live in that seed that is blessed for evermore.

And be diligent in all your meetings, and see to the setting forth of apprentices, all fatherless and poor Friends' children; and that all the poor widows be carefully looked after, that nothing may be lacking among you; then all will be well.

And keep your testimony against all the filthy rags of the old world; and for your fine linen, the righteousness of Christ Jesus. . . .

And train up all your children in the fear of the Lord, and in his new covenant, Christ Jesus; as the Jews did their children and servants in the old covenant, and so do you admonish your children.

No. 263. General Epistle on Property and Marriages, 1668. (The parts of this had appeared at various times since 1657, according to the Annual Catalogue.)

Friends, keep at a word in all your dealings, without oppression. And keep to the sound language: Thou to everyone.

And keep your testimony against the world's vain fashions.

And keep your testimony against the hireling priests, and their tithes and maintenance.

And against the old mass-houses, and the repairing of them.

And against the priests and the world's joining in marriages.

And your testimony against swearing, and the world's corrupt manners.

And against all looseness, pleasures and profaneness whatsoever.

And against all the world's evil ways, vain worships and religions, and to stand up for God's.

And to see that restitution be made by everyone, that hath done wrong to any.

And that all differences be made up speedily, that they do not fly abroad to corrupt people's minds.

And that all reports be stopped that tend to the defaming one another. . . .
And let no man or any live to themselves, but in that love that seeks not her own. . . .

And if any one hath anything to say, in opposition to the matter of marriages, propounded by any to the meeting, such Friend or Friends to make it known (what they have against the parties) to such as are appointed by the meeting, to enquire into the clearness of the parties, who laid their intentions before the Meeting. And such Friends as have intentions of marriage first to lay it before the men and women of the Monthly Meeting they belong to, and to see that things are clear, before they are brought to the Two Weeks Meeting.

And if any difference arise, either about marriages, or any other case, in the Two Weeks Meetings, that the business be presently referred to six Friends, to have a hearing of the matter another day, or else for them to go forth and determine it presently, and not to discourse it in the open meeting.

And if any legacy be left by any deceased Friend, to a particular use, as to putting forth apprentices, and breeding up poor Friends' children; that the said money be kept distinct, as a stock for the said use, and a particular account thereof to be kept. And the Quarterly or Six Weeks Meetings to see, that the said monies be disposed of to the uses as aforesaid. And if any of the principal money so given, be at any time made use of to any other use, that it be again made up by the Meeting of Friends in general. And though the money be left or given to any particular Friend for the use aforesaid; yet the same to be paid to two or three persons, whom the Quarterly Meeting or Six Weeks Meeting shall appoint to receive such money; that so the Meeting may have the ordering and disposing of the said money to the best advantage, and the use intended.

And that Friends do keep in their testimony against the vain fashions of the world, and all looseness and uncleanness whatsoever; and against all profane, idle tippling, and taking tobacco in coffee-houses and ale-houses, which is an ill savour: And against all strife and contention whatsoever.

And that some Friends be appointed at every Meeting to keep the doors, to keep down rude boys and unruly spirits; that so the Meetings may be kept civil and quiet.

And if one Friend hath anything against another, let him not treasure it up, till the time of his marriage, and then cast it upon him publicly; but let him presently speak to the Friend, and also to them, that the meeting hath appointed to see after his clearness, &C. And that things may not be deferred too long at the Two Weeks Meeting concerning marriage; but that they may be answered in a short time, lest they be put to a strait in the matter. . . .

Read this in the men and women's meetings in the fear of the Lord, as often as you see occasion, and record it in your book.

No. 304. To Friends in Virginia; from Worcester Jail, June, 1674

Dear Friends, W. Benson,[53] to whom is my love, I am glad to hear of the increase of truth amongst you. And the Lord prosper his work, and increase

[53] T. W. Denison, in the list of Fox's *Epistles*, according to Cadbury.

people in his knowledge, who will fulfil his promise, ... And in his name keep your men's and women's, and all your other meetings, that you may feel him in the midst of you, ... I am glad to hear of some of your diligence, in taking that great journey to Carolina through the woods; for if you visit them sometimes, it would do well: And there is a people at that place you call New-Country, as you go to Carolina, which had a great desire to see me, amongst whom I had a meeting. I received letters, giving me an account of the service some of you had with and amongst the Indian king and his council; and if you go over again to Carolina, you may enquire of Capt. Batts, the old governor, with whom I left a paper to be read to the Emperor and his thirty kings under him of the Tuscaroras, who were to come to treat for peace with the people of Carolina: Whether he did read it to them or not, remember me to Major General Benett, and Col. Dew, and the rest of the justices that were friendly and courteous to me, when I was there, and came to meetings;[54] and tell them, that I cannot but remember their civility and moderation, when I was amongst them. And so the Lord redouble it into your hearts, and theirs, the love and kindness which they and you showed unto me. I have been a prisoner here about these eight months, and now I am premunired, because I cannot take an oath; but the Lord's seed and power is over all, blessed be his name for ever, and glory and honour to him, who is over all, and is worthy of all.

Read this amongst Friends in the meetings. G.F.

No. 340. To Friends Colonizing West Jersey, 1676. Among the patterns of organization that Fox urged Friends to set up, the exchange of newsletters between Yearly Meetings was to become important for later Quaker history.

My dear Friends, in New Jersey, and you that go to New Jersey, my desire is, that you may all be kept in the fear of God, and that you may have the Lord in your eye, in all your undertakings. For many eyes of other governments or colonies will be upon you; yea, the Indians, to see how you order your lives and conversations. And therefore, let your lives, and words, and conversations be as becomes the Gospel, that you may adorn the Truth, and honour the Lord in all your undertakings: Let that only be in your eye, and then you will have the Lord's blessing and increase, both in basket and field and store house; and at your lyings down you will feel him, and at your goings forth and comings in. So that you may answer the Light, and the

---

54 Cf. Wm. Edmondson, *Journal,* p. 62.

Truth, in all people, both by your godly lives and conversations, serving the Lord, and being valiant for his Truth, with a joyful heart upon the earth, and the glorious name in whom you have salvation.

And keep up your meetings for worship, and your Men and Women's Meetings for the affairs of Truth, both Monthly and Quarterly: And, after you are settled, you may join together and build a Meeting House. And do not strive about outward things; but dwell in the love of God, for that will unite you together, and make you kind and gentle one towards another; and to seek one another's good and welfare, and to be helpful one to another; and see that nothing be lacking among you, then all will be well. And let temperance and patience and kindness and brotherly love be exercised among you, so that you may abound in virtue, and the true humility; living in peace, showing forth the nature of Christianity, that you may all live as a family and the Church of God, holding Christ your heavenly head, and he exercising his offices among you and in you. And hold him the head, by his Light, power and Spirit, and that will keep your minds over the earthly spirit up to God; for the earth, and the sea, and all things therein, are his, and he gives the increase thereof.

And therefore be not over eager after outward things, but keep above them in the Lord's power, and seed Christ Jesus, that is over all; in whom you have all life, election and salvation.

And write over yearly, from your Meetings, how you are settled, and how your affairs go in the Truth, and how your men and women's meetings are settled.

And my desires are that we may hear that you are a good savour to God, in those countries: So that the Lord may crown all your actions with his glory. So with my love to all.

Swarthmore, the 4th of the 1st month, 1676.   G.F.

The First Friends in Germany [from later copy in Haverford Library]. London, 8th of 1st Month, 1682-83. Fox wrote to Amsterdam Friends in 1683. (See Epistle No. 374 and *Annual Catalogue*.)

Dear Peter H[endricks] & J[an] C[lauss]

With my love to you and your wives, and all the rest of Friends, both in Holland and Germany and elsewhere.

I rec'd thy letter dated the [blank space], and I was glad to hear of the prosperity of Truth and the unity that is amongst Friends; the Lord preserve it; for it is the mind of the Lord that all his people should be in fellowship with him and one another in his Light.

Now, thou writing how Friends have set up a Yearly Meeting in Danzig, which I like very well, which may sound the Truth and the Gospel, the power of God in these parts of the world. And if they had it one year at Fredrickstadt, I think it would not do amiss, and the other year at Danzig. But that I shall leave to you as you shall feel or see meet. Or an half-yearly Meeting at Fredrickstadt, once in the summer, after your Yearly Meeting in Holland. Which then if any Friends come from England they might visit them. And 'tis very well that there is a Monthly Meeting settled at Hamburg, and so they should do at Fredrickstadt, and have a Monthly Meeting there, if they have not one; not of the same month that Hamburg's is of; that if any Friend should visit Hamburg Monthly Meeting, that they might then visit next Fredrickstadt. And so they ought to have a Monthly Meeting at Danzig of all the faithful, if they have not one; and to see that all things are kept sweet and clean in the power and Spirit of the Lord Jesus Christ; that righteousness, virtue and holiness may flow over all, and that God's vineyard and garden may bring forth holy and righteous fruits to the glorifying of him; and the lamps and candles may be burning night and day in every one's tabernacle, that all may dwell with the everlasting burning and with God, who is a consuming fire, to consume all the wicked, so that no wickedness may be in his camp or holy generation. And so if they have not a Monthly Meeting in the Palatinate, they ought to have one. And wherever Friends are gathered, the faithful should have a Monthly Men- & Women's-Meeting, for that will follow naturally in the divine life and heavenly unity of the Spirit & communion in the Holy Ghost. And so my desire is that all Friends may be faithful and valiant for God's Truth upon the earth, and spread it abroad, and keep an heavenly intelligence and a correspondence and fellowship in the Holy Spirit one with another in all places. And spread books up and down, where you hear of any tenderness.

And as for passages here, sufferings attends Friends in most places, and imprisonments very much, but the Lord with his power doth support his faithful people to stand for his glory. I hear that they have very precious Meetings in Wm. Penn's Country and in New Jersey, & Meetings are pretty quiet in other parts of America and in New England, and in Scotland and Ireland. But in Barbados they keep them out in the street; but there Friends are prettily well, I understand by letters. And the Lord keep and preserve all Friends chaste in his power, as virgins with oil in their lamps, that they may enter in with the Bridegroom, and not only so, but be married unto him, Christ Jesus, and keep in him the Sanctuary. Amen.   G.F.

And I have not yet received the books, but it's like, when they come, I shall receive them.

497

Here is a paper concerning marriage, & an Epistle of mine concerning magistrates, which you make what use you will of them.

Roger Longworth is present, and remembers his love to you all.

And another paper concerning the Seed of Abraham which you may print & send it among all Friends.

No. 386. Fox to Friends in Charleston, Carolina, 1683. Friends were at one time as active in South Carolina as farther north; there John Archdale, though a Friend, served as governor.

Dear Friends, of the Monthly Meeting of Charles-Town, in Ashley Cooper River in Carolina: I received your letter, dated the sixth day of the eighth month, 1683, wherein you give an account of your Meeting, and of the country, and of your liberty in that province, which I am glad to hear of, though your Meeting is but small. But, however, stand all faithful in Truth and righteousness that your fruits may be unto holiness; and your end will be everlasting life: And that you may be patterns of virtue, modesty, chastity and sobriety, showing forth the fruits and life of Christianity in your lives and conversations, that they may preach righteousness, truth and holiness to all people in that dark wilderness, that you may answer the Truth both in them that are called Christians, and in the Indians. And my desire is that you may prize your liberty, both natural and spiritual, and the favour that the Lord hath given you, that your yea is taken instead of an oath; and that you do serve both in assemblies, juries, and other offices, without swearing, according to the doctrine of Christ; which is a great thing, worth prizing. And take heed of abusing that liberty, or losing the savor of the heavenly salt, which seasons your lives and conversations in truth, holiness and righteousness. For you know, when the salt hath lost its savor, it's good for nothing but to be trodden under the foot of men. For we here are under great persecution, betwixt thirteen and fourteen hundred in prison, an account of which hath lately been delivered to the king, besides the great spoil and havoc which is made of Friends' goods, by informers; and besides the great spoil upon the two-thirds of our estates, and upon the twenty-pound-a-month Acts, and for not going to the steeple-house; and besides many are imprisoned and pre-munired for not swearing allegiance, both men, women, widows and maids; and many are fined and cast into prison, as rioters, for meeting to worship God. And we are kept out of our meetings in streets and highways in many places of the land, and beaten and abused. And therefore prize the liberty, both natural and spiritual, that you enjoy. And many are cast into prison because they cannot pay the priests' tithes; and also many are cast into prison by the bishops' writs, De Excommunicato Capiendo. So, that at present we are under great sufferings, persecutions and imprisonments: But the Lord's power is over all, and that supports his people.

But in Ireland, Scotland, Holland, Germany and Danzig, we hear that Friends are in peace and quietness; and therefore you that have great liberty, both natural and spiritual (as aforesaid) be valiant for God's Truth upon the earth, and spread it abroad, both among them that are called Christians and Indians, turning them from darkness to light, Christ Jesus, the saviour, whom God hath set up for an ensign among the Gentiles or heathen, and to be his salvation unto the ends of the earth. So seek the good of all, and the profit of all, and the salvation, and the glory of God above all, and the exalting of his name and Truth in your day and generation; and live in love, and in the Truth, and the love of it; and overcome evil with good; and hold fast that which is good, then you can try all things.

And so with my love to you all in the holy seed of life, Christ Jesus, that reigns over all, who is your sanctuary, in whom you have all life, and peace, and salvation, in him, the Lord God Almighty preserve and keep you all holy, pure and clean, to his glory, Amen.

London, the 23rd of the 12th month, 1683.

No. 396. To the Suffering Friends at Danzig, 1684

Dear Friends, Dan'l Abrams, Nic. Rust, C. Ruttel, with my love in the Lord Jesus Christ to you, . . .

Now, dear Friends, we do hear and understand, that the magistrates have cast you into prison again in Danzig; and that they have proffered you your liberty, upon condition that you would go away, or forsake your common meeting-place, or divide yourselves into several little meetings. Truly, Friends, we have had many of these proffers made to us within this twenty or thirty years, but we never durst make such bargains or covenants, to forsake the assembling of ourselves together, as we used to do; but did leave our suffering cause wholly to the Lord Christ Jesus, in whose name we were gathered, who has all power in heaven and earth given unto him. And the Lord at last did and hath tendered the hearts of many of our prosecutors both in England and other places. And therefore in the spirit and power of the Lord Jesus Christ, it is good to be faithful; who is God all-sufficient to support and supply you all in whatever you do, and strengthen you in all conditions. For if that should get a little advantage upon you, and get you into weakness, it would not rest so, but get more upon you. And therefore it is good to stand fast in the liberty in Christ Jesus, the second Adam, the Lord from heaven, who hath made you free out of the snares, and bondage, and limitations of the wills of the sons of old Adam. . . .

No. 420. To the Quaker Captives at Meknes, Algeria, 1690. Though Fox dictated about ten more letters before his death on 12/11/1690 (see *Annual Catalogue*), it is appropriate to close the record of his ministry with this message to English Friends, who even as slaves maintained their witness.

Dear Friends, with my love to you all in the Lord Jesus Christ, in whom you have life and salvation, and rest and peace with God; and the Lord God almighty with his eternal arm and power uphold and preserve you in Christ, in whom you have rest and peace; though in the world troubles, and though you be in captivity, from your wives and children, and relations and friends, yet the Lord is present with you by his Spirit of grace, light and truth. And so feel him at all times, and stand in his will. Do not murmur nor complain, but stand still in the faith and power of God, that you may see your salvation. For by faith the Lord delivered his people out of Egypt by his power; and by faith Enoch and Noah were preserved, and Abraham, Isaac and Jacob; and by faith the prophets were delivered out of many perils; and Daniel out of the lion's mouth. And you may see how the righteous were delivered by faith, in *Heb.* 11.

And it would be very well, if you that be captives and Friends could have meetings as they had at Algiers, to the comforting and refreshing one another. And you may speak to your patrons, of your meeting together to worship God that created heaven and earth, and made all mankind, and gives you breath, life and spirit, to serve and worship him.

And my desires are to the Lord, that you in his Truth and power may answer the Truth in all, both king, and prince, and Turks and Moors, that you may be a good savor among them all, and in them all; manifesting that you are the salt of the earth, and the light of the world; and a city set on a hill, that cannot be hid: So that they may see your good works, and glorify your Father, which is in heaven.

And what do you know, but the Lord hath set you there to preach in life, and word, and good conversation? Therefore while you are there, mind your service for God, who hath all things in his hand: And a sparrow cannot fall to the ground without his providence. And Christ is the mountain that filleth the whole earth; and so you will feel him there.

500

And therefore keep in the word of power, and in the word of patience, and the word of wisdom, that will give you dominion over all. Amen.

London, the 25th of the 8th month, 1690.

Postscript

You may petition the emperor, or king, and your patrons, whose captives you are, that you may have one day in the week to meet together to worship and serve the great God (that made you) in Spirit and Truth. For you worship no representation, image, or likeness, neither in heaven nor in the earth, but the great God, who is Lord over all, both in heaven and earth; and is manifest by his Spirit in his people; from you, poor captives, who desire their good here, and their eternal happiness hereafter.

And you may draw up a paper to this effect, and get it translated into their language, and send it to the emperor and his council, and your patrons; and set your hands to it with all speed, after the receipt of this.

10. George Fox's Sermon[54a] at Wheeler Street, London, at the General Meeting of 1st of 4th Month, 1680

Friends preached as they felt they were led by the Spirit. We have few surviving texts of Quaker sermons. Most that survive belong to Fox's and Penn's last and most orthodox years.

[54a] This sermon was originally taken down in shorthand, the text of which seems to be lost. Manuscript versions (cf. Henry Cadbury, *Annual Catalogue of George Fox's Papers*, p. 169) include (1) SMS 5:121, written close to the original date, and SMS 6:124, directly copied from it about 1800; and (2) a copy made somewhat hastily about 1750 by Claude Gay (born a Catholic in Lyons, France; converted to Quakerism by reading Barclay's *Apology* on the Isle of Jersey about 1745, and after banishment from Jersey a resident in London, who taught French there and translated Quaker books into French). Gay's copy came into the hands of George Dillwyn (1738-1820 or '21) of Philadelphia and Burlington, N.J., a Quaker merchant who traveled as a minister among English Friends from 1784 to 1791 and 1793 to 1802; it is now at Haverford.

The only printed version of this sermon appeared in 1825 as the appendix to a doctrinal pamphlet comparing the sermons on Christ of Thomas Story of Philadelphia (1737) and Elias Hicks, and published by S. Potter of Chestnut Street, Philadelphia, The printed version, however, is not based either on the SMS or the Gay copies, but apparently on an anonymous copy (also at

This sermon, which shows Fox's understanding of the Quaker term Seed, was partly intended to establish the role of women among Friends. It shows also Fox's quick mind and inventive use of Scripture.

Blessed be the Lord God of heaven and earth, who has preserved his people to this day, and hath given us this blessed opportunity that every one may be sensible of his mercy and may feel the blessed power and spirit of life and glory, etc.

God placed man in a blessed habitation in the beginning in a blessed and happy state, who taught man how to serve God, when he made him, and made him good, and blessed him, and made him perfect, and set him in dominion over all the works of his hands, & not only set him in dominion but bid him have dominion and keep dominion. God said to them "have dominion;" he did not say to them "do thou have dominion without thy wife," but he said to *them* "have dominion", to *them* "be fruitful", etc., and to them all was blessed and good and they good also. Here was a blessed concord and unity. Man was blessed and so was woman, and all things was blessed unto them. Man was perfect, God is perfect, all that he made was perfect; God is holy and pure. How came the loss then? Why, by the Serpent, he said. What, he? He, an enemy, a Satan, an adversary to man's prosperity, a devil, a destroyer; he came after God Almighty made man and woman, and had blessed them above all the works of his hands, and set them in Paradise his garden of pleasure, and gave them a liberty to eat of every tree of the garden freely (excepting the Tree of Knowledge). "In the day thou eatest thereof thou shalt surely die. Tho' it is good in itself, yet if thou eat thereof thou shalt die." Here God taught man, and limited him from this tree.

Now this Serpent, adversary, enemy, Devil, destroyer, he came to the woman first. The Serpent said to the woman, "hath God said, 'in the day ye eat thereof ye shall die'?" Then when he had got the woman down that was

Haverford) of (3) a copy sent in 1772 by Richard Shackleton (headmaster of Ballitore School, later the seedbed of Irish liberal Quakerism in Hannah Barnard's and Job Scott's days) to Morris Birkbeck, Sr. ([1734-1816], son of William and Sarah Morris Birkbeck of Lancaster, who traveled in America in 1773, and purchased land in North Carolina, but later returned to England. His son Morris Birkbeck, Jr. [1764-1825], left Quakerism when Hannah Barnard was disowned, moved to America in 1817, founded the town of New Albion, Illinois [1818], and drowned in the Little Wabash after a visit to Robert Owen at New Harmony, Indiana). Shackleton's copy (now at Swarthmore College) may be based on (4) the one at Dublin. The following reconstructed text follows SMS in the main, but Shackleton's and Gay's copies wherever comparison shows them more likely to be correct.

made of a rib of man, the beam was down, and now having got the beam down all the house came down. Then man entering into the temptation also, they both lost the blessed estate, the concord and the dominion. Adam and Eve had dominion over the Serpent, for they had dominion over all that God made, then very well might they have [had] dominion over him that was out of the truth. "In the day thou eat thereof thou shalt die," saith the God of truth. Saith the God of the world, that is out of the truth, "in the day ye eat thereof ye shall not die." O false liberty. Here came the false liberty; the Serpent's doctrine is contrary and opposite to God's. Now, man, whom wilt thou believe? Thy maker, who created thee in his own image, clothed thee with righteousness and holiness, or the Serpent, the adversary?

So man did eat: the eye out, the ear out, at last the mouth out too. But before they came to this, there was a farther thing: ye shall be as Gods, high up, higher puffed up above their condition. Pray how much higher would they be, than to be in the image of God, above all things that God made. You shall be as God, knowing good and evil. How can dead man know good and evil? So see the Serpent's doctrine and his text: he did not make this his text, be fruitful and multiply and have dominion etc., He did not make any of God's commandments his text; but he made that his text which he thought would destroy them and kill and devour them. So after a time (you see) the eye went out to the tree, thinking to be made wise; but here was another wisdom gone into, besides that wisdom Adam had, to know all that God made and to give names to them. So they got this wisdom by which the world knows not God. Now after Adam and Eve had eaten, they were naked, and hid themselves in the trees of the garden. Then they heard the voice of the Lord God, in the Cool of the day: "Adam, where art thou? While thou keptst in my image thou wert my Friend"—(as Abraham was called God's Friend). Where art thou now, Adam? Hast thou eaten of the tree? "The woman gave me." "Woman, what sayest thou?" "The Serpent beguiled." Then God passed sentence upon them. So here, you see, Adam died, Eve died according to God's word, they did not come to be as Gods according to the Serpent's word, but here begot a wisdom by which in process of time they knew not God. And here came the Lamb to be slain from the foundation of the world (tho' there is more in that).

Man and woman came then to be driven out of the garden, and a flaming sword placed every way with two edges to keep the way of the tree of life. So every one must come through this two-edged flaming sword before they can come into the Paradise of God. They must know this sword to cut down the transgressing life and earthly wisdom and to burn it up, before man can come to inherit life. And this I knew by experience, before I went out to declare the truth, as it is said: he that overcomes shall inherit all things. So here Adam died and Eve died. Thou may say they did live and had children. How

503

could they be dead and have children? Yes, inwardly dead. What died they from? From the purity, holiness and innocence, pure and good estate in which God placed them. So Adam died and Eve died and all died in Adam. Sad words. All are baptized into the death of Adam, into death from God by their unclean spirit, by their unclean ghost. Baptized, what is that? Plunged into Adam's death and imperfection and darkness; here all are baptized into Adam's death.

Now it's said: "the seed of the woman," not the seed of the man, for the woman was first in the transgression, the seed of the woman (who was first in the transgression) shall bruise the Serpent's head. Now the Serpent was got head in man, not God, for he was gone from God and his ordinance. The seed of the woman shall bruise the Serpent's head. This was the first Gospel promise, in which all the faithful did believe in and hope that this should come to pass. Therefore you see the Apostle, in the 11th to the Hebrews, reckons up Enoch and Abraham and Abel and all these died in the faith, not receiving the promise; that is, the Seed was not yet come. But to us and in our day, the Apostles' day, the Seed did come that inherits the promise, and the saints in the Apostles' days enjoyed that Seed that was come to bruise the Serpent's head; and by faith in this Seed every age had access to God and came up to God, and came atop of the Serpent's head. And so through Christ we're reconciled to God; and therefore is he called the rock of ages. And Abraham saw his day, and Jacob saw his star, and the rock that followed Israel was Christ. So the Seed came in the Apostles' days: "A Virgin shall conceive a son," etc. The Apostle said: "I permit not a woman to speak in the Church." But the Law did not keep down Deborah and Huldah, though there be a distinction between good women and bad women. The Apostle saith: I permit not a woman, yet he appointed Titus to ordain elders, and the elder women must be teachers of good things. So he ordains the elder women; then he did not stop them. So the elder women must teach good things: that is their duty incumbent upon them. So it must be in every family. Have your children in subjection. Men and women are to train up their children to walk in the New Covenant, as the Jews did in the Old Covenant. So that they may be plants of God round about their tables, all growing up to the praise of the pure God. So here is the particular service of every man in his family and every woman in her family. So going through this in your families, you grow in truth, in the life in all sobriety and righteousness and purity. So first, here is a duty in families; then come to take care of the church of God; then fathers and mothers in Israel which comes farther than fathers and mothers in a family.

What is Jacob? He was a supplanter. He supplanted Esau the first birth. So every man and woman must first know a supplanting in themselves. Afterwards he was called Israel, a Prince of God, and had power with God, and a prevailer with man. So here you are children of a Prince of God, the heavenly Israel, children of a Prince a prevailer with God.

Now it is from this Seed of the Woman that you have your wisdom for your particular exercises in your family, and for your more general service in the Church of God. The Seed of the Woman, etc.: This was the gospel to Adam. This was the gospel to Abraham: "In thy seed all nations shall be blessed." So all nations shall come to the blessing of this Seed. This seed is Christ that was promised to break the Serpent's power. This Seed is come, glory to God forever, born of a virgin: the Seed of the Woman, who suffered and tasted death for every man that was and is in death. So when Christ was risen, the woman that was first in the transgression, the women went first to declare the Resurrection out of death, out of the grave. Now, they said, "certain of our company came and told us he was risen." Certain *women* they were, disciples, learners and followers of Christ. This seemed as idle tales, but when they came into the belief of it, male and female believed: so both are one in Christ Jesus, and all can praise God together.

So here, in the resurrection and restoration of man up again into the image of God, Christ, (who bruiseth the Serpent's head that defiled man, and sanctifies and renews up into the heavenly image, as Adam and Eve were in before they fell); here they come to be meet helps; Not as it was in the fall: the woman was first in transgression, then Adam was set over the woman; now here is unity, here is the headship in Christ Jesus. Now the Serpent said Adam and Eve should be as gods if they would eat. They did eat and did not become gods as the Serpent said. In process of ages and times we see the Serpent set Father Adam's sons and daughters to make gods. He told Father Adam and Mother Eve they should be gods; in process of time he put them upon making Gods of wood and stone and molten & graven images. Yea, the Jews were so foolish after God brought them out of Egypt that they took the jewels and things they brought with them and made them a god. Therefore take heed of that ye brought out of "spiritual Egypt," that ye make not a God of it, and fall down in your hearts and worship it. Aaron took the jewels and he made them a god. And the people were naked. So Adam and Eve, when they had transgressed, they were naked, and they sewed fig leaves together to make them aprons. A sunshine day might dry their aprons to powder. So God found them making aprons; as [in] all the religions in the world in transgression they are stitching or sewing one thing or other together to make them a covering. So when Christ came to the Jews they cried: "What must we do? What will we stitch and sew together to make a covering, as Father Adam and Mother Eve did?" [omitting a long paragraph on making gods, making coverings, and making a "body" for Christ]

Now "Christ is the same today as he was yesterday": can we get any farther? Yes: "and forever, and to all eternity." Then come up to the Seed that is blessed, that lives and reigns over all for ever. Now the Devil will confess that he was, but not that he is; but Christ is revealed in the hearts of his people; and being ingrafted into him, he is their treasure of wisdom and knowledge. And the apostle John saith: he who was, is, and will be to all eternity.

Now when Christ came, according to the promises, prophecies, figures and shadows, John went before, a fore-runner: he prepared the way. And before Christ came saith John: "he that cometh after me is greater than I; he is preferred before me: for he was before me." He is greater in his birth, greater in his baptism, greater in his miracles, and greater in his death, who tasted death for every man. So did not John. Now in Adam all died, and so were plunged into his death and imperfection. Now comes Christ, the second Adam, of whom it is said: he shall baptize you with fire and with the Holy Ghost. People have been baptized with a foul unclean Spirit and unholy Ghost in old Adam. Now people must be circumcised and put off the body of death and sin; for Adam and Eve had no body of sin and death before transgression; but this came in by the Serpent. Now here is the baptism of Christ by fire: this Holy Spirit to plunge down the foul spirit and power that is got into man, which fills him with chaff and corruption. This baptism destroys him and his work in man, and burns him up and his chaff with his fire. So man and woman have had this chaff in them, with which the god of the world hath fed them. Now every one must know this baptism with the Spirit before they can come up into the garden in Paradise again; every man and woman must know this without book, in their own particulars. Mere humility, lowliness and quietness is known; here is work enough for every one in his own house to come to.

Now after Christ was come, saith he: "Moses was faithful as a servant in all his house;" he made no higher. The Son is *over* his house in the New Testament; Moses a faithful servant *in* his house in the Old Testament. Now to distinguish between these two covenants, these two testaments and houses, Moses' house and the Son of God's house, whose house ye are, saith he: the Son of God's house. Come, is there any tithes in your house? "Nay, it is in the servant's house, and Levi is our priest." In the New Testament our priest made higher than the heavens, he came not after the tribe of Levi, but of the tribe of Judah. There's no tithes in the Son's house; the tithes were in Moses' house. They had a priesthood of the tribe of Levi in the Old Testament. Now in Christ's house in the New Testament, they are all called a royal priesthood: not a tribe only, but all. What said Moses in the Old Testament: "the priest's lips shall preserve the people knowledge." Well said. What sayest thou now in the New Covenant? "I confess the law served till the Seed came." What Seed is that? Christ is the Seed of the Woman; Christ the high-priest, made higher than the heaven. He may well call it the New Testament. The old priest-hood had his pulpits and tithes, for they were to have no lot of the land. [omitting a half paragraph on tithes] What, will you not go to Temple now, will you? Nay, while Moses was read, the veil was over the heart; Christ is come, and he hath set up his Temple. Christ said the Temple should be thrown down, not one stone left upon another; and Stephen saith: the Most High dwelleth not in temples made with hands. Again in Acts the 17th, Paul comes forth with a thunder: the Most High, saith he, dwelleth not in temples made with hands. What, were not the Jews to pray towards the Temple in their captivity; and did not Solomon make a large prayer; and was not Daniel an honest man, and did he not pray towards Jerusalem? Now this was well till Christ came, who is come to fulfill these things. Now, what saith the New Testament?: your bodies are the temples of the Holy Ghost and God and Christ will dwell in you. Here is praying in the Spirit in the Temple. Here is the New Testament, not according to the Old. "I will make a new covenant not according to the old. I'll put my fear in the hearts." So now come to make a distinction.

So in Moses' house, here is an outward Temple, altar, priest and a Jew. In the New Testament, in the Son's house, here is the Jew in Spirit, the temple of the living God. So now the Lord saith: "I will make a new covenant with the house of Israel and Judah, not according to the old, when I took them by the hand, and led them out of the land of Egypt. I'll write my law in their hearts." Here is the new covenant. In the Old Testament thou must bring thy offering to the priest, and he was to circumcise the children, and his lips were to preserve knowledge. In the New Testament, Christ ministreth circumcision, and he circumciseth by his Spirit, and cuts off the body of sin and death got up in the transgression, which must be cut off before Christ presents man and woman perfect to God. In the Old Testament, the offering of the blood of bulls, rams and goats; in the New Testament, the blood of Jesus Christ. And under the law it was death to eat the blood: either thou must spill it on the ground, or offer it upon the altar; for that was the life of the clean beasts that went for the sins of the people. So the life of Christ, the spiritual man, the second Adam, that goes for man. In Adam all are dead, except ye eat the flesh, and drink the blood of Christ the Son of God. For by eating came death, and by eating comes life again, if ever a man have it. Moses sprinkled the blood, the life, upon the people; hath Christ given you his life? Give your lives to him; the blood of the Lamb without spot. O, the weight of it! Few understand or come to the sense of it. Here is the blood of the new covenant. Now drink his blood that is life. Now come further: what saith Moses? "If there be a difference between two, you are to go to the high-priest": he puts the oath to you, and if you be not subject to the high-priest, it is death. So now this oath is put between you two, and this ends the strife. Now what saith Moses: "thou shalt keep thy oath." This is the servant. What saith the Son's house: is there any swearing in your house? Nay, Christ who is the truth itself, the life itself, he is come. So there is no swearing in his house, for he saith: "swear not at all." Have you any order in your house? Yes, the order of the Gospel from the Prince of Life. All living glory and honor and praises to his name. We are of the Son's house. How happy had it been if all had kept here, in the Son's house. Have you any tithes in your house? No: "freely receive, freely give. Go without bag or staff." Now see what family you are of. But I hope you observe days and times and feasts, don't you? In Moses' house we did observe these things, till Christ came. But what day do you observe now? The everlasting day, the day of Christ Jesus. Some there were in the apostles' days, that came to the Son's house, and then they went to observe days, which made Paul say: "I am afraid of you, that I have labored in vain." What's become of all Paul's labors, in Christendom that observes days?

Now Moses he made servants; he could make no higher than he was. The Son of God he makes sons: to as many as believe he gives power to become the sons of God, a royal priesthood offering up spiritual sacrifice to God who is a spirit. They offered the natural in the Old Testament; in the New they offer the spiritual sacrifice. So in Moses' house you had a carnal sword and weapons and armor; but have you this armor and carnal weapons in the Son's house? What armor have you there? Our armor is spiritual, our weapons are spiritual not carnal, but mighty through God to the pulling down the strongholds. So the weapons are spiritual as Paul saith; and was not Paul of the Son's house, think you? We are come, say they, to the Son's house. We are come to the New Jerusalem, Jerusalem that is above, the mother of us all, to Jesus the mediator; to God the judge of all the earth. Here is the Son's house, the heavenly Jerusalem. Have you a temple in your Jerusalem? Yes, the Lord God Almighty and the Lamb is the temple, and the Lamb is the Light of the temple. Here needs no sun nor moon here. So now have a distinction between the new covenant and the old; and have a distinction to know what family you are of; and so be substantial and grounded in the Spirit of Light and Life in Christ Jesus the rock of ages. And many great and weighty things might be spoken as to this; but here is a veil of darkness over the hearts of this people which hinders the opening of these things.

So all keep in the New Testament, in the grace, in the Light and power of God in the heavenly unity, where the Devil cannot come. So here's Jerusalem from below and Jerusalem from above. Christ is the one offering that puts an end to the outward offerings. He is our offering and our sacrifice, that tasted death for every man; and not only so, but plungeth down the foul spirit

508

wherewith people have been baptised into Adam, and bruiseth the head of the Serpent, which has gotten into man and woman by transgression, and so baptizeth them with his Holy Spirit.

Now while Moses is read there is a veil over the heart. What veil? Outward offerings and sacrifices is a veil; tithes, swearing and observation of days, and the priests' lips is a veil; but now this veil of figures and shadows is done away by Christ. The veil has been over all nations; it hath been over the Jews.

Now thou art come to the new covenant, not according to the old, and comes to see the veil done away, and so comes to see Jesus Christ with open face, to the glory of God, who was glorified with the Father before the world began; and so thou comest to be changed from glory to glory, till thou comes up into the image of God. So thou dost see not only the veil of worldly corruption done away, but the veil of Moses done away, through Christ; and this I knew and experienced, before ever I knew the name of a Quaker was in England; and since I came abroad to declare the everlasting truth, I have been a sufferer very much at times, above these thirty years in gaols and prisons, and my body has been spoiled for the testimony of Jesus; so that I am not able to travel as I have done, and it was hard for me to come this journey; but I was moved of the Lord to come, etc. Now what I have suffered for, I can not but clear it, the God of heaven knows my heart: my sufferings have been against and for not joining with the relics of stinking popery: things which have not come from Christ. And what have Friends suffered for? For not paying of tithes. Did Christ set up these things or the Pope? "Wilt thou swear, thou schismatic? Wilt thou not sprinkle thy children with the cross, thou heretic? Wilt thou not marry by a priest?" Where had you these things from, from Moses, from Christ, or from the Pope? Search the scriptures, like the noble Bereans, and see what you can find there for these things. Marriage with a priest and with a ring, this is not an ordinance of God but of man; and when the Lord brought the children of Israel out of Egypt he gave them a charge not to follow the customs and manner of the Egyptians and Canaanites. Now that which I have suffered for, both in the former powers' days and in these, hath been as I said before against the relics of stinking popery. So if any say we are popishly affected, I say no, we are Christ affected; we are true Protestants and follow the practice of our fore-fathers and mothers, the holy men and women, and so have the scriptures on our side.

Now let all Friends be careful to keep in the holy chaste life over all lust and uncleanness of filthy fornication; for it was for uncleanness that the children was put out of the congregation. Now those that profess the truth should know more virtue and dominion over the filthy lusts, and keep their bodies clean till the day of their marriage and time of death, that all may be kept in chasteness and purity to God's glory.

And now in your proceedings to marriage let all be done to the praise and glory of God. For there were three things under the law for which marriage was divorceable: viz. fornication, marrying in the kindred, and marrying in nonage. If a young woman have a father or mother or guardian, go to them first, and lay the matter before them, that the matter may go on with their consent and approbation, and let it be done in the Light and not in the dark but upon the house top. And when things are clear before all parties, lay it twice before the women's Meeting and twice before the men's, that all may be clear in the sight of God and man. But there is another objection: the men being in one room and the women in another. This is a separation, say they. No; for saith the apostle, though we be absent in the body, yet we are present in the Spirit, enjoying and beholding your spiritual order. So this spiritual sight beholds the heavenly order and communion. And, saith he, "the steadfastness of your faith," which faith was heavenly received from the heavenly man. So this is no separation, for men to be in one room and women in the other, because they are present in spirit: one man may be here, another may be at Jamaica, Scotland or Ireland or in any nation of the world, absent in body yet present in spirit. But separated from the Spirit in Cain and Corah's way, when envy and prejudice appears, here is separation, and there it began in the apostles' days; for when they went from the Spirit of God, then they began to separate and persecute and kill about religion, and then get up the priest of Balaam that preached for reward; and so the apostasy entered. Now as ye come to the new covenant and into the order of the glorious gospel, there is a coming up again from this apostasy and beholding one another's comely order in the gospel of life and salvation though they be absent. So this religion is pure and undefiled and keeps from the spots of the world; into which the devil cannot get. Had all kept in this pure religion they had never thought of nor invented a Purgatory. So all walk in the wisdom of God.

Now in the new covenant we are of the Son's house, whose house ye are. Here every one keeps on his spiritual armor, the sword of the Spirit, the helmet of salvation that keeps and preserves the head. So here every one is shod with the preparation of the gospel of peace. The outward Jews' shoes did not wax old nor wear out. So these shoes wherewith the Jews inward are shod, they wax not old. Here thou may trample upon all the rocks and briars and brambles: you need not fear pricking your feet. So here you may see the Son's house in which you are to be shod in your spiritual travel towards the land of rest. So in old Jerusalem the trumpet sounded, so in New Jerusalem the heavenly trumpet sounds out of Zion, which gives a certain sound. So let all come to have a sense betwixt the house of Moses the servant and the house of Jesus Christ the Son of God, the substance who abolisheth the old and so makes all things new, all the shadows being done away in him. So here thou art a true Protestant: therefore protest against tithes and swearing and all the popish trumpery that is not from Jesus Christ the heavenly head.

The law in the Old Testament came from Mount Sinai, but the law of the New Testament comes out of Sion, which law is not written on tables of stone, but in the fleshly tables of the heart, according to the promise in the new covenant: "I will write my law in their hearts." In the Old Testament, the Lord poured out of his Spirit upon the Jews, but in the New Testament he said: "I will pour out of my Spirit upon all flesh, so that none can escape the spirit of burning."

And in the Old Testament God spoke to the Fathers by the prophets, but in the New Testament the apostle saith God hath spoken to us by his Son who is the one head and speaks to his people, to whom all are to keep. So ye have but one speaker, one mother, begotten of one Father to whom I commit and commend you, that you may receive the milk of the word, for there is no milk that will satisfy but from this word. All children of one Father, no milk below heaven, no bread below heaven. Look up and have the wine of the kingdom and receive the spring of life from heaven, even the milk of the word of life. Here all the children of this word are beautiful, and are all known by their fine countenance, being clothed with fine raiment; and these have their bread from heaven, all looking upwards and not downwards, as the ox or cow to the earth. For those that look downwards look for their bread in the house of old Adam, for it is leavened with the sour leaven that makes the heart burning one against another. But in the Son's house, the second Adam, there is living unleavened bread. And as the law came by Moses, so grace and truth came by Jesus Christ. Where is it come? It is come into thy heart and inward parts: from Christ, from whom you receive your heavenly bread and milk which feeds and suckles your heavenly babes. Many will say: have I been looking out and is it in my heart? O here is the truth in my inward parts, come from Christ who is the truth and the life. So Christ is my way, my truth, and my life, who is the rock of ages. So, Friends, take heed of a false liberty. For Adam and Eve were in a good state, till they entered into false liberty. But now Christ hath made you free from this false liberty. Therefore stand fast in the liberty wherewith Christ hath made you free; and, saith the apostle: "the grace of God which brings salvation hath appeared until all men, teaching us to deny ungodliness and worldly lust and to walk soberly in this present evil world:" it is not only talking of godliness, but to live godlikely and righteously, for we are required to walk humbly with God.

Be you want wisdom? Here is a treasure: our God is a god above all gods; his order is in the life and in the truth above the devil the god of disorder. So to him I commit and command you all, that you may have the upper and the nether springs, the blessings from above and from below. So if you want bread, look to him, for it is in his house, that nothing may be between you and the Lord but Jesus Christ; that living praises may ascend to the pure living God over all for ever.

511

And so the Lord God of power arm you and strengthen you by his power against whatever may come that is contrary to him, and so you may grow up in faithfulness and in the grace and truth that comes by Jesus Christ.

And so the God of all glory keep and preserve you, who is the first and the last, over all, blessed for ever.

11. Robert Barclay's *Anarchy of the Ranters* (1674) on the Bases of Church Order

Fox's defensiveness at Wheeler Street about the role of women (p. 504) carries us back to the years of crisis in the development of Quaker organization, 1666-76. On these events some modern liberal Friends would pin the blame for the transforming of Quakerism from a movement into a Society or even into a sect. The issues then raised are indeed still challenging and dividing Friends. Yet without the organizational steps, Quakerism might not have survived those years of persecution following the death of Nayler, Howgill and Burrough, Camm and Audland, Hubberthorne, Farnworth, and Fisher. The organizers—Fox, Penn, and Barclay—tended to link the individualism of their challengers with that total lack of test or restraint upon claimed impulses of the Spirit which they ascribed to the Ranters and to Nayler's faction at the time of his "fall."

Five years after Nayler's ride into Bristol, John Perrot returned in 1661 from the Inquisition's prisons in Rome, preceded by flowery, self-deprecating, and seemingly spiritual letters. He soon proclaimed a "leading" forbidding the removal of men's hats in prayer (unless by the man who prayed), and rejecting the handshake customary between Friends. He opposed fixed times and places of worship, which (like the similar flexibility of Wilkinson and Story a decade later) made it easier to avoid arrest and imprisonment by the Restoration sheriffs. Perrot's stress on openness to the Spirit convinced not only Nayler's old friend Robert Rich but such leading Quakers as Benjamin Furly, William Salt, and for a while Isaac Penington, Thomas Ellwood, John Crook, and a majority of the Friends of Maryland and Virginia, that he had new Light. Fox, Farnworth, and Dewsbury, who opposed Perrot, were angry that he deserted his wife for long periods; and their doubts of his ethical strength were confirmed when he first ac-

512

cepted voluntary banishment to Barbados, and then in Jamaica wore a sword as a civil magistrate. By 1674, Penington, Ellwood, and the Marylanders had confessed their mistake (the Londoners at a reconciliation meeting in 1667 [cf. p. 222], the colonists after Fox's voyage of 1671-72).

Meanwhile, however, Barclay had found the same spirit in the extravagant claims of Spirit-led inspiration by the non-Quaker Lodowick Muggleton (whom he and other Scots Friends and John Gratton visited in 1674), and in a 1673 tract (*The Spirit of the Hat*) by William Mucklow that revived the issues Perrot had raised.

The first such issue was the mere fact of outward organization. The work of local Meetings in supervising marriages, education, and the needs of members, and the use of national committees for printing books and helping prisoners, had already begun in the mid-1650's. But in May, 1666, Farnworth, just before his death, wrote an epistle to all Friends (which ten other leaders countersigned), urging stricter unity in spirit, acceptance of leadership by Elders, supervision of Quaker writing, and disowning of the unworthy. Fox, who was in Scarborough Castle dungeon at the time, may not have read it before he wrote his own similar epistle (No. 248), but he spent most of the summer and autumn of 1667, during the lull between persecutions, in traveling throughout England urging the setting up of county-wide "Quarterly" Meetings and of regular "Monthly" Meetings for business at the local level. In these same years there were annual meetings of the traveling Quaker ministers from 1666 to 1668; these led to a decision to hold Yearly Meetings, representing all Friends throughout the country, beginning in 1670. Fox had persuaded London Quaker women to meet in the "Box Meeting" and "Two Weeks' Meeting" since 1656 (cf. p. 147) for aid to Friends in need. Now in 1671 he urged all Monthly Meetings to set up parallel Women's Meetings. He meant to use women's abilities to the fullest, though women ordinarily played little or no part with the men in Monthly, Quarterly, and Yearly Meetings for Business. Fox also arranged for a "Six Weeks' Meeting" of the London men and women leaders jointly. The weekly "Second Day Morning Meetings" of traveling Quaker ministers in London became a publications committee, even vetoing a tract by Fox himself in 1676, to his exasperation. The monthly Meeting for Sufferings became eventually the most famous of all and collected forty-four folio volumes of records sent up by local Meetings. All this organization had seemed to

Perrot and Mucklow to depend too much on human will and imposed unity. Unity itself must come only from the Spirit.

As Barclay's book makes clear, however, the issue ran deeper. Along with shared plans for collective action, these Meetings supervised the life and morals of their members. William Rogers of Bristol and his Westmorland friends John Wilkinson and John Story after 1675 led their followers into splitting from the main body of Friends over this issue. They distrusted women's meetings. They agreed to common action and relief of needs; yet they felt that no outward group, but only the Spirit within each man, should have authority in matters of faith. To this in principle all Friends agreed, and no creed or dogma was ever laid down upon early Friends. Nevertheless the immorality of a few Friends, and the divergence of others from a common testimony about tithes, public meetings, or war, were felt to show that they were not truly led by the Spirit of Christ. Whatever they might believe, they were "disowned" as not led by the same Spirit as other Friends, which was expected to be consistent (cf. p. 405).

Finally, in the setting up of Meetings and the administering of disciples, the question arose *how* the Spirit would lead the group. Friends early and consistently rejected head-counting and externalized decision processes, expecting the group as a whole to be led into unanimity by the Spirit that would produce the sense of the Meeting. But when in fact disagreement arose, the more individualistic Friends assumed that the Spirit might lead different Friends divergently; while Barclay, Penn, and Fox stressed unity by accepting the leading of the older and more continuously distinguished Friends who were more likely to be authoritatively led. The concept of the "weighty Friend" had arrived. Along with this we find in Barclay's arguments the assumption that the Spirit will produce verbal agreement on ideas and doctrines, and that the words of scripture and the practice of the early apostles, being led by the Spirit, are also models for today. Thereby he comes at times perilously close to changing the Bible and tradition from tests of the Spirit into independent external authorities. Barclay never intended this, but he never fully solves the question he raises, how an individual can be reassured that he is personally responding to the Spirit in accepting and obeying its "leadings" or messages to other men.[55]

[55] For details on the rise of Quaker organization, and on the Perrot, Mucklow, and Wilkinson-Story-Rogers protests and separations, see William

THE ANARCHY OF THE RANTERS
AND OTHER LIBERTINES,

The Hierarchy of the Romanists, and other pretended Churches, equally refused and refuted, in a two-fold Apology for the Church and People of God called in derision QUAKERS.

Wherein they are vindicated from those that accuse them of disorder and confusion on the one hand, and from such as calumniate them with tyranny and imposition on the other; showing that as the true and pure principles of the Gospel are restored by their testimony, so is also the ancient apostolic ORDER of the Church of Christ reestablished among them, and settled upon its right basis and foundation.

By Robert Barclay

Phil. *2*:3; Hebr. *13*:7. [both quoted in full]

Printed in the year 1676.

The Preface to the Reader

Such is the malignity of man's nature in his fallen state, and so averse is he from walking in the straight and even path of truth that at every turn he is inclinable to lean either to the right hand or the left; yea, such as by the work of God's grace in their hearts, and powerful operation of his spirit, have obtained an entrance in this way, are daily molested, and set upon on all hands, some striving to draw them the one way, some the other; and if through the power of God they be kept faithful and stable, then are they calumniated on both sides, each likening or comparing them to the worst of their enemies.

[2] Those that are acquainted with the holy scriptures may observe this to have been the lot of the saints in all ages, but especially those whose place it hath been to reform and restore the ruins of the house of God, when decayed, or any considerable time have been liable to such censures. Hence those that set about repairing of the walls of Jerusalem were necessitated to work with the one hand, and defend with the other.

Christ is accused of the Jews as a Samaritan, and by the Samaritans quarrelled for being a Jew. The apostle Paul is whipped and imprisoned by

C. Braithwaite, *Second Period of Quakerism*, chs. 8-12; *JFHS*, XXXI, 36-37; Arnold Lloyd, *Quaker Social History*, chs. I-III and Conclusion; D. Elton Trueblood, *Robert Barclay*, ch. III; Richard Vann, *Social Development of English Quakerism*, ch. III; etc.

the Gentiles and upbraided with being a Jew, and teaching their customs; the same Paul is hated and ready to be killed by the Jews for breaking the law, and defiling the temple with the Gentiles. The like hath also befallen these faithful witnesses and messengers, whom God has raised up in this day to witness for his truth, which hath long been in a great measure hid, but now is again revealed, and many brought to be witnesses of it, who thereby are come to walk in the light of the Lord.

This people, thus gathered, have not wanted those trials that usually accompany the church of Christ, both on the right hand and on the left, each characterizing [3] them in such terms as they have judged would prove most to their disadvantage. From whence, as the testimony of the false witnesses against their Lord did not agree, neither do these against us. Some will have us to be foolish mad creatures; others, to be deep subtle politicians. . . .* Divers professors will have us to be only pensioners of the Pope, undoubtedly papists; but the papists abhor us as heretics. Sometimes we are a disorderly confused rabble, leaving every one to do as they list, against all good order and government; at other times, we are so much for order, as we admit not men to exercise the liberty of their own judgments. Thus are our reputations tossed by the envy of our adversaries, which yet cannot but have this effect upon sober-minded people, as to see what malice works against us, and how these men, by their contradictory assertions concerning us, save us the pains, while they refute one another.

[4] True it is, we have laboured to walk amidst these extremities, and upon our appearing for the truth we have found things, good in themselves, abused upon both hands; for such hath always been the works of an apostasy, to keep up the shadow of certain truths, that there-through they might shelter other evils. Thus the Jews made use of the law and the prophets to vindicate their abuses, yea, and to crucify Christ. And how much many Christians abuse the scriptures and the traditions of the apostles, to uphold things quite contrary to it, will in the general be readily acknowledged by most.

But to descend more particularly, there be two things especially, both of which in their primitive use were appointed, and did very much contribute towards the edification of the Church. The one is,

"The power and authority which the apostles had given them of Christ, for the gathering, building up and governing of his Church; by virtue of which power and authority they also wrote the holy scriptures."

---

*John Owen charges us with so much ignorance, that though he writes against us in Latin, he fears we will not understand it. And Thomas Danson about the same time accuses us of being Jesuits, sent from abroad under this vizard.

The other is, "That privilege given to every Christian under the Gospel to be led and guided by the Spirit of Christ, and to be taught thereof in all things."

Now, both these in the primitive Church wrought effectually towards the same end of edification, [5] and did (as in their nature they may, and in their life they ought to do) in a good harmony very well consist together; but by the workings of Satan and perverseness of men, they are made to fight against and destroy one another. For on the one hand, the authority and power that resided in the apostles, while it is annexed and entailed to an outward ordination and succession of teachers, is made use of to cloak and cover all manner of abuses, even the height of idolatry and superstition; for by virtue of this succession, these men claiming the like infallibility that was in the apostles (though they be strangers to any inward work or manifestation of the spirit in their hearts) will needs oblige all others to acquiesce and agree to their conclusions, however different from or contrary to the truths of the Gospel; and yet for any to call such conclusions in question, or examine them, is no less than a heinous heresy, deserving death, etc. Or while the revelation of God's mind is wholly bound up to these things already delivered in the scriptures, as if God had spoke his last words there to his people, we are put with our own natural understandings to debate about the meanings of it, and forced to interpret them not as they plainly speak but according to the analogy of a certain [6] faith made by men; not so much contrived to answer the scriptures as the scriptures are strained to vindicate it. Which to doubt of is also counted heresy, deserving no less than ejection out of our native country, and to be robbed of the common aid our nativity entitles us to. And on this hand we may boldly say both Papists and Protestants have greatly gone aside.

On the other hand, some are so great pretenders to inward motions and revelations of the Spirit, that there are no extravagancies so wild which they will not cloak with it, and so much are they for everyone's following their own mind, as can admit of no Christian fellowship and community, nor of that good order and discipline which the Church of Christ never was nor can be without. This gives an open door to all libertinism, and brings great reproach to the Christian faith. And on this hand have foully fallen the German Anabaptists, so called, viz. John of Leyden, Knipperdolling, etc., in case these monstrous things committed by them be such as they are related; and some more moderate of that kind have been found among the people in England called Ranters. As it is true the people called Quakers hath been branded with both of these extremes, it is as true it hath been and is their work to avoid them, [7] and to be found in that even and good path of the primitive Church, where all were no doubt led and acted by the holy Spirit, and might all have prophesied one by one. And yet there was a subjection of

517

the prophets to the spirits of the prophets. There was an authority some had in the Church, yet it was for edification, and not for destruction. There was an obedience in the Lord to such as were set over, and being taught by such, and yet a knowing of the inward anointing, by which each individual was to be led into all truth. The work and testimony the Lord hath given us is to restore this again, and to set both these in their right place, without causing them to destroy one another. To manifest how this is accomplished and accomplishing among us is the business of this treatise, which I hope will give some satisfaction to men of sober judgments, and impartial and unprejudicate spirits, and may be made useful in the good hand of the Lord, to confirm and establish Friends against their present opposers, which is mainly intended and earnestly prayed for

by

The 17th of the 8th month, 1674   Robert Barclay

[Table of Contents, omitted]

[9] Section First
The Introduction and Method of this Treatise

After that the Lord God in his own appointed time had seen meet to put an end to the dispensation of the law, . . . it pleased him to send his own Son, the Lord Jesus Christ, in the fulness of time; who, having perfectly fulfilled the Law, and the righteousness thereof, gave witness to the dispensation of the Gospel. And having approved himself, and the excellency of his doctrine by many great and wonderful signs and miracles, he sealed it with his blood, and . . . he cherished and encouraged his despised witnesses, who had believed in him, in that he appeared to them after he was raised from the dead, comforting them with the hope and assurance of the pouring forth of his Spirit, by which they were to be led and ordered in all things, in and by which he was to be with them to the end of the world. . . . By which Spirit come upon them, they being filled, were emboldened to preach the Gospel without fear; and in a short time thousands were added to the Church, and the multitude of them that believed were of one heart and of one soul, and great love and zeal prevailed, and there was nothing lacking for a season.

But all that was caught in the net did not prove good and wholesome fish; some were again to be cast in that ocean from whence they were drawn; of those many that were called, all [10] proved not chosen vessels, fit for the Master's use. . . . There were not only such as did backslide themselves, but sought to draw others into the same perdition. . . .

Moreover, as to outwards, there was the care of the poor, of the widow, of the fatherless, of the strangers, etc. therefore the Lord Jesus Christ, . . . did in the dispensation and communication of his Holy Spirit minister unto every member in a measure of the same Spirit, yet diverse according to operation, for the edification of the body, some apostles, some teachers, some pastors, some elders. . . .

[11] Now the ground of all schism, divisions or rents in the body is; whenas any member assumes another place than is allotted it, or being gone from the life and unity of the body and losing the sense of it lets in the murmurer, . . . and then, instead of coming down to judgment in itself, will stand up and judge its fellow-members, . . . Such suffer not the word of exhortation, and term the reproofs of instruction (which is the way of life) imposition and oppression, and are not aware how far they are in the things they condemn others for, . . . Yet if they be but admonished themselves, they cry out as if their great charter of Gospel-liberty were broken.

Now, though such and the spirit by which they are acted be sufficiently seen and felt by thousands, . . . yet there are [some men] who cannot so well withstand the subtlety and seeming sincerity some such [schismatics] pretend to. . . . And some there are, that through weakness, and want of true discerning, may be deceived, and the simplicity in them betrayed for a season. . . .

Therefore having, according to my measure, received an opening in my understanding as to these things from the Light [12] of the Lord, and having been for some time under the weighty sense of them, I find at this instant a freedom to commit them to writing, for the more universal benefit and edification of the Church of Christ.

Now, for the more plain and clear opening and understanding of these things, it is fit to sum up this treatise in these following general heads, to be considered of:

First, "From whence the ground and cause of this controversy is, the rise and root of it."

Secondly, "Whether there be now any order and government in the Church of Christ?"

Thirdly, "What is the order and government which we plead for, in what cases, and how far it may extend; in whom the power decisive is, and how it differeth, and is wholly another than the oppressing and persecuting principality of the church of Rome, and other antichristian assemblies."

Section Second
Concerning the Ground and Cause of this Controversy

Whenas the Lord God by his mighty power began to visit the nations with the dawning of his heavenly day (for thus I write unto those that have received and believed the Truth) . . . he sent forth his instruments, whom he had fitted and prepared for his work, having fashioned them, not according to the wisdom and will of man, but to his own heavenly wisdom and counsel. . . . But their words and testimony pierced through into the inner man in the heart, and reached to that of God in the conscience, whereby as many as were simple-hearted, and waited for the redemption of their souls, received them as [13] the messengers of the most high God. . . . For in the receiving and embracing the testimony of truth through them, they felt their souls eased, and the acceptable day began to dawn in and upon them. Now what evidence brought these men to make their testimony to be received? Did they entice? Did they flatter? Did they daub up? Did they preach liberty to the flesh, or will of man? Nay verily, they used no such methods: Their words were as thunder bolts, knocking down all that stood in their way, and pouring down the judgment of God upon the head of the transgressor everywhere. Did they spare the zealous professor more than the open profane? Nay, yet wanted they not regard to the tender seed and plant of God in either. Did they give way? Did they yield to the wisdom of man . . . saying "I must stay until I be convinced of this, and that, and the other thing; I see not yet this to be wrong, or the other thing to be my Duty?" How did they knock down this manner of reasoning, by the Spirit of God which wrought mightily in them, showing and holding forth, that this is the Day of the Lord that is dawned; that all are invited to come. . . . Is there not a cloud of witnesses, who felt the Enemy thus reasoning to keep us in the forms, fellowships, false worships and foolish fashions of this world? But we felt as we were obedient, all these things to be for condemnation, and that as we obeyed the pure manifestation of the light of Jesus in our hearts, there was no hesitation. We might and should have parted with all those things at the first, and what occasioned such scruples, was but that which drew back, [14] through being unwilling to give pure obedience to the Cross of Christ. For as many as gave obedience, and believed in the light, found no occasion of stumbling. . . . And many were brought in from the hedges and the highways, and the Truth was received by thousands with great cheerfulness, and a readiness of mind, . . . and subjection to the power, both in themselves, and in those who were over them in the Lord, and had gathered them into the Truth.

But as it was in the gatherings of old, so it also fell out in this day, all kept not their first love, as among these multitudes which were gathered by the apostles, there were many who continued not faithful to the end. . . . Some embraced the present world; some again separated themselves, being sensual and without the Spirit, despising dominion, and speaking evil of dignities, [15] their mouths speaking great swelling words, being puffed up and not abiding in these things which they were taught of the apostles. So it is to be lamented, that among these many thousands whom the apostles and evangelists, whom God raised up in this day, . . . some could not bear the tribulations, sufferings and persecutions which came for the Truth's sake, and the

Seed in them was soon scorched with the heat of the day. And some not abiding in subjection to the Truth in themselves were not contented with that place and station in the Body, which God had placed them in, but became vainly puffed up in their fleshly minds, intruding into those things which they have not seen, and would needs be innovators, given to change, and introducing new doctrines and practices, not only differing, but contrary to what was already delivered in the beginning; . . . and denying, despising and reviling the apostles and messengers of Christ, the elders of the Church, who . . . through much care, and travail, and watchings, and whippings, and bonds, and beatings, in daily jeopardy gathered us by the mighty power of God in the most precious Truth. Yet in all this there hath nothing befallen us, but what hath been the ancient lot of the Church of Christ in the primitive times.

Now he that was careful for his Church and people in old times hath not been wanting to us in our day; but as he has again restored the Truth unto its primitive integrity and simplicity, . . . [16] the Lord hath also gathered and is gathering us into the good order, discipline and government of his own Son the Lord Jesus Christ. Therefore he hath laid care upon some beyond others, who watch for the souls of their brethren, as they that must give account. . . .

And how are the saints perfected and the Body of Christ edified, of those who come under the cognizance and as it were the test of this order and government? I may chiefly sum them up in three sorts: . . .

The first is those that turn openly back to the world again, through finding the way of Truth too narrow; these have not been capable to do us any considerable hurt; for, being as salt that has lost its savour, they mostly prove a stink among those to whom they go. And I never knew any of them that proved any ways steadable to those to whom they go. I find other professors make but small boast of any proselytes they got out from among us. I hear little of their proving champions for the principles of others against us. And indeed, for the most part they lose all religion with the Truth; for I have heard some of them say that if ever they took on them to be religious, they would come back again to the Quakers, etc.

Secondly, those who through unwatchfulness, the secret corruption of their own hearts, and the mysterious or hidden temptations of the Enemy, have fallen into his snares; and so have come under the power of some temptation or other, either of fleshly lusts or of spiritual wickedness; who being [17] seasonably warned by those that keep their habitation, and faithful overseers in the Church, have been again restored by unfeigned repentance, not kicking against the pricks; but have rejoiced that others watched over them for their good, and are become monuments of God's mercy unto this day.

Thirdly, such who being departed from their first love, ancient zeal for the Truth, become cold and lukewarm, and yet are ashamed to make open apostasy, and to turn back again so as to deny all the principles of Truth; . . . and giving way to the restless imaginations of their exalted and wandering minds, fall out with their brethren, cause divisions, begin to find fault with everything and to look at others more than at themselves, . . . While they are far from living up to the life and perfection of this present, . . . [they] cry out of formality and apostasy because they are not followed in all things. And if they be reproved for their unruliness, according to the good order of the Church of Christ, then they cry out, "Breach of liberty, oppression, persecution; we will have none of your order and government, we were taught to follow the Light in our consciences, and not the orders of men." Well, of this hereafter; but this gave the rise of this controversy, which leads me to that which I proposed in the second place.

---

[18] *Section Third*
Whether there be now to be any Order or Government in the Church of Christ

In answer to this proposition, I meddle not at this time with those that deny any such thing as a Church of Christ. I have reserved their plea to another place, neither need I so be at much pains to prove the affirmative, to wit, "That there ought to be government and order in the Church of Christ," unto the generality of our opposers, both papists and protestants, who readily confess and acknowledge it, . . .

These then, to whom I come to prove this thing are such, who having cast off the yoke of the Cross of Christ in themselves, refuse all subjection or government, denying that any such thing ought to be, as disagreeing with the testimony of Truth; or those, who not being so wilful and obstinate in their minds, yet are fearful or scrupulous in the matter, in respect of the dangerous consequences they may apprehend, such a thing may draw after it. . . .

I judge the truth of these following assertions will sufficiently prove the matter; which I shall make no great difficulty to evidence.

First, that Jesus Christ the King and head of the Church, [19] did appoint and ordain that there should be order, and government in it.

Secondly, that the apostles and primitive Christians, when they were filled with the Holy Ghost, and immediately led by the Spirit of God, did practise and commend it.

Thirdly, that the same occasion and necessity now occurring which gave them opportunity to exercise that authority, the Church of Christ hath the same power now as ever, and are led by the same Spirit into the same practices.

As to the first, I know there are some, that the very name of a Church, and the very words order and government, they are afraid of. Now this I suppose hath proceeded because of the great hypocrisy, deceit and oppression that hath been cloaked with the pretence of these things. But why should the Truth be neglected because hypocrites have pretended to it? The right institution of these things, which have been appointed and ordained by God, must not, nor ought not to be despised, because corrupt men have abused and perverted them? . . . [Barclay here quotes Matthew 18:15-18.] [20] From which Scripture it doth manifestly and evidently follow, first, that Jesus Christ intended there should be a certain order and method in his Church, in the procedure towards such as transgress. Secondly, that he that refuseth to hear two [church members] is become more guilty (as hardened) than in refusing to hear him that first reproved alone. Thirdly, that refusing to hear the judgment of the Church, or whole assembly, he doth thereby exclude himself, and shut out himself from being a member, and is justly judged by his brethren as a heathen and a publican.

And lastly, that the Church, gathering, or assembly of God's people has power to examine, and call to an account such as, . . . owning the same faith with them, do transgress; and in case of their refusing to hear, or repent, to exclude them from their fellowship. And that God hath a special regard to the judgment and sense of his people, thus orderly proceeding; so as to hold such bond in heaven, whom they bind on earth, and such loosed in heaven, whom they loose on earth. . . . If it be reckoned so great a crime to offend one of the little ones, that it were better for him that so did, that a millstone were hanged about his neck, and he were drowned in the depth of the sea, without question to offend and gainsay the whole flock, must be more criminal, and must draw after it a far deeper judgment.

Now if there were no order nor government in the Church, [21] what should become of those that transgress? How should they be again restored? Would not this make all reproving, all instructing, all caring for, and watching over one another void and null? Why should Christ have desired them to proceed after this method? Why doth he place so much weight upon the judgment of the Church, as to make the refusing of hearing it, to draw so deep a censure after it? . . . There lies the same obligation upon the transgressor to hear that one, as well as all; for that one adviseth him to that which is right and good, as well as the whole. . . . Yet Jesus Christ, who is the author of order and not of confusion, will not have a brother cut off or reputed a publican for refusing to hear one or two, but for refusing to hear the Church. . . .

Secondly, that the apostles and primitive Christians did practice order and government, we need but to read the history of the Acts; of which I shall mention a few pregnant and undeniable testimonies, as we may observe in

[22] the very first chapter of the Acts, from verse 13 to the end, where at the very first meeting the apostles and brethren held together after the ascension of Christ, they began orderly to appoint one to fulfill the place of Judas. It may be thought this was a needless ceremony, yet we see how the Lord countenanced it. I hope none will say, that the apostles' appointing of these two men, or of him upon whom the lot did not fall, contradicted their inward freedom, or imposed upon it; but both agreed very well together. . . .

Moreover, after they had received the holy Ghost, you may read Acts 6, . . . how they wisely gave order concerning the distribution of the poor, and appointed some men for that purpose. So here was order and government according to the present necessity of the case. . . .

Thirdly, when that the business of circumcision fell in, whether it was fit or not to circumcise the gentiles, we see that the apostles saw not meet to suffer every one to follow their own minds and wills, they did not judge as one confusedly supposeth, that this difference in an outward exercise would commend the unity of the true faith. Nay, they took another method. It is said expressly, Acts 15:6. "And the apostles and elders came together to consider of this matter;" and after there had been much disputing about it (no doubt, then, there was here diversities of opinions and judgments) the apostles and elders told their judgments, and came also to a positive conclusion. Sure, some behoved to submit, else they should never have agreed. So those that were the elders gave a positive judgment, and they were bold to say, "that it pleased not only them [23] but the Holy Ghost." By all which it doth undeniably appear that the apostles and primitive saints practised a holy order and government among themselves. And I hope none will be so bold as to say, they did these things without the leadings of the Spirit of God, and his power and authority concurring and going along with them.

And that these things were not only singular practices, but that they held it doctrinally, (that is to say, it was a doctrine which they preached that there ought to be order and government in the Church) is manifest from these following testimonies: I Cor. 4:15, 16, 17. . . . No doubt there were apostates and dissenting spirits in the Church of Corinth that gave Paul occasion thus to write, as he testifies in the beginning of the chapter. . . . Might not they have judged the beloved Timothy to be far out of his place? Might they not have said, "it seems it is not God that moved thee and sent thee here by his Spirit, but lordly Paul that seeks dominion over our faith"? . . . [24] I question not but there was such a reasoning among the apostate Corinthians. Let such as are of the same kind among us examine seriously, and measure their Spirits truly hereby. . . . Because his ways and example was no other than the Spirit of God in themselves would have led them to, if they had been obedient, therefore he found it needful to charge them positively to follow him. . . . We see then that the Lord hath and doth give such whom he hath furnished and

524

sent forth to gather a people unto himself care and oversight over that people, yea, and a certain authority in the power over them to bring them back to their duty, when they stray at any time; and to appoint, [25] yea, and command such things as are needful for peace and order and unity's sake; and that there lies an obligation upon such as are so gathered, to reverence, honour, yea, and obey such as are set over them in the Lord. [Barclay also quotes I Corinthians 4:8; 5:3-4; Galatians 14:15; II Corinthians 2:9; 7:13, 15.]

Now this will not at all infer as if they . . . sought dominion over their brethren's faith, or to force them to do any thing beyond, far less contrary, to what the Lord leads us to by his Spirit. But we know, as they did of old, that the enemy lies near to betray under such pretences; and that (seeing in case of difference the Lord hath, and doth and will reveal his will to his people, and hath and doth raise up members of his Body, to whom he gives a discerning, and power and authority to instruct, reprove, yea, and command in some cases), the Spirit of God leads them to have unity and concur with their brethren. But such as are heady, and high minded, are inwardly vexed that any should lead or rule but themselves, and so it is the high thing in themselves that makes them quarrel others for taking so much upon them, pretending a liberty, not sinking down in the Seed to be willing to be of no reputation for its sake. Such, rather than give up their own wills, will study to make rents and divisions, not sparing the flock, but prostrating the reputation and honour of the Truth even to the world, ministering to them an occasion of scorn, and laughter, to the hardening them in their wickedness and atheism.

[26] Besides these Scriptures mentioned, I shall set down a few of many more that might be instanced to the same purpose. [Barclay quotes in full]: Ephes. 5:21; Phil. 2:3, 29; 3:17; 4:9; Coloss. 2:5; I Thess. 5:12-14; II Thess. 2:15; 3:4, 6, 14; II Cor. 10:8; Hebr. 13:7, 17; Jude 8. . . .

[27] I might at length enlarge, if needful, upon these passages, any of which is sufficient to prove the matter in hand, but that what is said may satisfy such as are not wilfully blind and obstinate. For there can be nothing more plain from these testimonies than that the ancient apostles and primitive Christians practised order and government in the Church; that some did appoint and ordain certain things; condemn and approve certain practices as well as doctrines by the Spirit of God; that there lay an obligation in point of duty upon others to obey and submit; that this was no encroachment nor imposition upon their Christian liberty, nor any ways contradictory to their being inwardly and immediately led by the Spirit of God in their hearts; and lastly, that such as are in the true feeling and sense will find it their places to obey, and be one with the [28] Church. . . .

Thirdly I judge there will need no great arguments to prove the people of God may and do well to exercise the like government upon the very like occasion ... especially if we have the testimony of the same Spirit in our hearts, not only allowing us, but commanding us so to do. It is manifest (though we are sorry for it) that the same occasions now fall in. ... If there be such as walk disorderly now, must not they be admonished, rebuked and withdrawn from, as well as of old? or, is such to be the condition of the Church in these latter times, that all iniquity must go unreproved? Must it be heresy or oppression to watch over one another in love, to take care for the poor, to see that there be no corrupt, no defiled members of the Body, and carefully and christianly deal with them, for restoring them, if possible, and for withdrawing from them, if incurable? ...

[29] We confess indeed we are against such, as from the bare letter of the Scripture ... seek to uphold customs, forms, or shadows, when the use for which they were appointed is removed or the substance itself known and witnessed, as we have sufficiently elsewhere answered our opposers in the case of water Baptism and bread and wine, etc.; so that the objection as to that doth not hold. And the difference is very wide, in respect of such things the very nature and substance of which can never be dispensed with by the people of God so long as they are in this world, yea, without which they could not be his people. For the doctrines and fundamental principles of the Christian faith we own and believe originally and principally because [30] they are the truths of God, whereunto the Spirit of God in our hearts hath constrained our understandings to obey and submit. In the second place we are greatly confirmed, strengthened and comforted in the joint testimony of our brethren the apostles and disciples of Christ, who by the revelation of the same Spirit in the days of old believed and have left upon record the same truths. ... And we deny not but some, that from the letter have had the notion of these things, have thereby in the mercy of God received occasion to have them revealed in the life. For we freely acknowledge (though often calumniated to the contrary) that whatsoever things were written aforetime, were written for our learning, that we through patience and comfort of the Scriptures may have hope. So then, I hope ... none will be so unreasonable as to say, I ought not to do it, because it is according to the Scriptures. Nor do I think it will favour ill among any serious solid Christians, for me to be the more confirmed, and persuaded that I am led to this thing by the Spirit, that I find it in itself good and useful; and that upon the like occasions Christ commanded it, the apostles and primitive Christians practised and recommended it.

Now seeing it is so that we can boldly say with a good conscience in the sight of God that the same Spirit which leads us to believe the doctrines and principles of the truth ... doth now lead us into the like holy order and government to be exercised among us as it was among them, ... what can any Christianly or rationally object against it? ... [31] So that we conclude, and that upon very good grounds, that there ought now, as well as heretofore, to be order and government in the Church of Christ. That which now cometh to be examined in the third place is,

First, what is the order and government we plead for?

Secondly, in what cases, and how far it may extend, and in whom the power decisive is?

Thirdly, how it differeth, and is wholly another than the oppressive and persecuting principality of the Church of Rome, and other antichristian assemblies?

Section Fourth
Of the Order and Government Which We Plead for

It will be needful, then, before I proceed to describe the order and government of the Church, to consider what is or may be properly understood by the "Church": for some, as I touched before, [32] seem to be offended, or at least afraid of the very word, because the power of the Church, the order of the Church, the judgment of the Church and such like pretences, have been the great weapons wherewith Antichrist and the apostate Christians have been these many generations persecuting. . . .

The word Church in itself, and as used in the Scriptures, is no other but a gathering, company, or assembly of certain people, called or gathered together, for so the Greek word signified, . . . [Barclay interprets *ecclesia* in Acts 19:41.]

A church, then, in the scripture phrase, is no other than a meeting or gathering of certain people, which (if it be taken in a religious sense, as most commonly it is) are gathered together in the belief of the same principles, doctrines and points of faith; whereby as a body they become distinguished from others, and have a certain relation among themselves, and a conjunct interest to the maintaining and propagating these principles they judge to be right; and therefore have a certain care, and oversight over one another, to prevent and remove all occasions that may . . . hinder the propagation of it, or bring infamy, contempt, [33] or contumely upon it, or give such as . . . may be banded together to undo them just occasion against them, to decry and defame them.

Now the way to distinguish that church, gathering, or assembly of people whereof Christ truly is the head, from such as falsely pretend thereto, is by considering the principles and grounds upon which they are gathered together. . . .

Forasmuch as sanctification and holiness is the great and chief end among true Christians, which moves them to gather together, therefore the apostle

527

Paul defines the Church in his salutation to the Corinthians, I Cor. *1*:2: "Unto the church of God which is at Corinth, them that are sanctified in Christ Jesus, called to be saints.". . .

The power and authority, order and government we speak of, is such as a church, meeting, gathering or assembly claims towards those that have or do declare themselves members, who own, believe and profess the same doctrine and principles of faith with us, and go under the same distinction and denomination; whose escapes, faults and errors may by our adversaries justly be imputed to us, if not seasonably and christianly, reproved, reclaimed, or condemned. For we are not so foolish, as to concern ourselves with those who are not of us, . . . so as to reprove, instruct, or reclaim them as fellow members or brethren. Yet with a respect to remove the general reproach from the Christian name, with a tender regard to the good of their immortal souls, . . . and for the exaltation and propagation of his everlasting Truth and Gospel in the earth, we have not been wanting with the hazard of our lives to seek the scattered ones, . . . and inviting and persuading all to obey the Gospel of Christ, and to take notice of his reproofs as he makes himself manifest in and by his Light in their [34] hearts. So our care and travail is and hath been towards those that are without, that we may bring them into the fellowship of the saints in Light; and towards those that are brought in, that they may not be led out again or drawn aside, either to the left hand or the right, by the workings and temptations of the Enemy.

These things being thus cleared and opened, we do positively affirm, that we being a people gathered together by the power of God . . . into the belief of certain principles and doctrines, and also certain practices and performances, (by which we are come to be separated and distinguished from others so as to meet apart and also to suffer deeply for our joint testimony), there are and must of necessity be, as in the gathering of us, so in the preserving of us while gathered, diversities of gifts and operations for the edifying of the whole body. . . . [Barclay quotes and comments on I Timothy 5:17.]

Secondly, forasmuch as all are not called in the same station, [but] some rich, some poor, some servants, some masters, some married, some unmarried, some widows, and some orphans, and so forth, it is not only convenient, but absolutely needful that there be certain meetings at certain places and times, as may best suit the conveniencies of such who may be most particularly concerned in them, where both those that are to take care may assemble, and those who may need this care may come and make known their necessities, and receive help, whether by counsel, or supply, according to their respective needs. This doth not at all contradict the principle of being led inwardly and immediately by the Spirit; else how came the Apostle in that day of the powerful pouring forth of the Spirit of God to set apart men for this purpose? Sure this was not to lead them from their inward guide; yea, of the

528

contrary it [35] is expressly said, "Look ye out among you seven men of honest report, full of the Holy Ghost and wisdom, whom we may appoint over this business." Sure they were not to undertake a business being full of the Holy Ghost, which might import a contradiction to their being led by it. So we see it is both fit, and suitable to the apostles' doctrine to have "Meetings about Business." Now if any should be so whimsical or conceited, as to scruple their being at set places and times, though these be nothing relative to the essential parts, but only circumstances relating to the conveniency of our persons, which we must have regard to so long as we are clothed with flesh and blood. . . . Yet shall we not scruple to make it appear that it is not without very good ground that we both appoint places and times. And first, as to the place, I say as before, it is with our bodies we must meet, as well as with our spirits; and so of necessity we must convey our bodies unto one place, that we may speak and act in those things we meet for. And that must be in some certain place, where all must know where to find it, having herein a regard to the conveniencies and occasions of such as meet. . . . Nay surely, God hath not given us our reasons to no purpose, but that we should make use for his glory, and the good of our brethren; yet always in subjection to his power and Spirit. And therefore we have respect to these things in the appointing of our meetings, and do it not without a regard to the Lord, but in a sense of his fear. And so the like as to times, which is no contradicting of the inward leading of the Spirit. . . . [He cites I Corinthians 16:2]. [36] I know not how any in reason can quarrel set times for outward business, it being done in a subjection to God's will, as all things ought to be. We appoint no set times for the performance of the worship of God, so as to appoint men to preach and pray at such and such set times, though we appoint times to meet together in the name of the Lord, that we may feel his presence. And he may move in and through whom he pleaseth without limitation, which practice of meeting together, we are greatly encouraged to by the promise of Christ, and our own blessed experience. And also we are severely prohibited to lay it aside by the holy Apostle, and also on the other hand by the sad experience of such as by negligence or prejudice, forsake the assemblies of God's People, upon many of which is already fulfilled, and upon others daily fulfilling the judgments threatened upon such transgressors. (Read Heb. *10*: from ver. 23. to the end). . . . And therefore having so much good and real ground for what we do herein, together with the approbation and encouragement of Christ and his apostles, both by command and practice; we can . . . faithfully affirm in good conscience, that God hath led us by his Spirit, both to appoint places and times where we may see the faces one of another, and to take care one for another, provoking one another to love and good works. . . . [37] And it is constantly confirmed to us, both by the testimony of God's Spirit in our hearts, and by the good fruits and effects which we daily reap thereby, as a seal and confirmation **that** God is well pleased therewith, and approveth us in it.

Having thus far proceeded to show that there ought to be order **and** government among the people of God, and that, that which we plead for **is,** that there may be certain meetings set apart for that end, it is next to **be** considered in what cases, and how far it may extend.

Section Fifth
In What Cases, and How Far this Government Extends, and
First, as to Outwards and Temporals

I shall begin with that which gave the first rise for this order among **the** apostles, and I do verily believe might have been among the first occasions that gave the like among us, and that is, the care of the poor, of widows **and** orphans. Love and compassion are the great, yea, and the chiefest marks **of** Christianity.... [He quotes John 15:7 and James 1:27.] For this then, **as** one main end do we meet together, that inquiry may be made, if there **be any** poor of the household of faith, that need, that they may be supplied, that **the** widows may be taken care of, that the orphans and fatherless may be bred **up** and educated.... [38] Nor is this a practice any ways inconsistent **with** being inwardly and immediately led by the Spirit; for the Spirit of God **doth** now as well as in the days of old lead his people into those things which **are** orderly, and of a good report. For he is the God of order, and **not of** confusion, and therefore the holy apostles judged it no inconsistency **with** their being led by the Spirit to appoint men full of the Holy Ghost **and of** wisdom over the business of the poor....

Moreover, we see, though they were at that time all filled with the **Spirit,** yet there was something wanting before this good order was established. "There was a murmuring that some widows were neglected in the **daily** ministration;" and we must not suppose the apostles went about to remedy this evil that was creeping into the Church without the counsel of God **by his** Spirit, or that this remedy they were led to, was stepping into the apostasy. Neither can it be so said of us, we proceeding upon the like occasion.

If then it be thus needful, ... that every one, as God moves their **hearts,** and hath prospered them, without imposition, force or limitation, may **give** toward these needful uses. In which case these murmurers at our good **order** in such matters may well think strange at the apostle, ... in ... I Cor. *16*:1, 2, and the 8th and 9th chapters of the 2nd Epistle throughout.

Now though he testifies to them elsewhere that "they are the temples **of** the Holy Ghost, and that the Spirit of God dwells in [39] them," yet **ceaseth** he not to entreat and exhort, yea, and to give them certain orders in this matter. . . .

The fruits and effects of it . . . hundreds can witness to, whose needs have been supplied, and themselves helped through diverse difficulties, and the testimonies of . . . many more orphans and fatherless children who have found no want neither of father nor mother, or other relations through the tender love and care of God's people in putting them in trades and employ-ments and giving them all needful education. Which will make it appear ere this age pass away, to those that have an eye to see, that these are not the mere doings and orders of men, but the work of him who is appearing in ten thousands of his saints to establish not only truth but mercy and righteous-ness in the earth.

And for that end, therefore in the second place this order reacheth the taking up and composing of differences as to outward things, which may fall out betwixt friend and friend. For such things may fall out through the intricacies of diverse affairs, where neither hath any positive intention to injure and defraud his neighbor, as in many cases might be instanced; or if through the workings and temptations of [Satan], any should step aside as to offer to wrong or prejudice his neighbour, we do boldly aver, as a people gathered together by the Lord unto the same faith, and distinguished from all others by our joint testimony and sufferings, that we have power and authority to decide and remove these things among ourselves, without going to others to seek redress. . . . For if we be of one mind concerning faith and religion, and that it be our joint interest to bring all others unto the same truth with us, . . . what confidence can we have [40] to think of reclaiming them, if the Truth we profess have not efficacy as to reconcile us among ourselves in the matters of this world. If we be forced to go out to others for equity and justice, because we cannot find it among ourselves, how can we expect to invite them to come among us, when such virtues as which still accompany the Truth, are necessarily supposed to be wanting? Should we affirm otherwise it were to destroy the Truth and faith we have been and are in the Lord's hand building up; and indeed the spirit and practice of such as oppose us herein, hath no less tendency.

Moreover, besides the enforcing and intrinsic reason of this thing, we have the concurrence, approbation and comfort of the apostles' testimony, I Cor. 6. . . .

If it be objected, "Do you reckon all unjust that are not of you? Think ye all other people void of justice?" I answer: . . . There was no doubt moral and just men among the heathen. And therefore the same Paul commends the nobility of Festus, [yet] he reckons them there unjust in respect of the saints, or comparatively with them, as such as are not come to the just principle of God in themselves to obey it and follow it. . . . [41] And therefore such as have a tender regard that way, would rather suffer [from brethren] what to their apprehensions may seem wrong. For in matters wherein two parties are opposite in the case of *Meum* and *Tuum,* it is somewhat hard to please both, except where the power of Truth, and the righteous judgment thereof reaching to that of God in the conscience hath brought to a true acknowledgement him that hath been mistaken, or in the wrong; which hath frequently fallen out among us, to the often refreshing and confirming our souls. . . .

Now suppose any should be so pettish or humorous, as not to agree in such matters to the judgment of his brethren, and to go before the unbelievers (for though I reckon them not such unbelievers as the heathen of old, because they profess a faith in God and Christ, yet I may safely say, they are unbelievers, as to these principles and doctrines which we know are the Truth of God, and in that sense must be unbelievers as to him that so appealeth to them from his brethren) I say, such as so do, first commit a certain hurt and evil in staining the honour and reputation of the Truth they profess, which ought to be dearer to us than our lives. And even in that outward matter, for which they thus do, they run a hazard, not knowing whether things shall carry as they expect. . . .

Indeed if there be any such, have been or appear to be of us, as suppose there is not a wise man among us all nor an honest man that is able to judge betwixt his brethren, we shall not [42] covet to meddle in their matter, being persuaded that either they or their cause is naught. Though (praise to God) amongst those that have gone from us, either upon one account or other, I never heard that any were so minded towards us; but the most part of them . . . have had this unanimous testimony concerning us that generally we are an honest and upright people. . . . We can confidently testify in good conscience, that God hath led us hereunto by his Spirit. And we see the hand of the Lord herein, which in due time will yet more appear, that as through our faithful testimony in the hand of the Lord that antichristian and apostatized . . . National Ministry hath received a deadly blow by our discovering and witnessing against their forced maintenance and tithes, (against which we have testified by many cruel sufferings of all kinds, as our chronicles shall make known to generations to come), . . . so on the other hand, do we by coming to righteousness and innocency, weaken the strength of their kingdom who judge for rewards, as well as such as preach for hire. . . . For as Truth and righteousness prevails in the earth, by our faithful witnessing and keeping to it, the nations shall come to be eased and disburdened of that deceitful tribe of lawyers, as well as priests, who by their many tricks, and endless intricacies, [43] have rendered justice in their method burdensome to honest men, and seek not so much to put an end, as to foment controversies and contentions, that they themselves may be still fed and upheld, and their trade kept up. Whereas by Truth's propagation, . . . when any difference ariseth, the saints giving judgment without gift or reward, or running into the tricks and endless labyrinths of the lawyers, will soon compose them. And this is that we are persuaded the Lord is bringing about in our day; though many do not, and many will not see it . . . who are now despising Christ in his inward appearance, because of the meanness of it, as the Jews of old did him in his outward. Yet, notwithstanding, there were some then that did witness and could not be silent, but must testify that he was come; even so now are there thousands that can set to their seal that he hath now again the second time appeared, and is appearing "in ten thousands of his saints," in and among whom (as a first fruits of many more that shall be gathered) he is restoring the golden age, and bringing them "into the holy order and government of his own son," who is ruling and to rule in the midst of them, setting forth the counsellors as at the beginning, and judges as at first, and establishing truth, mercy, righteousness and judgment again in the earth, Amen, Hallelujah.

Thirdly, these meetings take care in the case of marriages, that all things be clear, and that there may nothing be done in that procedure, which afterwards may prove to the prejudice of Truth or of the parties concerned. Which, being an outward thing that is acknowledged in itself to be lawful, . . . Therefore it doth very fitly among other things when it comes to be considered of by the people of God, when met to take care to preserve all things right and savory in the household of faith. [44] We do believe our adversaries that watch for evil against us would be glad how promiscuously or disorderly we proceeded in this weighty matter, that so they might the more boldly accuse us, as overturners of all human and Christian order. . . .

First, that we cannot marry with those that walk not in, and obey not the Truth, as being of another judgment, or fellowship, or pretending to it walk not suitably and answerably thereto.

Secondly, nor can we go to the hireling priests to uphold their false and usurped authority, who take upon them to marry people without any command or precedent for it from the Law of God.

Lastly, nor can we suffer any such kind of marriages to pass among us, which either, as to the degree of consanguinity or otherwise in itself is unlawful, or from which there may be any just reflection cast upon our way. . . . As to the first, besides the testimony of the Spirit of God in our hearts, which is the original ground of our faith in all things, we have the testimony of the Apostle Paul, II Cor. 6:14. "Be ye not unequally yoked together, etc." Now if any should think it were much from this scripture to plead it absolutely unlawful . . . [45] whether it be lawful or not, I can say positively, it is not expedient, neither doth it edify, and as that which is of dangerous consequence, doth give justly offence to the Church of Christ. And therefore no true tender heart will prefer his private love to the good and interest of the whole body.

As for the second, in that we deny the priests their assumed authority and power to marry, it is that which in no wise we can resile from. Nor can we own any in the doing of it, . . . seeing none can pretend conscience in the matter (for they themselves confess, that it is no part of the essence of marriage). If any pretending to be among us should through fear, interest, or prejudice . . . bow to that image, have we not reason to deny such slavish and ignoble spirits, as mind not Truth and its testimony?

Lastly, seeing if any walking with us, or going under the same name, should hastily or disorderly go together, either being within the degrees of consanguinity which the Law of God forbids, or that either party should have been formerly under any tie or obligation to others, . . . can any blame us for taking care to prevent these evils, by appointing that such as so design make known their intentions to these churches or assemblies where they are most known, [and] if any know just cause of hindrance, either by stopping it, if they can be brought to condescend, or by refusing to be witnesses and concurrers with them in it, if they will not? For we take not upon us to hinder any to marry otherwise than by advice, or disconcerning ourselves. Neither do we judge that such as do marry contrary to our mind, that therefore their marriage is null and void in itself, or may be dissolved afterwards. Nay, all our meddling is in a holy care for the Truth. For if the thing be right, all that we do is to be witnesses, and if otherwise, that we may say for our [48] vindication to such as may upbraid us therewith, that we advise otherwise, and did no ways concur in the matter; that so they may bear their own burden, and the Truth and people of God be cleared. . . .

Fourthly, there being nothing more needful than to preserve men and women in righteousness after they are brought into it, and also nothing more certain than that the great Enemy of man's soul seeks daily how he may draw back again and catch those who have in some measure escaped his snares and known deliverance from them, therefore do we also meet together, that we may receive an opportunity to understand if any have fallen under his temptations that we may restore them again if possible, or otherwise separate them from us. Surely if we did not so we might be justly blamed, as such among whom it were lawful to commit any evil unreproved. Indeed this were to be guilty of that libertinism, which some have falsely accused us of, and which hath been our care all along, as became the people of God, to avoid. . . . We desire not to propagate hurt, and defile people's minds with telling them such things as tend not to edify. Yet do we not so cover over or smooth over any wickedness, as not to deal roundly with the persons guilty, and causing them to take away the scandal, in their acknowledgment before all to whose knowledge it hath come. . . .

And therefore I conclude, that our care as to these things also, is most needful, and a part of that order and government which the Church of Christ never was nor can be without, as doth abundantly appear by diverse scriptures heretofore mentioned.

Section Sixth
How Far this Government Doth Extend in Matters Spiritual, and Purely Conscientious

Thus far I have considered the order and government of the Church, as it respects outward things. . . . [summary of previous section]

Now I come to consider things of another kind, which either verily are, or are supposed to be matters of conscience, or at least wherein people may lay claim to conscience in the acting or forbearing of them. In which the great question is: "How far in such cases the Church may give positive orders, or [48] rules? How far her authority reacheth, or may be supposed to be binding, and ought to be submitted to?" For the better clearing and examination of which, it will be fit to consider.

First, whether the Church of Christ have power in any cases that are matters of conscience, to give a positive sentence and decision, which may be obligatory upon believers?

Secondly, if so, in what cases and respects she may so do?

Thirdly, wherein consisteth the freedom and liberty of conscience, which may be exercised by the members of the true Church diversely without judging one another.

And lastly, in whom the power decisive is in case of controversy or contention in such matters, which will also lead us to observe the vast difference betwixt us and the papists, and others in this particular.

As to the first, whether the Church of Christ have power. . . . [etc.]

I answer affirmatively, she hath, and shall prove it from divers instances, both from scripture and reason; for first, all principles and articles of faith, which are held doctrinally are in respect to these that believe them matters of conscience. We know the Papists do out of conscience, such as are zealous among them, adore, worship and pray to angels, saints and images, yea, and to the eucharist, as judging it to be really Christ Jesus, and so do others place conscience in things that are absolutely wrong. Now I say, we being gathered together into the belief of certain principles and doctrines without any constraint or worldly respect, but by the mere force of Truth upon our understanding and its power and influence upon our hearts; these principles, and doctrines and the practices necessarily depending upon them, are as it were the terms that have drawn us together* and the bond by which we became centered into one body and fellowship, and distinguished from others. Now [49] if any one or more so engaged with us should arise to teach any other doctrine or doctrines contrary to these which were the ground of our being one, who can deny but the body hath power in such a case to declare, this is not according to the Truth we profess. And therefore we pronounce such and such doctrines to be wrong, with which we cannot have unity, nor yet any more spiritual fellowship with those as hold them. And so such cut themselves off from being members, by dissolving the very bond by which they were linked to the Body. Now this cannot be accounted tyranny and oppression, no more than a civil society, if one of the society shall contradict one or more of the fundamental articles upon which the society was contracted, it can be reckoned a breach or iniquity in the whole society to declare that such contradictors have done wrong and forfeited their right in that society, in case by the original constitution the nature of the contradiction implies such a forfeiture. . . . Suppose a people really gathered unto the belief of the true and certain principles of the Gospel, if any of these people shall arise and contradict any of those fundamental truths, whether has not such a stand good right to cast such a one out from among them, and to pronounce [50] positively, "this is contrary to the Truth we profess and own. . . . And is not this obligatory upon all the members, seeing all are concerned in the like care, as to themselves, to hold the right, and shut out the wrong? I cannot tell if any man of reason can well deny this, however, I shall prove it next from the testimony of the Scripture. . . . [He quotes in full Galatians 1:8; I Timothy 1:19, 20; and II John 10.]

What is to be the place of those that hold the pure and ancient Truth? Must they look upon these perverse men still as their brethren? Must they cherish them as fellow members, or must they judge, condemn and deny them? If we must (as our opposers herein acknowledge) preserve and keep those that are come to own the Truth by the same means they were gathered and brought into it, we must not cease to be plain with them, and tell them when they are wrong. . . . [51] If the apostles of Christ of old, and the preachers of the everlasting Gospel in this day, had told all people, however wrong they found them in their faith and principles, our charity and love is such, "we dare not judge you, nor separate from you, but let us all live in love

---

*Yet this is not so the bond, but that we have also a more inward and invisible, to wit, the life of righteousness, whereby we also have unity with the upright seed in all, even in those whose understandings are not yet so enlightened. . . .

together, and every one enjoy his own opinion, and all will be well," how should the nations have been, or what way now can they be brought to Truth and righteousness? . . . If it was needful then for the apostles of Christ, in the days of old, to reprove, without sparing to tell the high priests and great professors among the Jews that they were stubborn and stiff-necked, and always resisted the Holy Ghost, . . . [so] also for those messengers the Lord raised up in this day to reprove and cry out against the hireling priests, and to tell the world openly, both professors and profane, that they were in darkness and ignorance, out of the Truth, strangers and aliens from the commonwealth of Israel. If God has gathered a people by this means into the belief of one and the same Truth, must not they that turn and depart from it be admonished, reproved and condemned? Yea, rather than those that are not yet come to the Truth, because they crucify afresh unto themselves the Lord of Glory, and put him to open shame. . . . [He quotes Titus 1:10 and draws the same conclusion from it.] [52] Were not this an inlet to all manner of abominations, and make void the whole tendency of Christ and his apostles' doctrine, and render the Gospel of none effect, and give a liberty to the unconstant and giddy will of man, to innovate, alter and overturn it at his pleasure? So that from all that is above-mentioned, we do safely conclude. . . [the doctrinal issue resummarized] ; for otherways, if this be denied, farewell to all Christianity, or to the maintaining of any sound doctrine in the Church of Christ.

But secondly, taking it for granted that the Church of Christ or assembly of believers, may in some cases that are matter of conscience, pronounce a positive sentence and judgment without hazard of imposition upon the members, it comes to be inquired: in what cases and how far this power reached?

I answer, first, [to] that which is most clear and undeniable in the fundamental principles and doctrines of faith, in case any should offer to teach otherways (as is above declared and proved). But some may perhaps acknowledge that indeed, "if any should contradict the known and owned principles of Truth, and teach otherways, it were fit to cast out and exclude such; but what judgest thou as to lesser matters, as in principles of less consequence, or in outward ceremonies or gestures, whether it be fit to press uniformity in these things?" For answer to this, it is fit to consider:

First, the nature of things themselves.

Secondly, the spirit and ground they proceed from.

And thirdly, the consequence and tendency of them.

[53] But before I proceed upon these, I affirm, and that according to Truth, that as the Church and assembly of God's people may and hath power to decide by the Spirit of God in matters fundamental and weighty (without which no decision nor decree in whatever matters is available) so the same Church and assembly also in other matters of less moment . . . with a respect

537

to the circumstance of time, place and other things that may fall in, may and hath power, by the same Spirit . . . being acted . . . to pronounce a positive judgment; which no doubt will be found obligatory upon all such who have a sense and feeling of the mind of the Spirit, though rejected by such as are not watchful, and so are out of the feeling and unity of the life. And this is that which none that own immediate revelation, or a being inwardly led by the Spirit, to be now a thing expected or dispensed to the saints, can without contradicting their own principle deny, far less such who claim . . . "that they being moved to do such things, though contrary to the mind and sense of their brethren, are not to be judged for it," adding, "why may it not be so, that God hath moved them to it?" Now, if this be a sufficient reason for them to suppose as to one or two, I may without absurdity suppose it as well to the whole body.

If it be such a thing, . . . in and through which there may a visible schism and dissension arise in the Church, by which Truth's enemies may be gratified, and itself brought into disesteem, then it is fit for such whose care is to keep all right, to take inspection in the matter, to meet together in the fear of God, to wait for his counsel, and to speak forth his mind according as he shall manifest himself in and among them. And this was the practice of the primitive church, in the matter of [54] circumcision. . . . [He discusses the dispute in the early church with scripture quotation from Acts 15; Romans 12:16; I Corinthians 1:10; Ephesians 5:21; and Philippians 2:2 and 3:15ff.]

[55] And thus far as to the nature of the things themselves.

Secondly, as to the spirit and ground they proceed from: Whatsoever innovation, difference or diverse appearance, whether in doctrine or practice, proceedeth not from the pure moving of the Spirit of God, or is not done out of pure tenderness of conscience, but either from that which being puffed up affecteth singularity (and therethrough would be observed, commended and exalted), or from that which is the malignity of some humors and natural tempers. . . . [56] I say, all things proceeding from this root and spirit, however little they may be supposed to be of themselves, are to be guarded against, withstood and denied, as hurtful to the true Church's peace, and a hindrance to the prosperity of Truth.

If it be said, "how know ye that these things proceed from that ground?" for answer, I make not here any application as to particular persons or things. But, if it be granted (as it cannot be denied) that there may arise persons in the true Church, that may do such things from such a spirit, though pretending conscience and tenderness, then it must also be acknowledged, that such to whom God hath given a true discerning by his Spirit, may and ought to judge such practices, and the spirit they come from, and have no unity with them, . . . without being accounted imposers, oppressors of conscience, or enforcers of uniformity contrary to the mind of Christ, against which the Apostle also guardeth the churches of old.

... [He discusses Philippians 2:3, 4 and lists a dozen other passages on unity in the early church.]

[57] As to the third, concerning the consequence and tendency of them, it is mostly included in the two former, for whatsoever tendeth not to edification, but on the contrary to destruction, and to beget discord among brethren, is to be avoided, according to that of the Apostle, Rom. *16*:17 [quoted in full]....

And since there is no greater mark of the People of God than to be at peace among themselves, whatsoever tendeth to break that bond of love and peace, must be testified against. Let it be observed I speak always of the Church of Christ indeed, and deal with such as are of another mind, not as reckoning only false churches not to have this power, but denying it even to the true Church of Christ, as judging it not fit for her so to act, as in relation to her members. For though Christ be the prince of peace, and doth most of all commend love and unity to his disciples, yet I also know he came not to send peace, but a sword, that is, in dividing man from the lusts and sins he hath been united to. And also it is the work of his disciples and messengers to break the bonds and unity of the wicked, wherein they are banded against God and his Truth.... [Here follows a long exposition of I Corinthians 12.]

---

[66] *Section Seventh*
Concerning the Power of Decision

Seeing then it may fall out in the Church of Christ, that both some may assume another place in the body than they ought, and others may lay claim to a liberty, and pretend conscience in things they ought not, and that without question the wrong is not to be tolerated, but to be testified against, however specious its appearance may be, and that it must and ought to be judged, the question will arise, "who is the proper judge or judges in whom resideth the power of deciding this controversy?" And this is that which I undertook in the next place to treat of, as being the specific difference, and distinguishing property of the Church of Christ from all other antichristian assemblies and churches of man's building and framing. To give a short, and yet clear and plain answer to this proposition: "The only proper judge of controversies in the Church, is the Spirit of God, and the power of deciding solely lies in it, as having the only unerring, infallible and certain judgment belonging to it, which infallibility is not necessarily annexed to any persons, person, or places whatsoever, by virtue of any office, place or station any one may have, or have had in the Body of Christ." That is to [deny] that any have ground to reason thus, "because I am or have been such an eminent member, therefore my judgment is infallible, or because we are the greatest number, or that we live in such a noted or famous place" or the like. . . . And now if I should go on no further, I have said enough to vindicate us from imposition, and from the tyranny, whether of popery, [67] prelacy or presbytery, or any such like, we have or may be branded with, as shall after appear.

But to proceed, herein lies the difference betwixt the dispensation of the Law and the Gospel or New Covenant. For that of old all answers were to be received from the priests in the Tabernacle. . . . But under the Gospel we are all "to be taught of God," that is, none are excluded from this privilege, by not being of the tribe of Levi, or of the children of the prophets, though this privilege is as truly exercised in some by assenting and obeying to what God commands and reveals through others, they feeling unity with it in the life. . . . So that we say, that with very good ground, that it is no ways inconsistent with this sound and unerring principle to affirm that the judgment of a certain person or persons in certain cases is infallible, or for a certain person or persons to give a positive judgment, and pronounce it as obligatory upon others, because the foundations and ground thereof, is not because they are infallible, but because in these things and at that time they were led by the infallible Spirit. And therefore it will not shelter any in this respect to pretend "I am not bound to obey the dictates of fallible man; is not this popery, I not being persuaded in myself?" . . . And, one or more, their not being persuaded, may as probably proceed from their being hardened and being out of their place, and in an incapacity to hear the requirings, as that the thing is not required of them, which none can deny but it may as well be supposed as the contrary. But for the further clearing of this matter before I conclude [68] I shall not doubt both to affirm and prove these following propositions.

First, that there never will nor can be wanting in case of controversy, the Spirit of God to give judgment through some or other in the Church of Christ, so long as any assembly can properly, or in any tolerable supposition, be so termed.

Secondly, that God hath ordinarily, in the communicating of his will under his Gospel, employed such whom he had made use of in gathering of his Church, and in feeding and watching over them, though not excluding others.

Thirdly, that their *de facto* or effectually meeting together and giving a positive judgment in such cases will not import tyranny and usurpation, or an inconsistency with the universal privilege that all Christians have, to be led by the Spirit, neither will the pretences of any contradicting them or refusing to submit upon the account they see it not or so excuse them from being really guilty of disobeying God. For the first, to those that believe the Scripture there will need no other probation than that of Mat. *28*:20 . . . and ver. 18. . . .

Now if the Church of Christ were so destitute of the Spirit of God that in case of difference there were not any found that by the infallible Spirit could give a certain judgment, would not then "the gates of Hell" prevail against it? For where is strife and division, and no effectual way to put an end to it, there not only the gates, but the courts and inner chambers of darkness prevail; for where envying and strife is, there is confusion, and every evil work. But, that there may be here no ground of mistake, or supposition that we were annexing infallibility to certain persons, or limiting the Church to such, I understand not by the Church, every particular country or city. For I will not refuse, but divers of them, both apart and together, if not established in God's power, may err. Nor yet do I lay the absolute stress upon the General Assembly of persons, as such, picked and chosen out of every one of these particular [69] churches, as if what the generality or plurality of those conclude upon were necessarily to be supposed to be the infallible judgment of Truth. . . . Yet nor yet do I understand by the Church every gathering or assembly of people, who may hold sound and true principles, or have a form of Truth. For some may lose the life and power of godliness, who notwithstanding may retain the form or notion of things, but yet are to be turned away from. . . . But by the Church of Christ I understand all those that truly and really have received and hold the Truth as it is in Jesus, and are in measure sanctified or sanctifying in and by the power and virtue thereof working in their inward parts; and this may be made up of diverse distinct gatherings or churches in several countries or nations. I say, so long as these or any of them do retain that which justly entitles them the Church or Churches of Christ (which they may be truly called) though there may fall out some differences, divisions or schisms among them, (as we may see there was no small dissension in the Church of Antioch, and yet it ceased not to be a Church, Acts *15*:2 and I Cor. *1*:11. . .) so long I say, as they truly retain this title of the Church of Christ, as being really such, there will never be wanting the certain Judgment of Truth. For which, besides the positive promises [70] of Christ before mentioned, which is not without blasphemy to be called in question or doubted of.

I shall add these reasons: that seeing the Church of Christ is his Body, of which he is the Head, it were to make Christ negligent of his Body, who styles himself the good shepherd. . . . Next, we never find, in all the Scripture since the Gospel, that ever this was wanting, but that God still gave infallible judgment by his Spirit in some of the respects above mentioned, . . . There might be some scattered ones here and there one in a nation, and now and then one in an age who by the power and virtue of the Spirit of Life working in them might be truly sanctified, yet these were but as "witnesses in sack cloth," no ways sufficient to give these assemblies in which they were engrossed the appellation of the Church of Christ. . . . And thus much to prove that where there is any gathering or assembly, which truly and properly may be called the Church of Christ, the infallible judgment will never be wanting in matters of controversy.

Secondly, that ordinarily God hath in the communicating of his will under his Gospel employed such whom he had made use of in gathering of his Church, and in feeding and watching over them though not excluding others. For as in a natural Body to which the Church of Christ is compared, the [71] more substantial and powerful members do work most effectually, and their help is most necessary to supply any defect or trouble in the body, so also if there be diversities of gifts in the Church, as is above proved, and some have a greater measure and some a lesser, these that have the greater are more capable to do good and to help the body in its need, than others that are weaker and less powerful. Such are more able when the Enemy besets to resist, having already overcome, than others who are but yet wrestling and not conquerors. Now every controversy and dissension in the Church comes from the besetments of the enemy, yet if any of these strong or young men, or powerful members go from their station, it is not denied, but that they are as weak as any; and it is presupposing their faithfulness in their place, that I thus affirm, and no otherwise. . . . Yet we see the Lord doth ordinarily make use of the strong to support the weak, and indeed when such as may be termed weak are so made use of, it alters the nature of their place. Though the Apostles were mean men among the Jews, yet they were such as were Apostles of the Lord of Glory, instruments to gather the lost sheep of the House of Israel, and to proclaim the Day of the Lord. . . .

Now, then, let us consider whom the Lord makes use of in the affairs of the primitive Church, and through whom he gave forth his infallible judgment. Did he not begin first by Peter? He was the first that spoke in the first meeting they had (Acts *1*), and who first stood up after the pouring forth of the Spirit, and who first appeared [72] before the Council of the Jews and spoke in behalf of the Gospel of Christ. Though I am far from calling him as some do the Prince of the Apostles; yet I may safely say, he was one of the most ancient and eminent, and to whom Christ in a manner somewhat more than ordinary had recommended the feeding of his flock. We see also he was first made use of in preaching to the gentiles, and what weight his and James's words had in the contest about circumcision, towards bringing the matter to a conclusion (Acts *15*). Yet that we may see infallibility was not infallibly annexed to him, he was found blameable in a certain matter (Gal. *2*:11), notwithstanding his sentence was positively received in many particulars. So also the Apostle Paul argues from his gathering of the churches of Corinth and Galatia that they ought to be followers of him, and positively concludes in divers things, and upon this supposition exhort the churches both he and Peter, in many passages heretofore mentioned: "to obey the Elders that watch for them, to hold such in reputation," ... (I Cor. *16*:15, 16). ... [example from Revelation 1-2] And indeed I mind not where under the Gospel Christ has used any other method but that he always, in revealing his will, has made use of such as he himself had before appointed Elders and officers in his Church, though it be far from us to limit the Lord so as to exclude any from this privilege. Nor yet on the other hand will the possibility hereof be a sufficient warrant to allow every obscure member to stand up and offer to rule, judge and condemn the whole Body; nor yet is it without cause that such an one's message is jealoused and called in question, unless it have very great evidence and be bottomed upon some very weighty and solid cause and foundation. And God doth furnish those whom he raises up in a singular manner. ...

[73] Now as to the third: "That any particular person *de facto* or effectually giving out a positive judgment is not incroaching nor imposing upon their brethren's conscience," is necessarily included in what is said before. Upon which, for further probation, there will need only this short reflection: that for any member or members in obedience to the Lord to give forth a positive judgment in the Church of Christ is their proper place and office, they being called to it; and so for them to exercise that place in the Body which the Head moves them to is not to usurp authority over their fellow-members. As on the other hand to submit and obey, it being the place of some so to do, is not a renouncing [of] a being led by the Spirit, seeing the Spirit leads them so to do; and not to obey (in case the judgment be according to Truth and the Spirit lead to it) is no doubt both offensive and sinful. And that all this may be supposed in the Church of Christ without absurdity, and so establish the above mentioned propositions, will appear by a short review of the former passages.

If that Peter and James their giving a positive judgment in the case of difference in divers particulars did not infer them to be imposers, so neither will any so doing now, being led to by the same authority. Every one may easily make the application; and on the contrary, if for any to have stood up and resisted their judgment, ... things being concluded with an "it seemed good to the Holy Ghost and to us;" ... will not the like case now [74] occurring the same conclusion hold? ...

Moreover we see how positive the Apostle Paul is in many particulars throughout his epistles, insomuch as he saith (II Thess. *3*:14) "if any man obey not our word by this epistle, note that man, and have no company with him, that he may be ashamed." And in many more places before mentioned, where he commands them both to obey him and several others who were

543

appointed (no doubt by the Spirit of God) to be rulers among them. And yet who will say that either the Apostle did more than he ought in commanding, or they less [than] they were obliged to in submitting. And yet neither were to do any thing contrary or more than the Spirit of God in themselves led them to or allowed them in. And if the Church of God bear any parity or proportion now in these days with what it did of old, (as I know no reason why it should not), the same things may now be supposed to take effect than did then, and also be lawfully done upon the like occasion proceeding from the same Spirit and established upon the same basis and foundation. And thus much . . . to show "in whom the power of decision is;" which being seriously and impartially considered is sufficient to clear us from the tyranny either of Popery or any other of that nature; which those that are not wilfully blind or very ignorant of popish principles may observe. But seeing [that] to manifest that difference was one of those things proposed to be considered of, I shall now come to say something of it in its proper place.

---

[75] *Section Eighth*
How this Government altogether differeth from the oppressing and persecuting Principality of the Church of Rome, and to her Antichristian Assemblies:

[Barclay concludes with a detailed and well-informed statement of the principles of authority in the Roman Church, and presents historical and theological arguments in refutation.]

12. John Crook's *Epistle to Young People* (1686)

The changes in the style and spirit of Quaker life, both those which necessitated the formal organization of local and national Meetings and those which resulted from organizational authority, are reflected in Crook's wistful epistle. He was an appropriate leader to remember the early days. He was among the earliest to be convinced as a Quaker in the South of England, and from 1654 onward the estate he bought with his earnings as a Cromwellian officer and Justice at Beckerings Park in Bedfordshire became a frequent meeting-place of Fox and other traveling Quaker preachers (cf. p. 489). He had been in prison, had briefly followed John Perrot, and knew and shared the early Quaker spirit, already fading in the last years of persecution.

His letter may also represent the other Quaker writings on what would today be called Christian Education. The best known of these are Penn's aphorisms, particularly those in *Fruits of Solitude* (1693) and especially in *Fruits of a Father's Love* (1726, though written in 1699). Since Penn's maxims have often been and may soon again be printed, we may limit our acknowledgment of these paternalistic but deeply concerned books to a single excerpt from the latter work:[56]

> I will begin here also with the beginning of time, the morning. So soon as you wake, retire your mind into a pure silence, from all thoughts and ideas of worldly things, and in that frame wait upon God, to feel his good presence, to lift up your hearts to him; and commit your whole self into his blessed care and protection. Then rise, if well, immediately. Being dressed, read a chapter or more in the Scriptures, and afterward dispose yourselves of the business of the day, ever remembering that God is present, the overseer of all your thoughts, words and actions. . . . And if you have intervals from your lawful occasions, delight to step home,—within yourselves, I mean,—and commune with your own hearts and be still. . . . This will bear you up against all temptations, and carry you sweetly and evenly through your day's business, supporting you under disappointments and moderating your satisfaction in success and prosperity. The evening come, read again the Holy Scripture, and have your times of retirement before you close your eyes, as in the morning. So the Lord may be the Alpha and Omega of your lives.

Out of respect, not simply out of sobriety, Quaker children were treated like weaker adults from the beginning. Thus Crook wrote:

AN EPISTLE to Young People Professing the TRUTH

Dear Friends,
Knowing that many which fear the Lord, and think upon his name, have had (for some time) a concern upon their minds for the declining conditions of many young people that are among us; saying often one to another, "What will become of the next generation, considering the youth of this are so degenerated from those that received the truth at the beginning?"; . . . it

---

56 See Tolles and Alderfer, *Witness of William Penn,* p. 196, and in general pp. 163-202.

came into my heart, . . . to bring people to the beginning, that as they received Christ Jesus the Lord, so to walk in him; which is the drift and end of this epistle to young people and others professing the truth.

Many are yet alive who from their own knowledge can testify the [2] humility, mortification and self-denial of the youth at the beginning, . . . their words few and savory, their countenances grave and serious, in their places diligent and faithful [cf. p. 81, etc.] ; being examples of temperance and sobriety to neighbours and acquaintance; in the worship and service of God attentive and watchful, carefully improving all opportunities to increase their communion and acquaintance with God in Christ Jesus the Light. . . .

Let children inquire of their parents (that were eye witnesses from the beginning) and they can tell them; let servants ask their faithful masters, and they can inform them what manner of people the younger sort of Quakers (so called) were at the beginning: Nay, there were few such strangers in the places where the Truth first took place, but they could declare these things; by all which (as in a glass) many now professing the same truth may see themselves bearing another image; therefore ought diligently to make inquiry what is the cause, and whence the disparity ariseth. . . .

It's to be feared, those that are thus fallen have received another gospel, or the Gospel perverted, or turned upside down, as the apostle speaks, seeing those at the beginning began in the Spirit, but since that many that began well think to be made perfect by the flesh, where too many hold the truth in unrighteousness. But my design is not to accuse, but to inform those that are out of the way if possible they may be reclaimed before the evil day overtake them.

I know some of the younger are ready to blame the elder, and some children their parents, and some servants their masters' examples; to all which I say, that such as are justly guilty thereof shall bear their own burden, and shall not escape the righteous judgment of God. But you that make this plea "know that the soul that sins shall die"; and the witness of God in your own consciences (if hearkened unto) will convince you of the vanity of this fig-leaf covering, and the [3] deceitfulness of your own hearts in thinking that the evil example of others will be an excuse for your backsliding.

For those that in their youth received the truth at the beginning were surrounded with evil examples on every hand, so that if examples could have prevailed to continue them in worldly vanities, they could never have broken through those oppositions from acquaintance and nearest relations; for if they had looked outward, all hopes of preferment in this world were wholly gone, and looking inward, there appeared such strong holds of Satan, as seemed impossible ever to be overcome; the Truth itself being such a stranger in the earth, that almost everybody was backward to give it entertainment, especially if they had anything in the world to lose for harboring of it.

Whereas the youth and others of latter times found the Truth ready proved, [this was] successfully defended against the subtle arguments and wits of those professing times in which it at first brake forth, ... not by the might and power of wit, or outward learning, but by simplicity and godly sincerity, accompanied with holiness of life and conversation; which was a great confirmation to the first publishing of it, together with the meek and patient ... suffering [of] the loss of all for the truth as it is in Jesus; by which, in a great measure, the rough way was worn smooth, and the passage made much more easy to those that followed than it was at the beginning. For those that were as gazing stocks at the beginning, of latter time came to be well known, and that estrangedness to persons and principles came to vanish away, and a good esteem of the truth and of those that professed it sprang up in divers persons, so mightily grew the word of God, and prospered at the beginning.

But alas, ... [it is] as if the sins of "Sodom," which were pride, carelessness, excess and contempt of the poor, were become the vices of Sion, many young people and others getting into those things again which their parents, relations, and acquaintances, for good conscience sake, were forced to lay aside; as if in these latter times the efficacy of Truth was not the same as at the beginning, and as if the cross of Christ, that was so powerful then, was now become of no effect.

[4] Little do the wanton youth of this age think what sighs and tears their godly parents, and friends that love them, pour out in secret for them, both because of their eternal estates hereafter, and the dishonor they bring here unto the blessed name and truth of God; whereby it's become a saying among ancient people, "That the Quakers nowadays are not like those at the beginning."

What watchfulness, what carefulness, what diligence therefore ought every one to use, lest by bad company and examples, they should be ensnared before they are aware, and so by degrees be drawn to such inconveniences, as afterward they will find very hard to withstand.... Even strangers in our meetings are more serious, and tenderness of heart sooner procured in them, than in many who have frequented our assemblies from their childhood unto men's and women's estates, so evil and catching are the bad examples of others to them whose hearts are not kept tender to God.

Be serious, therefore, all you that make profession of the truth in your tender years, and examine yourselves how you came to make profession of it. Was it for some by-ends and sinister respects; or was it by education from your parents or others only? I say unto all such careless ones, I pity your condition; . . . therefore let the time past suffice that you have spent your precious time to no purpose; and rest no longer in an easeful mind, above the cross, but sink down in deep humility to the oppressed seed of God in you, which he hath left as a witness for himself, . . .

Parents and others that fear the Lord are bound in duty to God, to use all means they can to impress the tender minds of their children, and youth, with the sense of God's power, and in so doing they shall not lose their reward from God, although their children when grown up, turn their backs upon it; for parents at the beginning looked upon [5] the Truth as the best portion for their children, not so much heeding their preferment in this world, if by any means they might have an interest in that which is to come. . . .

Children and others ought to know that there is no standing at a stay or stop in religion, "for not to go forward therein, is to go backward"; hence it is that the scripture saith: [Hebrews 6:4-8, quoted in full]

If there be therefore any consolation in Christ the Truth, if any comfort of love, if any fellowship of the Spirit, if any bowels of mercies, you that live carelessly and wantonly upon the earth, consider your conditions, and examine yourselves, how far the fore-mentioned scripture affects you, for I have a deep concern upon my heart for you all that have forsaken your first love, and bear another image than those young people I have mentioned bore at the beginning.

Suppose by your conformity to the vanities of this present world you should gain a large share therein, which but few obtain; what will it avail when terrifying death looks you in the face? . . . [the example of Moses]

[6] Come let us reason together; and let God's witness speak: Wanted you anything while you kept your integrity? Did you not witness one day in God's presence better than all the delights that ever you have since your minds by looseness and vanities have been estranged from him? Did your pleasure and companions in folly ever afford you that comfort and inward contentment and peace, which sometimes you have felt among God's people? . . .

Many of the youthful people and others among us need not say, "What is truth?" because I know it has often proved itself to their consciences beyond all outward demonstration.

Come away therefore and tarry no longer in lying vanities, and let none say they cannot leave them, for that is the language of your soul's Enemy to discourage you; wherefore resist him steadfastly in the faith, and he will fly from you, . . . watch therefore to the Light of Christ Jesus that discovers all the twistings of that crooked serpent; and take up the daily cross to those evils that so easily beset you, and you will find, as you have often heard, the armor of light at hand to defend you against all your youthful lusts; as, blessed be God, there are yet a cloud of witnesses alive that can from good experience testify the same.

[7] Postscript

Let none despise these lines for their plainness, for we were a plain people at the beginning. I know some of the younger sort are apt to be taken with fine words and fashionable language, as with other things in fashion, but experience shows that that which tickles the outward ear commonly stops there, very seldom coming so low as to the truth in the inward parts; therefore this epistle is sent abroad in so plain a dress on purpose, answerable to a plain seed in them that are puffed up, but ought rather to have mourned; which seed being reached, and the souls relieved, my end is answered.

Luton, the 18th of the
    6th month 1686.   John Crook.

13. Yearly Meeting Epistles (1688 and 1691)

The stages by which the London Yearly Meeting evolved out of meetings of the traveling Quaker preachers naturally produced a parallel evolution from the formal epistles of Fox and the ministers to those from the Yearly Meeting itself. Regional or "General" meetings had met and issued such epistles under the Commonwealth. An important one for establishing the responsibility of local Meetings along the lines Fox had advised came from a meeting of the Elders of Meetings in Yorkshire, Lincoln, Derbyshire, and Notts, in November, 1656;[57] it included clauses advising

1). that Meetings for worship be on Sundays, those for business on week-days;
2). that new Meetings could be set up and organized as needed;
3). warnings by individuals, by local Meetings, and if necessary by the national Quaker leaders, to those who lived contrary to Quaker standards;

[57] Cf. BBQ, pp. 311-14; the original, preserved in the records of Marsden Monthly Meeting, may have been unobtainable even in Braithwaite's time.

4). ministry to be only as led by the Spirit;

5). collections for the poor and prisoners; 6). care for their families; 7). regulation of marriages; 8). and of records of births and deaths; 9). advice to husbands, wives, parents, children, 10). servants and masters; 11). mutual duties of servants and masters; 12). care for widows and orphans;

13). obedience to magistrates' summons; 14). willingness to take public office; 15). prompt payment of debts; single prices;

16), 17), 18), 19). mutual oversight, not gossip.

It closed: "Dearly beloved Friends, these things we do not lay upon you as a rule or form to walk by, but that all with the measure of Light which is pure and holy may be guided, and so in Light walking and abiding, these may be fulfilled in the Spirit."

At another meeting of representative and leading Friends in the northern countries, part of an annual series at Scalehouse in Yorkshire in the last four years of the Commonwealth, the first Quaker fund for foreign missions was set up, to expand and partly supersede the work of the Kendal Fund (see Taylor's letter, p. 474).

EARLY EPISTLES

At a meeting of Friends out of the northern counties of York, Lincoln, Lancaster, Chester, Nottingham, Derby, Westmorland, Cumberland, Durham, and Northumberland, at Scalehouse, the 24th of the fourth month, 1658.

Having heard of great things done by the mighty power of God, in many nations beyond the seas, whither he hath called forth many of our dear brethren and sisters, to preach the everlasting Gospel; by whom he hath revealed the mystery of his Truth, which hath been hid from ages and generations, who are now in strange lands, in great straits and hardships, and in the daily hazard of their lives;—our bowels yearn towards them, and our hearts are filled with tender love to those precious ones of God, who so freely have given up for the Seed's sake, their friends, their near relations, their country and worldly estates, yea, and their own lives also; and in the feeling we are [have] of their trials, necessities and sufferings, we do therefore in the unity of the Spirit and bond of Truth, cheerfully agree, in the Lord's name and power, to move and stir up the hearts of Friends in these counties, (whom God hath called and gathered out of the world,) with one consent, freely and liberally, to offer up unto God of their earthly substance, according as God hath blessed every one,—to be speedily sent up to London, as a free-will offering for the Seed's sake; that the hands of those that are beyond the seas in the Lord's work, may be strengthened, and their bowels refreshed, from the love of their brethren. And we commit it to the care of our dear brethren of London, Amor Stoddart, Gerrard Roberts, John Bolton, Thomas Hart and Richard Davis, to order and dispose of what shall be from us sent unto them, for the supply of such as are already gone forth, or such as shall be moved of the Lord to go forth, into any other nation; of whose care and faithfulness we are well assured.

And such Friends as are here present are to be diligent in their several counties and places; that the work may be hastened with all convenient speed.

Signed by many Friends; amongst them are

Thomas Aldam, John Killam, Thomas Bewley, Thomas Taylor, Geo. Tayler, Sam. Watson, Antho. Pearson, Tho. Killan, Tho. Brocksopp, [and thirty-four others].

By 1688, when the Yearly Meeting had met regularly for a decade, and sent out regular epistles since 1681, certain standard forms had come into use. The tone had also changed. Though James II was not dethroned until William III landed in November, 1688, he had already moved toward toleration in 1687, and but for fears of what Catholics would do with it, liberty would already have been certain.

Epistle XI. [From the book of *Epistles from the Yearly Meeting*, printed in 1757.] From the Yearly Meeting in London, held the 4th, 5th, and 6th of the fourth month, 1688. To the Quarterly and Monthly Meetings in England and Wales, and elsewhere.

Dearly beloved Friends and Brethren, we salute you in the dear and tender love of God, rejoicing in the communion and holy fellowship of the spirit of life, by which we are quickened together in Christ Jesus, that we may walk together in him acceptably to God the Father; to whom be glory and praise, throughout all the churches of Christ everywhere, world without end. Amen.

Dear Friends, we give you to understand, that according to the wonted kindness of our tender and merciful God, we have had a very living and refreshing assembling together, and the glory of the divine power and presence of God hath shined upon us from day to day, to our great consolation;

and a sweet harmony, love and concord hath appeared amongst us; and many living testimonies were brought forth, through the springings of life in many, both in respect to the ancient universal doctrine of the Light and grace of God, and also in particulars, relating to the holy and harmless conversation of those who have believed, exhorting all to walk as becomes the Gospel of Christ, that the profession thereof may shine forth more and more, and the beauty of holiness may be seen upon you, and upon your families.

I. And in the first place we do earnestly desire you all, in your several Monthly and Quarterly Meetings, to stir up and exhort Friends to diligence in their meetings on the week-days, as well as on the first-day; . . .

II. And also that Friends everywhere be put in mind to keep under the leadings and guidance of the Spirit of Truth, in their outward habits and fashions thereof; not suffering the spirit of the world to get over them, in a lust to be like unto them in things useless and superfluous; lest it prevail upon them (by giving a little way to it) till it leads them from the simplicity and plainness that becomes the Gospel; . . .

III. And for the prevention of these things, we do intreat and desire all you our dear Friends, Brethren, and Sisters, that are parents and governors of families, that ye diligently lay to heart your work and calling in your generation for the Lord, and the charge committed to you; not only in becoming good examples unto the younger sort, but also to use your power in your own families, in the educating your children and servants in modesty, sobriety, and in the fear of God; curbing the extravagant humor in the young ones, when it doth appear, and not to indulge it, and allow of it. For you are set in your families as judges for God, and it is you that must give an account of the power committed to you. And when you see a libertine wanton spirit appear in your children or servants, that lusteth after the vain customs and fashions of the world, either in dressings, habits or outward adornments, . . . O then look to yourselves, and discharge your trust for God and for the good of their souls, exhorting in meekness and commanding in wisdom; that you so may minister and reach to the witness, and help them over their temptations, in the authority of God's power. . . .

IV. And dear Friends, as it hath pleased God to bring forth a day of liberty and freedom to serve him, in which he hath stopped the mouths of the devourers, in a great measure, for his name's sake; O therefore let everyone have a care so to use this liberty, as the name of God may be honored by it; and not an occasion taken by any, because of the present freedom, to launch forth into trading and worldly business beyond what they can manage honorably and with reputation, among the sons of men, and so that they may keep their word with all men and that their yea may prove yea indeed, and their nay may be nay indeed; for whatever is otherwise cometh of the evil one. And such who make themselves guilty by thus dishonouring God and the

552

holy profession of his name and Truth, such are for judgment by the Truth; and the judgment of Truth ought to be set over them; that the Truth and those that abide and walk in it may be clear of their iniquities.

V. And dear Friends, as concerning those who through letting in the enemy of their souls have lost their part of this our heavenly unity, and sought to break the sweet harmony of the church and churches of Christ in some few places [presumably the remaining members of the Wilkinson-Story faction], we let you know the power of the Lord in righteous judgment is come over their evil works, and they cannot proceed. But divers, who were for a time beguiled and darkened by them, have received mercy from God, and Light to see whither they were going; and are returned to the shepherd's fold, to the comfort of their souls, and the praise of God. And concerning them that remain still under the influence of that evil separating spirit in any measure (being betrayed at unawares), we desire they may be gained upon in a Christian tenderness of spirit, and that bowels of compassion may be exercised towards them, for their recovery (if possible) out of the snare. . . .

VI. Farther we give you to understand that several good epistles from divers parts of the world were read amongst us; as from Holland, Scotland, Ireland, Wales, Barbados, Virginia, Maryland, Jamaica, Long Island, Rhode-island, and from sundry parts of this nation, signifying the prosperity of Truth, and the increase of Friends, and their great concord and unity in the blessed Truth, to our great comfort and joy in the Lord.

VII. And that the Friends appointed to inspect the accounts did report to us, that they found the accounts well and fairly kept, and the balance thereof not much different from what it was last year; so that there was no need of any farther collection this year. . . .

VIII. And we give you to know that the six Friends of this city, that are entrusted for this year with the accounts, are John Etridge, Benjamin Antrobus, Thomas Barker, Thomas Cox, Thomas Hudson and John West.

XI. And it is the desire of Friends generally, that you all be careful, in your Monthly and Quarterly Meetings, in collecting the sufferings of Friends by priests and impropriators for their testimony against tithes and what goods are taken away from them upon that account, with the value thereof as also about repairs of steeple-houses, or about not swearing, and all other sufferings on Truth's account and let them be carefully recorded and witnessed, and copies sent up to London, from your Quarterly Meetings to your correspondents; that the sufferings of Friends for their testimonies may not be lost.

X. It was agreed by Friends with one consent that this Meeting be continued the next year, at the usual time, as the Lord shall please to make way for it; and that in order thereunto, two sound faithful Friends in every county, may be desired to come up, that know the state of Friends, and their sufferings, in their respective counties; to whom we leave it to give a farther account of this Meeting, and of the glorious presence of the Lord manifested with us here.

XI. Finally, dear Friends, we tenderly, in the love of our God, recommend you all to the word of his grace and wisdom, . . . in the peaceable Spirit of our Lord Jesus Christ. And we tenderly desire and advise that all Friends everywhere keep peaceable and quiet in their spirits, and inoffensive in their conversations and discourses, that none let in, entertain, or mix with that jealous evil-surmising spirit, that is at work in some sorts of ungrateful prejudiced persons, who will not see the present providence of God, and mercy we enjoy under the king and his government; eyeing their own interests more than the public good, or peace of the church of Christ.

God almighty preserve you, and be with you and us all in Christ Jesus. Amen.

Signed in behalf of our said Meeting, by

Richard Richardson.

The "inoffensive," "harmless," "peaceable" spirit that the 1688 Epistle advised became the dominant mood of Quakerism after 1688. By keeping their resistance nonviolent, Friends had earned their right to toleration and their countrymen's respect. When toleration ended the defensive phase of "the Lamb's War," however, the spirit of peaceableness, added to decades of weariness, worked to prevent Friends from reopening the all-out attack upon evil throughout the world that had characterized Friends in the 1650's. The truce the world offered became a permanent peace. The Epistle of 1691, six months after Fox's death, shows Friends becoming a worldwide yet self-sufficient community gradually turning inward.

Epistle XIV. From the Yearly Meeting in London, held the 1st, 2d, 3d, and 4th of the fourth month, 1691. To the Quarterly and Monthly Meetings in England and Wales, and elsewhere.

Dear and faithful Friends and Brethren, we tenderly salute you all in our Lord Jesus Christ, and blessed union of his precious life; who hath eminently appeared among us and with us in this our heavenly solemnity; still ministering fresh encouragement unto us, by his divine power and counsel, to persevere in faithfulness and diligence in his work and service to the end of our days, and finishing our course with joy, as many of his dear ancient and faithful servants have already done. Blessed be his glorious name forever.

We are much comforted at this our weighty assembly, in the many good accounts given as heretofore of Truth's prosperity, and the increase of Christ's kingdom, and the abounding of love, peace and unity, among Friends; and the decrease and dying of the spirit of division and enmity in divers places where it has entered; and that meetings are increased, and many people's hearts opened to hear and receive the Truth: and that in some places new Meeting-houses are erected, and others about preparing and building; which are and will be of great advantage for Truth's promotion, we doubt not, as experience hath long and clearly shown: and that good order and christian care in your meetings aforesaid, is, and we hope will be, continued in the service of Truth and one another, to the honour of God, and exaltation of his holy name and Truth, and the strengthening and encouraging of Friends in general, and one another in the service thereof; which our souls earnestly desire, and hope you will ever be mindful of; that our God may have his praise, and you all your lasting peace and comfort.

We perceive the suffering that chiefly remains on faithful Friends in divers counties, by imprisonment and spoil of goods, doth increase, for our ancient christian testimony against the old and grand oppression of tithes; we having now account of about eighty Friends prisoners on that account; whose faithfulness the Lord will reward. And we desire that the same christian testimony may be duly kept up; and such as are unfaithful to Christ Jesus; that they may not strengthen the persecutors' hands, increase others' sufferings, nor make void Truth's testimony therein, which so many have offered up and laid down their lives for.

These things are also recommended to your godly care; and it is our tender and Christian advice, for the Lord's sake, and his blessed name and Truth's sake, that Friends be diligent in keeping their week-day meetings as duly as on First-days, in his worship and service: and that you do encourage the faithful Women's Meetings, and the settling them where they are wanting, and may with convenience be settled; knowing their service, and what need there is also of their godly care in the church of Christ in divers weighty respects, proper to them. And that great care be taken about marriages, for the consent of parents, due and orderly publication thereof, and solemnizing of them in a meeting appointed for that end and purpose; which method is convenient and commendable, as it has been lately made appear in the eye of the government, and well resented. And that Friends be reminded of this Meeting's former advice against marriage with near kindred, and against marrying by priests, and with persons of the world, unequally yoking with unbelievers; and against too early and unsavoury proceedings in second marriages after the death of husband or wife, contrary to the due method and practice of faithful Friends in Truth, and tending to the dishonour and reproach thereof.

And that Friends take care to keep to Truth and plainness, in language, habit, deportment and behaviour; that the simplicity of Truth in these things may not wear out nor be lost in our days, nor in our posterity's; and be exemplary to their children in each, and train them up therein; that modesty and sobriety may be countenanced, and the fear of the Lord take place and increase among them: And to avoid pride and immodesty in apparel, and extravagant wigs, and all other vain and superfluous fashions of the world; and in God's holy fear watch against and keep out the spirit and corrupt friendship of the world; and that no fellowship may be held or had with the unfruitful works of darkness, nor therein with the workers thereof. And to avoid unnecessary frequenting taverns, ale-houses, all looseness, excess and unprofitable and idle discourses, mis-spending their precious time and substance, to the dishonour of Truth, and scandal of our holy profession. Let your godly care and earnest endeavours be to stop and prevent all reproaches and scandals in these or any other cases. And that all Friends watch over their children; and none to indulge or suffer them in pride, or corrupt liberty; whereby they become exposed to the world, to be ensnared either in their marriages, or evil conversation tending to their hurt and ruin. And that Friends keep to their wonted example and testimony against the superstitious observation of days.

It is also the advice of this Meeting that all and every your Meeting-houses, and mansion-houses where Meetings are or may be, be entered upon record, as the law directs; each particularly: we having seen both the service and safety thereof, and the hurt and danger that may come by the omission. And that care be taken in each Monthly Meeting, that Friends who have estates to dispose of, by will or otherwise, be particularly advised to make their will, or settle their estates, in due time; to prevent the inconveniences, loss and trouble, that may follow upon their relations and friends, and injury to the poor, through their dying intestate. Delays and omissions in this case having been very prejudicial in divers respects.

We are glad to hear that care is taken in some places, according to former advice, for the providing school-masters and mistresses who are faithful Friends, to instruct Friends' children in such method as Truth allows. And we desire that Friends go on in that care to promote such education and schools, for the advantage of their children and posterity.

Divers good epistles and accounts were read in this Meeting from foreign parts; as Ireland, Scotland, Amsterdam, Dantzick, Jamaica, Nevis, Maryland, Rhode Island (and two from Friends, captives at Mequinez [Meknes] in Barbary, under the emperor of Morocco) [cf. p. 500] intimating the prosperity of Truth, and the peace and unity of Friends among themselves, and their love to Friends in this nation; and in many places their want of faithful laborers; and their desire for the spreading of Truth as much as may be, both by Friends' books and ministry; and also to be furnished with books, as Friends can send them.

There yet remain nine English Friends captives at Mequinez and three at Murbay: who have received the Truth there (it being three or four days' journey distant), who correspond with each other by letters. One Friend (to wit, Joseph Wasey) being lately redeemed, and newly come over, gave a large account to this Meeting of their miserable hard usage in captivity; having no lodging but under arches, in deep places on the cold ground, winter and summer; only water for their drink; and no bread allowed them by the king, but of old rotten stinking barley; and no clothes, but a frock once in two years; and forced to hard labour (except three days in a year); and more especially on the sixth day of the week (which is their day of worship) they are compelled to carry heavy burdens on their heads, running from sun rising to sun-setting, with brutish black boys following with whips and stripes at their pleasure. Many of the other captives perish and die, through their extreme hardships, and want of food to sustain them: as in all likelihood Friends there had, if Friends and their relations here had not sent them some relief: ... Joseph Wasey also signified, that Friends' day-time being taken up with hard servitude, they are necessitated to keep their meetings in the night-season to wait upon God. And that the aforesaid captive Friends were very thankful for the relief sent from hence; which was very refreshing to them.

An epistle from Friends Half-Year Meeting in Ireland was read, giving an account, that notwithstanding Friends' great suffering and exercise in that kingdom, Friends there have been well supported by the Lord's power under the same; having yet left them wherewithal to relieve them that stand in need and are impoverished. And accordingly our dear and ancient Friend William Edmondson (who lately came from Ireland, having with his family undergone deep suffering) also acquainted the Meeting, that although Friends there have undergone great suffering and losses,[58] yet care is taken that no Friends need now come from thence for want of a present supply or without a certificate from Friends of some meeting there. Wherefore, if there be necessity here-after to minister to their relief when they are capable to receive and make use thereof, it is left to the care of the Meeting here for sufferings to give you notice thereof in its time and season, when further necessity shall require.

We do also acquaint you that the Friends appointed by this Meeting to inspect the account, report back to this Meeting that they find them truly stated and fairly kept; and nothing of what was contributed towards captives'

58 In 1690, following the effort of James II to regain his throne through a rebellion in Ireland, William III defeated him at the Battle of the Boyne, still remembered with bitterness by Catholics and Protestants in Ireland.

redemption is disbursed this year past; no opportunity having yet presented for their redemption, though much endeavoured; but sixty pounds added, being repaid by Leven Buskin, who was a captive redeemed from Algiers some years since. But that the contribution, intended for the ease and relief of suffering and necessitous Friends, is wholly expended and in debt, by reason of the urgent occasions to endeavour the ease and relief of Friends that do or may suffer in divers general cases (and also the charity bestowed upon divers of our suffering Friends and Brethren of Ireland, both thefe and here); wherein our Friends of London have been very industrious, and intend not to be wanting therein, as the Lord shall yet afford opportunity. Whereupon they offer it to this Meeting as their judgment, that it is needful there should be a further supply, by a general contribution among Friends, for the like service, to be made this year. Which being duly and weightily considered, this Meeting agrees unanimously that a contribution be made by Friends throughout all the several meetings of Friends in England and Wales, for the supply and service of Friends and Truth, as aforesaid. And it is recommended by this Meeting to the Quarterly and Monthly Meetings aforesaid; who are desired to take care therein with as much convenient speed as may be; and to return the collections to the six Friends of the city, who are intrusted this year with the accounts; namely, Thomas Lacy, Thomas Cooper, George Green, Hercey Wilson, Jos. Wright, and Cornelius Mason, or any of them.

14. George Whitehead's "Christian Doctrine" (1693), from William Sewel's *History* (1722), pp. 642-649

This tract introduces two of the prominent Friends of the second generation, though both men had been convinced of Quakerism within the first decade. George Whitehead, a Westmorland Friend whose *Christian Progress* later became one of the most-read early journals, moved to London about 1670, at the height of the persecutions; and in the 1690's, since Penn was preoccupied and Fox, Barclay, and Dewsbury dead, he emerged as the leader and spokesman of the Yearly Meeting. Earnest, honest, devoted if not inspiring, he wrote dozens of tracts in answer to anti-Quakers, one of which is here reproduced from Sewel's *History*. William Sewel of Amsterdam, whose mother was a Friend and active speaker from 1657, had visited England in 1668 and became a lifelong friend of Penn; but he only became well known late in life when his *History of the People Called Quakers* (1717 in Dutch, 1722 in English) became the first full-length history of Friends by a Quaker, taking its place with Barclay's *Apology,* Besse's *Sufferings,* and Fox's *Journal* as for two hundred years the authoritative sources on the movement.

Whitehead's "Christian Doctrine" might seem to belong with doctrinal works, where it would rank among the more orthodox and unimaginative; but its importance is in reflecting the conflict with George Keith. A fellow-Scot and for decades friend and colleague of Barclay, Keith, too, had been convinced by 1662, traveled widely as a Quaker minister, and presented theological tracts that foreshadowed Barclay's. Settling in 1689 as a schoolteacher in Philadelphia, however, he broke with the Pennsylvania leaders, perhaps over personality as much as doctrine, was disowned by the Philadelphia Yearly Meeting, and returned to London. There, too, he was disowned in 1694, partly as a result of this tract; and after forming for a few years a "Christian Quaker" group in London, he went over in 1700 to the episcopal Church of England and became one of the first missionaries of its Society for the Propagation of the Gospel in the colonies. The Anglican Charles Leslie and three other ex-Quakers—Francis Bugg, William Rogers, and John Pennyman—were in the same years outdoing even Keith in their volume of anti-Quaker tracts. But the latter two were ultra-individualists of the Perrot-Story type, while Bugg was much less clear and creative than Keith in charging Friends with unorthodoxy by Christian standards. The issue had to do with Christ, and Whitehead and others had no trouble in showing that Friends held to all the traditional doctrines of Christianity. The subtler issues Keith raised, such as whether Friends came to the historic Christ by way of the Spirit, rather than vice versa, still divide Quakers today. Liberal Friends notice differences between Quaker language in the 1650's and in Whitehead's answer. A similar defense of Quaker orthodoxy, Fox's *Letter to the Governor of Barbados,* is still much quoted by evangelical Friends. In any case their efforts to answer Keith drove Quakers into a conservative and doctrinal style of thinking just in the decades when Anglican and Puritan thought were moving towards rationalism and even Deism. Quakerism was guarded against these, but at the cost of having no creative theological life to undergird its period of quietism and mysticism in the eighteenth century.

The Christian Doctrine and Society of the People called Quakers cleared &c.
(1693).

Whereas divers accounts have been lately published in print of some late division and disputes between some persons under the name of Quakers in Pennsylvania, about several fundamental doctrines of the Christian faith, (as is pretended by one party), which being particularly mentioned and thereupon occasion very unduly taken by our adversaries to reproach both the Christian ministry and whole body of the people commonly called Quakers, and their holy and Christian profession, . . . to the amusing and troubling the world therewith, and giving occasion to the loose, ignorant, and prophane, to slight and condemn the Truth, and the interest of the tender religion of our Lord Jesus Christ;—we are, therefore, tenderly concerned for Truth's sake, in behalf of the said people . . . to use our just endeavors to remove the reproach, and all causeless jealousies concerning us, touching those doctrines of Christianity, or any of them pretended (or supposed) to be in question in the said division. In relation whereunto we do in the fear of God and in simplicity and plainness of his Truth received, solemnly and sincerely declare what our Christian belief and profession has been, and still is, in respect to Jesus Christ the only begotten Son of God, his suffering, death, resurrection, glory, light, power, great day of judgment, &c.[59]

We sincerely profess faith in God by his only begotten Son Jesus Christ, as being our Light and life, our only way to the Father, and also our only mediator and advocate with the Father.

That God created all things, he made the worlds, by his Son Jesus Christ, he being that powerful and living Word of God by whom all things were made, and that the Father, the Word, and the Holy Spirit are one, in divine being inseparable; one true, living and eternal God blessed forever.

Yet that this word, or Son of God in the fulness of time, took flesh, became perfect man, according to the flesh descended and came of the seed of Abraham and David, but was miraculously conceived by the Holy Ghost, and born of the Virgin Mary. And also farther, declared powerfully the Son of God, according to the Spirit of sanctification, by the resurrection from the dead.

That in the word (or Son of God) was life, and the same life was the light of men; and that he was that true light which enlightens every man coming into the world, and therefore that men are to believe in the light, that they may become children of the Light. Hereby we believe in Christ the Son of God, as he is the light and life within us; and wherein we must needs have

[59] Whitehead buttresses every sentence from here onward with scripture texts.

sincere respect and honour to (and belief in) Christ, as in his own unapproachable, and incomprehensible glory and fulness, as he is the fountain of life and light, and giver thereof unto us; Christ, as in himself, and as in us, being not divided. . . . As man, Christ died for our sins, rose again having, in his dying for all, been that one great universal offering and sacrifice for peace, atonement and reconciliation between God and man; and he is the propitiation not for our sins only, but for the sins of the whole world. We were reconciled by his death, but saved by his life.

That Jesus Christ who sitteth at the right hand of the throne of the majesty in the heavens; yet is he our king, high-priest and prophet in his Church, a minister of the sanctuary and of the true tabernacle. . . . He is intercessor and advocate with the Father in heaven, and . . . also by his Spirit in our hearts, he maketh intercession according to the will of God, crying Abba, Father.

For any whom God hath gifted and called sincerely to preach faith in the same Christ, both as within and without us, cannot be to preach two Christs, but one and the same Lord Jesus Christ; having respect to those degrees of our spiritual knowledge of Christ Jesus in us, and to his own unspeakable fulness and glory, as in himself in his own entire being, wherein Christ himself and the least measure of his light or life as in us or in mankind are not divided or separable. . . . His fulness cannot be comprehended, or contained in any finite creature, but in some measure known and experienced in us, as we are capable to receive the same, as of his fulness we have received grace for grace. Christ our mediator received the Spirit, not by measure, but in fulness; but to every one of us is given grace according to the measure of his gift.

That the Gospel of the grace of God should be preached in the name of the Father, Son, and Holy Ghost, being one, in power, wisdom, and goodness, and indivisible, (or not to be divided) in the great work of man's salvation. We sincerely confess (and believe in) Jesus Christ, . . . and that he is the author of our living faith in the power and goodness of God, as manifest in his son Jesus Christ and by his own blessed Spirit (or divine unction) revealed in us; whereby we inwardly feel and taste of his goodness, life and virtue. The inward sense of this divine power of Christ and faith in the same and this inward experience is absolutely necessary to make a true, sincere and perfect Christian in spirit and life.

That divine honor and worship is due to the Son of God; and that he is in true faith to be prayed unto, and the name of the Lord Jesus Christ called upon (as the primitive Christians did) because of the glorious union or oneness of the Father and the Son; and that we cannot acceptably offer up prayers and praises to God, nor receive a gracious answer or blessing from God, but in and through his dear Son Christ.

That Christ's body that was crucified was not the godhead, yet by the power of God was raised from the dead; and that the same Christ that was therein crucified, ascended into heaven and glory is not questioned by us. His flesh . . . did not corrupt, but yet doubtless his body was changed into a more glorious and heavenly condition than it was in when subject to divers sufferings on earth; but how and what manner of change it met withal after it was raised from the dead, so as to become such a glorious body (as it is declared to be) is too wonderful for mortals to conceive, apprehend or pry into. . . .

True and living faith in Christ Jesus the Son of the living God, has respect to his entire being . . . also an eye and respect to the same Son of God as inwardly making himself known in the soul, in every degree of his Light, life, Spirit, grace and truth. He is both the word of faith, and a quickening spirit in us whereby he is the immediate cause, author, object, and strength of our living faith in his name and power, and of the work of our salvation from sin, and bondage of corruption: And the Son of God cannot be divided from the least or lowest appearance of his own divine Light (or life in us or in manking) . . . and where the least degree or measure of this light and life of Christ within is sincerely waited in, followed and obeyed, there is a blessed increase of light and grace known and felt, . . . and thereby a growing in grace, and in the knowledge of God, and of our Lord and savior Jesus Christ, hath been, and is truly experienced. And this Light, life or Spirit of Christ within (for they are one divine principle) is sufficient to lead unto all Truth, having in it the divers ministrations both of judgment and mercy, both of law and Gospel (even that Gospel which is preached in every intelligent creature under heaven:) It does not only, as in its first ministration, manifest sin, and reprove and condemn for sin, but also excites and leads them that believe in it to true repentance, and thereupon to receive that mercy, pardon, and redemption in Christ Jesus, which he has obtained for mankind in those Gospel-terms of faith (in his name), true repentance and conversion to Christ thereby required.

So that the light and life of the Son of God within, truly obeyed and followed . . . does not leave men or women (who believe in the Light) under the first covenant, nor as sons of the bondwoman, as the literal Jews were, (when gone from the Spirit of God, and his Christ in them) but it naturally leads them into the new covenant, into the new and living way, and to the adoption of sons, to be children and sons of the free-woman, of Jerusalem from above . . . wherever Christ qualifies and calls any to preach and demonstrate the mystery of his coming, death, and resurrection, &c. even among the Gentiles, Christ ought accordingly to be both preached, believed and received.

Yet supposing there have been, or are such pious and conscientious

Gentiles, in whom Christ was and is as the seed or principle of the second or new covenant, the Light, the word of faith, (as is granted) and that such live uprightly and faithfully to that light they have, or to what is made known of God in them, and who therefore in that state cannot perish, . . . and supposing these have not the outward advantage of preaching, scripture, or thence the knowledge of Christ's outward coming, being outwardly crucified and risen from the dead, can such . . . be justly excluded Christianity, or the covenant of grace, (as to the virtue, life, and nature thereof) or truly deemed no Christians? Or must all be excluded any true knowledge or faith of Christ as without them? No sure, for that would imply insufficiency in Christ and his Light as within them, and to frustrate God's good end and promise of Christ, and his free and universal love and grace to mankind, in sending his Son. We charitably believe the contrary, that they must have some true faith and interest in Christ and his mediation, because of God's free love in Christ to all mankind and Christ's dying for all men and being given for a Light of the Gentiles, and for salvation to the ends of the earth. And because of their living up sincerely and faithfully to his Light in them, their being pious, conscientious, accepted and saved, (as is granted) we cannot reasonably think a sincere, pious, or godly man, wholly void of Christianity (of what nation soever he be) because none can come to God or Godliness but by Christ, by his light and grace in them. Yet we grant if there be such pious sincere men or women, as have not the Scripture or knowledge of Christ, as outwardly crucified, &c. they are not perfect Christians in all perfections, as in all knowledge and understanding, all points of doctrine. They are better than they profess or pretend to be, they are more Jews inward and Christians inward than in outward show or profession. There are Christians sincere and perfect in kind or nature, in life and substance, though not in knowledge and understanding. A man or woman having the life and fruits of true Christianity, the fruits of the Spirit of Christ in them that can talk little thereof, or of creeds, points, or articles of faith (yea many that cannot read letters) yet may be true Christians in spirit and life. And some could die for Christ, that could not dispute for him; and even infants that die in innocency are not excluded the grace of God, or salvation in and by Christ Jesus. . . .

And though we had the holy Scriptures of the Old and New Testament, and a belief of Christ crucified and risen, &c. we never truly knew the mystery thereof, until we were turned to the Light of his grace and Spirit within us. We knew not what it was to be reconciled by his death, and saved by his life, or what it was to know the fellowship of his sufferings, the power of his resurrection, or to be made conformable unto his death (we knew not) . . . until he opened our eyes, and turned our minds from darkness unto his own divine Light and life within us.

Notwithstanding, we do sincerely and greatly esteem and value the holy Scriptures, preaching and teaching of faithful, divinely inspired, gifted and qualified persons and ministers of Jesus Christ, as being great outward helps, and instrumental in his hand and by his Spirit for conversion, where God is pleased to afford those outward helps and means, as that we neither do nor may oppose the sufficiency of the Light or Spirit of Christ within to such outward helps or means, so as to reject, disesteem, or undervalue them; for they all proceed from the same Light and Spirit, . . . being sent to turn people to the same Light and Spirit in them.

'Tis certain that great is the mystery of Godliness in itself. in its own being and excellency, namely, that God should be, and was manifest in the flesh, justified in the Spirit, seen of angels, preached unto the Gentiles, believed on in the world, and received up into glory.

And 'tis a great and precious mystery of Godliness and Christianity also, that Christ should be spiritually and effectually in men's hearts, to save and deliver them from sin, Satan, and bondage of corruption. . . . And therefore this mystery of Godliness, both as in its own being and glory, and also as in men (in many hid and in some revealed) hath been and must be testified, preached, and believed, where God is pleased to give commission (and prepare people's hearts for the same) and not in man's will. . . .

1. For the doctrine of the resurrection: If in this life only we have hope in Christ, we are of all men most miserable, I Cor. xv. 19. We sincerely believe, not only a resurrection in Christ from the fallen sinful state here, but a rising and ascending into glory with him hereafter; that when he at last appears, we may appear with him in glory; but that all the wicked, who live in rebellion against the light of grace, and die finally impenitent, shall come forth to the resurrection of condemnation.

And that the soul or spirit of every man and woman shall have its proper body, as God is pleased to give.

. . . Howbeit we esteem it very unnecessary to dispute or question how the dead are raised, or with what body they come. But rather submit that to the wisdom and pleasure of almighty God.

2. For the doctrine of eternal judgment: God hath committed all judgment unto his Son Jesus Christ, and he is both judge of quick and dead, and of the states and ends of all mankind. That there shall be hereafter a great harvest, which is the end of the world, a great Day of Judgment, and the judgment of that great day the holy scripture is clear. . . .

A Postscript relating to the Doctrine of the Resurrection and Eternal Judgment.

"Whosoever do now wilfully shut their eyes, hate, condemn, or shun the light of Christ, or his appearance within, shall at last be made to see, and not be able to shun or hide themselves from his glorious and dreadful appearance from heaven with his mighty angels, as with lightning and in flaming fire, . . . And though many now evade and reject the inward convictions and judgment of the light, and shut up the records or books thereof in their own consciences, they shall all be at last opened, and every one judged of these things recorded therein, according to their works.

Signed in behalf of our Christian profession and people aforesaid.

George Whitehead, Ambrose Rigge, William Fallowfield, James Parke, Charles Marshall, John Bowater, John Vaughton, William Bingley.

15. Margaret Fell's Last Epistle to Friends, from Swarthmoor Hall, 4th Month, 1698. The freedom of the Spirit from outward uniformity. From her *Works* (*A Brief Collection of Remarkable Passages,* London, 1710), pp. 534-35. We give the last word to a woman, who in her old age still personified the free spirit of early Friends.

Dear Friends, Brethren and Sisters:

God the Father of our blessed Lord and Savior Jesus Christ is a universal God of mercy and love to all people. And in that blessed love he visited us, "in an acceptable time and in a day of salvation, etc." And he that early brought unto us the glad-tidings of the gospel of peace, [i.e. George Fox], continued in the body amongst God's Plantation up and down forty years; and we had from him certain directions and instructions upon many weighty accounts and occasions. He hath left us several writings and records, to be practised according to the Gospel which he preached amongst us; and we have lived under the teaching of that blessed eternal Spirit of the eternal God, which he directed us to, unto this day. And now it is good for us all to go on and continue hand in hand in the unity and fellowship of this eternal Spirit, in humility and lowliness of mind, each esteeming others better than ourselves; and this is well-pleasing unto God.

And let us all take heed of touching anything like the ceremonies of the Jews; for that was displeasing unto Christ, for he came to bear witness against them, and testified against their outside practices, who told him of their long robes and of their broad phylacteries, . . . So that we may see how ill he liked their outward ceremonies. So let us keep to the rule and leading of the eternal Spirit, that God hath given us to be our teacher; and let that put on and off as is meet and serviceable for every one's state and condition. And let us take heed of limiting in such practices; for we are under the Gospel leading and guiding and teaching, which is a free spirit, which leads into unity and lowliness of mind the saints and servants of Christ, desiring to be established in the free Spirit, not bound or limited. Legal ceremonies are far from gospel freedom: let us beware of being guilty or having a hand in ordering or contriving that which is contrary to Gospel-freedom; for the Apostle would not have dominion over their faith in Corinth, but to be helpers of their faith. It's a dangerous thing to lead young Friends much into the observation of outward things, which may be easily done; for they can soon get into an outward garb, to be all alike outwardly, but this will not make them true Christians: it's the Spirit that gives life; I would be loth to have a hand in these things. The Lord preserve us, that we do no hurt to God's work; but let him work whose work it is. We have lived quietly and peaceably thus far, and it's not for God's service to make breaches.

Margaret Fox.

Appendix: Types of Quaker Writings by Year – 1650-1699

by David Runyon for Hugh Barbour

The first entry under each year and type shows the number of new Quaker tracts or other works printed (reprints, translations, and collected works are listed separately; joint works of several authors are listed only once).

The second entry under each year shows the number of "sheets" printed in the works of this type during that year (as listed in Joseph Smith, *Catalogue of Friends' Books*); generally folio volumes were printed 4 pages to a sheet, quarto 8 pp., octavo 16 pp., duodecimo 24 pp., if the reverse sides are counted. Since print size was not related to the size of the page, no more accurate total is available. Fractions of sheets are not given on the chart but are added into the totals.

Source: J. Smith, *Catalogue of Friends' Books,* checked against D. Wing, *Short-Title Catalogue.*

Key to classification system:

P = proclamation, prophetic judgment, and other preaching to non-Quakers
A = autobiographical tract
AJ = autobiographical journal
DP = doctrinal, or dispute with the Puritans
DE = dispute with the Church of England
DC = dispute with the Roman Catholics
DQ = dispute among the Quakers
DB = dispute with Baptists and other sects
S = sufferings of Quakers described or tabulated
ST = toleration tract, usually combined with appeal for the sufferers
X = exhortation, or appeal to non-Friends about specific moral issues
XS = appeal to the political leaders or Parliament
T = ethical testimony, or ethical defense
E = epistle to or by groups of Friends or Meetings
L = letter by individual Friend
M = memoir or testimony to the memory of a deceased Friend
R = reprinted or translation, other than collected works
I = scientific, scholarly, or technical tract
W = Collected Works (often including journal)

567

		P	A	AJ	DP	DE	DC	DQ	DB	S	ST	X	XS	T	E	L	M	R	I	W	Total
1650	Works																				
	sheets																				
1651	Works																				
	sheets																				
1652	Works													1	1						2
	sheets													7	1						7
1653	Works	24			9					5		3	3	1	5	3					53
	sheets	62			42					37		4	3	2	10	1					161
1654	Works	33	3		20		2		2	9		1	7	1	4	4		2			88
	sheets	76	18		72		5		6	14		2	11		2	6		12			224
1655	Works	43	2		34		5		4	13		3	3	2	6	1					135
	sheets	98	4		122		14		21	26		3	3	5	6						345
1656	Works	37	5		24		2		3	17		4	4	1	4						132
	sheets	85	14		92		13		9	62		18	6		15						377
1657	Works	31			12		3		4	13	1	3	6	6	5		1				102
	sheets	139			73		10		13	82	5	11	13	16	10						397
1658	Works	39	1		10		4		4	9	3	4	4		7	1			1		98
	sheets	111	2		48		28		18	31	4	5	10		11				2		298

		P	A	AJ	DP	DE	DC	DQ	DB	S	ST	X	XS	T	E	L	M	R	I	W	Total
1659	Works	59	5	1	7		4	1	11	22	1	13	36	13	16	1			1		210
	sheets	212	15	26	37		24		34	60	2	20	104	38	28	1			2		687
1660	Works	68	3		27	10	5		8	8	7	18	33	21	27	6			1		278
	sheets	262	3		75	23	7		16	23	29	40	36	104	40	1			5		742
1661	Works	38			11	3	1	1	2	11	6	10	18	13	28	1		36	1		180
	sheets	87			51	2	7	6	4	26	22	27	35	29	70			90	15		471
1662	Works	27	1		20	4	6		4	20	8	8	17	7	22	3	2	18		1	168
	sheets	46	2		40	4	12		10	106	14	7	22	44	31		4	47		18	411
1663	Works	42	1		16	4		1		7	1	3	7	12	37	1	4	10	1	1	149
	sheets	96	2		61	14				15	3	21	7	20	43		3	78	1	63	429
1664	Works	20	2		8		1			11	10	6	7	3	23	1	3	10	1		106
	sheets	47	4		13		5			28	28	10	10	21	31		4	18	5		224
1665	Works	24			2		2		22	6	7		6	4	24	2	1	17	1	1	99
	sheets	46			14		15		23	25	11		6	12	32		1	58	1	17	261
1666	Works	6	1		4	1				4		3	7	3	9	1	1	10		1	51
	sheets	6	1		9	1				6		2	9	16	8			7		193	258
1667	Works	14	2		7		3	1		7	2	1		1	4	1	1	4			48
	sheets	57	2		33		23	3		35	7	1		3	7			10			181

	P	A	AJ	DP	DE	DC	DQ	DB	S	ST	X	XS	T	E	L	M	R	I	W	Total
1668 Works	6	1		15						1	2	1	3	4			12	1		46
sheets	29	1		129						6	2	3	17	6			40	2		235
1669 Works	5	1		11	3	1	1		2				3	5	3	2	9	1		47
sheets	15	5		56	9	1	3		6				22	5	2	3	59	6		192
1670 Works	18			11	2	1		2	1	6		11	5	10	2		10		1	80
sheets	42			39	2	5		4	1	15		11	24	10			41			194
1671 Works	9			8	1	3	1	1	1	1		1	6	4	1	8	12		1	58
sheets	36			63	3	9	7	7	28			1	45	8	1	9	72		43	332
1672 Works	6			6		1		6	2	1	2	3	1	6	1	2	7	1	1	47
sheets	15			65				12	20	5	2	4	1	10		2	13	7	240	396
1673 Works	9	2		12	1	3		5	1		4	2	12	4	1		6	1		63
sheets	20	4		59	7	10		127	10		10	6	44	8	3		16	1		325
1674 Works	12			20	2		2	10				2	4	5	4		5	1		67
sheets	31			200	4		6	34				2	5	7	3		12	7		311
1675 Works	8			12	3		2		6	4	1	7	9	7	1	4	17	2	3	86
sheets	15			34	11		5		10	21	1	11	42	7	1	4	81	9	321	572
1676 Works	8			30	1	2			5	3	2	4	4	10	1	12	5	3		90
sheets	19			240	2	4			7	8	2	2	10	15	2	14	33	102		460

Year		P	A	AJ	DP	DE	DC	DQ	DB	S	ST	X	XS	T	E	L	M	R	I	W	Total
1677	Works	6	2		16	2	1		1	5	1	2	6	4	9		2	6			63
	sheets	17	6		66	21	1		2	13	6	5	11	9	10		5	18			190
1678	Works	7	1		11		1	2	1	3	1	1	1	1	2	1	1	4			38
	sheets	19	1		194		3	6		5	1	2	3	36	9		1	19			299
1679	Works	6			8	1	6		2	4	1	2	2	2	5	3	4	10	1	2	59
	sheets	63			60	13	31		65	22	2	5	5	15	5	2	1	67	12	226	594
1680	Works	5	1		7		3	2		8	1	3	5	10	9	3	11	4	1		72
	sheets	7	1		117		5	2		64	1	16	7	46	34	3	20	13	8		343
1681	Works	5			12		1	2		2	2	2	2	2	9	1	23	3	4	1	72
	sheets	46			44		1	2		2	1	11	1	3	16		22	11	6	221	388
1682	Works	6			13			2		12	3		1	3	19		5	4	6		74
	sheets	12			134			36		19	2		1	5	38		5	39	45		336
1683	Works	3			18		1	3		10	3	1	2	6	10	4	19	10	1	1	92
	sheets				76		2	14		22	38	2	4	12	12	7	21	59	1	48	318
1684	Works	4	1		12			1		3		1	5	3	10	3	3	22	4	5	77
	sheets	4	1		99			3		3		1	5	6	15		2	40	4	121	304
1685	Works	7			11	1		1	1		2	2	8	4	11	2	5	5	3	1	64
	sheets	10			31	1		4	4		2	2	11	6	10	8	7	27	7	27	157

571

		P	A	AJ	DP	DE	DC	DQ	DB	S	ST	X	XS	T	E	L	M	R	I	W	Total
1686	Works	5			6			3					3	1	9		5	4			36
	sheets	5			12			58					11	2	9		16	21			134
1687	Works	4			1			1		4	7	1	3	3	6	6	3	5	1		45
	sheets	19			8			4		3	14	1	3	14	7	12	4	37			128
1688	Works	1			6		2			2	3	1	1	1	6	5	4	7			39
	sheets				18		6			2	8	1	3	3	9	12	5	8			75
1689	Works	3		1	6			1		3	2		5	1	4	3	11	4	2	3	49
	sheets	12		3	110			2		2	3		8	2	6	6	10	4	1	109	278
1690	Works	2	1	1	5		1			1	2		4	1	11	2	10	5		2	48
	sheets	8		11	35		6				2		4		13	1	16	6		23	125
1691	Works	2			7			2				2		3	6	2	12	4	3		43
	sheets	5			20			3				5		15	15	5	31	22	14		135
1692	Works	6	1	2	10			3	3	1		2	4	3	13		9	2	1	2	62
	sheets	31	3	12	16			15	7	1		10	4	11	24		16		14	36	200
1693	Works	4			11			1		3		1			7	1	5	4	2		39
	sheets	8			31			4		10		1			6		4	18	7		89
1694	Works	5	2		10	1	1	5		1		1		1	9		4	3	3	1	47
	sheets	10	97		26	1	23	11				1			24		5	47	7	13	265

APPENDIX

	P	A	AJ	DP	DE	DC	DQ	DB	S	ST	X	XS	T	E	L	M	R	I	W	Total
1695 Works	2		3	13	1		3		1			3	4	5		1	6	2	1	45
sheets	57		216	47	3		20		1			2	10	9		3	38	4	12	422
1696 Works	4	1		16	2		4		1		1	2	5	12			8	1		58
sheets	2	2		57	9		19		3		7	1	4	15			36	2		157
1697 Works	4			5	1		3						1	4	1	8	11	2	1	41
sheets	17			38	1		5						8	7		4	54	1	54	189
1698 Works	2	1		11	2		1					3	5	16	1	1	6	1	1	51
sheets	3	1		22	10		1					2	9	12		2	36	7	144	249
1699 Works	3	1		15	9		2	1	4	1		3	4	7			10	2		62
sheets	20	13		93	28		1	7	13			1	9	11			42	4		242
1700-1710 Works			3														49		10	62
sheets			105														189		449	743
1711-1725 Works			3														25		4	32
sheets			58														188		144	390
Works Totals to 1700			9														469		31	3759
sheets			270														1670		1929	14107
Totals by Class	682	41	15	556	56	66	53	77	248	91	114	252	202	476	80	187	543	57	45	3853
sheets	2027	198	433	3021	169	270	246	423	843	259	258	402	752	727	79	244	2047	309	2522	15239

Conclusions:

The results of the chart can be seen more clearly in the graph on page 575: certain ambiguities in the charted groups are magnified when they are further grouped into the five main categories that correspond to the sections of this book:

(a) Many tracts fall into two or more classes, such as apocalyptic or proclamation-type exhortations for statesmen; apologies against persecution, which may also include doctrines; ethical-testimony tracts, which usually cover many topics; and reprints and collected works, which were meant mainly for Friends but cover a variety of genres, including notably the journals and autobiographical material.

(b) It has been difficult to know whether to list writings by the date of publication (as we have done with journals, memorials and epistles) or by the date of writing (as we did, following Smith, with a few items); in many cases memorials do not appear as separate items at all in catalogues such as Wing, since they were generally prefaced to collected works, etc.

Most striking is the overall rise and fall of all classes of Quaker writings according to the political situation and resulting persecutions: the years of harshest persecution were 1656-57, after Nayler's "fall"; early 1661 after the "Fifth Monarchist" revolt; 1662-65 and in part through 1669, the main pressure of the Clarendon Code; 1670-72 under the Second Conventicle Act; 1676-77 and 1681-84, under Tory pressure during the period of political infighting.

Another unexpected result was the peak of many kinds of writing output in 1658-62, the years of political crisis when hopes and fears were highest.

Proclamation tracts were highest in the early decade but fade only gradually throughout the whole period, as the appeal for total change of life and will became less hopeful.

Autobiographical tracts and journals are surprisingly few, though averaging the largest volumes per item; in addition to the records only found within collected works (e.g., Margaret Fell's), their role in the early years was mainly fulfilled by private letters and reports to Swarthmoor (see the biographical index).

Doctrinal and dispute tracts are as a group also prominent from the beginning, and only a handful are not in some sense a response to challenges by non-Quakers, though these include key items like Barclay's *Apology*. At first, they are naturally mainly answers to Puritans of the parish system, or to Baptists and other separatist sects; debates against maverick Quakers are mainly a feature of the later years, though Bugg, Pennyman, and Keith eventually have to be classified among the non-Quaker opponents. There were flourishes of debate against the Baptists at the end of the Commonwealth, and in 1672-74 under the Declaration of Indulgence, etc. In the 1690's the classes of opponents are less distinct.

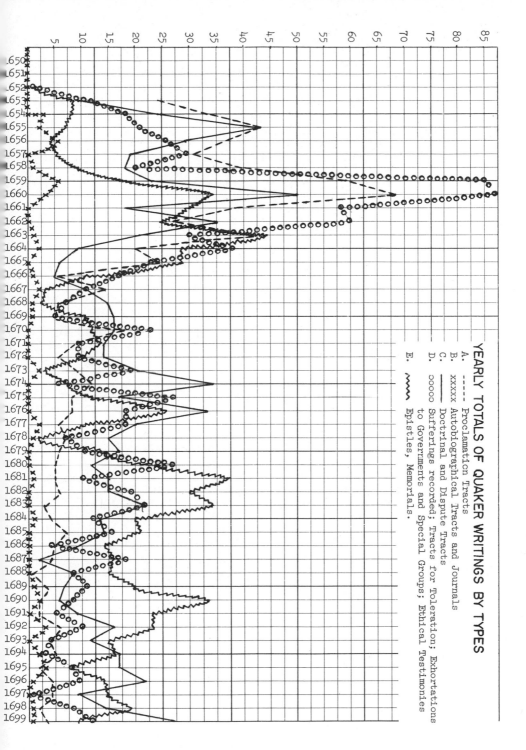

YEARLY TOTALS OF QUAKER WRITINGS BY TYPES

A. ------ Proclamation Tracts
B. xxxxx Autobiographical Tracts and Journals
C. ——— Doctrinal and Dispute Tracts
D. ooooo Sufferings recorded; Tracts for Toleration; Exhortations
       to Governments and Special Groups; Ethical Testimonies
E. ∿∿∿ Epistles, Memorials.

575

Ethical and suffering tracts include exhortations and appeals to rulers in times of hope, as well as records of the great imprisonments in dark years; defenses of specific Quaker ethical norms or "testimonies" are not always coupled with issues of toleration. Thus the subheadings in this group are more significant than most, and vary independently.

Epistles were naturally most numerous in times of stress (1662-63, 1682-84, etc.), but other subheads in this group show reverse correlations. Reprints came mostly in peaceful times, except in 1659 when a new attempt was made to win all England, and collected works belong mainly to the years after 1688; memorials often only in connection with these.

Introductory Bibliography:

The basic tools for research into early Quaker primary sources are those listed in the Abbreviations, pp. 577ff. The standard history of Quakerism is still the "Rowntree Series," namely the Braithwaite and Rufus Jones works on that list plus Jones' *Later Periods of Quakerism* and *Spiritual Reformers of the 16th and 17th Centuries.* For Fox's *Journal,* Barclay's *Apology,* and Penn's works see p. 13. Students with no previous contact with Quakerism may find one of the following one-volume histories helpful:

Brinton, Howard H. *Friends for 300 Years* (New York: Harper, 1952).
(Foulds), Elfrida Vipont. *The Story of Quakerism* (London: Bannisdale, 1954).
Russell, Elbert. *The History of Quakerism* (New York: Macmillan, 1942).
Sykes, John. *The Quakers: A New Look at Their Place in Society* (Philadelphia: Lippincott, 1959).
Trueblood, D. Elton. *The People Called Quakers* (2nd ed.; Richmond, Ind.: Friends United Press, 1971).
Williams, Walter R. *The Rich Heritage of Quakerism* (Grand Rapids, Mich.: Eerdmans, 1962).

Abbreviations

Ann. Cat.	*Annual Catalogue of George Fox's Papers,* ed. Henry J. Cadbury (Philadelphia, 1939); covers unprinted writings only.
ARBMS	A. R. Barclay Manuscripts (London: Friends House), available on microfilm; many of them reprinted in *JFHS* (Nos. 1-13, Vol. XXVII; 14-20, XVIII; 21-30, XXXI; 31-40, XXXII; 41-51, XXXIII; 52-60, XXXV; 61-71, XXXVII; 72-79, XLIII; 80-92, XLIV; 93-105, XLVI; 106-112, XLVII; 113-140, XLVIII; 141-148, XLIX; 149-157, L).
Besse	*Collection of the Sufferings of . . . Quakers,* ed. Joseph Besse (London, 1753); from seventeenth-century local records.
BBQ	Braithwaite, Wm. C., *Beginnings of Quakerism,* 2nd ed. (Cambridge, 1961).
BFHA	*Bulletin of the Friends Historical Association* (Philadelphia, from 1906; called *Quaker History* since 1962).
Bowden	Bowden, James, *The History of the Society of Friends in America* (London, 1850).
Bronner	Bronner, Edwin B., *William Penn's Holy Experiment* (New York: Temple Univ., 1962).
BSP	Braithwaite, Wm. C., *Second Period of Quakerism* (Cambridge, 1919).
Carroll	Carroll, Kenneth, *Quakerism on the Eastern Shore* (Maryland Historical Society, 1960).
CJ	*The Journal of George Fox,* ed. Norman Penney (Cambridge, 1911).
CNP	Cadbury, Henry J., *Narrative Papers of George Fox* (Richmond, Ind.: Friends United Press, 1972).
CR	*Calamy Revised,* ed. A. G. Mathews (Oxford, 1934).
DNB	*Dictionary of National Biography,* ed. Stephen (London, 1937f).
DQB	Haverford College Library's "Dictionary of Quaker Biography," in typescript (a parallel index is at Friends House, London); edited by William Bacon Evans.

577

EQL	*Early Quaker Letters from the Swarthmore MSS to 1660,* indexed and annotated by Geoffrey F. Nuttall (copies at major libraries).
ESP	*Extracts from State Papers Relating to Friends,1652-1672,* ed. Norman Penney (London, 1913).
FPT	*First Publishers of Truth,* ed. Norman Penney (London, 1907); *JFHS* Supplements.
HLH	Hodgkin, L. V., *A Quaker Saint of Cornwall: Loveday Hambly and Her Guests* (London: Longmans, Green, 1927).
HQA	Hull, William I., *The Rise of Quakerism in Amsterdam, 1655-1665* (Swarthmore College Monograph No. 4, 1938).
HWP	Hull, William I., *William Penn and the Dutch Quaker Migration to Pennsylvania* (Swarthmore College Monograph No. 2, 1935).
JFHS	*Journal of the Friends Historical Society* (London, from 1903).
JLP	Jones, Rufus M., *The Later Periods of Quakerism,* 2 vols. (London: Macmillan, 1921).
JQA	Jones, Rufus M., *The Quakers in the American Colonies* (2nd ed.; New York: W. W. Norton, 1966).
Jorns	Jorns, Auguste, *The Quakers as Pioneers in Social Work,* trans. T. K. Brown (Port Washington, N. Y., 1931).
LEF	*Letters of Early Friends,* ed. A. R. Barclay (London, 1841).
Lloyd	Lloyd, Arnold, *Quaker Social History, 1669-1738* (London: Longmans, Green, 1950).
LWD	*Letters to William Dewsbury and Others,* ed. Henry J. Cadbury (London, 1948); a *JFHS* Supplement.
NSE	Nuttall, Geoffrey F., *Studies in Christian Enthusiasm* (Pendle Hill, 1948).
PP	*Piety Promoted,* ed. Jn. Tomkins and Jn. Field, etc. (London, from 1701).
Riewald	Riewald, J. G., *Reynier Jansen of Philadelphia, Early American Printer* (Groningen: Wolters-Noordhoff, 1970).
SJ	*Short Journal and Itinerary Journals of George Fox,* ed. Norman Penney (Cambridge, 1925); like *CJ* and *EQL* it has good biographical notes and a good index.
Smith	Smith, Joseph, *Catalogue of Friends' Books* (London, 1867 and Supplement, 1893); note also *Bibliotheca Anti-Quakeriana,* 1873. (Note: "nnn in Smith" refers to numbers of titles written by author in question as listed in Smith, including those after 1700 if not previously published.)
SDA	*Swarthmore Documents in America,* ed. Henry Cadbury (London, 1940).
SMS	Swarthmore Manuscripts, mostly the same called earlier Devonshire House MSS; in seven portfolio vols., at Friends House, London; copies available on microfilm. (Note: the second number given for letters in Vols. 1, 3, and 4 [e.g., SMS 3:2=97] refers to the chronological sequence as indexed by Nuttall in *EQL, q.v.*)
TQA	Tolles, Frederick B., *Quakers and the Atlantic Culture* (New York: Macmillan, 1960).
TVS	Taylor, Ernest, *The Valiant Sixty* (London, 1947).

Biographical Index

Only the authors of tracts included in this volume and a few other major Quaker figures are described here carefully. Individuals mentioned only once or in one document are usually described more fully in footnotes than here. For each writer, only the major works in short title and the most important letters for biographical purposes have been cited (omitting also items reprinted or referred to in this volume). Women are listed by their surnames at the time of convincement.

Abrams, Daniel. Danzig Friend; cf. *BFHA* 41 (1952), 81ff. **499.**

Aldam, Thomas (1616-60). Yeoman of Warmsworth, Yorkshire, "a strong rugged man, lacking in elasticity, and with no suspicion of humor" (NSE, 28); from imprisonment in York Castle was organizer of local Friends and Quaker publication, as previously while a separatist leader; released in 1654 by Cromwell, before whom he later rent his cap "as a sign" that "his counsels should be rent in pieces"; traveled to Scotland and Ireland, and heavily fined for tithes; wrote three entries in Wing and six in Smith, including parts of composite works by York prisoners: *Searching out of Deceit, Brief Discovery of Threefold Estate of Antichrist;* see Besse, BBQ, *CJ,* CNP, *DNB, DQB, EQL, FPT, PP, SJ,* ARBMS 2-11, 15-17, 70-71, 113, 121-22, 125, *SDA* 14 and 16, SMS 1:373=4, 3:36=5, 3:40=7, 3:43=22, 3:39=43, 3:42=57, 3:44=71, 4:89=91 (cf. p. **471**), 3:37=96, 3:38=136 on the visit to Cromwell; see also 1:216=95 and on York prison 1:112=236, and 3:94=238 on Aldam's efforts for release of Friends imprisoned in Devonshire; 4:156=299 on Tithe trial; and esp. short biographies in NSE and his son's *Short Testimony* (1690) to him (father and son are confused by Wing). **33, 49, 64, 85, 161, 163n, 253n, 262, 289, 358-62, 385, 471-73, 473-74, 551.**

Alleine, Richard. Puritan pastor and writer. **38.**

Ames, William. Puritan "covenant" theologian. **108n.**

Ames, William (d. 1662). Gloucestershire Royalist soldier but a Baptist who turned Quaker in Ireland in 1655; became with Will Caton the missionary for Quakerism in Holland; learned Dutch and wrote in it, convinced the Sewel family, and probably knew Spinoza at Amsterdam; traveled through Germany, Poland, etc. and died in Amsterdam; cf. Besse, BBQ, BSP, *CJ*, CNP, *DNB, DQB, EQL, FPT,* HQA, HWP, Riewald, and esp. Benjamin Furley; he wrote five entries in Wing and thirty-two in Smith, including twenty-four in Dutch, one German, one Polish (miscalled Swedish in Smith), one French, *The Light upon the Candlestick* and *A Sound Out of Zion* (both 1663), and the autobiographical *Declaration of the Witness of God* (1656), SMS 4:28=384, ARBMS 2-11, 126; see also SMS 4:27=310, 1:323=562. **36, 38.**

Andrewes, Lancelot. Anglican bishop, prayer-writer, and Bible-translator. **17.**

Antrobus, Benjamin (1645-1715). London linen draper, active in Yearly Meeting affairs; wrote poetry (one book); see Besse, *CJ, DQB, FPT, SJ.* **553.**

Archdale, John. Quaker governor and a proprietor of Carolina; was elected Member of Parliament for Wycombe, Buckinghamshire, but was disbarred over oath; wrote ARBMS 68 and Howarth MS No. 2 (London: Friends House); cf. BSP, *DNB,* HWP; *JFHS* II, VIII, IX, XIX; *SJ.* **498.**

Askew, Mary. Servant in Swarthmoor household, mentioned in family documents and many SMS letters; probably related to Margaret Fell, with whom she traveled to London, etc., 1660ff; see *EQL,* Isabel Ross, *Margaret Fell.* **61.**

Atkinson, Christopher, of Kendal, Westmorland. For three years one of the dozen most active Friends in preaching and writing, he "was opened in a living Testimony, and labored zealously for a time in the service of 'Truth' " (*FPT,* 260); imprisoned at Kendal, and later in 1654 in Norwich, where he "committed lewdness with a servant-maid who served Thomas Simmonds" (George Whitehead, *Christian Progress,* p. 35); since anti-Quaker writers such as Weld cited his conduct, he was made to condemn it himself and then disowned; see Besse, BBQ, *CJ,* CNP, *DQB, EQL;* he wrote four entries in Wing and five in Smith, all in 1653-55, debates with Puritans; also SMS 1:354=116, 1:345=117, 1:347=133 (his fall); figures in twenty-four other letters, half from mission colleagues. **85, 475n.**

Audland, Anne Newby, later **Camm** (1672-1705), of Kendal. Married John Audland, joined his Westmorland separatist group, and with them became Quaker; preached with her husband, Jane Waugh, and others around Burham and Bristol, 1654; tried for blasphemy at Banbury, 1655, and jailed; married, after John's death, his colleague's son Thomas Camm, 1666; wrote a tract (1655) and SMS 1:13=201 on her trial; see also 1:391=183, BBQ, BSP, *CJ, DNB, DQB, EQL, PP.* **61, 117.**

Audland, John (1630-63/64). Yeoman from Preston Patrick, Westmorland, separatist leader; in 1654 with a dozen other Friends undertook mission based at Pearson's home in County Durham; then with Camm via London to Bristol where great mission lasted to mid-1655, broken by trip home and conferences of Quaker ministers in Bedfordshire and Leicestershire; journeyed into Wales, 1656; conciliator on Nayler and other Friends; homesick and died of TB; wrote four titles in Wing = five in Smith; collected works = *Memory of the Righteous Revived,* with Camm's (1689), mainly debates with

Puritans; also ARBMS 110, 116, 157, SMS 3:186=18, 1:7=114, 1:391=183, 1:5=205, 1:9=285, 1:10=377, 1:12=303; mentioned in forty-six other SMS (cf. *EQL*) from colleagues on many journeys; cf. Besse, BBQ, *CJ, DQB, EQL.* **35, 38, 60f, 78ff, 167, 479n, 512.**

Austin, Anne (d. 1665), of London. With Mary Fisher, first Friends in Massachusetts via Barbados; cf. Besse, BBQ, *CJ, DQB.* **125.**

Ayrey, Agnes or Anne, also Vayera. Married John Spooner; cf. *JFHS* X (1910), 19; SMS 4:1=65. **475.**

Bache, Humphrey (d. 1662). London Quaker goldsmith who gave up making jewelry, died in crowded jail; wrote two tracts in Wing and in Smith, esp. *A Few Words to Parliament* (1659); see Besse, BBQ, CNP, *DQB.* **86, 210.**

Bains, Joseph, of Stangerthwaite, Westmorland; wrote tract with John Blaykling; see Besse. **60.**

Baker, Daniel, of London. Tried to free Katharine Evans and Sarah Cheevers from Malta; fourteen titles in Smith, thirteen in Wing; cf. BBQ, Besse, *CJ,* CNP. **84n.**

Banks, John (1637-1710), wife **Anne** Littledale and second wife **Hannah.** Farmer and teacher from Cumberland; traveled in Ireland and England; wrote six titles in Wing, nine in Smith; letters included in his *Journal* (1712); see Besse, BSP, *CJ, DQB.* **7, 50, 141, 153, 155, 180-96, 208, 209, 253n, 479.**

Barclay, A. R. Nineteenth-century editor of *Letters of Early Friends.* **470n.**

Barclay, John (1797-1838), of Surrey. Brother of A. R. Barclay, editor of Penington's letters and Alexander Jaffray's Diary, *Select Series,* etc. **234, 238, 239, 240, 241.**

Barclay, Robert (1648-90). Son of Col. David Barclay, squire of Ury; after studying under a Jesuit uncle in Paris, attended University of Aberdeen, after becoming Friend, with his father, in 1666; debated with theological students and "went naked for a sign"; wrote the *Apology* in Latin (1676) and English (1678), prepared for by Catechism (*q.v.;* 1673) and *Theses Theologicae* (1676), all often reprinted and becoming normative of Quaker thought; became important for Quaker organization (see under *Anarchy of Ranters*) and missions to Holland and Germany; wrote eighteen titles, eighty-three editions in English in Smith, plus twelve Latin, five French, three Dutch, three Danish, three German, Spanish, Arabic, Welsh, and unpublished journal; twenty-four in Wing (two Latin); *Works,* 1692, 1717, 1831; see BSP, *CJ,* CNP, *DNB, DQB,* HWP, *JFHS passim;* and esp. D. Elton Trueblood, *Robert Barclay* (1968); J. P. Wragge, *Faith of Robert Barclay* (1948). **5ff, 13f, 27, 30, 41, 52, 54, 161n, 208n, 246f, 249f, 263, 298, 311n, 314-49, 463f, 469n, 501n, 512-44, 558ff.**

Barker, Thomas. London Friend from Seething Lane, center of 1683 court case; cf. Besse, *FPT, SJ.* **553.**

Barnard, Hannah (1757-?). Liberal and strangely pacifist American Friend; disowned in 1800 during travel in Britain. **502n.**

Barton, Nathaniel. Puritan colonel, Justice, and preacher of Derby; member, Parliament of Saints, 1653. **78, 148n.**

Bateman, Miles. Yeoman of Tullythwaite near Kendal; traveled in Ireland and Cornwall, where imprisoned, but later left Quakerism; see Besse, BBQ, *CJ, EQL, FPT,* SMS 1:112=236, 1:360=258, etc. **476n.**

Bauman, Richard. Contemporary historian of Pennsylvania. **45.**

Bauthumley, Jacob. Ranter antinomian of Commonwealth period. **25.**

Baxter, Richard (1615-91). Puritan pastor of Kidderminster, and organizer of Worcestershire Association of puritan ministers; after 1661 lived in semi-retirement, sometimes jailed, near London; outstanding puritan author, with 280 titles in Wing, twenty-one listed as anti-Quaker by Smith; cf. *DNB;* Geoffrey Nuttall, *Richard Baxter.* **19, 38, 43, 152, 247, 249, 262-89, 290-98.**

Bayly, William (also Bailey) (d. 1675), of Poole, Dorset. Shipmaster baptist lay preacher convinced by Fox in 1656; married Mary Fisher (*q.v.*); wrote forty-two titles in Smith, thirty-one in Wing, in all genres, esp. proclamations of Lamb's War, Day of Lord, exhortations to Friends; *Works,* 1676; see Besse, *CJ,* CNP, *DQB,* SMS 1:12; Margaret Hirst, *Quakers in Peace and War.* **86.**

Bealing, Benjamin. Recording clerk of London Yearly Meeting in 1690's and collector of documents in *FPT,* Besse, etc.; always the footnote, never the author (but three titles in Smith, two in Wing); see CNP. **57, 146n.**

Belcher, Mary. Bristol Quaker banished in 1664, but evidently imprisoned, not deported; see Besse. **480.**

Bellers, John (1654-1725), of London. Cloth merchant and son of a wealthy grocer, he was active in Meeting for Sufferings and took over Meade's key role in an Employment Fund to buy flax to keep poor Friends employed; with wife **Frances** from Gloucestershire lived in Penington's former Buckinghamshire home, then in her father's manor-house; wrote nineteen titles in Smith, eight in Wing, many on the poor; see BSP, and esp. A. Ruth Fry, *John Bellers* (1935). **7, 408n, 418n, 430, 451-59.**

Benson, Gervase, and first wife **Dorothy** (d. 1679 and c. 1660). Puritan colonel, Justice, and squire, of Sedbergh, ex-mayor of Kendal, one of few north-country gentry convinced as Friend in 1652; home a Quaker center; six titles in Wing, Smith; cf. BBQ, *CJ, DQB, EQL, FPT,* SMS 4:69, 4:33, 4:35, 4:162, 1:63, 4:243, 4:230, 4:231, 4:156, 3:78; also 3:80, etc., on his mediation in London for Friends in prison. **35, 60, 209, 470.**

Berkeley, Sir George (later Lord). Courtier friend of Charles II, James II and Penn; English proprietor of West Jersey. **409.**

Besse, Joseph. Eighteenth-century Colchester teacher; became London editor of Quaker reports on seventeenth-century sufferings; forty-one titles in Smith, either on sufferings or theological controversy; see CNP, HWP. **8, 43, 117n, 119ff, 145n, 162n, 381n, 387n, 559.**

Bewley, Thomas (b. 1595). With wife Dorothy and sons Thomas and George had been quiet, thoughtful Separatists when they entertained and were convinced by Fox, June 1653, at their home, Haltcliff Hall, Cumberland; this became regular Meeting site, though he bought Meetinghouse near Carlisle, and spent fourteen years in prison; cf. Besse, *DQB, CJ, EQL, FPT,* SMS 3:171=48, 1:214=126. **476, 551.**

Billing, Edward (also Byllinge, Bylynge, etc). Cromwellian officer (from Cornwall?) turned London brewer and Friend after convincement by Fox in Scotland; organizer, with Penn, Lucas, Lawrie, and Fenwick, of colony of West New Jersey; seven titles in Smith and Wing; cf. Besse, CNP, *DQB,* and esp. H. Brinton, *Children of Light;* J. E. Pomfret, *Province of West New Jersey.* **7, 388, 407-21, 422-29, 441.**

Bingley, William (1651-1715). Yorkshireman later portrayed by Bugg as weighty London Friend; traveled in Ireland and Holland, and published five epistles, two warnings to non-Friends, ARBMS 81; see BSP, *CJ, JFHS* V, VI, X. **565.**

Birkbeck, Morris, Sr. and Jr. Eighteenth-century English Friends traveling in America. **502n.**

Birkhead, Christopher (also Burket, Birkett). Shipwright convinced in 1654 and imprisoned at Bristol, as also in La Rochelle, France, and Middelburg, Holland, described (in Dutch) in his only tract; see *CJ, EQL,* HQA, SMS 4:44=479, 4:256=507. **480.**

Bishop, George (d. 1668), of Bristol. Cromwellian captain, secret service agent, and secretary and puritan politician, convinced at Bristol, 1654, or Reading, 1655; active against Nayler and for Massachusetts martyrs; wrote thirty-three titles in Smith, thirty-five in Wing, plus two perhaps before convincement, including *New England Judged* and many to king or Parliament; cf. BBQ, BSP, Besse, *CJ,* CNP, *DQB, EQL, ESP.* **8, 35, 79, 117n, 123, 134n, 137n, 408n, 481-85.**

Blackborow, Sarah, also Blackbury, Blackberry, of London (d. 1665). Friend of Nayler, noted Quaker preacher; wrote three tracts in Smith and Wing; cf. BBQ, *CJ,* CNP. **86, 147f.**

Blaugdone, Barbara (c. 1609-1704), of Bristol. Had worked as governess until convinced, 1654; emotionally intense, often in prison (paid her own way), two trips to Ireland; wrote *Journal,* also SMS 3:194; cf. 3:133, 4:75. **79, 478n, 479-80.**

Blaykling, Anne, also Blackley, and brother **John** (1625-1705). Lived at Draw-Well farm near Sedbergh, site of early meetings; both traveled widely preaching across southern England; she was imprisoned in Cambridge, Cornwall, and Suffolk, he in York and Tynemouth; mediated in

Wilkinson-Story conflict; he wrote one tract jointly with others; see BBQ, BSP, *CJ, DQB, EQL, FPT* on both; also SMS 4:159 by him; 4:33, 1:89, 4:5, 1:2, 1:166, 4:10 on her imprisonments and trials and temporary defection from Friends; on their father **Thomas Blaykling** and a puritan pastor brother Richard, cf. *EQL.* **60, 163.**

Boehme, Jacob. Early seventeenth-century German mystic. **21, 268n.**

Bolton, John. London goldsmith; visited Fox at Launceston prison, 1656, and Nayler en route; see Besse, BBQ, *EQL.* **551.**

Booth, George. Led 1659 Royalist rebellion. **398.**

Booth, Mary, of London. Sister of Rebecca Travers, friend of James Nayler and of John Perrot; imprisoned (*FPT*); wrote *Milk for Babes;* cf. BBQ, BSP, *FPT.* **86.**

Bourne, Edward (d. 1708). Physician of Worcester, often jailed; wrote up Worcester report for *FPT* (*q.v.*), also eleven tracts in Smith, ten in Wing; cf. Besse, BSP. **263.**

Bousfield, Major Miles. Separatist of Garsdale, NW Yorkshire; entertained Fox and Friends, and visited Edmondson in Ireland, but never fully a Friend; cf. BBQ, BSP, *FPT.* **60.**

Bowater, John, or Boweter, of Bromsgrove, Worcestershire, and later a weighty Friend of London. Traveled widely in America; wrote six titles in Smith; cf. Besse, BSP, *CJ, CNP.* **565.**

Bowden, James. Nineteenth-century historian and Clerk of London Yearly Meeting. **117n.**

Braithwaite, William C. Early twentieth-century Quaker historian; see under BBQ, BSP. **15, 469, 515n, 549n.**

Brend, William (also Brand; d. 1676). Londoner already old when convinced; sailed to America in 1656, and again with *Woodhouse,* 1657, staying despite tortures in Boston until 1661, back to London for more jails; wife stayed home; wrote six tracts in Smith and Wing, mostly for Friends; cf. Besse, Bowden, *CJ,* JQA, SMS 1:82. **121ff.**

Brinton, Howard H. Twentieth-century Quaker historian. **151n, 154, 408n, 486.**

Brocksopp, Thomas, of Normanton near Chesterfield, Derbyshire. Early convinced by Elizabeth Hooton with whom his wife **Joan** traveled in America; fined and imprisoned four times after 1660; she wrote one tract; cf. Besse, *EQL; BFHA II,* 56; SMS 1:374=129; E. Manners, *Elizabeth Hooton.* **551.**

Bronner, Edwin. Librarian, Haverford College, and Quaker historian. **408n, 441n, 464n.**

Brown, Ruth, of London. Wife of William Crouch. **84.**

Browne, Robert. Elizabethan Separatist. **17.**

585

Bugg, Francis (1640-1724?). Suffolk wool-merchant; suffered as Quaker, but after 1680 left Quakerism and spent next forty years writing endlessly repetitive anti-Quaker tracts on "New Rome," most as dull as Bugg's *Bomb* (1703); seventy-two titles in Smith, forty in Wing. **43, 262, 467, 559.**

Bullock, Noah. Puritan magistrate of Derby. **49, 381-82.**

Bunyan, John. Separatist-Baptist preacher and writer of *Pilgrim's Progress.* **24, 151, 171n, 180, 262, 295.**

Burden, Anne, of Bristol and for a while a Bostonian. Expelled as a Separatist, she returned as a Quaker, but was forbidden right to settle husband's estate; see *EQL*, SMS 3:102=348 (at convincement), 1:68=366, 1:79=387, 3:98=467, 1:104, 1:101=1664. **122.**

Burket (see Birkhead).

Burnyeat, John (1631-90). Like Banks, a Cumberland yeoman convinced in 1653 and author of a major journal (*Truth Exalted*, 1691), but deeper background in puritan experience; traveled to Scotland and Ireland, 1658-59, two long visits throughout American colonies, 1664-67 and 1670-74; debated with Roger Williams (*New England Firebrand*, 1679); wrote four other tracts; cf. BSP, *CJ*, CNP, *DNB*, *DQB*, *ESP*, *FPT*, HWP, JQA. **41, 153f.**

Burrough, Edward (1634-62). Young farmer and separatist preacher of Underbarrow near Kendal when convinced in 1652; before and after Nayler, the greatest Quaker preacher in London; went with fellow-worker Howgill to begin Irish Quakerism, 1655; died in Newgate prison; best-known early tract-writer on Quaker doctrine and politics; *Memorable Works* collected and printed, 1672; wrote story of convincement in *Warning from the Lord to Underbarrow* (1654), eighty-nine titles and editions (plus fifteen contemporary reprints and Dutch translations) in Smith, seventy-nine in Wing (fourth most among Friends, after Fox, Penn, and Keith); besides those printed here, see *To the Camp of the Lord* (1655), the *Trumpet of the Lord* (1656) (Calvert was arrested for printing it), *The Case of Free Liberty of Conscience* (1661), SMS 3:14=49, 3:34=70, 1:89=55, 4:170=62, 4:144=72, 3:17=179, 3:16=227, 1:1=248, 3:133=253, 1:164=260, 1:272=262, 1:274=273, 1:148=439, ARBMS 37, 61, 65, 176, 54, many in *LEF* (he also wrote many letters, now lost, to George Taylor of Kendal, whose gist he forwarded to Margaret Fell); cf. also BBQ, BSP, Besse, *CJ*, *DNB*, *FPT*, TVS, and esp. *EQL* and Elisabeth Brockbank, *Edward Burrough*. **7, 13, 21, 35, 38, 50, 79, 83ff, 90-92, 93, 117n, 134n, 137-40, 153, 160ff, 163n, 164, 167, 180, 197, 209, 221, 245, 246, 262, 294, 298-304, 306, 357, 363-71, 388f, 469, 476-78, 479n, 512.**

Buskin, Leven. For the virtually unrecorded story of the Algiers captives see BSP. **558.**

Buttery, Isabel. Yorkshire friend of Nayler; perhaps first Quaker in London (1653-54) where later jailed; cf. BBQ, *EQL*, *FPT*. **83f.**

586

Buttivant, Samuel. Yorkshire Friend, prison-mate of Aldam; wrote one 1653 tract, parts of others. **359n, 474.**

Cadbury, Henry J. Twentieth-century Quaker historian. **6, 16, 49, 55, 61, 141n, 145n, 153n, 381n, 470n, 480n, 486ff, 501n.**

Calvert, Giles (1612-63). Born in Somerset, but from apprenticeship on was printer in London, publishing over three hundred Quaker tracts; never fully a Friend (but cf. SMS 1:162=167); arrested briefly in 1655-56 and in 1660, when his wife and his assistant Robert Wilson carried on his press; cf. *EQL; JFHS* VIII, 148-50; XXXV (1938), 45-49; and Altha E. Terry's Master's thesis (Columbia, 1937), "Giles Calvert." **35, 90ff, 94ff, 167, 225, 251f, 306n, 359n, 386, 390, 411, 434n, 475f.**

Camm, John (1605-57/58), with his wife **Mabel** and son **Thomas,** of Camsgill farm, Preston Patrick, Westermorland. Convinced at Firbank in 1652, with two of their maids, Jane and Dorothy Waugh; oldest and least articulate of "big 10" "First Publishers of Truth"; with John Audland *(q.v.)* began Quakerism in Bristol (1654) and continued there (with interlude home) until health failed (TB) in 1656; after his death, Mabel married Gervase Benson and Thomas married Anne Audland *(q.v.);* works collected in *Memory of the Righteous Revived* with Audland's (1689) by son Thomas; two tracts published; see Besse, BBQ, *CJ,* CNP, *DQB, EQL, FPT,* and esp. 3:15=52, 3:34=70, 4:120=144, 4:119=156, 1:238=198, 1:178=232, 4:116=233, ARBMS 158, 20, 127, 39. **38, 53, 78ff, 83, 167, 382-85, 479n, 512.**

Canby, George, of Selby, Yorkshire. Dramatically convinced by Dewsbury, 1652; cf. BBQ, *FPT.* **58f.**

Carroll, Kenneth. Contemporary historian of American Quakerism. **36.**

Cater, Samuel. Littleport, Cambridge/Ely Friend, ex-Baptist; traveled in Essex, and with Nayler to Exeter and Bristol; see BBQ, *FPT.* **162n, 208, 483n.**

Caton, Will (1636-65). Secretary to Margaret Fell at Swarthmoor and companion to her son George when convinced in 1652; traveled esp. with John Stubbs, in Kent and Scotland, and from 1655 almost constantly in Holland, where he married Annekin Dericks, 1662; on visit home to Swarthmoor, 1659, sorted and copied letters of Friends (Will Caton collection, later part of ARBMS); wrote one of the earliest and sunniest *Journals* (1689); nineteen titles in English in Smith (many joint), eighteen in Dutch (singlehanded) and in Wing; also wrote SMS 4:234=124, 1:375=176, 1:336=251, 4:257=269, 3:187=270, 1:387=286, 1:313=291, 1:314=356, 1:315=364, 1:316=372, 1:317=448, 4:269=469, 4:267=493, 4:279=498, 4:268=503, 1:318=514, 4:261=525, 4:271=546, 4:272=557, 1:323=562; see also Besse, BBQ, BSP, *CJ,* CNP, *DQB, FPT,* HQA, HWP. **38, 61, 154, 155, 405, 470n.**

Chaundler, Thomas (or Chandler), of Chadwich, Worcestershire. Imprisoned, 1655, for challenging Baxter; cf. Besse. **269.**

Cheevers, Sarah (d. 1664), of Wiltshire. Set out with Katherine Evans for Jerusalem, 1659; spent 2½ years as prisoner of Inquisition, Malta; cf. Besse, BBQ, CNP. **84.**

Christison, Wenlock (d. 1681). Salem Quaker arrested in Boston, 1660, and sentenced to death, 1661, but reprieved by Charles II's "missive" brought by Shattuck; scourged at Boston, 1664; imprisoned in England, 1666; settled in Maryland in 1670 at Tredhaven, and sat in legislature; his widow sold his slaves; see Besse, Carroll, JQA. **137n, 140.**

Clark, Mary. Wife of London merchant John Clark; sailed on *Woodhouse,* 1657; flogged in Boston; cf. Besse, JQA. **122.**

Claus, Jan, also Claas. Dutch merchant convinced and imprisoned in 1664 while living in London, later a key Amsterdam Friend, interpreter and guide for Fox's, Penn's and Barclay's travels in Holland and Germany; wrote four epistles, etc., included in other men's books; translated English Quaker books for his own press; published Sewel and helped Croese with his *History;* cf. Besse, BSP, CNP, HQA, HWP, Riewald, *SJ.* **496.**

Claypoole, Elizabeth (1629-58). Second daughter of Oliver Cromwell; a religious seeker to whom Fox wrote; see *CJ, DNB.* **152.**

Cleaton or Clayton, Richard, and sister **Anne.** On staff at Swarthmoor (but he had a small estate); traveled as Quaker minister, he in England, Scotland, and Ireland, she at least twice to America, 1657-59 and 1669; cf. BBQ, *CJ, EQL,* SMS 1:27=125, 4:62=130, 1:121=139, 1:29=154, 1:30=164, 3:133=253, 1:360=258, 1:31=297, 1:28=445 (Richard), 1:310=186, 1:398=217, 1:380=246 (Lancaster jail), 1:165=289, 1:81=300, 4:36=352, 1:28=445, 1:72=459, 4:182=460; each published a small tract. **61, 476n.**

Clement, Walter (also Clements), of Olveston, Gloucestershire. Convinced in 1652 and imprisoned over tithes, 1656-57; host to many Quakers between Bristol and Swarthmoor, which he visited at least twice; wrote SMS 1:178=184, 187, 319, 185, 321, *EQL* 232, 287, 312, 321, 343, 456, 489, 492, 515, 521, 529; see Besse, BBQ, *EQL.* **79.**

Coale, Josiah (1633-69), of Bristol and nearby Winterbourne. Convinced in 1654; traveled with Thomas Thurston from Virginia (imprisoned) and Maryland to New England, later to Barbados, Holland; through England "to sound Trumpet of the Lord"; in prison, 1664, 1665; wrote nine tracts in Wing, fourteen in Smith, besides eleven epistles to Friends printed in *Books and Divers Epistles of J.C.* (1671); *SDA* 24, 25; SMS 1:377=422, 3:85=458, 1:62=512; cf. 3:7=426, 4:18=527, ARBMS 13, 44, 53, 63, 64, 87, 89, Besse, CNP, *DQB, EQL, FPT.* **79, 86.**

Cook, Edward. Cromwellian officer in Ireland; convinced by Howgill, traveled with Burrough, often in Dublin jails in 1660's; wrote six titles in Smith, three in Wing; see Besse, CNP, *DQB.* **478n.**

Cooper, Thomas, of London. One of twelve Quaker proprietors of East Jersey, 1682; fined for refusing tithes and arms, 1683-85; cf. Besse, *SJ.* **558.**

Copeland, John (or Coupland), of Holderness, Yorkshire. Sailed to Boston, 1656, and again on the *Woodhouse*, 1657, preaching throughout Massachusetts and Connecticut, losing ear; returned to London but later settled in Chuckatuck, Virginia; see Besse, Bowden, *DQB,* JQA, SMS 1:82=454, 4:182=460, Log of *Woodhouse*. **117n, 121, 122, 138.**

Cox Thomas. Wealthy London vintner, active in Friends' Business; see *CJ, SJ.* **553.**

Cradock, Walter. Radical puritan pastor and Cromwellian chaplain. **21.**

Cragg, Gerald C. Contemporary historian of Puritanism. **38.**

Creasey, Maurice. Contemporary Quaker theological writer. **16.**

Crisp, Stephen (1628-92). Though only a prosperous bays-maker of Colchester, was among the best-educated of early Friends; after his convincement by Parnell and travels in Essex and Scotland he began a series of visits to Holland and Germany (1663, 1671, 1677, etc.—his mother and his second wife were Dutch); active in London Quaker affairs; wrote twenty-one books and tracts, besides five in Dutch, French, and German translations; journal, allegory, many letters, and five books of sermons published posthumously; see Besse, BSP, *CJ, DNB,* HQA, HWP; C. Fell-Smith, *Steven Crisp and His Correspondents, 1657-1692;* L. Wright, *John Bunyan and Stephen Crisp;* SMS 4:268=503. **14, 23, 41, 50, 86, 153, 154, 163-66, 196-208, 479.**

Croese, Gerard. Dutch pastor, never a Friend but a friend of Dutch Quakers; his *General History of the Quakers* (Latin 1695, English 1696) was the first extensive history of Friends based on Quaker writings; cf. CNP, HWP. **55, 145.**

Cromwell, Henry. Fourth and ablest son of Protector Oliver Cromwell and Lord-Deputy of Ireland. **91, 476n, 479n.**

Cromwell, Oliver. Puritan squire turned cavalry general and statesman; secured victory of radical Puritans, 1647-49, by victories at Preston, Dunbar, Worcester; from 1653 to 1658 ruled England, Scotland, etc., as Protector through Council of State. **18ff, 36, 53f, 76, 83, 87, 91, 119, 146, 253, 260f, 363ff, 382, 384ff, 396ff, 408, 410, 414n, 417ff, 465, 473, 475f.**

Cromwell, Richard. Oliver's third son and briefly successor, 1658-59. **36, 146, 388, 397f, 408.**

Crook, John (1617?-99). North-country Cromwellian; bought confiscated Royalist estate at Beckerings Park, Buckinghamshire, center for many meetings of Fox with Quaker preachers; thereby lost post as Justice; lost estate after famous trial, 1662; wrote thirty-five tracts in Smith, twenty-seven in Wing, including *Journal;* see Besse, BBQ, BSP, *CJ, DNB, DQB, EQL, FPT; JFHS* VII (1910), 200; SMS 1:161=140, 3:9=187, 1:177=443, 3:87=470, etc. **35, 86, 512, 544-49.**

Crouch, William (1628-1710). From Penton, Hampshire, but apprenticed in London; married once before becoming Friend and marrying Ruth Brown, 1659; lived near Calverts until London fire; wrote book on Covetousness and *Posthuma* (pp. **82-90**); cf. Besse, *DQB, SJ.*

Curtis, Thomas, and his wife **Anne,** daughter of Royalist Sheriff Yeamans of Bristol. Lived at Reading; hosts there to Fox (1656 and 1659) and pillars of Meeting until joining Wilkinson-Story faction; he was a puritan captain and woollen-draper; convinced Peningtons; wrote memorials, ARBMS 86, *SDA* 25, SMS 3:87=470; see also ARBMS 28, Besse, BBQ, BSP, *CJ, DQB,* Ellwood, HLH, SMS 1:361=302, 1:168=496, etc. **79, 290.**

Danson Thomas. Puritan pastor and writer against Quakerism. **262, 295, 516n.**

Davis, Richard. Shopkeeper of London (not Richard Davies of Welshpool); helped distribute Quaker funds; died in prison, 1662; see Besse, BBQ, BSP, *CJ.* **86, 551.**

Dell, William. "Spiritual puritan" pastor and writer. **21, 466.**

Dewsbury, William (1621-88). Weaver from Allerthorpe, Yorkshire; had served in puritan army and left; had reached own inner experience of Light when he and wife were won as colleagues by Fox in moonlight walk, 1651; preached throughout Midlands, with long imprisonments at York and North-ampton (also Derby, London, Leicester) and nineteen years at Warwick, his later home (with second wife Alice); helped heal Fox-Nayler split; wisest of letter-writers in counseling, apocalyptic in tracts and thundering sermons; twenty-six printed epistles and proclamation tracts in Wing, besides three Dutch and Works; twenty-five in Wing; also SMS 4:130=33, 4:132=37, 4:131=63, 4:135=68, 4:144=72, 4:133=74, 4:140=80, 3:22=106, 3:25=107, 3:23=108, 4:139=180, 4:141=189, 4:154=218, 4:143=275, 4:137=280, 4:138=389, 3:24=390, 4:146=457, 4:153=466, 4:134=517; *JFHS* VIII (1911), 28-29; and esp. *LEF, LWD;* see also Besse, BBQ, BSP, *CJ,* CNP, *DNB, DQB, EQL, FPT, SJ,* etc. **7, 21, 33, 41, 55, 57ff, 86, 93-102, 122, 152, 167, 197, 359, 470n, 512, 558.**

Dillwyn, George. Eighteenth-century Philadelphia Quaker; made two journeys to Europe (sixteen years); cf. *DQB,* JLP. **501n.**

Donne, John. Anglican preacher, poet, and dean. **17.**

Downer, Ann, later married Benjamin Greenwell and George Whitehead *(q.v.)* (1624-86). Oxfordshire parson's daughter; convinced of Quakerism on arrival at London, 1654; went to Cornwall to cook and take shorthand for Fox and other Launceston prisoners, 1656; co-authored two tracts; twenty-eight testi-monies to her were printed in 1686 as *Piety Promoted;* see Besse, BBQ, *CJ,* CNP, *DQB, EQL, FPT,* SMS 4:15=429. **84f.**

Dring, Robert and brother **Simon** of Moorfield, London (Simon earlier of Watling Street). Linen draper; their homes were first sites of London Meet-ings, drops for mail, news, petitions, tracts to publish; wrote SMS 1:285=252, 1:137=256; cf. 3:93=69, BBQ, *DQB, EQL, FPT.* **83f, 252n, 390.**

Dyer, Mary. Martyr in Massachusetts (1660); from Barret family of Quen-don, Essex, but born in London, where she served at Court, and married (1633) William Dyer of Somerset family, apprenticed to importer Black-borne; he settled as milliner in Boston, where he became friend of Roger

Williams, she of Anne Hutchinson and Wm. Coddington, whose antinomian-
ism was blamed by Winthrop and Puritans for "monster" (deformed stillborn
child) of Mary, 1638; settling at Aquidneck, Rhode Island, were involved in
factional feud, to settle which William sailed to England, 1651; William
returned in 1653, Mary only 1656 and as a Quaker; her son William, later in
Delaware, tried to intercede when she was imprisoned in Boston; see Stephenson, Bishop, Besse as cited, Bowden, *DQB*, JQA, biographies of Williams by
Brockunier, Ernst, Winslow; H. Rogers, *Mary Dyer* (1896); much of this data
privately from Polly Lee. **122, 131, 132f, 136-40.**

Edmondson, William (1627-1712). Puritan ex-soldier and carpenter; born in
Westmorland, where convinced of Quakerism (1653) on home visit from new
shop and home in Lurgan, Ulster; first wife and children were at Mount-
mellick (Dublin) home too when house burned around them during 1687-89
wars; he traveled widely in Ireland, three times to American colonies; children
by second wife named Hindrance and Trial; wrote five tracts in Smith (one in
Wing) besides *Journal*, ARBMS 103, SMS 3:177=196, 4:77=282; cf. also
1:27=125, 4:62=130, 1:31=297; *JFHS* XXX (1936), 32-34; Besse, Bowden,
BBQ, BSP, *CJ, DNB, DQB, EQL*, Record of Friends Travelling in Ireland,
1656-1765," reproduced in *JFHS* X (1913), 157-80, 212-62, and esp. Frank
Edmondson, "William Edmondson" in *BFHA* 42 (1953), and Leon Camp,
"Rhode Island Debates" in *Quaker History*, 52 (1963). **154f, 476n, 495n,
557.**

Edwards, Jonathan. Eighteenth-century American preacher and theologian.
15, 22, 151, 250.

Elgar, Sarah. Perhaps wife of Sandwich, Kent, shopkeeper Thomas Elgar;
convinced, 1666; fined, 1675 and 1682, for tithes and pacifism; imprisoned,
1684; see Besse, *FPT*. **240.**

Ellwood, Thomas (1639-1713). Son of Crowell, Oxfordshire Justice; schooled
at Thame; convinced (1659) at Peningtons'; often imprisoned thereabout or
in London; married Mary Ellis; frequently clerk of Quarterly Meeting, later
chief editor of Fox's *Journal* and other works; wrote thirty-one titles in
Smith, twenty-one in Wing, and many doctrinal debates, but also *Sacred
History* of biblical events, *Davideis* (an epic poem inspired by his secretaryship
to Milton), a posthumously published book of poems, and *Life*, many
MSS in Friends House, London; see also BSP, *CJ*, CNP, *DNB, DQB*. **7, 13f,
35, 41, 43, 145, 148n, 154, 155, 208-24, 225, 230, 437-40, 469n, 477n, 486,
512f.**

Endicott, John. Puritan governor of Massachusetts. **131f, 137, 138.**

Erbury, Dorcas. Adoring disciple of Nayler, who had raised her (from
swoon?); shared in Bristol events, and lived there c/o Margaret Thomas; see
BBQ, *CJ;* Ralph Farmer, *Satan Inthron'd* (1657); SMS 1:12=303, 1:294=337.
483.

Etridge, John (also Edridge). London haberdasher; his home was used for
Meeting for Sufferings; suffered jail in 1680's; cf. Besse, *SJ.* **553.**

Evans, Katharine (d. 1692). With Quaker husband **John** lived at Englishbatch, Somerset; preached and was persecuted at Salisbury, on Isle of Man, and especially on Malta by Inquisition during eastward trip with Sarah Cheevers, described in their *Short Relation* and its reworkings; wrote one other tract, SMS 1:394=261; cf. 4:184, BBQ, *CJ, DQB;* Whiting, *Persecution Exposed.* **84.**

Everard, John. "Spiritual puritan" pastor, translator of Boehme. **21.**

Fallowfield, William (1639-1719), of Strickland-head, Westmorland. Son of puritan minister, later married and settled in Leek, Staffordshire, after period of traveling ministry as Friend; see *EQL, FPT,* SMS 1:244=166; wrote one testimony. **565.**

Farnworth, Richard (also Farnsworth) (d. 1666). Yeoman from Tickhill (Balby), Yorkshire; had been Puritan, Separatist, and virtually Quaker before enlistment by Fox, 1651; "leader in the north" in 1650's; preached widely, often from Revelation, especially in Westmorland and Worcestershire; imprisoned at Banbury; wrote forty-nine titles in Smith, forty-four in Wing, including many of earliest Friends' tracts, also theological disputes (e.g., with Muggleton), autobiography *Heart Opened by Christ* (1654), ARBMS 38, SMS 1:372=3, 4:229=6, 3:58=12, 3:45=13, 4:83=20, 3:46=25, 3:53=34, 3:50=51=35, 3:49=75, 3:54=109, 3:55=146, 3:57=149, 3:48=152, 3:56=296, *LWD* 3; cf. 3:40=7, 1:3=98, 4:88=157, 1:391=183, 4:137=280; see also BBQ, BSP, *CJ, DNB, DQB, EQL, FPT,* NSE. **33, 55, 57, 64n, 86, 167, 197, 263, 264, 269, 278, 358nf, 512f.**

Feake, Christopher. "Fifth Monarchist" radical. **410.**

Fell, Henry (c. 1630-c.1674). As young clerk to Judge Fell at Swarthmoor (apparently no kin), was convinced by Fox, 1652; around London and Bristol, 1655-56, then sailed for Barbados, when his newsletters give much data on New England missions, which he briefly joined; also visited Surinam, 1658/59; after returning to London and Barbados again, set out in 1661 with Stubbs, Baker, and Scosthrop to deliver epistles of Fox to Prester John and Emperor of China, but forced to return from Alexandria; settled in Barbados where he evidently died after 1674; wrote five proclamation tracts (three in Wing), SMS 4:167=138, 4:260=268, 4:265=271, 1:81=300, 1:65=301, 1:42=305, 1:66=329, 1:67=345, 1:68=366, 1:69=381, 1:79=387, 1:70=410, 1:71=417, 1:72=459, 4:182=460, 4:181=497, 1:73=530, 1:74=538, 1:77=545, 1:78=560, letter in *CJ* II, 256-58; Thirnbeck MS 4 (*JFHS* IX [1912]); see Besse, Bowden, BBQ, CNP, *DNB, EQL,* Luke Howard MS 11, and Caton's *Journal.* **123n.**

Fell, Leonard (1624-1701). Another Swarthmoor retainer (no kin?); traveled to preach and visit Friends from Scotland and Durham to Devonshire; several Lancashire imprisonments; wrote three tracts, SMS 1:116=112, 1:121=139, 1:122=145, 1:113=158, 1:136=161, 3:175=177, 1:118=199, 1:114=208, 1:119=277, 1:120=292; see Besse, BSP, *CJ, EQL.* **61.**

Fell, Margaret (1614-1702). From 1632 wife of Justice Thomas Fell; from

Askew family, also of Furness; after 1669 married to George Fox but seldom saw him; made her Swarthmoor Hall home center for Quaker itinerants, relief funds, and newsletters (Swarthmore MSS, see p. **469**); ten visits to London, mostly to plead for imprisoned Friends; two long imprisonments at Lancaster castle, 1664-68 and 1670-71; her seven daughters all traveled as Friends and married Quakers: **Margaret,** who married John Rous, **Bridget** Fell Draper, **Isabel,** who married Yeamans and Morrice, **Sarah,** wife of William Meade, **Mary,** wife of Thomas Lower, **Susanna** Fell Ingram, **Rachel** Fell Abraham; Judge Fell's son **George Fell** remained Anglican but thereby protected family claim on Swarthmoor; she wrote twenty-eight tracts (twenty-three in Wing) including one in Dutch and three to Dutch Jews; her works=*A Brief Collection* include autobiography; also wrote ARBMS 105, *SDA* 23, SMS 1:308=433; see Besse, BBQ, BSP, *CJ,* CNP, *DNB, DQB, EQL,* HLH; Isabel Ross, *Margaret Fell;* and older H. G. Crosfield and Maria Webb biographies. **8, 33ff, 37f, 61f, 152, 160f, 195n, 209, 382, 405, 469, 470-71, 471-73, 474-76, 476-78, 481-85, 565-66.**

Fell, Thomas (1598-1658). Puritan Justice and Parliament member, owner of Swarthmoor Hall and host to Friends, though never fully convinced; see BBQ, *DNB.* **61, 66, 68, 251, 387n.**

Fenwick, John, from Bracknell, Berkshire. Arrested in Buckinghamshire Meeting, 1666; provided funds for purchase of West Jersey and set up at Salem his settlement of New Caesarea, 1675; subject of a verbal and tract debate with Penn's friends; see Besse and esp. Pomfret. *West Jersey.* **409.**

Fisher, Mary (1623?-98), wife of William Bayly *(q.v.)* (1662), and of John Cross (1678). Servant in Tomlinson home, Selby, Yorkshire, when convinced (1652); after York Castle imprisonment, traveled with Elizabeth Williams to Cambridge (1654), with Anne Austin to Barbados (1655), to Boston (1656), to West Indies (1657-58), and to visit Sultan at Adrianople (overland) (1660); with her second family settled and died in South Carolina; wrote SMS 4:193=234; see also Besse, Bowden, BBQ, *CJ, DNB, DQB, EQL,* JQA, TQA. **120, 358-62.**

Fisher, Samuel (1605-65). Oxford-trained vicar of Lydd, Kent, son of Northampton shopkeeper; renounced his living to turn Baptist (1649) and then Quaker (1655), yet much of his voluminous writings (*Testimony of Truth Exalted,* 800 pp., 1676) outdid puritan scholars to prove the "Rustick's" superiority; exuberant lover of words and ideas, he went reluctantly on mission to Germany, Rome, and Venice with Stubbs, but died of plague during third imprisonment; wrote sixteen works including one in Dutch; see also Besse, BBQ, *CJ, DNB, DQB, EQL,* SMS 3:160=379, 3:152=405, 3:124=414. **7, 12, 31, 49n, 86, 153, 250, 262, 295, 304-14, 405, 479n, 512.**

Fletcher, Elizabeth (c. 1638-58). "Of a considerable family" in Kendal; traveled preaching to Oxford with Elizabeth Leavens (went "naked for a sign" and brutally beaten up) and alone in Ireland, 1655 and 1657; wrote one tract, SMS 4:99=409; see also 4:1=65, 1:192=77, 1:193=86, 1:197=175, 3:16=227, 1:198=319, 4:23=401, BBQ, *CJ, EQL, FPT.* **477f.**

Fowler, Robert. Shipowner-captain of Bridlington, Yorkshire, whose small

Woodhouse carried eleven Quakers to New England in 1657, stopping over at Portsmouth, England (where they "gathered sticks and kindled a fire," i.e., a Meeting), and New York before entering Hell's Gate; voyage described in his *Quaker's Sea-Journal* and ARBMS 1; see also Bowden, CNP, JQA, SMS 4:126=391. **117n, 122.**

Fox, George (1624-91). Son of "righteous" Christopher Fox, puritan weaver of Fenny Drayton, Leicestershire, and Mary, b. Lago; teen-age years of wandering obscure; from 1650 his *Journal* gives almost weekly detail in retrospect; more than any other, founded Quaker movement and led establishment of its organization, esp. 1664-79; married widowed Margaret Fell, 1669; besides his *Journal* (*v.* p. **153**), *The Great Mistery* (pp. **289-94**), and his *Epistles* (pp. **486-501**), many of his tracts were collected and printed by Ellwood (*Gospel Truth Demonstrated*, 1706, etc., usually called Fox's *Doctrinals*); he wrote (usually dictated) about 250 tracts (266 in Wing, including testimonials and parts of composite works, besides twenty in Dutch and five German never printed in English, and thirteen Dutch, thirteen Latin, and five French translations in his lifetime); these shift in emphasis from proclamation to exhortations to rulers (1656-62) to general epistles for Friends and doctrinal disputes; his notebooks and unpublished MSS have been edited as CNP, *Annual Catalogue, GFS Book of Miracles,* etc., by Henry Cadbury; Fox also wrote personal letters (most of *SDA*, SMS, Vol. 7, and 3:186=17; ARBMS 98, 109, etc.), yet many may have been destroyed; biographies of him were written by A. Neave Brayshaw (1933), Paul Held (1950), Samuel N. Janney (1853), Rufus Jones (1930), Rachel Knight (1923), Hanna D. Monaghan (1970), W. Vernon Noble (1953), Arthur Roberts (1959), Harry E. Wildes (1965), etc., but none can yet be called definitive. **5ff, 13f, 21ff, 25f, 33ff, 41ff, 58ff, 64ff, 74f, 78, 84f, 93, 116, 117, 123n, 141n, 144-48, 153ff, 161, 173, 189, 194, 196, 209, 223, 245f, 247ff, 251-62, 289-94, 296, 298, 305, 359, 371, 381, 384, 385-88, 405-07, 408, 429-33, 433-37, 441, 463f, 465ff, 469f, 475n, 479-80, 480-81, 486-501, 501-12, 512ff, 544, 549, 558f, 565.**

Fox, George, "the Younger" (d. 1661), of Woodbridge, Suffolk. Evidently a veteran puritan soldier moved by "Fifth Monarchists" and Levellers, convinced by George Whitehead, 1655 (hence "younger" in Truth, not years, than his namesake); soon preaching at Norwich, jailed at Bury St. Edmunds, and esp. in 1660 at Harwich and London; wrote twenty-five tracts (besides four Dutch and one French translations), mostly political exhortation; his works—*A Collection of the Several Books* (1662)—was the first such Quaker compilation; cf. *EQL, FPT,* SMS 4:93=254, 4:92=486, 4:178=500, 3:179=526, 4:18=527. **86, 89, 153n, 164, 357, 388-404, 410f.**

Foxe, John. Elizabethan puritan recorder of "Martyrs." **152, 270.**

Furly, Benjamin (1636-1714). Prosperous linen merchant of Colchester and (from 1658) Amsterdam and Rotterdam, where he, Ames, Caton, and Stubbs built up Dutch Quakerism; here also he, Stubbs, and Fox wrote *The Battle-Door for Singular & Plural,* showing pronouns in thirty-five languages, and most of his six English, eight Dutch, and two French tracts; corresponded with Bayle, van Helmont, Locke, Sidney, and Penn; briefly followed John

Perrot; sale-catalogue of his 4,400-book library was also published; see William I. Hull, *Benjamin Furly and Quakerism in Rotterdam* (1941); C. Fell-Smith, *Crisp; DNB, DQB,* HWP, Riewald, *SJ.* **512.**

Gay, Claude. Eighteenth-century Frenchman convinced as Friend and exiled to England. **501n.**

Gibbons, Sarah (1635?-59), of Bristol. Sailed for Boston (1656), and again (1657) (via the *Woodhouse*) where jailed and whipped; expelled from Connecticut (1658); on third trip drowned off Providence, Rhode Island; see Besse, *DQB,* Fowler MS, JQA, SMS 4:58=293, 1:82=454, 4:182=460, Robinson's last letter to GF 5/12/1659. **121.**

Giles, John. London tailor, early convinced; preached at Oxfordshire (1659); died in Newgate prison (1662); see Besse, *FPT.* **86.**

Goodaire, Thomas (d. 1693), of Selby. Convinced near Wakefield, Yorkshire (1651), with Nayler; important early Quaker preacher, esp. in Yorkshire moors, Midlands; jailed at Worcester, Northampton, Oxford (praemunired), Warwick; wrote three tracts; cf. Besse, BBQ, BSP, *CJ, DQB, FPT,* ARBMS 159, SMS 1:372=3, 4:83=20, 1:3=98, 3:55=146, 3:57=149, 3:48=152, 4:88=157, 1:243=371, etc. **57, 263, 264, 269, 274, 278.**

Gould, Anne, also Gold. Early London Friend; traveled in Essex, Ireland; cf. Besse, BBQ, *FPT.* **86.**

Gould, Daniel. Newport, Rhode Island, Friend; imprisoned in Boston (1659), traveled to Virginia with Burnyeat (1671); see Bowden, Bishop, JQA; his letter was later reprinted. **129.**

Gratton, John, of Monyash, Derbyshire (c. 1643-1712). Convinced (1670) by humble local Friends after ten-year prilgrimage among Baptists and Muggletonians; 5½ years in Derby prison, 1680ff.; wrote five tracts and a classic journal; see Besse, BSP. **513.**

Green, George. London Friend; imprisoned (1660), but evidently a wealthy merchant when fined (1682); see Besse. **558.**

Greenway, Richard (d. 1666). Tailor of Blackfriars, London; traveled through Essex, Oxfordshire, and by sea; wrote five tracts; cf. Besse, BBQ, *FPT.* **86, 193.**

Grotius, Hugo. Seventeenth-century scholar, founder of modern International Law. **355.**

Halhead, Miles (c. 1614-90). Yeoman of Mountjoy, Underbarrow, Westmorland; convinced (1652); traveled to Devon with Salthouse (1656); wife complained, "I would to God I had married a drunkard, I might have found him in the Alehouse"; he told her their son's death was judgment for her rebelliousness; see autobiography *Book of Some Sufferings* (1690); also Besse, BBQ, BSP, *CJ, EQL, FPT,* HLH, SMS 3:171=48, 3:14=49, 3:73=73, 1:89=81, 4:120=144, 1:220=147, 1:162=167, 1:259=194. **154, 476n.**

Haller, William. Contemporary historian of Puritanism. **16, 151n, 152n.**

Hambly, Loveday Billing (c. 1604-82), of Tregangeeves, Cornwall. Cousin or aunt of Billing, friend of Rous, Lowers and the Fells, hostess to all traveling Friends, and "mother of Quakerism in Cornwall"; subject of L. V. Hodgkin, *Quaker Saint of Cornwall;* see also BBQ, *EQL,* epistle, printed posthumously, and SMS 4:185=490. **408.**

Harrison, Thomas. Outstanding Cromwellian officer; let Fifth Monarchist radicals, from 1653. **387n, 410.**

Hart, Thomas. London Quaker treasurer; wrote SMS 3:7=442 to George Taylor; see *EQL.* **551.**

Hartas, George (d. 1670?), of Ulrome, Yorkshire. Convinced (1651); imprisoned and died at York Castle (1660-70?), leaving his wife and ten children in prison; cf. Besse, *CJ, FPT.* **58.**

Harwood, John. Early convinced in eastern Yorkshire, pushed "proclamation" to limit; imprisoned at York in 1652, then at Bury St. Edmunds and in Bastille, Paris (1658); wrote SMS 3:96=446 and eight tracts, the last denouncing Fox, who called him "dirty fellow" for planned non-Quaker marriage to widow (1660); see Besse, BBQ, *CJ, EQL,* SMS 4:94=170, 4:9=419, 4:174=563. **474n.**

Haselrig, Sir Arthur. Puritan politician, leader in Long Parliament. **408.**

Hendricks, Pieter. Dutch button-maker at Danish town Glockstadt on Elbe (perhaps a Mennonite); convinced in 1658 by William Ames; by 1661 in Amsterdam (and jailed) and thenceforth a pillar of Dutch Quakerism, in organizing, corresponding, traveling (e.g., to Friesland with Caton, 1661, and with Fox and Penn, 1677), translating, writing, publishing (eight tracts in Dutch, two English, ARBMS 140; his wife Elizabeth wrote five in Dutch and one in English, ARBMS 140-44); see Besse; Hull, *Benjamin Furly;* HQA, HWP, Riewald, *SJ,* and esp. Wm. I. Hull, *William Sewel,* and *BFHA* 41 (1952), 81ff; 44 (1955), 3ff. **208, 496.**

Hicks, Elias. Early nineteenth-century New York State Quaker educator; traveled much to minister; his liberal Christology led to Hicksite split throughout America. **6, 501n.**

Hicks, Jane, of Chadwich, Worcester. Imprisoned (1655) for challenging priest; cf. Besse. **269.**

Higginson, Francis (1619-73). New England-bred puritan pastor of Kirkby Stephen, Westmorland; ejected in 1663, but reinstated when he conformed to Anglicanism. **7, 63-78.**

Holder, Christopher (1631-88), of Winterbourne, Gloucester. Well-educated, prosperous family; sailed to Boston, 1656; returned there via *Woodhouse,* 1657; wrote in jail there one of earliest Quaker statements of faith, 1658; on third visit ear cut off; married Ann Hutchinson's niece Mary Scott, 1660; second wife also Rhode Islander; later imprisoned and died in England; wrote one tract; cf. Besse, Bowden, *CJ, DQB,* JQA, SMS 4:58=293, 4:126=391, 3:110=441, 4:82=454, 1:319=515. **121f, 128f, 134.**

Hollister, Dennis (d. 1676). Bristol grocer and member of Parliament; Baptist, convinced in London, host to traveling Friends; wrote two tracts against Baptists; cf. *CJ*, CNP, SMS 1:391=183, 3:9=187; R. S. Mortimer, *Quakerism in Seventeenth Century Bristol.* **483n.**

Holme, Thomas (1627?-66). Emotional young Kendal weaver; convinced, 1652; preached and jailed in Lancashire and Cheshire; married fellow-traveler Elizabeth Leavens *(q.v.)*, mildly embarrassing Friends who helped via Kendal Fund; thereafter they were first and leading Quaker preachers in South Wales; he sang in Meetings; wrote SMS 1:189=55, 1:190=58, 1:191=67, 1:192=77, 4:249=78, 4:248=79, 1:193=86, 1:195=89, 4:250=105, 1:2=120, 4:244=171, 1:197=77, 1:194=207, 1:200=230, 4:247=239, 1:201=245, 1:203=264, 1:205=276, 1:204=281, 1:198=319, 4:28=384, 1:199=418, 4:252=518, 4:253=519; see BBQ, BSP, *CJ, DQB, EQL, FPT,* and continuation in *JFHS* XXXI (1934), 3-19; NSE. **475n.**

Holmes, Jane. Following her preaching at Matton, Yorkshire "awakening," 1652, was imprisoned in York Castle where she became ill and "high" or rebellious in spirit; still a prisoner in 1654; see BBQ, *EQL,* and SMS 1:373, 3:36, 4:229, 3:42 (*EQL* 4-6, 57). **358-62.**

Hookes, Ellis (c. 1630-81), from Odiham, Hants. Shy, humble, "the salaried secretary of Friends for twenty-four years," collecting data on Friends' sufferings used later by Besse and immediately in petitions and tracts; he wrote nine tracts, besides thirteen testimonies, etc., SMS 4:117=544, Thirnbeck MSS 5 and 6 (*JFHS* IX), and many in SMS later volumes; cf. 3:146=533, BSP, *CJ,* CNP, *EQL, FPT, JFHS* I (1903), 12-22; edited the works of Burrough, Samuel Fisher, Howgill, Parnell, and William Smith, boarded with a Southwark widow, worked in room at "Bull & Mouth Meetinghouse." **41, 118, 405.**

Hooton, Elizabeth (c. 1600-71/72). Lived in Ollerton; joined separatist group at nearby Mansfield, Nottinghamshire; was perhaps first to take Fox as leader, later followed by husband and son, both Oliver (one wrote a lost MS history); preached and interrupted pastors; hence jailed four times by 1655 in Derby, York, and Lincoln; so sailed twice to Massachusetts, where repeatedly flogged; wrote one tract, ARBMS 14, 16, and accounts given in Emily Manners, *Elizabeth Hooton* (*JFHS* Suppl. XII, 1914); see also ARBMS 14, 97, 153, Besse, BBQ, BSP, *CJ,* CNP, *DNB, DQB,* SMS 3:36=5. **8, 49, 358-62, 381-82.**

Howgill, Francis (1618-68/69) and first wife **Dorothy** (d. 1655-56), daughter Abigail. Lived at their farm near Grayrigg, Westmorland; he was well schooled, perhaps for ministry; patriarch and leader of separatist groups in Sedbergh-Firbank-Kendal area before whole group was won by Fox; Burrough was his preaching partner in London (three periods) and Ireland; imprisoned at Appleby in 1652, and again for the last five years of his life; wrote forty-four works (many jointly with other Friends; thirty-four in Wing) besides three Dutch and one Latin translation, mostly long, gentle, and doctrinal; works collected (1676) as *Dawning of the Gospel Day;* also wrote ARBMS 18, 19, 20, 21, 31, 33, 34, 39, 60, 61, 65, 83, 84, 85, 90, 91, 92, 93, 104, 114, 117, 118, 127, 155-56; many in *LEF; SDA* 9; SMS 1:89=81,

1:161=140, 1:86=162; Dorothy wrote ARBMS 30, 32, SMS 1:376=241; see also Fox and Nayler, *Saul's Errand;* Will Hayes, *Gray Ridge: the Book of Francis Howgill* (1942); Besse, BBQ, BSP, *CJ, DNB, DQB, EQL, ESP, FPT, JFHS* X (1913), "Records of Fds in Ireland"; many other details in SMS (cf. *EQL*). **78f, 83ff, 90f, 153, 154, 160ff, 163n, 164, 167-79, 180, 197, 208, 246, 382-85, 437, 467, 475n, 476n, 477nf, 479n, 512.**

Hubberthorne, Richard (1628-62). "Rational, calm-spirited" little puritan ex-captain from Yealand, near Kendal; after convincement in 1652 preached in Wales (jailed), Cambridge, Norwich, and later in London, where he helped reconcile Fox and Nayler, and in 1660 got Charles II to promise toleration; died in London prison; write thirty-six tracts (many jointly, twenty-nine in Wing), especially appeals to fellow ex-soldiers; works as *A Collection* (1663); also largest group of SMS (except for Fox and George Taylor): 4:4=1, 3:1=2, 1:341=32, 1:339=41, 1:340=47, 4:1=65, 1:343=66, 4:5=83, 4:235=94, 4:8=100, 4:6=103, 1:356=110, 1:354=116, 1:345=117, 4:2=118, 1:346=122, 1:347=133, 1:344=142, 4:3=160, 1:30=164, 1:106=184, 1:348=190, 4:7=209, 1:350=210, 1:351=279, 3:153=315, 4:11=340, 1:352=341, 4:14=373, 1:353=393, 4:9=419, 4:15=429, 4:13=434, 4:12=435, 4:10=440, 4:16=449, 1:342=451, 1:349=501, 4:17=505, 4:261=525, 4:18=527, 4:19=539, 4:20=540, 4:21=541, Abraham MSS 4 and 5 (*JFHS* XI), *FPT,* suppl. in *JFHS* XVIII (1921), 22ff; see also Besse, BBQ, *CJ, DNB, DQB, EQL, FPT, JFHS* XXVI (1929), 11-15, and esp. the biographies by Ernest Taylor and Elisabeth Brockbank. **35, 85, 89, 153, 154, 155-60, 164, 167, 197, 208, 235, 390, 405, 475n, 512.**

Hudson, Thomas (c. 1624-97). London shipmaster and helper of Quaker prisoners; see *CJ,* SMS 1:56, 1:150. **553.**

Hudson, Winthrop. Contemporary American historian of Puritanism. **465n.**

Hutchinson, Ann. Boston Puritan disowned by John Cotton and driven out of Massachusetts to become a co-founder of Rhode Island. **119.**

Hutton, Thomas (d. 1695), of Rampside, Furness, near Swarthmoor. Preached in Scotland; cf. *CJ, SJ,* SMS 1:301=408. **61.**

James, William. Early twentieth-century student of religious experience and psychology. **23.**

Jones, Rice (or Rhys Johns). Baptist of Nottingham, who joined Fox's circle (c. 1650) but had already pulled away by 1654, leading "proud Quakers"; cf. BBQ, *CJ,* CNP, SMS 7:104. **463f.**

Jones, Rufus M. Quaker historian and mystic (1863-1948). **15, 21, 25, 32, 268n, 465n.**

Jones, T. Canby. Contemporary Quaker teacher and theologian. **16, 104.**

Keith, George (1638-1716). Scottish Quaker theologian; but for his swing away from Quakerism after 1689, he would be seen as a Quaker thinker as central as his friend and fellow-student at Aberdeen, Robert Barclay, whom he much influenced; persecuted around Aberdeen, 1664-79; preached in Scotland, Barbados, New England; with his wife Elizabeth went as one of Quaker "big 4" (Fox, Penn, Keith, and Barclay) to Holland and Germany (visit to Princess Elizabeth), 1677; taught Quaker schools near London, 1682-84; prosecuted; surveyor to New Jersey, 1684; schoolteacher in Pennsylvania, 1689-92, but conflict over his desire for creed led to disownments at Philadelphia (1692) and London (1694); meanwhile Keith's "Christian Quakers" split Pennsylvania; after 1700, when he turned to Church of England, came to America as first S.P.G. missionary, returned to be vicar in England, kept up pamphlet barrage; wrote 117 works, mainly theological (besides two in Dutch and one in Latin), the majority against Quakerism; see BSP, Bronner, *CJ*, CNP, Carroll; Hull, *Benjamin Furly; JFHS* XLVI (1954), 59-63; JQA; Lloyd; J. Pomfret, *W. New Jersey;* Riewald, and esp. E. W. Kirby, *George Keith* (1942). **41, 43, 145, 262, 478n, 559.**

Killam, John and brother **Thomas** (d. 1690). Yeomen of Balby and leaders of a separatist group at Balby, near Doncaster, Yorkshire, who were already close to Quakerism when Fox won them in 1651; both preached through Yorkshire; John was jailed with Aldam in York; planned Swannington meeting, December 1654; hosted 1660 General Meeting in their orchard; wrote ARBMS 123, SMS 4:85=14, 4:86=15, 4:87=19, 1:3=98, 4:88=157; cf. 3:58=12, 3:9=187, 1:243=371, BBQ, *CJ, EQL, FPT.* **359, 551.**

Killam, Margaret (d. 1672) and sister **Joan**. Sisters of Thomas Aldam (who married Mary Killam) and wives of John and Thomas Killam; Margaret traveled widely to preach, esp. to Devon with John; co-authored a tract and wrote SMS 1:2=84, 1:374=129, 3:94; cf. 1:112=236; BBQ, *CJ, EQL.* **359.**

Knappen, Marshall. Twentieth-century historian. **16n, 151n.**

Lacey, Thomas. London tobacconist; imprisoned four times and heavily fined, 1660-85; for vivid account of fire destroying his Tower Hill shop, see *ESP;* cf. also Besse. **558.**

Lambert, John. Leading radical Puritan among Cromwell's generals. **386, 388, 395n, 396n, 398n, 408.**

Lancaster, James (d. 1699), of Walney Island, Furness, Lancashire. Ferried and protected Fox on first visit; traveled with him through Cumberland and later to Ireland; preached in London, Norwich (jailed), Scotland, Ireland; wrote five tracts, mostly jointly authored (one in Wing); see BBQ, *CJ, DQB, EQL, FPT,* SMS 4:8=100, 4:6=103, 1:121=139, 1:161=144, 1:301=408, 1:28=445. **61ff, 475n, 476n.**

Larkham, George. "Founder of Independency in Cumberland" and pastor of a Congregational church in Cockersmith; ejected, 1660. **186.**

Laud, William. Charles I's Archbishop of Canterbury. **17.**

Lawrie, Gawin (also Gawan, Gavin; d. 1687). London Quaker merchant; later lived in Hertfordshire; heavily fined, 1682; trustee and later a proprietor for

Billing's West Jersey venture; later unskillful Deputy Governor under Barclay for East Jersey, 1684-87, where he died at Elizabeth; wrote one tract; see SMS 4:127=483, Besse, *CJ, EQL;* Pomfret, *W. New Jersey* and *E. New Jersey; SJ.* **409, 422-29.**

Lawson, John (1615/16-89). Shopkeeper of Lancaster (also schoolmaster [?] ; cf. Wing on tracts of 1644 and 1646); early received Fox; preached at Lancashire, Cheshire (jailed), Derby, Wales; wrote one Quaker tract, SMS 4:66-69=38, 121, 50, 39; cf. Besse, *CJ, EQL, FPT,* and its supplement in *JFHS* XXXI (1934), SMS 1:189=55, 1:193=89, 3:30=134. **262.**

Lawson, Thomas (1630-91). Son of Sir Thomas, Cambridge educated, parson of Rampside, Furness, Lancashire, when he invited Fox to preach there; became Quaker schoolmaster of Great Strickland; mainly unhurt through 1660's by friendship with bishop and gentry; reputation as "most noted herbalist in England"; wrote ten tracts (eight in Wing), ARBMS 42, SMS 1:241-245=371, 168, 371, 166, 44; cf. 1:1=248, ARBMS 139, BBQ, *CJ, DQB, EQL;* M. Webb, *Fells of Swarthmoor.* **61, 253n, 408n, 418n, 430, 474n.**

Leake, John (or Leeke; d. 1685) and **Ann** (d. 1653), of Selby, Yorkshire. Convinced while visiting Fox in Derby prison, 1651; himself imprisoned at least twice (7 years?) and fined, 1660-82; see Besse, BBQ, *CJ.* **58.**

Leavens, Elizabeth (d. 1665). Married Thomas Holme (1654) immediately on release together from jail in Chester; many preaching trips together and apart; had three children; saw visions; emotionally intense; see Holme's SMS newsletters, also 4:1=65, 1:162=167, 1:255=181, 1:301=408, Besse, BBQ, *CJ, EQL, FPT.* **475n.**

Leddra, William (d. 1661). Cornish settler in Barbados; convinced there by Henry Fell; came to New England with Rous, 1657-58; whipped, jailed, banished; returned to Boston, 1660; tried and executed; see Besse; Bishop, *New England;* Bowden, JQA. **122, 140.**

Leeming, Thomas, of Weeton-in-the-Wolds, Yorkshire. Jailed, 1660, and fined, 1659, 1671; cf. Besse. **126.**

Leslie, Charles. Anglican clergyman and anti-Quaker writer. **43, 559.**

Lilburne, John (1614?-57), of London. Puritan journalist, lieutenant-colonel and reformer, leader of "Levellers" and manifesto writer, for which jailed both by Charles I and Cromwell; after return from Channel Islands to Dover Castle, turned quietist and Quaker; added his *Resurrection* to his 109 pre-Quaker tracts; note his Thirnbeck MS 2 (*JFHS* IX); see *DNB, FPT,* SMS 4:14=373, and esp. biographies: Mildred A. Gibb, *John Lilburne* (1947); Pauline Gregg, *Free-born John* (1961). **122, 410.**

Lloyd, Arnold. Contemporary historian. **53, 116, 468n, 515n.**

Lloyd, David (1656-1731), from Manoron, North Wales. Educated in law in England, came to Pennsylvania in 1686 as Penn's Attorney-General, but opposed life-long the centralizing power in hands of proprietor and his governor and council; his "impudence" in opposing provincial Court of

Admiralty led to loss of office (1700), but he continued to lead Assembly and to be (along with James Logan of proprietary party) most powerful man in province; wanted political power and economic freedom for small farmers and traders, but was a landowner in Chester and Philadelphia, where he set up Jansen's press; see Bronner, JQA; *JFHS* III (1906), 47-55, 96-106; E. W. Kirby, *George Keith;* Burton A. Konkle, "David Lloyd, [etc.]" (Swarthmore Collections); Roy N. Lokken, *David Lloyd, Colonial Lawmaker* (1959); Riewald. **45.**

Loe, Thomas (d. 1668). Tradesman of Oxford; convinced by Camm (1654); there and in Ireland (1667) convinced Penn; also visited Ireland, 1655, 1657, 1660, etc.; jailed at Oxford and Marlborough; wrote SMS 4:238=547; cf. Besse, BBQ, BSP, *EQL, FPT, LEF,* biographies of Penn. **210, 478n.**

Longworth, Roger (1640?-87). Shoemaker from Longworth, Lancashire; apprenticed to and convinced by James Harrison; imprisoned for Quaker Meetings three times, 1669-75, when he went to Silesra and Saxomy in vain effort to win Boehmanists and Schwenkfelders; revisited Holland, Emden, Fredenrstadt and other German cities in 1677, 1678, 1679, 1681, then England and Ireland; became Penn's agent (1682), recruiting Dutch and German colonists; traveled in America, Pennsylvania to New England (1682-85), and again in 1686-87 after visit to Danzig; wrote many letters; see Pemberton MSS (Historical Society of Pennsylvania) and esp. HWP. **498.**

Lower, Humphrey or Humfry (d. c. 1672). Magistrate, of Tremecre House, St. Tudy, Cornwall; convinced while visiting Fox in Launceston dungeon, 1656; his wife Margery was sister of Loveday Billing Hambly and probably related to Edward Billing *(q.v.);* they made their homes centers for traveling Friends and Meetings; see *CJ, DQB, EQL,* and esp. HLH, SMS 4:145=416, 3:174=558. **195n.**

Lower, Thomas (1633-1720). Doctor and son of Humphrey and Margery Lower *(q.v.);* owned homes both at Pennance, near Creed, Cornwall, and Marsh Grange, Furness, Lancashire; his second wife was Mary Fell, daughter of Thomas and Margaret Fell *(q.v.),* m. 1668; traveled with Fox in Cornwall and beyond, arrested with him at Worcester, 1673, where Fox dictated to him his *Journal* (cf. p. **153**) and related documents; see *CJ;* wrote one tract; cf. Besse, BBQ, BSP, *CJ, CNP, DNB, DQB, EQL; JFHS* X (1913), 144-45, and esp. HLH. **41, 195.**

Lucas, Nicholas (d. 1688). Hertford Maltster and one of Billing's trustees for West Jersey financing (1675-83); tried under Conventicle Act (1664) but led in building new Hertford Meetinghouse next to his home on Butchery Green (1667-73); wrote one debate tract (1664), and joined Wilkinson-Story faction; see Besse; Pomfret, *West New Jersey,* and Violet A. Rowe, *First Hartford Quakers.* **409.**

Luff, John (also Luffe, Love; d. 1658), from Limerick, Ireland; had preached in New England, Spain, and Smyrna, before arrest, trial and death in Rome; see BBQ, *CJ.* **222.**

Lurting, Thomas. Seaman of London, impressed into navy, refused to fire guns at attack on Barcelona; imprisoned for attending Meeting in London; his

Fighting Sailor Turned Peaceable Christian was published in 1710 and often after; cf. Margaret Hirst, *Quakers in Peace and War*. **357.**

Marsden, William (also Marston). Hampton, Massachusetts, Puritan; fined for owning Quaker book; see Besse. **93, 172.**

Marshall, Charles (1637-98) and wife **Hannah.** Convinced (1654) by Camm and Audland, whose works he later edited; lived at Bristol until c. 1683, then at London; traveled widely visiting Meetings, 1670-71; wrote fifteen tracts (eleven in Wing), most to Friends, one medical; many other epistles printed with journal in his works, *Sion's Travellers* (1704); cf. BSP, *FPT, SJ.* **78-82, 565.**

Marshall, William. Cambridge-trained puritan vicar of Lancaster; ejected, 1660; later physician in London. **66.**

Mason, Cornelius. London Friend, fined (1685); see Besse. **558.**

Meade, William (1628-1713). From landowning family in Essex, to which he returned buying estate of Gooseyes in 1670, after achieving wealth as London cloth merchant; in same year famous with Penn for Gracechurch Street Meeting trial, establishing Juries' rights; in 1681, his second marriage was to Sarah Fell; thereafter often assisted Fox; wrote jointly six tracts; see Besse, *CJ.* **118, 441.**

Milner, Gregory, of Cottam, Yorkshire. Imprisoned at York in 1659 over tithes; cf. Besse. **126.**

Milner, James (d. 1662). Tailor of Baycliff, Furness, Lancashire; with wife Elizabeth made apocalyptic prophecies; resulting odium led Friends to compel the Milners to condemn these, 1655; cf. BBQ, *CJ.* **67.**

Milton, John. Puritan poet, secretary to Cromwell. **212, 221f, 355, 437.**

Monk, George, later Duke of Albemarle. Commanded Cromwellian garrison in Scotland, leading it south to restore King Charles II in 1660. **37, 396n, 408, 411.**

Mucklow, William, of Mortlake and London (1631-1713). Imprisoned with Ellwood, 1662; joined Perrot's faction by *Spirit of the Hat* and two other tracts (all 1673) against Fox's leadership; see *CJ*, BSP. **215, 513f.**

Muggleton, Lodowick. Tailor, sect-founder, prophet of 1660's, who debated in tract and in person with Penn, Farnworth, Thomas Taylor, Penington, etc. **262, 347, 513.**

Myers, Richard (d. 1654), of Baycliff, Furness. Joined Milner in prophecies; cf. *CJ, EQL,* SMS 1:63=225. **61, 158.**

Nayler, James (1618?-60). Born at Ardsley, he lived nearby at Wakefield, Yorkshire, until he served as Quartermaster and lay preacher of Lambert's puritan regiment; leader of separatist group at Woodkirk until he felt called to follow Fox into Northwest (cf. p. **68**); after Fox the best-known and strongest Quaker preacher, and the best theologian before Barclay, yet kept simplicity of shepherd (cf. p. **209**) or butcher; after peak of London mission, Exeter jailing led to Bristol scandal (p. **481**) and final years in London prison, where he wrote the best of his sixty-six tracts (sixty-one in Wing); earlier ones more controversial and/or jointly with Fox; works as *A Collection* (1716) include famous "dying words"; wrote also letters—*JFHS* X (1913), 18ff.; SMS 3:3, 67=8, 3:69=9, 1:85=10, 3:65=11, 3:66=21, 3:2=27, 3:62=28, 3:60=29, 3:61=30, 3:59=31, 3:5=45, 3:4=53, 3:70=56, 3:71=60, 3:192=192, 3:73=73, 3:74=92, 3:81=163, 3:80=195, 3:76=265, 3:82=274, 3:83=437, 3:84=438, until 1656, mostly to Fox rather than Margaret Fell; also received many letters; see *DNB*, biographies of him by Mabel Brailsford, Emilia Fogelklou Norlind; on Friends' response to his "fall" see *EQL* 334-35; *JFHS* XXVI (1929), 11ff.; on Puritans' response, see W. K. Jordan, general Nayler bibliography; on background see R. A. Marchant, *Puritans and the Church Courts in the Diocese of York* (1940). 7f, 21, 33ff, 38, 54f, 64ff, 67f, 68ff, 72, 76, 78, 83, 102-16, 162n, 183n, 209, 245f, 251-62, 262-89, 294, 296, 298, 359, 371, 385-88, 463f, 470-71, 475n, 476n, 477n, 480-81, 481-85, 488, 513.

Neway, Richard, of Worcestershire. **264.**

Nicholson, Benjamin, of Tickhill, Yorkshire. Wrote four tracts; died in York Castle, 1660; cf. SMS 3:52=36. **289, 358-62, 385, 388, 474.**

Nicholson, Joseph and wife **Jane.** Convinced by Fox in their home church at Bootle, Cumberland, 1653; sailed to Boston, 1659, after local ministry; described trial, jail, birth of child in prison in tract, *The Standard of the Lord* (1660) and SMS 1:124 and 4:107-9=*EQL* 447, 520, 535-36; settled in Settle but visited America; see BBQ, *CJ, EQL.* **138, 140.**

Nickalls, John L. Twentieth-century Quaker historian and librarian. **13, 145n, 152n, 153n, 405n, 408n, 465n, 467n, 468n.**

Niclaes, Hendrik, also as Niclas, Henry Nicholas, etc. Dutch mystic and founder of the "Family of Love" or "Familists"; fifteen of his books (twenty-five editions) had appeared in English by 1656. **266.**

Norton, Humphrey, of Durham and London. Contact man for the Kendal Fund; went to Cromwell, 1656, to offer to take Fox's place in Launceston dungeon; also preached in Essex and in Ireland, and visited Swarthmoor; sailed on *Woodhouse,* 1657; repeated sufferings throughout New England (branding too) described in *New England's Ensign* (1659); he also wrote three short tracts; left Quakerism soon after (over sex?); cf. Besse, BBQ, Bowden, *CJ,* JQA; Smith, *Cat.;* SMS 1:255=181, 1:350=210, 1:392=358, 1:10=377, 4:126=391, *Woodhouse* MS=ARBMS 1, 4:108=536. **117n, 120n, 122.**

Norton, John. Hertfordshire puritan pastor who became Teacher of Boston, Massachusetts, Church, published anti-Quaker tract, and inspired act imposing death-penalty on Friends. **122.**

Nuttall, Geoffrey. Contemporary master-historian of Friends and Congregationalists. **16, 53, 245, 247, 270n, 470n, 479n, 480.**

Oakley, John. London Friend of Wheeler Street. **86.**

Ollive, Thomas (also Olive, Olliffe), of Brampton, Northamptonshire. Convinced by Dewsbury (1655), disowned by father (1658), but appears as Northampton Quaker treasurer (1675); twice fined, sailed to West Jersey (1677), where he became deputy governor (1684) and died (1692); wrote a proclamation tract (1666) and SMS 4:166=646 (the Thomas Ollive of Aylesbury (1654-1726) who married Dorothy D'Oyley, Oxfordshire Quaker heiress, was presumably his son or unrelated); see Besse, *CJ, EQL,* JQA. **422-29.**

Ovy, John, of Buckinghamshire. No other data. **211.**

Owen, John. Puritan pastor, key Congregational leader, vice chancellor of Oxford University. **262, 295, 516n.**

Padley, William, of North Cave, Yorkshire. Fined in 1678; cf. Besse, *DQB.* **126.**

Parke, James (d. 1696). Perhaps from Lancashire and Morgan Lloyd's Wrexham separatist group; became weighty Friend in London, still traveled widely (debate at Lancaster vs. Col. Wigan), and spoke at Fox's funeral, January 1690/91; wrote ARBMS 57, twenty tracts, including sermons, three in Dutch; cf. Besse, BSP, *CJ, FPT.* **565.**

Parker, Alexander (1628-89). The most under-noticed early Friend, probably well educated and from a landed family of Chipping, Bowland (West Yorkshire near Lancashire), though called "butcher"; cf. Nuttall on his "freedom from fanaticism"; after convincement at Lancaster became Fox's commonest traveling partner; preached alone in Lancashire, Scotland, Midlands, Herefordshire (confronted baptist pillar Tombes), Cornwall, Somerset; often link with Quakers in jail; later settled in London, married widow Prudence Wager, went to Holland with Fox, 1684; wrote thirteen tracts (eleven in Wing) besides memorials, SMS 1:163=85, 4:234=124, 1:161=140, 1:162=167, 1:161a=231, 1:1=248, 1:164=260, 1:165=289, 1:166=304, 1:167=314, 3:140=425, 3:142=472, 3:144=476, 1:84=485, 4:143=488, 1:168=496, 1:169=516, 3:146=533, 3:145=542, 1:170-2=550, 553, 554, 3:147=555, all compact with news; see also Besse, BBQ, *CJ, DNB, DQB, JFHS* VIII (1911), 30-32; John Whiting, *Persecution Exposed.* **85, 470.**

Paget, Nathan. Puritan minister's son; "physician to the Tower" of London. **212.**

Parnell, James (1636-56), of Retford, Nottinghamshire. Joined Balby separatist group, then Friends, after visit to Fox in Carlisle prison; for preaching mission in Cambridge and Ely see p. **160;** for work and death at Colchester see pp. **164f, 203;** wrote thirteen tracts (twelve in Wing) besides seven reprints, three Dutch and one German translation in his short lifetime, ARBMS 58; works as *A Collection* (1675) also included epistles; see Besse, BBQ, *CJ, DNB, EQL, FPT,* SMS 3:52=36, 1:192=77, 1:89=81, 4:5=83, 1:2=84; *JFHS* VI (1909), 41; XXXIV (1937), 85-86. **119, 153, 160-63, 163-66, 180, 203, 387.**

Parr, Ellen (of Kendal family?). **471.**

Pears, William, of Yorkshire. Shared Aldam's imprisonment, and died there in 1654, after going naked as a sign; see SMS 3:36=5; E. Manners, *Elizabeth Hooton.* **358-62, 387n.**

Pearson, Anthony (1628-65/66). Born at Cartmel, Furness; lived at Rampshaw Hall, County Durham; the most prominent of gentry won to Quakerism; convinced as Justice trying Nayler at Appleby, 1653; thereafter made his home a center for Quaker preachers northward, interceded in London for all imprisoned Friends, was active against Royalist revolt, 1659; hence, and also because he had been legal secretary to Sir Arthur Haselrig in Parliament from 1648, had served on puritan confiscation commissions, and was friend of Sir Harry Vane (*q.v.*), he kept status by turning Anglican from 1660; wrote four tracts (three in Wing) including *The Great Cast of Tythes* (1657), often reprinted, SMS 1:87 and 3:33=23=*LEF* 10, 3:35=51, 3:34=70, 1:216=95, 4:162=160, 3:78=335; see also 3:64=26, 3:61=30, 3:14=49, 3:70=56, 3:192=61, 3:44=71 and ARBMS 121, many SMS newsletters by George Taylor and esp. SMS 3:80=195 by Nayler at Court, London; later letters concerning a debt dispute with Lancelot Wardell; see BBQ, *CJ, DNB, EQL, FPT,* and esp. *DQB, Durham Univ. Journal* (June, 1944); *JFHS* XLVIII (1957), 119-22; II (1965), 77-96; and *The Friend* (1860), p. 206; (1912), p. 478. **55, 209, 260ff, 384, 475f, 551.**

Pearson, Peter. Yorkshire Quaker; came to Barbados and New England with Marmaduke Stephenson, 1658, where he was also the first to suffer under the "Cart and Whip Act" of Boston, 1661; wrote SMS 4:128=508; cf. 4:182=460, Besse, Bowden, *EQL,* JQA. **125f, 134-36.**

Penford, John, of Kirby, Leicestershire. Fined under Conventicle Act, 1670, 1672, 1679; became one of "London settlers" in West Jersey, where he was appointed a commissioner, 1677; see BBQ; Pomfret, *West Jersey.* **422-29.**

Penington, Isaac (1616-79). Son of puritan Lord Mayor of London; turned back himself from mysticism and Ranters to Quakerism, 1658, moving from London to quiet Chalfont, Buckinghamshire, where his home became a center for Quaker travelers, Ellwood and Penn; diligent theological writer (eleven pre-Quaker books, sixty-six Quaker works [fifty-nine in Wing]), including one Dutch, many often reprinted, esp. in four editions of works (1681, 1761, 1784, 1861-63); sensitive sternness shown in letters of counsel (*v.* pp. **234ff**); see also BSP, *CJ,* CNP, *DNB, EQL;* Ellwood, *Story of the Life;* SMS 1:106=184, 3:144=476, 3:179=526, and esp. *JFHS* II (1965), 30-53. **7f, 14, 25, 31, 54, 117n, 152, 153, 154, 209, 211f, 224-41, 246, 262, 355, 357, 371-80, 466, 475nf, 512f.**

Penington, Mary (1625?-82). Daughter of Sir John Proude of Kent; married Sir William Springett of Sussex, and after his death (1644) and the birth of Gulielma Springett (*v.* as wife of Penn), married Isaac Penington, 1654; on her mysticism cf. p. **225n** and her manuscript (*Events,* 1910); Maria Webb, *Penns and Peningtons,* lives of Penn, etc. **209, 224f.**

Penn, William (1644-1718). The Renaissance Quaker; named for his father, the genial, unreflective Admiral under Cromwell and Charles II; raised in

London and in Ireland (his mother's home at the death of her Dutch first husband) and at Oxford; he lived at Worminghurst, Sussex; London; and Penn Mayor, Pennsylvania; was convinced by Loe; married **Gulielma Springett** (1672, just after Penn-Meade trial), and after her death Hannah Callowhill of Bristol (1696); his life-style, his friendship with James II (earlier Duke of York), and his involvement in Whig politics were criticized by more radical Friends; but Pennsylvania and West Jersey colonies owed their existence to his work and vision; Wing lists 109 works by Penn, plus forty-four reprints before 1700; Smith lists 134 works, including some prefaces, epistles, and memorials not printed separately and his works of 1700-11, also five Dutch, two German, and two Latin originals and six translations in his lifetime; the Historical Society of Pennsylvania has photocopies of all extant Penn manuscripts; *DQB's* bibliography of secondary works on Penn runs to thirty typed pages. **5ff, 13f, 30f, 35, 41, 45, 54, 91, 118, 154, 180, 181, 208n, 209, 225, 262, 295, 314, 355, 357f, 388, 408n, 409f, 422-29, 430, 441-51, 452, 463, 470n, 478n, 497, 501, 512, 514, 544, 545, 558f**; Gulielma Penn: **209, 223, 225n.**

Penney, Norman. Quaker historian of early twentieth century and greatest editor of Quaker documents; cf. all references to *CJ, FPT, SJ*, etc. **13, 57, 153n.**

Pennyman, John (1628-1706). Yorkshire gentleman's son; lived as London woollen-draper after serving in Royalist army; became Friend c. 1658, joined Perrot faction, and was disowned, 1670, whereupon he married with pomp his dead wife's sister Mary (cf. "The Quaker's Wedding" ballad, SMS 1:395); wrote one Quaker tract, later published eight letters and twenty-three tracts, mostly against Friends, esp. Penn and G. Whitehead; Mary wrote one; cf. *CJ*, BSP, Smith. **43, 164, 262, 559.**

Perkins, William. Elizabethan puritan pastor and counselor of consciences. **152n, 171.**

Perrot, John (d. 1665), of Waterford, Ireland. Perhaps illegitimate grandson of Henry VIII; convinced in 1655 and jailed at Dublin in 1656 during Irish mission; returning from Near East mission with John Love or Luff, thrown for three years into insane asylum in Rome; on return (1661), his "imaginative mysticism" and martyr spirit won following for his ultra-individualism, clashing with Fox's leadership; sailed to Barbados and Virginia, where he won most Friends, but died broke and worldly in Jamaica; wrote twenty-nine symbol-clashing tracts, mostly from 1660-63, also letters in *JFHS* VIII (1911), 21-24; XXIX (1932), 29ff.; XXXI (1934), 36-38, etc.; cf. IX (1912), 95; Besse, BBQ, BSP, *CJ, DNB, DQB*, SMS 3:127=398, 3:7=442, 4:269=469, 1:2=477, 6:125, 6:157, 6:83, and esp. Kenneth Carroll, *John Perrot, Early Quaker Schismatic* (*JFHS* Suppl. No. 33, 1971). **42, 222, 305n, 463f, 512ff, 544, 559.**

Peters, Hugh. Radical puritan pastor and Cromwellian army chaplain. **21.**

Pool, William. Young Quaker convert whose "mind run out"; after his suicide, Susanne Pearson tried vainly to revive him from grave; cf. *EQL*, SMS 1:217=368. **62.**

Prince, Mary, of Bristol. Traveled with seven other Friends to Boston in 1656, and with Mary Fisher to Turkey in 1657, back via Venice; wrote SMS 4:58=293 in adoration of Fox; cf. Besse, Bowden, BBQ, *EQL,* JQA. **121.**

Pursglove, Richard, of Cranswick, Yorkshire. Puritan captain; received Fox, 1651; fined as Quaker, 1684; between wrote SMS 3:119 and a tract (with others, 1663); cf. Besse, *CJ, FPT.* **57.**

Rawlinson, Thomas (d. 1689). Gentleman, of Graythwaite, Furness, Lancashire; separatist, convinced in 1652 and disowned by family; preached at Durham, Midlands, Exeter (jailed), London, Sussex; wrote two tracts and SMS 3:15=52, 3:9=187, 3:12=307, 3:11=375, 3:10=479; cf. 3:60=29, 1:161=140, 4:120=144, 1:81=300, 1:21=303, 1:40, 3:12, 1:314=356, BBQ, *CJ, EQL, FPT,* and continuation in *JFHS* XXXI (1934), 11, 13. **182n.**

Rawson, Edward. Puritan clerk of Massachusetts General Court. **122.**

Rich, Robert (d. 1679). Long-haired London merchant; convinced, 1654; preached and arrested at Banbury, 1655; shared Nayler's imprisonment and led Bristol ride; later joined Perrot faction; settled in Barbados, 1659-79; eleven of his epistles and proclamations were printed; see *CJ, DNB, EQL.* **512.**

Richardson, Richard (1623?-89). Lived, married (1676), and died in Bow and neighboring Ratcliff, London, suburb; over two years prisoner under Second Conventicle Act, then taught London Quaker school; in 1681 succeeded Ellis Hookes as paid Clerk of Meetings and Quaker committees in London, recording sufferings, lives and deaths of Quaker ministers and writing ten "learned" tracts against Bugg and periwigs; cf. Besse, BSP, *CJ,* CNP, *JFHS* I (1904), 60-68. **41, 551-54.**

Rigge, Ambrose (c. 1635-1705). Eighteen-year-old schoolteacher of Bampton and Grayrigg, Westmorland, when convinced at Firbank; joined "Valiant Sixty" in mission to south Kent, Sussex, Isle of Wight (jailed), Southampton (jailed), Dorset (jailed), home visit to Grayrigg (misunderstood)—then settled as schoolteacher in Gatton, Surrey (married in Horsham jail), and later Reigate; elegant handwriting as Meeting clerk; also wrote thirty-six tracts covering a balance of all major genres (four reprinted; twenty-five in Wing), his works compiled as *Constancy in Truth* (1710), SMS 4:84=353, 4:80=465, 4:81=502, 4:82=543; cf. 1:16=167, 4:205=213, 1:285=252, 4:200=267, 7:141, ARBMS 169, *LEF* 226f, Besse, BBQ, BSP, *CJ, DNB, EQL, FPT.* **197, 565.**

Roberts, Gerrard (c. 1621-1703). Wine-merchant of London; convinced early; from 1658 to the Great Fire of 1666 his house "at the Sign of the Fleur de Lys" was center for Quaker publications, meetings of ministers, clearing of funds; wrote jointly two tracts, SMS 3:127=398; cf. 3:9=187, 3:76=265, 3:18=406, 3:7=442, 4:20=540, Besse, BBQ, BSP, *CJ, DQB, EQL, FPT.* **86, 147, 405, 551.**

Robinson, Richard, of Brigflats, Sedbergh, Yorkshire (d. 1673). His home became Meetinghouse. **60.**

Robinson, William (died young, 1659), from Cumberland. "Bred up with a merchant in Crooked Lane, London, being convinced at the first appearing of Truth in London" (*FPT* 159), preached and jailed in Essex, sailed on *Woodhouse,* hanged in Boston; wrote the epistles later used in New England martyrologies, SMS 4:126=391; cf. 1:169=516; 1:319=515, 4:107=520, Besse, Bowden, BBQ, *CJ, EQL, FPT,* JQA. **117n, 122, 124f, 128-32, 133-34, 134-36, 138.**

Rogers, William (d. c. 1709). Bristol merchant and weighty Friend; drawn into Wilkinson-Story split with Fox, which Rogers hopelessly embittered in 1678, thereafter writing seven hostile tracts against Fox and Whitehead; cf. BSP. **43, 262, 514, 559.**

Roper, Richard (d. 1658), of Cartmel, Furness, Lancashire. Puritan turned Quaker; traveled in Lancashire, London, and Ireland, and probably in Germany, to preach; jailed also for tithes, but died at home; wrote ARBMS 23, 24, and 57, SMS 3:135=226, 3:131=324, 3:134=395, 4:23=401, 3:132=431; cf. 4:260=268, 4:99=409, Besse, BBQ, *CJ, EQL, FPT,* and supplement in *JFHS* XXXI (1934), 12. **478n.**

Rous, John (d. 1694/95). Son of puritan lieutenant and sugar-planter, the Quaker first-fruits on Barbados; in 1657 went with William Leddra and Thomas Harris to New England, where after repeated trials he lost his ear; visited Nevis in 1658 and England in 1659, where he settled as (sugar?-) merchant in London and Kingston-on-Thames and married Margaret Fell, Jr. (*q.v.*); in 1671-72 returned to Barbados, Jamaica, Virginia, and New England with Fox, etc.; drowned after later trip to his plantation; wrote seven tracts (three in Wing), mostly on New England; Abraham MSS 9-11, 14, 29 (cf. 32 on death) (*JFHS* XI [1914]), ARBMS 46-49, 80, 137, SMS 1:90=400, 1:82=454, Thirnbeck MS 3 (*JFHS* IX [1912], 59ff.); see also Besse, Bowden, BBQ, BSP, *CJ,* CNP, *DNB, EQL,* JQA; M. Webb, *Fells.* **117n, 122, 471.**

Row, Henry. Bristol Friend convinced in 1654; owned inn where Nayler's procession ended, 1656; cf. BBQ, *FPT.* **483n.**

Rudd, Thomas (c. 1643-1719). Miller of Wharfs, near Settle, Yorkshire; continued to proclaim prophetic woes on missions through southern England, after 1689; jailed at Canterbury, 1702; fined under Conventicle Act; wrote five tracts; see Besse, BSP. **118.**

Rudyard, Thomas (d. 1692 in Barbados). London lawyer, first arrested as Quaker in 1664 and again in 1670; went to Holland with Penn, etc., 1671; to East Jersey as deputy governor replacing Lawrie, 1682-85, after being a proprietor and promoter of West Jersey; wrote nine tracts against the Baptists, 1670-74; cf. *CJ, DQB,* JQA, and esp. Pomfret, *E. Jersey* and *W. Jersey.* **422-29.**

Rust, Nicholas, of Danzig. Probably convinced by William Ames, 1661, but first on list of jailed in 1677; exiled to London, and perhaps lived there or in Holland until 1693 when he reported for Danzigers to London Yearly Meeting; for sources see Ruttel. **499.**

Ruttel, Christian, should be Puttel or Pittel. Arrested in Friends' Meeting,

Danzig, 1670; exiled to London; some time after 1677 returned and died after further persecutions in Danzig; for Rust and Puttel see Besse; *JFHS* VII (1910), 136-39; *BFHA* 41 (1952), 81-92. **499.**

Salt, William. London Friend; went with Fox to Cornwall, 1656, jailed with him at Launceston and at Morlaix, France, 1659; wrote two tracts supporting Perrot, 1660 and 1663, hence disowned; see BBQ, *CJ, EQL, SDA* 7, HLH. **117, 512.**

Salter, Hannah. See Stranger.

Salthouse, Thomas (1630-91). Son of shoemaker of Dragleybeck; became "steward" of nearby Swarthmoor Hall, where convinced, 1652; preached in Furness with Burrough, Cumberland with Halhead, London with Caton, then long mission into Devon and Cornwall, broken by jailing and notable trials at Plymouth, Exeter, and Ilchester; after trips to London and home, settled in Cornwall, where he married Anne Upcott, vicar's daughter of St. Austell, in 1668, and joined in her draper's shop (disowned by dad) between further missions; wrote eleven tracts of all genres (eight in Wing) including *Wounds of an Enemie* (autobiography), also Abraham MS 6 (*JFHS* VII [1910], 140-41), ARBMS 142, SMS 3:171=48, 1:112=236, 3:188=308, 3:158=311, 3:157=331, 3:162=333, 3:165=342, 3:185=357, 3:183=369, 3:173=375, 3:156=377, 3:163=380, 1:320=524, 3:179=526, 3:168=528, 3:190=531, 3:167=534, 3:166=552, 3:174=558; cross-references in many other SMS; see also Besse, BBQ, *CJ*, CNP, *DNB, EQL, FPT*, and supplement in *JFHS* XXXI (1934); XLIX (1960), 137-47; and esp. HLH. **61f, 85.**

Saltmarsh, John. Spiritual puritan pastor and writer. **21, 465.**

Sawrey, John. Puritan Justice from Ulverston; member of "Parliament of Saints." **62, 66f.**

Sewel, William (1654-1720). Born at Amsterdam, son of Jakob and Judith Zinspenning Sewel, Mennonites and first Dutch leaders (1657-64) of Friends; grandson of Kidderminster Separatist; visited England, 1668-69; lived as author (ten books including dictionary, three grammars) and esp. translator (ten Quaker books, esp. Penn's; twenty-two non-Quaker, including Boyle, Juvenal, Congreve, Burnet); helped sympathetic non-Quaker pastor Gerard Croese gather MSS and data for first history of Quakers; ended writing his own fuller, more accurate *History of the Rise, Increase & Progress of . . . Quakers;* see BSP, *CJ,* and esp. HWP and Wm. I. Hull, *William Sewel* (1934). **55, 145, 558-65.**

Shackleton, Richard. Eighteenth-century Quaker schoolmaster of Ballikore, Ireland. **502n.**

Shattuck, Samuel, of Salem dissenters' circle. Tried to help Holder, 1657; convinced, banished, and arrived at Bristol for 1660 persecutions; sent back to Boston with Charles I's "missive" of pardon, 1661; see Besse, JQH. **117n, 137n, 138.**

Simmons, Thomas (also Simmonds, Simons) and wife **Martha** (1623/24-65), sister of Giles Calvert. He was printer of London, produced three hundred

Quaker works, also Baxter's, etc.; she was from Colchester, joined Friends in 1655, and was known mainly for key role in Nayler's Exeter quarrel with Fox and "fall" at Bristol; died on voyage to Maryland, 1665; wrote three apocalyptic tracts; cf. BBQ, *CJ, DQB, EQL, FPT,* SMS 3:153=315, 3:194=317, 1:181=321, 3:193=322, 3:129=403, and biographies of Nayler. **35, 125, 290, 297, 304, 430;** Martha: **86n, 104, 481, 483f.**

Simpson, William (1627?-70/71), of Lancashire. Preached at Cumberland; went "naked as a sign" through Oxford, Cambridge, and London and "for 3 yrs. in the days of Oliver"; wrote *Going Naked, A Signe* and four other tracts; see BBQ, *CJ,* CNP, *EQL, DNB, FPT, PP,* SMS 1:336=251, 4:114=370, 1:170=523. **161n.**

Smith, Elizabeth (d. 1668), of Hazel, Gloucester. Preached in Ireland in 1655 with Elizabeth Fletcher; married Miles Hubbersty (*q.v.*); died at Kendal; cf. BBQ, *CJ, FPT,* SMS 3:16=227, 1:370=523. **477n, 484.**

Smith, Humphrey (1624?-63). Herefordshire farmer, separatist preacher, and from 1654 Quaker; active in Gloucester, 1654-55, and in Worcester and Devon, 1657; singlehanded gatherer of many Dorset Meetings, 1657; between and later jailed at Evesham, Exeter, Dorchester, and in Winchester until he died there; wrote forty-two tracts (thirty-two in Wing) including many short prophetic warnings and sufferings tracts; combined works issued as *A Collection* (1683); cf. Besse, BBQ, *CJ,* CNP, *DNB, FPT; JFHS* XII (1915), 98; SMS 1:12=303. **8, 140-44.**

Smith, Joseph. Nineteenth-century bibliographer of Quakerism. **14, 28** and *passim.*

Smith, Margaret, of Salem. Convinced c. 1658, imprisoned and whipped (1659) and again (1660), leading to convincement of husband John; for his letter, see Besse; both were in prison until general pardon of 1661. **139.**

Smith, Richard, of Southampton, Long Island, New York. Convinced by Dewsbury on visit home to England, returning in time to welcome Quaker preachers and join Massachusetts invasion, 1654; cf. Besse, Bowden, JQA. **121, [422-29?].**

Smitten, Sarah, of Bristol. No other data. **480.**

Sonnemans, Arent, called Aaron Sonmans in England (d. 1683). Prosperous Rotterdam merchant won to Quakerism by "familiar friend" Benjamin Furly (*q.v.*), whom he helped in pamphlet war vs. Collegiants; he helped Fox set up Yearly Meeting at Amsterdam, 1677; settled and married near Edinburgh and Barclay, with whom he was en route to London, intending visit to his large holdings in East and West Jersey when killed by highwayman; HWP; Wm. I. Hull, *Furly;* D. E. Trueblood, *Barclay;* Pomfret, *E. Jersey, W. Jersey.* **409n.**

Spoden. Early Quaker preacher, perhaps the same as John Snowden of Yorkshire; see *EQL, FPT,* and SMS 3:53=34, 4:144=72. **65.**

Spooner, John, of Windermere, Westmorland. In Appleby jail, 1654; married Agnes Ayrey (*q.v.*) before priest; cf. *JFHS* X (1913), 18-19. **475.**

Stephenson, Marmaduke (d. 1659). Plowman of Market Weighton, Yorkshire;

his own account of his call to preach in Barbados and suffer in New England is almost only data; see Besse, Bowden, JQA. 7, 117n, 123-24, 126-28, 132, 134-36.

Sterry, Peter. Radical puritan pastor and lively Cromwellian chaplain and bureaucrat. 21.

Stoddart, Amor (d. 1670). Friend of Elizabeth Hooton; met Fox in Nottinghamshire, 1647, but was still captain in Cromwell's cavalry, 1651; to London, 1653; with Fox in East Anglia, Yorkshire, and Worcester, 1654-55; related to Solomon Stoddard and Jonathan Edwards of eighteenth-century Massachusetts; with Davis and Roberts, London distributors of Kendal Fund, 1658; jailed at London, 1660; died at Enfield c/o Samuel Newton; no record between but three tracts; see Besse, BBQ, BSP, *CJ, FPT,* SMS 3:52=36, 4:35=76, 3:9=187, 1:297=385, 4:134=517, ARBMS 160; W. C. Abbott, *W. & S. Oliver Cromwell,* p. 398; E. Manners, *Elizabeth Hooton.* **83f, 359n, 405, 473-74, 551.**

Storer, William. His reply to Baxter, 1679, was never published; see Smith, *Bibliotheca Anti-Quakeriana.* **294.**

Storr, Marmaduke (d. 1679). Farmer from Ostwick, East Yorkshire; tried and imprisoned at Northampton, 1655; attended General Meeting at Scalehouse, 1658; wrote one tract and ARBMS 129; see Besse, BBQ, *CJ, EQL,* SMS 4:139=180. **126.**

Story, Christopher (1648-1720/21). Farmer (?) of Kirklinton, Cumberland, on Scots border, where he hosted Meetings, 1672; became preacher; two periods in Ireland; the *Brief Acc't of [His] Life* was printed in 1726; see BSP, *CJ, DQB, FPT.* **181, 463f.**

Story, John, also **Storey** (all these three names from Viking stor?) (d. 1681). Farm laborer of Preston Patrick, Westmorland; convinced at Firbank, 1652; went south with "Valiant Sixty" in 1654 with John Wilkinson (*q.v.*), founding Meetings through Wiltshire, traveling in "broad-brimmed beaver hat, periwig," and silver belt-buckle; in 1672 returned from South to lead protest of Preston Patrick Friends against Fox's leadership in new Women's Meetings, and against the bold Quaker stand under Second Conventicle Art urged by London leaders; resulting separation, 1675 (briefly healed in 1677), won leaders of Meetings of Bristol, Reading, Wiltshire, and of Underbarrow and other northern towns; died in midst of conflict with Thomas Camm at Kendal, but schism lasted through century; wrote two tracts, ARBMS 119; memorials to him printed, 1692; cf. BSP, also BBQ, *CJ, EQL, FPT,* SMS by John Wilkinson, also 1:5=206, 1:9=285, 3:129=403, 3:166=552, Rogers and Bugg tracts; *JFHS* IV (1907), 119-21; I (1903), 57-61. **42, 512, 514, 553, 559.**

Stranger, Hannah (also Stringer) and later married Salter. Wife of London combmaker, John Stranger; both became disciples of James Nayler, fellow-prisoners at Exeter, leaders in Bristol "fall"; in 1666 she formally repented; cf. BBQ, *CJ.* **481, 483.**

Stuart, Anne. Queen of England, Scotland, Ireland, etc., 1702-14; daughter of James II. **40.**

Stuart, Charles I. King of England, 1624-49; son of James I. **18, 88f.**

Stuart, Charles II. King of England, etc.; son of Charles I; reigned, 1660-85, after exile under Commonwealth. **37ff, 137n, 206, 389ff, 399n.**

Stuart, James I. King of England, 1603-24; son of Mary, Queen of Scots. **17.**

Stuart, James II. Brother of Charles II; formerly Duke of York; reigned from 1685 to 1688. **39.**

Stuart, Mary. Daughter of James II; with her husband-cousin **William of Orange** ruled England, Scotland, Ireland, etc., as William III and Mary II, 1688-1702, also Holland as Stadtholder. **39, 120.**

Stubbs, John (1618?-74). Cromwellian soldier at Carlisle when convinced by jailed Fox, 1653; refused oath, so discharged; became schoolmaster at Lancaster; thence south with Will Caton to Kent (won Fisher and Luke Howard), 1654 and 1655; Holland, 1655; with Ames to Amsterdam, 1656; on to Flanders, Barbados (?), Bristol, and Dublin; with difficulty persuaded Fisher of their joint call to mission to Turkey via Holland, Germany, Leghorn, Venice, Rome, and back via Heidelberg, 1657-58; went with Henry Fell to Alexandria, 1660, failing to reach China; arrested at Swarthmoor, 1664; with Fox to Ireland, 1669; with Fox's group to Barbados and American colonies, 1671-73; meanwhile his Quaker wife Elizabeth raised their girls at Ulverston and later Durham (he died at London); wrote jointly five tracts, esp. *A Battle-Door* on "thee- and- thou" in thirty-five languages, also ARBMS 12, 97, Abraham MS 3 (*JFHS* XI), Etting MS 42; *SDA* 61, SMS 3:151=135, 4:24-27=354, 272, 316, 310, 3:160=379, 3:152=405, 3:124=414; see references in other SMS, Besse, Bowden, BBQ, BSP, *CJ*, CNP, *EQL*, *FPT*, HWP; L. V. Hodgkin, *Shoemaker of Dover;* and esp. HQA. **36, 85, 405.**

Sykes, William. Early Knottingly Yorkshire Friend; convinced while already imprisoned at York for tithes, 1652, and died in prison; cf. Besse, BBQ, *EQL*, SMS 4:229=6. **387.**

Taylor, Christopher (c. 1615-86). Oxford graduate; born at Craven, West Yorkshire; pastor of Chapel-in-the-Briars near Halifax; convinced by his brother; jailed at Appleby; taught school at Hertford; first head of Friends School at Waltham Abbey, 1672-82; sailed to Pennsylvania, where he was a leader; wrote fifteen tracts (nine in Wing) including Latin grammar and translation of Fox's Primer; see Bowden, BBQ, BSP, *CJ, DNB, FPT*. **57, 475n.**

Taylor, George (d. 1696). Kendal ironmonger; served (with Willan) as treasurer of Kendal Fund; author of many newsletters to Margaret Fell, 1654-59 (when discharged?), i.e., SMS 1:210-12, 214, 218, 220, 236-40, 247-52, 257-72, 278, 282, 288-303 (see *EQL* for sequence numbers); cf. also BBQ, *CJ*. **469, 474-76, 551.**

Taylor, Thomas (c. 1617-82), of Craven or Ravenstonedale, West Yorkshire. Brother of Christopher, also Oxford graduate; puritan curate, but turned separatist preacher of groups at Preston Patrick (Westmorland) and Richmond, Yorkshire; convinced, 1653, at Swarthmoor, gave up salary, and traveled preaching throughout Northwest and Midlands; jailed at Appleby,

Vann, Richard. Contemporary sociologist of early Quakerism. **24, 35, 44, 53, 151n, 154, 155n.**

Vaughton, John (1644-1712). Fined for tithes, militia dues, and preaching in Meeting, 1672, 1674, 1682, 1684, 1685; one sermon published; debated against Keith; traveled to Ireland, 1698; weighty committeeman; cf. Besse, *CJ, JFHS* V (1908). **565.**

Vokins, Joan (d. 1690), of White-Horse Vale, Berkshire. Preached in Nevis (and Barbados?); wrote two tracts and one of the first full journals—*God's Mighty Power* (1691). **154.**

Waller, Richard (d. 1657). Married fellow-servant and Congregationalist at Stockport, Cheshire; moved to Cartmel, Furness, Lancashire; arrested and jailed at Lancaster, 1655; preached in Westmorland and Ireland, 1656; again (also Isle of Man) with Roper, 1657; jailed at Waterford; wrote ARBMS 23-27, SMS 132-4=431, 253, 395; see Besse, *CJ, EQL.* **478n.**

Walwyn, William. London merchant, chief theoretician and major writer of the Levellers. **410.**

Watson, Samuel (c. 1618-1708), of Knight Stainforth, Gigglesworth, Yorkshire. Convinced while prisoner at York Castle, 1654; became prominent Quaker regionally; imprisoned and put in stocks (1659) for interrupting pastors; imprisoned in 1660 and 1682 over oaths; wrote SMS 1:389=392 and six tracts, including *A Short Account of the Convincement* (1712); see Besse, BBQ, *EQL, SJ,* and his collection of Early Quaker MSS at Friends House, London. **551.**

Waugh, Dorothy (b. 1636) and sister **Jane** (d. 1674), from Hutton, Westmorland. Servants in Camm's home when convinced, 1652; Jane preached at Manchester (jailed), Cambridge (jailed), and Danbury (jailed), married Thomas Whitehead, and settled in Somerset; Dorothy traveled through Cumberland and Lancashire, Norwich (jailed), 1654; Basingstoke and Cornwall (jailed at Truro), 1655; Berkshire, 1656 (jailed at Reading); then sailed for Boston (jailed); returned on *Woodhouse,* 1657; jailed at Nieuw Amsterdam; returned to Boston twice via Rhode Island and Barbados, 1658; married William Lotherington of Whitby, Yorkshire; cf. Besse, Bowden, BBQ, *CJ, CNP, EQL,* SMS 1:189=55, 1:2=84, 1:391=183 (on Jane); (on Dorothy) 1:344-6=142, 117, 122, 1:285=252, 4:58=293, 3:183=369, 3:173=375, 3:163=380, 1:82=454, 4:108=536. **121f, 163.**

Wesley, John. Greatest eighteenth-century evangelical preacher. **22, 151, 182n, 249.**

West, John, of Hertfordshire and/or Olveston, Gloucester. Quaker farmer; distrained for tithes, 1659; arrested and jailed for refusing oaths in Lancashire and Kent, 1660; longer imprisonment at Hertfordshire for Meetings, 1662; distrained at Gloucester, 1678; cf. Besse (are all the same man?). **553.**

West, William. Puritan colonel. Justice, mayor of Lancaster, member of Parliament of Saints, friend of Fells, and defender of Quakers at Lancaster

oned as outlaw at Lancaster, 1654-56, but released by writ of Justice West; wrote SMS 1:43=16 (spiritual autobiography; cf. *Life & Death of . . . Widders,* 1688), 4:100=113, 4:31=132, 1:307=216, 4:41=221, 4:29=222, 4:30=223, 4:102=224, 4:101=240; cf. 3:14=49, 3:15=52, Besse, Bowden, BBQ, BSP, *CJ,* CNP, *DQB, EQL, FPT, JFHS* IX (1912), 5-39. **182n.**

Wilkinson, Agnes. Jailed at York for forty days for confronting pastor, 1652; cf. Besse, *EQL, FPT,* SMS 3:39=43. **471f.**

Wilkinson, John (d. c. 1683). Farmer of Millholme, New Hutton, Westmorland; convinced at Firbank, 1652; traveled with John Story (*q.v.*) in Wiltshire, 1654ff.; jailed at Gloucester, 1655; joined Story's separatist group at Preston Patrick; wrote part of tract and SMS 1:32-36=102, 249 (1661), 197, 174; see fuller story of separation in BSP, also BBQ, *CJ, DQB, EQL, FPT.* **42, 189, 485, 512, 514, 553.**

Wilkinson, John (d. 1675). Puritan pastor of Brigham, Cumberland; convinced, 1653; helped Meetings throughout Northwest; see BBQ, *CJ, FPT.* **471.**

Willan, Thomas, of Underbarrow, near Kendal. He and George Taylor (*q.v.*) were treasurers of "Kendal Fund" for Quaker preachers; hence also wrote newsletters to Swarthmoor along with accounts: SMS 1:256, 209, 222, 213, 235, 255, 247, 274, 280, 283, 287, 275, 217 (in chronological order; see numbers in sequence in *EQL*); see BBQ, *CJ, EQL, FPT.* **474-76.**

Wills, Daniel. Northampton Quaker doctor, writer of two debate tracts and one of original Commissioners of West Jersey, enthusiastic settler, continuing as magistrate even under Andros, 1687; disciplined by Meeting, 1692; see Pomfret, *West Jersey.* **422-29.**

Wilson, Anne. Fiery Quaker preacheress, who denounced Thomas Ayrey's weakness near Kendal in 1656; was jailed at Cambridge, 1655, and later in London; see *EQL,* ARBMS 37, SMS 4:209=99, etc. **478.**

Winstanley, Gerrard (1609-76?), from Lancashire. Settled as tradesman of London by 1640; in 1649 began communitarian "Digger" group camping on St. George's Hill common, Kingston, broken up by troopers; before and after he praised man and soil in pantheistic tracts; may have died a Quaker; see *JFHS* L (1962), 65-68, and George Sabine's edition of *The Works of Gerrard Winstanley* (1941). **465f.**

Woolman, John. Mid-eighteenth-century Quaker reformer, minister, and tailor. **6, 13, 41, 358.**

Wortevale, Philadelphia (also Worthevale). Married Cornish landowner, not Quaker. **408.**

Wright, Joseph. London Friend; imprisoned at Newgate, 1684-85; see Besse. **558.**

Wright, Luella. Early twentieth-century student of Quaker literature. **14, 27, 153n.**

Index of Topics, Issues, Groups and of Counties or States

(For towns except London, Bristol, and Reading, see corresponding region.)

618